Expert .NET 1.1 Programming

SIMON ROBINSON

Apress®

Expert .NET 1.1 Programming

Copyright © 2004 by Simon Robinson

ISBN (pbk): 1-59059-222-0

Printed and bound in the United States of America 9 8 7 6 5 4 3 2 1

Trademarked names may appear in this book. Rather than use a trademark symbol with every occurrence of a trademarked name, we use the names only in an editorial fashion and to the benefit of the trademark owner, with no intention of infringement of the trademark.

Lead Editor: Dominic Shakeshaft
Technical Reviewers: Gwyn Cole, Mitch Denny, Jeroen Frijters, Jim Hogg, Christian Nagel,
    Valery Pryamikov, Morgan Skinner, Gavin Smyth, Helmut Watson
Editorial Board: Steve Anglin, Dan Appleman, Ewan Buckingham, Gary Cornell, Tony Davis,
    Jason Gilmore, Chris Mills, Dominic Shakeshaft, Jim Sumser
Project Manager: Beth Christmas
Copy Edit Manager: Nicole LeClerc
Copy Editor: Kim Wimpsett
Production Manager: Kari Brooks
Production Editor: Janet Vail
Compositor: Gina M. Rexrode
Proofreaders: Sachi Guzman and Katie Stence
Indexer: Michael Brinkman
Artist: Kinetic Publishing Services, LLC
Cover Designer: Kurt Krames
Manufacturing Manager: Tom Debolski

Distributed to the book trade in the United States by Springer-Verlag New York, Inc., 233 Spring Street, 6th Floor, New York, New York 10013 and outside the United States by Springer-Verlag GmbH & Co. KG, Tiergartenstr. 17, 69112 Heidelberg, Germany.

In the United States: In the United States: phone 1-800-SPRINGER, fax 201-348-4505, e-mail orders@springer-ny.com, or visit http://www.springer-ny.com. Outside the United States: fax +49 6221 345229, e-mail orders@springer.de, or visit http://www.springer.de.

For information on translations, please contact Apress directly at 2560 Ninth Street, Suite 219, Berkeley, CA 94710. Phone 510-549-5930, fax 510-549-5939, e-mail info@apress.com, or visit http://www.apress.com.

The source code for this book is available to readers at http://www.apress.com in the Downloads section.

Contents at a Glance

Contents

About the Author

Dr. Simon Robinson is editor-in-chief of ASP Today, the leading Web site for intermediate- and advanced-level Web developers, and is a freelance programmer based in Lancaster, United Kingdom. He has a varied background, having graduated with a doctorate degree in theoretical physics in 1992. He then spent a couple of years working as a physics researcher, mostly doing mathematical modeling of certain types of superconductor, before he realized there was more money to be made doing straight computer programming!

He worked for a period at Lucent Technologies, doing a mixture of programming and research into new technologies, before taking up a career in full-time writing and freelance development. He wrote or contributed to a large number of books, before finally settling down as the ASP Today editor. He's extremely keen on .NET and the way it's revolutionizing programming. He mostly codes these days in C# and sometimes in VB or C++.

Besides his ASP Today work, he's currently working on private projects concerned with .NET developer utilities, as well as his long-standing pet project, a computer game, which he has resolved to complete sometime in ~~2002.~~ ~~2004.~~ 2005.

As far as personal life is concerned, Simon's outside interests include performing arts, current affairs, and politics, and he retains a keen interest in physics. He is unmarried, and his immediate aim after finishing this book is to relearn the delicate art of starting a conversation by saying "Hello," instead of "using System;."

You can visit Simon's Web site at http://www.SimonRobinson.com.

Acknowledgments

Almost any book can of course only be written with the involvement of quite a few people, and this is certainly true of this book. For a start, this book wouldn't have been what it is without the hard work of the reviewers. And I don't think I've ever before had the privilege to work with such a highly qualified set of reviewers. Particular thanks are owed to Jim Hogg and Morgan Skinner at Microsoft for suggestions and advice that went well beyond the bounds of normal reviewing. As far as editors are concerned, I'd like to mention Julian Skinner, who was the main editor on the first edition of the book. It was Julian who had the original idea for this book back in the summer of 2001 and pushed the idea through, keeping it going through several delays when I was tied up with other work. Julian wasn't involved with the second edition, but thanks are deserved to John Franklin and Dominic Shakeshaft for their hard work in taking the book through a change of publishers to make a second edition, as well as to Gary Cornell for providing the inspiration and Beth Christmas for the coordination/administrative work.

Then on the personal side, thanks go to my girlfriend Anne for putting up with my being glued to the computer for the three months of writing the first edition and various other friends for, much to my surprise, remembering what I look like after I had written it. I'm hoping they'll achieve the same remarkable feat when this second edition is complete....

Introduction

This is a book about getting the best out of .NET. It's based on the philosophy that the best approach to writing good, high-performance, robust applications that take full advantage of the features of .NET is to understand what's going on deep under the hood. This means that some chapters explore the .NET internals and in particular Common Intermediate Language (CIL), and other chapters have a practical basis, covering how to use specific technologies such as threading, dynamic code generation, and Windows Management Instrumentation (WMI).

This book isn't a purely theoretical book for geeks, but it also isn't one of those purely problem-solving books that tells you how to write some code to do something without explaining how and why it works. Rather, I've sought to combine the twin aspects of practical technology: showing how to create specific applications while also diving under the hood of the Common Language Runtime (CLR). I believe that the true advanced .NET developer needs both. So a lot of the book is devoted to showing how .NET works; I'll go way beyond the MSDN documentation in places—and generally beyond most other .NET books currently available. But I never go into some abstract feature just for the sake of it. I always focus on the fact that understanding this CLR implementation detail can in some way help you to write better code. And some chapters show you how to write better applications in specific areas such as Windows Forms, how to take advantage of .NET features such as security, and how to better optimize for performance.

Just as it says on the cover, this is a book about *expert* .NET programming. It's a book for people who are already familiar with the principles of writing applications targeted at the .NET Framework and who want to understand more. This is perhaps to get an idea of exactly what the Just-in-Time (JIT) compiler is looking for when it assesses whether your code is type safe. Perhaps it's to be able to look at the CIL emitted by your compiler so you can understand some of the optimizations and use the knowledge to write better-performing code. Or perhaps it's because you need to use some of the more advanced features of .NET in your code, such as dynamic code generation, or you need more information about setting up code access security to enable your application to function correctly without being abused by other, malicious code.

The advanced nature of this book is illustrated by the fact that the first thing you'll do, in Chapters 1 and 2, is to start learning Intermediate Language (IL). You have no way out of that if you really want to get the best from this book—you'll need it so you can look at how certain high-level language features of VB, C#, and C++ work under the hood.

This is an advanced book, so I won't spend any time telling you any of the basics of .NET, other than occasionally in the form of a quick background review. So, for example, if you don't yet know what a JIT compiler is, or what the difference between a value and reference type is, then this isn't the book for you—because I assume you already know all that that. Similarly, I assume that you're fluent in at least one high-level .NET-compliant language, such as Managed C++, Visual Basic .NET, or C#. You should in particular be comfortable with reading C# code since that's the language in which most of the examples are presented, but at the same time I'll occasionally swap languages if a good reason exists for a particular sample to be coded in another language. To read this book you should also be comfortable with the principles of implementation- and inheritance-based object-oriented programming.

As an example, I cover assemblies in this book. If you want to understand why Microsoft introduced the concept of the assembly, what metadata is, or how assemblies solve versioning issues and enable all the information needed to use the assembly in one place, you *won't* find that information in this book. Lots of books already on the market can give you that kind of information. Since this is an advanced book, I assume you already know all that stuff. Instead, my chapter about assemblies starts by presenting the binary format for an assembly—reviewing how the IL code and metadata is laid out in it and how this helps with performance. Then it goes on to cover how you can extract information and metadata from the assembly programmatically, following up with how you can use assemblies and resources in your assemblies to make sure your applications are correctly localized and ready for those worldwide sales for which you're looking.

What This Book Covers

The following sections go over what the book covers, chapter by chapter.

Intermediate Language (Chapters 1 and 2)

The first two chapters of the book introduce you to IL. It isn't possible to cover the whole of IL in just two chapters, but I'll go over the basic concepts, including the principles of programming using the evaluation stack, declaring and instantiating value and reference types, and interacting with unmanaged code. The emphasis in the chapters is on using IL as a tool to enhance your understanding of the CLR and to enable you to improve the C++/C#/VB code you write. I even finish Chapter 2 by comparing the IL code generated by the C++, C#, and VB compilers. The appendix contains a comprehensive guide to the IL instruction set, which you can reference if you encounter IL instructions not covered in Chapters 1 and 2.

Inside the CLR (Chapter 3)

This chapter examines a number of aspects of the internal workings of the CLR that are often not covered by introductory .NET texts. In particular you'll consider the following:

- **JIT compiler**: You'll examine the way the JIT compiler processes your code.

- **ECMA**: I'll cover the ECMA standard for a Common Language Infrastructure (CLI) and its relationship to the Microsoft .NET implementation.

- **Type safety**: Type safety is often seen a black box. Code either is or isn't type safe, but few sources explain many of the factors behind what makes your code pass or fail verifiability. I'll work through the algorithms used to verify code, explaining how the tests work.

- **Managed and unmanaged code**: I'll discuss how managed and unmanaged code can work together and what happens at the managed/unmanaged boundary. This coverage should help C++ developers understand some of the restrictions that the C++ compiler imposes on mixing managed and unmanaged code and how to get the best out of applications that cross the boundary.

Assemblies and Localization (Chapter 4)

I'll cover in some detail at assemblies, considering the following:

- The basic structure of an assembly and how the metadata and IL is embedded in it. Here I'll focus particularly on how assemblies have been designed to assist performance.

- The relationship between assemblies and modules.

- Programmatic manipulation of assemblies.

- How resources are embedded in assemblies and how to localize your applications using resources. This means I'll also give an overview of the support for globalization in .NET.

Garbage Collection (Chapter 5)

You're no doubt familiar with the basic principles of garbage collection in .NET. In this chapter I'll go into some detail about the way the garbage collector works. I'll examine how the garbage collection algorithm has been designed with performance in mind and how the garbage collector interacts with the threads in your code. I'll also cover some advanced topics related to garbage collection such as weak references.

Performance (Chapter 6)

Performance is an important consideration when designing code, and much of the material in other chapters touches on the performance implications of the architecture of .NET. In Chapter 6, I'll take the opportunity to focus exclusively on performance, covering both some of the ways that performance has been designed into the .NET Framework and how you can take advantage of this to write higher-performance code. In particular I'll cover the following:

- I'll cover the performance implications for writing managed as opposed to unmanaged code. Generally speaking, managed code scores extremely well on performance, and that's going to get even better in the future; however, Microsoft's .NET publicity doesn't tell you about certain issues, and I'll cover some of these.

- I'll discuss what JIT optimizations are provided at JIT compilation time and how to control these in code.

- I'll cover tips for improving performance when writing your code.

Profiling (Chapter 7)

Optimizing performance goes hand in hand with being able to measure the performance of your code. In Chapter 7, I'll cover how to profile managed code. Specifically, I'll cover the following:

- .NET-related performance counters and the PerfMon tool

- How to write and use custom performance counters

- Advanced use of the Task Manager and other profiling tools

Dynamic Code Generation (Chapter 8)

Let's get one thing straight here: Dynamic code generation is not just for compiler writers. In some situations this technique can be a useful tool for improving performance. For example, it's used extensively in the System.Text.RegularExpressions classes to give high-performance regular expression analysis. It's also quite easy, although a little tedious, to code. In this chapter, I'll cover the basic principles of code generation, including the following:

- The System.CodeDom and System.CodeDom.Compiler namespaces and how to use them to control generation and compilation of source code. I'll also cover the facilities available for specific language compilers.

- The System.Reflection.Emit namespaces and dynamic generation of assemblies.

Threading (Chapter 9)

In some ways, threading has become a lot easier with managed code, since now classes are available that implement such things as thread pools, which were important but hard to implement with unmanaged code. In another way, however, threading has become more complicated, since more choices are available for threading models—particularly with the easy availability of thread pools or asynchronous execution of methods. In this chapter, I'll discuss the options available for writing multithreaded managed code and for controlling communication and synchronization between threads.

Management Instrumentation (Chapter 10)

.NET offers powerful facilities for interacting with both the operating system and the actual hardware on which your code is running. These facilities come through the classes in the System.Management and System.Management.Instrumentation namespaces that allow you to connect .NET applications to WMI providers. WMI is a useful technology that's often poorly understood and therefore little used by developers. Chapter 10 is devoted to rectifying that problem. In that chapter I'll cover the following:

- The concepts behind WMI, including how to architect WMI providers and consumers, the range of tasks you can achieve using WMI, and how to find out about logical drives on your system to programmatically detect when the screen resolution changes.

- How the relevant .NET base classes interact with WMI and how to code managed applications that use WMI to find out about or even control the operation of your hardware.

Advanced Windows Forms (Chapter 11)

You've no doubt written basic applications using Windows Forms by putting a few controls on a form, maybe even using GDI+ to perform custom drawing. This chapter takes you further. I'll cover the following:

- The underlying Windows message architecture that underpins Windows Forms and Windows Forms events. I'll show how you can use an understanding of this architecture to achieve more complex tasks such as accessing some useful events that aren't directly accessible through the usual Windows Forms event mechanism and using multithreading to allow the user to cancel lengthy operations.

- More advanced windowing to impress your users, such as nonrectangular forms and owner-drawn controls.

- Performance issues for drawing with GDI+.

Security (Chapter 12)

One of the big promises of .NET is the way that its enhanced security features will give you better control over what code is allowed to do, allowing you to be more confident about the code you choose to download and run. In this chapter I'll show you how to take advantage of .NET evidence-based security. I'll cover the following:

- How evidence-based security works

- How .NET security interacts with W2K/XP security

- How to control your security settings using tools such as `mscorcfg` and `caspol`

Cryptography (Chapter 13)

Cryptography is about secure communication, especially across the Internet: making sure that unauthorized users aren't able to view or tamper with your data. Microsoft has provided a rich set of classes that allow you to use cryptographic services, such as hashing, message authentication, and public-private key generation. In this chapter I'll cover both how these concepts work in principle and how to use the classes in the `System.Security.Cryptography` and related namespaces to work with cryptography facilities.

LANGUAGE-SPECIFIC TERMS

One problem with addressing an audience of programmers from different languages is that in many cases the terminology for various OOP or .NET constructs differs from language to language. And since I have to use some terminology in the book, I can't avoid some language bias here, as well as the risk that developers from other languages may not be familiar with the terms used. In this book, I'll generally adopt C# terminology, in accordance with my decision to present most code samples in C#.

Conventions

I've used a number of different styles of text and layout in this book to help differentiate between different kinds of information. This section contains examples of the styles I used and an explanation of what they mean.

Code has several fonts. If it's a word that I'm talking about in the text—for example, when discussing a for {...} loop—the word will appear in this monospaced font. If it's a block of code that can be typed as a program and run, then it will appear in bold typeface, such as this:

```
ldstr    "Hello, World!"
call     void [mscorlib]System.Console::WriteLine(string)
```

Sometimes you'll see code in a mixture of styles, like this:

```
.method static void Main() cil managed
{
    .maxstack 1
    .entrypoint

    ldstr    "Hello, World!"
    call     void [mscorlib]System.Console::WriteLine(string)
    ret
}
```

In cases such as this, the code that isn't in bold typeface is code you're already familiar with; the code in bold typeface is a new addition to the code since you last looked at it.

CHAPTER 1

■ ■ ■

Introducing Intermediate Language

Intermediate Language (IL)—which is also known as *Common Intermediate Language* (CIL) and as *Microsoft Intermediate Language* (MSIL)—lies at the core of .NET. Whatever language you use to write your source code in, it will, if it's to run under the auspices of the .NET Framework, end up as IL. So if you want to understand at an advanced level how .NET works, then knowing a bit about IL is a huge advantage. If you understand some IL, you'll be able to do the following:

- Understand better how the managed code you write works under the hood. You'll have two sources of information: you can read the documentation, or you can examine the IL code generated by your compiler—which may give you insights that aren't covered by the documentation.

- Examine the code that the compiler for your usual language (such as C++, C#, or Visual Basic [VB]) emits, which sometimes can help you in debugging or in designing code that's optimized for performance. It may also help you understand some of the finer points of how your chosen language works.

- Actually write some code directly in IL—it's probably not that often that you'll want to do this, but you may occasionally find it useful to be able to take advantage of IL features not implemented in your normal language, in much the same way that in pre-NET days people writing high-performance C or C++ code would occasionally drop to native assembly language to improve the performance of some particular function.

Obviously, if you're writing developer tools such as compilers or debuggers, understanding IL is a prerequisite!

Because of the importance of IL, I've decided to introduce the language before I do anything else in this book—which I'll do in this and the next chapter. In this chapter, I'll concentrate on the basics. You'll learn basic IL assembly syntax; how the *abstract stack machine*, on which IL is based, works; and how to code procedural flow control in IL. Finally, you'll look at IL errors and how to debug IL source code. Then in Chapter 2, I'll build on all this by showing how to code classes and structs and invoke instance methods. In that chapter I'll also cover some more advanced topics such as working with delegates and exceptions and calling into unmanaged code.

I won't go into every nuance of the language, and I won't cover some of the more advanced, and rarely used, features. This is, after all, a book about advanced .NET programming in general, not a book about IL programming. I'm not expecting you to start writing all your code in IL—for most purposes that would be a pretty silly thing to do, and the only significant result would be to multiply your development and debugging time considerably. Rather, I'm working on the basis that understanding IL will help you get the most out of the .NET Framework in your high-level language development. So, while I'll inevitably have to cover IL syntax, the emphasis in these chapters is on teaching you the basic concepts sufficiently so that you can read IL. Another motivation is that high-level managed languages do sometimes hide or give a misleading impression of how the .NET Framework implements certain tasks. C++, C#, and VB are all guilty of this to some extent. High-level languages tend to hide such implementation details in order to make things easy for you, but IL, the language that the Just-in-Time (JIT) compiler has to deal with, can hide nothing—so by learning IL, you can get the true picture of what is happening.

You'll find this chapter starts at a fairly gentle pace in terms of IL concepts. I'm not assuming you've had any experience of programming in IL (or native machine code for that matter). I do, however, assume you're experienced in your high-level language and understand object-oriented programming and the basic principles of the .NET Framework. At the end of these two chapters, you should have a good enough grasp of IL to be able to read most of the IL code generated by your compiler. In addition, this book's appendix gives a comprehensive list of the meanings of every IL instruction, along with the corresponding opcodes, which you can refer to if you encounter any IL instructions not mentioned in this chapter.

I should also remind you that you don't strictly have to read these IL chapters—most of the code samples throughout the rest of the book are in C#, so as long as you can read C# you'll be able to get through most of the rest of the book. If you really feel daunted at the prospect of reading assembly code, feel free to skip ahead to Chapter 3. But I do think that if you have a sound grasp of the principles of IL, then your advanced .NET programming will benefit.

Introducing IL Assembly

IL itself has a binary format. Just as with native assembly language, an IL instruction is actually stored in its containing assembly as a binary number (an *opcode*), which means that it would be pretty pointless to use a text editor to read a file containing IL. However, just as with native executable code, an assembly language has been defined for IL that consists of textual mnemonic codes to represent the IL commands. This language is known as *IL assembly*—though since this is a long name, you'll often hear it conveniently, albeit not strictly accurately, referred to just as IL, or sometimes as *ILAsm* or as *IL source code*. For example, the IL instruction to add two numbers together is the opcode 0x58 (88 in decimal—in this book I follow the usual practice of prefixing hexadecimal numbers with 0x), but this instruction is represented in IL assembly by the string add. For obvious reasons, I'll use assembly rather than the native IL code in this book. In effect, I'll be teaching you IL assembly rather than straight IL. However, because of the obvious one-to-one correspondence between the IL assembly instructions and the IL instructions, this means for all practical purposes you'll be learning IL as well. In this chapter, don't worry too much about the actual format of how the opcodes are represented in assemblies—I'll deal with that issue in Chapter 4, where you'll examine assembly format in more detail. I'll mention, though, that keeping file size small was one of the main design priorities for the binary format. Hence, most opcodes occupy just 1 byte, although some more rarely used opcodes occupy 2 bytes. Quite a few of the instructions also take *arguments*—numbers occupying anything from 1 to 4 bytes that follow the instruction in the assembly and provide more information about that instruction. For example, the call instruction, which invokes a method, is followed by a *metadata token*—a number that indexes into the metadata for the module and can serve to identify the method to be invoked.

Of course, the .NET runtime can't actually execute ILAsm: .NET assemblies contain straight IL. So if you start writing ILAsm code, you'll need some way to convert it to IL. Fortunately, Microsoft has provided a command-line tool for this purpose; it's an IL assembler, which confusingly is also called `ilasm`. You run the assembler by running the file `ilasm.exe`.

■**Tip** The dual use of the name *ilasm* is unfortunate. In this book, when I use the name as shorthand for IL assembly, I'll always capitalize it as ILAsm, as opposed to `ilasm` for the assembler tool. Also, don't confuse *IL assembly* (IL source code stored in text files, usually with the extension `.il`) with the term *assembly* (the binary `.exe` or `.dll` file that contains assembled IL).

In some ways, this idea of assembling ILAsm code looks like the same process as compiling a higher-level language, but the difference is that the IL assembly process is far simpler, being little more than a substitution of the appropriate binary code for each mnemonic (although the generation of the metadata in the correct format is more complex). Not only that, but in the case of IL, a disassembler tool exists to perform the reverse process— a command-line tool called `ildasm.exe`, which converts from IL to IL assembly. You've probably already used `ildasm` to examine the metadata in assemblies that you've compiled from high-level languages. In this book, you'll be using it to generate ILAsm files.

Figure 1-1 summarizes the various languages and the tools available to convert between them. The shaded boxes show the languages, and the arrows and plain boxes indicate the tools that convert code between the languages.

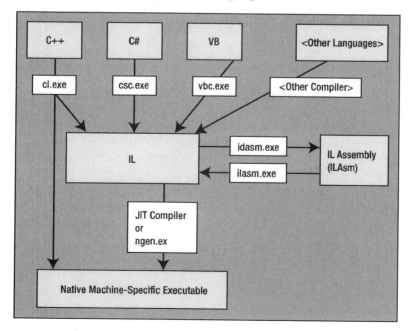

Figure 1-1. *Converting between different languages*

Creating a HelloWorld IL Program

Since the days of C programming back in the 1970s, it has been traditional that the first program you write when learning a new language displays the phrase *Hello, World* at the command line. I'm not going to break with that tradition in this book, so I'll start with a HelloWorld example—an IL program that displays *Hello, World*. Unfortunately, Visual Studio (VS) .NET doesn't offer any intrinsic support for writing programs directly in IL assembly, so you'll have to fall back on a plain-text editor, such as Notepad. Therefore, open Notepad and type the following code into it:

```
// HelloWorld.il
// This is our first IL program!
.assembly extern mscorlib {}

.assembly HelloWorld
{
    .ver 1:0:1:0
}

.module HelloWorld.exe

.method static void Main() cil managed
{
    .maxstack 1
    .entrypoint

    ldstr    "Hello, World"
    call     void [mscorlib]System.Console::WriteLine(string)
    ret
}
```

If you want to try this, you can type in this code, or you can download the code from the Apress Web site—all the samples in this book are available in the Downloads section at http://www.apress.com. If you type in this file, give it the name HelloWorld.il. Then you can compile—or perhaps *assemble* is a better term—the file into an assembly using the ilasm tool; in general you do this by typing ilasm <*FileName*> at the command prompt. In this case, this produces an assembly called HelloWorld.exe, which you can now run. The following output shows what happens when you assemble and run the program at the command prompt:

```
C:\>ilasm HelloWorld.il

Microsoft (R) .NET Framework IL Assembler.  Version 1.1.4322.573
Copyright (C) Microsoft Corporation 1998-2002. All rights reserved.
Assembling 'HelloWorld.il' , no listing file, to EXE -> 'HelloWorld.EXE'
Source file is ANSI

Assembled global method Main
Creating PE file
```

```
Emitting members:
Global  Methods: 1;
Writing PE file
Operation completed successfully
```

C:\>HelloWorld
```
Hello, World
```

If you don't supply any parameters to `ilasm`, it produces an executable assembly with the same name as the `.il` file but with the `.exe` extension. In this case you get a file called `HelloWorld.exe`, which is of course the file that gets executed when you type `HelloWorld`. If you actually need a DLL, you just specify the `/dll` flag when running `ilasm`, like so:

ilasm /dll MyLibrary.il

No command-line flag exists to specify a Windows (as opposed to a console) `.exe`. If you want to generate a Windows application, you need to indicate this in the IL code inside the `.il` file. You do this using the `.subsystem` directive and specifying the value 2 for a Windows application, like so:

```
.assembly MyAssembly
{
    .ver 1:0:1:0
}
```

```
.module MyAssembly.exe
```
.subsystem 0x00000002

Now let's look at that IL source code. As you can see, the syntax bears some similarity to C#/C++ syntax in several aspects.

- Curly braces delimit regions of code. In the `HelloWorld.il` example, curly braces mark the beginning and end of a method, but in general they can group together any instructions for readability.

- Excess whitespace is also ignored, which allows you to indent the code to make it easier for you to read.

- IL supports the `//` syntax for single-line comments. IL also supports the `/* ... */` syntax for comments that are spread over multiple lines or over just a part of a line. The assembler completely ignores any text that follows a `//` on the same line or that comes between a `/*` and the following `*/`, exactly as in C++ or C#.

On the other hand, IL terminates instructions by whitespace, not by semicolons as in C-style languages. In general you'll probably want to place statements on separate lines because it makes the code a lot easier to read.

I'll now work through the code in a bit more detail. At this stage, don't expect to understand everything about it—you'll see just enough to get a rough idea of what's happening.

The first uncommented line is the `.assembly` directive. This directive is qualified by the keyword `extern`.

```
.assembly extern mscorlib {}
```

`.assembly extern` indicates other assemblies that will be referenced by the code in this assembly. You can have as many `.assembly extern` directives as you want, but you must explicitly name all the assemblies that will be directly referenced. Strictly speaking, you don't need to declare `mscorlib`—`mscorlib.dll` is such an important assembly that `ilasm.exe` will assume you want to use it and supply the directive for you anyway, but I've included it here just to make it explicit.

Next you come to another `.assembly` directive, but this one isn't marked as `extern`.

```
.assembly HelloWorld
{
    .ver 1:0:1:0
}
```

This directive instructs the assembler to insert an assembly manifest, which means the file produced will be a complete assembly (as opposed to a module that will later be incorporated into an assembly). The name of the assembly will be the string following the `.assembly` command. The curly braces can contain other information you want to specify that should go in the assembly manifest (such as the public key or the version number of the assembly)—for now you simply supply the version using the `.ver` directive. Since this is the first time for writing this assembly, I've gone for version 1:0:1:0—major version 1, minor version 0, build 1, revision 0.

You'll notice that `.assembly` is one of a number of items in the `HelloWorld.il` file that's preceded by a dot. This dot indicates that the term is a *directive*: IL distinguishes between statements, which are actual instructions to be executed when the program is run (for example, `ldstr`, which loads a string), and directives, which supply extra information about the program. While statements map directly into IL instructions and are part of the formal definition of IL, directives are simply a convenient way of supplying information to the `ilasm.exe` assembler about the structure of the file and the metadata that should be written to the assembly. *Keywords*, such as `static` in the previous `HelloWorld` example, serve to modify a directive but don't have a preceding dot.

The next directive is `.module`; this declares a module and indicates the name of the file in which this module should be stored.

```
.module HelloWorld.exe
```

Note that you supply the file extension for a module since this is a filename, in contrast to the `.assembly` directive, which is followed by the assembly name rather than a filename. All assemblies contain at least one module; since this file will assemble to a complete assembly, strictly speaking you don't need to explicitly declare the module here—`ilasm.exe` will assume a module with the same name as the assembly if none is specified, but I've put the directive in for completeness.

The next line contains the .method directive, which you won't be surprised to learn instructs the assembler to start a new method definition.

```
.method static void Main() cil managed
```

■**Tip** What may surprise you if your .NET programming has been entirely in C# is that the method declaration doesn't come inside a class. C# requires all methods to be inside a class, but that's actually a requirement of the C# language, not a requirement of .NET. IL, just like C++, has no problem defining global methods. The Common Language Runtime (CLR) has to be able to support global methods in order to support languages such as C++ or FORTRAN.

A couple of extra keywords here provide more information about the nature of the Main() method. It's a static method and will return a void. static in IL usually has the same meaning as in C# and C++ (or the Shared keyword in VB)—it indicates that a method isn't associated with any particular object and doesn't take a this (VB .NET: Me) reference as an implicit parameter. IL syntax requires that global methods should also be marked as static, in contrast to many high-level languages, which often require only the static keyword for static methods that are defined inside a class. The method name in IL assembly is followed by brackets, which contain the details of any parameters expected by the method (but this example's Main() method has no parameters). The string cil managed following the method signature indicates that this method will contain IL code. This is important because .NET also supports methods that contain native executable code instead of IL code.

Once you get into the method definition, you'll see two more assembler directives before you come to any actual instructions. The .entrypoint directive tells the assembler that this method is the entry point to the program—the method at which execution starts. ilasm.exe will flag an error if it can't find a method marked as the entry point (unless of course you've used the /dll flag to indicate you're assembling to a DLL). You don't worry about the .maxstack directive for now.

Now let's move onto the code.

```
ldstr    "Hello, World"
call     void [mscorlib]System.Console::WriteLine(string)
ret
```

It shouldn't be too hard to guess what's going on here. The code starts by loading the string "Hello, World". (You'll examine exactly what I mean by *loading the string* soon; for now I'll say that this causes a reference to the string to be placed in a special area of memory known as the *evaluation stack*.) Then you call the Console.WriteLine() method, which you'll be familiar with from high-level programming. Finally, the ret command exits the Main() method and hence (since this is the .entrypoint method) the program altogether.

The previous IL assembly code has the same effect as this C# code:

```
Console.WriteLine("Hello, World");
return;
```

However, the syntax for calling the method is a bit different in IL. In C#, as in most high-level languages, you specify the name of the method, followed by the names of the variables to be passed to the method. In IL, by contrast, you simply supply the complete signature of the method—including the full name, parameter list, and return type of the method. What's actually passed as the parameters to the method at runtime will be whatever data is sitting on top of the evaluation stack, which is why you loaded the string onto the stack before calling the method.

The HelloWorld program should have given you a small flavor of the way IL works. You'll now leave HelloWorld behind and examine the principles behind how IL works in more detail—in particular how the evaluation stack works.

Understanding IL Principles

IL is based on the concept of a virtual machine. In other words, the language is based on a conceptual, fictional machine architecture. This architecture in fact bears little resemblance to the physical processors that your programs run on, but it has been designed in a way as to support type-safe programming while also allowing highly efficient JIT compilation to machine code. Because this virtual machine is important to the basic structure of an IL program, you need to examine it first.

The IL Virtual Machine

When you're coding in a high-level language, you'll be aware that certain types of memory are available to use. For example, when writing unmanaged C or C++ code, you can allocate variables on the stack or on the heap. For C#, VB .NET, or MC++ code, value types are allocated on the stack (or inline inside objects on the heap), and reference types are placed on the managed heap (and in the case of MC++ you can additionally place unmanaged instances on the unmanaged heap). Not only that, but most high-level languages make the distinction between local variables, instance fields, static (shared) fields, global variables, and data that has been passed in as an argument to a method.

Although you'll be accustomed to thinking of all these types of data in different ways, in terms of the underlying Windows operating system and the hardware, these forms of data are simply different regions of the machine's virtual address space. In a sense, the high-level languages have abstracted away the actual hardware configuration, so while you're programming, you think in terms of different types of memory that in reality don't exist. This abstraction is of course convenient for developers—being able to work with concepts such as local variables and parameters without worrying that at the assembly-language level such concepts don't always exist makes for much easier programming. And the compiler for each language of course deals with translating the view of memory presented by the language into the physical hardware.

If you've ever only used high-level languages before, chances are you've naturally worked with this abstraction without even thinking about it. But it's a concept that's important to understand if you start working with IL, because the IL definition formalizes the concept into what's known as the *IL virtual machine*. Figure 1-2 summarizes what the computer looks like as far as IL is concerned—in other words, the virtual machine. The boxes in the figure show the areas of memory, and the arrows indicate the possible paths that data can flow along.

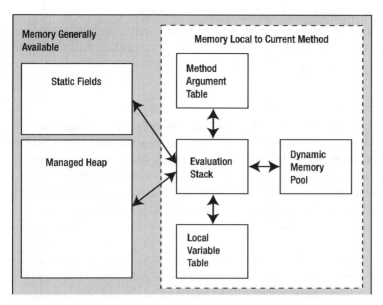

Figure 1-2. *The virtual machine seen by IL*

You can get an idea of the importance of the evaluation stack—any transfer of data always has to go through it. It's also the only place where you can perform any modifications to data.

In all, Figure 1-2 shows that several areas of memory are available to you that are local to the method currently being executed.

Local variable table: This is the area of memory in which local variables are stored. It has to be declared at the beginning of each method.

Argument table: This area of memory contains those variables that have been passed to the method as arguments. This memory area also includes the `this` reference if the current method is an instance method—the `this` object is strictly speaking passed to the method as the first argument.

Local memory pool: This is the area of memory that's available for dynamic allocation. Like the local variable and argument tables, it's visible only within the scope of the current method and is reclaimed as soon as the method exits. However, the difference between the pool and the local variable table is that the amount of memory required for the pool can be determined at runtime. By contrast, each variable in the local variable array has to be indicated explicitly in the IL code. The pool is the area of memory that will be used, for example, when a C# `stackalloc` statement is executed.

Evaluation stack: The evaluation stack is arguably the most crucial area of memory, because it's the only area in which actual computational operations can be calculated. For example, if you want to add two numbers, you must first copy them to the evaluation stack. If you want to test the value of a variable, you first have to copy it to the evaluation stack and then perform the test. Also, if you call a method, then any parameters to be passed to that method are taken from the evaluation stack. The name of the evaluation stack is no coincidence; it really works just like a stack. You push elements onto it and pop elements off it, but you can only ever access the topmost element. In other words, if an IL command pushes the integer 27 onto the stack and then another IL command pushes a reference to the string "Hello, World" onto the stack, it's not possible to access that value of 27 again until the string reference has been removed from the stack.

■Tip The evaluation stack is commonly referred to simply as the *stack* when it can't be confused with that other meaning of *stack*—the machine or processor stack—which is the whole area of memory where value types, local variables, arguments, and the stack frame are stored. I'll often use this shorthand terminology in this book, so you'll need to be aware of these two distinct meanings of the term *stack*. Usually there's little risk of confusion since the evaluation stack is an abstract concept that exists only in IL—once the assembly has been JIT compiled and is actually running, there's no such thing as an evaluation stack anymore.

Also, two areas of memory have longer lifetimes—they can be accessed from the method currently executing and will continue to be around after the method exits. These areas of memory shouldn't need any introduction, as they're the same areas of memory that high-level languages see.

- **Managed heap**: This is where reference data types and boxed value types are stored. In IL, as in most .NET high-level languages, you rarely access this memory directly but instead manipulate object references that refer to the managed heap.

- **Static fields**: The currently executing method can of course also access static member fields of any classes that are loaded. Static reference types will of course be stored on the managed heap, but the references to these objects will be stored, along with static value type instances, in a separate area of memory.

It's worth pointing out that IL does support unmanaged pointers. Since a pointer contains a numeric address, it can point to any location whatsoever in the process's virtual memory space, including the memory that holds the previous sets of data. For type-safety reasons you should generally avoid using unmanaged pointers if possible—and you'll find that you rarely need them.

It's important to understand that every time a new method is invoked, for all practical purposes that method gets a clean slate of local memory. The managed heap, and of course any memory accessed through pointers, is available throughout your code, but the areas of memory for locals, arguments, local dynamic memory, and the evaluation stack are all effectively visible only to the currently executing method.

Example: Adding Two Numbers

In this section, I'll illustrate how the IL virtual machine model works with a couple of programs that add numbers together. I'll start with a program called AddConsts.il, which embeds the numbers to be added as hard-coded constants within the code. As usual, you can either download the files from the Apress Web site or type the program yourself into a text editor.

```
// AddConsts sample
.assembly extern mscorlib {}

.assembly AddConsts
{
    .ver 1:0:1:0
}

.module AddConsts.exe

.method static void
Main() cil managed
{
    .entrypoint
    .maxstack 2
    ldstr       "The sum of the numbers is "
    call        void [mscorlib]System.Console::Write(string)
    ldc.i4.s    47
    ldc.i4      345
    add
    call        void [mscorlib]System.Console::WriteLine(int32)
    ret
}
```

■Note I realize that a program that adds two hard-coded constants together doesn't exactly look like a best-selling, state-of-the-art, killer application, but be patient. Moving from a high-level language to IL involves a lot of relearning basic programming concepts—and you need to get through a lot of concepts before you can write some useful IL code.

In this code I've just highlighted what has changed since the previous sample. The declaration of the assembly and of the Main() method are the same as the earlier HelloWorld application—other than the (trivial) change of name of the assembly.

You're now in a position to understand the purpose of that .maxstack directive: It indicates how big the evaluation stack for that method needs to be. And for the Main() method in this program, you make it size 2, like so:

```
.maxstack 2
```

This directive will cause ilasm.exe to write information into the assembly that tells the JIT compiler there will never be more than two items simultaneously on the evaluation stack for this method—having this information can in principle make JIT compilation more efficient, because it means the JIT compiler will know in advance how much memory it needs to allocate for the evaluation stack, potentially saving it one pass through the code. I say *in principle* because the JIT compiler in the CLR is relatively sophisticated, and I'm informed it completely ignores the .maxstack size (other than for verification)! However, the definition of IL requires this directive to be present in order to support basic JIT compilers, such as Rotor's FJIT. It's therefore regarded as an error if the sequence of instructions in the method can place more than the number of elements specified by .maxstack on the evaluation stack while the method is executing. The JIT compiler will detect if this can occur when it analyzes the program and if so will refuse to compile it.

■**Tip** Note that the size of the stack isn't measured in bytes or any fixed unit—it's measured by the number of variables. Hence, the .maxstack 2 directive means that only two variables can be simultaneously placed on the evaluation stack, but it doesn't place any restriction on the type or size of those variables.

Now let's work through the instructions in the Main() method to see in detail what they do.

When execution of the Main() method starts, the evaluation stack will be empty (recall that each method always starts with a clean evaluation stack). After the ldstr command has been executed, the evaluation stack will have one item on it—a reference to the string. The IL assembly syntax here is a bit misleading since it gives the impression the string itself is embedded in the code. In fact, the string is stored in the metadata for the module, and in the actual binary IL, the opcode for ldstr is followed by a 4-byte token that identifies the location of the string in the metadata. When ldstr is executed, it will cause a copy of this string to be placed in the runtime literal string pool, and it's a reference to this copy that's placed on the evaluation stack.

In the documentation, it's common practice to indicate the effect that a command has on the evaluation stack. This is usually described by a *stack-transition diagram* and occasionally also by an integer known as the *stack delta*. The stack-transition diagram shows the changes that occur to the evaluation stack when the instruction is executed, and the stack delta is the number of items by which the evaluation stack grows.

For ldstr, the stack-transition diagram looks like this:

    ... → ..., string

In the diagram, the ellipsis (...) represents any data that was on the stack before the command was executed and that isn't affected by the instruction being executed. The items to the left of the arrow indicate the state of the evaluation stack before the instruction is executed, and the items to the right of the arrow indicate its state afterward. The diagram makes it clear that ldstr doesn't remove any items from the stack but pushes one item, a string reference, onto it. Although this stack-transition diagram names the type of data being loaded (string), no hard-and-fast rules exist about how you describe the items on the stack that are affected by the instruction in the stack-transition diagrams. As you'll see in the other diagrams I present, it's more common for the text in a stack-transition diagram to indicate the meaning of the value rather than its type.

The stack delta for ldstr is 1, since one item is placed on the stack. If an instruction causes the number of items on the evaluation stack to fall, its stack delta will be negative.

The next instruction to be executed is the `call` instruction.

```
call        void [mscorlib]System.Console::Write(string)
```

This instruction indicates that you're to call a `System.Console` method. It also indicates that this method requires a string and returns a void. As mentioned earlier, parameters to the method are taken from the stack, and any return value will have been pushed onto the stack when the method returns. Since this overload of `Write()` takes one parameter, just one parameter (a string) will be removed from the stack. And since it returns nothing, no return value will be put on the stack. The stack delta for this line of code is therefore -1, and the diagram looks like this:

```
..., string → ...
```

■Tip Although the stack delta is -1 in this case, `call` has a variable stack delta since it depends on the signature of the method called. In general, the stack delta will be minus the number of parameters for a method that returns `void` and will be one minus the number of parameters for a method that returns some value.

It's important to understand that the parameters to be passed into a method are always actually popped off the evaluation stack in the caller method (and appear in the argument table of the called method). Hence, if you subsequently want to reuse any of those values in the caller method, you'll have to reload them onto the evaluation stack. This is generally true of most IL commands—the process of using a value from the evaluation stack causes it to be popped off the stack.

In this case, the evaluation stack will be empty after the execution of the `call` instruction, since no other values are on it.

The next two instructions each load a constant value onto the evaluation stack.

```
ldc.i4.s  47
ldc.i4    345
```

These instructions appear to have a different syntax, but they both do basically the same thing: They take a constant numeric value (which will be embedded inline in the IL code as an argument that immediately follows the instruction) and copy it onto the evaluation stack. You may be surprised to see dots in the mnemonic text, but don't worry about this—`ldc.i4` and `ldc.i4.s` really are simply the mnemonics for two different commands. The reason I'm using two different instructions has to do with making the assembly as small as possible; `ldc.i4.s` loads a 1-byte signed integer and so can't load a number outside the range (-128,127), which means you can't use it to load the number 345. However, `ldc.i4` loads a 4-byte signed integer, meaning that it doesn't have this restriction but takes up more bytes in the generated assembly. I'll explain more about the dotted mnemonic notation and the idea of having different variants of commands in the section "Variants of Instructions," but I'll finish going through the sample code first.

The ldc.i4.s and ldc.i4 command both have a stack delta of 1, and their effect on the stack can be represented like this:

```
... → ..., value
```

In this diagram, value represents whatever constant value was specified as the argument to the load-constant instruction.

■**Tip** You may be confused about the terms *argument* and *operand* as applied to IL instructions. Terminology in this area isn't generally consistent, even within the partition documents, which means that in the documentation you'll often need to deduce the meanings of the terms from the context. However, to provide some consistency, in this book I'll always use the term *argument* to indicate any hard-coded data (such as a token or a branch offset) that follows the opcode in the instruction stream in the assembly, and I'll use the term *operand* to indicate any value that the IL instruction reads from the evaluation stack when executing. Note that argument also has a separate meaning of argument (parameter) of a method (as opposed to an IL instruction—but it will normally be clear from the context which meaning is intended).

So, after executing both instructions, the stack will have two int32 values on it—47 and 345. And the evaluation stack is now at the maximum size indicated by the .maxstack directive.

The next instruction in the sample code adds together the two numbers you've loaded onto the stack.

```
ldc.i4.s  47
ldc.i4    345
add
```

The add instruction is the first of the arithmetic operation instructions that you'll encounter. It adds two numbers together, and, as always for IL operations, it expects to find the numbers on the stack. To be precise, it pops the top two items off the evaluation stack (these must both be of the same numeric data type), adds them together, and pushes the result onto the evaluation stack. Hence, the add command has a stack delta of -1 and is represented by the following diagram:

```
..., value, value → ..., result
```

In the example program, the only item on the evaluation stack after executing this command will be the integer 392 (which is what you get when you add 47 and 345). This item will be popped off the stack when you call Console.WriteLine(). This means that when you hit the ret statement, the evaluation stack will be empty. That's important because the definition of IL requires that the evaluation stack is empty when you return from a void method. (As mentioned earlier, if the method isn't void, then the evaluation stack should contain one item, the return value, when you return from the method.)

More About the Evaluation Stack

The idea of having to load everything onto the evaluation stack may seem a bit strange and unfriendly if you're used to dealing with high-level languages, but it's a common concept in lower-level languages and language compilers. An even more formal name for the abstract conceptual processors that languages such as IL work with exists: *abstract stack machines*. Java bytecode is another example of such a language. The real advantage of the abstract stack machine architecture is that it makes it easier to write front-end compilers that convert high-level languages into the abstract stack language. However, using the abstract stack concept does have an extra advantage in that it makes it easy to enforce type safety. Recall that one of the goals of .NET is to ensure that programs can easily be checked for type safety so that there's no risk of them doing anything bad such as overwriting memory that doesn't belong to them. Forcing all operations to go through the evaluation stack makes it relatively simple to check whether a program is verifiably type safe. The JIT compiler can easily see what data types the IL code will cause to be loaded onto the stack, so it can check that these data types are consistent with whatever you're going to do with them. Indeed, one of the basic points about type safety is that the JIT compiler can always figure out how many values are on the evaluation stack and what their data types are at any particular point in the program. I'll say more about how you verify type safety in IL code in Chapter 3.

IL Data Types

In this section I'll briefly review the data types that IL supports. One of the strengths of the .NET Framework is the way it has provided language interoperability—and a key aspect of that is its unified type system. I'd have to say, though, that one of .NET's weaknesses is its failure to provide any simple, language-independent way of describing those types that makes it easy to remember what's what. Take, for example, the simple, 32-bit, signed integer: In C# and MC++ that's an int; in VB it's an Integer. But then you have to remember that really, behind the scenes, it's just an instance of the type System.Int32. And you also need to be aware that int/Int32 is one of the Common Language Specification (CLS)–compliant types, which means it should be available from any language. That's of course unlike System.UInt32, which isn't CLS compliant, isn't recognized by VB .NET, and is known as uint in C# and unsigned int in MC++. By the way, in IL, the signed one is called int32, and the unsigned one is called unsigned int32. However, sometimes in instruction mnemonics they're referred to as .i4 and .u4. Confused yet?

So the bad news is that you have a whole new set of names to learn for types that you're probably familiar with from your high-level language programming. And it gets worse....

> The set of types that are recognized as part of IL isn't the same as the CLS types. (There's no real reason why it should be, but it would have been nice...). The CLS types are selected to offer interlanguage operability, which means they include some types that aren't primitive types. On the other hand, the IL types are the types that Microsoft decided it was sensible to define as primitive types—most likely on hardware grounds.

> Although the primitive types include integer types of various sizes from 1 byte upward, the CLR internally expects to operate only on 4-byte or 8-byte integers. IL will therefore always promote any type that occupies less than 4 bytes into a 4-byte type when loading

it onto the evaluation stack and truncate types if storing from the evaluation stack into a memory location that's declared as holding a smaller value. The promotion occurs by zero-extending unsigned types and sign-extending signed types, so values are always preserved.

The only redeeming feature of this is that if you're learning IL only so you can read IL code and you're not intending to write direct IL yourself, you can almost certainly get by without understanding the finer points of IL typing. And if you do write IL code, after a while it will become apparent that good reasons exist for all the various rules, and these rules will eventually start to make sense intuitively (even if the multiplicity of different names for the same underlying types doesn't).

You'll look at those points in more detail soon, but first Table 1-1 lists the IL types.

Table 1-1. *The IL Types*

IL Name	Corresponding .NET Base Type	Meaning	CLS Compliant?	Can Store on Evaluation Stack Without Promotion?
void	<no data>	Only used for method return types	Yes	No
bool	System.Boolean	Boolean value— true or false	Yes	No
char	System.Char	Sixteen-bit Unicode character	Yes	No
int8	System.SByte	One-byte signed integer	No	No
int16	System.Int16	Two-byte signed integer	Yes	No
int32	System.Int32	Four-byte signed integer	Yes	Yes
int64	System.Int64	Eight-byte signed integer	Yes	Yes
native int	System.IntPtr	Signed integer	Yes	Yes
unsigned int8	System.Byte	One-byte unsigned integer	Yes	No
unsigned int16	System.UInt16	Two-byte unsigned integer	No	No
unsigned int32	System.UInt32	Four-byte unsigned integer	No	Yes
unsigned int64	System.UInt64	Eight-byte unsigned integer	No	Yes
native unsigned int	System.UIntPtr	Unsigned integer	No	Yes
float32	System.Single	Four-byte floating-point value	Yes	No
float64	System.Double	Eight-byte floating-point value	Yes	No
object	System.Object	Reference to an object on the managed heap	Yes	Yes
&		Managed pointer	Yes	Yes
*	System.IntPtr	Unmanaged pointer	No	Yes

Table 1-1. *The IL Types (continued)*

IL Name	Corresponding .NET Base Type	Meaning	CLS Compliant?	Can Store on Evaluation Stack Without Promotion?
typedref	System.Typed Reference	Special type that holds some data and explicitly indicates the type of the data	No	Yes
array	System.Array	One-dimensional zero-indexed array (also known as a *vector*)	Yes	Yes
string	System.String	Reference to a System.String instance on the managed heap	Yes	Yes

The types listed in Table 1-1 are those types recognized by IL and by the CLR as primitive types. This means the names in the first column of Table 1-1 are keywords in IL assembly. For example, you can use these keywords to identify the types as parameters or return types in method signatures:

```
.method static int32 DoSomething(int16, float32, object)
```

Contrast this with the way you pass nonprimitive types to methods. Consider this C# code, which invokes the Rectangle.Intersect() method, like so:

```
// assume rect1 and rect2 are of type System.Drawing.Rectangle
rect1.Intersect(rect2);
```

The corresponding IL is this:

```
call instance void [System.Drawing]System.Drawing.Rectangle::Intersect(
                    valuetype [System.Drawing]System.Drawing.Rectangle)
```

As illustrated by this code, in IL you always explicitly fully specify the type of nonprimitive types—even to the point of explicitly indicating the referenced assembly in which a type is defined. IL simply won't understand a reference to, for example, Rectangle; it needs the fully qualified type name, including the assembly name for any type not defined in the current assembly. Notice also that when calling instance (as opposed to static) methods, you need to use the keyword instance when indicating the method signature.

Besides the difference in IL assembly syntax, details of primitive types are stored in a different format in the assembly metadata.

The second and third columns in Table 1-1 indicate the .NET base type that formally represents this type (if one exists) and the meaning of the type. Then the fourth column tells you whether this type is compliant with the CLS—the only relevance of this is that a "No" in this column means you shouldn't use this type in any position where it could be visible outside your assembly, because it could prevent other code written in some languages (such as VB!) from using your library.

The final column is more interesting: A "No" in this column indicates that, although this type is recognized in the definition of IL, it must be widened to a 4-byte type before it can be operated on. As mentioned earlier, this widening will happen automatically when instances of the type are loaded onto the evaluation stack.

A couple of other points are worth bearing in mind.

In general, signed and unsigned data types have no difference, other than how the value in them is interpreted. Although a number of unsigned types are marked as storable on the evaluation stack, in reality they're stored there in the same format as if they were signed types, but instructions are available that interpret them as unsigned. Instructions that interpret a value as signed will treat the highest value (leftmost) bit of the value as the sign bit, and instructions that interpret a value as unsigned will treat that bit as a high-value numeric bit.

The typedref type is mostly present to support languages such as VB. VB has a free style that doesn't always require the programmer to be very explicit about the types being used. The result is that sometimes the VB compiler doesn't have sufficient type information to emit IL code to invoke methods using the usual techniques—typedref is a special type designed to support this situation. However, code that uses typedrefs is still fully type safe because of late type checking (at a performance cost).

The array type isn't really so much a data type as a generic. (Whoever said that .NET doesn't have generics?) In other words, when instantiating an array, you need to indicate the type of data that each element will hold. You'll examine arrays in Chapter 2.

You'll see three pointer types: object, &, and *. The object pointer is a type in its own right, but & and * have to be qualified by the type that they point to, such as int32 & or int32 *. You'll look briefly at each of these types now.

Object References

object is a reference to an object on the managed heap. It's pretty much equivalent to object in C#, System.Object* in MC++, and Object in VB, and so on, and you use it in much the same way, for example, to call methods on reference types. For example, this C# code:

```
MyClass myClass = new MyClass();    // MyClass is reference type
myClass.DoSomething();
```

will be converted to IL code that uses object references.

Managed Pointers

& is IL notation for a managed pointer. You'll typically use it when passing values by reference to methods. In other words, when you compile this C# code:

```
int x = 30;
DoSomething (ref x);
```

then the IL code emitted will use managed pointers.

Managed pointers differ from object references to the extent that they can legally refer to data either on the managed heap or on the stack, but object will always refer to an object on the managed heap (unless it contains the value null or has somehow been corrupted by unsafe code!). Also, managed pointers are designed to point to the data in the object instance itself, but object actually points to some header information that precedes the instance data for each reference object. (You'll look at the structure of reference types in Chapter 3. Suffice to say here that each reference instance contains not only the data forming its fields but also a pointer to that type's method table—equivalent to the vtables of unmanaged C++ code—and a sync block index that's used for internal CLR purposes including thread synchronization. Value types don't have headers—each instance of a value type occupies only the memory needed for its data.)

Managed pointers have one other use—if you're calling methods on value types such as `Int32.ToString()`, you'll need to call the methods through managed pointers rather than object references.

Unmanaged Pointers

Unmanaged pointers are designed to point to literally anything, which means they will be what you'll need to use if you need to refer to some arbitrary unmanaged types by address. You'll find that you manipulate them in much the same way as managed pointers and often using the same IL commands in your IL code. The garbage collector will pay no attention to unmanaged pointers, but it will pay attention to managed pointers when deciding what objects can be garbage collected, and it will update managed pointers when it moves objects around on the heap. Also, any dereferencing of unmanaged pointers in your code will instantly make it fail the .NET type-safety checks—this isn't normally the case for managed pointers. Be aware that if you push an unmanaged pointer onto the stack, it will be regarded for typing purposes as a `native int` by IL instructions that expect a signed type and as a `native unsigned int` by IL instructions that expect an unsigned type. (However, it's tracked as a * by the verification process.)

IL Types and the Evaluation Stack

You're probably wondering why Microsoft would go to the trouble of having IL recognize all the types listed earlier but then decree that quite a few of these types have to be autoconverted to wider types before they can be used on the evaluation stack. This is because of the conflicting demands of modern hardware, which is generally based on 32-bit processing, and the needs of developers, who generally find it convenient to work with shorter types such as Booleans and characters. C++ developers, for example, will be familiar with using the C++ `bool` data type, which can store only the values `true` and `false`. However, on a modern 32-bit machine, `bool` will almost invariably be treated at an executable level as a 32-bit integer when it's loaded into registers—with the C++ compiler making sure that any nonzero value of this integer will be interpreted as `true` and zero as `false`. The .NET Framework works on the same principle. Although you're free to store short data types in memory (for example, as local variables, fields, or parameters passed to methods), this data has to get promoted to 32 bits if you want to actually do anything with it. Hence, any of the data types `bool`, `int8`, or `int16` will automatically get converted to `int32` as they're loaded onto the evaluation stack. Conversely, if an IL command needs to pop an item off the evaluation stack into some memory location that requires a short data type, it will truncate it. These conversions happen automatically and, in the ruthlessly type-safe IL language, are the only type conversions that ever happen implicitly. If you want to do an explicit conversion, you can use a large number of IL conversion commands, which all have mnemonics beginning with `conv`.

As a rule, this padding and truncating of numbers happens quietly behind the scenes and doesn't really affect your life as a developer. The only time you need to be aware of it is if truncating some integer on the evaluation stack may cause data loss. I won't deal with this situation in the book, but if you do encounter it, the relevant conv.* commands are detailed in the appendix.

I've just described the situation for integers. For floating-point numbers, similar principles hold, except that all floating-point arithmetic is done using a native representation of floating-point numbers defined in the ISO/IEC standard, IEC 60559:1989. When float32 or float64 values are stored as static or instance member fields (including as array elements), the CLR reserves the 32 or 64 bytes for them, but everywhere else (including not just the evaluation stack but also locals and arguments), floats will be stored in the native, processor-specific format. When necessary, conversions will be made automatically when IL instructions cause floats to be copied. Note that the native representation is always greater than 64 bytes, so no data loss occurs.

■**Tip** For the most part, this automatic conversion of floating-point numbers isn't a problem—few people will object to having their floating-point arithmetic done to a greater accuracy than they need (because of modern processor architecture, there's generally no performance loss). However, some mathematical algorithms specifically require intermediate results to be computed to the same accuracy as the precision to which the results are stored. This will occur only for a small minority of code, and if you haven't encountered those issues before, then you almost certainly don't need to worry about this. If these issues affect your code, you'll need to look up the IL conv.r4 and conv.r8 commands.

One other point you need to be aware of is that the format used to store floating-point numbers includes special representations for plus or minus infinity and for "not a number" (NaN—which is what you get if you try to do something such as divide zero by zero). These special values aren't Microsoft specific—they're defined in the IEEE 754 standard. They will generally behave in the normal intuitive way in comparison and arithmetic operations; for example, adding anything to NaN gives NaN as a result.

IL Instruction Variants

I said earlier that I'd give you a closer look at the way that IL has groups of similar instructions. Quite a few cases in IL exist where several different instructions have a similar effect, and this is normally reflected in the IL assembly mnemonic codes for those instructions. You can see this by using a couple of examples. First you'll see a relatively simple example—the add instruction. add has three variants, as shown in Table 1-2.

Table 1-2. *Variants of* add

Mnemonic	Opcode and Argument(s)	Purpose
add	0x58	Adds the top two items on the stack
add.ovf	0xd6	
add.ovf.un	0xd7	

I'm not really concerned about opcodes in this chapter, but I've included them in Table 1-2 to emphasize that these really are different instructions. It just happens that because their meanings are similar, they've all been given mnemonics that begin with add. The difference between them is that add does plain addition. It's the one to use for performance, but you should bear in mind that it will take no action if an overflow occurs—your program will just carry on working with the wrong results from the addition. add.ovf does the same as add, but it will detect if an overflow has occurred and throw a System.OverflowException. Obviously, this automatic overflow detection carries a performance hit. Addition operations in languages such as C# and MC++ will normally by default compile to IL code that contains add, but VB normally generates add.ovf. The mnemonic add.ovf.un is similar to add.ovf, but it assumes the numbers are unsigned.

Where groups of instructions perform similar tasks, I'll often refer to them as *instruction families* and use a generic .* suffix for the mnemonic. Thus, I'll write add.* to denote any of the instructions add, add.ovf, and add.ovf.un.

Similar instructions perform the other main arithmetic operations—mul.* and sub.*, as well as rem.* to take the remainder. On the other hand, div, the division instruction, has no .ovf version. You'll find full details of these and similar bitwise operations in the appendix.

So far, so good. Now let's look at the ldc.* family of instructions, for which the situation is a bit more complex. The ldc.* instructions all push a constant value onto the evaluation stack. So far you've met two such instructions: ldc.i4 and ldc.i4.s. Amazingly no fewer than 15 instructions push a constant numeric value onto the stack. Table 1-3 shows the full list.

Table 1-3. *Variants of* ldc

Mnemonic	Opcode and Argument(s)	Purpose
ldc.i4.0	0x16	Pushes the value 0 onto the stack
ldc.i4.1	0x17	Pushes the value 1 onto the stack
ldc.i4.2	0x18	Pushes the value 2 onto the stack
ldc.i4.3	0x19	Pushes the value 3 onto the stack
ldc.i4.4	0x1a	Pushes the value 4 onto the stack
ldc.i4.5	0x1b	Pushes the value 5 onto the stack
ldc.i4.6	0x1c	Pushes the value 6 onto the stack
ldc.i4.7	0x1d	Pushes the value 7 onto the stack
ldc.i4.8	0x1e	Pushes the value 8 onto the stack
ldc.i4.m1 or ldc.i4.M1	0x15	Pushes the value -1 onto the stack
ldc.i4.s ldc.i4 ldc.i8 ldc.r4 ldc.r8	0x1f <int8> 0x20 <int32> 0x21 <int64> 0x22 <float32> 0x23 <float64>	Pushes the argument onto the stack
ldnull	0x14	Push the null reference onto the stack (this is of type object)

Let's go over these instructions in detail. The first instruction, ldc.i4.0 (opcode 0x16), pushes zero onto the stack. Because this instruction is so specific, it doesn't need an argument. If the JIT compiler encounters the opcode 0x16, it knows you want the value zero pushed onto the stack. The numbers up to 8 and -1 have similar instructions. (The opcode 0x15 has two mnemonics, ldc.i4.m1 and ldc.i4.M1; this simply means ilasm.exe will recognize either mnemonic and convert it to the opcode 0x15.) The implication of all this is that if you want to push an integer between -1 and 8 onto the stack, you can get away with a command that occupies just 1 byte in the assembly. If the constant you need to push onto the stack is larger in magnitude but can still be represented in 1 byte, you can use the ldc.i4.s command—opcode 0x1f. If the JIT compiler encounters the opcode 0x1f, it knows that the following byte contains the number to be loaded. On the other hand, if your number is larger still but can be represented as a 4-byte integer (int32), you can use ldc.i4—and the instruction will occupy a total of 5 bytes in the assembly. Finally, as far as ints are concerned, ldc.i8 occupies 9 bytes but can put an int64 onto the stack. ldc.r4 and ldc.r8 will do the same thing, but their arguments are interpreted as floating-point numbers. This has two consequences: First, they will be converted to a native-size floating-point format as they're passed to the stack. Second, and more important, the JIT compiler knows that the top slot on the evaluation stack contains a float—which is important for type checking.

So why do we have all these instructions? Is it really worth having ldc.i4.0 and ldc.i4.1, and so on, when ldc.i8 will serve the same purpose? The answer comes in the ".NET" part of the Microsoft .NET marketing publicity. Remember, one of the motivations of the .NET Framework is to make it easy for us to do network-based programming—and in particular this means the framework contains a lot of support for deploying applications remotely and for downloading code or updated versions of assemblies on demand. For such code, the download time—and hence the assembly size—is an important contributor to the performance of the code. And if the most commonly used IL instructions have compact versions, then those bytes saved in the assembly can all add up and make a real difference.

In general, the suffixes that are put on the mnemonic have a fairly regular pattern, so you can easily tell what a variant of an instruction is for, as listed in Table 1-4.

Table 1-4. *IL Mnemonic Suffixes*

Suffix	Meaning
.ovf	This instruction detects overflows and throws an exception if one occurs.
.un	This instruction interprets its data as unsigned.
.s	This is a short version of the instruction. Its argument occupies fewer bytes than normal, which restricts its range but saves assembly file size.

Also, some suffixes indicate the data type that a particular variant of the instruction interprets its data to be. Unfortunately, these suffixes aren't the same as the IL assembly keywords for the primitive data types. Table 1-5 shows the suffixes.

Table 1-5. *IL Mnemonic Suffixes That Represent Data Types*

Suffix	Data Type
.i1	int8
.i2	int16
.i4	int32
.i8	int64
.u1	unsigned int8
.u2	unsigned int16
.u4	unsigned int32
.u8	unsigned int64
.ref	object
.r4	float32
.r8	float64

Note that not all primitive types have corresponding suffixes. You have no need, for example, to have a suffix representing a typedref, because no instructions have a special form for taking typedref arguments.

Programming IL

In the following sections, you examine how you can perform various tasks using IL (yes—you can finally get down to doing some programming!).

Defining Types and Namespaces

The samples I've presented so far contain just one global method, Main(). Of course, as we all know, .NET is supposed to be about object-oriented programming (OOP), and one of the principles of OOP is that global functions aren't really that desirable. If you code in C#, you have to put the Main() method inside a class, and if you code in any language, it's considered good .NET practice to define a namespace for your data types. So you'll now modify the HelloWorld program so that the entry point method is a static method of a class. This new sample is called HelloWorldClass. You'll call the class EntryPoint, and you'll put this class in a namespace, Apress.ExpertDotNet.ILChapter. I've also decided, just for this sample, to call the entry point method DisplayHelloWorld() rather than Main(), just to emphasize that nothing is significant in the name Main()—it's the .entrypoint directive that indicates the startup method. Here's the new file:

```
// This is a HelloWorld app with a class!
.assembly extern mscorlib {}
.assembly HelloWorldClass
{
    .ver 1:0:1:0
}
```

```
.module HelloWorldClass.exe

.namespace Apress.ExpertDotNet.ILChapter.HelloWorldClass
{
    .class public auto ansi EntryPoint extends [mscorlib]System.Object
    {
        .method public static void DisplayHelloWorld() cil managed
        {
            .maxstack 1
            .entrypoint
            ldstr    "Hello, World"
            call     void [mscorlib]System.Console::WriteLine(string)
            ret
        }
    }
}
```

The HelloWorldClass program is almost identical to HelloWorld—I've just highlighted the differences.

The HelloWorldClass code shows that the syntax for declaring classes and namespaces is almost identical to that for high-level languages. In IL you use the .namespace and .class directives. You use the extends keyword to indicate a base class. Notice that the base class must be specified fully, including the name of the assembly in which it's contained. As you saw earlier when invoking the Console.WriteLine() method, IL has no equivalent to C#'s using statement or VB's Import statement. All names, including namespace names, must always be given in full.

I've applied a couple of other flags to the EntryPoint class in this code.

public has the same meaning as in C++ and C#, and as Public in VB, and I've applied it to both the class and the DisplayHelloWorld() method. It indicates that this type is visible outside the assembly in which it's defined (as opposed to private types that are visible only within that assembly).

auto specifies the way that the class will be laid out in memory. You have three options here. auto allows the loader to lay the class out in whatever manner it sees fit—which normally means the class will be laid out to minimize its size while remaining consistent with hardware byte alignment requirements. sequential will cause the fields to be laid one after the other in memory (this is how unmanaged C++ classes are laid out). explicit indicates that the relative offset of each field is explicitly specified. These options are equivalent to applying the StructLayout attribute in high-level source code.

ansi indicates how strings will be converted to native unmanaged strings if this is required by any P/Invoke calls associated with this class. ansi specifies that strings will be converted to ANSI strings. Other options are unicode (strings will be left in Unicode format) and autochar (the conversion will be determined by the platform on which the code is running).

Since auto and ansi are the default specifiers for classes, the explicit inclusion of them here doesn't actually have any effect—I could have omitted them, but I wanted to be explicit about what was going on in the code and what options IL gives you. Similarly, marking the EntryPoint class as public won't really change anything, since you aren't intending to invoke methods in this assembly from any other assembly.

Just as for most high-level languages, the IL assembler will assume [mscorlib]System.Object is the base class if you don't specify it explicitly. In place of the previous code, you could have written the following for the class definition:

```
.class public ansi auto EntryPoint
{
```

If you want to define a value type instead of a class, you must declare [mscorlib]System.ValueType as the base class. In this case, you should also explicitly mark the class as sealed—since the .NET Framework requires value types to be sealed.

```
.class public ansi auto sealed EntryPoint extends [mscorlib]System.ValueType
{
```

So far you've seen how to define classes that contain static methods. And, using Console.WriteLine() as an example, you've seen how to invoke static methods. That's actually all you'll be seeing of classes in this chapter. Dealing with instance methods is more complex, since that involves actually instantiating an object and passing an object reference to the method, so I'll leave that for the next chapter. Also, to keep the code displayed simple, for the remainder of this chapter I'll often not show the class and namespace that contains the Main() method, although it's present in the code downloads.

Member Accessibility Flags

You've seen that types can be public or private. Members of types (fields, methods, and so on) of course have a much greater range of accessibilities. The accessibilities allowed in IL are broadly the same as those in high-level languages; however, the names may be different, and IL has a couple of additional accessibilities that aren't available in languages such as C# and VB.

Table 1-6 lists the various flags available in IL.

Table 1-6. *IL Member Accessibility Flags*

Accessibility	Visible To	C# Equivalent	VB Equivalent
public	All other code	public	Public
private	Code within the same class only	private	Private
family	Code in this class and derived classes	protected	Protected
assembly	Code in the same assembly	internal	Friend
familyandassem	Code in derived classes in this assembly		
familyorassem	Code in derived classes and any code in the same assembly	protected internal	Protected Friend
privatescope	Same as private, but privatescope items can have the same name and signature		

As noted in Table 1-6, the `privatescope` accessibility is similar to `private` but allows two methods to have the same signature or two fields to have the same name. You may wonder how this can work—it works within a single module because methods are always referred to in the actual PE file (the file that stores the final assembly) by an integer token, not by their signatures (recall that the text-based name is just an artifact of the IL source code or of the high-level language). `privatescope` is really intended for internal use by compilers; I don't recommend you ever use it when coding directly in IL.

You can also apply the previous accessibilities to types that are defined inside other types, if you prefix the accessibility with `nested`, like so:

```
// Public class containing nested inner class, inner class only
// visible in this assembly
.class public OuterClass
{
    .class nested family InnerClass
    {
        // etc.
```

Conditional Statements and Branches

IL offers a number of commands to perform branching. These commands are equivalent to `if`, `else if`, and similar commands in higher-level languages.

Unconditional Branches

The simplest branching command is `br`, which performs an unconditional branch to a labeled statement. You can also use the shortened form `br.s`.

```
br    GoHere    // or you can use br.s    GoHere
//
// Any other code here will be skipped after the br command
//
GoHere:
// The statement here will be the first one executed after the br command
```

The syntax for labeling statements is similar to that in many high-level languages: You can label any statement by preceding it with some string (the *label*) followed by a colon. The colon isn't included in references to the label.

This IL assembly syntax to some extent hides the way branching works in actual IL. The labels are present only in IL assembly and aren't propagated to the binary assembly. IL itself has no concept of a statement label. In the assembly itself, branching commands are actually followed by a signed integer that indicates the relative offset—how many bytes in the `.exe` or `.dll` file by which the execution flow should jump. This number will be positive if you're branching to a point further on in the method or negative if you're branching to a command further back near the beginning of the method. An offset of zero will cause execution to immediately follow the statement following the branch command, as if the branch command wasn't there.

However, working out the value of the offset is something that the ilasm assembler handles, so you don't need to worry about it. (If you prefer, you can indicate the numerical offset in the IL assembly code instead of supplying a label, but because of the difficulties of trying to work out manually what the offset is, that approach isn't recommended.)

■**Tip** The br statement and other branch statements I present here can be used only to branch within a method. You can't transfer control to a different method (which makes sense, since that would cause problems about what to do with the contents of the evaluation stack, which is supposedly local to each method, as well as what to do about method arguments).

The br command allows for an offset between minus 0x80000000 bytes and plus 0x7fffffff bytes. If you know that the target of the branch is within -128 or +127 bytes of the branch statement, you can take advantage of the br.s statement, a shortened form of br, which takes an int8 instead of an int32 as its offset. Obviously, you should use br.s in your IL assembly code only if you're fairly sure the offset is less than 128 bytes. If you do use br.s, and ilasm.exe computes the offset to be too large, it will refuse to assemble the file.

The br command has no effect on the stack contents, so it has a stack delta of 0, as follows:

$$\ldots \;\rightarrow\; \ldots$$

Conditional Branches

IL offers a number of instructions that perform conditional branching, dependent on the contents of the top elements of the evaluation stack. I'll illustrate how these commands work by showing how to use the ble command, which compares two numbers on the stack and transfers execution if the first number is less than or equal to the second. The following code snippet loads two integers onto the stack and then branches if the first is less than or equal to the second. Since the first number in this sample, -21, is less than the second number, +10, the condition is satisfied, and the control flow will branch. After the ble command is executed, the next statement to be executed will be whatever statement follows the FirstSmaller label.

```
ldc.i4    -21
ldc.i4    10
ble       FirstSmaller

// Intervening code. Any code here will not be executed after processing the
// ble command

FirstSmaller:
// More code
```

You may have guessed by now that in the process of taking the comparison, the `ble` command will pop the top two elements off the stack, so it has a stack delta of -2, as follows:

```
..., value, value → ...
```

To use this command, you need to understand what's meant by *first item* and *second item*. The first item is the one that was pushed onto the stack first, and the second item is the one that was pushed onto the stack second. If you think about how the stack works, you'll see that this means the second item is the one that's at the top of the stack.

This is a general rule that applies to all IL commands that take more than one operand from the evaluation stack: The last operand will be the one right at the top of the stack—the one that can get popped off first. The same principle also applies for methods that take multiple parameters. The parameters are supplied by taking the final one from the top of the stack and working back to the first parameter. This means that if you're calling a method that takes multiple parameters, you must load the numbers onto the stack in the same order as the order of the parameters.

Besides the `ble` command, IL offers conditional branches based on all the usual arithmetic comparisons.

In all cases you can also use an abbreviated command that's written by appending `.s` to the mnemonic for the usual form of the statement: `ble.s`. Just as with `br.s`, the shortened form restricts the offset to being within -128 or +127 bytes of the branch. Not only that, but all the comparative branch commands have unsigned versions. *Unsigned* refers to the operands you're comparing, not the relative offset. In the previous example, the `ble` code snippet would branch; the following code, on the other hand, which uses the unsigned version of `ble`, will not branch because it will treat the two values as if they were unsigned numbers. This means it will treat the sign bit as if it was the most significant bit and will therefore conclude the first number is greater.

```
ldc.i4   -21
ldc.i4   10
ble.un   FirstSmaller

// Intervening code. This code will be executed since ble.un will not
// branch here.

FirstSmaller:
// More code
```

Unsigned comparison of signed numbers will always yield the (incorrect) result that a negative number is bigger than a positive number. So don't do unsigned comparison unless you know you're manipulating unsigned types!

Table 1-7 lists the conditional branches based on comparing two numbers.

Table 1-7. *Binary Conditional Branch Instructions*

Commands	Program Flow Will Branch If...
beq, beq.s, beq.un, beq.un.s	First operand == second operand
bne, bne.s, bne.un, bne.un.s	First operand != second operand
bge, bge.s, bge.un, bge.un.s	First operand >= second operand
bgt, bgt.s, bgt.un, bgt.un.s	First operand > second operand
ble, ble.s, ble.un, ble.un.s	First operand <= second operand
blt, blt.s, blt.un, blt.un.s	First operand < second operand

Also, a couple of branch instructions exist based on an examination of just the top element of the evaluation stack. These will branch according to whether the top element is 0, as shown in Table 1-8.

Table 1-8. *Unary Conditional Branch Instructions*

Commands	Program Flow Will Branch If...
brfalse, brfalse.s	The top item on evaluation stack is zero.
brtrue, brtrue.s	The top item on evaluation stack isn't zero.

I'll illustrate the use of the branch statements by writing another program, which I'll call CompareNumbers. This program will invite the user to input two numbers and will inform the user which number is greater. This code will not only illustrate branching, but it will also show how you can use the evaluation stack efficiently. To make this code simpler, it contains the absolute minimum in terms of assembly and module directives that you can use. Here's the code:

```
.assembly CompareNumbers {}
.method static void Main() cil managed
{
    .maxstack 2
    .entrypoint

    ldstr   "Input first number."
    call    void [mscorlib]System.Console::WriteLine(string)
    call    string [mscorlib]System.Console::ReadLine()
    call    int32 [mscorlib]System.Int32::Parse(string)
    ldstr   "Input second number."
    call    void [mscorlib]System.Console::WriteLine(string)
    call    string [mscorlib]System.Console::ReadLine()
    call    int32 [mscorlib]System.Int32::Parse(string)
    ble.s   FirstSmaller
    ldstr   "The first number was larger than the second one"
    call    void [mscorlib]System.Console::WriteLine(string)
    br.s    Finish
```

```
FirstSmaller:
    ldstr   "The first number was less than or equal to the second one"
    call    void [mscorlib]System.Console::WriteLine(string)

Finish:
    ldstr   "Thank you!"
    call    void [mscorlib]System.Console::WriteLine(string)
    ret
}
```

It's quite instructive to work out what's happening to the evaluation stack as this program executes. Let's suppose that the user enters -21 for the first number and 10 for the second number. The program first loads a reference to the string Input first number to the stack and writes this string to the console. Calling Console.WriteLine() removes the string reference from the stack, which will now be empty. Then you call Console.ReadLine(). Since this method returns a string reference, the evaluation stack will now have a reference to a string on it. Calling Int32.Parse() to convert the string to an integer will pop the string reference from the stack and push the integer result onto the stack (the return value from this method call). Then you go through the process again for the second number, but in this case, the first number—the -21—will sit unaffected on the stack while you input and parse the second string. When you come to the ble.s command, the stack will contain just the two numbers, -21 and 10. Since -21, the first number, is smaller, the branch will occur. Table 1-9 shows the contents of the stack as each statement is executed (note that for clarity I've abbreviated most statements in this table into a form that isn't syntactically correct IL).

Table 1-9. *Stack Contents*

Statement	Stack Contents After Executing Statement
ldstr "Input first number."	Ref to "Input first number."
call Console.WriteLine()	<Empty>
call Console.ReadLine()	"-21"
call Int32.Parse(string)	-21
ldstr "Input second number."	-21, Ref to "Input second number."
call Console.WriteLine()	-21
call Console.ReadLine()	-21, "10"
call Int32.Parse(string)	-21, 10
ble.s FirstSmaller	<Empty>
... Branch happens	
FirstSmaller:	
ldstr "The first number was less than or equal to the second one"	Ref to "The first number was less than or equal to the second one"
call Console.WriteLine()	<Empty>
Finish:	
ldstr "Thank you!"	Ref to "Thank you!"
call Console.WriteLine()	<Empty>
ret	

the CompareNumbers sample I've neatly arranged the code so that the
lly stored on the evaluation stack in the correct order, so you haven't
se any local variables to store any intermediate results. (This is just as
n't covered declaring local variables in IL yet!) This sample is actually
of how small and efficient you can make your IL if you code it by
s worth writing the same program in your favorite high-level language,
ildasm to examine the IL code produced. You'll almost certainly find
ger—when I tried it in C# I found several intermediate results being
s. Whether this would lead to significantly higher performance after JIT
mple case as this small sample is doubtful since the JIT compiler itself
timizations, but it does illustrate the potential for optimizing by

---

mparison, be sure to do a release build—debug builds place a lot of extra code in
nded solely for debugging purposes. You should also use a debugger such as
T because VS .NET may turn off optimizations. I'll show you how to examine opti-
pter 3.

Defining Methods with Arguments

So far, all the samples have contained only one method, the main entry point to the program,
and this method hasn't taken any parameters. Although you've seen examples of calling a
method that takes one parameter, you haven't seen how to define such a method or access its
arguments from within the method body. That's the subject of this section.

You're going to create a new sample, CompareNumbers2, by modifying the CompareNumbers
sample so that the processing of figuring out which number is larger is carried out in a separate method, which will be invoked by the Main() method. For this purpose you'll define a new
class, MathUtils, which will contain one static method, FirstIsGreater(). This method takes
two integers and returns a bool that will be true if the first parameter is greater than the
second. Here's what the class definition and method body look like:

```
.namespace Apress.ExpertDotNet.CompareNumbers2
{
    .class MathUtils extends [mscorlib]System.Object
    {
        .method public static bool
        FirstIsGreater(int32 x, int32 y) cil managed
        {
            .maxstack 2
            ldarg.0
            ldarg.1
            ble.s       FirstSmaller
                ldc.i4.1
                ret
```

```
FirstSmaller:
            ldc.i4.0
            ret
        }
    }
}
```

The actual definition of the method shouldn't contain any surprises in syntax: I simply listed the parameter types in the brackets after the method name. Hence, as far as at this method is concerned, the first argument is simply argument 0, and the second is argument 1. Also, be aware that these arguments are passed by value—the same as the default behavior in C#, C++, and VB .NET.

Within the method you indicate the maximum size of the evaluation stack as usual, and you use a couple of new commands, ldarg.0 and ldarg.1, to load the two arguments onto the stack, like so:

```
ldarg.0
ldarg.1
```

This is where the first surprise occurs. The arguments aren't referred to by name but only by index, with the first argument being argument 0. The ldarg.0 command copies the value of the first argument onto the evaluation stack, and ldarg.1 does the same thing for the second argument. Having done that, you're back to roughly the same program logic as in the previous sample: You check to see which value is greater and branch accordingly. In this case you want to return true if the first argument is greater than the second. To do this, you simply place any nonzero value onto the stack and return the following:

```
ldc.i4.1
ret
```

Since the FirstIsGreater() method returns a value, the definition of IL requires that this value should be the only item on the stack when the method returns—as is the case here. If you need to return false, then you simply place zero onto the evaluation stack and return the following:

```
FirstSmaller:
            ldc.i4.0
            ret
```

The bool return value is of course stored as an int32 on the evaluation stack. You use the usual convention that zero is false, and a nonzero value (normally 1) is true.

Now let's examine the code you use to invoke this method:

```
.method static void Main() cil managed
{
    .maxstack 2
    .entrypoint
    ldstr    "Input first number."
    call     void [mscorlib]System.Console::WriteLine(string)
    call     string [mscorlib]System.Console::ReadLine()
```

```
        call    int32 [mscorlib]System.Int32::Parse(string)
        ldstr   "Input second number."
        call    void [mscorlib]System.Console::WriteLine(string)
        call    string [mscorlib]System.Console::ReadLine()
        call    int32 [mscorlib]System.Int32::Parse(string)
        call    bool Apress.ExpertDotNet.CompareNumbers2.
                        MathUtils::FirstIsGreater(int32, int32)
        brfalse.s FirstSmaller
          ldstr   "The first number was larger than the second one"
          call    void [mscorlib]System.Console::WriteLine(string)
          br.s    Finish

FirstSmaller:
          ldstr   "The first number was less than or equal to the " +
                  "second one"
          call    void [mscorlib]System.Console::WriteLine(string)

Finish:
        ldstr   "Thank you!"
        call    void [mscorlib]System.Console::WriteLine(string)
        ret
    }
```

This code is pretty similar to the Main() method in the previous CompareNumbers sample, so I've highlighted only the differences. After the user has typed in his chosen numbers, you call the FirstIsGreater() method. Notice how I've left the two numbers on the evaluation stack in the correct order to be passed to the method. Then you use the brfalse.s command to separate the execution paths according to whether the method returned true or false in order to display an appropriate message.

More About Method Arguments

Let's look at those method arguments and also at the ldarg.* commands in more detail. The first observation to make is that, since you never actually used the names of the arguments in the method body of the FirstIsGreater() method, there wasn't strictly speaking any need to supply names. The sample would have compiled and worked just as well if you had declared the method like this:

```
.method public static bool FirstIsGreater(int32, int32) cil managed
{
```

Indeed, if the method had been declared as private, privatescope, assembly, or familyandassem, it could have been advantageous to declare it like this (at least in a release build), on the basis that the less information you supply in the assembly, the harder it is for someone else to reverse-engineer your code. The lack of names also knocks a few bytes off the assembly size. However, for methods that are declared public, you really want the names of the parameters there in order to provide documentation for other people who may want to use your code (actually, this argument is really relevant more for a library than an executable assembly, but you get the idea anyway).

Tip A good tip if you want your IL source code files to be easy to maintain without giving away variable names to users of your assembly is to add comments in your IL source code that give the names of variables. Since ilasm.exe will ignore the text of the comments, the information in them will not be propagated to the assemblies that you ship.

The ldarg.* family of commands includes several instructions, based on the usual principle of having the smallest commands for the most frequently used scenarios. Four commands—ldarg.0, ldarg.1, ldarg.2, and ldarg.3—are available to load the first four arguments onto the stack. For arguments beyond that, you can use ldarg.s, which takes one unsigned int8 argument specifying the parameter index and hence can load method parameters with an index up to 255. For example, to load parameter 4 (the fifth parameter since the index is zero based) of a method onto the stack, you could do this:

```
ldarg.s    4
```

If you have more than 255 parameters, ldarg is for you—this command takes an int32 as an argument, which gives you—shall I say—a lot of parameters. But if you do write a method where you actually have so many parameters that you need to use the ldarg command, please don't ask me to debug it for you!

Incidentally, if you do name your parameters, ilasm.exe gives you the option to specify the parameter name with the ldarg.s and ldarg commands, like so:

```
.method public static bool
FirstIsGreater(int32 x, int32 y) cil managed
{
    .maxstack 2
    ldarg.s    x
    ldarg.s    y
```

ilasm.exe will automatically convert the names into the parameter indexes when it emits the assembly. This may make your code easier to read but will obviously (at least for the first four parameters) increase the size of the assembly, since ldarg.s takes up more space than ldarg.0, and so on.

Storing to Arguments

As a quick aside, I'll mention one feature that can occasionally be useful. Besides loading a method argument onto the stack, you can also pop a value from the stack into an argument. The instructions that do this are starg.s and starg. These instructions both require an argument that gives the index of the argument whose value should be replaced. For example, to write 34 into the first argument, you'd do this:

```
ldc.s    34
starg.s  0
```

However, it's important to understand that because arguments to methods are always passed by value (and yes, I do mean *always*), the value so stored will not be passed back to the calling function. Using `starg` in this way amounts to using a slot in the argument table as a cheap way of providing an extra local variable, on the assumption that you no longer need the original value of that parameter—exactly like the following C# code (and this isn't always good programming practice anyway):

```
void DoSomething(int x)
{
    // some code
    x = 34;   // using x like a local variable
```

If you actually do want to return a value to a calling method via a parameter that's passed by reference, then you'll need to use the `stind` instruction, which you'll examine in the section "Passing by Reference."

Because `starg` isn't such a widely used instruction, no shorthand `starg` versions exist. For example, no `starg` equivalent exists that's comparable to `ldarg.0`, `ldarg.1`, and so on.

This aside brings up the obvious question, how do you declare and use genuine local variables?

Local Variables

You declare and use local variables using a directive, `.locals`, at the beginning of a method. Here's how you'd declare a void static method that takes no parameters but has two local variables, an `unsigned int32` and a `string`:

```
.method static void DoSomething() cil managed
{
    .locals init (unsigned int32, string)
    // code for method
```

Just as for parameters, you don't need to name local variables. You can do so if you want, but since local variables are *never* seen outside the method in which they're defined, you have no reason to make any names available to people who use your libraries. Therefore, for confidentiality reasons you'll probably want to leave local variables unnamed in release code—and for this reason high-level language compilers usually leave locals unnamed in release builds.

The `init` flag following the `.locals` directive will cause `ilasm.exe` to mark the method in the emitted assembly with a flag that tells the JIT compiler to initialize all local variables by zeroing them out. I suggest you always set the `init` flag. If you don't, you may gain a tiny performance benefit, but your code will become less robust and will be unverifiable. Without the initialization flag set, you'll be responsible for making sure you initialize each variable explicitly before you use it; you always have the risk that when you next modify your code you'll make a mistake and end up with code that reads an uninitialized variable. As far as verifiability is concerned, it's possible in principle for a verifier to check that all variables are set before they're used, and it's always possible this may get added in a future version of .NET. But as of version 1.*x*, the .NET runtime takes the easy way out and says that if any method is invoked that doesn't have the `init` flag set, the code isn't type safe.

Lecture about initialization aside, using a local variable happens in much the same way as for a parameter. The instructions are `ldloc.*` to load a local variable to the stack and `stloc.*` to pop the value off the stack into a local variable. The actual `ldloc.*` and `stloc.*` instructions available follow the same pattern as `ldarg`. You have a choice between `ldloc.0`, `ldloc.1`, `ldloc.2`, `ldloc.3`, `ldloc.s`, and `ldloc`. Similarly for storing, you have `stloc.0`, `stloc.1`, `stloc.2`, `stloc.3`, `stloc.s`, and `stloc`. I'm sure by now you can guess the difference between these variants. And just as for `ldarg`, I trust that as an advanced .NET developer, you'll never, ever, write a method so complex that you need to use the full `ldloc` and `stloc` commands.

As a quick example, the following code snippet copies the contents of the second local variable into the fifth local variable (for this code snippet to be verifiable, the types of these variables must match):

```
ldloc.1     // Remember that locals are indexed starting at zero
stloc.s 4
```

Loops

In high-level languages, you'll be used to using a number of quite sophisticated constructs for loops, such as `for`, `while`, and `do` statements. IL, being a low-level language, doesn't have any such constructs. Instead, you have to build up the logic of a loop from the branching statements that you've already encountered. In this section I'll present a sample that demonstrates how to do this. The sample will also have the bonus of illustrating local variables in action.

For this sample, I'll add a new method to the `MathUtilities` class, called `SumBetween()`. `SumBetween()` takes two integers as parameters and then adds all the numbers between the first parameter and the second. In other words, if you invoke `SumBetween()`, passing it 6 and 10, it will return the value 40 (because 6+7+8+9+10=40). If the first number is bigger than the second, you'll get zero back. So `SumBetween()` does the same as the following C# code:

```
int CSharpSumBetween(int lower, int higher)
{
   int total = 0;
   for (int i=lower; i<=higher; i++)
      total += i;
   return total;
}
```

■**Note** For the purposes of this sample, I'll pretend I don't know that a mathematical formula is available to compute the sum: `(higher*(higher+1)-lower*(lower-1))/2`. This formula has the advantage of performance but has the disadvantage that it can't be used in a sample to demonstrate a loop.

The following is the IL code for the method (note that, as with all the IL code in this chapter, this is code I've written by hand—it's not been generated by compiling the previous C# code):

```
.method assembly static int32
SumBetween(int32 lower, int32 higher) cil managed
{
   .maxstack 2
```

```
    .locals init (int32, int32)
    // local.0 is index, local.1 is running total

    // initialize count
    ldarg.0
    stloc.0

Loop:
    ldloc.0
    ldarg.1
    bgt Finished
    // increment running total
        ldloc.0
        ldloc.1
        add
        stloc.1

        // increment count
        ldloc.0
        ldc.i4.1
        add
        stloc.0
        br.s    Loop

Finished:
    ldloc.1
    ret
}
```

This code doesn't have any new concepts, but the manipulation I'm doing is a bit more complex than anything I've shown up to now, so I'll go over the code briefly. As usual, I start with the method signature and .maxstack declaration (two again—it's amazing how far I've gotten in this chapter without wanting to put more than two items simultaneously on the evaluation stack). I've also declared two int32s as local variables, which will, respectively, store the index and the running total (equivalent to i and total in the C# code I previously presented).

The first thing I need to do in this code is initialize the count—it needs to start off having the same value as the first, I hope lower, parameter.

```
// initialize count
ldarg.0
stloc.0
```

The next statement is labeled Loop because that's where you'll need to keep branching back to until the loop is complete. You load the count and the second parameter—what should be the upper bound for the loop—and compare them. If the count is bigger, you've finished working out the sum and can jump to the final bit of code, in which you load the value of the sum you want to return and call ret to exit the method. Otherwise, you need to go round the loop: You increment the total by adding the value of the count to it. Then you add one to the value of the count before using the `br.s` command to branch back to the comparison to test if you've completed the loop yet. And that's it! It's so simple it almost makes you wonder why we ever needed `for` loops….

The full sample, including a suitable `Main()` method to call the loop, is downloadable as the `SumBetween` sample.

Passing by Reference

In this section you're going to start playing with managed pointers. You'll investigate how you can use parameters to pass values back to calling methods—what in high-level languages you call *passing by reference*. This is going to bring in several new topics and IL instructions: you'll be manipulating managed pointers, you'll be loading addresses of variables, and you'll be using a `stind` instruction to do some indirect memory addressing.

I titled this section "Passing by Reference" with some reluctance, because, strictly speaking, there's no such thing as passing by reference. When you call a method—any method—the values of the parameters are always copied across—that's to say passed by value. In high-level languages such as C#, C++, and VB, we often talk about *passing by reference* (and despite all my denials I'll use the same terminology here, as does some of the IL documentation), but what this actually means is that you're passing the *address* of a variable by *value* into the method. In other words, the method takes a copy of the address of some data in the calling method and can dereference this address to get at and possibly modify that data. C++, C#, and VB are all guilty of using some nifty syntax to hide what's actually happening, such as the `ref` keyword in C# and the `ByRef` keyword in VB. But in IL no such hiding exists. In IL, if you want the behavior that in high-level languages is termed *passing by reference*, then you'll have to explicitly declare and use the addresses of the variables to be passed—which means using managed pointers.

Suppose you have a C# method declaration with a signature that looks like this:

```
static void DoSomething(int x, ref int y)
{
```

The equivalent IL code will look like this:

```
.method static void DoSomething(int32 x, int32 & y) cil managed
{
```

As you can see, the first parameter in the C# version, an `int` passed by value, maps smoothly onto the `int32` type—which is just IL's name for the same type. However, the second parameter, an `int` passed by reference, has turned into an `int32 &` in IL—in other words, a managed pointer to an `int32`. Recall that earlier in the chapter, when I listed the IL data types in Table 1-1, I indicated that & denoted a managed pointer.

■**Caution** C++ developers should beware: C++ uses the & syntax just like IL. But, like the C# `ref` keyword, C++ is using & as a bit of clever syntax to hide what's actually happening: & in C++ doesn't have quite the same meaning as & in IL. In IL, & really does mean you're declaring a pointer—to that extent, & in IL is closer in concept to * in C++.

That's the theory, so how do you use it? It's probably easiest for me to demonstrate the principle in action, so I'll present another sample. For this sample I'll keep with the MathUtils class name but this time add a method called Max(). This method is somewhat unusual—it takes two integer parameters, works out which is the bigger of them, and returns the index of the larger one—0 or 1 (it will return -1 if the two integers are the same). However, it also maximizes the integers. Whichever one is the smaller one will get reset to the value of the larger one. In other words, if I call Max(), passing it two variables containing 45 and 58, the first variable will get changed to 58, and I'll get 0 as the return value. Because I'm expecting Max() actually to change the value of the data I pass to it, I'll have to pass in managed pointers. Or, to use the parlance of high-level languages, I'll have to pass the integers in by reference.

■**Note** I'll admit this is a slightly odd definition for a method. It's not totally unreasonable, though—Max() is the sort of short method I may write for my own use in code as a private or assembly-visible method if I know I need to do something like what Max() does in several places in my code. So, to make the sample a bit more realistic, I've defined Max() to have assembly accessibility.

The following code actually invokes Max(). It's my Main() method, and it asks the user for two numbers, passes them to Max() to get them both maximized, and then displays the results.

```
.namespace Apress.ExpertDotNet.ILChapter.Max
{
    .class EntryPoint extends [mscorlib]System.Object
    {
        .method static void Main() cil managed
        {
            .maxstack 2
            .locals init (int32, int32)
            .entrypoint

            ldstr     "Input First number."
            call      void [mscorlib]System.Console::WriteLine(string)
            call      string [mscorlib]System.Console::ReadLine()
            call      int32 [mscorlib]System.Int32::Parse(string)
            stloc.0

            ldstr     "Input Second number."
            call      void [mscorlib]System.Console::WriteLine(string)
            call      string [mscorlib]System.Console::ReadLine()
            call      int32 [mscorlib]System.Int32::Parse(string)
            stloc.1

            ldloca.s 0
            ldloca.s 1
```

```
        call       int8 Apress.ExpertDotNet.ILChapter.Max.MathUtils::Max(
                                                   int32 &, int32 &)

        ldstr      "Index of larger number was "
        call       void [mscorlib]System.Console::Write(string)
        call       void [mscorlib]System.Console::WriteLine(int32)

        ldstr      "After maximizing numbers, the numbers are:"
        call       void [mscorlib]System.Console::WriteLine(string)
        ldloc.0
        call       void [mscorlib]System.Console::WriteLine(int32)
        ldloc.1
        call       void [mscorlib]System.Console::WriteLine(int32)
        ldstr      "Thank you!"
        call       void [mscorlib]System.Console::WriteLine(string)
        ret
    }
}
```

This code starts in a similar manner to code in previous samples that asks the user to enter two numbers. However, it has one crucial difference: In previous samples, you've been able to get away with permanently leaving the two numbers the user types in on the evaluation stack, without having to store them anywhere else. You can't do that here. Now the numbers that the user types in will have to be stored in local variables because you need to pass the addresses of these variables to the Max() method. IL gives you no way to get an address for data on the evaluation stack for the very good reason that the evaluation stack is no more than a useful IL abstraction and doesn't actually exist anymore once the code has been JIT compiled! The only way you can get addresses is actually to store these integers somewhere. Hence, the code first declares two local variables and then goes on to ask the user for the numbers. As before, you grab the first string from the user and use Int32::Parse() to convert the string to an integer. But this time you store the result in the first local variable, like so:

```
ldstr      "Input First number."
call       void [mscorlib]System.Console::WriteLine(string)
call       string [mscorlib]System.Console::ReadLine()
call       int32 [mscorlib]System.Int32::Parse(string)
stloc.0
```

Then you do the same thing for the second number, this time storing it in the second local variable.

Next comes a new instruction that you haven't encountered before, ldloca.s.

```
ldloca.s 0
ldloca.s 1
call       int8 Apress.ExpertDotNet.ILChapter.Max.MathUtils::Max(int32 &, int32 &)
```

ldloca.s is similar to ldloc.s. However, where ldloc.s pushes the value of the specified local variable onto the stack, ldloca.s instead loads the address of that variable, as a managed pointer. As you'll no doubt guess, `ldloca.s` is the short form of `ldloca`, and you can use `ldloca.s` for locals with an index less than 256.

It's important to understand how IL treats the types here. In this code, the local variable 0 is of type `int32`. The JIT compiler will see this and will therefore know that ldloca.s 0 will load a managed pointer to `int32`—`int32 &`. Hence, after executing this instruction, as far as the JIT compiler is concerned, the top item on the stack is an `int32 &`. And type safety requires this is how you treat the data. The same thing applies to the second ldloca.s statement in the previous code snippet. The JIT compiler will complain about any attempt to use the data on the stack as anything else (for example, as an `int32` instead of an `int32 &`). Fortunately, you're OK because the next command is a call to invoke `Max()`. `Max()` will be defined as expecting two `int32 &` parameters, which will be popped off the stack, at entry, with the return value left on the stack when `Max()` has exited. During its execution, the `Max()` method may or may not use the managed pointers now in its possession to modify the data in the two local variables.

The rest of the code for the `Main()` method is relatively straightforward. You simply display the return value from `Max()` along with the values of the local variables, like so:

```
call     int8 Apress.ExpertDotNet.ILChapter.Max.MathUtils::Max(int32 &,
                                                    int32 &)
ldstr    "Index of larger number was;"
call     void [mscorlib]System.Console::Write(string)
call     void [mscorlib]System.Console::WriteLine(int32)
```

The only point I will draw your attention to is the cunning way I've used the evaluation stack to avoid having to create a third local variable to hold the return value from `Max()`. You leave this value on the stack, push a string onto the stack above this value, and then pop the string off again as you display it so that the return value from `Max()` is once again at the top of the stack, ready to be passed to the `Console.WriteLine()` call.

Next you'll look at the implementation of `Max()`.

```
.class MathUtils extends [mscorlib]System.Object
{
    // Max() works out which of two numbers is greater,
    // returns the index of the greater number
    // or -1 if numbers are equal,
    // and sets lower number to equal higher one
    .method assembly static int8 Max(int32 &, int32 &) cil managed
    {
        .maxstack 2
        .locals init (int32, int32)

        // Copy argument values to locals
        ldarg.0
        ldind.i4
        stloc.0
        ldarg.1
        ldind.i4
        stloc.1
```

```
        // Now start comparing their values
        ldloc.0
        ldloc.1
        blt.s      FirstIsLess

        ldloc.0
        ldloc.1
        bgt.s      FirstIsBigger

        // Both numbers are equal
        ldc.i4.m1
        ret

FirstIsLess:
        ldarg.0
        ldloc.1
        stind.i4
        ldc.i4.1
        ret

FirstIsBigger:
        ldarg.1
        ldloc.0
        stind.i4
        ldc.i4.0
        ret
    }
```

Let's go through this code in detail. This method also defines two local variables, which I'm using to store local copies of the integers I want to maximize. The reason for taking local copies is that I'm going to have to push them onto the evaluation stack several times, and I don't want to have to go through the process of dereferencing managed pointers every time. The first thing you're going to do is dereference those managed pointers and copy the result into the local variables, like so:

```
// Copy argument values to locals
ldarg.0
ldind.i4
stloc.0
ldarg.1
ldind.i4
stloc.1
```

You use ldarg.0 to copy the first parameter onto the evaluation stack. Now recall that the first parameter passed to this method is the address, of type int32 &. So after executing this command, the stack will contain one item, of type int32 &. Next is a new instruction, ldind.i4. ldind stands for *load indirect* and takes the top item on the stack, which must be a pointer, pops that item off the stack, dereferences it, and loads the data at that address.

```
..., address → ..., value
```

So, after executing the ldind.i4 instruction, the stack will contain a copy of the first number the user typed in, which you then copy to your first local variable using stloc.0. Then you do the whole thing again for the second number.

ldind.i4 is just one of a whole family of ldind.* instructions, including ldind.i1, ldind.i2, ldind.i4, ldind.i8, ldind.r4, and ldind.r8, as well as unsigned equivalents and a couple of others—the full list is in the appendix. The difference between these instructions lies in the data type they're expecting to dereference. For example, ldind.i4 is expecting to find an int32 & (or an unmanaged pointer to int32, int32*) on the stack, dereference it, and store it in a local variable of type int32. If you had used (for example) ldind.r4, which expects a float32 &, in the code instead, the JIT compiler would refuse to compile it. This is both because the wrong pointer data type is on the stack and because local variable slot 0 would be of the wrong data type. IL may be a low-level language, but it's still exceedingly type safe.

The next instructions don't contain anything particularly new. You simply load the newly stored local variables on the stack and test first of all to see if the first one is smaller than the second and then to see if the first one is bigger than the second. You have two tests because you need to distinguish three cases: the first is bigger, the first is smaller, or both numbers are the same.

```
// Now start comparing their values
ldloc.0
ldloc.1
blt.s FirstIsLess

ldloc.0
ldloc.1
bgt.s FirstIsBigger
```

If the two numbers are equal, then both tests in the previous code will fail, and you can go straight to returning a value of -1 to the calling routine.

```
// both numbers are equal
ldc.i4.m1
ret
```

However, if one number is bigger, you need to modify the value of the smaller number in the dereferenced parameter to the method. I'll present only one of the cases since the logic is the same in both cases. This is how you do it if the first number is smaller:

```
FirstIsLess:
        ldarg.0
        ldloc.1
        stind.i4
        ldc.i4.1
        ret
```

You need to change the value of the first number and return 1, which is the index of the larger number. To change the dereferenced first parameter, you need a new instruction, `stind.i4`. `stind.i4` is similar to `ldind.i4`, except that it stores data to a given address rather than loading the data at the given address. This means it will pop two values off the stack: the data to be stored and the address at which it will be stored.

```
..., address, value  →  ...
```

You set up the evaluation stack ready for `stind` by first pushing the address onto the stack (that's obtained from `ldarg.0`) and then pushing the data onto the stack (that's the value of the second local variable). Then you call `stind.i4`, before finally pushing the return value of 1 onto the stack and returning.

Like `ldind.i4`, `stind.i4` is one of a family of `stind` instructions, each of which deals with a different data type. And once again, the full list of instructions is in the appendix.

Debugging IL

If you do start writing IL code, you'll want to debug it. And even if you've compiled code from a high-level language, you may want to step through the corresponding IL code for debugging purposes or to understand the code better. Debugging IL code isn't hard to do using VS .NET, but you need to do a bit of preparatory work to set up the required VS .NET solution. I'll illustrate how it works by using the `Max` sample from the previous section.

Debugging with VS.NET

The first thing you need to do is assemble the `Max.il` IL source code file and generate a program database file. You do this by supplying the `/debug` flag to `ilasm.exe`, like so:

```
C:\>ilasm max.il /debug
```

Besides the executable assembly, you'll also find that a program database file, `max.pdb`, has been created. A `.pdb` file contains information that links the executable code to the source code. In general, when a debugger attaches itself to a process, it looks for the presence of this file and loads it if present. It's the `.pdb` file that tells the debugger which source code instructions correspond to which executable instructions, and which variable names correspond to which addresses in memory, thus allowing you to debug by setting breakpoints and examining variables using the original source code.

Now you should launch VS .NET and select File ➡ Open Project from the menu. Navigate to the folder in which the newly compiled `max.exe` file is located, and select `max.exe` as the solution to debug—yes, VS .NET really will let you do that. It will accept `.sln` files and `.exe` files as valid solutions.

Next, open the `max.il` file as an individual file (not as a solution). You can now set breakpoints in this file in the normal way and then hit the F5 key or use the main menu to start debugging. VS .NET will recognize from the .pdb file that the max.il file is the source code for the executable it's required to run. You'll also find that when you tell VS .NET to start debugging, it will prompt you to create a new .sln solution file that describes this relationship. The next time you want to debug this IL file, you can just open this .sln file directly (although you'll still have to compile from the command line if you make changes to the .il file).

The really great thing about it is that, besides the source window, VS .NET provides the Disassembly window—this allows you to see the actual native code that's generated from the IL by the JIT compiler (see Figure 1-3).

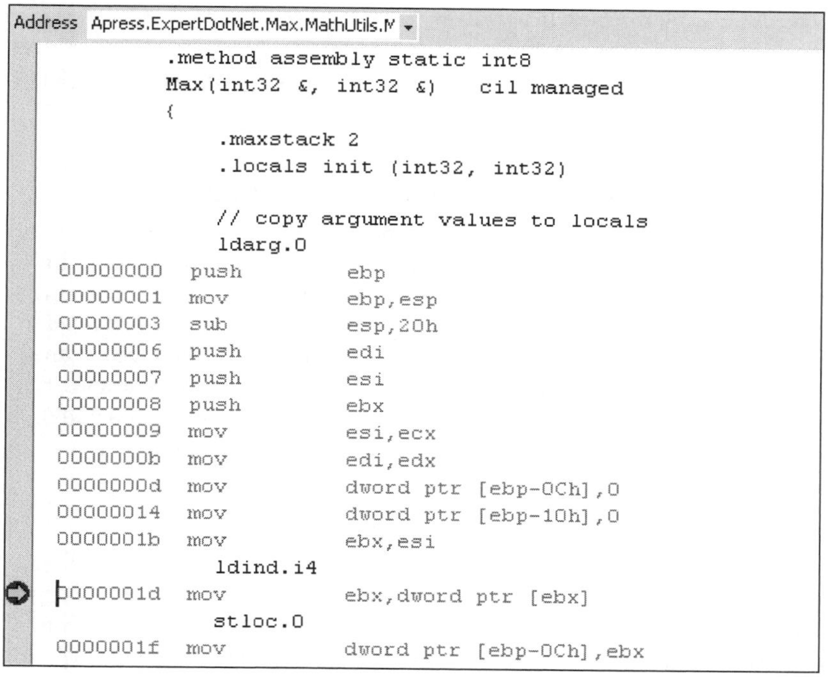

```
Address  Apress.ExpertDotNet.Max.MathUtils.M ▾

               .method assembly static int8
               Max(int32 &, int32 &)    cil managed
               {
                      .maxstack 2
                      .locals init (int32, int32)

                      // copy argument values to locals
                      ldarg.0
  00000000  push         ebp
  00000001  mov          ebp,esp
  00000003  sub          esp,20h
  00000006  push         edi
  00000007  push         esi
  00000008  push         ebx
  00000009  mov          esi,ecx
  0000000b  mov          edi,edx
  0000000d  mov          dword ptr [ebp-0Ch],0
  00000014  mov          dword ptr [ebp-10h],0
  0000001b  mov          ebx,esi
                      ldind.i4
⇨ 0000001d  mov          ebx,dword ptr [ebx]
                      stloc.0
  0000001f  mov          dword ptr [ebp-0Ch],ebx
```

Figure 1-3. *VS .NET Disassembly window*

It's also possible to use the various watch windows to track the values of variables. If variables have been named, then you can use the supplied names to examine them. However, in the Max() method of the Max sample, neither the local variables nor the arguments have been given names. In this situation, you can use the Locals window and type in the names V_0, V_1, and so on, for the local variables (V_0 = local 0, V_1 = local 1, and so on) and A_0, A_1, and so on, for the arguments. VS .NET will automatically match these pseudo-names to the appropriate variable or argument. Figure 1-4 shows the situation after the first stloc.0 command in the Max() method has been executed, with 34 and 25 input as the two numbers.

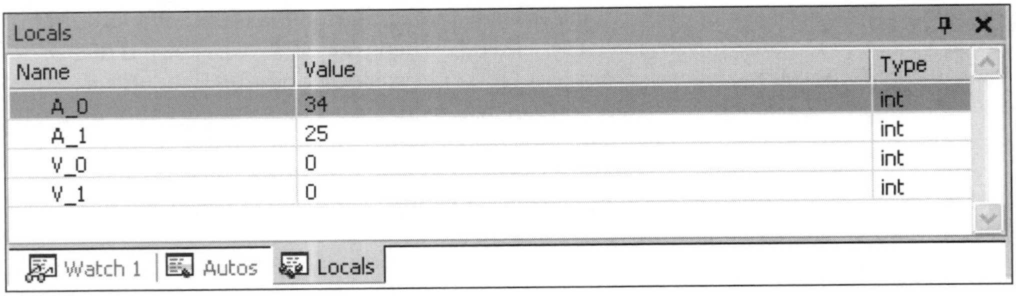

Figure 1-4. *VS .NET Locals window, tracking IL variables*

The two arguments have the correct values, and the first argument has just been stored in local variable 0.

Debugging IL Compiled from High-Level Languages

The previous technique works fine for IL that you've written yourself, but sometimes you may have written some code in a high-level language that you need to debug. Unfortunately, the Disassembly window in VS .NET for high-level language projects shows the source code and the native assembly but not the IL code—so if you want to debug at the IL level, you'll need to fool VS .NET into thinking that the IL is the source code. One way to do this is to take advantage of the ildasm.exe/ilasm.exe round-tripping facility (this will work only in C# and VB, not in C++, because round-tripping doesn't work for assemblies that contain unmanaged code). To do this, you simply compile the code as normal. Then, once you have the compiled assembly, you can disassemble it using ildasm.exe, like so:

```
ildasm MyProject.exe /out:MyProject.il
```

Applying the out flag to ildasm.exe will cause it to disassemble the IL and send the output to the named file instead of running its normal user interface. Now that you have an IL source file, you can proceed as before: use ilasm to assemble the IL source, specifying the /debug option, and then start VS .NET, specifying the executable as the solution.

Other Debuggers: CorDbg.exe

Besides VS .NET, you may want to try two other debuggers: DbgClr.exe and CorDbg.exe.

DbgClr.exe is essentially a cut-down version of the debugger that comes with VS .NET, though with a few modifications. DbgClr can be a convenient tool to use to debug IL code, but compared to VS .NET, it has fewer features. I won't consider it further here. If you do want to try it, you can find it in the FrameworkSDK\GuiDebug subfolder of your VS .NET installation folder.

CorDbg.exe is a command-line debugger designed to debug managed source code (either IL code or high-level language code). One thing that may make CorDbg.exe particularly interesting to advanced .NET developers is that it comes complete with its (unmanaged C++) source code, so if you're interested, you can find out how it works or use it as a basis for writing your own debuggers. You can find the source code in the Framework SDK\Tool Developers Guide subfolder of your VS .NET installation folder—or you can just run cordbg directly by typing cordbg at the VS .NET command prompt. As far as ease of use goes, a command-line tool is never going to match the facilities offered by VS .NET, but CorDbg.exe has one plus: You can explicitly tell it to work in optimized mode, allowing you to debug optimized JIT-compiled code. You'll use this facility in Chapter 6 to examine the optimized native assembly generated by the JIT compiler. I don't have space to go into full details of cordbg here, but I'll give you enough information to get you started.

To debug with cordbg, you need an assembly that has been compiled with the /debug option to generate a .pdb file, either from a high-level language or from IL assembly. Then you simply type cordbg <AssemblyName>.exe at the command prompt.

```
C:\>cordbg max.exe
Microsoft (R) Common Language Runtime Test Debugger Shell Version 1.1.4322.573
Copyright (C) Microsoft Corporation 1998-2002. All rights reserved.

(cordbg) run max.exe
Process 3976/0xf88 created.
Warning: couldn't load symbols for
c:\windows\microsoft.net\framework\v1.1.4322.573\mscorlib.dll
[thread 0x5ac] Thread created.

020:    ldstr    "Input First number."
```

cordbg will stop on the first instruction. If a .pdb file is available, cordbg will use it to display the source code. Don't worry about the warning about not being able to load certain symbols. You'll always get that unless you've installed the debug version of the CLR, but it won't stop you from debugging your own code.

You can show the surrounding source code with the sh command, specifying how many lines around the current location you want to see, like so:

```
C:\>cordbg max.exe
Microsoft (R) Common Language Runtime Test Debugger Shell Version 1.1.4322.573
Copyright (C) Microsoft Corporation 1998-2002. All rights reserved.

(cordbg) run max.exe
Process 3976/0xf88 created.
Warning: couldn't load symbols for
c:\windows\microsoft.net\framework\v1.1.4322.573\mscorlib.dll
[thread 0x5ac] Thread created.
```

```
(cordbg) sh 4
016:    {
017:    .maxstack 2
018:    .locals init (int32, int32)
019:    .entrypoint
020:*   ldstr    "Input First number."
021:    call     void [mscorlib]System.Console::WriteLine(string)
022:    call     string [mscorlib]System.Console::ReadLine()
023:    call     int32 [mscorlib]System.Int32::Parse(string)
024:    stloc.0
```

The asterisk (*) indicates the current point of execution.

You can then set a breakpoint at the appropriate line using the br command and use the go command to continue execution to a breakpoint, like so:

```
(cordbg) br 22
Breakpoint #1 has bound to E:\IL\max.exe.
#1      C:\ExpertDotNet\ILIntro\max.il:22 Main+0xa(il) [active]
(cordbg) go
Input First number.
break at #1     C:\ExpertDotNet\ILIntro\max.il:22 Main+0xa(il) [active]

022:    call string [mscorlib]System.Console::ReadLine()
```

You can also display the values of variables with the p command or display the contents of machine registers with the reg command. However, I'll leave the introduction to cordbg there; you can find full details of the various cordbg commands on MSDN.

Compile-Time Errors in IL

Debugging code is all well and good, but it depends on you being able to run the program in the first place. In a high-level language, you'd expect a program to run if it doesn't have any compile-time errors. But if you're used to coding in high-level languages, then you'll find that the types of build-time errors you get in IL are somewhat different. Therefore, it's worth spending a couple of pages discussing the categories of errors you can get from IL source code.

Even in high-level languages, the categorization of build-time errors depends to some extent on the language and environment. For example, C++ developers will be familiar with both compile and link errors. In a typical link error, the code is syntactically correct but refers to a method or class for which the correct library hasn't been made known to the compiler. The same type of error can occur in C# or VB .NET if you fail to reference a required assembly, but in this case this is considered a straight compile-time error since these languages don't have separate compile and link phases (these compilers query assembly metadata for referenced types as they compile, but C++ simply throws in external references to be resolved later by the linker).

Table 1-10 shows the types of errors that can occur in IL source code and that will prevent the code from running (note that for IL code the definition of compile-time extends to JIT compilation time).

Table 1-10. *Types of IL Errors*

Nature of Error	Symptom	Usual Technique to Identify Error
Syntax error	ilasm.exe refuses to assemble the IL source code.	Examine the .il file for the error.
Invalid program	InvalidProgramException thrown as soon as the JIT compiler tries to compile the method that contains the error.	Run peverify on the binary assembly.
Unverifiable program	Fully trusted code has no symptoms; the program will run fine. But if the code is being executed in certain partially trusted contexts (such as from the Internet or a network drive), the JIT compiler will throw an exception when it encounters the error. You can use peverify to check whether an assembly contains unverifiable code.	Run peverify on the binary assembly.

Table 1-10 indicates that a tool called peverify is useful for helping to track down many of these errors. peverify.exe is a command-line program that you'll examine shortly. I'll first review the three categories of errors listed.

Table 1-10 doesn't mention one other possible error condition: the condition where one of the tokens in the instruction stream that refers to a method, field, or type, and so on, turns out not to be a valid token that can be resolved. Because different implementations of the Common Language Infrastructure (CLI), which is the ECMA standard for the .NET Framework, may in principle find it more convenient to trap this error at different stages in the execution process, the ECMA standard doesn't specify when such errors should be caught. It may happen at JIT compilation time, or it may occur through an exception thrown when code actually tries to access that token. However, this type of error is easy to understand, and I won't discuss it further.

Syntax Errors

A syntax error is conceptually the simplest to understand. It occurs if something is wrong with your IL source file that prevents ilasm.exe from understanding it. For example, the following code contains the nonexistent instruction ldsomestr (which presumably should be ldstr):

```
ldsomestr "Hello, World"    // error. Should be ldstr
call      void [mscorlib]System.Console::WriteLine(string)
ret
```

Syntax errors manifest themselves pretty clearly when you run ilasm, since ilasm will simply refuse to assemble the code.

Problems that will give rise to an error on assembly include (but are not limited to) the following:

- A nonexistent IL instruction

- Failing to provide a .EntryPoint method in an executable assembly

- Some problem with the structure of the file (such as omitting an opening or closing brace)

Invalid Program

An invalid program is an assembly that contains errors in the binary IL code that prevent the JIT compiler from being able to understand the code. The C#, VB, and C++ compilers have of course been thoroughly tested, so they should never emit an assembly that contains invalid code; however, if you're using a third-party compiler, an invalid program error may arise if the compiler is buggy.

What may surprise you, however, is that it's perfectly possible for ilasm.exe to generate invalid code. The reason is that ilasm performs only the minimum of checks that it needs to perform its task—in other words, that the .il file is structurally sound and all the commands in it can individually be understood. However, the IL definition also lays down various other requirements for code to be valid—in particular, it must be possible for the JIT compiler to determine the state of the stack at any given execution point. Not only that, but certain instructions (such as ret) require the stack to be in certain states. Checking these kinds of constraints is a nontrivial task, since it requires working through every possible path of execution of the code to see what types would be placed on the evaluation stack for each path, and ilasm.exe doesn't perform these checks. This means that if your code contains these kinds of errors, then this will be detected only when you attempt to execute (or peverify or ngen) the code.

■**Tip** The question of what constitutes an invalid program is a subtle one. I'll point out some of the ways this can happen now, but I'll postpone a full discussion of how the compiler checks that a program is valid until Chapter 3. For the time being, I just want to make sure you know what the different types of error are, in case you encounter them when writing IL assembly code.

The following code provides an example of a program that successfully assembles but is nevertheless invalid. This code is downloadable as the Invalid sample.

```
.assembly extern mscorlib {}
.assembly Invalid {}
.module Invalid.exe

.method static void Main() cil managed
{
    .entrypoint
    .maxstack 2

    ldc.i4    47
    ldc.r8    32.4
    mul
    call      void [mscorlib]System.Console::WriteLine(int32)
    ldc.i4    52
    ret
}
```

This code actually has two problems, either one of which is sufficient by itself to render the code invalid. In the first place, this code leaves a value on the evaluation stack when the method returns. In this code, the evaluation stack will be empty immediately after the call to `Console.WriteLine()`. You then load an integer onto it and return. However, the IL definition requires that a method that returns void must leave an empty evaluation stack when it returns.

The other problem is that you've attempted to multiply an integer by a floating-point number. Look at the first instructions in the `Main()` method. You start by loading the value 47 as a 4-byte integer onto the evaluation stack; then you load the value 32.4 as an 8-byte floating-point number, and you try to multiply these numbers together. Now, the IL `mul` command is quite happy to perform either integer or floating-point arithmetic, but it must be presented with consistent data types. It can't multiply one data type (an integer) by another data type (a float). And recall that, unlike some high-level languages, IL never performs any implicit conversions for you (other than widening or narrowing when loading 1- or 2-byte numeric types to or from the evaluation stack). If you want to cast data types, you must explicitly use a `conv.*` instruction.

If you try to run the invalid code presented earlier, you'll normally see the exception shown in Figure 1-5.

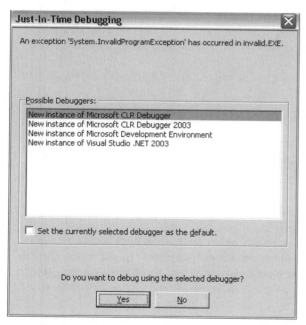

Figure 1-5. *Result of running an invalid program*

You'd have little point using any of the debuggers listed in the dialog box since they wouldn't be able to show you any executable code, because the JIT compiler hasn't actually managed to JIT compile any of your code! So the easiest option is to click No, in which case you'll get a message that tells you roughly where the error occurred but doesn't give you much more information.

```
Unhandled Exception: System.InvalidProgramException:
Common Language Runtime detected an invalid program.
   at Main()
```

Unfortunately, the statement "invalid program" doesn't help very much in identifying the error. If you want to gain more information about errors without resorting to debugging the code, the easiest way is to use the peverify tool, as I'll discuss soon.

Typical examples of problems that will give rise to invalid code include the following:

- Performing an arithmetic operation on incompatible types

- Having code that places more items on the evaluation stack than was specified in the .maxstack directive

- Leaving data of the wrong type on the evaluation stack when a method returns

Unverifiable Code

You'll no doubt be aware that the CLR imposes so-called type-safety checks, which are designed to identify code that may be able to perform dangerous operations by accessing memory outside the areas of memory specifically allocated to store that program's data. Unverifiable code is code that fails the CLR's type-safety checks. I'll discuss type safety and the verification algorithms in more detail in Chapter 3, but for now I'll just point out that a program will fail type safety if it contains certain potentially dangerous IL instructions or sequences of IL instructions.

Typical examples of issues that will cause your code to fail verifiability include the following:

- Attempting to pass the wrong types to a method call

- Using certain IL opcodes that are formally regarded by the CLR as unverifiable or that are regarded as unverifiable in certain conditions, when those conditions are true

- Any instruction that treats an item on the evaluation stack as if it was the wrong type

- Any code that dereferences unmanaged pointers

Obviously, I've made sure that the IL samples I've written for this book (other than the Invalid sample) are verifiable. The VB compiler will always generate verifiable code, and the C# compiler will always generate verifiable code unless you've declared any C# unsafe blocks. The C++ compiler at the time of writing can't generate verifiable code. Code written in C++ will always fail verifiability.

The interesting thing is that although failing type safety is formally considered an error, the JIT compiler is still able in principle to convert the IL to native executable, and the code will still execute provided it has the security permission SkipVerification. That is why Table 1-10 indicated that there may not be any symptoms for unverifiable code. Indeed, sometimes you may want your code to be unverifiable (for example, if some operation can be performed more efficiently than would have been the case using only verifiable code). Precisely which code has the SkipVerification permission will depend on your security policy. By default when you install .NET, assemblies run from your local machine have this permission, but assemblies run from the Internet or a network share don't. You'll examine those issues in more detail in Chapter 12.

If you do attempt to execute code that doesn't have the SkipVerification permission, and that fails verifiability, then you'll see something like this:

```
Unhandled Exception: System.Security.VerificationException:
 Operation could destabilize the runtime. at Main()
```

Using peverify

peverify has been described as the compiler writer's best friend. It's a tool that examines an assembly and reports any problems that would cause the code either to be invalid or to fail verifiability. The great thing about it is that it will report all such errors—unlike the JIT compiler, it doesn't terminate after it hits the first error. The two main uses of peverify are for checking code you've written in IL and assembled using ilasm.exe and for developers writing compilers to use peverify to check that their compiler is emitting verifiable code.

It's simple to run peverify—you simply type peverify followed by the name of the assembly to be checked. If you run peverify on the invalid.exe sample, this is the result:

C:\>peverify invalid.exe

```
Microsoft (R) .NET Framework PE Verifier  Version 1.1.4322.573
Copyright (C) Microsoft Corporation 1998-2002. All rights reserved.
[IL]: Error: [C:\ExpertDotNet\ILIntro\invalid.exe :
<Module>::Main] [offset 0x0000000E] [opcode mul]
Int32 Double Non-compatible types on the stack.
[IL]: Error: [C:\ExpertDotNet\ILIntro\invalid.exe :
<Module>::Main] [offset 0x00000019] [opcode ret]
Stack must be empty on return from a void function.
2 Errors Verifying invalid.exe
```

If you write your own IL source code, it's a good idea to always run peverify on the generated assembly.

Summary

In this chapter I presented an introduction to IL and to IL assembly syntax. I covered the way that IL is based on the concept of an abstract stack machine and went over how to write simple methods that use this architecture—covering flow control, local variables, arguments, and indirection. Finally, you saw how to debug IL source code, both using VS .NET and using the command-line cordbg utility, and you looked at the various types of error that can arise when you compile or execute IL source code.

You now have a basis to move onto more advanced IL code, including instantiating objects; looking at reference and value types, enums, delegates, and exception handling; and calling unmanaged code. I'll cover all these in Chapter 2.

CHAPTER 2

■ ■ ■

Intermediate Language: Digging Deeper

In this chapter, I'll carry on where I left off at the end of Chapter 1. In Chapter 1 you learned many of the principles on which IL is based: IL assembly syntax, the concept of the evaluation stack, and how to code a simple procedural program in IL. However, I haven't yet introduced object-oriented programming in IL. In the previous chapter, everything you did was essentially procedural. You did see how to define classes, but in the examples in Chapter 1, I was generally careful to use only static methods. This chapter will rectify that by discussing how to define and use types in IL, including defining instance fields, methods, properties, and constructors. I'll also show you how to code some more advanced .NET constructs such as delegates—and the chapter will end by applying what you've learned and then examining and compare the IL emitted by the C#, VB, and C++ compilers.

So in this chapter I'll cover the following:

- Instantiating objects of both value and reference types, invoking instance methods, and defining fields and properties

- Using enums

- Using arrays

- Using P/Invoke

- Handling exceptions

- Invoking methods through delegates

- Marking code items with custom attributes

- Comparing the IL code generated by compilers in C#, VB, and C++

Working with Objects and Value Type Instances

In the following sections I'll introduce objects and value types. I'll cover how IL treats the differences between value and reference types, which means that you'll get a feel for how value and reference types look from the point of view of CLR internals. You'll also learn how to instantiate objects and define instance methods, fields, properties, and constructors—in other words, all the usual basic aspects of classes and objects but from an IL point of view. Although most of the concepts will be familiar to you from your MC++, C#, or VB programming experience, you'll see that IL and the CLR do throw up a few surprises.

■**Caution** Strictly speaking, in the context of managed code, the term *object* specifically means an instance of a reference type. However, in practice the term is often also used informally to indicate a value type instance, and in keeping with common usage this book will do so too when the context is clear.

In the following sections I'll gradually develop an application based on a clock. The clock is represented initially by a value type, called Clock. Later I'll convert Clock to a reference type to show how this affects the code, but for now I'll stick with a value type to keep things simple. I'll use Clock to gradually introduce the various object-based operations: declaring fields and instance methods, using constructors, instantiating objects, and calling instance methods.

Instance Fields

I'll start by presenting the first version of the Clock type. It's very simple: It just contains one unsigned int8 (System.Byte) field that indicates the time of day in hours. It's crude, but when you're dealing with a low-level language such as IL, believe me, this struct will easily be sufficient to show all the main programming features. Here's the ILAsm file, Clock.il:

```
.assembly extern mscorlib {}
.assembly Clock
{
    .ver 1:0:1:0
}


.module Clock.dll

.namespace Apress.ExpertDotNet.ClockSample
{
    .class public ansi auto sealed Clock extends [mscorlib]System.ValueType
    {
        .field public unsigned int8 Hours
    }
}
```

This code immediately tells you how to declare a field in IL. So far not really anything is new apart from the syntax. Notice, however, that I haven't declared the field explicitly as either instance or static. When declaring members of classes, the default is for items to be instance members unless you explicitly say they're static—this is in common with most high-level languages. The code also rather clearly illustrates a pretty bad programming practice, in that I've declared a public field, but that's just temporary. As soon as I've covered how to declare properties, I'll put this field back to private.

In the previous chapter I used only one file for each sample to keep things simple. In this chapter, I'll try and inject a bit more realism into the samples by having the Clock class itself in one assembly and the client code to test Clock in another. This arrangement also gives you the flexibility to test your IL code using clients written in high-level languages—you'll use this later in the "Value Type Initialization in C#" section.

You assemble Clock.il like this:

```
ilasm Clock.il /dll
```

Now create a separate file, TestClock.il, that contains the Main() method. This is where things get interesting. The following is the file, containing a Main() method that instantiates a Clock instance as a local variable, sets its Hours field to 6, and displays the value of the field to make sure everything is working properly. In this assembly I've specifically indicated the version of the Clock assembly I want to reference. That's because, for added realism, I'll keep the assembly name the same but increase its version number as I develop the Clock sample.

```
// I've compacted the .assembly extern Clock directive to one line for
// simplicity, but I could have spread it over several lines if I wanted.
.assembly extern mscorlib {}
.assembly extern Clock { .ver 1:0:1:0 }

.assembly TestClock
{
    .ver 1:0:1:0
}

.module TestClock.exe

.namespace Apress.ExpertDotNet.ClockSample
{
    .class EntryPoint extends [mscorlib]System.Object
    {
        .method static void Main() cil managed
        {
            .maxstack 2
            .locals init (valuetype
                        [Clock]Apress.ExpertDotNet.ClockSample.Clock clock)
            .entrypoint

            // Set Hours to 6
            ldloca.s clock
            ldc.i4.6
            stfld    unsigned int8 [Clock]
                                Apress.ExpertDotNet.ClockSample.Clock::Hours

            ldstr    "Hours are "
            call     void [mscorlib]System.Console::Write(string)
            ldloca.s clock
```

```
        ldfld     unsigned int8 [Clock]
                            Apress.ExpertDotNet.ClockSample.Clock::Hours
        call      void [mscorlib]System.Console::WriteLine(int32)
        ret
      }
    }
}
```

■**Note** Notice that in this sample the final call to Console.WriteLine() passes in an int32, even though I loaded an unsigned int8 onto the stack. That's fine because of the way that shorter integers will always be promoted when being pushed onto the stack. Because any number that can be stored in an unsigned int8 can also be stored in an int32, you have no overflow or sign issues. I had to pass in int32 because there's no overload of Console.WriteLine() that takes unsigned int8 (System.Byte).

This sample is the first time you've declared a local variable that isn't a primitive—which means that the declaration must give the type's fully qualified name. Also, since this type is a value type, its declaration must be prefixed by the word valuetype (for a reference type, as you'll see later, you use class instead of valuetype).

```
.locals init (valuetype [Clock]Apress.ExpertDotNet.ClockSample.Clock clock)
```

In this sample I've given the local variable the name clock, but, as always, naming variables is optional. My real reason for naming this variable is simply so I can refer to it more easily in the text!

Notice that the definition of the Clock type includes the assembly name—you need to do this because Clock is defined in a separate assembly. This name by the way is case sensitive.

That's actually all you need to do to have the type available as a local variable—it really is as simple as that. Because you've explicitly indicated the init flag for local variables, clock will automatically be initialized by being zeroed. Note that no constructor has been called (or even defined) for Clock. For performance reasons, the .NET Framework won't call constructors on value types unless the IL code explicitly tells it to do so.

Now you need to set the Hours field of clock to the integer 6. To do this, you need a new instruction, stfld. stfld expects to pop two items from the evaluation stack: a reference to the object for which you're going to set a field and the actual value to be written to the field.

```
        ..., address, value → ...
```

For reference types, the reference would be an object reference, but since this is a value type you need a managed pointer instead—which you can get by using the ldloca.s instruction. In the following code I've explicitly named the variable to be loaded, but I could supply the index instead (ldloca.s 0); ilasm.exe will replace the variable name with the index in the emitted IL anyway. ldloca works just like the ldloc.* instructions in this regard.

```
// Set hours to 6
ldloca.s clock
ldc.i4.6
stfld     unsigned int8 Apress.ExpertDotNet.ClockSample.Clock::Hours
```

Notice that `stfld` also takes an argument—a token indicating the type and field in which you're interested. As with all tokens, in ILAsm this is a rather long string, but in the IL emitted by `ilasm.exe` it will simply be a 4-byte integer (token) that indexes into the appropriate entry in the module metadata.

Retrieving the field value so you can display it involves another instruction, `ldfld`, which pretty much does the reverse of `stfld`: It loads a field onto the evaluation stack. Like `stfld`, `ldfld` needs a token identifying the field as an argument and expects to find the address of the object concerned on the stack as either a managed or an unmanaged pointer or an object reference.

..., address → ..., value

This all means that you can retrieve and display the field with this code:

```
ldloca.s clock      // Could write ldloca.s 0 here instead
ldfld     unsigned int8 Apress.ExpertDotNet.ClockSample.Clock::hours
call      void [mscorlib]System.Console::WriteLine(unsigned int8)
```

Although I won't be using them here, I'll note a couple of related commands.

- `ldflda` is like `ldfld`, but it retrieves the field's address as a managed pointer, instead of retrieving the field's value. You can use it if you need to get the address in order to pass the field by reference to another method.

- `ldsfld` and `stsfld` work, respectively, like `ldfld` and `stfld`, but they're intended for static fields—which means they don't need any object address on the stack. `ldsfld` simply pushes the value of the field onto the stack, and `stsfld` pops the value off the stack into the relevant field, in both cases without making other changes to the stack.

To compile the `TestClock.il` file (after compiling `Clock` using `ilasm Clock.il /dll`), type in this command:

ilasm TestClock.il

Unlike the compilers for many high-level languages, `ilasm.exe` doesn't need a reference to `Clock.dll` to be specified at the command prompt: `ilasm` can figure out referenced assemblies from the `.assembly extern` declarations in the file being assembled.

Defining Instance Methods and Properties

Now that you've got a basic handle on how to manipulate fields of value types, you'll look at improving the `Clock` struct by wrapping that public field in a property. This means you'll be able to kill two birds with one stone as far as learning IL syntax: I'll cover both declaring instance methods and declaring properties. This is because in IL the get and set accessors of properties are actually declared as methods, and a separate .property directive links these methods to indicate that they constitute a property. The code for this sample is also contained in files called Clock.il and TestClock.il, but if you download the sample code you'll find the files for this sample in the Clock2 folder. In general, successive Clock samples in this chapter are numbered sequentially upward.

I've also kept the same namespace name as the previous example Apress.ExpertDotNET.ClockSample. Since this is really development of existing code, rather than a completely new sample, it makes more sense simply to increase the version number of the assembly, as I noted earlier. Since you're making a substantial change to the public interface of the class, you should change the major version number from 1 to 2.

```
.assembly Clock
{
    .ver 2:0:1:0
}
```

Next you change the declaration of the field to make it private. While you're at it, change its name from Hours to hours to keep with the normal camel-casing convention for private fields and to free up the name Hours for the property. Start with the method declaration for the get accessor. That means adding this code to the Clock struct:

```
.class public ansi auto sealed Clock extends [mscorlib]System.ValueType
{
    .field private unsigned int8 hours

    .method specialname public instance unsigned int8 get_Hours()
                                                        cil managed
    {
        ldarg.0
        ldfld    unsigned int8 Apress.ExpertDotNet.ClockSample.Clock::hours
        ret
    }
```

I emphasize that this so far is a plain, ordinary method. The main difference in its declaration from the methods you've defined up to now is that instead of declaring the method as static, you've declared it as instance.

The previous code has another new keyword—specialname. And this keyword is present only because you intend to use this method as a property accessor. specialname in this context is there to inform developer tools (such as VS .NET and the C++, C#, and VB compilers) that this method actually forms part of a property and should therefore be treated using the property syntax. In general, the purpose of specialname is to indicate that an item may be of significance to developer tools—though how the tools interpret it in a given context is up to them. specialname here has no significance to the CLR.

You must remember one crucial point when invoking the method: Since this is an instance method, it has an extra hidden parameter—the address of the object against which it has been called. You never need to worry about the extra parameter in high-level languages because the compilers take care of it for you, but in IL you need to take it into account. Hence, although get_Hours() is declared without any parameters, when invoked it will always expect one parameter—the variable that in VB you think of as the Me reference and that to C++/C#

people is the this reference. Hence, within any instance method, the instruction ldarg.0 will load the this/Me reference. If any explicit parameters existed, you'd need to remember to index those parameters starting at 1 instead of 0. Bearing all this in mind, you can see that the code presented previously simply loads the hours field and returns its value.

Now for the set accessor: This is an instance method that also takes an explicit parameter. You'll name the parameter value in accordance with the usual practices for property set accessors. However, since value is an ILAsm keyword and would hence cause a syntax error if used by itself as a variable name, enclose the name in single quotes. This is ILAsm's equivalent of preceding a variable name with the @ sign if the variable name clashes with a keyword in C# or if enclosing the name in square brackets in VB.

```
.method specialname public instance void set_Hours(
                                   unsigned int8 'value')
{
   ldarg.0
   ldarg.1
   stfld    unsigned int8 Apress.ExpertDotNet.ClockSample.Clock::hours
   ret
}
```

set_Hours() uses the stfld command to copy the parameter to the hours field.

So far, all you've got is two methods that happen to have been tagged specialname and happen to follow the same signature and naming convention that you'd expect for property accessors. To actually have metadata placed in the assembly that marks these methods as property accessors, you need to add the following code to the Clock struct:

```
.property instance unsigned int8 Hours()
{
   .get instance unsigned int8 get_Hours()
   .set instance void set_Hours(unsigned int8 'value')
}
```

This code formally declares to the .NET runtime that there's a property called Hours and that these two methods should be interpreted as accessors for this property. Notice that the .property directive doesn't itself have public or private or any other accessibility. Whether you can get/set a property depends upon the accessibility of the relevant accessor method. Note, however, that to be CLS compliant, the accessibility of the get accessor method must be the same as that of the set accessor method.

Although you now have a property definition, you should be aware that this definition is useful only for the following two situations:

- It means that if reflection is used to examine the Clock class, Hour and its accessor methods will correctly be reported as a property.

- High-level languages that use a special syntax for properties (and that includes C#, MC++, and VB) will be able to use their own property syntax for invoking the accessor methods. (High-level language compilers can do this because they recognize the .property directive and the specialname tag on the accessor methods).

As far as the .NET runtime is concerned, the accessors remain normal methods. You can see this when you examine the new version of the `Main()` method in the new version of the `TestClock.il` file, which invokes these methods. The following code completes the `Clock2` sample. It performs the same as the `Clock1` sample but now using the properties instead of the fields to set and read the hour stored in the `Clock` instance. The changed code is in bold—as you can see, the calls to `ldfld` and `stfld` have been replaced by calls to invoke the accessor methods.

```
.method static void Main() cil managed
{
    .maxstack 2
    .locals init (valuetype [Clock]Apress.ExpertDotNet.ClockSample.Clock clock)
    .entrypoint

    // Initialize
    ldloca.s clock
    ldc.i4    6
    call      instance void [Clock]Apress.ExpertDotNet.ClockSample.Clock::
                                                    set_Hours(unsigned int8)

    ldstr     "Hours are "
    call      void [mscorlib]System.Console::Write(string)
    ldloca.s clock
    call      instance unsigned int8 [Clock]
                          Apress.ExpertDotNet.ClockSample.Clock::get_Hours()
    call      void [mscorlib]System.Console::WriteLine(int32)

    ret
}
```

Initialization and Instance Constructors

Now you'll extend the `Clock` value type to add a couple of constructors to it: one that doesn't take any parameters (this type of constructor is often called a *default constructor*) and that initializes the hours to 12 (you'll assume midday is a suitable default value) and one that takes an `unsigned int8` parameter that indicates the initial hour.

■**Note** In this chapter I'll focus on instance constructors—don't worry about static constructors. So bear in mind that when I refer to constructors, I'm normally talking specifically about instance constructors.

Constructors, especially constructors of value types, are an area where high-level languages often impose various rules or syntaxes of their own, which don't reflect the underlying mechanism in .NET. So you may find you need to forget quite a bit of what you've learned about constructors in your high-level language.

So how do constructors work in .NET? The following are a couple of points that apply to constructors in general, irrespective of whether you're dealing with value types or reference types:

- Instance constructors are methods that have the name .ctor and return void (static constructors are called .cctor). They also need to be decorated with two flags—specialname, which you've already encountered, and a new flag, rtspecialname. Other than this, constructors are treated syntactically as normal methods and can be called whenever you want, not just at object initialization time, though in most cases it's not good programming practice to invoke them at any other time—doing so may make your code unverifiable.

- You can define as many different constructor overloads as you want.

- For reference types, you ought always to call the base class constructor from every possible code pathway inside the constructor. Failing to do so will cause the program to fail verification because of the risk of having uninitialized fields inherited from the ancestor types (although the constructor will still constitute valid code). Although the formal requirement is merely that every code pathway should call the base constructor, in practice the best solution is almost always to do this as the first thing in a constructor, before you do anything else. Note that this requirement is for reference types only. For value types, invoking the base constructor isn't only unnecessary but is pointless: the base type is always System.ValueType, which doesn't contain any fields to initialize!

- It's illegal to define a constructor as virtual.

- Constructors of reference types are always invoked automatically when a new object is instantiated. Constructors of value types, however, are never automatically invoked. They're invoked only if you explicitly call them from your IL code.

Having learned the principles of constructors in .NET, let's briefly review a couple of the gotchás that will catch you if you just blindly assume the rules for constructors are what your favorite high-level language would have you think.

- Many high-level languages prevent you from declaring a constructor return type. In IL, constructors must be specifically given their true return type—void.

- Some high-level languages such as C# will not let you define a parameterless constructor for value types. This is a restriction of the language, not the .NET runtime. IL has no syntactical problem about declaring such a constructor, but you should think carefully before defining one. Occasionally a default constructor may be useful, but as you'll see later, default value type constructors can cause some subtle runtime bugs that you'll need to take care to avoid (I stress this applies only to parameterless value type constructors, not to constructors of reference types or to constructors that take parameters).

- Many high-level languages automatically insert IL code in a constructor to call the base class constructor. For example, C# will automatically insert a call to the base class default constructor as the first item of code in a constructor, unless you explicitly supply a constructor initializer in your code, indicating that some other constructor should be called instead. This is useful because it forces good programming practice. As you've seen, IL itself doesn't put such stringent restrictions on code in constructors.

Adding a Default Constructor

That's the theory—now for the code. You'll first add a default (that is to say, parameterless) constructor to the Clock type (this will constitute the Clock3 sample in the code download). I know I hinted that doing this can be a bad idea for value types, but you still need to see the syntax for declaring a default constructor. Besides, you'll soon be converting Clock to a reference type, and then the default constructor will be important.

To add the constructor, you add this code inside the Clock definition:

```
.method public specialname rtspecialname instance void .ctor()
{
   ldarg.0
   ldc.i4.s 12
   stfld    unsigned int8 Apress.ExpertDotNet.ClockSample.Clock::hours

   ret
}
```

Now you'll invoke the constructor. You need to add the following code to Main() to have the Clock initialized to its default value of 12 instead of explicitly initializing the hours field:

```
Main() cil managed
{
   .maxstack 2
   .locals init (valuetype Apress.ExpertDotNet.ClockSample.Clock clock)
   .entrypoint

   // Initialize
   ldloca.s clock
   call     instance void [Clock]Apress.ExpertDotNet.ClockSample.Clock::
                                                          .ctor()

   ldstr    "Hours are "
   call     void [mscorlib]System.Console::Write(string)
   ldloca.s clock
   call     instance unsigned int8 [Clock]
                      Apress.ExpertDotNet.ClockSample.Clock::get_Hours()
   call     void [mscorlib]System.Console::WriteLine(int32)

   ret
}
```

This code emphasizes that constructors of value types always have to be explicitly invoked if you want them to be executed.

Adding a Constructor That Takes Parameters

Finally, having seen how to write a parameterless constructor, you'll write one that takes one parameter that determines the initial time. So you'll add the following code (this will form the Clock4 sample):

```
.method public specialname rtspecialname instance void .ctor(
                                                unsigned int8 hours)
{
    ldarg.0
    ldarg.1
    stfld    unsigned int8 Apress.ExpertDotNet.ClockSample.Clock::hours
    ret
}
```

Adding this code is all you strictly need to do to implement this constructor. However, you now have two constructors that separately initialize the hours field. Normally, in this situation, good programming practice dictates that you should keep the initialization code in one place and have the constructors call each other. So, you'll modify the code for the default constructor as follows:

```
.method public specialname rtspecialname instance void .ctor()
{
    ldarg.0
    ldc.i4.s  12
    call      instance void Apress.ExpertDotNet.ClockSample.Clock::.ctor(
                                                        unsigned int8)
    ret
}
```

Lastly, you'll modify the code for Main() to call the one-parameter constructor (for simplicity, the test harness will test only this constructor), as follows:

```
.method static void Main() cil managed
{
    .maxstack 2
    .locals init (valuetype Apress.ExpertDotNet.ClockSample.Clock clock)
    .entrypoint

    // Initialize
    ldloca.s clock
    ldc.i4   9
    call      instance void [Clock]Apress.ExpertDotNet.ClockSample.Clock::
                                            .ctor(unsigned int8)

    ldstr    "Hours are "
    call      void [mscorlib]System.Console::Write(string)
    ldloca.s clock
    call      instance unsigned int8 Apress.ExpertDotNet.ClockSample.Clock::
                                                        get_Hours()
    call      void [mscorlib]System.Console::WriteLine(int32)

    ret
}
```

Value Type Initialization in C#

You'll now see how the principles I've been discussing translate to a high-level language by examining how C# deals internally with the initialization of value types. In the process you'll see why default constructors for value types can cause problems, especially for clients in high-level languages.

Let's quickly write a C# program to consume the Clock value type. Here's the file (it's called CShTestClock.cs):

```
using System;

namespace Apress.ExpertDotNet.ClockSample
{
   class EntryPoint
   {
      static void Main()
      {
         Clock clock = new Clock();
         Console.WriteLine(clock.Hours);
      }
   }
}
```

To start with, place this file in the same folder as the Clock4 sample files—the previous sample that contains constructors for Clock—and compile it using the /r flag to reference the Clock.dll assembly. Then run it.

```
C:\ExpertDotNet\ILDeeper>csc cshtestclock.cs /r:clock.dll
Microsoft (R) Visual C# .NET Compiler version 7.10.3052.4
for Microsoft (R) .NET Framework version 1.1.4322
Copyright (C) Microsoft Corporation 2001-2002. All rights reserved.


C:\ExpertDotNet\ILDeeper>cshtestclock
12
```

You'll see no surprises here. The parameterless Clock constructor has been invoked, so the clock has been initialized to 12.

Now let's do the same thing, but this time placing the C# source file in the folder that contains the first Clock sample, for which Clock didn't have any constructors. Interestingly, despite that you've used a constructor syntax in C# against a struct that has no constructors, the code compiles fine. However, with no constructors, the Hours field clearly won't get initialized to 12. In fact, it turns out to be initialized to zero.

```
C:\ExpertDotNet\ILDeeper>csc cshtestclock.cs /r:clock.dll
Microsoft (R) Visual C# .NET Compiler version 7.10.3052.4
for Microsoft (R) .NET Framework version 1.1.4322
Copyright (C) Microsoft Corporation 2001-2002. All rights reserved.
```

```
C:\ExpertDotNet\ILDeeper>cshtestclock
0
```

Evidently the C# compiler is up to something behind the scenes. And examining the emitted IL using ildasm shows what's going on.

```
.maxstack 1
.locals init (valuetype [Clock]Apress.ExpertDotNet.ClockSample.Clock V_0)

IL_0000:  ldloca.s V_0
IL_0002:  initobj  [Clock]Apress.ExpertDotNet.ClockSample.Clock
IL_0008:  ldloca.s V_0
IL_000a:  ldfld    unsigned int8 [Clock]
                              Apress.ExpertDotNet.ClockSample.Clock::Hours
IL_000f:  call     void [mscorlib]System.Console::WriteLine(int32)
IL_0014:  ret
```

■**Tip** Don't worry about the IL_* labels attached to each instruction. That's an artifact of ildasm. ildasm labels each instruction with a string that indicates the relative offset in bytes of the instruction compared to the start of the method in case you need the information and to make it easier to see where the targets of branch instructions are.

The key is in that initobj instruction. You haven't encountered initobj yet, but its purpose is to initialize a value type by zeroing out all its fields. It requires the top item of the stack to be a reference (normally a managed pointer) to the value type instance to be initialized, and it takes a token indicating the type as an argument (the argument determines how much memory the type occupies and therefore needs to be zeroed).

The C# compiler detects whether a value type to be instantiated has a default constructor defined. If it does, it compiles the new() operator to invoke the constructor. If it doesn't, the new() operator calls initobj instead. You may get a possible small performance hit because you're initializing the object twice—once through the init flag on the .locals directive and once through the initobj command. You could avoid this hit by coding in IL directly, though it's undocumented whether the JIT compiler would detect this and optimize it away anyway.

The Problem with Default Value Type Constructors

Now you're in a position to see exactly why default constructors for value types can cause problems. The problem is that it's quite possible for value types to be instantiated without any constructor being invoked—unlike the case for reference types, which, as you'll see soon, simply can't be instantiated without at the same time specifying one of the available constructors that will be executed. That means that if you write a value type that depends on its constructor always having been executed, you risk the code breaking.

Related to this is a risk of version brittleness. If you compile C# code, for example, against a value type that has no default constructor, the client code will initialize the instance using initobj. If you subsequently modify the value type to add a constructor, you'll have existing client code that initializes the object in the "wrong" way.

Another issue is that the usual expectation among .NET developers is that the statement SomeValueType x = new SomeValueType(); will initialize x by zeroing it. If you supply a default constructor that does something else, you're running against the expectations of developers, which clearly means bugs are more likely in their code. On the other hand, if you're aware of these issues and prepared to work around them, you may be justified for defining a default constructor for some value type in certain situations (for example, if your type has the access level nested assembly and will be used only from your own code).

Working through the emitted IL code in this way demonstrates the potential for gaining a deeper understanding of what's going on in your high-level language if you're able to read the IL emitted by the compiler.

Instantiating Reference Objects

Now that you've seen how value types are instantiated and initialized, you'll move onto examining the instantiation of reference types. So, for the next sample (Clock5), let's change Clock to a reference type that derives from System.Object. To do this, you need to change its definition, like so:

```
.class public ansi auto Clock extends [mscorlib]System.Object
{
    .field private unsigned int8 hours
```

You'll also need to modify the one-parameter constructor so that it calls the System.Object constructor—recall that I mentioned earlier that constructors of reference types must call a base class constructor. This is the new one-parameter constructor for Clock:

```
.method public specialname rtspecialname instance void .ctor()
{
    ldarg.0
    call    instance void [mscorlib]System.Object::.ctor()

    ldarg.0
    ldarg.1
    stfld   unsigned int8 Apress.ExpertDotNet.ClockSample.Clock::hours

    ret
}
```

Notice that the call to the base class constructor is the first thing you do. If you had initialized the hours field first, the code would still pass verification—but in most cases it's not good programming practice to do anything else before calling the base class constructor: you risk the possibility of manipulating fields inherited from the base class that haven't been initialized.

The default constructor, which simply invokes the one-parameter constructor, is completely unchanged.

```
.method public specialname rtspecialname instance void .ctor()
{
   ldarg.0
   ldc.i4.s 12
   call     instance void Apress.ExpertDotNet.ClockSample.Clock::.ctor(
                                                 unsigned int8)

   ret
}
```

Notice that this constructor doesn't invoke the base constructor directly, but it does so indirectly via the call to the one-parameter constructor. The verification process is nevertheless able to detect that the base constructor is invoked, so the code is still verifiable.

Now for the Main() method in the TestClock.il file. Again, the code that has changed is in bold. For this test, you invoke the default constructor, like so:

```
.class EntryPoint extends [mscorlib]System.Object
{
   .method static void Main() cil managed
   {
      .maxstack 2
      .locals init (class [Clock]Apress.ExpertDotNet.ClockSample.Clock)
      .entrypoint

      newobj   void [Clock]Apress.ExpertDotNet.ClockSample.Clock::.ctor()
      stloc.0

      ldstr    "Hours are "
      call     void [mscorlib]System.Console::Write(string)
      ldloc.0
      call     instance unsigned int8 [Clock]
                        Apress.ExpertDotNet.ClockSample.Clock::get_Hours()
      call     void [mscorlib]System.Console::WriteLine(int32)

      ret
   }
}
```

The first difference is that in this definition of the local variable's type that will store the object reference, you prefix the name of the type with class rather than with valuetype. This informs the JIT compiler that it needs to reserve space only for a reference rather than for the actual object. Interestingly, this program would work equally well if you declared the local variable as simply being of type object, although for obvious type-safety reasons, it's better practice to supply as much information as you can about the type in the IL code.

```
.locals init (object)      // This would work too
```

More specifically, the advantage of declaring the type explicitly is that if there was a bug in your code that caused the wrong type of object to be instantiated, it could potentially be detected and an exception could be raised earlier—when the object reference is first stored in the local variable rather than the first time a method on it is called.

The next difference comes when you instantiate the object—and this is the crucial difference. Whereas for a value type, the space to hold the object was allocated in the local variable table at the start of the method, when you declared it as a local variable; now you need a new command to instantiate the object on the managed heap—newobj. newobj takes one argument, which must be a token to the constructor you want to call. Note that you don't need a separate token to indicate the type because that information can be deduced from the constructor you're invoking. Any parameters required by the constructor will be popped off the stack, and an object reference to the newly created object is pushed onto the stack.

..., parameter1, ..., parameterN → ..., object

In this case, since you're calling the default constructor, no parameters will be popped from the stack. All you need to do once you've instantiated the object is store the reference to it using stloc.0.

```
newobj  void Apress.ExpertDotNet.ClockSample.Clock::.ctor()
stloc.0
```

You need to make one more change to the code. When loading the object reference onto the evaluation stack in order to call its get_Hours() method, you use ldloc.0 instead of ldloca.s 0.

ldloc.0
```
call    instance unsigned int8 Apress.ExpertDotNet.ClockSample.Clock::get_Hours()
```

The reason for this change is that invoking an instance method requires a reference to the object to be on the stack. Previously, the local variable held the object itself when it was a value type, which meant you needed to load its address using ldloca.s in order to obtain a managed pointer suitable for use as the reference. Now, however, the local variable already contains an object reference. Using ldloca.s would result in the evaluation stack containing an unusable managed pointer to a reference. ldloc.0 is sufficient to put the correct data on the stack.

Finally, just for the sake of completeness, I'll show how you'd need to change the code to instantiate the Clock instance using its one-parameter constructor (this code is downloadable as the Clock6 sample). The only change you'll need to make is to ensure that the value to be passed to the constructor is on the stack prior to executing newobj and, obviously, to ensure that the argument to newobj is the correct constructor token.

```
.maxstack 2
.locals init (class Apress.ExpertDotNet.ClockSample.Clock)
.entrypoint
```

ldc.i4.s 6   // To initialize hours to 6
newobj   void [Clock]Apress.ExpertDotNet.ClockSample.Clock::.ctor(unsigned int8)
stloc.0

Virtual Methods

In the following sections you'll examine how to declare, override, and invoke virtual methods in IL.

Declaring Virtual Methods

Declaring and overriding virtual methods is no different in principle in IL compared to higher-level languages, although you have a certain amount of freedom of expression in how you define and invoke the methods. I'll demonstrate this through a new sample, Clock7, in which you override the ToString() method in the Clock class to return the time in hours followed by "O'Clock" (such as "6 O'Clock"). Here's the override:

```
.method public virtual hidebysig string ToString()
{
    ldstr    "{0} O'Clock"
    ldarg.0
    ldflda   unsigned int8 Apress.ExpertDotNet.ClockSample.Clock::hours
    call     instance string unsigned int8::ToString()
    call     string string::Format(string, object)
    ret
}
```

This method uses the two-parameter overload of the String.Format() method to format the returned string. Recall that the first parameter to this overload of String.Format() is a format string, and the second parameter is an object whose string value will be inserted into the format string. The previous code is roughly equivalent to this C# code:

```
public override ToString()
{
    return String.Format("{0} O'Clock", this.hours.ToString());
}
```

You should take note of a couple of points in the implementation of ToString(): the way I've invoked unsigned int8.ToString() (or equivalently, System.Byte.ToString()) using a managed pointer and the virtual hidebysig attributes in the method declaration.

As far as calling Byte.ToString() is concerned, notice that I've used the ldflda instruction to load the address of the hours field onto the evaluation stack—so you end up with a managed pointer to the Byte against which ToString() is to be invoked. That's important because when you call an instance method, you need a reference to the this pointer for the method on the stack. In the case of calling methods of value types in general, and the CLR primitive types in particular (such as Byte, Int32, Int64, and so on), the methods expect a managed pointer (not an object reference). This is quite nice for performance since it means you have no need, for example, to box the types. If you want to call Byte.ToString(), you just provide the address in memory of the unsigned int8 to be converted onto the evaluation stack, and you're ready to invoke the method. That unsigned int8 can literally be anywhere—field, local variable, argument, and so on.

Now let's look at the virtual and hidebysig attributes.

You'll get no surprises in the virtual keyword. It's exactly equivalent to virtual in C++, to Inheritable or Overrides in VB, and to virtual or override in C#. Notice, however, that ILAsm doesn't have separate terms such as override/Overrides to distinguish whether this method is already overriding something else, as C# and VB do.

hidebysig is another of those flags that actually has no effect whatsoever as far as the runtime is concerned, but it's there to provide extra information to compilers and developer tools for high-level languages. hidebysig tells you that this method—if it's to hide any method—should be interpreted by compilers as hiding only methods that have the same name and signature. If you omitted hidebysig, the method would hide any method that has the same name. In high-level languages, you never get a choice about hidebysig behavior: C# always uses it. VB uses it for Overrides methods but not for Shadows methods. MC++ never uses it. These days, hidebysig seems to be regarded as a better object-oriented approach, but MC++ doesn't use it because the ANSI C++ standard uses hide by name. As you can see, the meaning of hidebysig is subtle—and it provides an example of the fine degree of control you get by coding directly in IL.

Before showing how to invoke virtual methods, I'll quickly list some other flags related to override behavior that may be useful. For these flags, the only new thing you have to learn is the ILAsm keywords—there's no difference in meaning from the high-level language equivalents (see Table 2-1).

Table 2-1. *Flags for Overriding*

IL Keyword	C# Equivalent	VB Equivalent	MC++ Equivalent	Meaning
newslot	new	Shadows	new	This method takes a new slot in the vtable. It doesn't override any base class methods even if some base methods have the same name.
final	sealed	NotOverrideable	__sealed	It isn't permitted to further override this method.
abstract	abstract	MustOverride	__abstract	No method body is supplied. This method must be overridden in nonabstract derived classes.

Invoking Virtual Methods

To invoke a virtual method, you won't normally use the IL call instruction. Rather, you'll use a new instruction, callvirt. The syntax of callvirt is identical to call: It takes a token as an argument that indicates the method to be called. However, callvirt can't be used to call static methods, which means it always requires a this reference for the method to be on the evaluation stack. callvirt also does a bit more work than call. First, it checks that the item it pops off the evaluation stack isn't null—and throws an exception if it's null. Second, it calls the method using the method table (vtable) of the object on the stack. In other words, it treats the method as a virtual method—you get the small performance hit of an extra level of indirection to locate the method to be invoked but the security of knowing you're calling the appropriate method for the given object.

Here's the code in TestClock.il to display the value of the clock variable:

```
.method static void Main() cil managed
{
    .maxstack 2
    .locals init (class [Clock]Apress.ExpertDotNet.ClockSample.Clock)
    .entrypoint

    // Initialize
    newobj   void [Clock]Apress.ExpertDotNet.ClockSample.Clock::.ctor()
    stloc.0

    ldstr    "The time is "
    call     void [mscorlib]System.Console::Write(string)
    ldloc.0
    callvirt instance string [Clock]Apress.ExpertDotNet.ClockSample.Clock::
                                                        ToString()
    call     void [mscorlib]System.Console::WriteLine(string)

    ret
}
```

The interesting thing about IL is that you get a choice each time you invoke a method whether you invoke the method using a virtual or nonvirtual technique. In high-level languages, you don't always get that choice (though in C++ you can use the ClassName::MethodName() syntax to indicate which override you need). But in IL, you can always choose to call a method using call or callvirt. Both of these instructions can be used to call either virtual or nonvirtual methods. To see the difference more clearly, let's change the previous code to this:

```
ldloc.0
callvirt instance string [mscorlib]System.Object::ToString()
```

Here you invoke Object.ToString(). However, because you're using callvirt, the specification of the object class won't make any difference. The method to be invoked will be taken by looking up ToString() in the method table for the object reference on the evaluation stack, which of course will identify Clock.ToString() as the method to be invoked. On the other hand, this code:

```
ldloc.0
call     instance string [mscorlib]System.Object::ToString()
```

will cause Object.ToString() to be invoked, even though the top of the evaluation stack contains a reference to a Clock instance.

Incidentally, although a performance hit is associated with using callvirt rather than call, this is only very small. And the C# team decided it was small enough to be worth paying in just about every method call. If you examine code generated by the C# compiler, you'll see that `callvirt` is used almost exclusively, even for nonvirtual methods. The reason? It's because of the extra code robustness you gain because `callvirt` checks for a `null` pointer. The Microsoft C# compiler works on the philosophy that the extra debugging check is worth the slight performance loss.

Boxing and Unboxing

Boxing value types is fairly easy in IL: You simply use the `box` instruction. For example, if you had an integer type stored in local variable with index 0 and want to box it, you could use this code:

```
ldloc.0
box     int32
```

As usual for primitive types, I've used the relevant IL keyword (in this case, `int32`) as shorthand for the fully qualified type name. Obviously, for nonprimitive types you'd have to indicate the type explicitly, like so:

```
ldloc.0 // This is a Color instance
box     [System.Drawing]System.Drawing.Color
```

`box` will leave an object reference on the stack. The stack-transition diagram looks like this:

..., value → ..., object ref

Unboxing is quite simple, too. You use the `unbox` instruction, which expects a token identifying the type, pops an object reference off the stack, and returns a managed pointer to the data.

```
unbox   int32
```

`unbox` has the following stack-transition diagram:

..., object ref → ..., managed pointer

Notice that the diagram for `unbox` isn't the reverse of that for `box`. Where `box` takes the value type instance, `unbox` leaves an address on the stack—a managed pointer. And this reflects an important point you need to understand. Unboxing isn't really the opposite of boxing. Boxing involves copying data, but unboxing doesn't. Boxing a value type means taking its value (which will be located on the stack for local variables or inline on the heap for value-type instances that are members of objects), creating a new boxed object on the managed heap, and copying the contents of the value type into the boxed object. Because of this, it's common for high-level language programmers to assume that unboxing means extracting the value from the boxed object and copying it onto the stack. But it doesn't mean that—all that unboxing involves is figuring out the address of the data on the managed heap and returning a managed pointer to that data. Figure 2-1 shows the difference.

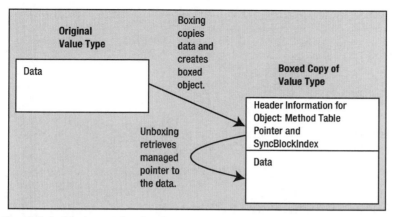

Figure 2-1. *Boxing and unboxing*

It really comes down to the difference I indicated earlier between an object reference and a managed pointer. Recall that I said that where a managed pointer points to the first field in an object, an object reference contains the address of the object's method table pointer. So when you unbox an object, all you're effectively doing is adding a few bytes (OK, let's be specific—4 bytes in version 1.*x* of the .NET Framework) onto the object reference and interpreting the result as a managed pointer.

The confusion typically arises from this kind of code:

```
// C# code
int someNumber = 12;
object boxedNumber = someNumber;    // Box the integer

// Do some processing on object

int copy = (int)boxedNumber;        // Unbox and copy the integer
```

In this code, the statement in which I declare and initialize the boxedNumber variable is correctly described as *boxing the integer*. Later I take a copy of the boxed value—and this procedure is often loosely described by C# developers as *unboxing the value*. In fact, this last line of code unboxes *and* copies the value.

Suppose now that what you want is to unbox a value *and* take a local copy of it in IL—the equivalent of the (int) cast in the previous C# code. How do you do it? The answer is you go back to the ldind.* instructions to convert the managed pointer to data and hence retrieve the actual value of the data. The following code snippet shows you how to do that:

```
// Top of stack contains an object reference to a boxed int32.
// You need to store the value of the int32 in local variable 0.
unbox     int32
ldind.i4
stloc.0
```

Finally, before I present a sample that illustrates boxing, I just want to warn you about a potential catch. The following code, which I've called the BoxWrong sample, loads an integer, boxes it, and then uses System.Int32.ToString() to convert its value to a string and display the value:

```
.method static void Main() cil managed
{
   .maxstack 1
   .entrypoint

   ldstr      "The number is "
   call       void [mscorlib]System.Console::Write(string)
   ldc.i4.s   -45
   box        int32
   call       instance string int32::ToString()
   call       void [mscorlib]System.Console::WriteLine(string)
   ret
}
```

If you think this code will display the value -45, you're in for a shock. It displays the following:

```
C:\ExpertDotNet\ILDeeper\BoxWrong Sample>boxwrong
The number is 2042169096
```

So what has gone wrong? The answer is quickly revealed if you run peverify on the code.

```
C:\ExpertDotNet\ILDeeper\BoxWrong Sample>peverify boxwrong.exe

Microsoft (R) .NET Framework PE Verifier  Version 1.1.4322.573
Copyright (C) Microsoft Corporation 1998-2002. All rights reserved.

[IL]: Error: [c:\ExpertDotNet\ILDeeper\boxwrong sample\boxwrong.exe :
Apress.ExpertDotNet.BoxWrong.EntryPoint::Main] [offset 0x00000011]
[opcode call] [found [box]value class 'System.Int32'] [expected address of Int32]
 Unexpected type on the stack.
1 Errors Verifying boxwrong.exe
```

The problem is that you're using an object reference to call a method on a boxed value type—and you have an object reference instead of a managed pointer on the stack. Remember I said earlier that you should use a managed pointer, not an object reference, to invoke members of value types. The same applies to boxed value types. Because int32 is a value type, its ToString() implementation expects the first parameter passed in to be a managed pointer to the int32 that needs to be converted. If the method had to do additional processing to figure out whether what it had been given was actually an object reference, performance would be pretty badly affected. In the case of the previous code, Int32.ToString() will dereference the object reference, which (at least for .NET version 1.x) will lead to the value (address) sitting in the object's method table pointer, and convert that to a string. Not surprisingly, the result isn't very meaningful.

Fortunately, this program is easily corrected by inserting an unbox command. The corrected code is downloadable as the BoxRight sample.

```
ldc.i4.s   -45
box        int32    // Assuming you need to box for some other reason
unbox      int32
call       instance string int32::ToString()
call       void [mscorlib]System.Console::WriteLine(string)
```

And the moral is that if you're calling a method defined in a value type, give it a pointer to a value type—not an object reference to a boxed value type.

■**Caution** Note that the `BoxRight` sample is based on the supposition that you have some good reason for wanting to box your `int32`—presumably connected with something else you intend to do to it (for example, passing it to a method that expects an object as a parameter). As the code stands, it'd be a lot more efficient not to box at all but to store the integer in a local variable and load its address using `ldloca`. But then I couldn't demonstrate boxing to you.

Declaring Enumerations

Now you'll examine how to declare enumerations in IL. Enumerations are relatively straight-forward—no fundamental new concepts are involved, but the .NET Framework imposes various restrictions on enums.

In high-level languages, you'll be used to declaring enums like this:

```
// C# code
enum TimeOfDay { Am, Pm }
```

And you'll no doubt be aware that what you're actually declaring is a type that's derived from System.Enum, with System.Enum providing all that clever stuff you're used to, such as converting the values to or from a string. However, an awful lot of what's going on is hidden by the special enum syntax of high-level languages. In practice, some of the support for defining enums in languages such as C#, MC++, and VB falls naturally out of the class structure and the methods implemented by System.Enum, but the .NET Framework also provides some help because it has some specific knowledge of enums hard-coded into it.

The following are supplied by the class structure:

- Each enum you define is in fact a value type that derives from System.Enum.

- Methods such as ToString() and Parse() are implemented by System.Enum and hence inherited by your enum.

- The enumerated values (Am and Pm in the previous example) are public static literal fields of your enumeration class. These fields must be of the same type as the enum in which they have been defined (in other words, with the previous example, Am and Pm are each public static literal TimeOfDay fields; literal in IL means the same as const in C# or C++ and Const in VB).

- There's also a private instance field, which is the "value" of any instances of the enum you declare and is always called value__. The type of this field is the underlying type (if your enumeration class is based on int32, the default underlying type, the value__ field will also be of type int32).

The following are supplied by the .NET runtime:

- The runtime knows about the value__ instance field. (This field must be decorated with the specialname and rtspecialname flags.)

- The runtime knows that types derived from System.Enum form a special category of types, and it imposes restrictions on them to ensure they conform to the enum model. In particular, each enum must implement the value__ instance field and can't implement any other instance members.

In addition to all this, VS .NET supplies extra user-interface features such as enum-specific IntelliSense to assist in programming with enums.

Let's see how all this works by writing a short IL program that defines an AmOrPm enum as previously shown, instantiates it, and prints the value of the AmOrPm instance. Here's the enum definition:

```
.namespace Apress.ExpertDotNet.EnumDemo
{
    .class public auto ansi sealed AmOrPm extends [mscorlib]System.Enum
    {
        .field public specialname rtspecialname int32 value__
        .field public static literal valuetype Apress.ExpertDotNet.EnumDemo.AmOrPm
                                                        Am = int32(0x0)
        .field public static literal valuetype Apress.ExpertDotNet.EnumDemo.AmOrPm
                                                        Pm = int32(0x1)
    }
}
```

The code for the definition essentially illustrates the points I've already made. The value__ field represents the value of an instance of the enum, and the various enumerated values exist as static fields. When declaring literal (const) values in IL, the actual literal value is always supplied after the = sign, in a format that should be clear from the previous code.

Now let's see how you use the enum.

```
.method static void Main() cil managed
{
    .maxstack 2
    .entrypoint
    .locals init (valuetype Apress.ExpertDotNet.EnumDemo.AmOrPm time)

    // Initialize the local variable to 1 (=Pm)
    ldc.i4.1
    stloc.0
```

```
// Write out time as a number
ldstr    "Value of enum (as number) is "
call     void [mscorlib]System.Console::Write(string)
ldloc.0
call     void [mscorlib]System.Console::WriteLine(int32)

// Write out time as a string
ldstr    "Value of enum (as string) is "
call     void [mscorlib]System.Console::Write(string)
ldloc.0
box      Apress.ExpertDotNet.EnumDemo.AmOrPm
call     instance string [mscorlib]System.Enum::ToString()
call     void [mscorlib]System.Console::WriteLine(string)

ret
}
```

Notice first that you initialize the enum from an int32 value that you've pushed onto the stack.

```
ldc.i4.1
stloc.0
```

This code looks at first sight like it breaks type-safety rules: It pushes an int32 into a memory location occupied by an AmOrPm object. The fact that it passes peverify is an example of the support for enums that's built into the CLR. The CLR knows that enums are for all practical purposes just integers (or whatever the underlying type is), so the verification process considers an enum as being equivalent to its underlying type.

Next you load the enum and pass its value to Console.WriteLine() to display its numerical value. Given what I've just said about the CLR, this part of the code shouldn't surprise you. But a surprise is in store in the code that invokes Enum.ToString(): you box the value before calling System.Enum.ToString()—apparently in direct contradiction to what I said earlier about not passing object references to boxed value types to methods.

```
ldloc.0
box      Apress.ExpertDotNet.EnumDemo.AmOrPm
call     instance string [mscorlib]System.Enum::ToString()
```

The reason for this apparent discrepancy is quite simple: Although types that are derived from System.Enum are always automatically enumerations and therefore value types, System.Enum itself is a reference type! So, because you're calling a method (Enum.ToString()) defined on a reference type, you need to box the enum instance and pass in an object reference to the method. The same oddity occurs for other value types: Any type derived from ValueType (apart from System.Enum) is a value type, but System.ValueType itself is a reference type. Although this sounds counterintuitive, good reasons exist for this. In particular, ValueType and Enum need to be reference types in order to allow you to derive other types from them. You'll explore this issue in more detail in Chapter 3, when you examine how to implement value, reference, and boxed types in practice.

Working with Arrays

I was quite surprised and pleased when I first started playing with arrays in IL. I had read lots of documentation for managed high-level languages that told me repeatedly that arrays were nothing more than instances of the System.Array class—and I had vaguely gathered that arrays must be implemented as instances of that class, and therefore the CLR had no built-in support for arrays. I couldn't have been more wrong! It's true that if you want to do something fancy, such as have a VB 6–style array that isn't zero indexed, then you're on your own and will need to work by explicitly invoking System.Array methods, but if you just want a simple zero-indexed one-dimensional array (known in metadata as szarray and more generally as a *vector*), then you'll find considerable built-in support through several specific IL commands.

Arrays are declared using a similar syntax as for C#, using square brackets. For example, a one-dimensional array of int32s would be denoted int32[], and a two-dimensional rectangular array of objects would be denoted object[,]. Note, however, that for multidimensional arrays, beyond the availability of this syntax, IL has little built-in support. Again, you're best off explicitly manipulating System.Array methods.

For the rest of this section you'll concentrate on manipulating vectors. Table 2-2 describes the IL commands available for manipulating vectors.

Table 2-2. *IL Commands to Manipulate Vectors*

Instruction	Meaning
newarr	Instantiates an array (vector) object
ldelem.*	Loads a given element of an array onto the evaluation stack
ldelema.*	Loads the address of the given element of an array onto the evaluation stack
stelem.*	Pops the top element of the evaluation stack into the given array element
ldlen	Loads the length of an array onto the evaluation stack

■**Caution** Somewhat confusingly, although zero-indexed one-dimensional arrays are technically known as *vectors*, the instruction names and surrounding documentation continues to refer to them as *arrays*. For consistency, I'll follow the same practice here.

newarr works much like newobj, except that it instantiates an array. The type of each element of the array is supplied in the argument to newarr. Like newobj, it pushes a reference to the array onto the stack.

```
..., no. of elements → ..., array ref
```

ldelem.* expects the stack to contain a reference to the array and the index of the element. It pushes a copy of the element (or of the reference if the element type is a reference type) onto the stack.

```
..., array ref, index → ..., value
```

You can use different `ldelem.*` instructions according to the data type of the element. For example, you can use `ldelem.i4` to retrieve elements of `int32[]` arrays, `ldelem.i1` for `int8[]` arrays, and `ldelem.ref` for `object[]` arrays and arrays of reference types. You'll find the full list of `ldelem.*` instructions in the appendix. `ldelema` works like `ldelem.*`, but it loads the address of the element as a managed pointer instead of its value.

For each `ldelem.*` instruction you'll find a corresponding `stelem.*` instruction, such as `stelem.i4`, `stelem.i1`, and `stelem.ref`.

```
..., array ref, index, value → ...
```

Finally, the `ldlen` instruction expects the top item on the stack to be an array reference, which it replaces with the length of the array.

```
..., array ref → ..., length
```

You'll use all these instructions (apart from `ldelema`) in the following sample, which illustrates the use of arrays. It sets up an array of `int32` of length 10. It then populates the array by setting element 0 to 0, element 1 to 4, element 2 to 8, and so on. Finally, it displays the value of element 3 (12), and the length of the array (10).

The following code is quite long, so I'll present it and then go over it in some detail:

```
.method static void Main() cil managed
{
    .maxstack 10
    .locals init (int32 counter, int32[] thearray)
    .entrypoint

    // Set up array
    ldc.i4.s   10
    dup
    stloc.0

    newarr     int32
    stloc.1

Loop:
    // Test if you have counted down to zero yet
    ldloc.0
    brfalse.s Finish

    // Decrement counter
    ldloc.0
    ldc.i4.1
    sub
```

```
        stloc.0

        ldloc.1
        ldloc.0

        // Get stack ready to store element
        dup
        ldc.i4.4
        mul
        stelem.i4

        br.s        Loop

Finish:
        // Display element no. 3 of array
        ldstr       "Element no. 3 is "
        call        void [mscorlib]System.Console::Write(string)
        ldloc.1
        ldc.i4.3
        ldelem.i4
        call        void [mscorlib]System.Console::WriteLine(int32)
        // Display length of array
        ldstr       "Length of array is "
        call        void [mscorlib]System.Console::Write(string)
        ldloc.1
        ldlen
        call        void [mscorlib]System.Console::WriteLine(int32)

        ret
    }
```

Other than using the array commands I've just described, this code has little that's new. However, its use of the evaluation stack is considerably more complex than anything you've seen before—as evidenced by the .maxstack value of 4. This sample also includes the first use of the dup instruction. dup is really simple—it simply duplicates the top item of the stack. It has a stack delta of +1, and after executing it the top two items of the stack will have identical contents. It's useful if you want to store the top item of the stack somewhere but want to leave a copy of that data on the stack as well.

The first part of the code deals with setting up the array. To make things clearer, I'll present the code as a table, showing the contents of the evaluation stack after executing each instruction. In the table, the symbol "array ref" denotes an object reference to the array (see Table 2-3 and Table 2-4).

Table 2-3. *Stack Contents*

Instruction	State of Evaluation Stack After Executing	Comments
ldc.i4.s 10	10	
dup	10, 10	dup puts an extra 10 on the evaluation stack so you can store it in local 0 and still leave 10 on the stack.
stloc.0	10	
newarr int32	array ref	
stloc.1	<EMPTY>	

You first load the constant 10 onto the stack—this is how big you want the array to be.

Now for the loop: The loop will be executed quite a few times with different values for the count. You'll use "counter" in the table to indicate that value. Notice that you're counting down from ten rather than up to ten. Counting down saves a local variable, makes for more compact code, and may slightly improve performance since at native-executable level (rather than IL level), because testing a value for zero is faster than comparing it to ten (you have to subtract ten, then compare it to zero).

Table 2-4. *Stack Contents (Continued)*

Instruction	State of Evaluation Stack After Executing	Comments
Loop:		
ldloc.0	counter	
brfalse.s Finish	<EMPTY>	If counter has reached zero you've finished and can go display the results.
ldloc.0	counter	
ldc.i4.1	counter, 1	
sub	counter – 1	
stloc.0	<EMPTY>	
ldloc.1	array ref	
ldloc.0	array ref, counter – 1	
dup	array ref, counter – 1, counter – 1	
ldc.i4.4	array ref, counter – 1, counter – 1, 4	
mul	array ref, counter – 1, 4 * (counter – 1)	4 * (counter – 1) is the value to be stored in element (counter - 1).
stelem.i4	<EMPTY>	
br.s Loop	<EMPTY>	

Notice in this code that the stack is empty immediately after executing the brfalse.s statement and immediately before executing the final br.s statement. It's significant that the same number of items (zero) is on the stack at these two points. If a net change happened, that would signal some invalid code. Suppose, for example, that you had done something wrong in the code so that between the brfalse.s Finished and the br.s Loop statements there was a net stack delta of 1. That would mean that every time you go round the loop, the stack would have one more element than previously. The JIT compiler would refuse to compile such code because it'd be unable to determine in advance the details of the types on the stack for each instruction (you wouldn't have been able to present a table such as the previous one—which amounts to the same thing). So quickly adding the stack deltas on a loop provides a good check on your code.

I won't go over the final part of the code for the sample, which displays the results; that code is relatively straightforward.

Calling Unmanaged Code with P/Invoke

You'll examine how you can call unmanaged code using the platform invocation (P/Invoke) mechanism. P/Invoke is something that's well supported natively by the CLR. As a result, you'll have little new to learn in terms of concepts—calling unmanaged code through P/Invoke looks pretty much the same in IL as it does in high-level languages, other than obvious syntactical differences. You will, however, spend a little time looking at what actually happens under the hood.

I'll illustrate P/Invoke by developing a small sample called PInvoke, which uses the platform invocation mechanism to display a message box using the Windows application programming interface (API) MessageBox() function. In real life, of course, you wouldn't use P/Invoke to do this because you can more easily use System.Windows.Forms.MessageBox. However, this sample is good for illustrating the principles, which you can then apply to calling other API functions that have no managed equivalents.

The native MessageBox() function has the following C/C++ signature:

```
int MessageBox(
    HWND hWnd,          // Handle to owner window
    LPCTSTR lpText,     // Text in message box
    LPCTSTR lpCaption,  // Message box title
    UINT uType          // Message box style
);
```

The first parameter (hWnd) is a Windows handle, which indicates any parent window of the message box. The second and third parameters are pointers to C-style unmanaged strings. The final parameter, uType, is a 32-bit unsigned integer (= unsigned int32 in IL), which indicates the type of message box required and the buttons on it. For example, a value of zero here indicates the message box should just have an OK button. A value of 1 (which you'll use) indicates it should have OK and Cancel buttons. The return type is a 32-bit integer that indicates which button the user pressed to quit the message box.

So that's what a message box looks like to unmanaged code. This is how you define a managed wrapper method for it:

```
.method public static pinvokeimpl("user32.dll" winapi) int32 MessageBox(
    native int hWnd, string text, string caption, unsigned int32 type) {}
```

The previous IL code corresponds to this C# code:

```
[DllImport("user32.dll")]
extern static int MessageBox(IntPtr hWnd, string text, string caption,
                             uint type);
```

In this code I've replaced the names of the parameters in the native MessageBox() method with .NET-style names, and I've replaced the native types with suitable corresponding managed types (for example, LPCTSTR with string). Notice too that all imported functions must be declared static.

The important new keyword here is pinvokeimpl. This keyword indicates that you aren't going to supply an implementation for this method but are requesting the .NET runtime to create a method whose implementation is to perform any relevant marshaling/data type conversion, then call the specified native method, and finally to perform any relevant marshaling on the return values. Of course, you don't have any equivalent to IL's pinvokeimpl in high-level languages, but you can instead use an attribute, DllImportAttribute. How this gets converted into pinvokeimpl when C# code is compiled is something you'll examine later in this chapter in the "Specifying Attributes" section.

The pinvokeimpl keyword must be followed by parentheses in which you supply the filename of the DLL that implements the function. You also need to indicate the calling convention of the native function, in this case winapi.

■Tip If you're not familiar with calling conventions, don't worry too much. Calling conventions are rules governing the precise details in memory of how parameters are passed to methods and whether the caller or callee is responsible for cleaning up any memory allocated for the parameters. For purely managed code, the CLR handles all that, so you don't have to worry about it. In native code, compilers will still handle the calling convention, so developers don't need to worry about the details. However, unlike the CLR, for historical reasons several different calling conventions are used in native code on Windows, such as cdecl and winapi, so if you're going to call a native method from managed code, you need to tell the CLR which calling convention to use. In almost all cases when using P/Invoke for Windows API functions, this will be winapi. If a particular API function takes a different calling convention, this will be indicated in the documentation for that function.

Native methods don't have metadata, which means the CLR has no way to obtain any information concerning what data a given method is expecting. The only information the CLR can extract from the unmanaged DLL is at which address the method is located. So instead, you the developer have to look up the parameter types and calling convention in the documentation and then tell the CLR what to expect by supplying an appropriate list of arguments in the declaration of the pinvokeimpl method. The arguments you indicate are, of course, managed types, but the CLR has its own list of rules for how it converts managed types to unmanaged types. It's up to you to choose a managed type that will be converted into the correct unmanaged type for the method. In the previous example, I picked native int

(System.IntPtr) as the first parameter to MessageBox() because I know that native int is the type that will be correctly marshaled to the native type, HWND. MSDN documents the full list of conversions.

The CLR will convert System.String instances to C-style strings and figure out the appropriate pointer to pass to the native code. Numeric items such as int32 will be passed without conversion. User-defined structs will be marshaled by breaking up into the individual fields and marshaling each field separately. The main work involved in the marshaling process (other than converting strings) is to make sure the fields are laid out in memory in the way expected by the native function. And the real benefit to you is that you can use .NET types.

The CLR will carry out one extra task: A number of API functions come in two versions— an ANSI version and a Unicode version. MessageBox() is one of those. User32.dll actually contains two functions, MessageBoxA() and MessageBoxW() (W stands for *wide* and indicates the Unicode version). P/Invoke can identify the correct version to be called. It's possible to specify the version in the pinvokeimpl declaration, but if this information is missing (as is the case for this sample), the CLR will instead work using whichever marshaling flag was applied to the definition of the type in which the pinvokeimpl method was defined. That's just the ansi, unicode, or autochar flag that I described in the previous chapter.

Let's now look at the code for the PInvoke sample (as usual for clarity I haven't shown the .assembly directives, and so on):

```
.method public static pinvokeimpl("user32.dll" winapi)
int32 MessageBox(native int hWnd, string text, string caption, int32 type)
{
}
.namespace Apress.ExpertDotNet.PInvokeDemo
{
    .class public auto ansi EntryPoint extends [mscorlib]System.Object
    {
        .method static void Main() cil managed
        {
            .maxstack 4
            .entrypoint

            ldc.i4.0
            ldstr    "Hello, World"
            ldstr    "Hello"
            ldc.i4.1
            call     int32 MessageBox(native int, string, string, int32)
            pop
            ret
        }
    }
}
```

The EntryPoint class specified the ansi flag, which means that string instances will be marshaled to ANSI strings. This is the option you'll normally use if you know that your code is to run on Windows 9*x* or if for some reason the unmanaged functions you're calling specifically expect ANSI strings (as may be the case for some third-party components). In most cases, on later versions of Windows, you'll get better performance by specifying unicode or autochar, but I'll stick with ansi here just so I illustrate some real data conversion. This means that for this sample, the CLR will make sure that it's MessageBoxA() that's ultimately invoked.

I've defined the MessageBox() wrapper method outside the namespace. You don't have to do this, but I think it can make things clearer for P/Invoke methods. In any case, namespaces apply only to types and have no effect on global functions.

The code to invoke MessageBox() in the Main() method is relatively simple. You just load the types specified by the wrapper onto the stack, in order. Note that you're not interested in the return value from MessageBox() here, so you just pop this value off the stack before returning. This involves another new IL instruction, pop, which simply removes the top value from the stack and discards it. You have to call pop here to get rid of the return value from the MessageBox() call, because the stack must be empty when returning from a void method.

Running the sample from the command line gives the result shown in Figure 2-2.

Figure 2-2. *Running the PInvoke sample*

One interesting point about the previous code is that it actually passes type safety despite its use of a P/Invoke method.

```
Microsoft (R) .NET Framework PE Verifier  Version 1.1.4322.573
Copyright (C) Microsoft Corporation 1998-2002. All rights reserved.

All Classes and Methods in pinvokedemo.exe Verified
```

The reason for this is that type safety measures only what's happening in the managed code. So calling into unmanaged code using P/Invoke doesn't formally affect verifiability. However, to call unmanaged code, code must have the SkipVerification security permission, which will obviously be granted only to trusted code—so in practice this doesn't cause a security loophole.

Defining Literal Binary Data

In this section I'll show you a useful technique in IL that allows you to embed hard-coded binary data in an assembly. Such data is specifically placed in a section of the PE file known as the .sdata section—it's not placed with the module's metadata. (Note that all assemblies follow the PE file format—you'll examine this issue in Chapter 4.) In general, this technique is most useful in your own IL code for arbitrary binary data (blobs). However, to demonstrate the technique, I'll use embedded native strings as the data and develop the previous

PInvoke() sample into an application that displays a message box but passes in unmanaged ANSI strings instead of relying on the platform invoke mechanism to marshal managed strings.

In general, embedding unmanaged strings in an assembly isn't a technique I'd recommend if you're writing your own IL code—it will make your code more complex and therefore harder to debug. In some situations, doing this can give a marginal performance improvement (for example, if you're passing ANSI strings to unmanaged code—in this case by storing the strings as ANSI strings, you save the cost of the Unicode-to-ANSI marshaling conversion). In any case, using embedded strings saves the initial string copy involved in an ldstr. However, the performance benefit from these is likely to be marginal, and in most cases code robustness is more important. However, if you port unmanaged C++ code to the CLR, the C++ compiler will need to use this technique in order to cope with any unmanaged strings in the original C++ code (since this is compiler-generated code, code maintainability isn't an issue— the code will definitely be correct!). It's therefore quite likely that if you work with C++, you'll see embedded unmanaged strings in your assembly—which is why I've chosen strings as the data type to illustrate the embedded blob technique.

Embedding and accessing the data requires a few new keywords. The easiest way to see how to do it is to examine some of the code you'll use in the sample.

```
.class public explicit sealed AnsiString extends [mscorlib]System.ValueType
{
    .size 13
}
.data HelloWorldData = bytearray(48 65 6c 6c 6f 2c 20 57 6f 72 6c 64 0)

.field public static valuetype Apress.ExpertDotNet.DataDemo.AnsiString
HelloWorld at HelloWorldData
```

This code has the following three stages:

You define a placeholder value type that you can use to hold data. For this example, the new type is called AnsiString.

You reserve space for the data in the .sdata section of the PE file using the .data directive. The previous code indicates that the name HelloWorldData will be used to refer to this data.

You declare a global variable called HelloWorld, of type AnsiString, and indicate that the location of this variable is in the .sdata section, at the HelloWorldData address. This is an unusual variable declaration: No new memory is allocated for the variable, and the variable isn't initialized. You just indicate that this existing and pre-initialized block of memory is to be interpreted as forming the HelloWorld instance. This effectively means that the variable name, HelloWorldData, has for all practical purposes simply become a reference into the .sdata section.

When you define the AnsiString type, you don't define any member fields or methods. Instead, you use the .size directive to indicate how many bytes each instance of the type should occupy.

```
.class public explicit sealed AnsiString extends [mscorlib]System.ValueType
{
    .size 13
}
```

This means that the type is assumed to take up 13 bytes (and if you ever instantiate it without using the at keyword, the CLR will reserve 13 bytes of memory for it). I've chosen 13 because that's how many bytes are needed to hold the string "Hello, World" as a C-style string—12 characters plus a terminating zero.

The .data directive that initializes the block of memory in the .sdata section indicates the data to be placed in the memory using a byte array.

```
.data HelloWorldData = bytearray(48 65 6c 6c 6f 2c 20 57 6f 72 6c 64 0)
```

The bytearray keyword simply indicates that you're explicitly specifying the numerical value to be placed in each byte. The values are given in hexadecimal though without the prefix 0x that you'd normally expect. It may not look obvious that my bytearray contains "Hello, World", but I promise you it does. Notice the trailing zero, which native API functions will interpret as indicating the end of a string.

Now you can present the code for the sample. Here's the new definition of the MessageBox() wrapper:

```
.method public static pinvokeimpl("user32.dll" winapi) int32 MessageBox(
    native int hWnd, int8* text, int8* caption, unsigned int32 type)
{
}
```

This is what I think is one of the amazing things about P/Invoke: It's the same underlying native method but a different definition for the wrapper—and it will still marshal over correctly. Instead of defining the second and third parameters as strings, you've defined them as int8*—your first-ever use of an unmanaged pointer in IL in this book. Why int8*? It's because int8 is the equivalent of an unmanaged ANSI character. C-style strings are, as I've said, basically pointers to sets of these characters, so what the native MessageBoxA() method is expecting is actually a pointer to an 8-bit integer (the first character of the string).

Now let's examine the rest of the code, starting with the data definitions. You're actually defining two lots of data, represented by the variables HelloWorld and Hello, to store the two strings that will be passed to MessageBox(). Notice that both sets of data are padded out to the 13 characters.

```
.namespace Apress.ExpertDotNet.DataDemo
{
    .class public explicit sealed AnsiString
                            extends [mscorlib]System.ValueType
    {
        .size 13
    }

    .data HelloWorldData = bytearray(48 65 6c 6c 6f 2c 20 57 6f 72 6c 64 0)
    .data HelloData = bytearray(48 65 6c 6c 6f 0 0 0 0 0 0 0 0)
```

```
.field public static valuetype Apress.ExpertDotNet.DataDemo.AnsiString
                                        HelloWorld at HelloWorldData
.field public static valuetype Apress.ExpertDotNet.DataDemo.AnsiString Hello
                                        at HelloData
```

The following is the `Main()` method:

```
.method static void Main() cil managed
{
    .maxstack 4
    .entrypoint

    ldc.i4.0
    ldsflda   valuetype Apress.ExpertDotNet.DataDemo.AnsiString HelloWorld
    ldsflda   valuetype Apress.ExpertDotNet.DataDemo.AnsiString Hello
    ldc.i4.1
    call      int32 MessageBox(native int, int8*, int8*, unsigned int32)
    pop
    ret
  }
}
```

This looks similar to the `Main()` method for the previous sample in that all you're doing is loading the four parameters for `MessageBox()` onto the evaluation stack and then calling `MessageBox()`. The second and third parameters are different, though—instead of loading strings using `ldstr`, you're loading the addresses of the two ANSI strings stored in the metadata. You do this using `ldsflda`. Recall that `ldsflda` loads the address of a static field, as a managed pointer. Since `ldsflda` needs no information other than the token supplied in the argument to identify the field, it doesn't pop any data off the stack.

This sample when run will do the same thing as the previous sample. On Windows 9*x*, the new sample will run slightly faster. However, you'll pay a price (beyond the greater complexity of the code): You're never going to get this sample through a type-safety check. Just look at what you're doing. You load two items onto the stack as managed pointers to `AnsiString` structs, and then you pass them off as if they were unmanaged `int8*`s when invoking the method! The JIT compiler will compile the code—it's valid code, since the type on the stack is defined at each point. But because you then interpret the types on the stack incorrectly in the call method, the code will fail type safety. In fact, if you run `peverify` on the sample, you'll get quite a few type-safety failure messages.

Introducing Exception Handling

Exception handling is quite an important topic when writing managed code, so you may have expected quite a large section on the subject in this chapter. However, in fact I won't spend that much time going over exceptions. The reason is that exception handling in IL isn't very different from high-level languages. Even the syntax in IL assembly is similar to the syntax in C# or VB. Just as in high-level languages, you can define `try`, `catch`, and `finally` blocks. And exceptions are thrown using the IL `throw` command. You can use the `rethrow` command inside catch blocks that rethrow the current exception. Two new types of block are *fault* and *filter* blocks, which I'll explain soon. As in high-level languages, try blocks are also known as *guarded* or *protected blocks.*

The Structure of IL Exception Handling Code

Typical code that uses exception handling would look a bit like this in IL assembly:

```
.try
{
    .try
    {
        // Code inside the try block or methods called from here,
        // which will likely contain some throw statements
    }
    catch [mscorlib]System.Exception
    {
        // Code for the catch block.
    }
}
finally
{
    // Code for the finally block
}
```

The previous IL code corresponds to the following C# code:

```
try
{
    // Code inside the try block or methods called from here,
    // which will likely contain some throw statements
}
catch (Exception e)
{
    // Code for the catch block.
}
finally
{
    // Code for the finally block
}
```

Although the syntax is quite similar in IL and C#, notice that the IL version contains two try blocks, where C# has only one. In fact, in C# and other high-level languages, the compiler would add a second try block to the emitted IL when compiling the previous code. The reason is that in IL, if a guarded block is associated with a finally (or fault) handler, then it can't have any other associated handler blocks. So it's not possible to have one guarded block that's associated with both a catch and a finally block, as is common in high-level languages. You need instead to insert a nested try block, which will be associated with the catch block.

In IL, `.try` is a directive (as you can see because it has a preceding dot), but `catch` and `finally` are simple keywords associated with the `.try` directive. `.try`, `catch`, and `finally` have the same meanings as in C#, MC++, and VB. In the previous code snippet I've supplied a `catch` block that handles `System.Exception`, but obviously you can specify whatever class you want—the normal rules about the system searching until it finds a suitable `catch` handler for each exception thrown apply. Be aware, however, that the exception doesn't have to be derived from `System.Exception`—that requirement is imposed by languages such as C# and VB but isn't a requirement of the CLR. Obviously, however, it's good programming practice to throw exceptions derived only from `System.Exception`.

It's worth remembering that the concept of guarded blocks doesn't exist in the JIT-compiled native code, since native assembly language doesn't have any concept of exceptions. The JIT compiler will internally sort out all the logic behind how to convert the `try`, `catch`, and `finally` blocks and the `throw` statements into suitable branch and conditional branch instructions at the native executable level.

That's the basics, but you need to be aware of some other IL-specific issues.

- `fault` blocks are similar to `catch (...)` in C++ and `catch` without supplying an exception type in C# but with one subtle difference: A `fault` block is *always* executed if any exception is thrown from the guarded block. In other words, if an exception is thrown, the program will first execute the `catch` block that most closely matches the exception type, if one is present; then it will execute the `fault` block, if present, and lastly it will execute the `finally` block if present. If no exception is thrown, execution goes straight to any `finally` block after leaving the guarded block.

- `filter` is similar to `catch`, but it provides a means of checking whether to actually execute the `catch` handler. Using a `filter` provides an alternative to placing a `rethrow` command in a `catch` block. The VB compiler actively uses `filter` blocks, since VB allows constructs such as `Catch When x > 56`. That kind of code can be translated into a `filter` block. However, C# and C++ don't expose any similar feature.

I won't go into `fault` or `filter` in detail in this book. If you're interested, they're detailed in the documentation for IL.

The following are also a couple of other restrictions on the use of the guarded blocks:

- The evaluation stack must be empty when entering a `.try` block. When entering or leaving most of the other blocks, it must contain only the relevant thrown exception. However, you have no evaluation stack restrictions when exiting a `finally` or `fault` block.

- It isn't possible to use any of the branch instructions you've met so far to transfer control into or out of exception handling blocks. Instead, you can use a new command, `leave`, and the equivalent shortened form, `leave.s`, to exit `.try`, `catch`, and `filter` blocks.

- The only way you can leave a `finally` or `fault` block is by using an IL instruction, `endfinally`/`endfault`. This is a single instruction with two mnemonics, and you should use whichever one is most suitable. (Common sense dictates that if you use it in a `finally` block, then using the `endfault` mnemonic will not help other people to understand your code!) `endfinally`/`endfault` works in a similar way to `br` (it doesn't empty the evaluation stack). However, since the JIT compiler knows where the end of the `finally` block is and where control must therefore be transferred to, endfinally/endfault doesn't need an argument to indicate where to branch. This instruction therefore only occupies 1 byte in the assembly.

leave works almost exactly like br—it's an unconditional branch, taking an argument that indicates the relative offset by which to branch. The difference between br and leave is that before branching, leave clears out the evaluation stack. This means that leave has quite an unusual stack-transition diagram.

$$... \rightarrow \text{<empty>}$$

All these restrictions are really for the benefit of the JIT compiler. Converting throw statements and exception handling blocks into straight branch instructions as required in the native executable code isn't a trivial task, and writing an algorithm to do this would become ridiculously complicated if the JIT compiler had to cope with possible different states of the evaluation stack as well.

Exception Handling Sample

To illustrate exception handling, you'll return to the CompareNumbers sample from the previous chapter. Recall that CompareNumbers asked the user to type in two numbers and then displayed a message indicating which one was the greater one. Because CompareNumbers didn't do any exception handling, if the user typed in something that wasn't a number, the program would simply crash and display the usual unhandled exception message. (The exception would actually be thrown by the System.Int32.Parse() method if it's unable to convert the string typed in by the user into an integer.) Here you'll modify the code to add appropriate exception handling:

```
.method static void Main() cil managed
{
    .maxstack 2
    .entrypoint
    .try
    {
      .try
      {
         ldstr    "Input first number."
         call     void [mscorlib]System.Console::WriteLine(string)
         call     string [mscorlib]System.Console::ReadLine()
         call     int32 [mscorlib]System.Int32::Parse(string)
         ldstr    "Input second number."
         call     void [mscorlib]System.Console::WriteLine(string)
         call     string [mscorlib]System.Console::ReadLine()
         call     int32 [mscorlib]System.Int32::Parse(string)
         ble.s    FirstSmaller
         ldstr    "The first number was larger than the second one"
         call     void [mscorlib]System.Console::WriteLine(string)
         leave.s Finish
FirstSmaller:
```

```
            ldstr   "The first number was less than or equal to the second one"
            call    void [mscorlib]System.Console::WriteLine(string)
            leave.s Finish
        }
        catch [mscorlib]System.Exception
        {
            pop
            ldstr   "That wasn't a number"
            call    void [mscorlib]System.Console::WriteLine(string)
            leave.s Finish
        }
    }
    finally
    {
        ldstr   "Thank you!"
        call    void [mscorlib]System.Console::WriteLine(string)
        endfinally
    }
Finish:
    ret
}
```

The code contains two nested .try directives, one that's associated with the catch block and one that's associated with the finally block. finally blocks are usually there to do essential cleanup of resources, but it's a bit hard to come up with a small IL sample that uses much in the way of resources, so I've had the finally block display a *Thank you!* message. Recall that putting code in a finally block ensures that the code will always be executed irrespective of whether an exception has been thrown.

You should be able to follow the logic of the code fairly well. However, notice that the concluding ret statement is located outside the .try blocks. That's because ret, in common with other branch instructions, can't be used to leave a guarded block. The only way to leave a guarded block is with a leave or leave.s instruction. Because of this, you leave the .try or catch blocks with leave.s—specifying the Finish label as the branching point. Of course, in accordance with the normal rules for always executing finally, when execution hits the leave.s Finish instruction, control will actually transfer to the finally block. Execution will leave the finally block when the endfinally is reached—and at that point control will transfer to the destination of the leave.s instruction.

One other point to notice is that the catch block starts with a pop instruction. That's because when entering a catch block, the CLR will ensure that the caught exception is placed on the evaluation stack. You're not going to use this exception object here—all you're going to do is display a message, so you pop it from the stack before you do anything else.

One final point I should mention: You may be wondering how a .try directive can appear in the middle of the instruction stream for a method, when .try, being a directive rather than an instruction, doesn't have an opcode. The answer is that it doesn't. The syntax I've been using for .try blocks is supported by ILAsm but isn't really related to the actual representation of guarded blocks in the assembly. Instead, separate structures appear at the end of the definition and code for each method that define any guarded blocks (one token for each .try directive), and these tokens indicate the relative offsets in the method of the beginnings and ends of the guarded blocks, as well as any associated handler blocks. It's possible to write ILAsm code that uses a syntax that more directly maps onto this representation, but it's not recommended because it makes your code harder to read. Full details of the alternative syntax are in the ECMA standard's Partition III documentation for IL.

Specifying Attributes

Viewed from high-level languages, attributes tend to fall into two informal categories, which are often known as *custom attributes* and *Microsoft attributes*. The syntax in the high-level languages is identical, but attributes are typically viewed as custom attributes if they've been defined in some code that wasn't written by Microsoft! Since the Microsoft compilers can't have any awareness of individual third-party attributes, the sole effect of such attributes is to cause metadata to be emitted to an assembly. On the other hand, Microsoft-defined attributes are normally assumed to have some other effect on the code—for example, the Conditional attribute may cause certain code not to be compiled.

This common view of attributes isn't really accurate; it's more accurate to divide attributes into the following three categories:

Custom attributes: These are attributes whose sole purpose is to cause metadata to be emitted in assemblies. Other managed code may of course read the metadata data using reflection and change its behavior based on the presence of these attributes. All non-Microsoft attributes will fall into this category, but some Microsoft-defined attributes also do so, such as STAThreadAttribute.

Distinguished attributes: These exist in assemblies as metadata, but they're additionally recognized by the CLR itself, and the CLR will take some action if it sees these attributes.

CLS attributes: These are similar to custom attributes but are formally defined in the CLS. It's expected that certain developer tools will recognize these attributes.

Although I've listed three categories of attributes, it's important to understand that as far as IL is concerned, they have no differences. Only one type of attribute is at the level of IL: the *custom attribute*. Every attribute in existence is a custom attribute, and every attribute is introduced in IL source code with the same syntax, using the .custom directive.

```
.custom instance void [mscorlib]System.STAThreadAttribute::.ctor() =
                                                    (01 00 00 00)
```

Another category is *pseudo-custom attributes*. Pseudo-custom attributes aren't really attributes at all, though. They're certain predefined flags in the metadata. However, they're represented in high-level languages by attributes—a representation that's useful, though misleading, since when this code is compiled, the emitted IL will contain these flags rather than any attributes.

Obviously, I can't present a full list of attributes since new attributes are certain to get added over time, but to give you an idea, Table 2-5 shows some of the attributes that Microsoft has defined.

Table 2-5. *Selection of Microsoft-Defined Attributes*

Category	Attributes
Custom	BrowsableAttribute, DefaultPropertyAttribute, SoapAttribute, EditorAttribute
Distinguished custom	SecurityAttribute, ObsoleteAttribute, SerializableAttribute
CLS custom	AttributeUsageAttribute, CLSCompliantAttribute, ObsoleteAttribute

Table 2-6 gives some of the pseudo-custom attributes, along with their corresponding flags in IL.

Table 2-6. *Selection of Pseudo-Custom Attributes*

Attribute	Flag(s)
DllImport	pinvokeimpl
StructLayoutAttribute	auto/explicit/sequential
MarshallAsAttribute	ansi/unicode/autochar

If you're interested, you can find the full list of distinguished, CLS, and pseudo-custom attributes as of version 1.*x* in the Partition II specifications. However, in most cases you don't need to know which category an attribute falls into in order to use it, since the syntax is the same for all categories in high-level languages and for all categories except pseudo-custom attributes in IL assembly.

The concept of pseudo-custom attributes is quite cunning, since it provides a way that Microsoft can in the future, if it so decides, define more flags or directives in IL and have support for these new directives automatically propagated to all high-level languages. Take the DllImport attribute as an example. You've already seen how you can mark a method as [DllImport] in your C#, VB, or C++ source code and have this converted to a method marked pinvokeimpl in the emitted IL. In fact, the compilers themselves know nothing of this attribute—they will simply pass it through their normal attribute syntax checks. However, the compilers will internally call up some code called the *unmanaged metadata API* to emit the metadata into the compiled assemblies. (If you're interested, this API is documented in the Tool Developers Guide subfolder of the .NET Framework software development kit [SDK]). The metadata API will recognize DllImportAttribute and know to emit a pinvokeimpl flag instead of an attribute into the metadata when it encounters DllImport. You can probably see where this is heading. If Microsoft decides it wants to make some other IL flag or directive available to high-level languages, all it needs to do is define a corresponding pseudo-custom attribute and update the metadata API to recognize the new attribute, and instantly all high-level languages will gain support for the directive via the attribute. Clever, huh?

Let's quickly look in more detail at the IL syntax for defining custom attributes. As noted earlier, you can define attributes using the .custom directive. Here's an example of an attribute that has been applied to a method:

```
.method public static void  Main() cil managed
{
  .entrypoint
  .custom instance void [mscorlib]System.STAThreadAttribute::.ctor() =
                                        (01 00 00 00)
```

The attribute in question here is the STAThread attribute, which indicates the COM threading model to be applied to a method if it calls into COM interop services. The .custom directive is followed by a token indicating the constructor of the attribute—in this case [mscorlib]System.STAThreadAttribute::.ctor(). Clearly, the CLR can deduce from the constructor what type the attribute is intended to be. The constructor token is followed by binary data, which will be embedded into the metadata and which indicates the data that should be passed to the constructor if the attribute needs to be instantiated (this will occur if some other application or library uses reflection to instantiate the attribute). You may wonder why the previous code shows 4 bytes being passed to a zero-parameter constructor. The answer is that the blob of data supplied with the .custom directive is set in a format defined in the Partition II document, and this format requires certain initial and terminating bytes that must always be present. The 4 bytes you see in this code are just those bytes.

The position of the .custom directive tells ilasm.exe to which item the attribute should be applied. For items that have some scope that's marked by braces (such as types and methods), you can place the directive inside the scope. For other items, such as fields, that don't have any scope, the .custom directive should be placed immediately after the declaration of the item (the opposite position to high-level languages, which normally place attribute declarations immediately before the item to which the attribute should be applied).

The following alternative syntax, in which the .custom directive is qualified by a token indicating the object to which it should be applied, therefore allows the directive to be placed anywhere in the .il file:

```
.custom (method void NamespaceName.ClassName::Main())instance void
[mscorlib]System.STAThreadAttribute::.ctor() = (01 00 00 00)
```

This latter syntax corresponds better to the internal representation of the attribute in the actual assembly: In the binary assembly, attributes are listed in the metadata, along with the token of the object to which they refer. Being able to place attributes next to the item they decorate in IL assembly code is a convenience permitted by the ilasm.exe assembler.

Delegates and Events

Delegates have a similar status in the CLR to enums: You saw earlier that to define an enum, you simply declare a type that's derived from System.Enum. The CLR will recognize from the base type that this is a special class and will therefore process it in a special manner. The same thing happens with delegates. You just derive a class from System.MulticastDelegate, and the CLR will recognize that it's a delegate and treat it accordingly. This means in particular that the CLR imposes certain restrictions on your definition of delegate-derived classes.

- They aren't permitted to contain any fields, and the only methods they can contain are the methods you'd normally expect a delegate to have: Invoke(), the constructor, and optionally the BeginInvoke() and EndInvoke() methods.

■**Note** `BeginInvoke()` and `EndInvoke()` are used for invoking delegates asynchronously. It isn't compulsory for delegates to implement them, but in practice most high-level language compilers will add support for `BeginInvoke()` and `EndInvoke()` automatically. I'll postpone discussion of these methods until Chapter 9, when I discuss threading.

- You're not permitted to supply implementations for any of the member methods, because the CLR does that for you—and the CLR's implementation involves all sorts of internal hooks into the execution engine to make delegates work correctly. You do, however, have to declare these methods to make sure the appropriate tokens get put in the metadata to refer to the methods so that other code can call them.

To illustrate the principles, I'll quickly show the code for a simple delegate. I'll assume you want a delegate that allows a string to be output in some manner (for example, to the console, to a file, or in a message box). In other words, the following is a delegate you'd define in C#:

```
public delegate void WriteTextMethodCSh(string);
```

The simplest possible definition of a delegate with the previous signature in IL would be as follows:

```
.class public auto ansi sealed WriteTextMethodIL
    extends [mscorlib]System.MulticastDelegate
{
    .method public specialname rtspecialname
        instance void .ctor(object, native int) runtime managed
    {
    }
    .method public virtual instance void Invoke(string text) runtime managed
    {
    }
}
```

I've named the IL delegate `WriteTextMethodIL`. I've given it a different name from the earlier C# delegate definition because the previous IL code isn't quite the same as what you'd get if you compiled the C# delegate definition—most notably, the C# compiler would add `BeginInvoke()` and `EndInvoke()` methods. As noted, the fact that `WriteTextMethodIL` derives from `System.MulticastDelegate` is sufficient to identify this type as a delegate. The two member methods you define are both marked `runtime managed`—a designation you haven't seen before. `managed` of course means that it contains managed code; `runtime` indicates that the CLR knows about this method and will supply an implementation for you. Also, notice that the sole means of indicating the signature of the delegate in IL is through the signature of the `Invoke()` method.

In C# to instantiate a delegate, you have to pass in details of a method. For the following example, suppose you're using the delegate to wrap the Console.WriteLine() method:

```
WriteTextMethod myDelegate = new WriteTextMethodCSh(Console.WriteLine);
```

In C#, a lot of what's going on is hidden. However, the new keyword gives away the fact that a constructor is being called—in IL, the .ctor() method. At the IL level, all delegate constructors take two parameters, of types object and native int, respectively. The object is the object reference to the object against which the delegated method is to be invoked. This will of course be null for static methods such as Console.WriteLine(). The native int is a pointer to the entry point of the method that the delegate will wrap. You haven't seen native int used like this before, but it's legal IL—it's even verifiable provided you use the correct technique to obtain the function pointer, which you'll see soon.

The Invoke() method is of course used on the delegate to invoke the method that's wrapped by this instance of the delegate. It has to have the correct signature—and as I remarked earlier, this signature is the only means the CLR has available to figure out what type of method this delegate can be used to invoke.

Now let's see how a delegate is actually used. You'll code some IL that's equivalent to this C# code:

```
WriteTextMethod myDelegate = new WriteTextMethodCSh(Console.WriteLine);
myDelegate("Hello, World");
```

This code instantiates the delegate and uses it to display *Hello, World* in the console window. Here's what the IL code to instantiate the delegate looks like (note that this code assumes the WriteTextMethodIL delegate is defined in a namespace, DelegateDemo):

```
ldnull
ldftn    void [mscorlib]System.Console::WriteLine(string)
newobj   instance void DelegateDemo.WriteTextMethodIL::.ctor(object,
                                                             native int)
```

This code contains a couple of new commands. ldnull loads a null object reference onto the stack. It's identical in its behavior to ldc.i4.0, except that the zero on the stack is interpreted as an object reference instead of an int32. You want null on the stack for the first parameter to the constructor, since you're passing a static method to it. For an instance method, the ldnull would be replaced by an instruction to put an object reference onto the stack, such as ldloc.0 (if local variable 0 contains the object reference).

ldftn is another new command. It's the instruction that supplies the function pointer. It takes as an argument a token indicating a method and places the address where the code for that method starts onto the stack.

Then, with the parameters on the stack, you can call the actual constructor, which will leave a reference to the newly created delegate on the stack.

Next you invoke the delegate. This code assumes that a reference to the delegate object is stored in local variable 0 and that the delegate is in the DelegateDemo namespace.

```
ldloc.0
ldstr    "Hello, World"
callvirt instance void DelegateDemo.WriteTextMethod::Invoke(string)
```

You load the delegate reference (the `this` reference as far as the `Invoke()` method is concerned), then load the one parameter that must be passed to the delegate, and finally use `callvirt` to invoke the method.

One interesting point to note from all this is the way that type safety works here: The standard phrase is that delegates provide a type-safe wrapper for function pointers. You may wonder how type safety can be enforced here—after all, what's to stop you from just loading any old number onto the stack in place of `null` or the method address, passing it to the delegate, and as a result having some code that shouldn't be executed invoked through the delegate? The answer is that Microsoft has defined certain standard IL instruction sequences for use when invoking delegates, which will all ensure that the `native int` passed to `Invoke()` is the address to an appropriate method. The previous code is an example of one of these sequences. The JIT compiler will recognize these sequences and accept them as verifiable, but the verification algorithm will reject any other sequence. Obviously, high-level language compilers will emit only known verifiable sequences to invoke delegates.

One last point: While I'm on the subject of delegates, I'll quickly mention events. The relationship between an event and a delegate is similar to the relationship between a property and a method. Just like properties, the CLR has no intrinsic knowledge or support for events. As far as IL is concerned, an event is declared with the `.event` directive. But all `.event` does essentially is the equivalent of attaching a flag to a specified existing delegate to indicate that high-level languages may want to interpret that delegate as an event and use any special supported high-level language event syntax in association with it. That's pretty much analogous to the situation for properties. Since there's no new .NET or CLR concepts to be understood by examining events, I won't cover events further.

Disassembling IL and Round-Tripping

You've spent virtually the whole of this chapter and the previous one examining hand-written IL assembly code. However, it's also possible to examine and edit IL assembly that has been generated by disassembling existing assemblies using the `ildasm` utility. For the rest of this chapter, you'll examine code that has been generated in this way.

I mentioned earlier that one difference between IL and higher-level languages is the ease with which IL can be disassembled into IL assembly. In fact, it's perfectly possible both for `ilasm.exe` to read `ildasm.exe` output (provided there was no embedded native code in the original assembly) and for `ildasm.exe` to read `ilasm.exe` output. One of the specific aims Microsoft had when designing `ilasm` and `ildasm` was the ability to perform round-trips. At the end of the previous chapter, I demonstrated one possible use for this: It enables the debugging of IL code generated from a high-level language, with the debugger being used to view the IL rather than the high-level source code. Also, you have the following other uses for round-tripping:

- You can hand-modify a compiled assembly. If you have an assembly (for example, one that was generated by the C# or VB .NET compiler), you can use `ildasm` to convert its contents to ILAsm text, make whatever changes you want to make to it, and then use the `ilasm` tool to convert the results into a binary assembly.

- You'll also need to use round-tripping if you want to create a single file that contains IL code generated from multiple languages. The technique is to compile the segments written in each language separately and then use `ildasm` to disassemble the assemblies. You can then hand-edit the `.il` files produced to merge them into one file and use `ilasm.exe` to convert this back into an assembly.

I won't illustrate these techniques in detail here, since anything I write concerning the details may change in the near future. At present none of the .NET tools support automating the process of round-tripping and editing IL code. And none of the Microsoft compilers support writing embedded IL code in your high-level source code—something that would have made it much easier to use IL when you want to do so. Currently, it seems unlikely that any such support will be added in the near future, but it's likely that third-party tools on the Web will appear to assist in automating the round-tripping process, so if you're thinking of doing that, it'd be worthwhile to check what's available.

It's also worth pointing out that some tools are available on the Internet that not only disassemble assemblies but that convert (decompile) the IL into equivalent high-level code, making it a lot easier to read. The best known of these is almost certainly the free tool anakrino, which is available at `http://www.saurik.com`. If you do decide to try anakrino or similar tools, however, be aware of licensing issues—your software licenses will almost certainly not permit you to run this type of tool on many of the assemblies installed on your machine. In many cases this restriction will apply to running `ildasm.exe` on assemblies as well.

In the following sections, you'll use `ildasm.exe` to examine the IL generated by the C#, VB, and MC++ compilers—this will both teach you a little more IL and start to familiarize you with some of the differences between the compilers.

■**Caution** The samples you'll look at here were generated with version 1.1 of the .NET Framework. Although the general principles should still hold, you may find that you get slightly different IL code from that presented here if you try these samples using a later version of the framework, since it's always possible that Microsoft will make improvements either to the compilers or to the `ildasm.exe` utility.

Comparing IL Emitted by C#

For this test, have VS .NET generate a C# console application called `CSharp` for you and modify the code so that it looks like this:

```
using System;

namespace CSharp
{
    class Class1
    {
        [STAThread]
        static void Main(string[] args)
        {
```

```
        string helloWorld = "Hello, World!";
        Console.WriteLine(helloWorld);
    }
  }
}
```

You then compile this program, making sure you select the release configuration in VS .NET, since you don't want the IL you examine to be cluttered with debugging code (or if you're doing this at the command line, specify that optimizations should be turned on with the /o flag).

The full listing file produced by ildasm.exe is too long to show in full. I'll just present some highlights from it.

Before the Main() method is defined, you encounter the following empty class definition:

```
//
// ============== CLASS STRUCTURE DECLARATION ==================
//
.namespace CSharp
{
  .class private auto ansi beforefieldinit Class1
        extends [mscorlib]System.Object
  {
  } // end of class Class1


} // end of namespace CSharp
```

One aspect of IL assembly I haven't mentioned is that it's possible to close and reopen class definitions within the same source file (although this is purely a feature of IL assembly—this structure isn't persisted to the binary IL). ildasm.exe emits ILAsm code that takes advantage of this feature. Doing so serves the same purpose as forward declarations in C++—it prevents certain possible issues related to types being used before they're defined, which could confuse ilasm.exe if it's called on to regenerate the assembly.

Then you come to the actual definition of Class1, the class that contains the Main() method.

```
.namespace CSharp
{
  .class private auto ansi beforefieldinit Class1
        extends [mscorlib]System.Object
  {
    .method private hidebysig static void
            Main(string[] args) cil managed
    {
      .entrypoint
      .custom instance void [mscorlib]System.STAThreadAttribute::.ctor() =
                                                    ( 01 00 00 00 )
      // Code size       13 (0xd)
      .maxstack  1
      .locals init (string V_0)
```

```
    IL_0000:  ldstr      "Hello, World!"
    IL_0005:  stloc.0
    IL_0006:  ldloc.0
    IL_0007:  call       void [mscorlib]System.Console::WriteLine(string)
    IL_000c:  ret
  } // end of method Class1::Main

  .method public hidebysig specialname rtspecialname
          instance void  .ctor() cil managed
  {
    // Code size       7 (0x7)
    .maxstack  1
    IL_0000:  ldarg.0
    IL_0001:  call       instance void [mscorlib]System.Object::.ctor()
    IL_0006:  ret
  } // end of method Class1::.ctor

} // end of class Class1
```

You should notice several points about this code. The actual class definition is marked with several flags that you've already encountered, as well as one that you haven't: beforefieldinit. This flag indicates to the CLR that there's no need to call a static constructor for the class before any static methods are invoked (though it should still be called before any static fields are invoked). The flag seems a little pointless in this particular case since Class1 doesn't have any static constructors anyway but can be a useful performance optimizer where a static constructor exists but no static method requires any field to be pre-initialized.

This code contains several comments, indicating the start and end of various blocks. These comments aren't of course emitted by the C# compiler or present in the assembly—they're generated by ildasm.exe. The same applies for the name of the local variable, V_0, and for the statement labels that appear by every statement. These give what amounts to a line number—the offset of the opcode for that instruction relative to the start of the method.

The Main() method contains a local variable, which holds the string to be displayed. You or I could easily see from a simple examination of the C# code that this variable isn't actually required and could be easily optimized away. The fact that it's present in IL illustrates a feature of both the C# and the VB compilers: to a large extent, they leave optimization to the JIT compiler, performing very little optimization of the code themselves.

Another related aspect of the Main() method isn't immediately obvious but deserves comment. Look at how the ILAsm instructions match up to the C# instructions.

```
string helloWorld = "Hello, World!";
    IL_0000:  ldstr      "Hello, World!"
    IL_0005:  stloc.0
Console.WriteLine(helloWorld);
    IL_0006:  ldloc.0
    IL_0007:  call       void [mscorlib]System.Console::WriteLine(string)
(Return implied)
    IL_000c:  ret
```

Do you notice how there's a neat break and how each set of IL instructions corresponding to a C# statement leaves the stack empty? That's a general feature of how many high-level compilers work. I haven't yet observed any code generated by the C# or VB compilers that doesn't follow this practice, although the C++ compiler does seem to use the stack in a slightly more sophisticated way. This has performance and security implications. On the performance side, it means these compilers won't perform optimizations that cause the stack to contain values that are used between different high-level language statements. The JIT compiler will probably perform these optimizations anyway, but at a cost of a tiny performance penalty the first time each method is executed. On the security side, this feature of high-level compilers makes it particularly easy for decompilers to reverse-engineer IL code—you just look for the points where the stack is empty and you know that's the boundary between high-level statements. However, you'll observe that in the IL code that I've written by hand for the samples in this and the previous chapter, I've generally made much more sophisticated use of the evaluation stack (for example, loading data onto it that will be used only several operations later). The potential implications for improved performance and security against reverse engineering if you hand-code methods in IL should be obvious.

The [STAThread] attribute that's applied to the Main() method by the VS .NET wizard when it generates the code for a C# application has made it through to the IL code. STAThreadAttribute (which indicates the threading model that should be used if the method makes any calls to COM) is an example of a custom attribute that's largely ignored by the CLR. It comes into play only if COM interop services are called on.

One other point to observe is that the IL code contains a constructor for the Class1 class, even though none is present in the C# code. This is a feature of C#: If you don't supply any constructors for a class, then the definition of C# requires that the compiler supply a default constructor that simply calls the base class. This is actually quite important. Although in this code so far you don't instantiate the Class1 class, you may in principle do so if you develop the code further. And as you saw when you examined the instantiation of reference types, newobj requires a constructor as an argument. So if the C# compiler didn't supply a default constructor to classes where you don't specify one yourself, then it'd be impossible to ever instantiate those classes.

Comparing IL Emitted by VB

Now let's examine the equivalent code produced by the VB compiler. Once again for this I've used a file generated by VS .NET. That's important, since in the case of VB, VS .NET maintains some information, such as namespaces to be referenced and the program entry point as project properties, to be supplied to the VB compiler as parameters, rather than as source code. The VB source code looks like this:

```
Module Module1

    Sub Main()
        Dim HelloWorld As String = "Hello, World!"
        Console.WriteLine(HelloWorld)
    End Sub

End Module
```

The VB code defines a module—which can be confusing since a VB module isn't remotely the same thing as an IL module. The VB `Module` keyword declares a sealed class that's permitted to contain only static methods (as opposed to a module in an assembly, which is a file that forms part of the assembly). You can see the difference from the ILAsm file. Here's what the `Module` declaration in VB has become:

```
.namespace VB
{
  .class private auto ansi sealed Module1
         extends [mscorlib]System.Object
  {
  } // end of class Module1

} // end of namespace VB
```

Although the `sealed` keyword is there, you have no way in IL to mark a class as only containing static methods—that's a requirement that's enforced by the VB compiler at the source code level.

Note that the IL code defines a namespace that isn't apparent in the VB code. This namespace originates in the VS .NET project properties—by default VS .NET gives VB projects a namespace name that's the same as the project name. You can change this using the project properties dialog box in VS .NET.

On the other hand, here's the "real" module declaration:

```
.module VB.exe
// MVID: {0E871D8A-FBDF-4925-B17C-E6EFDD5563B4}
.imagebase 0x11000000
.subsystem 0x00000003
```

As usual, the prime module (in this case the only module) has the same name as the assembly.

Now let's examine the code for the `Main()` method.

```
.method public static void  Main() cil managed
{
  .entrypoint
  .custom instance void [mscorlib]System.STAThreadAttribute::.ctor() =
                                                  ( 01 00 00 00 )
  // Code size       13 (0xd)
  .maxstack  1
  .locals init (string V_0)
  IL_0000:  ldstr      "Hello, World!"
  IL_0005:  stloc.0
  IL_0006:  ldloc.0
  IL_0007:  call       void [mscorlib]System.Console::WriteLine(string)
  IL_000c:  ret
} // end of method Module1::Main
```

This code is virtually identical to the code compiled from C#, illustrating that VB and C# have little difference in practical terms for those IL features that both languages implement—apart of course from the source-level syntax. However, a couple of points here illustrate minor differences between the approaches taken by the languages. Recall that I said earlier in the chapter that C# uses hidebysig semantics for all methods, but VB does so only when overriding. You can see that here—in C# the Main() method is marked as hidebysig; in VB it isn't. You'll also see evidence of the VB compiler's slightly greater tendency to hide some features from the developer—much less than in the days of VB 6 but still present to a small extent: The STAThreadAttribute has made its way into the VB-generated IL, even though it wasn't present in the source code. The C# compiler emits it only if it's there in source code. Which approach you prefer depends on precisely where you prefer to strike the balance between how much work you have to do and how fine a degree of control over your code you want.

Comparing IL Emitted by MC++

Now let's bite the bullet and look at the C++ code. I'll warn you that you can expect a more complex assembly because of the greater power of C++. In fact, I'll make things a bit more complicated still by putting two Console.WriteLine() calls in the C++ source code. One will take a string as a parameter, and the other one will take a C++ LPCSTR—a C-style string—or as close as I can get to a C-style string when using managed code. The reason I'm doing this is because I want to show you how the C++ compiler copes with LPCSTR declarations. It uses the technique I showed earlier for defining a class to represent binary data that's embedded in the metadata—and as you'll see soon, this can lead to some strange-looking entries when you examine the file using ildasm.

The following is the C++ code you'll use. Once again it's generated as a VS .NET project—in this case called CPP. For this I generated a C++ managed console application and then modified the code by hand to look like this:

```
#include "stdafx.h"
#include "Windows.h"

#using <mscorlib.dll>

using namespace System;

int main(void)
{
   LPCSTR pFirstString = "Hello World";
   Console::WriteLine(pFirstString);

   String *pSecondString = S"Hello Again";
   Console::WriteLine(pSecondString);

   return 0;
}
```

I also made one change in the stdafx.h file: VS .NET 2003 generates code that includes the standard template library iostream classes, which I don't actually use in the previous code.

This will result in a lot of unwanted additional metadata describing `pinvokeimpl` methods, and so on, to wrap the STL code, and believe you me, analyzing the assembly is going to be complicated enough for now without this additional metadata. So I commented out the offending line, like so:

```
//#include <iostream>
#include <tchar.h>
```

Now you're ready to examine the emitted IL. Before I show you the code for the `Main()` method, let's look at what `ildasm` shows you if you run it without any parameters (see Figure 2-3).

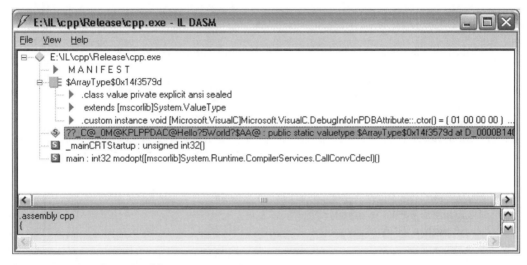

Figure 2-3. *IL code emitted from a C++ project*

Confusing, huh? I still remember I couldn't believe my eyes the first time I ever tried running `ildasm.exe` on a large C++ project. But rest assured there's a good reason for all the items here. Let's consider them in turn:

The structure named `$ArrayType$0x14f3579d` is a type that's defined as a placeholder for the binary data. It's the type that will be used to represent the "Hello World" string.

The global field called `??_C@_0M@KPLPPDAC@Hello?5World?$AA@` is the field that will be used to instantiate `$ArrayType$0x14f3579d`. The names of this data and class are pretty complicated, but that's because these names are generated internally by the C++ compiler. Obviously, the compiler wants to make sure that its names don't conflict with the names of any types you may want to declare—and `??_C@_0M@KPLPPDAC@Hello?5World?$AA@` and `$ArrayType$0x14f3579d` are the names it has chosen for this purpose. If you ever try porting an unmanaged C++ project to managed code and look at the results with `ildasm`, the chances are you'll see a huge number of types and static fields with these kinds of names, representing all the hard-coded strings in your application.

_mainCRTStartup() is the entry point for the application. However, it isn't the main() method that you think you have written. The C++ compiler works by generating a separate entry-point method called _mainCRTStartup(), which contains unmanaged code. This unmanaged function performs several tasks that can't be done from managed code and that are relevant only to C++ applications, such as making sure the C runtime library is initialized. Then it calls the method you thought you had told the compiler was the entry-point method. The existence of this method illustrates the greater range of resources that can be called on by the C++ compiler but also demonstrates clearly why the C++ compiler can't generate type-safe code (at least as of .NET version 1.*x*): The type-safety checks will fail at the very first hurdle—the entry-point method. This is likely to be fixed at some point in a future version of .NET, however.

main() is the method you wrote in the source code.

Now let's look at the actual code. Here's the true entry point:

```
.method public static pinvokeimpl(/* No map */)
        unsigned int32  _mainCRTStartup() native unmanaged preservesig
{
  .entrypoint
  .custom instance void
[mscorlib]System.Security.SuppressUnmanagedCodeSecurityAttribute::.ctor()
= ( 01 00 00 00 )
  // Embedded native code
  //  Disassembly of native methods isn't supported.
  //  Managed TargetRVA = 0x10d5
} // end of method 'Global Functions'::_mainCRTStartup
```

Clearly you can't deduce much from this. The native unmanaged flag attached to the method definition tells you that the method contains unmanaged code, not IL. ildasm can't generate IL source code for native code and has left comments to warn you of that fact instead. The preservesig flag is one you haven't encountered yet—it prevents the marshaler from modifying the signature of this method (so-called name-mangling is sometimes done for internal reasons on method names in unmanaged C++).

The method has the attribute SuppressUnmanagedCodeSecurityAttribute. This attribute is there for performance reasons—normally, any call into unmanaged code will trigger a so-called stack walk, in which the CLR examines this assembly and every calling assembly going up the call stack, to verify that all these assemblies have permission to call unmanaged code—which is great for security but not good for performance. This attribute suppresses the stack walk—you'll normally apply it to code that you think has been thoroughly tested and can't possibly open security loopholes.

This is the method that contains the interesting code:

```
.method public static int32
modopt([mscorlib]System.Runtime.CompilerServices.CallConvCdecl)
        main() cil managed
{
  .vtentry 1 : 1
  // Code size       27 (0x1b)
```

```
.maxstack  1
IL_0000:  ldsflda    valuetype $ArrayType$0x14f3579d
                                ??_C@_0M@KPLPPDAC@Hello?5World?$AA@
IL_0005:  newobj     instance void [mscorlib]System.String::.ctor(int8*)
IL_000a:  call       void [mscorlib]System.Console::WriteLine(string)
IL_000f:  ldstr      "Hello Again"
IL_0014:  call       void [mscorlib]System.Console::WriteLine(string)
IL_0019:  ldc.i4.0
IL_001a:  ret
} // end of method 'Global Functions'::main
```

You should be able to follow through this code without too much difficulty. One point I'll mention is that the C++ compiler does show slightly more intelligent use of the evaluation stack than the C# and VB compilers do: It doesn't use a local variable for either string, despite that the original C++ source code had local variables for both of them, but instead confines the strings to the evaluation stack. The two new keywords, .vtentry and modopt, present in this code smooth the internal operation of the unmanaged/managed transition: .vtentry indicates the entry in a table consisting of what are known as *vtable fixups*. This is simply a table of method addresses and is necessary to allow managed and unmanaged code to interoperate in the same assembly. The modopt keyword indicates the calling convention of a method for the benefit of unmanaged code. This quick examination of the code generated for simple HelloWorld applications in different languages does appear to bear out Microsoft's claims that the C++ compiler is more powerful than the C# or VB ones and can potentially give you higher-performance managed code. On the other hand, the IL code generated by the C++ compiler will have more work to do at program startup time as it performs various initializations of unmanaged libraries.

Working through these short programs, and compiling and disassembling them, also shows how much more extra information you can find out about your code when you understand a little IL.

Summary

In this chapter you've examined using IL to define classes and other more sophisticated constructs, going beyond basic program control flow and the use of the evaluation stack. You've seen how to define and instantiate both value and reference types, and you've seen how the CLR provides support for areas such as arrays and enumerations, as well as more advanced concepts such as exception handling, custom attributes, and delegates. Finally, you've put your understanding of IL into practice by using it to compare the output from compilers in different languages—and have in the process seen some evidence of the greater power of the C++ compiler as compared to the C# and VB compilers.

You've now finished your look at IL but not of the internal workings of the .NET Framework. In the next chapter you'll carry on with digging under the hood of the common language runtime to investigate how it supports a variety of services, including interaction with unmanaged code and support for type safety.

CHAPTER 3

■■■

Going Inside the CLR

In this chapter, you'll investigate certain aspects of how the CLR works under the hood. I won't try to be in any way comprehensive—that's hardly possible for a piece of software as powerful as the CLR. But I'll select a few key topics to explore in detail. And in choosing topics, I've deliberately emphasized areas that are frequently glossed over by other books or by the documentation.

The chapter will start by identifying the various parts of the .NET architecture—which leads you to examine the relationship between the formal ECMA definition of a common language infrastructure and Microsoft's implementation of that standard.

Note The full name of ECMA is *Ecma International–European Association for Standardizing Information and Communication Systems*. It's an organization that sets internationally recognized standards for aspects of computer technology.

Once I've outlined the ECMA standardization of the .NET Framework, you'll move onto examine the following:

The type system: I'll dig under the hood of the type system, show how value and reference types are actually represented in memory, and discuss some subtleties about using value types and boxed types. I'll also present a C++ sample that shows how you can find addresses of objects and access their in-memory representations.

Code validation and verification: You'll look at exactly what the JIT compiler does when it validates and verifies your code. You'll also examine the question of what exactly constitutes type-safe code. You probably learned at an early stage in your .NET programming career that type safety is important for preventing nasty things such as memory corruption. You'll learn in this chapter what kinds of conditions a program has to satisfy to count as type safe.

Managed and unmanaged code: You're used to the idea that you can use `DllImport` or COM interop to call up unmanaged code—and C++ developers will also know that they can use C++ to embed unmanaged code in an assembly. You'll examine how this is done and how the various techniques used to call unmanaged code (internal call, It Just Works [IJW], P/Invoke, and COM interop) work behind the scenes.

But first, let's look at the overall architecture of the CLR and the ECMA CLI standard.

Introducing the Relationship Between .NET Framework Components and ECMA Standards

In this book, I mostly follow the common informal usage as far as terminology is concerned, in which the terms *.NET Framework* and *CLR* are used roughly interchangeably to mean the whole set of software Microsoft has written that allows you to run managed code on Windows. The term *.NET Framework* possibly has a broader meaning, since it also includes support libraries and tools that are useful but not essential to run managed code and aren't part of the CLR. The CLR provides the runtime environment and consists of a number of components implemented by various DLLs, including `mscoree.dll`, `mscorjit.dll`, and so on.

Figure 3-1 shows the main components of the framework.

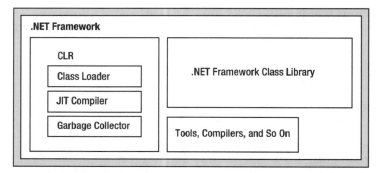

Figure 3-1. *The main components of the .NET Framework*

Many of the boxes in this figure will be familiar to you. For simplicity, I've marked only a few components of the CLR that are particularly relevant to code execution. Other aspects of the CLR include, for example, the code responsible for security and for reflection.

It's worth making the following observations:

- An important distinction between the CLR and the class library is that the CLR is written in unmanaged C++, and the framework classes are largely written in C#—in other words, they're written in managed code that depends on the CLR to execute.

- The class loader performs the first stage of processing when some managed code is to be executed. It reads the assembly, using the hash to check that the assembly hasn't been tampered with. It then reads the metadata and from the metadata works out how to lay out the types defined in the assembly in memory. For types that have been defined with `auto` layout (as opposed to `sequential` or `explicit`), it's the loader that decides in which order the fields will be arranged.

The ECMA Standard

What I've just described is the .NET Framework as implemented by Microsoft. You're no doubt aware that a core part of the specifications of the framework have been accepted as ECMA standard 335. This standard defines what's formally known as the *Common Language*

Infrastructure (CLI)—a set of minimum features that should be supported by any software product that implements the equivalent of the .NET Framework. The ECMA standard indicates the supported feature set, including the definition of IL, but doesn't define any particular implementation.

The ECMA standard has two components: the *Virtual Execution System* (VES), which is the actual environment under which the code should run, and the libraries. Hence, under this scheme, the .NET Framework is an implementation of the CLI, the CLR is an implementation of the VES, and the .NET Framework Class Library is an implementation of the ECMA specification for the libraries. However, the .NET Framework goes further than this: both the CLR and the .NET Framework Class Library implement many additional features that aren't defined in the ECMA specifications.

The following are among the features defined by the CLI:

- The common type system

- The file format for assemblies

- CIL (note that IL and MSIL are just alternative names for CIL)

- The extensible metadata system

The Partition Documents

The CLI is formally defined in five documents known as the *partitions*. You can find these documents at http://www.ecma-international.org/publications/standards/Ecma-335.htm. Alternatively, copies of the partitions are supplied as Word documents in the Tool Developers Guide\Docs subfolder in the .NET Framework software development kit (SDK). These documents cover the following areas:

Partition I, Architecture: This describes the architecture of the CLI.

Partition II, Metadata: This is the largest of the documents. It describes in detail not only the items of metadata in an assembly but also the PE assembly file format. It includes, for example, specifications of value and reference types, enums and delegates, method calling conventions, and so on. It also gives the syntax for IL assembly language and defines the IL source code directives.

Partition III, CIL: This partition specifies the instruction set for IL, along with some background information. It includes a complete list of CIL opcodes.

Partition IV, Library: This explains the difference between the kernel and compact profiles (defined shortly) and indicates the libraries required for each.

Partition V, Annexes: This contains information about various other topics, including good programming guidelines and some portability considerations.

Besides defining the CLI, these documents also specify (in Partition IV) two possible levels of implementation: a *compact implementation* and a *kernel implementation*. Software is said to provide a compact implementation if it implements everything defined in the CLI. A subset of particularly essential CLI features, known as the *kernel features*, is also defined, and it's acceptable to write software that provides a *kernel implementation*, which, as you may guess, means supporting only the kernel features. Having said that, though, a kernel implementation isn't much smaller than a compact implementation. In reality, the CLI has few nonkernel features, the most significant being that it has no requirement to support floating-point numbers in the kernel implementation.

As you may expect, the .NET Framework implements virtually everything as defined in the CLI, so it's for most practical purposes a compliant compact implementation—besides implementing a huge superset of features not defined in the CLI (a more sophisticated JIT compiler and garbage collector, many more class libraries, and so on). However, a few places in the documents indicate that the CLR doesn't implement some small feature that's strictly speaking a formal CLI requirement, at least in version 1.*x* of the .NET Framework. These few exceptions are relatively minor, and I imagine are likely to be addressed in future .NET Framework releases.

The ECMA Libraries

I've mentioned that the ECMA standard includes class libraries. The standard defines the classes, the signatures of their methods, and their purposes. The .NET Framework Class Library of course includes all the libraries in the ECMA definition, as well as a lot more. Here I'll briefly summarize which classes are defined by the ECMA libraries. Full details are available from the ECMA Web site.

A kernel implementation of the CLI should provide these libraries:

- The Runtime Infrastructure Library includes classes required by compilers that target the CLI.

- The Base Class Library contains many of the basic classes in the System, System.IO, System.Collections, and other namespaces, including classes to support string handling, primitive types, file I/O, and collections.

A compact implementation of the CLI should in addition provide these libraries:

- The Network Library, which contains classes to support networking.

- The Reflection Library, which contains classes to support reflection.

- The Xml Library, which contains some of the classes in the System.Xml namespace.

- The Extended Numerics Library, which provides support for floating-point arithmetic. For example, the System.Single and System.Double types count as being in this library.

- The Extended Array Library, which supports multidimensional arrays and arrays that aren't zero indexed.

I list these libraries here only for reference. When you're actually using the classes in them, you certainly don't need to worry about which library a particular class comes from—after all, many, if not most, .NET developers get by perfectly well without even being aware of the existence of the formal CLI libraries! The specifications of the CLI libraries may become relevant in the future, though, if .NET is ever ported to another platform and you need to start worrying about whether your code is portable.

Framework SDK Resources

For basic .NET programming, the information in the MSDN documentation is normally adequate as far as documentation goes. However, many of the topics covered in this book aren't documented on MSDN. Instead, you may find some resources in the Framework SDK useful. These include the following:

- The Tool Developers Guide, which consists of Microsoft Word documents that describe certain advanced features of .NET, as well as copies of the ECMA partition documents. This includes documentation for several unmanaged APIs that are exposed by the CLR, including the *debugging API* (which allows debuggers to attach to running managed processes), the *metadata API* (which allows compilers to generate metadata for assemblies), and the *profiling API* (which allows profilers to attach to running managed processes).

- Header files that define many of the constants and internal C structures used in .NET and in assemblies, as well as structures and interfaces required by the unmanaged APIs.

- A number of advanced samples.

You can locate all this information by browsing around the folder in which you've installed the .NET Framework SDK and its subfolders. If you installed the .NET Framework SDK as part of VS .NET, you'll most likely find this folder as a subfolder of your VS .NET install folder; for example, on my machine it's at `C:\Program Files\Microsoft Visual Studio .NET 2003\SDK`.

Shared Source CLI

Another source of invaluable resources for anyone who wants to understand the internal workings of the CLR is Microsoft's *Shared Source CLI* (code-named *Rotor*). Rotor is a complete implementation of the ECMA-standard CLI that will work on the Windows XP and the FreeBSD operating systems. The best bit of it is that it's free (subject to licensing restrictions), and it comes with source code! Microsoft has provided Rotor for the benefit of developers who want to experiment with .NET (for example, to see how a CLI should be implemented) or who want to use it for research purposes. Studying the Rotor source, or compiling it and playing around with it, will give you an idea of how things can be implemented at a logical level to conform to the ECMA standard. I'm also told that, although the JIT compiler and the garbage collector in Rotor are far simpler than those of the CLR, the remainder of the implementation closely matches the CLR itself. You can download the source code for Rotor at `http://www.microsoft.com/downloads/details.aspx?familyid=3a1c93fa-7462-47d0-8e56-8dd34c6292f0&displaylang=en`.

While I'm on the subject of alternative implementations, it's also worth mentioning the Mono project. This is an open-source community-based CLI implementation primarily aimed at the Linux platform, though it also runs on Windows, Solaris, and FreeBSD. You can find out about Mono at `http://www.go-mono.com/`.

Finally, I should mention DotGNU Portable.NET (`http://www.southern-storm.com.au/portable_net.html`), which is a CLI implementation targeted initially at Linux platforms. This forms part of the wider DotGNU project that includes other components and tools not related to the CLI and that aims eventually to comprise an "operating system for the Internet."

Investigating the Value/Reference Type System

In the following sections, you'll delve into the .NET type system, focusing on the differences between value and reference types. I assume you're familiar with the basic principles of value and reference types; you'll examine how the two categories of types are actually implemented.

Reference Types

One of the important features of .NET is that reference types are self-describing. This means that in principle, the CLR needs to have only the address of an object in the managed heap to be able to find out everything about that object, including its type, what fields and methods it implements, how much memory the object occupies, and how those fields are laid out in memory. This self-describing feature is important, and it's the reason why code like this will work:

```
// C# code
object obj = GetSomeObjectFromSomewhere();
Type type = obj.GetType();
```

If you actually look at an object in memory, you'll see it looks rather like Figure 3-2.

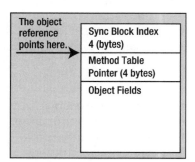

Figure 3-2. *The structure of a reference type*

■**Tip** Note that this figure is correct for version 1.*x* of the framework. Microsoft reserves the right to change the details in future versions, though the basic concepts as explained in this chapter are unlikely to change.

The reference to an object actually contains the first byte of a method table pointer—that's a 4-byte address that points to something called a *method table*. Details of the method table aren't documented, but you can expect that it's something like the vtable of unmanaged code. The method table is dependent only on the type, not the instance. Hence, two instances of the same class will contain identical values for the method table pointer. The method table will contain addresses that allow the CLR to locate the entry points of methods implemented by this type, and in particular to invoke the correct override for virtual methods. It also permits the CLR to look up the information concerning the type and size of the object. It's this pointer to the method table that enables the object to be self-describing.

Immediately before the method table pointer you'll find another word, which is occupied by something called a *sync block index*. This is an index into a table of sync blocks that's used for synchronizing threads. I'll cover the full theory of how this works in Chapter 9. Suffice to say that if any thread requests a lock on this object, then that object's sync block index will be modified to index into the table. In most cases, if you haven't created a sync block, this word will contain zero (in fact, I'd say that for most applications, virtually all objects will have this word set to zero most of the time—most real applications have vast numbers of objects but only a few locks active at any one time).

Value Types

A value type is much simpler than a reference type and occupies less memory. It can be located somewhere on the stack frame, or, if it's declared to be a member field of a reference type, then it will be stored inline in the managed heap inside that reference type. In terms of memory layout, it looks like Figure 3-3.

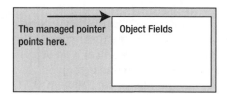

Figure 3-3. *The structure of a value type*

As the figure shows, the value type contains only its fields. Compared to a reference type that contains the same fields, a value type saves 12 bytes: the method table pointer, the sync block index, and the object reference. Twelve bytes may not be significant, but if you have a lot of objects, those bytes can accumulate. Depending on the situation, this can make value types much more efficient for storing and manipulating data. Also, you save because value types don't need to be garbage collected. But that all comes at the expense that these data structures aren't self-describing. This fact may come as a surprise—after all, we have pretty much been brought up to believe that all .NET types are self-describing; that's a fundamental principle of .NET and .NET type safety. However, in the case of value types, the CLR has other means to find out what's occupying the memory.

- For a value type that exists inline inside a reference type, the reference type is self-describing, and part of its definition will include the fact that this value type occupies a certain area of memory inside the reference object.

- For a value type that exists on the stack frame, the class loader, as part of the JIT compilation process, emits tables that indicate what data types will be occupying various memory locations at various points in the execution flow (these points are known as *safe points* for garbage collection). Do you recall that in the previous chapter I emphasized that a requirement of valid IL is that the JIT compiler should be able to work out what's on the evaluation stack at each point in the code? Given that the JIT compiler has this information, you can probably see that emitting tables showing what type occupies each memory location isn't going to be that hard a task. When required, the CLR uses these tables to identify types. One example of where this facility is used is during garbage collection: The garbage collector needs to know what value types are stored where so that it can locate references to objects that may be contained in those types. This all means, incidentally, that value types do still each have a method table, but each instance doesn't have a need to contain a pointer to it.

Boxed Types

Boxed types are formally recognized as reference types, and in almost all respects they're treated as such. It's also important to understand that for many purposes the boxed type is regarded as a different type from the underlying value type, even though it will share the same metadata. You even declare a boxed type in IL in the same way as you declare an object; the following .locals directive declares two locals, a System.Drawing.Point instance, and a boxed instance of the same struct. The declaration of the reference to the boxed object uses the object keyword, in the same manner as for declaring an object reference.

```
.locals(valuetype [System.Drawing]System.Drawing.Point,
        object [System.Drawing]System.Drawing.Point)
```

Boxed types are different from normal reference types in one aspect, however. In general, instance and virtual methods on reference types are expected to be implemented on the assumption that the first parameter passed in (in other words, the this reference) is an object reference. On the other hand, instance methods on value types are expected to be implemented on the assumption that the first parameter is a managed pointer to the first item of data in the type itself. Since boxed types share the implementations of all their methods with the corresponding unboxed value types, this means they too expect a managed pointer rather than an object reference as the first parameter to instance methods. Hence, as you saw in the previous chapter, you shouldn't pass an object reference to a method on a boxed type. Instead, you should unbox the reference and pass in a managed pointer, like so:

```
// stack contains a boxed reference to a Point instance
unbox
call    string [System.Drawing]Point.ToString()
```

System.ValueType and System.Enum

System.ValueType and System.Enum have quite a strange status in .NET. The framework has a special knowledge of these types, and it treats types derived from them in a way that's quite peculiar if you think about it. Derive from any other type, and you get the reference type you've defined. But derive from either of these two classes, and you get a (boxed) reference type *and* a stack-based value type. And although high-level programmers are accustomed to thinking of the value type as the "real" type and the boxed type as some kind of rarely used mutation, at the IL/CLR level, you'd probably get a better understanding of what's really going on if you looked at it the other way around—view the boxed type as the genuine type that has been derived from ValueType or Enum, and view the unboxed struct as a strange freeloader that you happen to get as a by-product.

As mentioned briefly in Chapter 2, System.ValueType and System.Enum are actually reference types. This is a fact that often comes as a surprise to people exploring IL for the first time. However, it makes a lot of sense. For simplicity, you'll examine the situation for ValueType here, but the same principles apply to System.Enum.

Notice that since boxed types are derived from ValueType, you can do all the normal reference tricks with them. For example, a ValueType reference can refer to a boxed type.

```
.locals (valuetype int32, object [mscorlib]System.ValueType)
ldloc.0
box       int32
stloc.s   1       // Valid and verifiable
```

You can also call virtual methods, just as you would for a class. The only restriction, of course, is that the only virtual methods that can possibly exist on the boxed type are the ones defined in System.Object/System.ValueType: Equals(), GetHashCode(), and ToString(). (Finalize() is also virtual, but you shouldn't be explicitly calling that method.)

```
// These instructions place the string "43" on the stack
ldc.i4.s   43
box        int32
callvirt   [mscorlib]System.ValueType.ToString()
// These instructions also place the string "43" on the stack
ldc.i4.s   43
box        int32
callvirt   [mscorlib]System.Object.ToString()
// But these instructions place the string "System.Object"
// on the stack
ldc.i4.s   43
box        int32
call       [mscorlib]System.Object.ToString()
```

But beware of this:

```
// These instructions place the string "43" on the stack
ldc.i4.s   43
box        int32
unbox                    // You MUST unbox in this case
callvirt   [mscorlib]int32.ToString()
```

What the previous sample shows is that if you explicitly specify the method as a member of int32, you need to pass a managed pointer—not an object reference—to the method. And not only that—this last construct will fail verifiability. All this happens despite that it's the same method that ultimately gets called.

The previous code snippets show that having ValueType as a reference type works quite well. Indeed, if Microsoft had done the opposite and made ValueType a genuine value type, it would have actually constituted a syntax error in mscorlib.dll. The reason? The CLR requires all value types to have some finite nonzero size, since otherwise it'd have—shall I say—an interesting task, figuring out how to reserve memory for them! Hence, you'll get a syntax error if you try to declare a value type that doesn't either have at least one field or have a size specified with the .size directive. ValueType, of course, has neither.

Another corollary of this is that an unboxed value type doesn't really behave as if it derives from anything at all. It's simply a plain set of fields, along with some metadata that allows you to call methods against this set of fields. This is in marked contrast to the boxed type, which derives from ValueType, and has its own method table index and sync block index, just like a proper class.

Field Alignment

So far I've covered the overall view of what types look like in memory, but I haven't said anything about how the individual fields of a type are organized. This clearly will depend on the layout flag that's indicated for the class in the assembly—whether the class is marked as explicit, sequential, or auto. (Or, equivalently, if you're using a high-level language: it will depend on whether the type has been decorated with StructLayoutAttribute and what value the StructLayoutAttribute.Value property has.)

Explicit layout is syntactically the most complicated to code but conceptually the simplest: The fields will be laid out at exactly the locations you specify in your code. The only proviso is that specifying offsets that overlap object references with other types will cause the class loader to refuse to load the type. Since this chapter is about concepts, not syntax, and since you can look up the syntax for the StructLayoutAttribute easily on MSDN, this chapter won't cover it further.

If you specify sequential layout, the fields will be laid out in the order of the class definition. However, they won't necessarily be packed next to each other: They may have some space between them. The reason for this has to do with something that's known as the *byte alignment*. The way modern hardware works, it's more efficient to load any primitive data type from memory into or from a register in the CPU if the data is aligned in a certain way in memory. And the rule is that the starting address of the data should be a multiple of the size of the data. What that means is that if you're trying to load an int16 (which occupies 2 bytes) from memory, then it's better if the starting address of that int16 is, for example, 2, 4, 6, 8, and so on. If the data type is an int32 (4 bytes), then it should be stored at an address 4, 8, 12, 16, and so on, and an int64 or float64 (8 bytes) should be stored at locations 8, 16, 24, 32, and so on. Values that are located at these optimal addresses are referred to as being *naturally aligned* or as having the correct byte alignment. If a machine needs to load or store data that isn't aligned correctly (for example, if it needs to load an int16 that's located at address 36917), then the load process will take longer and may not be atomic. If a type is to be laid out sequentially, it means that the fields will appear in the same order in which they've been defined but that padding may be inserted between them in order to ensure that each individual field is naturally aligned. This is the same scheme that's used by the VC6 compiler, which means that if you want types to be able to be passed directly to unmanaged code compiled from Visual C++ without having to be marshaled, sequential layout is the way to do it. (However, this isn't guaranteed to work with code compiled with other compilers, since other compilers may not lay out structures in the same way.) Types that have been laid out so that they require no marshaling are termed *isomorphic*.

auto layout is similar to sequential, except that the class loader won't be under any obligation to lay out the fields in the order in which they were defined. Instead, it will reorder them to find a layout that maintains byte alignment while minimizing the amount of memory that's wasted on padding.

Generally speaking, if your application uses only managed code, you'll usually get the best performance using the auto layout. On the other hand, if you're calling into unmanaged code, you may find that sequential layout for the types being passed to the unmanaged code serves you better because of the savings in marshaling.

Using C++ to Access Managed Heap Memory Directly

I'll now present some code in C++ that defines and instantiates a couple of simple classes and that uses unmanaged pointers to locate the objects on the managed heap and examine the memory they occupy. I've picked C++ for this example because C++ offers the greatest freedom to manipulate pointers. C# allows some use of pointers, but even in unsafe code blocks it places restrictions on their use, which would be awkward in the context of this example. VB would also not be an option here because VB doesn't allow any direct pointer manipulation at all. Apart from illustrating some of the principles I've just been discussing, this code will demonstrate some of the techniques you can use if you want to get at the memory occupied by an object directly.

■**Caution** Bear in mind, aspects of this code are highly unsafe. The code won't just fail verifiability; but if you use this technique in other code, you risk your code breaking if Microsoft changes the layout of fields. However, if you do want to do some deep digging into the internals of .NET, this code demonstrates a useful technique.

The code is contained in a sample called ObjectDig.

To start with, you define two classes, like so:

```
__gc class BigClass
{
public:
    int x;          // = IL int32
    double d;       // = IL float64
    bool b;         // = IL bool
    short s;        // = IL int16
    String *sz;     // = IL object reference
};

__gc class LittleClass
{
public:
    int x;
    int y;
};
```

These classes have no purpose other than to illustrate memory layout. LittleClass contains only two fields of the same size, so the loader has no reason to reorder the fields. BigClass, on the other hand, contains fields of several different sizes, and you'd expect the loader to rearrange these to maintain type alignment while keeping BigClass objects as small as possible. Normally, the fields will be arranged in decreasing size order, which means you'd expect the actual order of them to be d first (which occupies 8 bytes), then x and sz (4 bytes each), s (2 bytes), and finally b (1 byte).

Before you instantiate these classes, you need a helper global method that can display memory contents in a user-friendly format.

```
void WriteMemoryContents(unsigned char *startAddress, int nBytes)
{
    for (int i=0; i<nBytes; i++)
    {
        if (i % 8 == 0)
            Console::Write("Address {0:x}: ", __box((int)(startAddress) + i));
        if (startAddress[i] < 16)
            Console::Write("0");
        Console::Write("{0:x} ", __box(startAddress[i]));
        if (i % 4 == 3)
            Console::Write("  ");
        if (i % 8 == 7)
            Console::WriteLine();
    }
    Console::WriteLine();
}
```

This method takes a start address, supplied as unsigned char*, and the number of bytes from this address to write. The various if statements are simply to format the data in a readable way. It displays each byte of memory in hex format, with 8 bytes to a line on the console window and a bigger space after the fourth byte for readability. Each console line starts by indicating the address of the first of the 8 bytes.

Now here's the interesting code:

```
int _tmain(void)
{
    BigClass __pin *obj1 = new BigClass;
    obj1->x = 20;
    obj1->d = 3.455;
    obj1->b = true;
    obj1->s = 24;
    obj1->sz = S"Hello";
    LittleClass __pin *obj2 = new LittleClass;
    obj2->x = 21;
    obj2->y = 31;
    LittleClass __pin *obj3 = new LittleClass;
    obj3->x = 22;
    obj3->y = 32;

    unsigned char *x = (unsigned char*)(obj1);
    Console::WriteLine("Memory starting at &obj1 - 4:");
```

```
WriteMemoryContents(x - 4, 60);

Console::WriteLine("Memory starting at obj1->s:");
x = (unsigned char*)(&(obj1->s));
WriteMemoryContents(x, 2);
Console::WriteLine("Memory starting at obj1->sz:");
x = (unsigned char*)(&(obj1->sz));
WriteMemoryContents(x, 4);

return 0;
}
```

You start by instantiating one BigClass object followed by two LittleClass objects and by initializing the fields to values that you'll be able to identify when you examine the memory. Note that you declare all the objects using the __pin keyword. This does two things. First, it ensures that the garbage collector won't move the object while you're examining its memory. This is unlikely in such a small program but is a good safety feature, since having objects moved around would make it hard for you to inspect the correct memory contents! More important for these purposes, you have to declare obj1 as a pinned reference because otherwise the C++ compiler won't let you cast it to the unmanaged pointer that you'll need in order to examine memory. The C++ compiler lets you get away with a lot in terms of trusting you to know what you're doing, but it does have limits to its trust! Note also that the objects will be automatically unpinned when the references go out of scope as the function returns.

Having set up the variables, you declare an unsigned char* variable and initialize it to point to the first object allocated. This line is the key piece of code:

```
unsigned char *x = (unsigned char*)(obj1);
```

The key point about this line is that obj1 is, in IL terms, an object reference. This means it will point to the actual beginning of the object—its method table, not to its fields. By casting it to an unmanaged pointer, you have a pointer that you can basically do whatever you like with but that you know currently points to the managed object's method table. Now it's a simple line to call the WriteMemoryContents() helper function to display the memory not only for obj1 but also for obj2 and obj3, which follow it. Notice, though, that you give WriteMemoryContents() the address 4 bytes below the method table pointer to make sure you include the sync block index in the output.

```
unsigned char *x = (unsigned char*)(obj1);
Console::WriteLine("Memory starting at &obj1:");
WriteMemoryContents(x - 4, 60);
```

I've asked for 60 (= 0x3c) bytes of memory to be displayed. I'm cheating here a bit and using the fact that I happen to know this is exactly how much memory the objects are going to occupy. In most cases, asking for a bit too much memory to be displayed won't be a problem—you'll just get some extra bytes of garbage at the end. However, a small chance exists that if you attempt to display unused memory that crosses a page boundary, you'll get a memory access violation because of attempting to access memory that hasn't been committed. Chapter 7 will explore further the issue of how memory is managed and what it means for memory to be committed.

Finally, you call WriteMemoryContents() twice more, but this time you pass it unmanaged pointers that have been set up to point to particular fields in the obj1 instance. This will give you a confirmation of which memory is being used to store which fields, and it also illustrates how to get an unmanaged pointer to a field directly in C++.

Running the ObjectDig sample on my computer gives these results:

```
Memory starting at &obj1-4:
Address c71b64: 00 00 00 00   5c 53 94 00
Address c71b6c: a4 70 3d 0a   d7 a3 0b 40
Address c71b74: 4c 1b c7 00   14 00 00 00
Address c71b7c: 18 00 01 00   00 00 00 00
Address c71b84: e0 53 94 00   15 00 00 00
Address c71b8c: 1f 00 00 00   00 00 00 00
Address c71b94: e0 53 94 00   16 00 00 00
Address c71b9c: 20 00 00 00
Memory starting at obj1->s:
Address c71b7c: 18 00
Memory starting at obj1->sz:
Address c71b74: 4c 1b c7 00
Press any key to continue
```

These results may look at first sight like garbage, but they show the correct object layout. The first DWORD (I use DWORD as a convenient shorthand for a set of 4 bytes), starting at address 0xc71b64, contains the sync block index. This is zero currently, since no locks exist on this object in operation. The next DWORD (at address 0xc71b68) contains the address of the method table, and the following two DWORDs contain the double, obj1->d—since the double is stored in exponent-mantissa format, you won't be able to easily relate the bytes there to the represented value of 3.455. The fifth DWORD (at 0xc71b74) is what would be expected to be the sz pointer to the "Hello" string. It is—that's confirmed by the later display of obj1->sz, which contains the same value, 00c71b4c. (Note that the lowest order byte comes first in memory, in little-endian format, so you reverse the order of the bytes in giving the full address.)

Next you get to some data that you can easily identify. The sixth DWORD, starting at address 0xc71b78, contains 0x00000014, which is just 20 in decimal. That's what you set the obj1->x field to. Now you get two even smaller fields, which can be placed in one DWORD between them. The following 2 bytes contain the short, s, initialized to 24 (0x0018). Then comes the bool, occupying 1 byte and set to the value unity. The following single byte, which contains zero, is just padding. You can't use it for anything else without breaking byte alignment, since the object has no other 1-byte fields.

That's the end of the obj1 instance, so the next DWORD will contain the sync block index of the next object allocated—obj2. You won't be surprised to find this sync block index contains zero. This is followed by the address of the LittleObject method table. Reading this DWORD, you can see that the address of this method table is 0x009453e0. Looking further back in the output, the BigClass method table was indicated to be at 0x0094535c, which confirms that the two method tables are located fairly close together, as you'd expect. You can carry on this analysis to pick out the fields of obj2 and obj3, noting that they have the same method table address.

If you do try any code like this, bear in mind that the layout of objects may change with future versions of .NET, so don't write code that relies on a certain layout. If you want to access memory in an object directly (which you may want to do so you can pass it to unmanaged code and avoid the marshaling overhead), the recommended way of doing so is by accessing individual fields. In other words, do it this way:

```
short *pshort = &(obj1->s);
```

In C#, the restrictions on the use of pointers to objects on the managed heap ensure that this is the only way you can retrieve pointers to data on the heap.

This code will be translated into an IL `ldflda` command, which will continue to work correctly, no matter how the fields in the object are laid out by the loader. If you want your code to be robust against future implementations of .NET, you should obtain the address of each field separately and use each address only to examine or manipulate memory within that field. With this proviso, directly accessing memory on the managed heap can be a good way to improve performance in some situations. You can use it to perform direct manipulations on memory or to pass data to unmanaged code. Having said that, this kind of micro-optimization is worth doing only in a small number of cases. Usually you're better off sticking to robust type-safe code. Also, make sure you pin the objects concerned for as short a time as possible; otherwise you risk impairing the performance of the garbage collector, which may more than cancel out any performance gains from the direct memory access. Correctly managing the pinning looks something like this in C++:

```
MyClass __gc* __pin obj = DoSomethingToGetObjReference();
try
{
    // Do your processing with obj
}
finally
{
    obj = NULL;
}
```

In C#, correct management of the pinning means making sure that the C# `fixed` block extends over the minimum amount of code, like so:

```
fixed (MyClass obj = DoSomethingToGetMemberFieldReference())
{
    // Do your manipulation of fields in obj here
}
```

Incidentally, if you're marshaling isomorphic data via P/Invoke, the CLR will just give the unmanaged code the address of the original data rather than copying it and will automatically pin this data for the duration of the P/Invoke call.

JIT Compilation: Verifying and Validating Code

You'll now examine aspects of the operation of the JIT compiler. In particular, I'll cover the principles behind how it validates and verifies code before executing it.

In the previous chapter I indicated that the errors that could prevent managed code from executing include invalid code and unverifiable code. If the JIT compiler detects invalid code, it will fail the JIT for that method, causing an exception to be thrown, but if it detects unverifiable code it will merely insert some extra code into the relevant block of code, which will generate an exception if code doesn't have permission to skip verification. If the code does have SkipVerification permission, it will run without the exception, and the user has to hope that this trust in the unverifiable code is justified and that it won't accidentally trash the system. In the following sections, you'll examine in more detail what requirements a program must satisfy if it's to pass the valid code and verifiable code tests.

Validating Code

For IL code to be considered valid, it must have the following two requirements:

- Certain instructions require particular data types to be on the evaluation stack.

- It must be possible to work out the state of the evaluation stack at each point in the code in a single pass.

In Chapter 2, you saw a couple of examples that illustrate the first requirement: The ret command expects the evaluation stack to be empty for a void method or to contain one item, the return value, for a nonvoid method. Similarly, the mul command and other arithmetic commands require the top two data items on the stack to be consistent types. For example, an attempt to multiply an int32 by a float32 is considered invalid code.

It should be self-evident that the two previously listed requirements are closely related: If you can't work out the state of the evaluation stack, then you can't test whether the stack is in an appropriate condition for instructions such as a mul. However, the second requirement is a much more general condition, since it requires that even for instructions such as ldloc.0 and br.s, which don't care what's on the evaluation stack, the JIT compiler must still be able to establish the state of the stack at that point.

You also shouldn't forget those last few words on the second condition: *in a single pass.* These words ensure that IL supports simple JIT compilers. The requirement for the stack contents to be in principle calculable on a single pass is the reason for the .maxstack directive at the beginning of each method. By providing the maximum number of items to exist simultaneously on the stack first, you reduce the number of passes needed to analyze the code. As it happens, the CLR's JIT compiler is quite sophisticated and makes multiple passes, including passes to optimize the code. However, it will still fail as invalid any code that doesn't satisfy the formal definition of valid code (even though it, as a more sophisticated compiler that makes multiple passes, would have been able to compile that code).

An important point about valid code is that all you're effectively testing for when you test for validity is that the JIT compiler can work out what's on the stack. If it can't do that, then various reasons exist why it wouldn't be able to run the code in the .NET environment—for example, it wouldn't be able to generate the tables of the types that occupy the various memory locations to which the garbage collector may need to refer. That's why code has to be validated before it can run. By validating code, you're testing whether it's going to be possible in principle to compile and execute that code. However, what you *aren't* testing is whether the types are used in a consistent way (other than for certain specific IL instructions that require it). For example, if you try to pass an object reference to a method that's expecting a managed pointer, that won't be detected—for the simple reason that that may give you unexpected results but doesn't in principle stop the code from being executed. That type of condition will be tested for when you attempt to verify the code—you'll look at this shortly.

To test the condition of the evaluation stack, the ECMA standard specifies that the JIT compiler follows a simple algorithm: Starting with the first instruction in a method (for which the evaluation stack is empty), it follows every possible path from one instruction to the next, working out the effect that each instruction has on the evaluation stack and checking that the resultant stack state for the next instruction is consistent with that obtained from any other path that leads to that instruction. Described like that, the algorithm may sound hard to grasp, but it's actually roughly what you've done yourself several times in the previous couple of chapters—whenever I've presented a code sample and listed the state of the evaluation stack beside each line of code. When reading through the list, you'll almost certainly have gone through virtually the same process in your head—the process of saying, "This instruction does that to the stack, which means the next instruction will find this data on it." The only difference is that in the examples in the previous chapter, I occasionally inserted data *values*. The JIT compiler won't do that. When validating code, all it's interested in is what types will be placed on the stack—at this point in time it has no way of knowing and doesn't care anyway what values those types may contain.

In order to illustrate how validation works in practice, I'll now go through an example and manually validate some code, just the way the JIT compiler would do it. This should make it clear what the validation involves and what kinds of situation can cause a program to be invalid.

Note Although I'll describe some algorithmic details here, I don't as it happens have access to the code for the JIT compiler (much as I would like to have!). I can't say whether Microsoft's implementation follows how I do it here, but I can tell you that, however Microsoft has done it, it will be logically equivalent to the algorithm you're going to work through here.

Here's the method you're going to validate:

```
.method public static int32 GetNumber() cil managed
{
    .maxstack 1
    .locals init (int32)
    ldc.i4.s    23
    br.s        JumpThere
BackHere:
    ldloc.0
    ret
JumpThere:
    brtrue.s    BackHere
    ldloc.0
    ldc.i4.1
    add
    ret
}
```

This is actually a rather silly implementation of a method—all it does is return the value 0—but the code manages to jump all over the place in the process of getting the value. But then I've designed this method to illustrate a couple of points about validation, not as an example of good programming! Do you think this method will pass? Well, let's see. Imagine some conceptual boxes, one for each instruction. The JIT compiler wants to put in each box the details it's worked out of what type will be on the stack at that point. Figure 3-4 shows what you know before you start validating the method.

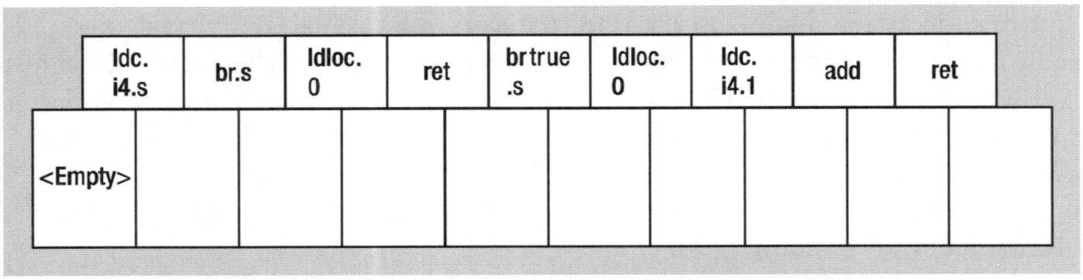

ldc. i4.s	br.s	ldloc. 0	ret	brtrue .s	ldloc. 0	ldc. i4.1	add	ret
<Empty>								

Figure 3-4. *Types known to be on the stack before validation*

Initially almost all the boxes are blank, indicating that you don't yet know what type goes in any of them, although you do know from the .maxstack directive that there will be at most one data item in each box. The only exception is that you know the first box contains nothing (I've written <empty> to indicate the fact). This box represents the start of the method, and methods always start with a clean evaluation stack.

The first instruction the JIT compiler examines is ldc.i4.s. That puts an int32 onto the stack. You know the value is 23, but all the validation algorithm cares about is that it's an int32. So int32 can go in the second box. Then you have a br.s instruction. That doesn't change the contents of the stack, but it does transfer control. So you need to place the correct stack contents into the box representing the target of the branch. Figure 3-5 shows what the stack contents look like so far.

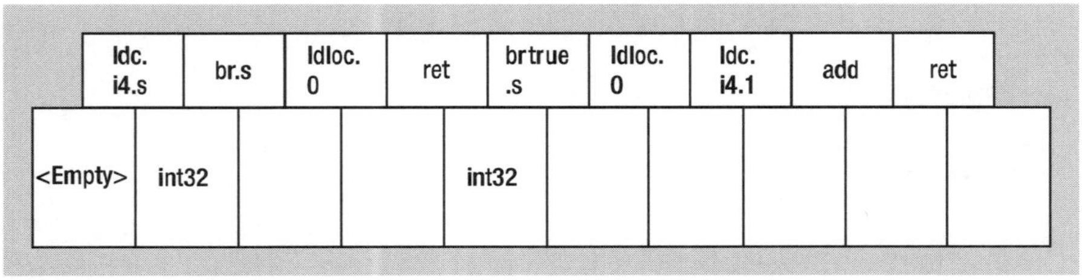

ldc. i4.s	br.s	ldloc. 0	ret	brtrue .s	ldloc. 0	ldc. i4.1	add	ret
<Empty>	int32			int32				

Figure 3-5. *Stack contents detected after evaluating the br.s*

Now you have a problem. Remember, you aren't following execution flow—instead you're doing a forward pass through the code, so the next instruction you need to consider is the first ldloc.0 command, the one that immediately follows the br.s and is attached to the BackHere label. What's the state of the stack that this command sees? You have no way of knowing, since you haven't yet seen any command that branches to here. So you'll have to assume the stack is empty at this point. The ECMA specifications actually say that if you hit a situation such as this, then you must assume that the evaluation stack is empty, and any later instructions that branch back here will have to live with that and be consistent with it. So you follow ldloc.0—that places an int32 on the stack, since local variable zero is of type int32. Next you come to the ret statement. This is the first statement for which the opcode has a requirement of its own about the stack contents. Since this is a nonvoid method, ret expects to find one item on the stack. Luckily that's what you have, so everything is consistent. Figure 3-6 shows the new information you've derived concerning the stack contents.

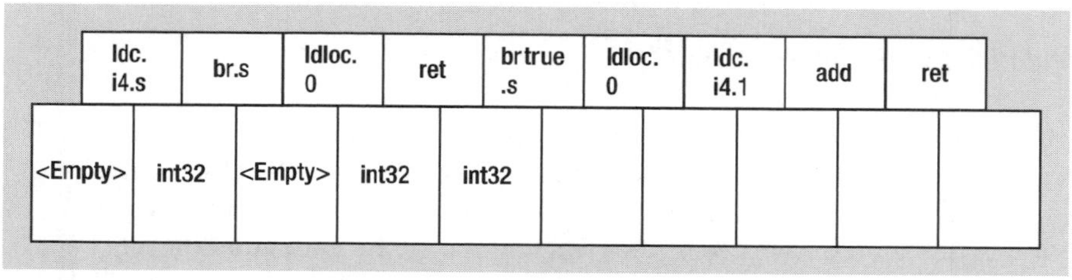

ldc. i4.s	br.s	ldloc. 0	ret	brtrue .s	ldloc. 0	ldc. i4.1	add	ret
<Empty>	int32	<Empty>	int32	int32				

Figure 3-6. *Contents detected after evaluating the first* ret

Now you have to consider the brtrue.s instruction, which branches if the top item of the stack is nonzero. And this instruction is an interesting one: brtrue.s expects to find at least one item of an integer type on the stack, and, since it's a conditional branch, it may theoretically send the control flow to either of two locations. (Yes, I know that you and I can tell just by looking at the code that the stack contains 23, the nonzero condition will always be satisfied, and the branch will always occur. But the JIT compiler can't tell that yet. Remember, it's looking at types, not values.)

To sort out this opcode, you first need to confirm the stack starts with an integer type as the topmost element. As it happens, you've already filled in the stack contents for this instruction—you did it when you analyzed the br.s. It's got one int32 in it, which is fine. brtrue.s will pop that off the stack, leaving it empty. So let's look at the two instructions that may get executed next. First, look at the following instruction (if the branch doesn't happen)—so you place <Empty> into the next box. Second, look at the target of the branch, the BackHere label. Ah—a potential problem exists. You've already filled in a stack contents for that point in the code. It'd better match. Luckily you filled in that box as <Empty>, which is what you want. If an inconsistency existed here, then the method would be deemed invalid on the grounds that it failed the test of being able to work out uniquely and consistently what data type occupies the stack at each point in the code.

Finally, you trawl on linearly through the code. You hit the last ldloc.0, which puts an int32 onto the stack. Then you hit ldc.i4.1, which puts another int32 onto the stack and—wait—that's torn it. The .maxstack directive told you that you needed to reserve space for only one item on the stack. You have no room for the new int32. It's so close to the end, and you've failed the test. This method isn't valid code and will be rejected by the Microsoft JIT compiler, as well as by any JIT compiler that conforms to the ECMA standard. Though, as you can probably see, if you had said .maxstack 2 instead, then the method would have passed (see Figure 3-7).

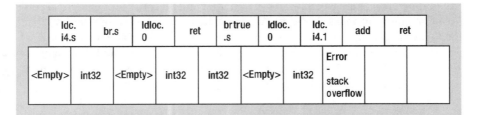

ldc. i4.s	br.s	ldloc. 0	ret	brtrue .s	ldloc. 0	ldc. i4.1	add	ret
<Empty>	int32	<Empty>	int32	int32	<Empty>	int32	Error - stack overflow		

Figure 3-7. *Validation failed after detecting a stack overflow*

The irony is that the code has failed because of some instructions that will never actually get executed anyway. But because you need to support a basic JIT compiler that wouldn't be able to spot things such as that, you still have to decree that this code isn't correct, valid, IL.

Going through this should have given you a feel for most of the issues that the JIT compiler will face when testing whether code is valid. Other than .maxstack problems, I'd imagine the most common reason for hand-written IL code not being valid is an inconsistency in the stack state detected at a branch target. For example, a loop that on balance adds one item to the stack on each iteration will cause this problem.

Incidentally, checking that types match on a branch target is a slightly more complex problem than the previous example illustrates. Suppose you have two branches that both target the same instruction. Clearly, for valid code, the number of items on the evaluation stack at the target must be the same for each branch. But what about the types? Suppose one branch instruction branches with a System.Windows.Forms.Control reference on the stack, where the other has a System.Windows.Forms.Form reference. Will that count as valid? The answer is "yes" in this case. The JIT compiler, if it sees different types, will try to find one type that can encompass both possibilities. In this example, you have no problem if you assume that the type on the stack is Control: Form is derived from Control, so a Control reference can happily refer to a Form object. On the other hand, if one branch instruction had Form on the stack, and the other had a System.Drawing.Color instance, that wouldn't be valid. No type exists that you can use to store both a Control reference and a Color instance—not even System.Object, since Color is a value type. (Of course, if it had been a reference to a boxed Color instance, then Object would do nicely, and the code would be valid.) I could go on with examples, but I think you get the picture. The Partition III document lists a complicated set of formal rules for resolving type discrepancies, but the rules just boil down to the common-sense criteria I've been using here.

By now you probably have a good idea of the principles used to identify valid code. It may look a bit remote from your high-level language programming—after all, all the Microsoft compilers will generate only valid IL code (if one of them did ever emit some invalid code even just once, I'd imagine there'd be some pretty red faces at Microsoft and some frantic efforts to fix the bug in the compiler!). However, if you do ever write your own IL code, I can virtually guarantee you'll quickly find yourself trying to work out why the JIT compiler has claimed your code is invalid when it looked perfectly logical to you. That's when you'll need to make sure you understand the contents of this section. You'll also need to understand it if you ever do compiler writing. Also, it may be useful if you look at the IL code emitted by your favorite compiler and wonder why the IL seems to be going through some unnecessary hoops in its control flow when you can see some obvious optimizations. A good chance exists that it's because of the need to keep to valid code.

■Tip Don't forget `peverify.exe`. This tool can be a great help, since it will point out the reasons why code fails validity as well as verifiability.

Verifying Type Safety

Now you'll examine in detail how .NET enforces type safety and, for that matter, what type safety actually means. You'll see that the verification algorithm is similar to the validation algorithm but imposes more stringent conditions on the state of the evaluation stack.

Type Safety: The Theory

I can't help thinking that the term *type safety* is in some ways a slightly unfortunate choice; it immediately makes you think of the type-safety restrictions enforced by many languages whose aim is to ensure you at all times treat the data with the correct data type assumptions. This is the kind of type safety that's aimed at preventing bugs by insisting, for example, that if you load an integer, you shouldn't manipulate it like it's a floating-point number. Although that kind of type safety is important in .NET, and is indeed the basis of the verification algorithm, it's more a means to an end. When I talk about verifying type safety, what I'm actually talking about is verifying that an application is well behaved and more specifically that it can't manipulate any memory that doesn't belong to it. In fact, enforcing classic type safety is one of the main weapons that ensures this can't happen. So somewhere along the line the terminology has arisen whereby managed code is *type safe*, when what we actually mean is that it won't try to do anything naughty as far as accessing memory that doesn't belong to it (because it doesn't misinterpret types in a way that could allow that to happen). But since *type safe* is the terminology in use, I'll stick to it here.

Type safety is in fact just one of two weapons in .NET's armory against badly behaved programs. You'll deal with the following two issues separately:

- Is the code in the assembly explicitly going to do things such as write to the registry using the registry access classes, write to your file system using the `System.IO` classes, or do some other potentially dangerous action you may not want it to do? This is really an issue of security and as such will be dealt with in Chapter 12.

- Is the code in the assembly going to do some unfortunate pointer arithmetic or something similar that results in it corrupting your memory or doing something to damage other applications? This is the concern of type safety. The difference between this and the previous bullet point is that here you aren't using any classes that have been designed to access data outside the application—you're accessing this data almost by mistake (for example, by faulty pointer arithmetic).

Many versions of Windows, of course, have built-in native security checks that will prevent code accessing some areas of memory or the file system to which the user account doesn't have access—but this security is based on the user ID of the process in which the code is running, so it can't help you if you're, say, the administrator wanting to run some code that you're not sure if you trust. For this reason I'll concentrate here on the additional security features built into the CLR.

Security against things such as the program explicitly and openly using the registry or the file system is fairly easy to achieve. This security is normally guaranteed because CIL doesn't have any instructions in its instruction set that can do those sorts of operations. Instead, such actions need to be done by instantiating various .NET Framework classes supplied by Microsoft, which will handle those tasks (internally using native code that has been thoroughly tested). The CLR will of course prevent an assembly from accessing those classes unless it thinks the code has sufficient security permissions (in .NET terms, *evidence*) to do so. You'll look in detail at how this security mechanism works in Chapter 12.

■Tip Incidentally, the ability to call into unmanaged code is covered by this same security mechanism. An assembly must have the UnmanagedCode permission to do that. Microsoft's assemblies such as mscorlib.dll always have this permission, because they have been strongly signed by Microsoft. But other assemblies may not have this permission—that depends on your security policy and on from where those other assemblies have come.

Security against the program corrupting memory or doing something else bad, simply because it uses poor (or malicious) coding practices, is a lot harder to achieve. This doesn't only mean corrupting memory or accessing memory belonging to a different process. If an assembly can start freely tampering with memory in its own process space, then it can in principle do just about anything else. For example, the CLR may have deemed that an assembly isn't sufficiently trusted to use the Microsoft.Win32 classes to write to the registry. But that by itself won't stop a malicious assembly from using some clever pointer arithmetic that locates the IL code for those classes in mscorlib.dll (which will almost certainly be loaded in the running process) and then using some IL command such as the indirect call command (calli) to invoke the code without the CLR having any means to identify which classes and methods this malicious code is actually invoking.

To guard against that, you need to be able to guarantee that code in an assembly won't under any circumstances do the following:

- Access any memory other than the variables that it has itself instantiated on the stack frame and managed heap

- Call into code in another assembly other than by using instructions such as call or callvirt, which allow the CLR to see at JIT compile time what methods are being called and therefore to judge whether the assembly is trusted to call those methods

And this is where you hit the problem. In an ideal world, a computer would be able to tell with 100 percent accuracy whether a particular program complied with these conditions. Unfortunately, in the real world that's simply not possible. A lot of mathematical theory lies behind computability, and it has been proven mathematically that it's impossible to come up with an algorithm that can, in a finite time, work out with 100 percent accuracy whether any program is type safe. Such an algorithm would be a mathematical impossibility, given the rich range of instructions available in CIL. The only way to tell for certain exactly what every program is going to do is to run it—and of course by then it's too late.

So you have to come up with the nearest best solution that's practical to achieve and accept that the solution will inevitably be imperfect. Any realistic solution is going to have to involve making some guesses about whether a given program is or isn't going to behave and therefore whether it's OK to run it. And performance is at a premium as well: this process of figuring out whether it's OK to run a program has to happen at JIT compilation time, which means it has to put as little overhead as possible on the JIT compiler.

Having established that there's going to have to be some approximation involved, what approximations can you make? If you're going to start guessing, then it's pretty clear that sometimes you'll guess wrong. It should also be clear that it'd be completely unacceptable if the algorithm had any possibility of passing a program that's in fact not type safe. If that happened, even once, it'd completely invalidate all the careful security systems that Microsoft has built up around .NET. So the algorithm has to err on the side of caution. And from this arises the concept of *verifiably type safe*. You come up with some algorithm that tests whether code is type safe. That algorithm is imperfect and will quite often fail code that would have been perfectly safe to run. But it will *never* pass any code that isn't type safe. Code that the algorithm passes is, at least as far as that algorithm is concerned, known as verifiably type safe or more commonly simply as *verifiable*. The situation looks like the Venn diagram shown in Figure 3-8.

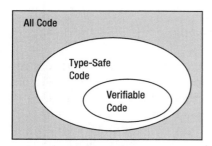

Figure 3-8. *Relationship between the set of type-safe code and the set of verifiably type-safe code*

The simplest such algorithm would be one that failed every program. An algorithm like that would be very quick to run, too! But unfortunately it wouldn't be very useful. However, from that trivially simple starting point, you can start to build tests into the algorithm— conditions that will prove that the code is type safe if it passes them. It should be clear that by making the algorithm more sophisticated, you can make the set of verifiably type-safe code come closer to matching the set of genuinely type-safe code. You can never get an exact match—that's mathematically impossible. And in any case, at some point the trade-off between how accurate you'd like the algorithm to be and how quickly you want it to run comes into play.

So that's the principle. Unfortunately, another potential problem exists. Although Microsoft has come up with an algorithm to test type safety, what happens if some other company implements a CLI, say, on Linux, and it doesn't use the same algorithm? You could end up in a situation in which code that's actually type safe gets verified on one platform but not on another platform. To avoid this situation, the ECMA standard for the CLI contains a specification of the algorithm to be used to test type safety. And it's a requirement that if some piece of code will pass verification using this standard algorithm, then any conforming implementation of the CLI must also pass that code. Notice my careful wording here. I haven't said that any conforming implementation of the CLI must actually use this algorithm. It's perfectly acceptable for some organization to develop a CLI implementation that uses a more sophisticated algorithm, which is capable of identifying type-safe code that would fail the ECMA algorithm, provided that algorithm doesn't fail any code that would pass the ECMA algorithm. And it's likely that this will happen in future releases of the .NET Framework as Microsoft refines the verification process performed by the JIT compiler. So now the situation looks more like Figure 3-9.

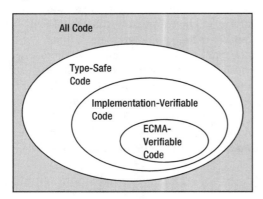

Figure 3-9. *Type safety: Meeting the ECMA standards for verifiability*

The existence of this standard algorithm is important. It means that it's possible to design compilers that will only ever emit code that passes this algorithm (such as the VB compiler, or the C# compiler when the source code it processes doesn't have any unsafe blocks). It's then possible to guarantee that code generated by those compilers will pass type safety on any future implementation of the CLI.

The peverify.exe tool in theory uses the ECMA definition of verifiability when it checks your code. That's why peverify is such an important tool: If your code passes peverify, you know it will run on any compliant implementation of the CLI. However, as of version 1.*x*, peverify has some problems of not picking up all errors (for example, it won't tell you if an explicit layout allows object references inside a type to overlap). For an absolutely complete check, you'll therefore need to run peverify and run an assembly in a manner that doesn't give it SkipVerification permission (with the default security policy, this could be from a network share, for example).

Implementing Type Safety: The Practice

Now you've seen the theory of what verifying type safety should achieve, let's look at what the ECMA algorithm actually involves. I don't have space here to go into any rigorous kind of analysis—what I describe is somewhat simplified, but it should give you an idea of how the verification process works. The algorithm has the following two aspects:

- Checking evaluation stack types

- Checking individual instructions

Let's look at these separately.

Checking Evaluation Stack Types

This ensures that no problems can occur through one type being interpreted as another type. This is a classic way in which memory can become corrupted. For example, suppose that a slot in local memory has been declared as holding `object`, and you try to store an `int32` in it.

```
.locals init (object, int32)
// Other code
ldloc.1
stloc.0
```

This code is syntactically correct IL, and it will pass validation. It loads the value stored in local variable slot 1 (an `int32`), and then the `stloc.0` instruction will cause this `int32` to be stored in a location that's supposed to hold an object reference. You now have an object reference that almost certainly doesn't now point to any valid object, since that `int32` could have been storing any value. And the cause of the problem is clearly wrong types: the previous code will fail verification at the `stloc.0` instruction, on the grounds that the wrong data type is on the stack.

The great thing about this check is that it's really just an extension of the checks on evaluation stack state that are performed by the JIT compiler to validate code anyway. Recall that to validate code, the JIT compiler makes sure it can identify the stack state at each point in the code, but it doesn't worry about whether that state is being used consistently. Hence, adding this check for verifiability doesn't add too much overhead to the JIT compilation process.

Checking Individual Instructions

Checking an individual IL instruction is more interesting. Microsoft has carefully studied all the IL commands, to check all the possible effects of these commands. And the commands break down into the following three categories:

- Some commands can never cause a program to violate memory. As an example, the `ldloc.0` command is always type safe. The action of loading the first local variable onto the evaluation stack can't possibly compromise memory integrity.

- Some commands can in principle cause memory to be violated if they're used in a certain way, but it's easy to identify conditions under which those commands will always be safe.

- A small group of commands may violate memory depending on the context in which they are used, but for these commands, no simple test exists that can distinguish whether they're being used in a type-safe manner. An example of this is the `initblk` command. `initblk` initializes a block of memory of a given size. Since the size is taken from the evaluation stack and could be huge, `initblk` could easily overwrite variables to which it shouldn't be writing.

You can probably guess what happens now. The verifier ignores instructions in the first category in the previous list. If it sees an instruction in the second category, then it checks if it has been used in one of the ways it knows about that guarantees type safety. If the instruction fails this test, then the method fails verification. And of course, if the verifier sees an instruction in the third category, then that's it. That block of code has failed verification straightaway. In that case, as I mentioned earlier, what will happen is that the JIT compiler will insert code that will throw an exception if you don't have the `SkipVerification` permission. Incidentally, this means that the method may be able to execute without this permission, provided that the flow of execution avoids the particular block of code in question.

I don't have space here to list details of which IL instruction falls into which category, but this book's appendix provides some information about each instruction. In addition, the Partition III document formally lists the exact situation in which each IL instruction is considered type safe.

Note that, just as for validating code, the verification algorithm examines only types—it never considers values. It has to be this way, because verification happens at JIT compile time, not when the code is being executed. So you don't have an easy way to tell what the values may be. For example, `initblk` may be used in a context in which only a few bytes of memory to a particular local variable are being written. But the verifier has no way of knowing that.

One other point—you may wonder why I haven't mentioned anything about arrays in connection with type safety. After all, array indexes out of bounds represent one of the most common reasons for memory corruption. The reason is that array access in IL is controlled either through the array-related commands, `newarr`, `ldelem.*`, `stelem.*`, and `ldlen`, which perform their own bounds checking and throw an exception if an index out of bounds is detected, or through the `System.Array` class. Most of the methods of this class are `internal-call` methods (implemented within the CLR and similarly implemented to perform bounds checking). Either way, no danger exists of memory violations caused by array overruns. Hence, arrays are simply not an issue as far as type safety is concerned.

Managed and Unmanaged Code

In the following sections, you'll examine some of the principles behind the interoperability of managed and unmanaged code and how managed code can call into unmanaged code. The focus here is on the underlying principles rather than on coding details.

Principles of Calling Unmanaged Code

You saw in Chapter 2 that it's possible to embed native executable code in an assembly. The trick is quite simply to indicate in a method's signature that this method contains native code rather than IL code. (It isn't possible to mix IL and native code within a method—either a method contains only native code or it contains only IL code.) This means you need a mechanism to call from managed into native code, and vice versa.

Managed code can call into unmanaged code in the following three ways:

- Internal call

- P/Invoke and IJW

- COM interop

Internal Call

The internal call technique is the most efficient way of calling into unmanaged code. It's a technique used inside some of the framework base classes. It's not that well documented, being mentioned briefly in the Partition II document, and it's not something you can use for your own code. I mention it here because you'll see it used a lot if you examine the IL for some Microsoft-defined classes. An `internalcall` method will be flagged as `cil managed internal-call`. For example, here's the definition in IL of `Object.GetHashCode()`:

```
.method public hidebysig newslot virtual
        instance int32  GetHashCode() cil managed internalcall
{
}
```

A method marked as `internalcall` will simply transfer control to some hard-wired helper function in the CLR itself. Because these functions are hard-wired, they're very efficient, and the CLR can skip most or all of the time-consuming checks on security, and so on, that have to be made when using other techniques to call unmanaged code.

As an example, many of the methods on `System.Object`, `System.Array`, `System.Type`, and `System.Threading.Monitor` are `internalcall`.

P/Invoke and IJW

The P/Invoke and IJW techniques are often presented as if they were different, but in fact IJW is simply a variant of P/Invoke that offers some additional benefits for C++ developers (the technique isn't available in VB or C#). For both P/Invoke and IJW, you define a method in the assembly with the `pinvokeimpl` flag, which contains native executable code. For example, here's a definition of a `pinvokeimpl` function called `MessageBox()`—you'd probably have code like this if you wanted to call the unmanaged `MessageBox()` Windows API function:

```
.method public hidebysig static pinvokeimpl("user32.dll" winapi)
        int32  MessageBox(int32 hWnd,
                               string text,
                               string caption,
                               unsigned int32 type) cil managed preservesig
{
}
```

As you saw in the previous chapter, the `pinvokeimpl` flag tells the JIT compiler to insert code to perform marshaling and also to perform certain tasks that are collectively known as *setting the execution context*. This includes setting up flags so that the garbage collector knows this thread is running unmanaged code (an item called a *sentinel* is placed on the stack frame—this is recognized by the garbage collector as marking the boundary between managed and unmanaged code). The P/Invoke mechanism also makes arrangements for any unmanaged exceptions that are thrown from the native code to be converted into managed exceptions. It will also nor-mally ask the CLR for a .NET security permission, `UnmanagedCodePermission`, though this step will be skipped if the `pinvokeimpl` wrapper method is marked with the `System.Security.SuppressUnmanagedCodeSecurityAttribute` attribute. Using this attribute improves performance, and you should mark calls to unmanaged code with it if you're certain there's no way any malicious code could abuse the call (for example, by passing in unexpected parameters to public methods in the assembly).

In terms of high-level languages such as C# and VB, the usual way you code the P/Invoke technique is to declare a method with the `DllImport` attribute, like so:

```
// C#
[DllImport("user32.dll")]
public static extern int MessageBox(IntPtr hWnd, string text,
                                    string caption, uint type);
```

This DllImport attribute definition is what compiles into the pinvokeimpl method in the emitted assembly. You saw how to use this technique when coding directly in IL in Chapter 2, when you examined coding with platform invoke. As you saw there, the advantage of explicitly declaring a method in this way is that you can specify what types the pinvokeimpl wrapper method expects and therefore have some control over how the marshaling happens.

In C++ it's possible to explicitly declare the DllImport method as well and with similar syntax to C#. However, C++ also offers as an alternative the IJW technique. IJW in C++ is literally just that. You don't have to explicitly declare the DllImport wrapper yourself, but instead you rely on the C++ compiler to automatically supply a pinvokeimpl wrapper method, based on the original unmanaged method declaration, which will of course be located in one of the header files you've included with #include (or possibly even in the same C++ file). Besides potentially saving you some work, the compiler is also able to supply a more sophisticated definition of the pinvokeimpl method in IL, which will save the CLR some work and so enhance performance when calling the method. On the other hand, you don't get the chance to specify which managed types should be passed in and marshaled: you have to supply unmanaged types to the method in your C++ code whenever you invoke it.

To compare the two approaches, let's quickly see what happens with a simple application that uses P/Invoke or IJW to call the MessageBox() API function. Here's the P/Invoke version:

```
[DllImport("user32.dll")]
extern int MessageBox(IntPtr hWnd, String *text, String *caption,
                      unsigned int type);


int _tmain(void)
{
    MessageBox(NULL, S"Hello", S"Hello Dialog", 1);
    return 0;
}
```

If you look at the MessageBox() method that's generated by compiling this code, you see the following relatively basic pinvokeimpl function:

```
.method public static pinvokeimpl("user32.dll" winapi)
        int32  MessageBox(native int hWnd,
                          string text,
                          string caption,
                          unsigned int32 type) cil managed preservesig
{
}
```

But here's what happens if I change the C++ code to use IJW:

```
#include "stdafx.h"
#include "windows.h"
#include <tchar.h>
```

```
#using <mscorlib.dll>

using namespace System;
int _tmain(void)
{
    MessageBox(NULL, "Hello", "Hello Dialog", 1);
    return 0;
}
```

I've included all the headers in this code to make it clear it doesn't contain a DllImport definition. The C++ compiler will pick up the definition of MessageBox() from Windows.h.

Now the emitted IL contains the following definition of MessageBox():

```
.method public static pinvokeimpl(/* No map */)
    int32 modopt([mscorlib]System.Runtime.CompilerServices.CallConvStdcall)
    MessageBoxA(valuetype HWND__* A_0, int8
    modopt([Microsoft.VisualC]Microsoft.VisualC.NoSignSpecifiedModifier)
    modopt([Microsoft.VisualC]Microsoft.VisualC.IsConstModifier)* A_1,
    int8 modopt([Microsoft.VisualC]Microsoft.VisualC.NoSignSpecifiedModifier)
    modopt([Microsoft.VisualC]Microsoft.VisualC.IsConstModifier)* A_2,
    unsigned int32 A_3) native unmanaged preservesig
{
  .custom instance void
[mscorlib]System.Security.SuppressUnmanagedCodeSecurityAttribute::.ctor() =
(01 00 00 00 )
  // Embedded native code
  //   Disassembly of native methods is not supported.
  //   Managed TargetRVA = 0xa2b8
} // end of method 'Global Functions'::MessageBoxA
```

I don't have the space to go through all this code in detail. But I want you to notice the following about the IJW version of this method:

- The C++ compiler has done the work of identifying the ANSI version of MessageBox(), MessageBoxA(), as the one to be called. That means the CLR doesn't have to do that work at runtime. This is shown both by the function name MessageBoxA() and by the appended flag preservesig.

- While both methods are pinvokeimpl, the IJW version is also native unmanaged and contains embedded native code. Unfortunately, ildasm.exe can't show you the native code, but you can make an educated guess that it implements some of the transition stuff that would otherwise have had to be figured out by the CLR.

- The IJW version declares SuppressUnmanagedCodeSecurityAttribute.

- The data types to be passed in with the IJW version are int32, int8, int8, and int32. In other words, they're exact, isomorphic types, so the P/Invoke mechanism doesn't need to do any marshaling.

Note that much of this code is devoted to modopt specifiers. However, the information supplied by modopt is largely aimed at developer tools, not at the CLR—and so isn't of interest to you here.

In conclusion, you shouldn't expect massive performance gains from using IJW because it still ultimately goes through the P/Invoke mechanism. Still, it may offer small improvements, and it may make your coding easier. Bear in mind, however, that performance when going over P/Invoke can easily be swamped by any required data marshaling. For IJW this marshaling doesn't happen during the method call, but you may have to perform explicit data conversions in your C++ code before calling the pinvokeimpl method. On the other hand, you can probably arrange your data types in your C++ code to minimize any data conversion over-head with better results than for P/Invoke marshaling.

COM Interoperability

The .NET COM interop facility is designed to allow managed code to call into legacy COM components and vice versa. Strictly speaking, you probably shouldn't view COM interop as an alternative to P/Invoke—it's more correct to view it as an additional layer. At some point when invoking a method on a COM component, the P/Invoke mechanism is still going to get called in to perform the managed to unmanaged transition, but that's all hidden from the developer. Because of this, COM interop transitions take longer than P/Invoke ones. Microsoft has suggested typically 60–70 native instructions, plus data marshaling time (as compared to 10–30 native instructions plus marshaling for plain P/Invoke).

COM interop in practice is based on a command-line utility, tlbimp.exe. tlbimp examines a COM type library and then creates a managed assembly that wraps the library. The assembly contains managed classes and managed interfaces that have similar definitions to the COM equivalents defined in the type library and implements the methods in the managed classes so that they internally use P/Invoke to call the corresponding methods in the component (with the constructor in the managed class presumably implemented to call CoCreateIn-stance()).

You can quickly see what roughly is going on in COM interop by creating a project in VB 6. Here's the code—it's a VB 6 Class Module (in other words, a COM component) called Doubler, and it provides a means by which you can perform that much sought after and terribly hard to implement task of doubling a number:

```
Public Function DoubleItVB6(x As Integer) As Integer
   DoubleItVB6 = x * 2
End Function
```

The code sample download for this project includes the source files and the compiled DLL, so you don't have to build the DLL yourself, which means you don't need VB 6 installed to run the sample (though you'll need to register the DLL with regsvr32.exe if you don't build it on your own machine). Next you run tlbimp on the file by typing this at the command prompt:

```
tlbimp Doubler.dll /out:ManDoubler.dll
```

This gives you the managed assembly, which implements all the code required to wrap the unmanaged code in Doubler.dll. If you examine the assembly using ildasm, you find quite a lot there (see Figure 3-10).

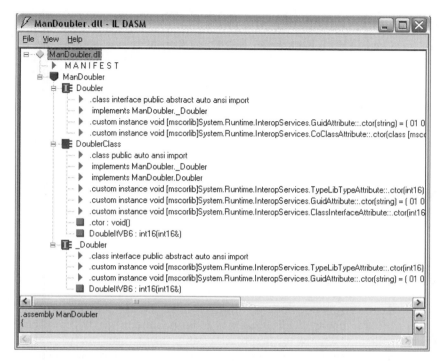

Figure 3-10. *Managed wrapper round a COM component—viewed with* ILDASM

ILDASM shows not one but two interfaces—the reason for the additional interface has to do with internal implementation details in VB 6, which normally generates two COM interfaces for its types, a public one and an internal one prefixed by an underscore. Figure 3-10 shows that tlbimp has wrapped literally everything and also has used some custom attributes to indicate information about the COM components.

Of course, the really interesting thing here is what happens if some managed code uses this wrapper to call the DoubleItVB6() method. Here's the wrapper's implementation of this method:

```
.method public hidebysig newslot virtual
        instance int16  DoubleItVB6([in][out] int16& x)
runtime managed internalcall
{
   .custom instance void
[mscorlib]System.Runtime.InteropServices.DispIdAttribute::.ctor(int32)
= ( 01 00 00 00 03 60 00 00
   .override ManDoubler._Doubler::DoubleItVB6
}
```

The crucial point in this code is the runtime managed internalcall flag on the method definition. In other words, this is a method that's implemented within the CLR itself. The CLR's implementation will essentially use P/Invoke to transfer control to the underling DoubleItVB6() method in the COM component.

Mixing Managed and Unmanaged Types

You'll now examine how the C++ compiler and the .NET Framework allow unmanaged and managed types (as opposed to isolated methods) to coexist in the same assembly and to hold pointers to and invoke methods on each other. In other words, you learn how it's possible to have this:

```
__nogc class UnmanagedClass
{
   // etc.
}

__gc class ManagedClass
{
   UnmanagedClass *pUnmanagedObject;
   // etc.
```

This is distinct from what you've been looking at up to now—so far you've seen that P/Invoke lets you call unmanaged *methods* from managed code, but now you're looking at entire unmanaged class definitions.

It's important to make the distinction between unmanaged objects and unmanaged methods. A method is of course managed if it contains IL code and unmanaged if it contains native code. This is controlled in MC++ by the preprocessor directives #pragma managed and #pragma unmanaged. On the other hand, a type is regarded as managed if the type is defined in metadata. This is shown in MC++ for reference and value types, respectively, by the __gc and __value keywords. By specifying __nogc, on the other hand, you're saying that you don't want any metadata made available to allow managed code in other assemblies to use this class, but you want instead to lay this type out in memory as an unmanaged type and want to be able to instantiate it either on the stack or on the unmanaged heap. (And obviously you may still want your C++ code in the same project to be able to access the methods on this class and to treat it as an unmanaged type.)

Mixing the two concepts is fine; for example, you can have an unmanaged class, all of whose methods are implemented as managed code, like so:

```
#pragma managed
__nogc class MyClass        // Unmanaged class
{
   void DoSomething()       // will compile to managed code
   {
      // etc.
```

This is indeed the default behavior for C++ code compiled with the /clr flag.

Unmanaged References in Managed Types

Let's see how you can have a managed type hold a reference to a C++ class compiled with __nogc. To understand this, you'll need to delve into the IL that's emitted when an unmanaged type is compiled. What actually happens is that for every unmanaged type, the C++ compiler generates a shadow-managed value type with the same name. If you compile a C++ project specifying the /clr flag, then *every* class and struct that you define will cause at least some corresponding metadata for a managed type to be emitted into the assembly. For classes that are marked __gc or __value, you'll get full metadata that lists all the members of that type, just as you would in C# or VB. For other classes, however, the metadata will simply define a shadow value type, which has sufficient space to hold all the fields of that type but no methods defined. The type will simply look like an opaque blob to the CLR. You may wonder how it's possible for managed code to call the methods on such a class. The answer is that for each method of a __nogc class that you define in the C++ source code, the compiler defines a corresponding global (static) method in IL. This method will contain IL code (for #pragma managed __nogc classes) or will be a pinvokeimpl method that calls up the real native code (for #pragma unmanaged __nogc classes). The next sample illustrates all these concepts. The sample is called the UnmanCombis (unmanaged combinations) sample, and it's a managed C++ VS .NET project that contains a number of simple types that mix different combinations of managed and unmanaged classes and methods and that has these types called from a managed entry point. This is the source code for the sample:

```cpp
#include "stdafx.h"
#include <tchar.h>

#using <mscorlib.dll>

#pragma unmanaged
__nogc class UnNoTest
{
public:
    UnNoTest(int x) { this->x = x; }
    int DoubleIt() { return 2 * x; }
private:
    int x;
};

#pragma managed
__nogc class ManNoTest
{
public:
    ManNoTest(int x) { this->x = x; }
    int DoubleIt() { return 2 * x; }
private:
    int x;
};

#pragma managed
__gc class ManGCTest
{
public:
    ManGCTest(int x) { this->x = x; }
    int DoubleIt() { return 2 * x; }
private:
    int x;
};
```

```
#pragma managed
int _tmain(void)
{
   UnNoTest *pUnNoTest = new UnNoTest(3);
   Console::WriteLine(pUnNoTest->DoubleIt());
   delete pUnNoTest;

   ManNoTest *pManNoTest = new ManNoTest(3);
   Console::WriteLine(pManNoTest->DoubleIt());
   delete pManNoTest;

   ManGCTest *pManGCTest = new ManGCTest(3);
   Console::WriteLine(pManGCTest->DoubleIt());
   return 0;
}
```

As you can see, this project contains three classes that have identical implementations:
They store an integer in their constructor and multiply it by two in a DoubleIt() method. The
difference between these classes is that UnNoTest is—at the C++ level—an unmanaged class with
native methods, ManNoTest contains IL methods but is an unmanaged type, and ManGCTest is a
fully managed type containing IL methods. The C++ compiler doesn't support the fourth combination, a managed type containing native methods. The entry point method simply instantiates
each of these classes in turn and invokes the DoubleIt() method for each of them.

Examining the compiled assembly with ildasm.exe reveals what's shown in Figure 3-11.

Figure 3-11. *The IL emitted from the* UnmanCombis *sample*

In this figure, you can see that the managed type, ManGCTest, has compiled in the way you expect, and details of all its methods are present in the metadata. You won't consider this type further. On the other hand, for each of the two unmanaged classes, you can see a value type—these value types are the shadow types, which are defined to look like opaque blocks of data to the CLR. For example, here's the definition of ManNoTest:

```
.class private sequential ansi sealed ManNoTest
        extends [mscorlib]System.ValueType
{
    .pack 1
    .size 4
    .custom instance void [Microsoft.VisualC]Microsoft.VisualC.
                        DebugInfoInPDBAttribute::.ctor() = ( 01 00 00 00 )
}
```

So what's the point of this shadow type? Well, presumably you're going to want managed classes to be able to refer to instances of this class in their methods. The only way that that's possible in IL is if this type exists in some kind of format that's recognizable to the CLR and can be described by metadata—simply in order to give you a TypeDef token that can be used in the IL stream. Because this class is really intended as an unmanaged class, however, no managed fields within it have been defined in the metadata. Instead, the type has been specified as having size 4—this means that instances of this type will be big enough to hold the (unmanaged) int member field that has been declared within the type. Details of accessing that int will of course be left to unmanaged code. The C++ compiler has also added an attribute to the type; this is for the benefit of the VS .NET debugger—it indicates where you can find debugging information for this type.

__nogc C++ classes are compiled to value types. That's important because unmanaged C++ allows types to be instantiated on the stack, just as with .NET value types.

On the other hand, for both the unmanaged types, you see the global managed methods that represent the instance methods you've declared—the constructor and the DoubleIt() method. The names of these methods contain embedded dots—for example, ManNoTest.DoubleIt() and UnNoTest.DoubleIt(); that's fine because IL syntax allows dots in names. Don't be fooled into thinking that these dots represent some kind of type information—they're there only for legibility to humans. ManNoTest.DoubleIt() really is the name of a global method. Here's what the IL code for this method looks like:

```
.method public static int32
    modopt([mscorlib]System.Runtime.CompilerServices.CallConvThiscall)
ManNoTest.DoubleIt(valuetype ManNoTest*
    modopt([Microsoft.VisualC]Microsoft.VisualC.IsConstModifier)
    modopt([Microsoft.VisualC]Microsoft.VisualC.IsConstModifier) A_0)
    cil managed
{
  .vtentry 2 : 1
  // Code size        5 (0x5)
  .maxstack  2
  IL_0000:  ldarg.0
  IL_0001:  ldind.i4
```

```
    IL_0002:  ldc.i4.1
    IL_0003:  shl
    IL_0004:  ret
}
```

Interestingly, the implicit this pointer that forms the first parameter to an instance method has been explicitly supplied here: The first parameter is a ManNoTest* pointer. And notice the * syntax—this is a genuine unmanaged pointer. No ldfld instruction exists to retrieve the x field of the ManNoTest*—because as far as IL is concerned, this type doesn't contain any field. Instead, the ldind.i4 command just dereferences the address of the object. Since x is the only field in ManNoTest, dereferencing the pointer will give you this field.

For reference, the following is the corresponding code for UnNoTest.DoubleIt(). This code doesn't tell you much, because you told the compiler to generate native methods for this class.

```
.method public static pinvokeimpl(/* No map */) int32
    modopt([mscorlib]System.Runtime.CompilerServices.CallConvThiscall)
UnNoTest.DoubleIt(valuetype UnNoTest*
    modopt([Microsoft.VisualC]Microsoft.VisualC.IsConstModifier)
    modopt([Microsoft.VisualC]Microsoft.VisualC.IsConstModifier) A_0)
    native unmanaged preservesig
{
    .custom instance void [mscorlib]System.Security.
          SuppressUnmanagedCodeSecurityAttribute::.ctor() = ( 01 00 00 00 )
    // Embedded native code
    //  Disassembly of native methods is not supported.
    //  Managed TargetRVA = 0x1010
}
```

This tells you how the CLR manages to pull off the trick of having managed code reference unmanaged types. To summarize, it declares a shadow value type and uses unmanaged pointers to reference that type. It also declares static methods corresponding to the members of that type—those static methods take an extra unmanaged pointer argument, giving them the same signature as a genuine instance member of the type would have had.

The code for the main() method of this sample is too long to present here in full. However, you'll find it quite revealing if you compile the sample as a release build and examine the IL. If you do, you'll find that a lot of extra IL has been generated around the use of the unmanaged types, mostly to guard against exceptions, and so on—an essential safety feature as far as the CLR is concerned, since it has no way of knowing what the unmanaged code is going to do. You'll also see explicit calls to new() and delete() to assist with the construction and destruction of the unmanaged objects. You'll also find that much of the IL code around the ManNoTest type—and in particular the call to ManNoTest.DoubleIt()—has been inlined, emphasizing the performance benefits of using C++.

Managed Pointers in Unmanaged Types

You've now seen how easy it is for a managed type to reference what in C++ terms is seen as an unmanaged type. However, going the other way involves a bit more work by the developer—it's not all handled by the compiler.

The fundamental problem with attempting to access a managed type from an "unmanaged" type is that at any point the garbage collector may get called in—and it needs to be able to locate all the references to managed reference types that are currently in existence so that it can update those references when it performs garbage collection. That's a problem because the garbage collector won't know about any data held by unmanaged types. So clearly, even if an unmanaged type were able to determine the address in memory at which some managed type was stored, it wouldn't be sensible simply to hold a pointer to this location, because that pointer may at any time become invalid as the object gets moved. While it's true that you can prevent this by pinning the object, doing so drastically reduces the efficiency of garbage collection. As I've already noted, because of the performance implications, pinning objects isn't a good idea; this is particularly important in this case because holding onto a reference to a type is something that could be done for a long time continuously—for example, a long-lived instance of an unmanaged type may maintain a pointer to a managed type as a member field. Because of this problem, C++ actually regards it as a syntax error if a managed pointer is declared as a member field of an unmanaged type.

Similar considerations also apply in the case of value types. Although the garbage collector doesn't move value types, it needs to know of them because value types may contain references to reference types that need to get updated when the reference types are moved.

Notice that all this is a problem only for member fields. No problem exists for local variables in unmanaged methods, because the lifetime of a local variable can't last beyond the return of the method. If the garbage collector does get called up while an unmanaged method is executing, the garbage collector will reroute the return address from the unmanaged code so that it can take over as soon as the unmanaged code returns. At that time, any local variables from the unmanaged code will go out of scope and so no longer be relevant to the collection. Hence, it's fine for managed pointers to be declared locally to unmanaged methods.

Of course, if you've done much managed C++ programming, you'll be familiar with what happens at the C++ source code level: You can completely solve the problem just by using the gcroot<> template (defined in gcroot.h) when you declare any member references to managed types as member fields. So for example, instead of writing this:

```
ListBox *listBox = new ListBox;
```

you use the following:

```
gcroot<ListBox> *listBox = new ListBox;
```

and you can then treat *listBox as if it was a ListBox pointer (even destruction will be handled automatically).

While that code is quite easy to follow (assuming you're used to C++ template syntax), it doesn't give you any idea what's actually happening to solve the garbage collection problem. That's what you'll investigate here.

Since pinning the managed pointer isn't really an option, what you need is some mechanism by which unmanaged code can hold a reference to a managed type while letting garbage collection know that this reference exists and somehow coping if the garbage collector moves the object. Fortunately, Microsoft anticipated this problem and provided a framework base class to deal with it. The class is GCHandle, and it's in the System namespace. The purpose of GCHandle is to maintain an Object reference—which can be either to a reference type or to a boxed value type—and to make this reference available to unmanaged code. How can it do this? It takes advantage of a loophole in the restrictions: Unmanaged code shouldn't hold any references to managed objects, but nothing is stopping unmanaged code from calling static members of managed types! Static members will never be touched by the garbage collector, so it's perfectly OK for unmanaged code internally to store pointers to static member methods or fields of managed classes.

GCHandle makes available some static methods, which allow unmanaged code to reference a handle—a System.IntPtr instance (or in IL terms, a native int). This handle is used in a similar way to those normal (unmanaged) Windows handles that C++ developers used for years before .NET came along—it doesn't give the address of an object, but it can identify the object to the GCHandle class. The idea is that whenever unmanaged code wants to call a method of a managed object, it passes the handle to a static GCHandle method—effectively saying, "You're a managed type so you're allowed to keep hold of the reference corresponding to this handle. Can I have it for a moment, please?" The unmanaged code gets the object reference just long enough to call the method it wants. As long as it uses this object reference only as a local variable inside a method, everything is fine. The way this works is illustrated by a sample called GCHandleDemo. This sample defines a class called ManTest, which is identical to the ManGCTest class from the previous sample:

```
__gc class ManTest
{
public:
   ManTest(int x) { this->x = x; }
   int DoubleIt() { return 2 * x; }
private:
   int x;
};
```

To demonstrate an unmanaged class wrapping a managed class, you'll define two unmanaged classes, each of which serves as an unmanaged wrapper around ManTest and needs to contain some reference to the embedded ManTest instance. One of these classes, called TemplateWrapper, does this using the gcroot<> template, and the other, RawWrapper, does the same thing but without using gcroot<>. Hence, TemplateWrapper demonstrates the syntax you'd normally use in this situation, and RawWrapper shows you what's actually going on under the hood.

Here's TemplateWrapper:

```
class TemplateWrapper
{
private:
   gcroot<ManTest*> pTest;
public:
   TemplateWrapper(int x)
   {
      pTest = new ManTest(x);
   }
   int DoubleIt()
   {
```

```
      return pTest->DoubleIt();
   }
};
```

And here's RawWrapper:

```
class RawWrapper
{
private:
   void *handle;

public:
   RawWrapper(int x)
   {
      ManTest *pTest = new ManTest(x);
      GCHandle gcHandle = GCHandle::Alloc(pTest);
      System::IntPtr intPtr = GCHandle::op_Explicit(gcHandle);
      handle = intPtr.ToPointer();
   }

   int DoubleIt()
   {
      GCHandle gcHandle = GCHandle::op_Explicit(handle);
      Object *pObject = gcHandle.Target;
      ManTest *pTest = __try_cast<ManTest*>(pObject);
      return pTest->DoubleIt();
   }
   ~RawWrapper()
   {
      GCHandle gcHandle = GCHandle::op_Explicit(handle);
      gcHandle.Free();
   }
};
```

Instead of storing a pointer to a managed class (which would be illegal), RawWrapper stores a void* pointer—this will contain the handle that GCHandle gives you to identify the ManTest object.

In the RawWrapper constructor you need to instantiate a managed ManTest object and obtain the handle required to identify the object. Instantiating the object is easy—you just use the new operator. The problem of course is that you're allowed only to store the pointer to this object as a local variable. So you pass this reference to the static GCHandle::Alloc() method, which creates a GCHandle instance that wraps the object. Since GCHandle is a value type, you can store it directly in your constructor—you don't need to access it via a pointer. You now invoke an operator defined on GCHandle, which returns an IntPtr (native int), which is the actual handle. You'll use this handle as a void*, so you convert it to that using the IntPtr.ToPointer() method. Note that, besides returning a GCHandle instance, GCHandle.Alloc() will store the reference to the object in some static internal data structure, the details of which are undocumented (most likely it'd be a dictionary-based collection). The fact that the reference is stored here will ensure that the garbage collector thinks that the object is in use, so it doesn't garbage-collect it.

Now let's examine that DoubleIt() method. Here you need to use the handle you've stored to retrieve a reference to the object; it's basically the reverse process to that for getting the handle. You call the static GCHandle.op_Explicit() method to instantiate a temporary GCHandle struct that corresponds to this handle/object reference—this method will of course retrieve the reference from GCHandle's own internal data structure. You then use an instance property, GCHandle.Target, to retrieve the actual object reference. You get the reference as an Object*, so you have to cast it to ManTest* before you can use it.

Finally, you need to make sure that when your wrapper class is destroyed, so is the managed Test object. The GCHandle.Free() method deals with that—it removes it from its internal data structure so that the object can be garbage collected.

Summary

In this chapter, you toured some of the internal workings of the CLR, focusing especially on some of its less well-documented aspects. You looked at the relation of the CLR to the ECMA standard CLI specification. You then studied some of the implementation details of value and reference types and looked at the differences between value and boxed types. You learned in detail about the algorithms used to validate and verify code and then examined how the CLR copes with embedded unmanaged code, the techniques for calling into unmanaged code, and how the C++ compiler arranges things to fit in with the requirements of the CLR when compiling projects that contain unmanaged code.

In the next chapter, you'll continue to focus on the workings of the CLR, but you'll look particularly at the implementation of assemblies.

CHAPTER 4

■ ■ ■

Understanding Assemblies

In this chapter you'll take a close look at assemblies, focusing in particular on the under-the-hood implementations of the basic concepts behind assemblies. I'll assume you're familiar with the purpose of an assembly as well as related concepts such as metadata, modules, and the broad differences between public and shared assemblies, as well as basic techniques for compiling high-level code into assemblies—so I'll go a bit beyond those topics and show the underlying structure of assemblies and the Global Assembly Cache (GAC).

In particular I'll cover the following:

- **PE files**: The concept of a portable executable (PE) file and how this concept has been extended to provide for assemblies.

- **Assembly files**: The types of file that can make up assemblies and the high-level structures and information contained in them: modules, the prime module, resource-only PE files, and other linked files.

- **Identity**: The component parts of an assembly identity: the name, version, key, and culture. You'll examine how these are used.

- **Metadata**: I'll give an overview of the main command-line tools that allow you to examine the information inside an assembly, as well as the two programmatic APIs for this purpose: the System.Reflection classes and the unmanaged reflection API.

- **The GAC**: The structure of the cache.

- **Probing**: You'll examine the rules that determine where the runtime searches for assemblies and how to customize the probing rules for your applications.

- **Resources**: How to compile resources and create satellite assemblies for localization purposes.

- **Assembly tools**: I'll briefly review the various command-line tools available for generating and manipulating assemblies: al.exe, gacutil.exe, and so on.

I'll finish the chapter with a short example that demonstrates the process of creating a relatively complex assembly. The actual code for this assembly will be quite short, but I've designed the example so that the assembly contains code written in two high-level languages, as well as requiring localized and nonlocalized resources. Also, the assembly needs to be signed and placed in the GAC. I'll illustrate how to generate this assembly both by using the command prompt and (as far as possible) by using VS .NET.

Note that although I'll mention a little about signing assemblies with a private key in this chapter, you can find more detailed information on this topic, as well as a discussion of the underlying theory, in Chapter 13, once I've covered the necessary background in cryptography theory.

You'll start now by examining the structure of a typical assembly, focusing on the PE and other files that may make up an assembly.

Introducing the Internal View: Assembly Physical Structure

As you'll be aware from your basic .NET programming experience, assemblies are the basic unit of code deployment. Microsoft likes to say that they form the logical security and version boundary for code, which is basically techno-speak for the same thing. You'll also be aware that an assembly can contain a number of files (with the exception of dynamic assemblies, which you'll examine in Chapter 8 and which exist in memory only). The possible files are as follows:

- A PE file containing the prime module (must be present)

- Any number of optional PE files that contain other modules

- Any number of optional resource files that contain data and can be in any format

You'll examine resource files in the section "Resources and Resource Files." For now, you'll concentrate on files that contain code—the PE files—and get a high-level look at the structure of these files and what kinds of information they contain. I won't go into too much detail—and don't worry, I'm not going to start showing the low-level binary details of the files (well, not much anyway). However, I want to give you some background information so you understand what information is contained in an assembly file.

■**Tip** The actual low-level binary format of the files is documented (if you can call it that) by a couple of C header files on your system, which define C structures that match the binary information in the PE files. You'll normally need this information only if you're writing applications that do some sophisticated low-level processing of assemblies. But if you do, you should look in `Windows.h` for the structures of the PE headers and in `CorHdr.h` in the .NET Framework SDK for the structure of the CLR headers and code. In addition, many of the constants used for such things as flags are defined in the .NET partition documents.

PE Files

The portable executable file isn't something that's new to .NET. PE files have been around ever since 32-bit programming first emerged on the Windows platform with the release of NT 3.1. The statement that a file is a PE file means that it contains certain specified items in an agreed-upon standard format.

A PE file doesn't only contain code: The file also contains information that indicates to Windows whether the code it contains represents a Windows form, a console application, or some other kind of application (such as a device driver). Furthermore, pre-initialized data structures that are associated with the application may exist. Other code may need to be brought in from libraries—a PE file needs to indicate which libraries it's dependant on, and it will also need to supply information about any functions it exposes to the outside world and the addresses in the file where they're located. (These are technically known as its *exports*. All DLLs obviously have exports, and some .EXE files also may do so, for example, to expose call-back functions.) Thus all in all, a PE file needs to supply a lot of data as well as code. The same principles hold true for other operating systems, although details of the data structures will be different. This means each operating system needs some agreed-upon format for how data should be laid out in an executable file—in other words, what items are located where—so that the operating system knows where to look for them (strictly speaking, the format depends on the loader rather than the operating system, but in practice, formats are associated with operating systems). To that extent, the assembly format, with its manifests and metadata, hasn't introduced any fundamentally new principles—it has just added to the information already present.

On Windows, the agreed-upon format is the PE format. However, other formats are around, such as `Elf`, which is generally used on Unix.

The PE format uses indirection extensively—a few header fields exist at fixed locations early in the file, and these headers contain pointers indicating where other structures in the file are located. These structures in turn contain pointers, and so on, until you get to the actual data and executable instructions that will be executed. One benefit of PE files is performance. They've been designed in such a way that they can be loaded into memory to a large extent as-is. Windows makes a few modifications to the copy of the file in memory (which I'll explain soon), but these are relatively small. For this reason, you'll also commonly hear PE files referred to as *image files*, or *images*, reflecting the idea that they can be thought of as file-based images of what sits in memory when the code actually runs.

The PE file format replaced several earlier formats for executable files on 16-bit Windows, and now essentially every executable, DLL, and static library file that runs on your system is a PE file. The *portable* in its name refers to the fact that this file is designed to run on any 32-bit version of Windows running on an x86-based processor. That's the remarkable feature that's quite often forgotten these days: the same files will execute on Windows 9*x* or on Windows NT/2000/XP, despite that these are completely different operating systems with different underlying core code.

You may also see the PE file format referred to as the PE/COFF format. COFF stands for *Common Object File Format*, and COFF files, also known as *object files*, are produced as an intermediate stage in generating PE files from source code by compilers for languages such as C++. The C++ compiler works by first compiling each source code file as an isolated unit and then matching all the type definitions, and so on, from the various source files—a process known as *linking*. The intermediate files are COFF files. COFF files contain executable code but aren't ready to be executed because the data and code that's intended for one PE file is still spread across several files (typically one COFF file for each source code file). To ease the work required by the linker, Microsoft defined a common format for both PE and COFF files. This does mean, however, that a few fields in the PE/COFF format are relevant only to COFF files and are therefore zeroed in PE files, and vice versa. Because of the indirection used in the PE/COFF format, though, the number of affected bytes in the file is small.

At a basic level, the PE file looks roughly as shown in Figure 4-1. Note that what I'm presenting here is the basic PE format: the information here is processed by the Windows operating system loader, so no data is directed at the CLR—that part comes later.

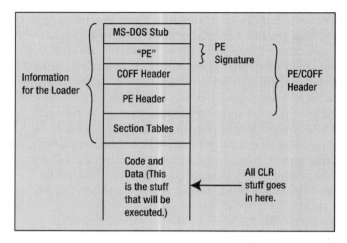

Figure 4-1. *Windows PE file structure*

This figure shows that the file contains a number of header structures, followed by the actual code and data. The initial structures—marked in the figure as "Information for the Loader"—are the stuff that the loader reads when Windows loads the file in order to determine basically what to do with the file.

The MS-DOS stub is what will be executed if the program runs under MS-DOS mode. For most PE files, and all assemblies, this is just a piece of code that displays a message telling you the file can't be executed in MS-DOS mode. For a modern, graphical user interface (GUI)–based Windows file, that's about all you can do. However, if Windows loads the file, it knows not to just jump in and start executing the file from here. Instead, Windows goes straight to the subsequent headers and starts processing them. For .NET assemblies, the ECMA standards for the CLI specify the actual values of the bytes to be placed in the MS-DOS stub, so all assemblies are identical in this regard.

The first item that Windows will process is the PE signature, which simply contains the two ANSI characters PE. This tells Windows that this really is a PE file, as opposed to a file in some other format.

Next comes the COFF header. Most of this data isn't relevant for assemblies, and the COFF header occupies just 20 bytes anyway.

Things start to get interesting with the PE header. This contains some quite important information, including the lowest-possible version number of the operating system on which this file is intended to run. The loader will abort loading the file if this version number is greater than that of the operating system actually running. The PE header also includes the SubSystem flag, which indicates whether the file should run as a Windows or as a command-line application or whether it's, for example, a device driver that has no user interface. Also embedded in the PE header is a structure known as the *data directory table*. This contains details of where to locate various tables of specific data in the PE file (two DWORDs respectively containing the size and a pointer to the start of each table). The data directory table lists a number of useful tables—some of the more interesting ones include the following:

- **Import table**: This details unmanaged symbols, and so on, that need to be imported from other files.

- **Export table**: This indicates the unmanaged symbols that this file makes available to other files.

- **Resource table**: This contains details of unmanaged resources.

- **Thread Local Storage (TLS) table**: This indicates details of data that's stored natively in thread local storage (note that this is separate from the parallel thread-local-storage facilities implemented by the CLR).

- **Relocation table**: I'll explain this table soon. Roughly speaking, it lists the locations of words in the file that may need to be modified when the file is loaded into memory.

Notice that although these tables contain information of relevance to an application, most of them are nevertheless geared toward unmanaged stuff. These tables don't, for example, contain any information about managed types imported or exported. And this really reflects the status of .NET. Perhaps one day, .NET will be a fully integrated part of Windows, but for the time being, .NET is in reality little more than an application that sits on top of Windows, acting as a layer between your managed code and Windows. The stuff you've looked at so far includes standard PE header file contents, which Windows itself is expecting to process. Only when Windows has done its work in loading the file can control be handed over to the .NET Framework to execute the file.

The relocation table is quite interesting, as it gives some insight into how the file is actually loaded. So far I've been loosely talking about pointers to items in the file. Pointers used by the loader are generally stored as file offsets—in other words, the number of bytes from the start of the file where an item is located. (Actually, it's more complicated than this because the file gets loaded in sections that don't necessarily follow directly from each other addresswise, because of constraints imposed by the disk operating system and the paging system. Corrections have to be made for this, but to keep things simple, I'll ignore that complication in the following discussion.) For example, if the file were always loaded at address 0 in virtual memory, then calculating virtual memory addresses would be easy. Address 232 in the physical file, for example, would correspond to address 232 in the loaded image (ignoring file sections as just mentioned). But of course this never happens. When the file is loaded, its contents get placed at some address in the process's virtual address space, and that address is never 0. Executables are usually placed at location 0x400000, for example. This means that these offsets won't give the correct address of items used when the program is running. That's not really relevant, however, for things such as pointers to the import table, because that information is used only while the file is being loaded.

What happens is that some default address is assumed for where the file is likely to be loaded—this assumed address is indicated in the PE header. Those addresses that are inside the executable code in the PE file that will be read when the program is running (such as pointers to pre-initialized memory) are stored in the file on the assumption that this address will be correct. However, if the file ends up getting loaded at a different location, then these addresses will need to be changed (this will happen to a DLL, for example, if another DLL has already been loaded at the preferred address). That's the purpose of the relocation table—it contains a list of which words in the file will need to be changed if the file gets loaded at the "wrong" address. Suppose your code contains an instruction to load some data, which has been hard-coded into the PE file X bytes from the start of the file. If the file is expected to be loaded at location Y, the instruction will have been coded to say, "Load the data at virtual address X+Y." If, however, the file actually gets loaded at address Z, then Z–Y will have to be added to this address—the instruction must be changed to say, "Load the data at virtual address X+Z." Note that the target of branch instructions in x86 native executables is always given relative to the location of the branch instruction, just as in the IL br.* commands, so branch targets don't need to be relocated.

Finally, the PE file has the actual data and code. And that's where the CLR-specific data comes in. Once all the stuff that Windows consumes is out of the way, this is followed by stuff that the CLR can read and use to figure out the assembly structure and contents. And that's what you'll examine next.

PE Extensions for the CLR

You've come a long way into the file without really seeing much in the way of CLR-specific stuff. And two reasons exist for that. One is backward compatibility. Windows 95/98/ME/ NT4/2000 is expecting PE files to contain certain data in a certain format. And short of .NET shipping with new loaders for unmanaged code, Microsoft can't realistically muck around with that data. The other reason, as I've mentioned, has to do with the way that .NET really sits on top of Windows just like any other application.

File Structure

Since the code in an assembly or .NET module conforms to the PE file format, it shares the same header information as unmanaged executables and DLLs. However, beyond the PE header, the data structures are different from an unmanaged file and contain information specific to the .NET Framework. Figure 4-2 shows a fairly simplified impression of what the files look like.

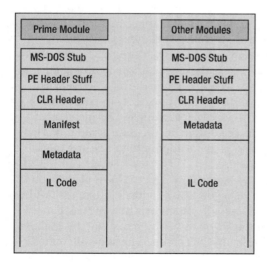

Figure 4-2. *Managed PE file structure*

As you can see, the structure of a module file is similar to that of the prime module file. The sole difference is the inclusion of the assembly manifest in the prime module file. The manifest is what makes a file into an assembly. It contains the information that's needed to identify all the other files in the assembly, as well as the information that's needed by other external code (in other assemblies) in order to access the types in this assembly. Another way of looking at it is that a module file contains metadata that describes the types in that module. An assembly (prime module) file, however, contains the metadata that describes the types in its own module, as well as a manifest that details the other files that are part of the assembly and the types that those modules make available to outside code (in other words, which ones have `public`, `family`, or `familyorassem` visibility). By storing a copy of this information in the prime module, it means that other code that accesses this assembly needs to open only one file to determine what types it can use, no matter which module actually implements those types. The performance benefit should be clear. Obviously, if the external code actually needs to invoke code in one of the other modules, that's when the relevant file(s) will be opened.

But I'm jumping ahead of myself. If you go through the various items of CLR data in more detail, you'll find regions of the file containing the following:

- The *CLR header* lists the version of the CLR that the assembly was built with and designed to work with. Among other things, it also indicates the managed entry point (if this is an executable assembly) and the addresses of other items of data, including the strong name, the signature (if present), and the table of the `vtfixups` that are used to indicate addresses for managed methods that are exported as unmanaged code.

- The *manifest* contains details of all files that make up this assembly, along with a copy of any metadata from other modules that's externally visible. The manifest is also important because it contains details of the identity of this assembly—the name, version, and so on, as well as a hash of the combined contents of all the files in the assembly from which file integrity can be verified. Basically, the manifest contains all the information needed to identify and describe this assembly to the outside world.

- The *metadata* is the data that defines all the types used in a given module. To a first approximation, it contains the information that's given in IL directives (as opposed to IL opcodes). It details the types defined in the module, as well as the member methods and fields of each type. For each method, it will also indicate the start point and length of the IL instruction stream for that method within the file (a consequence of this is that you have no need to embed any method header information within the instruction stream itself—that data can be found in the metadata). The metadata will also contain any string constants and details of which types and methods in other modules or assemblies are required by the code in this module.

- The *IL code* shouldn't need any explaining. It's quite simply the stream of IL instructions that make up the actual code to be JIT compiled in the assembly.

How the CLR Is Invoked

I've just reviewed the main items of data in the assembly that need to be processed by the CLR. But one problem exists: The PE file is loaded by Windows, not by the CLR. So how does the CLR get involved? The answer depends on what version of Windows you're running. For

Windows 2000 and earlier versions of Windows, Windows simply loads the file as normal, quite unaware that it's a managed file, and locates an (unmanaged) entry point, which will be specified in one of the fields in the PE/COFF headers. Once Windows has satisfied itself that it has loaded and initialized the file correctly, it has the appropriate thread of execution start running at this unmanaged entry point. However, in all managed assemblies, the code that's placed here is little more than a call into the library mscoree.dll (the ee presumably stands for *execution engine*). This DLL is responsible for loading and hosting the CLR. Once the thread of execution is inside mscoree.dll, that's it. The CLR is now in charge and will start reading through the manifest, metadata, and IL code in your file and will start processing it, beginning with wherever the "real" managed entry point is. A rather intriguing consequence of this is that all the IL code, which you and I think of as *code*, actually has the status of *data* as far as Windows is concerned. Windows never directly executes this code, obviously—instead it's read and processed by the (native) code inside mscoree.dll. Note also that these few unmanaged instructions at the start have no effect on the verifiability of your code, and the assembly doesn't need permission to execute unmanaged code in order to run this code—for the simple reason that at the point in time when this code is being executed, the CLR hasn't even been started. Clearly, until that initial call into mscoree.dll is made, there can be no verification or other .NET security checks!

In the case of assemblies generated by the C++ compiler, the startup procedure is somewhat complicated by the fact that the C++ compiler adds its own unmanaged Main() method, which is responsible for tasks such as initializing the C runtime library. The result is a curious hopping from unmanaged code into mscoree.dll (though at this point still executing unmanaged code whose purpose is to initialize the .NET environment) and then back into unmanaged code in the assembly to run the unmanaged Main() method—and finally back into mscoree.dll where the code that starts JIT compiling your managed entry point will start running.

If your assembly is running on Windows XP, the same principles hold, except that the initial unmanaged stub in the assembly isn't executed. That's because Windows XP was developed at about the same time as .NET, which means Microsoft was able to modify the PE file loader in Windows XP to explicitly check to see if this is a managed PE file and if so to call the startup code in mscoree.dll directly. The check happens by examining a field in the PE header called IMAGE_DIRECTORY_ENTRY_COM_DESCRIPTOR. It happens that this field isn't used and is always zero in unmanaged PE files. Microsoft has defined this field to be nonzero in managed assemblies. The benefit of this is that no unmanaged code needs to be executed initially, so the CLR's code access security mechanism is active from the start. This allows administrators to lock down a system more effectively and prevents any viruses that may infect the unmanaged entry point from executing.

Verifying File Integrity

Don't worry too much about the details of how file integrity is verified here, since I cover that topic in Chapter 13. However, for completeness I'll remind you of the basic idea. A hash of the entire assembly is computed and stored in the manifest. You can think of the hash as being a bit like those old cyclic redundancy checks but a lot more sophisticated. The hash is some number that's calculated by applying some mathematical formula to the data in the files that make up the assembly. The important point is that every byte in every file in the assembly is used in computing the hash—so if any corruption to even a single byte happens, then it's virtually certain that the hash computed from the corrupted file won't match the one that the uncorrupted file would have produced. So checking the value of this hash should for all practical purposes guarantee file integrity against random corruption. In addition, in assemblies that have a strong name, the hash is signed (encoded) using the assembly's private key, which is known only to the company that supposedly coded the assembly. Since no one else can encrypt the hash with that key, a successful decryption and matching of the hash proves that the file was produced by the correct company and so hasn't been deliberately changed.

The IL Instruction Stream

When you looked at IL assembly in Chapters 1 and 2, you got quite a good idea of what the CLR can actually do with your program and how the IL language works. However, because I was dealing with assembly language, you didn't get much idea at all of how the genuine IL binary data is stored in an assembly. That's what you'll examine here. In the process, you'll also see some other ways that the assembly has been designed with performance in mind.

■**Note** Don't confuse IL assembly (the textual IL source code) with assemblies (the binary files)! You may wonder whatever possessed Microsoft to call the unit of managed code storage an *assembly*, when (ironically) the one IL-related thing it doesn't contain is IL assembly!

Let's consider this IL assembly code sequence:

```
ldstr    "Hello, World!"
call     [mscorlib]void System.Console::WriteLine(string)
```

In the IL source file, all the items needed to understand this code are presented inline—including that "Hello, World!" string. However, that's not how it works in the assembly. Once assembled into opcodes, the previous lines look more like Figure 4-3.

Understanding this figure will probably be easier if I mention that 0x72 happens to be the opcode for ldstr, and 0x28 is the opcode for call. (Actually, it'd probably be more correct to say that ldstr is the mnemonic for 0x72, and so on, but you get the picture.)

The two opcodes are each followed by a token. As mentioned in Chapter 1, these tokens are essentially 4-byte numbers that index into some table into the metadata. The figure illustrates the use of two such tables: The string "Hello, World!" is contained in a table of strings, and the method Console.WriteLine() is contained in a table of what are known as MemberRefs—references to methods in other assemblies. In fact, the MemberRef entry itself basically consists of a number of tokens to such items as a TypeRef (which will identify the Console type) and a SignatureRef (which indicates the signature of a method).

The following are a couple of reasons why it's done this way:

Space: It's quite likely that the Console.WriteLine() method is going to be called from more than one location. If details of this method had to be repeated, that would bloat the assembly.

Performance: If the JIT compiler is to process the IL instructions quickly, then it's important that it knows exactly how many bytes are going to be taken up with each instruction.

If an instruction had to be followed by a `MethodRef` or by a string, there would be the complicating factor of sorting out exactly how many bytes are occupied by the argument to the instruction. But since the `ldstr` and call instructions are followed by 4-byte tokens, the JIT compiler immediately knows just from inspecting the opcode how many bytes will follow as an argument and how to interpret those bytes.

Metadata: One of the principles of assemblies is that the assembly is self-describing. That means not only that the information about the types used in the assembly is readily available but also that information about types referenced, and so on. By placing the `MethodDef` in the metadata, you ensure this principle.

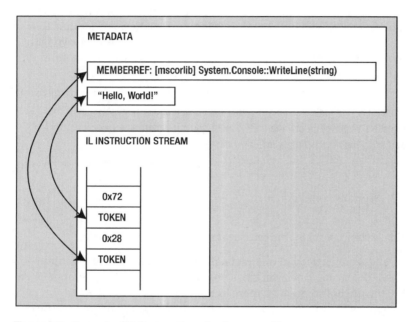

Figure 4-3. *Layout of IL instructions in the assembly*

It's apparent from the design of the IL instruction stream and the metadata that Microsoft was concerned about performance—the indirect indexing method using tokens provides one example of this. Another example is the way that the opcodes are designed. The majority of opcodes consume 1 byte; this means that examining that 1 byte of data is sufficient to tell the JIT compiler what the instruction is and how many bytes of argument follow. However, the less frequently used instructions have 2-byte opcodes. For these instructions, the first byte is always `0xFE`, so the JIT compiler knows that if it reads a byte and sees this value, then it needs to read the next byte to determine what the instruction is. Conversely, having all the rarely used instructions have the same first byte reduces the number of values that that first opcode byte needs to be tested for, making it faster to process the more common instructions. It also means you're allowing for future expansion: If at any point in the future an expanded IL were to contain more than 256 instructions, you already have the means to deal with that possibility. However, keeping all the commonly used instructions as 1 byte each keeps assembly file size down to a minimum, reducing load time and—more significantly—reducing download time if the assembly is to be downloaded.

Metadata Tables

So far you've seen an example that illustrated the tables of strings and of MemberRefs. The metadata actually has quite a few standard tables—more than 40 of them in fact, all stored in a highly compressed format and having such names as MethodDef, TypeDef, TypeRef, MethodPtr, AssemblyRef, and so on. The last three letters of each name give a clue about where entries in the table refer. Def means that it's a table of items that are defined in this assembly, which clearly means the metadata will need to supply the complete definitions. Ref indicates that it's a reference to something that's fully defined in another assembly, which means that the data in this assembly needs to contain only enough information to identify where the full definition can be found. However, the data in this assembly contains sufficient information, such as the signatures of methods, to allow the JIT compiler to perform basic type and verifiability checking without actually having to load the other assembly. A name ending in Ptr indicates some reference to another item in this assembly. Ptr items aren't found in well-organized assemblies—they exist to sort out the problems that can occur if types are (for example) referenced before being fully defined—their function is analogous to forward declarations in C++. Write your IL code carefully, and you won't get any Ptr items in your assembly.

Full details of the various tokens are listed in Partition II. However, just so you're familiar with some of the terms in use, Table 4-1 lists some of the more important tables in the metadata.

Table 4-1. *Some of the More Important Metadata Tables*

Table Name			Meaning
Def Type	**Ref Type**	**Ptr Type**	**Defines or Identifies...**
MethodDef		MethodPtr	A method
TypeDef	TypeRef		A type—class, struct, enum, and so on
AssemblyDef	AssemblyRef		The current assembly or a referenced assembly
ParamDef		ParamPtr	A parameter to a method
FieldDef		FieldPtr	A field in a type

For the actual tokens used in arguments in the IL instruction stream, certain high-value bits in each argument indicate which table the token refers to, and the remaining bits indicate the index in the table. For example, if the highest order byte in a token is 0x06, then the JIT compiler knows it's a MethodDef, and 0x0A indicates a MemberRef. Since you're not going into the binary details in this book, don't worry about which bit means what; again, the information is available in the Partition II document if you need it. Note that in many cases these high-order bits are redundant. For example, the token that follows the ldstr opcode can only ever refer to a string, and that following call or callvirt can refer only to either a MethodDef or a MemberRef.

Version Robustness

I'll finish this discussion of the file structure of executable modules with an observation about version robustness. You'll no doubt be familiar with the concept that assemblies do away with "DLL hell" because they allow assemblies with different versions to exist side by side. Assemblies help to ensure version robustness in another way, which is quite clever. It falls naturally out of the way metadata works but is nevertheless not so commonly publicized. Think about what happens if you bring out a new version of a DLL assembly, in which you've added some new fields and methods to a type. You ship this assembly, and various existing applications for whatever reason, shift to use the new version of your assembly. Now in the old unmanaged DLL days, adding fields could kill application compatibility straightaway unless you took care to add them at the end of the class definition. That's because existing fields would otherwise probably be moved to new offsets within the data structures so any client code that accessed fields as offsets against the address of an instance of a type would break dramatically. However, that can't happen in managed code because such references (for example, MemberRefs and TypeRefs) are explicitly stored by name rather than by offset in the dependant assemblies. That means the locations of fields are resolved at runtime by the .NET loader and the JIT compiler, so it doesn't matter if the layout of a class changes—the correct fields will always be accessed (provided of course you don't write unsafe code that uses pointer arithmetic to calculate field locations).

Resources and Resource Files

Finally, you need to consider the remaining type of file that can be part of an assembly: the *resource file*, which contains managed resources. Be aware that a managed resource file isn't the same as an unmanaged resource; an assembly is of course quite capable of reading either a managed resource file or an unmanaged resource, but in this book I'll cover only managed resource files.

A resource simply means any data—of course, other than the executable code and metadata—that forms part of an assembly. This means that .NET resources can include (for example) strings, bitmaps, icons, and so on; in fact, it can include any binary or textual data that's required by an assembly. A resource can even contain simple numeric types. An important reason for using resources is the issue of *localization*—the ability of an application to call different sets of resources (notably strings) according to the language in which it's running. The idea is that porting an application shouldn't require any changes in the actual code for the program—all language dependencies should be confined to the resources, so all that's needed is to load a different set of resources at runtime. I'll save discussing the question of how the .NET resource model supports localization until the section "Resources and Resource Files." For now, I'll focus on the principles of how resources can be included in an assembly.

Linking or Embedding

In fact, you need to consider two situations, and only one of these involves a separate resource file.

- Resources can be embedded in a PE file.

- Resource files can be linked to an assembly as separate files.

The case for which a resource file is linked as a separate file is conceptually the easiest case to understand, but in programmatic terms it's the least powerful model. The resource file can be literally any file—for example, a text file or a bitmap file. The file format has no restrictions. However, the lack of restrictions on the file format means that there can be little built-in .NET support for processing such resources. You'll link a resource file typically by using the /linkresource option of the assembly linker utility, al.exe.

All that happens when linking a file is that details of the filename are placed in the assembly manifest, and the hash of the assembly contents is of course calculated to incorporate the linked file. However, the linked file itself isn't modified. In practical terms, basically what you have is a separate file shipped with your assembly but with the hash used as an extra check that the contents of this file haven't been corrupted. The easiest way to load the data in such a file at runtime is still to treat it as if it were an independent file (for example, by calling Bitmap.LoadImage(<*filename*>) for a bitmap or using the StreamReader class for a text file). If you have files such as bitmaps or text files that you want to ship with your code and aren't modified at runtime, then linking them to the assembly in this way is probably a good idea simply because of the extra file integrity check you'll get.

Embedding a resource inside an assembly PE file has a disadvantage that the resource will automatically be loaded along with the code in that file—so you have less flexibility in terms of being able to delay loading the data until that data is actually required. However, the advantage you gain is a much more powerful programming model. The .NET Framework provides for a standard format in which resources can be embedded. This format is supported by various classes in the System.Resources namespace, notably ResourceManager, which is able to read the data embedded in an assembly.

In high-level terms, the format for a resource embedded in an assembly may look something like this:

Type: String	Name: Greeting	Value: "Hello, World"
Type: Boolean	Name: DrivesOnLeftSideOfRoad	Value: True
Type: Bitmap	Name: NationalFlag	Value: <Binary data>

The key point to note is that this format includes details of the type of object that each lump of data represents. You can probably guess what the benefit of this structure is. Taking the previous data as an example, you tell the resource manager to read the resource called Greeting from the table, and you get back a string (in other words, a System.String instance) that contains the value "Hello World". You tell the resource manager to read the resource called "NationalFlag", and you get a bitmap (System.Drawing.Bitmap) back. The .NET Framework is able to handle the work involved in identifying the nature of the resource and hence returning the appropriate managed type. The code you'd write looks a bit like this in C#:

```
// thisAssembly is a reference to the current executing assembly
ResourceManager resMan = new ResourceManager("MyFirstResourceSet", thisAssembly);
string greetingText = (string)resMan.GetObject("Greeting");
Bitmap diagram = (Bitmap)resMan.GetObject("NationalFlag");
```

By the way, for the particular case of strings, the `ResourceManager` class offers a simpler way of getting at the data.

```
string greetingText = resMan.GetString("Greeting");
```

The actual format of the data in the assembly is compact and fairly natural. The header information that identifies the resource is followed by the names of the items in the resource and their data types, stored as strings. Then the actual values follow as binary blobs, which can in many cases be loaded directly into memory to represent the object values.

■**Note** Simple data, such as individual strings or blobs, can also be embedded in the assembly using the `ldstr` command or the `.data` directive in IL. This technique isn't the same as using resources and doesn't implicitly support localization. I won't discuss that situation here, as this section focuses on the case where items are stored in the format that's supported by the .NET resource infrastructure. Chapter 1 discussed `ldstr` and `.data`.

Managed vs. Unmanaged Resources

As noted earlier, it's important to understand that managed resources aren't the same as unmanaged resources. The model used for resources in the .NET Framework is considerably enhanced compared to the facilities offered by Windows for unmanaged resources. Before the days of .NET, support for resources was available through various API functions, which were concerned with specific types of data, including the following:

- Bitmaps

- Menus

- String tables

- Accelerator tables

- Icons

- Cursors

For example, if you wanted to use a bitmap, either you could have the bitmap stored in a separate file or you could embed it as a resource in the PE file itself. In both cases you'd use the API function `LoadImage()` to actually load the bitmap and create a handle by which your code could reference the bitmap. The parameters passed to `LoadImage()` would indicate whether the bitmap was to be obtained from a file or as a resource.

Whereas unmanaged resources are embedded in the PE file in a manner that's known and recognized by Windows, managed resources are described in the assembly metadata and are therefore recognized only by the CLR. As far as Windows is concerned, the managed resources are just another block of opaque data in the PE file. A side effect of this is that it's perfectly legitimate to embed both managed and unmanaged resources in the same assembly. An obvious example of this is that if you want a custom icon to be associated with your application and displayed by Windows Explorer, you'd need to embed it as an unmanaged resource since Windows Explorer currently is unable to read managed resources. Using unmanaged resources is supported by the main Microsoft compilers (see, for example, the /win32res flag in C# and the /win32resource flag in VB), though VS .NET has little specific built-in support, other than within unmanaged C++ projects.

Once you've gotten used to the flexibility provided by managed resources, it's probably fairly unlikely that you'll want use unmanaged resources anyway, apart from legacy compatibility reasons—simply because the managed resource model is so much more powerful.

- If you want to store resources in separate files, then maintaining them as linked managed resource files means you get the automatic file integrity checking for free. For unmanaged resources, no support exists for this—if you want to use this technique, you just have to supply the file separately as a completely independent file.

- If you want to embed resources in the assembly PE file, then the format for managed resources allows you to embed and instantiate a large number of types from managed resources—and to use a simple but powerful programming model to instantiate that data as the appropriate managed types.

- If the CLR gets ported to other platforms, then this opens the possibility of platform-independent resources.

- Enhanced localization support. Windows does offer support for localization of unmanaged resources, but as you'll see soon the localization model offered by the .NET Framework for managed resources that are embedded into a PE file really does make localizing applications incredibly simple in concept (although the implementation details can still get a bit hairy).

As you can probably imagine, a fairly sophisticated API supports the generation of managed resources. This API comes partly from classes in the System.Resources namespace (of which ResourceManager is only one of a number of classes) and partly from some command-line utilities (which are for the most part implemented internally using these same classes!); VS .NET also provides some intrinsic support for managed resources. You'll see a lot more about managed resources later in the section "Generating Assemblies."

Introducing the External View: Assembly Logical Structure

At this point in the chapter, I've largely completed the discussion of the internal structure of assembly files. You're ready to examine assemblies on a higher level and to consider how to manipulate them. I'll kick off this part of the chapter with a brief review of the subject of assembly identity—in other words, the characteristics of an assembly that distinguish it from the other assemblies on your system.

Assembly Identity

The identity of an assembly consists of the following four items:

- The name

- The version

- The public key (provided that a private key was available when the assembly was signed)

- The culture

Assemblies that haven't been signed don't of course have a public/private key combination. They do, however, still have a hash of the assembly contents, which can be used to verify that the assembly hasn't been corrupted. The hash means you can detect if some random corruption has happened to the assembly or one of its files, though obviously it can't guard against the possibility of some malicious person replacing the entire assembly.

All four of the previous items form an essential part of the identity of an assembly. Two assemblies whose identity differs in any one of these items will be considered as completely different assemblies by the CLR.

The following sections quickly review these items.

Name

You should think of the name as the filename for the file that contains the prime module but without the .exe or .dll extension. Although the assembly name is stored separately inside the file, you should normally keep the assembly name the same as the name of the prime module file (minus the extension).

Version

The version has no surprises. The version of the assembly is simply a set of four numbers, known respectively as major version, minor version, build, and revision. For example, version 2.1.345.0 should be interpreted as version 2.1, with build number 345. The version is normally indicated as part of the assembly manifest and is indicated in this way in the IL source:

```
.assembly MyAssembly
{
    .ver 2:1:345:0
}
```

Dependent assemblies will normally specify that they require a particular version of the referenced assembly, like so:

```
.assembly extern SomeLibrary
{
    .ver 2:1:0:0
}
```

How you interpret the four numbers in your code is up to you. One good way of working is to use the major and minor version numbers to indicate breaking changes—and changes in build and revision number should be nonbreaking bug fixes. A typical use of the build and revision numbers may run something like this: The build number gets incremented each time a full build of the application happens, and the revision number will be modified if for some reason an unusual extra build takes place. For example, if it's normal practice in your group to do a new build of some large application each day, but on one day because of an unexpected bug an extra build needs to be done, then you indicate this with the revision number. However, these are only recommendations—in the end it's up to your organization how it treats these numbers.

Public/Private Key

This is the one aspect of an assembly's identity that's optional. For private assemblies, you can choose whether to sign the assembly with a key, but signing is compulsory for assemblies that are to be placed in the GAC and made publicly available to any application. Assemblies that have been signed are said to have *strong names*. The unusual aspect of the key is that it isn't stored in its entirety as separate data in the assembly manifest in the way that happens for other aspects of the assembly identity. Instead, only the public part of the key is stored. The private part of the key is instead used to encrypt the hash of the assembly contents using a technique known as *public key cryptography*. You'll examine how this technique works in Chapter 13. For now, I'll simply say that the public and private keys will be computed in such a way that decrypting the hash using the public key (which is readily available) will yield only the correct decrypted hash if the hash was originally encrypted with the correct private key. Assuming that an organization keeps its private key secret, then that provides a guarantee that the correct company produced the assembly.

Culture

Culture, roughly speaking, amounts to .NET's implementation of an old concept—that of indicating the intended language and area in the world in which an assembly is intended to be used. In pre-.NET days, the Windows locale ID provided this information. While the locale is still used as the way that Windows identifies the area, .NET has refined the concept into the culture, which not only identifies the language and the geographical region but also is supported by a number of .NET classes in the System.Globalization namespace.

As far as assemblies are concerned, the main use for the culture is to identify resources to be loaded. The way this is normally implemented in .NET is that the code for an assembly that contains code should have what's known as the *invariant culture*—a default culture that doesn't indicate any language or place in particular. But then resources such as strings that will be displayed by the application are stored separately in related assemblies known as *satellite assemblies*, each of which has an associated culture. An application therefore loads its main assembly containing the code, then based on the culture it's running under (usually taken by the .NET Framework from the locale ID (LCID) that Windows thinks it's running under), identifies the appropriate satellite assembly from which to load resources. This ensures, for example, that text is displayed in Japanese if the application is running on a Japanese installation of Windows or is displayed in French if it's a French installation of Windows. This all means that the main assembly should be able to run satisfactorily anywhere in the world.

The culture can consists of the following two parts:

- The language

- The region

These items are each indicated by two- or three-character strings. The first two letters, which indicate the language, are normally lowercase and are separated by a hyphen from the final letters, which indicate the geographical region and are normally in uppercase. For example, en-GB indicates English as used in the United Kingdom, en-US indicates English as used in the United States. The format for the strings used is an industrywide standard and is defined in Request for Comments (RFC) number 3066 at http://www.ietf.org/rfc/rfc3066.txt. The language codes are defined by ISO standard 639 at http://lcweb.loc.gov/standards/iso639-2/langhome.html. However, for the full list of cultures recognized by the relevant .NET classes, it's best to look at the MSDN documentation.

Although cultures can contain designations for both language and region, this isn't essential. For example, if you prefer, you can supply a satellite assembly in straight English (en) without further localizing it to the country. Cultures such as en are referred to as *neutral cultures*, and those such as en-GB as *specific cultures*. The region itself incidentally is used independently of the language to determine such things as the formatting of numbers, dates, and currencies by the relevant .NET classes.

Referencing Other Assemblies

Assemblies are normally referenced from other assemblies that depend on them—for example, an executable will contain references to the libraries that it uses—the so-called AssemblyRefs. An AssemblyRef is introduced into the IL source by the .assembly extern directive, as you saw in Chapter 1.

```
.assembly extern MyLibrary
{
    .ver 1:0:0:0
}
```

You won't necessarily include the entire identity of the referenced assembly in your IL or high-level language source code, although you can do so if you want. Provided you specify the name, high-level language compilers are generally quite capable of extracting the remaining information from the referenced assembly as they compile and inserting it into the emitted dependent assembly. You'll need to make sure that the version of the assembly located and checked by the compiler is the same as the version that will be loaded at runtime. (You'll examine how the compiler and CLR locate assemblies soon.) You'll also find that, even in the emitted assembly, the full public keys of referenced assemblies aren't stored. That's because they're quite large, so storing the full keys for all referenced assemblies would bloat an assembly (remember that an assembly can typically reference quite a few other assemblies). Instead, a *public key token* is stored—this contains 8 bytes of the hash of the key and is sufficient to verify with near certainty whether the referenced assembly that's loaded does in fact have the correct public key. Of course, each assembly stores its own public key in its entirety.

Reading Assembly Contents

In general, there are two situations where you'll want to read the contents of an assembly to see what the assembly contains—for example, what types are defined in the assembly, what methods are implemented, and so on.

- You may want to do this at development time, when you want to know more about the libraries your code may reference (or simply if you're exploring to find out more about the .NET Framework).

- Your code may need to do this at runtime, if its operation depends on reflection.

If you're working at development time, you'll want to use one of the utilities Microsoft has written to allow you to explore assemblies and PE files, but at runtime you'll need a programmatic API (which is what the utilities will use internally anyway).

In the following sections I'll quickly review some of the available Microsoft tools and APIs. Although third-party tools are available on the Internet, I'll confine the discussion to the tools that come with VS .NET or with the .NET Framework.

ildasm

`ildasm.exe` is probably the tool you've used most—indeed you've already been routinely seeing `ildasm` figures where appropriate in earlier chapters in this book. It's excellent for providing a relatively high-level, logical view of an assembly, including IL code and metadata.

You need to be aware of a few subtleties when using `ildasm`. One is that by default `ildasm` starts in basic mode, which means you don't get quite all the available options to view the file. To start it in advanced mode, you should use the `/adv` option.

```
ildasm /adv
```

This gives you a couple of extra options on the View menu to look at the statistics for the file (how many bytes each part of it occupies, and so on) and to look at the raw header information.

Another issue with `ildasm` is that it's unable to directly view assemblies that are in the assembly cache. Why Microsoft put in this restriction is frankly beyond me. If they meant it as a security precaution to protect the code in shared assemblies from being viewed, then it's so easy to circumvent as to be virtually worthless—it merely serves as a minor irritant if you want to examine such code.

If you want to use `ildasm.exe` to examine the DLLs in the assembly cache, then you have the following options:

Use the command prompt: If you know where the assembly you want is located, then you can navigate into the assembly cache with the command prompt and copy the file. Unfortunately, because of the strange folder names, it's not often that you'll know the location of the file you want.

Copy the assemblies out en masse: It takes a few minutes to write a short program in C# or VB .NET that recursively searches through all the folders in the assembly cache and copies every `.dll` or related file into some other folder of your choice.

Use the copies in the CLR system folder: This is the folder in which the .NET Framework is installed—in version 1.1, it's `%windir%\Microsoft.NET\Framework\v1.1.4322`. Obviously for future versions this version number will change. You'll find this folder contains all the unmanaged DLLs that implement the CLR (`mscorjit.dll`, `mscorwks.dll`, and so on), as well as many of the compilers and tools you're used to using (`csc.exe`, `ilasm.exe`, `gacutil.exe`). The folder also contains copies of every .NET Framework Class Library DLL (as you'll see soon, copies are needed here for compilers to look up when they resolve references in your code). You'll also incidentally find the only IL copy of `mscorlib.dll` here. This DLL is so fundamental to the operation of managed code that it's kept in the CLR's install folder and always loaded from there. The assembly cache contains only the ngen'd native version of `mscorlib.dll`.

DumpBin

`DumpBin.exe` is a useful utility supplied by Microsoft that displays the contents of PE files, as well as provides some degree of interpretation of them. It works at a lower level than `ildasm`—for example, if you want, it will display the raw binary data. Unlike `ildasm.exe`, `DumpBin` is designed for all PE and COFF files, not specifically for managed assemblies. This has the advantage that it lets you see all the PE header information that's skipped by `ildasm` (if you want to see that stuff, of course), and it has the disadvantage that it's able to do very little CLR-based interpretation of metadata, and so on. Microsoft has added a `/CLR` option to `DumpBin` that lets you view the CLR header, but the information you get from that is pretty limited. Another disadvantage is that `DumpBin` is a command-line, not a GUI-based, tool. Still, as an overall tool, `DumpBin` is useful for displaying the generic contents of a PE file. If you want to use this utility, simply type `dumpbin <filename>` at the command prompt.

Reflection

The .NET `System.Reflection` classes allow you to programmatically examine assemblies or types, as well as to instantiate instances of types and invoke methods on them. If you want to use reflection to examine an assembly, then your starting point is likely to be the `System.Reflection.Assembly` class, and in particular one of the static methods `Assembly.GetExecutingAssembly()`, `Assembly.LoadFrom()`, or `Assembly.Load()`, for example, to retrieve a reference to the currently executing assembly.

```
Assembly thisAssembly = Assembly.GetExecutingAssembly();
```

`GetExecutingAssembly()`, as the name suggests, returns an `Assembly` reference that can be used to find out about the assembly that's currently being executed, and `LoadFrom()` and `Load()` load an assembly given, respectively, its filename or assembly name. As is suggested by their names, they actually load the assembly into the current process if it's not already loaded. Analyzing the data in an assembly with this managed API requires the whole assembly to be loaded. You'll need to be aware of this, as it could cause your working set to rise considerably if you're loading and analyzing a large number of assemblies—and currently .NET doesn't support unloading of individual assemblies. You can avoid this problem by loading assemblies into a separate application domain and unloading the application domain.

I won't go into the Reflection classes in detail—they're adequately documented in MSDN and in many other .NET books. However, I'll present a quick example to show you how to get started analyzing an assembly.

The example is called ReflectionDemo. It's a simple C# console application that uses Assembly.LoadFrom() to load the System.Drawing.dll assembly from the folder that contains copies of shared assemblies for VS .NET's use and then displays a list of the types defined in that assembly. The code for the Main() method for this sample looks like this:

```
static void Main()
{
    string windir = Environment.GetEnvironmentVariable("windir");
    Assembly ass = Assembly.LoadFrom(windir +
                @"\Microsoft.NET\Framework\v1.1.4322System.Drawing.dll");
    foreach (Type type in ass.GetTypes())
        Console.WriteLine(type.ToString());
}
```

A quick sample of some of the output from ReflectionDemo (a small part of the output—the list of types goes on for several pages!) looks like this:

```
ThisAssembly
AssemblyRef
System.Drawing.SRDescriptionAttribute
System.Drawing.SRCategoryAttribute
System.Drawing.SR
System.ExternDll
System.Drawing.Image
System.Drawing.Image+GetThumbnailImageAbort
System.Drawing.Image+ImageTypeEnum
System.Drawing.Bitmap
System.Drawing.Brush
System.Drawing.Brushes
System.Drawing.Imaging.CachedBitmap
System.Drawing.Color
```

Once you have a Type reference, you can manipulate instances of the type, as detailed in the documentation for System.Reflection.

The System.Reflection classes are designed to support working with the various managed types defined in an assembly, and as such they don't include much support for examining the assembly at a lower level, such as examining its file structure or the CLR headers. As an example, you can't use reflection to find out whether an executable assembly is a console or Windows application. To obtain that kind of information, you'll need to manually examine the SubSystem field in the PE header. You can also gain some more low-level information using the unmanaged reflection API.

The Unmanaged Reflection API

The unmanaged reflection API consists of a small number of COM components that are able to examine and extract information from an assembly. It isn't nearly as sophisticated as its managed equivalent—for example, it doesn't support instantiation of objects. However, it does allow more access to the metadata and header information in an assembly—which means you can use the unmanaged reflection API to access information not available using the System.Reflection classes. It's the unmanaged reflection API, and not the System.Reflection classes, that's used internally by ildasm.exe.

The API isn't really documented in MSDN, but you can find a Word document, Metadata Unmanaged API.doc, that defines the components available as well as an example (the metainfo example) in the .NET Framework SDK, under the Tool Developers Guide folder. If the lack of documentation wasn't enough to dissuade you from using the unmanaged reflection API, the COM components it contains don't have an associated type library, which means that if you want to invoke methods in this API from managed code, you can't use tlbimp.exe or any of the built-in support in VS .NET for COM interop to help you. However, nothing is stopping you from using IJW to access these methods from managed C++ code or from writing some managed C++ wrappers around the components.

If you do want to use the unmanaged reflection API, then you'll find the starting point is to instantiate the COM object called the CorMetaDataDispenser using a call to CoCreateInstance()—you can then manipulate this object to extract metadata information and related objects from an assembly.

Exploring the Assembly Cache

The assembly cache contains the shared assemblies (in the GAC), as well as native images of assemblies that have been ngen'd, and it contains copies of assemblies that have been downloaded from remote machines to be executed, for example, from inside Internet Explorer.

The ShFusion View of the Cache

You'll no doubt be well aware that the assembly cache appears to Windows Explorer as a structure that contains assemblies but whose internal details are hidden. This is thanks to a shell extension, shfusion.dll, that's installed with .NET and that takes control of the user interface Windows Explorer presents for the files in this folder. Thus, opening Windows Explorer and navigating to the assembly cache gives you something like Figure 4-4.

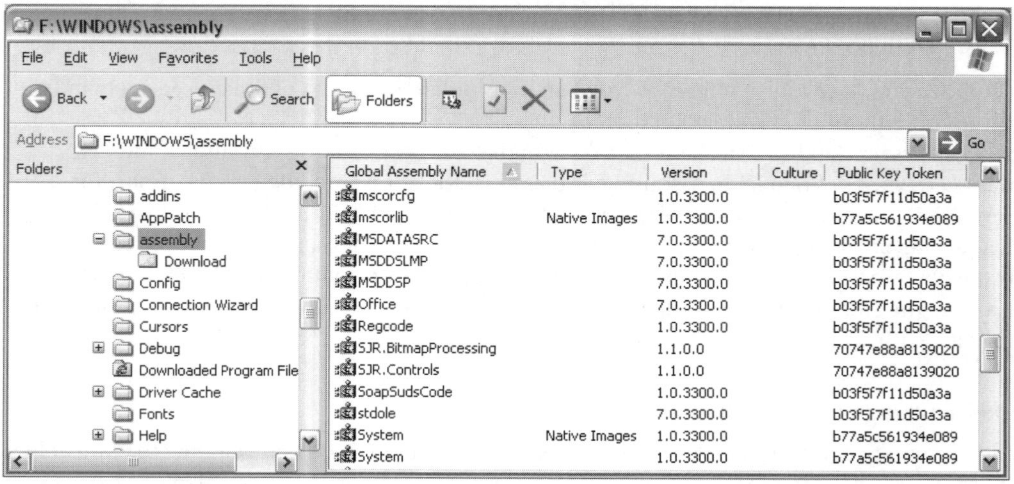

Figure 4-4. *The Windows Explorer view of the assembly cache*

The shell extension has of course been written for your own protection—it stops you from fiddling with GAC and breaking it! Beyond looking to see what files are there, the shell extension will let you do little with the cache. If you right-click an assembly, you get the option to either view the assembly's properties (basically the same information that's already in the list view) or delete the assembly—something I don't recommend doing for any of the Microsoft-supplied assemblies! The view supplied by the shell extension tells you the name and version of each assembly. You also get an indication if the assembly is actually a native image (that's to say, an ngen'd assembly). All ngen'd assemblies are here, whether shared or private. However, any such private assemblies located here can still be accessed only by the applications for which they were intended, since the native image has to be loaded in conjunction with the original assembly, which—if private—won't be in the assembly cache. The culture of each assembly and its public key token are also listed. Obviously, you need the public key token to be able to use the assembly. In Figure 4-4, most of the assemblies are the Microsoft framework base class libraries, which therefore have the same Microsoft public key. mscorlib has a different key—this is because mscorlib contains ECMA standard libraries and is therefore signed with the ECMA private key. In Figure 4-4 you'll also see a couple of assemblies of my own in the cache, and you'll see that two of the Microsoft assemblies are present as ngen'd files.

The shell extension also displays a "folder" called Download. You won't be surprised to learn that this is where assemblies downloaded from the Internet or intranets are placed. I say "folder" in quotes because (as you'll see soon) this isn't a real folder on the file system at all—it's rather a logical folder within the cache. In fact, the Download area maps to a user-specific location so that any one user can't see files downloaded by other users. If you examine this area, you'll find the information displayed is rather different from that for the shared assemblies (see Figure 4-5).

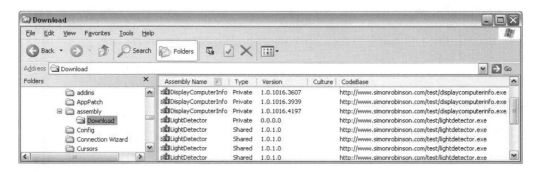

Figure 4-5. *The download section of the assembly cache*

Instead of the public key token you see a field termed CodeBase. This is simply the uniform resource indicator (URI) from which the file was downloaded. This URI is important as it forms a crucial part of the evidence that the CLR's security system uses to assess how far the application should be trusted and therefore which permissions it should be granted, as you'll learn in Chapter 12. The assemblies displayed here are the ones I've installed and then downloaded and executed from the Internet—I have multiple versions of them because I was testing and recompiling the assembly.

The Actual Assembly Cache Structure

While the GAC shell extension may be great for stopping people who don't know what they're doing from hacking into the cache, it's not so great if you want find out what the structure of the assembly cache is and how it works. If you want to do that, then you have the following options:

Windows Explorer: You can disable the shell extension for the assembly folder. The shell extension is in a file, `shfusion.dll`, that's located (in version 1.*x* of the framework) in the CLR system folder (as noted earlier, in version 1.1 of the framework, that's `%windir%\Microsoft.NET\Framework\v1.1.4322`). This file hosts a standard COM component, which means it can easily be unregistered by removing its COM-related entries from the registry. To do this you'll need to navigate to this folder and from the command prompt type `regsvr32 -u shfusion.dll`. When you've finished browsing the GAC, you should reinstall the shell extension by typing `regsvr32 shfusion.dll`.

Command prompt: You can use the command prompt, which is unaffected by the shell extension, but obviously you don't get such a convenient user interface.

Custom explorer: This is my favored technique. It's simple to write a Windows Forms application with a simplified Windows Explorer–style user interface, specifically for the purpose of navigating the assembly cache. An example of this type of application is included with the code download for this chapter. The example uses the `System.IO` classes to enumerate subfolders and is therefore impervious to the Windows Explorer shell extension. I won't present any of the code for this utility in the chapter, since it's the results rather than the code that's important here. But if you want to use it, it's called `GACExplore`. The example gives less information than Windows Explorer, but it saves you from having to keep unregistering the shell extension.

Windows Explorer via the run command: You can open Windows Explorer directly within the assembly cache (though without the treeview pane) by clicking the Start menu, selecting Run, and typing in the path to the assembly cache—usually `c:\Windows\assembly\gac`.

If you disable the shell extension, then your assembly cache in Windows Explorer will look like Figure 4-6.

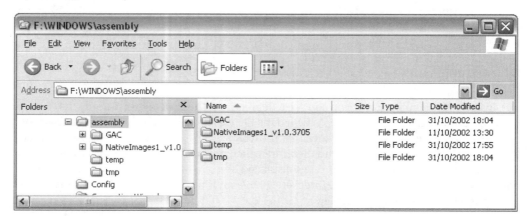

Figure 4-6. *Assembly cache—actual folder structure*

You can see that, besides a couple of temporary folders, the assembly folder contains two subfolders that hold public assemblies that have been installed to the GAC and native images (both private and shared). Drilling down into the GAC reveals the kind of structure shown in Figure 4-7.

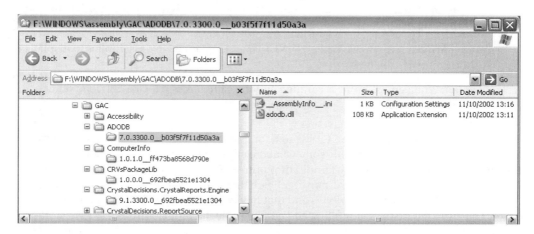

Figure 4-7. *Drilling further into the assembly cache*

This structure isn't too hard to figure out and is a lot less scary than you may have expected. Below the GAC folder is a folder for each assembly name—for example, the adodb.dll assembly is located somewhere under the folder ADODB. But you'll see a second folder level: Under the ADODB folder is a folder whose name reflects the version number of the assembly and its public key. In other words, all you have is an elaborate folder system to arrange assemblies according to their identities (Figure 4-7 doesn't show any subfolders for culture because all the assemblies here have neutral culture). The file structure of the GAC with the current version of .NET is nothing more than a simple hierarchy that allows assemblies with different versions and cultures to coexist side by side. And when you use gacutil.exe to place an assembly in the cache, gacutil.exe isn't doing any magic behind the scenes—it's just reading the name, public key, version, and culture of the assembly, creating the appropriate folders and copying the file across them.

One other file is packaged with each assembly: All assemblies have an associated file called __AssemblyInfo__.ini. This is just a short file that conveniently stores information about a couple of the properties of the assembly to make it slightly easier for the CLR to grab the information. The __AssemblyInfo__.ini file for the adodb.dll file shown in Figure 4-4 looks like this:

```
[AssemblyInfo]
MVID=4b18ed8eb3823d41a6633f1d2232e919
DisplayName=ADODB, Version=7.0.3300.0, Culture=neutral,
 PublicKeyToken=b03f5f7f11d50a3a
```

Although I haven't shown the structure for assemblies in the native image cache, you can probably gather that the folder structure for these assemblies is quite similar.

Locating Assemblies

I'll now answer the question, where will the system search for assemblies? A search for assemblies will be performed at three times, and each has different rules.

- **Compiling:** When a compiler is searching for assemblies that are referenced in the code it's compiling

- **Adding project references:** When VS .NET is working out which assemblies to display in its Add Reference dialog box

- **Loading:** When an assembly is running and the CLR needs to locate and load other referenced assemblies

The third item on this list, the CLR's search for assemblies to load into a process, is officially known as *probing*. It's arguably somewhat cheeky of me to include the other two cases in the same list since these cases aren't under the control of the CLR but are application specific. If you take into account all the third-party software that's around, other applications may exist that need to explicitly locate assemblies and that have their own rules for which folders they search. However, the cases of compiling and adding project references in VS .NET are situations you're likely to encounter frequently when writing managed code, so it seems sensible to consider those cases here.

You may wonder why Microsoft has gone for several sets of rules. Wouldn't it be simpler to have, for example, compilers look in the same places that the CLR looks in when loading an assembly? The trouble is of course that you're not normally talking about the same machine. The compiler is at work on the developer's machine, and the CLR is more likely to be loading an assembly on the end user's machine. The circumstances are different, and the rules for locating assemblies need to take account of that.

How the Microsoft Compilers Locate Assemblies

What I'm talking about here is when you type something like this:

```
csc /r:MyControl.dll /r:MyOtherControl.dll MyProgram.cs
```

Where is the compiler going to look for MyControl.dll and MyOtherControl.dll? Well, assuming you haven't actually specified the path in the csc command, it will search through the following locations in order:

- The working directory.

- The CLR system directory.

- If you've specified any folders using the /lib flag in the csc command (/libpath for the VB compiler), these folders will be searched.

- If the LIB environment variable specifies any folders, these will be searched.

If none of these folders yields the required assemblies, then the compiler will flag an error.

One interesting point to note here is that I haven't mentioned the GAC in the previous list. The assembly cache is something that's really the prerogative of the CLR itself, and although it'd in principle be possible for compilers to look there for libraries, Microsoft has chosen for them not to do so. Thus, any assembly that the compiler looks up will be a local copy rather than something in the assembly cache. That arguably makes sense because most likely many of the referenced assemblies are ones you're working on and debugging at the moment—and it'd add some considerable extra work to the build process if you had to install the most up-to-date copies of them all to the assembly cache every time you rebuilt the project.

This does of course mean that in many cases, the compiler won't be looking up the same copy of the assembly as is loaded at runtime. That's no problem as long as the copies contain identical metadata—since all the compiler is doing with the referenced assemblies is examining their metadata to make sure the types and methods, and so on, that your code refers to do exist and that your code has passed the correct number and type of arguments to the methods.

You should be aware of one other point. When you build a project, it's common to give the names of only referenced assemblies, as in the previous command-line operation (although you can specify a complete assembly identity if you prefer). If you specify only a name, then the compiler will use the first assembly it finds whose name matches, and it will read the full assembly identity out of this assembly (including the version, culture, and public key, if present) and place this information in the AssemblyRef token in the generated assembly. This means that when your assembly is executed, it will by default load the same version of any referenced assembly as the code was compiled against.

How VS .NET Locates Assemblies

When you build a project with VS .NET, VS .NET is of course invoking the same compiler you use from the command line to do the build, so the paths searched are the same as those listed previously. However, when you click Add Reference to open the Add References dialog box, the places that VS .NET searches in order to populate the .NET tab of that dialog box are rather different. Here's where VS.NET looks:

- The .NET Framework installation folder.

- In the following two registry keys:

  ```
  HKEY_LOCAL_MACHINE\SOFTWARE\Microsoft\VisualStudio\7.1\AssemblyFolders
   (for VS.NET 2002 replace 7.1 by 7.0) and
  HKEY_LOCAL_MACHINE\SOFTWARE\Microsoft\.NETFramework\AssemblyFolders
  ```

- In any subkeys of the previous keys. For any such key, VS .NET will look at the default value of the key, which is assumed to be a folder path. VS .NET will display any .dll assemblies (not executable assemblies—VS .NET won't let you add executables as references, though it's possible to do so when compiling from the command line) in all the folders so identified.

Notice that, once again, the assembly cache isn't searched for files. VS .NET will pick up all the .NET Framework Class Library DLLs, because copies of them are stored in the .NET Framework installation folder. So if you've ever registered an assembly in the GAC and wondered why VS .NET wouldn't display it in the Add References dialog box to let you add a reference to it, that's the reason.

If you do want some of your assemblies that aren't part of the VS .NET solution you're working on to be displayed in the Add References dialog box, then the best procedure is to add a subkey under the .NETFramework\AssemblyFolders registry key and set its default value to the folder containing your assemblies. Figure 4-8 shows you the idea in regedit—it shows that I've registered a folder, E:\IL\GroovyLibrary\bin\Release, as a location that contains assemblies for VS .NET to display in the Add References dialog box.

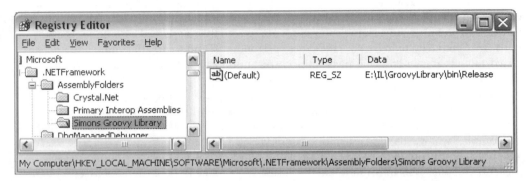

Figure 4-8. *Registry key that adds assemblies to the VS .NET Add References dialog box*

Note that the .NETFramework\AssemblyFolders key seems to be the one that's used by third-party software, with VisualStudio\7.1\AssemblyFolders intended for use by VS .NET itself to indicate its own DLLs. Also bear in mind that each time you compile your code, VS .NET will copy referenced files into the working directory—otherwise the compiler, with its different rules for where to look for assemblies, wouldn't be able to find them. The exception to this is any assemblies referenced from the CLR system folder—these don't need to be copied because compilers look in that folder anyway.

How the CLR Probes for Assemblies

After the complicated rules of compiler and VS .NET searches, you may be relieved to know that the way that the CLR searches for assemblies when it's loading them into a process to be executed is by default relatively simple. Only one or two locations are checked for each assembly (which, obviously, is good for runtime performance).

- If the identity of the requested assembly doesn't include a strong name, then the only place the loader will search is the application folder; this is the folder that contains the entry point assembly for the process that needs to load the referenced assembly.

- If the identity of the requested assembly contains a strong name, then the CLR will search in the GAC and in the application folder.

- mscorlib.dll is a special case and is always loaded from the CLR system folder.

- Satellite assemblies have separate rules, which I'll cover later in the section "Generating Assemblies."

These rules for assembly probing are of course the reason why it's normal to place all assemblies that form part of one application in the same folder.

Unfortunately, little in life is quite so simple. The complicating factor when probing for assemblies is that it's possible to override the default probing policy for any application—the mechanism for this is an Extensible Markup Language (XML) configuration file called `<AppName>.exe.config`, which is placed in the application folder alongside the main application assembly whose probing policy you want to modify. (In this filename, you should replace `<AppName>` with the name of the executable assembly.) You have quite a few possibilities for changing the probing rules, but I'll briefly summarize the most important points here.

The most common purposes of overriding the default probing policy for an assembly are as follows:

- To allow referenced assemblies to be located in different locations.

- To tell the CLR to load a different version of a referenced assembly from that indicated in the `AssemblyRef` token in the assembly that needs to load the new assembly. This will typically be done if you've just shipped a new version of some library and you want dependant assemblies to call up the new version, but you don't want to have to recompile and reship all the dependant assemblies (or perhaps some dependant assemblies are written by another company, so you don't have access to them to recompile them).

Although customization of probing policy for each application is controlled through the `.config` XML file, provided you're not doing anything too exotic, the easiest way to manipulate probing policy is to use a tool that generates the `.config` file for you. Such a tool is available— it's an MMC snap-in called `mscorcfg.msc`. The easiest way to run the tool is from the control panel; select Administrative Tools ➤ .NET Framework Configuration. `mscorcfg.msc` is a generic .NET configuration tool—you'll use it a fair amount in Chapter 12 when you examine the security policy.

If you run the snap-in to configure an assembly, you should navigate to the `Applications/Configured Assemblies` node, as shown in Figure 4-9. For assemblies in the GAC, you should navigate to the `Configured Assemblies` node.

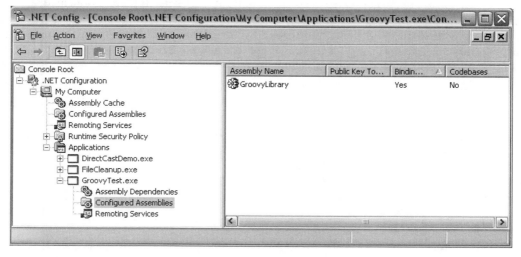

Figure 4-9. *Configuring assemblies with* `mscorcfg.msc`

Right-clicking the Applications node will open a context menu that allows you to add applications to configure. Figure 4-9 shows that I have three applications for which I've overridden the probing policy. In particular, for my assembly called GroovyTest, I've set up an override for the referenced assembly, GroovyLibrary.dll. Double-clicking this assembly in the listview allows you to set the custom probing rules for this assembly, as shown in Figure 4-10.

Figure 4-10. *Modifying the probing rules of an assembly*

In Figure 4-10, you can see that I've asked that if the GroovyTest.exe application requests to load any version of the library between 1.0.0.0 and 1.0.9999.9999, the CLR should load version 2.0 instead—making sure that a newer version of the library is used.

If I navigate to the folder containing GroovyTest.exe, I can see what mscorcfg.msc has actually done. Beside the GroovyTest.exe assembly is a new configuration file, GroovyTest.exe.config; it contains this code:

```xml
<?xml version="1.0"?>
<configuration>
  <runtime>
    <assemblyBinding xmlns="urn:schemas-microsoft-com:asm.v1">
      <dependentAssembly>
        <assemblyIdentity name="GroovyLibrary" />
        <bindingRedirect oldVersion="1.0.0.0-1.0.9999.9999"
                         newVersion="2.0.1.0" />
      </dependentAssembly>
    </assemblyBinding>
  </runtime>
</configuration>
```

The key XML element here is the <bindingRedirect> element—that's the one that tells the CLR to load version 2.0.1.0 of the GroovyLibrary instead of the one specified in the main assembly.

Redirecting a referenced assembly can be a powerful technique. I've only scratched the surface here, but that should be enough to point you in the right direction if you need to explore further.

Generating Assemblies

This is the point where this chapter becomes a lot more applied in nature. You've so far picked up quite a reasonable understanding of the internal workings of assemblies, both at the level of what information they contain and at the level of how that information is arranged within and between files. It's now time to start working toward applying that understanding to actually generate a couple of assemblies. In the following sections, you'll review some of the tools that are available to generate and modify assemblies—looking first at the big picture and then focusing on two areas that can cause particular confusion: signing assemblies to create a strong name and localizing assemblies. Finally, in the "Putting it All Together" section, you'll present two actual examples in which you work through the generation of some assemblies— in one case working at the command line, in the other case working with VS .NET.

Assembly Utilities

Quite a few permutations of assemblies, satellite assemblies, and related files exist, and therefore you can use quite a few commands at the command line to generate the various files. Figure 4-11 shows all the ways you can get from source files and resource files to actual assemblies.

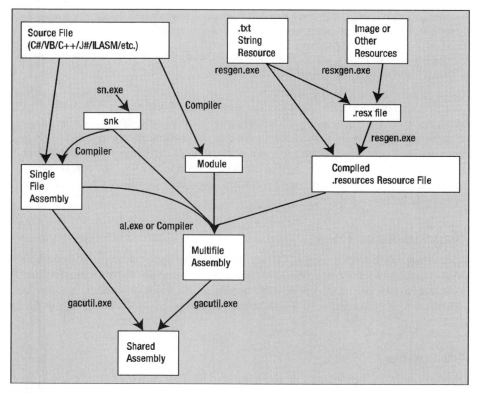

Figure 4-11. *The tools for generating assemblies*

You should treat Figure 4-11 as an overall roadmap, with the names alongside the arrows indicating which command-line utility can perform the conversion. The way to use the figure is to first work out what source files you're expecting to start with and then look at what type of assembly you want to create (for example, private or public, with or without a strong name and/or resources). Then you can use the figure to identify how to get that type of assembly generated.

Detailed usage instructions for, and lists of, the various parameters you can supply to the command-line utilities are of course available in the documentation. However, the following list summarizes the broad purposes of the command-line tools you'll most likely need to use, and you'll see examples of all these utilities in the samples in the "Putting It All Together" section:

- `al.exe` is the assembly linker, which is responsible for creating an assembly by linking various files that contain compiled code or resources intended to go in the assembly. It takes as input one or more assemblies, modules, or resource files, as well as related files such as key files, and it emits an assembly with the desired identity.

- `gacutil.exe` is the utility that's responsible for the assembly cache. Its main functions are to install assemblies to the cache and to remove them from the cache.

- `resgen.exe` is responsible for compiling resources from text-based files into the binary format used in assemblies. It's often used in conjunction with `resxgen.exe`, which can convert image files into XML-based text files that can be processed by `resgen`.

- `sn.exe` generates the public/private key combinations that `al.exe` uses to sign assemblies, as well as performing other tasks such as re-signing an assembly.

- Compiler tools, such as `csc.exe` (C#), `cl.exe` (C++), and `vbc.exe` (VB), are the programs that convert source files into assemblies or modules.

If you're using VS .NET, you'll find that VS .NET uses many of these tools in its build process, saving you from having to worry about the detailed command-line syntax in many cases. You may, however, still want to practice working at the command line in order to get a clearer picture of what's actually happening—something that VS .NET hides. Also, you'll find that the support for many options in VS .NET is limited, so even with a VS .NET project, you may find you need to use the command line for certain tasks (for example, VS .NET can't at present generate multifile assemblies).

Compiling Resource Files

You'll now get a closer look at the process of compiling resources. From now on, the discussion of resources will focus solely on embedded resources, as these are the ones that require compilation into a certain format. As previously mentioned, for linked resources, the file type is literally whatever type of file you want linked to the assembly—no modification of this file is performed.

Types of Resource Files

You probably noticed from Figure 4-11 that three types of files are relevant to embedded resources.

.txt Files

`.txt` files are designed for string-only resources. They have a simple format, allowing you to easily type in a resource by hand. For example, a typical `.txt` file that's destined to become an embedded resource may look like this:

```
FileMenu = File
FileMenuSave = Save
FileMenuOpen = Open
```

In other words, it contains a series of name-value pairs, allowing your code to load each string by name.

.resx Files

`.resx` files are actually XML files, which conform to a fairly strict schema. The advantage of a `.resx` file over a text file is that it can represent resources of any type. Whereas a text file simply contains a table of strings, a `.resx` file contains a table where each item may be a different type; the type of each item being indicated by XML tags. `.resx` files can be quite large, so you don't have space to present a full example, but to give you an idea, a few lines from within a `.resx` file may look like this:

```
<data name="greeting.Text">
  <value>Hello, World!</value>
</data>
<data name="btnShowFlag.Location" type="System.Drawing.Point,
System.Drawing, Version=1.0.3300.0, Culture=neutral,
PublicKeyToken=b03f5f7f11d50a3a">
  <value>16, 72</value>
</data>
```

This snippet is taken from the `.resx` file that VS .NET will generate in the example presented later in the "Putting It All Together" section. It defines the text for a `System.Windows.Forms.Panel` control called `greeting` and the location of a `Button` control called `btnShowFlag`. Notice the way that the `.resx` file defines, in plain-text format, not only the name but also the type of the data (which appears to default to `string`).

For types that require binary data, such as bitmaps, the XML file will contain base-64 encoding of the binary data. Base-64 encoding is a way of representing binary data in a purely text format. As you may guess, this is quite a verbose format (added to the XML file format, which is itself verbose), but you don't need to worry about that. Data is only stored in `.resx` files temporarily, prior to compilation, and resources aren't shipped in that format.

.resources Files

`.resources` files are the actual files incorporated into the assembly. Whereas `.txt` files and `.resx` files are formatted as text files in order to make it easy for the developer to modify them by hand, the corresponding `.resources` file contains the data in the actual binary format that will be embedded in the assembly. The process of generating a `.resources` file from a `.txt` or `.resx` file is known as *compilation* by analogy with the process of compiling source code. Thus, the `.txt` and `.resx` files play the role of the "source files" that the developer manipulates.

resgen.exe and resxgen.exe

The workhorse utility for compiling resources is resgen.exe. This utility is quite capable of compiling either a .txt file or a .resx file into a .resources file (and can equally well decompile a .resources file if passed the appropriate parameters, though you won't do that in this chapter). For example, to compile a .txt file, MyResource.txt, into the file MyResource.resources, you'd write the following:

resgen MyResource.txt

But to compile a .resx file, you'd write the following:

resgen MyOtherResource.resx

If you want, you can even use resgen to convert a .txt file into an XML .resx file, like so:

resgen MyResource.txt MyResource.resx

Using resgen, you can probably see quite easily how to generate a string resource. You type the .txt file, use resgen to compile it, and then use al to embed the resource in an assembly. However, other resources—for example, images—are trickier since you need to start off with a .resx file, which is harder to write from hand. If you want a resource that contains a mixture of types such as strings and primitive types, your best bet is simply to find some compiled .resources file on your system (such as a VS .NET–generated one), use resgen to decompile it into a .resx file and then rename and edit this file. However, that's not possible if you want to embed some binary data such as a bitmap into a resource. For that you'll need to programmatically generate the .resx file containing the base-64 encoded data. Although I won't go into details here, the relevant classes to do this are in the System.Resources namespace.

Fortunately, for the case of bitmaps, the most common scenario, Microsoft has made available a command-line utility that can generate a .resx file from a bitmap. It's resxgen.exe. Unusually, however, resxgen isn't a straight utility but is an example that you'll need to compile from C# source files. It's in the framework SDK samples, and as of version 1.*x* of the .NET Framework you can find it at <Framework SDK Folder>\Samples\Tutorials\resourcesandlocalization\resxgen. Here, <Framework SDK Folder> indicates the folder in which you've installed the .NET Framework SDK. You'll find two C# source files there, resxgen.cs and argparser.cs, along with a batch file to build the project, build.bat. You can either use this batch file or invoke the C# compiler directly, like so:

csc /out:resxgen.exe resxgen.cs argparser.cs

Once resxgen has been built, using it is quite simple.

resxgen /i:MyBitmap.bmp /o:MyBitmap.resx

Once you have your .resources file (or files), either you can use the assembly linker tool, al.exe, to convert them into a resource-only assembly, or you can pass the names of these files as parameters to your high-level language compiler to embed the contents of the files with the emitted code. You'll see how to use both of these techniques in the GreetMe example that I'll present in the "Putting It All Together" section.

Localization and Satellite Assemblies

You'll now examine the model used in .NET for localizing resources. The system is based on what are known as *satellite assemblies*, and the following typical file structure illustrates the principle:

Folders	Files in This Folder	
Name	**Name**	**Culture**
MainFolder	MyLibrary.dll	Invariant culture
MainFolder/en	MyLibrary.resources.dll	en (English)
MainFolder/de	MyLibrary.resources.dll	de (German)
MainFolder/en-CA	MyLibrary.resources.dll	en-CA (English in Canada)

In this file, I've shown the situation for a DLL, but the same principles hold true if MyLibrary was replaced by an EXE—the only thing that would change would be MyLibrary's file extension.

This file shows an assembly called MyLibrary.dll, which has to be localized into specific versions for English and German. In addition, the user interface for English-speaking Canadians has slight differences, so a version for English in Canada is supplied. This obviously represents only a small fraction of the number of localized versions that would be supplied in real life (for example, I've provided an en-CA version but haven't supplied anything for French speakers in Canada—quite a significant oversight), but it'll do to illustrate the principles.

The point to note is that for each localized version a subfolder beneath the folder contains the main assembly and has the same name as the corresponding culture string. Within each folder is another assembly—these are known as *satellite assemblies*—and each satellite assembly has the same base name as the main assembly but with the string .resource appended before the .dll extension. You'll need to keep strictly to these names because the ResourceManager class that handles loading the resources relies on these naming conventions being followed.

The main assembly should contain all the code, just as for nonlocalized applications. It should also contain a version of the resources that can be used in any country for which a specific version isn't supplied (which in practice usually means having strings in English, on the basis that English is the language most likely to be understood by the biggest number of computer users). As far as identity is concerned, the culture of the main assembly should be the invariant culture. The satellite assemblies should contain only resources—no code. If you do for some reason want to place code in a satellite assembly (for example, if you have code that's executed only for certain cultures), then you'll have to explicitly load that assembly to access and execute the code; the resources infrastructure won't help you.

Each satellite assembly should have its culture set to the appropriate culture and contain a version of the resources in that language that's appropriate to that country. Your application is now localized, and the ResourceManager.GetString() and ResourceManager.GetObject() methods will always retrieve a correctly localized resource. The implementation of these methods works like this: The ResourceManager first checks the user interface (UI) culture of the thread on which it's running. It then looks for a satellite resource with this culture and obtains the relevant string or other object from this resource. If it can't find it, then it'll just grab the corresponding object from the (culture-invariant) main assembly. That's the principle, but the process is slightly more sophisticated: Suppose the application is running with the UICulture set to en-US, and ResourceManager is asked to load a string from the resources. The resource manager will look for an en-US satellite assembly that contains the string in question. If it doesn't find this assembly, or if the assembly exists but doesn't contain the required string, it will look to see if there's a culture-neutral en satellite assembly that contains generic English-language resources and that contains the required string. If that fails, it'll look in the main assembly for the language-invariant resources, and finally if that doesn't yield the string, it'll throw an exception. A consequence of this architecture is that satellite assemblies don't need to contain all resource objects—each one needs to contain only those resources that are different from the corresponding object in the parent culture.

Tip I've referred specifically to CurrentUICulture. The Thread class has several culture-related properties, but it's beyond the scope of this chapter to go into them in detail. ResourceManager uses Thread.CurrentUICulture to determine which localized resources should be loaded. Several other .NET classes use a different property, Thread.CurrentCulture, to determine aspects of string formatting. But in most cases you'll allow both of these properties to have the same value anyway. If you don't set cultures explicitly, the values will be inherited from the operating system.

That's the theory; the only question is, how do you create a resource-only satellite assembly? The answer is that you use the assembly linker al.exe, just as you would to create an ordinary assembly that contains code. You just don't specify any code files as input. For example, if you have a file called MyResources.resources that contains the German (de) version of resources and that needs to be converted into a satellite assembly called MyLibrary.resources.dll, you'd do this:

```
al /res:MyResources.resources /c:de /out:MyLibrary.resources.dll
```

This command emits the assembly. The /c flag indicates the culture of the emitted assembly and must be set for the ResourceManager to be able to locate the assembly.

It's important to understand that the satellite assembly is still a portable executable file, containing all the relevant PE headers, as well as the assembly manifest. It just happens not to contain any IL code.

Signing Assemblies

The process of signing an assembly that's ready to place into the GAC is relatively straightforward in principle.

You generate the key using the utility sn.exe, like so:

```
sn -k OurKey.snk
```

The previous command generates a file called OurKey.snk, which contains the public and private key pair. You can now get the assembly signed by this key in two ways. The first way is to indicate this key using the /keyfile parameter to the assembly linker utility. Thus, taking the previous example, if you want the MyResources satellite assembly to be signed as well, you'd type the following:

```
al /res:MyResources.resources /c:de /keyfile:OurKey.snk
/out:MyLibrary.resources.dll
```

For compiled source code, the usual practice is to indicate the key file in the AssemblyKeyFile attribute in the source code. For example, in C#, you'd use this:

```
[assembly:AssemblyKeyFile("OurKey.snk")];
```

Although the previous procedure will get the assembly signed, it's probably not how you'll do it in practice in a real organization. Typically, companies won't want their developers to have access to the company's private key. In Chapter 13, when you examine cryptography, you'll see that the public/private key principle requires the private key to be absolutely confidential. Since executing the previous commands requires the OurKey.snk file containing the private key to be present, you'd end up in a situation where the developers would have to keep running to whomever the trusted person with the private key is (most likely one of the senior systems administrators or a security manager) every time they recompile their code. In Chapter 13, you'll examine an alternative procedure for delay-signing assemblies, which doesn't require access to the private key until the final build of the product ready for shipping takes place.

Once an assembly is signed, it can be placed in the GAC, like so:

```
gacutil /i MyLibrary.dll
```

One point to understand is that you can sign code without placing it in the assembly cache. Even for private assemblies, it's good practice to sign them with your organization's private key as an extra security precaution (provided of course that the private key really is kept confidential).

Putting It All Together

I'll now illustrate the process of generating an assembly that has a relatively complex structure by developing a short example called GreetMe (see Figure 4-12). The example is a Windows Forms control that displays a localized welcome message in the user's home language. To run and test the control, you'll also code a Windows form in which the control is embedded.

Figure 4-12. *The* GreetMe *sample, running under the* en-GB *culture*

As you can see, for the UK version (en-GB) I'm marketing the sample to people who like speaking Scouse (an informal Northern English dialect, mostly spoken around Liverpool). You probably wouldn't use such dialects in a real business application, but doing so here serves to better distinguish the different en cultures.

Clicking the button opens a dialog box that shows the flag of the user's home country, just in case the user wants to know what it looks like. In my case, since I'm from the United Kingdom, it's as shown in Figure 4-13.

Figure 4-13. *The* GreetMe *sample, showing the local flag for the* en-GB *culture*

I'll freely admit this isn't exactly the most useful application I've ever written in my life in terms of sales potential. However, you're going to develop it in a way that illustrates the following points:

- You'll have the control as a public assembly (in case any other applications need to display a welcome message to the user and need to use the services of this control to do so…). This means signing it and installing it to the GAC.

- The assembly is written in two languages: The initial welcome message was written by the company's C# team (that'd be me), and the job of coding that flag dialog was handed to the VB team (OK, that's me again, but you get the idea). So you need to compile the two modules (called GreetMe and FlagDlg) that make up the assembly separately.

- The assembly is localized using the .NET satellite assembly localization model.

You'll start by developing the example entirely at the command line with a command-line batch file so you can see what's actually happening. Then you'll redo the sample using VS .NET so you can see how to take advantage of VS .NET's built-in support for localization. By doing this, you'll see that although VS .NET makes it easy to support some localization, it runs into problems if you want to do anything particularly sophisticated. For this reason, the VS .NET version of the sample won't have quite the same features as the command-line version—in particular it won't have the dynamically constructed Flag: *<culture>* caption for the dialog box that displays the flag.

Command-Line GreetMe Example

In terms of assembly structure, the example should look like Figure 4-14.

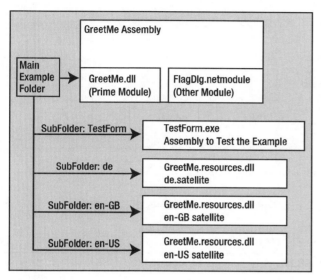

Figure 4-14. *Assembly structure of the* GreetMe *sample*

To develop the example, you first need to create the folder structure for the satellite assemblies. For this example I have satellites for en-GB, en-US, and de, so I have subfolders for those cultures. I also have a subfolder called TestForm, which will contain the form you'll be using to test the example—I wanted this form in a separate folder to make sure that when I run it, it will work correctly only if the sample has been correctly installed in the GAC. If the test form was in the same folder as the example, then CLR would be able to load the local, private copy of the example—which means that executing the example successfully would give you no clue as to whether the example was working correctly and picking up the file from the GAC.

Figure 4-15 shows the two files that will be used to generate the resources for the en-GB culture—a file with the strings and a file with the bitmap. Note the filename Strings.en-GB.txt carefully. Ignore the correct format for this filename (or any of the names of resource files for that matter), and your application won't localize properly. The name of the .jpg file doesn't matter because it won't be directly processed by resgen.exe—it has to be converted to a .resx file by resxgen first; it's the .resx file that will need to have a name in the correct format of <Resource-Name>.<Culture-Name>.resx (in this case Flags.en-GB.resx).

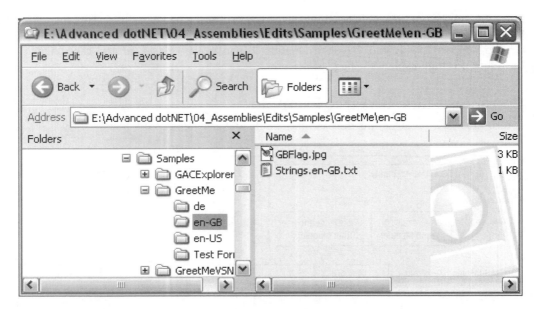

Figure 4-15. *File structure of the* GreetMe *sample source code*

The contents of the resource files are as follows. Table 4-2 shows the text files.

Table 4-2. *Resource File Contents for the Different Cultures*

Strings.en-US.txt	Strings.en-GB.txt	Strings.de.txt
Greeting = Howdy World!	Greeting = Ariite Wurld!	
	ButtonCaption = See yer flag	Greeting = Hallo, Welt!
		ButtonCaption = Flagge zeigen
		DialogCaption = Flagge:

You also have an invariant-culture version in the main project folder, Strings.txt (see Table 4-3).

Table 4-3. *Invariant Culture Version of the Resource Strings*

Strings.txt
Greeting = Hello, World!
ButtonCaption = See Your Flag
DialogCaption = Flag:
DialogFormatString = {0}: {1}

Notice how each culture-specific file contains only those strings that will differ from the parent culture-neutral or culture-invariant version. Also notice the DialogFormatString string.

This will be passed to `String.Format()` and used to format the caption of the dialog box (which will display messages such as Flag: en-US). It's important that you allow for the possibility of the format string itself being culture specific in order to take account of grammatical differences between languages. Having said that, even a localizable format string can be crude, and you may find you need to do some language-specific processing to insert names, and so on, into phrases in different languages in a grammatically correct manner, but I'll keep things simple here.

Now for the flags: The default assembly has a bitmap file called NoFlag, which contains a graphic saying that no flag is available, that's used for the invariant culture. Flags exist for Great Britain and the United States but not for Germany—it wouldn't be appropriate here since I have no resources specifically localized to Germany but only to the German language (which could, for example, mean Austria). Figure 4-16 shows the flags I've supplied.

Figure 4-16. *The flags supplied for* en-GB *(left),* en-US *(middle), and the invariant culture (right)*

The main project's GreetMe folder also contains a key file, ExpertDotNet.snk, that contains the public and private key for the assembly you'll generate. I created the key file by typing sn -k ExpertDotNet.snk at the command prompt.

The build process for this project is going to be complex since you have to build a total of seven resource files, as well as the source code files, and then sign most of the assemblies and add them to the assembly cache. The simplest way to do this is for a command-prompt batch file to do the work. The contents of that batch file are what this example is ultimately all about. Before you look at the batch file, you ought to have at least a cursory look at the source code that's going to get compiled.

Here's the VB code for the flag dialog box. This code is contained in a file called FlagDlg.vb.

```
Option Strict

Imports System
Imports System.ComponentModel
Imports System.Drawing
Imports System.Windows.Forms
Imports System.Reflection
Imports System.Resources
Imports System.Globalization
Imports System.Threading

Namespace Apress.ExpertDotNet.GreetMeSample
    Public Class FlagDlg Inherits Form
        Private FlagCtrl As PictureBox = New PictureBox()
```

```vb
        Public Sub New()
          Dim resManager As ResourceManager = New ResourceManager( _
              "Strings", [Assembly].GetExecutingAssembly())
           Me.Text = _
                 String.Format(resManager.GetString("DialogFormatString"), _
                 resManager.GetString("DialogCaption"), _
                 Thread.CurrentThread.CurrentUICulture.ToString())
          resManager = New ResourceManager("Flags", _
              [Assembly].GetExecutingAssembly())
          Me.ClientSize = New Size(150,100)
          FlagCtrl.Image = DirectCast(resManager.GetObject("Flag"), Image)
          FlagCtrl.Location = New Point(20,20)
          FlagCtrl.Parent = Me
        End Sub
    End Class
End Namespace
```

The dialog box, represented by the FlagDlg class, will contain a PictureBox instance that's used to actually display the flag. You first sort out the caption for the dialog box, which you want to be the localized equivalent of Flag: *<Your culture name>*. So you use the ResourceManager.GetString() method to read the DialogCaption string from the Strings resource—which will have been obtained by compiling the relevant Strings.*.txt file. (Notice by the way that the resource name has been picked up from the initial filename, Strings.*.txt.) Then you use the Thread.CurrentUICulture property to find out what your culture actually is so you can display it. Note that the only reason the code explicitly looks up the culture is to display the culture in the dialog box caption—it's not needed for loading the resources since the ResourceManager handles that automatically. Finally, you load the bitmap and set it to be the Image property of the PictureBox control.

The previous VB code will form part of the GreetMe assembly. The rest of the code in the assembly, as follows, comes from the C# file, GreetMe.cs, which contains the code to display the greeting and button:

```csharp
using System;
using System.Drawing;
using System.Windows.Forms;
using System.Reflection;
using System.Resources;
using System.Globalization;
using System.Threading;

[assembly: AssemblyVersion("1.0.1.0")]
[assembly: AssemblyCulture("")]
[assembly: AssemblyKeyFile("ExpertDotNet.snk")]


namespace Apress.ExpertDotNet.GreetMeSample
{
    public class GreetingControl : System.Windows.Forms.Control
```

```
{
    private Label greeting = new Label();
    private Button btnShowFlag = new Button();

    public GreetingControl()
    {
        ResourceManager resManager = new ResourceManager("Strings",
                                     Assembly.GetExecutingAssembly());
        this.ClientSize = new Size(150,100);
        greeting.Text = resManager.GetString("Greeting");
        greeting.Location = new Point(20,20);
        greeting.Parent = this;
        btnShowFlag.Text = resManager.GetString("ButtonCaption");
        btnShowFlag.Location = new Point(20,50);
        btnShowFlag.Size = new Size(100,30);
        btnShowFlag.Parent = this;
        btnShowFlag.Click += new EventHandler(btnShowFlag_Click);
        btnShowFlag.TabIndex = 0;
    }

    void btnShowFlag_Click(object sender, System.EventArgs e)
    {
        FlagDlg dlg = new FlagDlg();
        dlg.ShowDialog();
    }
}
}
```

This code follows similar principles to the VB code. You have two private fields—in this case for holding the Label control that will display the greeting and for the button. You then initialize the text for these controls to the appropriate values read in from the Strings resource. Finally, it contains an event handler to be invoked when the button is clicked—this event handler simply displays the flag dialog box.

You now need the following code for the test form, which will be used to test the sample:

```
using System;
using System.Windows.Forms;
using System.Globalization;
using System.Threading;

namespace Apress.ExpertDotNet.GreetMeSample
{
    public class TestHarness : System.Windows.Forms.Form
    {
        private GreetingControl greetCtrl = new GreetingControl();

        public TestHarness()
        {
```

```csharp
            this.Text = "GreetMe Test Form";
            greetCtrl.Parent = this;
        }
    }

    public class EntryPoint
    {
        static void Main(string [] args)
        {
            if (args.Length > 0)
            {
                try
                {
                    Thread.CurrentThread.CurrentUICulture = new
                                                CultureInfo(args[0]);
                }
                catch (ArgumentException)
                {
                    MessageBox.Show("The first parameter passed in " +
                                "must be a valid culture string");
                }
            }
            Application.Run(new TestHarness());
        }
    }
}
```

Much of this code is fairly standard code to define and display a form. The only note-worthy part of it is that the Main() method takes an array of strings as an argument and tries to instantiate a CultureInfo() object from the first string in this array. If successful, it sets the thread's UI culture to this culture. The reason for this is that it allows you to test the ability of the sample to be localized to different cultures without having to actually change the locale of your machine. You just type in something such as TestForm de to run the application under the German culture, no matter the locale to which your machine is set.

That's the source code files sorted out, so now you can look at the build process. The following is the Compile.bat batch file (bear in mind that the build process doesn't include the generation of the key, since the key needs to remain the same through all builds):

```
rem COMPILE DEFAULT RESOURCES
rem ------------------------
resgen Strings.txt
resxgen /i:NoFlag.jpg /o:Flags.resx /n:Flag
resgen Flags.resx

rem COMPILE SOURCE FILES
rem -------------------
vbc /t:module /r:System.dll /r:System.drawing.dll
    /r:System.Windows.Forms.dll FlagDlg.vb
```

```
csc /addmodule:FlagDlg.netmodule /res:Strings.resources /res:Flags.resources
    /t:library GreetMe.cs

rem COMPILE en-US RESOURCES
rem ----------------------
cd en-US
resgen Strings.en-US.txt
resxgen /i:USFlag.jpg /o:Flags.en-US.resx /n:Flag
resgen Flags.en-US.resx
al /embed:Strings.en-US.resources /embed:Flags.en-US.resources
    /c:en-US /v:1.0.1.0 /keyfile:../ExpertDotNet.snk  /out:GreetMe.resources.dll
cd ..

rem COMPILE en-GB RESOURCES
rem ----------------------
cd en-GB
resgen Strings.en-GB.txt
resxgen /i:GBFlag.jpg /o:Flags.en-GB.resx /n:Flag
resgen Flags.en-GB.resx
al /embed:Strings.en-GB.resources /embed:Flags.en-GB.resources
    /c:en-GB /v:1.0.1.0 /keyfile:../ExpertDotNet.snk /out:GreetMe.resources.dll
cd ..

rem COMPILE de RESOURCES
rem Note that there is no de flag because de could mean Germany or Austria
rem ----------------------------------------------------------------------
cd de
resgen Strings.de.txt
al /embed:Strings.de.resources /c:de /v:1.0.1.0
    /keyfile:../ExpertDotNet.snk /out:GreetMe.resources.dll
cd ..

rem INSTALL INTO GLOBAL ASSEMBLY CACHE
rem ---------------------------------
gacutil /i GreetMe.dll
gacutil /i en-US/GreetMe.resources.dll
gacutil /i en-GB/GreetMe.resources.dll
gacutil /i de/GreetMe.resources.dll

rem COMPILE TEST FORM
rem -----------------
cd Test Form
csc /r:../GreetMe.dll TestForm.cs
cd ..
```

The first thing this file does is to compile the culture-invariant resources that will be embedded in the main assembly.

```
rem COMPILE DEFAULT RESOURCES
rem ------------------------
resgen Strings.txt
resxgen /i:NoFlag.jpg /o:Flags.resx /n:Flag
resgen Flags.resx
```

This process should be fairly clear by now. You use resgen to compile Strings.txt into a Strings.resources file. You then do the same for the NoFlag.jpg bitmap—converting it to a Flags.resources file. For the .jpg file, the process is a two-stage one, since you need to use resxgen to create a resource .resx file containing the image first.

This means your culture-invariant resource files are now ready for inclusion in the main assembly when that gets built. Here's how that happens:

```
vbc /t:module /r:System.dll /r:System.drawing.dll
    /r:System.Windows.Forms.dll FlagDlg.vb
csc /addmodule:FlagDlg.netmodule /res:Strings.resources /res:Flags.resources
    /t:library GreetMe.cs
```

You first compile the VB code for the flag dialog box into a module. Then you compile the C# code for the rest of the assembly into a DLL, adding the module and embedding the resources as you go. The order of building is important here: The C# code references the FlagDlg defined in the VB code, which means the VB code has to be compiled first or you'd have unresolved references. Notice also that the C# compiler is able to automatically load the Microsoft base class assemblies System.dll, System.Drawing.dll, and System.Windows.Forms.dll, but the VB compiler needs to be informed explicitly of these references—hence you'll see a relative lack of references in the csc command.

Next the batch file changes directory and builds the satellite assemblies—starting with the en-US one. (The order of building the satellite assemblies, as well as whether the main assembly is built before or after the satellite ones, is immaterial.) The process is no different from that for compiling the resources for the main assembly, except that now you have the additional step of using al.exe to actually create an assembly from the resource files. In the following code, note the filenames and the change of folder:

```
cd en-US
resgen Strings.en-US.txt
resxgen /i:USFlag.jpg /o:Flags.en-US.resx /n:Flag
resgen Flags.en-US.resx
al /embed:Strings.en-US.resources /embed:Flags.en-US.resources /c:en-US
   /v:1.0.1.0 /keyfile:../ExpertDotNet.snk  /out:GreetMe.resources.dll
cd ..
```

Notice the explicit specification of the key file to be used to sign the assembly in the al command. That wasn't necessary when compiling the main assembly, since that assembly was created using csc from C# source code—and the C# code contained an assembly attribute to indicate the key file.

The en-GB and de satellites follow suit, with the difference that no .jpg file is included for the German satellite.

Finally, you install all the files into the GAC. You individually install each satellite, like so:

```
gacutil /i GreetMe.dll
gacutil /i en-US/GreetMe.resources.dll
gacutil /i en-GB/GreetMe.resources.dll
gacutil /i de/GreetMe.resources.dll
```

You then compile the test form in its separate folder, like so:

```
cd Test Form
csc /r:../GreetMe.dll TestForm.cs
cd ..
```

That completes the example. If you download the code from http://www.apress.com, you'll find that all you need to do is run the batch file and then run the TestForm.exe assembly.

Finally, I'll mention that a Cleanup.bat batch file comes with the example, which you can use to remove the sample from the GAC and delete all the files created when you compile the example. I won't go over the code in the Cleanup.bat file here in detail—it mostly consists of DOS Del commands. However, I'll point out the syntax for removing files from the GAC.

```
rem REMOVE FILES FROM GLOBAL ASSEMBLY CACHE
rem --------------------------------------
gacutil /u GreetMe
gacutil /u GreetMe.resources
```

When installing a file into the GAC, you simply specify the filename (such as GreetMe.dll). When removing an assembly, however, you need to specify the assembly identity. If you specify only the name part of the identity, as I've done here, then all assemblies with that name will be removed. Hence, since all the satellite assemblies have the name GreetMe.resources (the different identities of these assemblies being distinguished by their different cultures), the single command gacutil /u GreetMe.resources is sufficient to remove all the satellites from the cache.

VS .NET GreetMe Example

The previous example has shown you in principle how creating a complex assembly works and in particular how localization in .NET is implemented. However, you also probably noticed that trying to run everything from the command prompt can be tedious and prone to errors, even though it does have the advantage of giving you a fine degree of control, as well as the ability to automate the process through batch files. In this section, I'll develop an example analogous to the previous one, but I'll do so using VS .NET, so you can see how VS .NET can helps you. For this example, what I'm really interested in doing is showing you the mechanisms that VS .NET uses to assist with localization. Because of this, I'll work through only the things that are different in VS .NET. In particular, VS .NET can't really help you with the flag dialog box caption, which had to be generated from a localizable format string, and it can't install assemblies into the GAC (short of adding custom build steps). Therefore, the VS .NET example won't cover those areas.

This example has one other change. VS .NET at the time of writing doesn't support using more than one language in the code for the same assembly, so I'll instead create two separate assemblies—one for the flag dialog box (in VB again) and one for the greeting control (in C#, as before).

Thus, the project involves asking VS .NET to create a multiproject solution, containing the following:

- A C# Windows Forms project called TestForm for the main test form

- A C# Windows Control project called GreetMe for the greeting control

- A VB Windows Forms project called FlagDlg for the flag dialog box

In creating this project, I also changed the VB project settings from the VB default of an executable to a Class Library project, as well as changed its default namespace to Apress.ExpertDotNet.GreetMeSample. And I added all the namespaces you need to reference in the project properties (for the C# projects, you make these last two changes directly in the source code rather than project properties). I also made the usual changes to the project dependencies and project references to ensure that each project has the appropriate references to the assemblies it references.

I won't present the code for the TestForm project—all I did when creating this sample was modify the wizard-generated code so that it roughly matches that for the TestForm project in the previous sample.

The GreetMe project is more interesting—other than modifying the assembly attributes for the key file, version, and so on, and adding the event handler for the button, you have no code to add manually. I simply used the VS .NET Design View to drop a label and button onto the control and to add a Click event handler for the button. The code for the button click event handler is the same as in the previous sample, other than the wizard-generated event handler name.

```
private void btnShowFlag_Click(object sender, System.EventArgs e)
{
    FlagDlg dlg = new FlagDlg();
    dlg.ShowDialog();
}
```

The project must also be localized. For this project, localizing it simply means providing culture-specific strings for the text of the button and label controls—and the amazing thing is that VS .NET allows you to do this entirely using the Design View and Properties window. First, you locate the Localizable property in for the top level (GreetMe) control in the Properties window, and set it to True. This has quite a significant effect on the code in the wizard-generated InitializeComponent() method. Remember that when you first create a project, InitializeComponent() looks something like this:

```
private void InitializeComponent()
{
    this.btnShowFlag = new System.Windows.Forms.Button();
    this.SuspendLayout();
    //
    // btnShowFlag
    //
    this.btnShowFlag.Location = new System.Drawing.Point(40, 64);
    this.btnShowFlag.Name = "btnShowFlag";
```

```
this.btnShowFlag.TabIndex = 0;
this.btnShowFlag.Text = "Show Your Flag";
this.btnShowFlag.Click += new System.EventHandler(this.button1_Click);
```

I haven't presented the code for the whole method here—just enough of the part that sets up the Button control, btnShowFlag, to remind you what's happening. Many properties on Microsoft controls have VS .NET–recognized default values defined using the DefaultValueAttribute. Where any properties have default values defined with this attribute, and the developer explicitly sets different values using the VS .NET Properties window, VS .NET will add code to the InitializeComponent() method to initialize the values, which is what you can see has happened in the previous code snippet. (The assumption VS .NET makes is that if the required value happens to be the same as the default value, then the control will initialize this value itself, so VS .NET has no need to initialize it again in InitializeComponent().)

■Tip The DefaultValueAttribute doesn't automatically cause controls to be initialized with this value; it's purely to help VS .NET generate code. If you're writing your own controls that you want to be available to other developers, then you're normally recommended to set the default values of properties in the constructor for the control, and also to apply the DefaultValueAttribute to the relevant properties, to tell VS .NET what the default value is. This makes it easier for developers to manipulate your control using the VS .NET Design View.

Now look at the equivalent code when you set Localizable to True in the Properties window:

```
private void InitializeComponent()
{
    System.Resources.ResourceManager resources = new
        System.Resources.ResourceManager(typeof(GreetingControl));

    this.btnShowFlag = new System.Windows.Forms.Button();
    this.SuspendLayout();
    //
    // btnShowFlag
    //
    this.btnShowFlag.AccessibleDescription = ((string)(resources.GetObject(
        "btnShowFlag.AccessibleDescription")));
    this.btnShowFlag.AccessibleName = ((string)(resources.GetObject(
        "btnShowFlag.AccessibleName")));
    this.btnShowFlag.Anchor = ((System.Windows.Forms.AnchorStyles)(
        resources.GetObject("btnShowFlag.Anchor")));
    this.btnShowFlag.BackgroundImage = ((System.Drawing.Image)(
        resources.GetObject("btnShowFlag.BackgroundImage")));
    this.btnShowFlag.Dock = ((System.Windows.Forms.DockStyle)(
        resources.GetObject("btnShowFlag.Dock")));
    // etc.
```

VS .NET has added a *lot* more code than previously—I've shown only a small fraction of the code that sets up `btnShowFlag`. Two changes are apparent: First, the values of all the properties are being read in from a resource using the `ResourceManager` class, instead of being hard-coded into the program. Second, whereas before only those properties whose required values differed from the default values were set, now all properties are being set. (It has to be done like that because VS .NET has no way of knowing whether the resource will at runtime contain the default value.) Notice, however, that this means you do pay a considerable runtime performance penalty (as well as an assembly-size penalty) for using VS .NET: When I developed the application at the command line, I had the program load only those strings from a resource that I knew were going to be localized. With VS .NET, everything gets loaded that way.

What's happened is that VS .NET has created a default `.resx` resources file behind the scenes for you and written values into this resource for every property that's visible in the Properties window for every control that's visible in the Design View. This is the file you saw a small section of earlier in the chapter.

No magic is going on here although VS .NET has done so much work that it almost looks like magic. This is a perfectly normal `.resx` file that you could have written yourself if you had the time (quite a lot of time!) to do so. It's a `.resx` file rather than a `.txt` file, so it can be used to define properties that aren't strings (such as the sizes of controls). The file has been initially set up to contain the normal default values for each property, and you can now just edit these values using the Properties window. In the Properties window for the parent control (or form), you find the Language property for the form in its Properties window—initially it'll be set to Default, indicating the invariant culture. Just click to select a culture from the drop-down box, as shown in Figure 4-17.

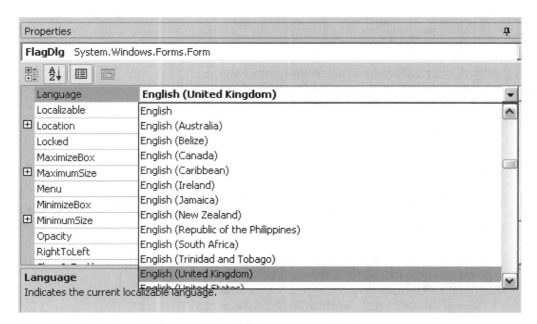

Figure 4-17. *Selecting a language in the VS .NET Properties window*

Now any changes you make in the Properties window either for that control (or form) or for all other controls displayed in the Design View will affect only the localized resources for that language. So with Figure 4-17 you can now use the Properties window to set up your localized text for en-US and then return to change the Language from this drop-down list to set up the text for some other language. For a project that isn't set to Localizable, changing properties in the Properties window causes VS .NET to directly modify the code in the InitializeComponent() method. For a Localizable project, the changes you make in the Properties window don't affect the source code but instead cause VS .NET to modify the relevant .resx file. Note that selecting a new culture in the Localization drop-down list will cause a new .resx file to be created if one for that culture doesn't already exist.

VS .NET will automatically handle compiling resources into correctly named satellite assemblies for you and will create the appropriate folder structure to hold these assemblies in the bin/debug (or bin/release) subfolder of the GreetMe project. However, you actually need this folder structure in the bin/debug (or bin/release) subfolder of the Test Form project, from where the executable will execute. Unfortunately, VS .NET appears to have a bug, where on some installations it fails to copy these folders across, preventing the application from localizing. If you find that problem affects you, you'll need to copy the folders and satellite assemblies over manually or add a custom build step in VS .NET to do so.

Finally, let's examine the code for the new FlagDlg project. Once again, you can let VS .NET handle most of the work. You use the Design View to create a picture box on the form, set Localizable property of the form to True, and then work through the cultures you're going to support, for each one setting the Image property of the picture box to the appropriate .jpg file for the flag. Note that the JPG files are supplied in the main folder for this project in the code download. That's the point at which I'll leave the example to you.

I haven't localized one resource: the caption for the FlagDlg dialog box. The reason is that although VS .NET will allow you to localize it to a constant string using the same technique as for all the other localized resources, that's not good enough in this case: You need to generate the caption dynamically with a localized formatting string. Unfortunately, VS .NET won't really help you there, so you'll need to fall back on defining your own resource files—which is likely to involve adding custom build steps to the VS .NET project.

If you start working with localization and VS .NET, you can check out another tool, winres.exe. I don't have space to go into its details here, but it's a dedicated resource editor, supplied with the VS .NET, and you can start it by typing winres at the VS .NET command prompt.

Summary

In this chapter, you examined how assemblies are implemented and saw the process for creating a complex, multimodule, strongly named assembly that has satellite resource assemblies. In more detail, I discussed the PE format of assembly files that contain IL code and showed how each assembly module is stored in a format that extends the classic portable executable format recognized by all 32-bit versions of Windows. I indicated some of the flexibility benefits that this format offers, and then you studied the structure of the GAC, as well as reviewed some of the techniques for extracting metadata and other information from assemblies, both at the command line and from within your code.

Finally, I went over the rich model for localizing resources and presented a couple of examples that illustrate building a complex, localized application that contains a group of assemblies.

■ ■ ■

CHAPTER 5

Understanding Garbage Collection

Memory management, and in particular cleaning up any resources that are no longer needed by an application, is an important service provided by the .NET Framework. The aim of this chapter is to make sure you understand at a fairly detailed level how the main .NET resource cleanup system, the garbage collector, works and how best to use the garbage collection services in your code. I'll also explain the best methods for implementing objects that can be cleared up by the garbage collector. In more detail, I'll cover the following:

- The main advantages of garbage collection vs. alternative techniques (in short, why Microsoft decided on garbage collection as the best solution)

- The way the garbage collector works, including details of the algorithm it currently uses and the way it hijacks your threads

- How to implement `Dispose()` and `Finalize()`

- Weak references

I'll start the chapter by presenting the advantages of garbage collection as compared to the alternatives.

■**Note** For most of the book, the term *resource* indicates some specific unmanaged or managed resource that's embedded in or linked to an assembly, such as a bitmap. However, in this chapter, I use the term *resource* more generically to mean any item that occupies memory or system resources. This could be, for example, a plain managed object, or on the unmanaged side it could be an unmanaged object or an external resource such as a file or window handle. It's also important in this context to differentiate between "normal" resources—such as managed memory—for which the garbage collector's collection mechanism is adequate, and "precious" resources, such as database connections, which really need to be cleaned up as soon as the program has finished with them.

Why Use Garbage Collection?

When it comes to cleaning up resources, the following three options are generally available:

Developer-controlled cleanup: This is the C/C++ model in which the developer explicitly indicates in the source code when a resource is no longer required and should be deleted, using a statement similar to `delete` in C++.

Reference counting: This is the model used in COM and COM+, since it's well suited to a client-server environment. VB 6 also used this model, partly because of its frequent dependence under the hood on COM. Objects are instantiated by clients, and it's the responsibility of the client to inform the object when it's no longer required. The object deletes itself when it detects that it's no longer required by any client.

Garbage collection: This is the system used in .NET, in which some specialist piece of software examines the memory in your process space and removes any object that it detects is no longer referenced.

.NET, of course, has gone for a primarily garbage-collected model, but with a developer-controlled element that's available when required, via the `IDisposable` interface.

■**Note** The algorithms used by the .NET garbage collector are also sometimes referred to as *exact*. Exact garbage collection is guaranteed to release the memory held by all dead objects. This is in contrast to older "conservative" garbage collection algorithms, which were simpler but couldn't always distinguish between pointers and other data types so therefore weren't guaranteed to release all unused memory.

Exact garbage collection has the potential to be an extremely efficient mechanism. However, it does impose some requirements on the system. In particular, it works only if every object is self-describing; in other words, if some way exists for the garbage collector to obtain details of the object's size and field layout, including which fields refer to other objects. Otherwise, the garbage collector has no way of working out from the state of the process's memory which objects are still being used.

In the particular case of .NET, this information is available because each object contains a field at a known location that points to other structs that contain this information (specifically, the first word in each .NET reference object points to a method table, which in turn points to an `EEClass` structure that holds the information). Garbage collection does, however, have a possible disadvantage in that it doesn't support *deterministic finalization*. Deterministic finalization means that an object will be destroyed and any associated destruction/finalization code will be executed at a well-defined point in time. When coding an application, deterministic finalization is significant because it means that when you write code elsewhere in the application, you know whether a certain finalizer had already executed.

■**Tip** The terms *finalizer* and *destructor* both indicate a method that's responsible for cleaning up an object (performing finalization or destruction). However, such a method is usually termed a *finalizer* if it's normally invoked by a garbage collector and a destructor if it's normally invoked in some other means.

The lack of deterministic finalization caused quite a few heartaches in the developer community when .NET was first released, for a couple of reasons. In the first place, developers were concerned that, on the face of it, it'd seem rather hard to write code if you don't know what other finalization code had already been executed. Developers were also concerned that there would be an unacceptable claim on resources because of objects that were no longer needed still being around waiting for garbage collection. In practice, both of these fears have proved unfounded for these reasons:

- Not knowing the order and timing in which finalizers are executed in practice affects only code written inside other finalizers. And the only restriction imposed by this lack of knowledge is that you must not write code that depends either on whether the finalizer for any other object has been called or on whether any other managed object exists. Since, as you'll see later in the chapter, the purpose of finalizers is as a last point of call to clean up *unmanaged* objects, absolutely no reason exists why finalizers should contain code that references other managed objects anyway. So this restriction is a moot point.

- As far as fears of objects hanging around too long are concerned, this would be an important issue if garbage collection were the only means available to delete objects. But Microsoft has anticipated the need for an additional deterministic element in the way in which certain objects are cleaned up and provided this via an optional IDisposable interface, which objects can implement if needed. If an object references a number of managed or unmanaged resources, and it's important that those resources are cleaned up as soon as possible, that class can simply implement IDisposable, thus allowing client code to explicitly indicate when that object is no longer required. Of course, this opens the possibility for bugs in which the client code fails to call Dispose() appropriately—but that situation is no worse than for the other memory management models. The C/C++ model has the risk of the developer forgetting to call delete on a dynamically allocated object, and the COM reference counting model has an equal risk of the developer of client code forgetting to insert the call to IUnknown.Release(). Indeed, the situation is arguably *worse* in those two models than the situation in a garbage-collected environment, since the consequences of bugs in the client are more serious. For the C/C++ models and for reference counting, such a bug will lead to a memory leak that will persist until the process ends, but with the garbage-collected model, you have a good chance that the "leak" (although not any associated unmanaged resources) will be removed earlier, during a future garbage collection.

The history of the debate on .NET garbage collection is quite interesting. When the .NET Framework was first released, a fair amount of discussion took place on the various .NET newsgroups, with a number of developers concerned that memory management was going to suffer because of the lack of deterministic finalization. As the months went on, this debate gradually died down, and the .NET garbage collection model became accepted. With hindsight, it was apparent that deterministic collection is something that, if you're used to having it, is easy to convince yourself that it's an absolutely vital part of your programming armory. However, in practice, once you've gotten used to doing without it, you find that it really makes no difference except on rare occasions (which are covered by IDisposable). If you're interested in the arguments in detail, look at the http://discuss.develop.com/archives/wa.exe? A2=ind0010A&L=DOTNET&P=R28572&I=3. This page consists of a detailed analysis by one of the lead programmers at Microsoft, Brian Harry, of the arguments that eventually persuaded Microsoft that garbage collection was the way forward. In this chapter, I won't go into too much detail about the arguments, but I'll summarize the advantages and disadvantages of the various systems.

The Pros and Cons of the Memory Management Models

In the following sections, I'll quickly review the three main memory management and cleanup models (the C/C++ style explicit delete calls, reference counting, and garbage collection), and I'll identify the main advantages and disadvantages of each.

C/C++ Style Cleanup

The advantage of this system has traditionally been performance. As the theory goes, the developer knows his own source code, and probably knows when data is no longer needed far better than any compiler or environment could determine. And he can hard-code that information into the program, via delete or equivalent statements, so the environment doesn't need to do any work whatsoever to figure out what needs deleting when. This means that none of the algorithms have any overhead to work out when to delete objects and also that resources can be freed virtually the instant they're no longer used.

The disadvantage is the extra work the developer has to do and the potential for hard-to-find memory leak bugs, as well as bugs in which objects are deleted too soon—which can lead to memory corruption issues in release builds that are often hard to find.

In general, if your code has been designed in such a way that an obvious life span–containment relationship exists between classes, then writing cleanup code is easy. For example, suppose you have an EmployerRecord class, which contains references to name and job description classes, and for some reason you need all these objects to be individually allocated dynamically.

```
// This is C++ code!
class EmployerRecord
{
   private:
      Name *pName;
      JobTitle *pTitle;
```

Assuming the Name and JobTitle instances can be accessed only through the EmployerRecord, cleanup logic simply involves propagating the delete operations.

```
~EmployerRecord
{
    delete pName;
    delete pTitle;
}
```

However, suppose you have a second way of accessing the names. Suppose another class, EmployerNameList, contains pointers to all the Name instances.

Now the process of, say, deleting an employer is a lot harder, because you need to track the deleted name through to the EmployerNameList and amend that object. And suppose the EmployerNameList offers the option to delete an employer, too—now the EmployerRecord destructor may have to figure out whether it's been invoked from the EmployerNameList or from elsewhere. You may think that's a bad architecture in this particular example, but this illustrates the kinds of problems you get manually writing destruction code if you have a complex set of interrelated objects. In this situation, it's easy to see how destruction-related memory bugs can occur.

Note When you come to examine the Dispose() method later in the "Implementing Dispose() and Finalize()" section, you'll discover similar difficulties, though to a much lesser extent.

Reference Counting

Reference counting was the favored solution in COM, and although it proved useful in COM, it has two problems: performance and cycles.

Performance

Look at any typical large application, and you'll find object references (or, in unmanaged C++, pointers) being copied everywhere. Without reference counting, copying a reference involves just that: copying a number from one memory location to another memory location. With reference counting, you have to check that the reference isn't null. If it isn't, you need to dereference it and increase that object's reference counter. And if you want to set a reference to null, or if the reference goes out of scope, you need to check whether the reference wasn't already null and, if it wasn't, decrease the reference count. If that kind of logic has to happen every time you do the equivalent of a = b; or a = null; for managed reference types, application performance will suffer heavily. So on performance grounds alone, reference counting for managed applications was never going to be an option.

On the other hand, as far as COM was concerned, reference counting was a suitable solution. But that's because reference counting in COM took place in a particular client-server context. Essentially, two big blobs of code existed—the client code and the COM object (server) code, and reference counting happened only for objects used across the boundary. Within each blob, it was likely to be C/C++ style memory management that was used—this minimized the performance hit but was a particular artifact of the COM environment that isn't really applicable to most managed code.

Cycles

Cyclic references represent the other big problem associated with reference counting. Cyclic references don't happen that often, but when they do, they can prevent deactivation of objects. Imagine, for example, that object A holds a reference to object B, B has a reference to C, and C a reference to A. The whole cycle was originally established because of another object, X, which was responsible for instantiating A. Now suppose this outside object (X) no longer requires A, so it reduces its reference count and releases A. This means that none of the objects A, B, and C are required anymore, so they should all be removed. The trouble is that A refuses to remove itself, because it thinks it's still needed: C still has a reference to A. Meanwhile, B refuses to die because A still exists, and C clings onto life on the grounds that it's still required (by B). You're stuck! The work-around for this situation was complex, involving something called a *weak reference* (no relation to the .NET weak reference, which you'll explore later and which has a different purpose). The cyclic reference problem would be a huge issue if reference counting were to be implemented in .NET. In COM, because of the client-server model, cyclic references tended not to occur quite as often, although even in COM the issue was a serious one.

Before leaving the topic of reference counting, I ought to note that reference counting has two variants: *autoreference counting*, as used in VB 6, and reference counting with *smart pointers*, as used for example in the Active Template Library (ATL) `CComPtr` class. Both of these variants work on the same principles as COM reference counting. However, with autoreference counting, the compiler works out where reference counts need to be decremented or incremented, without any programmer involvement. This takes the programmer error element out of reference counting but leaves the other disadvantages (as well as a potentially greater performance hit since the compiler may not notice some reference counting optimizations that the developer can see). Smart pointers are designed to give a similar effect to autoreference counting, but they work instead by classes defined in the source code that wrap pointers to reference-counted objects. The smart pointer classes automatically deal with the reference counts in their constructors and destructors.

Garbage Collection

Now you've seen the disadvantages that led Microsoft to avoid either reference counting or manual memory cleanup as the solution to resource management in .NET—and garbage collection is the only option left. But you shouldn't take that in a negative light. Garbage collection actually has a lot going for it in principle, and Microsoft has done a lot of work to provide a good-quality, high-performance garbage collector. For a start, as you've seen, garbage collection largely frees the developer from having to worry about resource cleanup. Given that one of the main goals of .NET was to simplify programming, that's important. Unlike reference counting, garbage collection has virtually no overhead until a collection has to occur—in which case the garbage collector pauses the program, usually for a tiny fraction of a second, to allow the collection. And the really great thing about garbage collection is that it doesn't matter how complex your data structures are or how complex the pattern of which objects link which other objects in your program. Because the sole test for whether an object can be removed is whether it's currently accessible directly or indirectly from any variables in current scope, the garbage collector will work fine no matter how objects are linked. Even cyclic references pose no problem and don't require any special treatment. Consider, for example, the cyclic situation discussed earlier in which objects A, B, and C maintained cyclic references to each other, with an outside object X holding a reference to A. As long as X holds this reference, the garbage collector will see that A is accessible from the program, and hence so are B and C. But when X releases its reference to A, the program won't have any references that can be used to access any of A, B, or C. The garbage collector, when next invoked, will see this and hence will know that all of A, B, and C can be removed. The fact that these objects contain cyclic references is simply irrelevant.

Another big advantage of garbage collection is the potential to create a more efficient heap. This is because the garbage collector has an overall view of the heap and can take control of the objects on it in a way that's not possible with either reference counted or C/C++ style heaps. In the case of the CLR, the garbage collector takes advantage of this by moving objects around to compact the heap into one continuous block after each garbage collection. This has two benefits. First, allocating memory for an object is fast, as the object can always be allocated at the next free location. The garbage collector has no need to search for free locations through a linked list, as happens with C/C++ style heaps. Second, because all the objects are compacted together, they will be closer together, which is likely to lead to less page swapping. Microsoft believes that as a result of these benefits, a garbage-collected heap may ultimately be able to outperform even a C++ style heap, despite the common perception that maintaining the latter seems to require less work. However, bear in mind that each pinned object (C#: fixed) will prevent this compaction process—which is the reason that pinning is regarded as such a potential performance issue.

The disadvantage of garbage collection is of course the lack of deterministic finalization. For the rare cases in which resource cleanup needs to be done sooner than the garbage collector will do it, Microsoft has provided the IDisposable interface. Calling IDisposable.Dispose() works in much the same way as calling delete in unmanaged C++, with the difference that you don't need to call Dispose() nearly as often—you just use it for those objects that implement this interface, not for every object. And if you forget to call Dispose(), the garbage collector and the Finalize() method are there as a backup, which makes programming memory management a lot easier and more robust than in C++.

■**Note**   Strictly speaking, the analogy between Dispose() and unmanaged delete is only approximate. Both Dispose() and delete call finalization code, which may cause contained resources to be cleaned up, but delete also destroys the object itself, freeing its memory—Dispose() doesn't do this. In terms of implementation, a better analogy is between Dispose() and explicitly calling an unmanaged destructor in C++, but in terms of usage, Dispose() really replaces delete.

How the .NET Garbage Collector Works

The aim of the garbage collector is to locate those managed objects that are no longer referenced by any variable that's currently in scope in the program. The theory is quite simple: If an object isn't referenced directly or indirectly by any object reference currently in scope, then your code has no legitimate way to ever get access to that object ever again, and therefore the object can be deleted. (By *legitimate way*, I mean by dereferencing managed object references. Theoretically, you could get access to one of these objects by doing some clever unmanaged pointer arithmetic, but the assumption is that you're not going to be silly enough to try anything like that.)

When a collection occurs, the garbage collector initially builds a list of all the objects that can be accessed from your code. It does this by systematically trawling through every variable that's in scope, recursively dereferencing every object it finds until it has the complete list. Once it has that list, it can compact the managed heap so that these objects form a contiguous block (though there may be gaps in the block if any objects have been pinned). That's the basis of the algorithm; it has various complications—in a number of places Microsoft has made the algorithm more sophisticated either for performance reasons or for allowing features such as finalization.

In the following sections, I'll go over the principles behind the .NET implementation of the garbage collector—how a collection is actually performed. The full details of the algorithm aren't publicly available, since Microsoft reserves the right to tweak details of it in future, but the rough outline has been documented. Understanding how garbage collections are performed can be important, partly because it helps you to understand how to implement finalizers that have as little adverse impact on performance as possible and partly because several concepts arise from the garbage collector, including generations and resurrection, that may under some situations affect your code.

■**Tip** The details presented here are specifically for Microsoft's implementation of the .NET garbage collector. Bear in mind that this isn't the only way of implementing a garbage collector, so don't assume that any other garbage collector you may encounter in the future is implemented the same way. Also, years of research have been put into optimizing garbage collection algorithms—so although some of the following discussion may give you the impression of a long, cumbersome task, in practice the actual algorithm and data structures used have been so finely tuned that the process of garbage collection really consumes very little time.

In the following discussion, I'll frequently refer loosely to the managed heap. In fact, two managed heaps exist because large objects are placed on their own heap, in a separate area of memory. What counts as large is presumably subject to change—tests by one of the reviewers of this chapter suggest the threshold is 80 kilobytes (KB), but you shouldn't rely on this figure staying unchanged through different .NET versions. This separate large object heap exists for performance reasons. As I've mentioned, the garbage collector normally compacts the (small object) managed heap by moving objects that are still in use around so they form one contiguous block. For small objects, the performance gain from having a small and contiguous heap outweighs the cost of performing the compaction. For sufficiently large objects, however, the cost of moving the objects is too great. So the large object heap isn't compacted. Obviously, for the vast majority of applications, only a tiny proportion of objects will be large enough to be placed on the large object heap.

Invoking the Garbage Collector

In principle, the system may automatically instigate a collection in two ways. Some background thread could continuously monitor memory usage and instigate a collection whenever it deems it appropriate, or alternatively a check can take place whenever an object is allocated (in which case no background thread is necessary). Microsoft has gone for the second approach.

This means that in .NET, whenever an object is allocated, a possibility exists that a collection may be performed—this will happen if the memory requested pushes the data occupied by objects on the managed heap up to a combined size at which the garbage collector deems it beneficial to perform a garbage collection—and if that's the case, then the garbage collector kicks in. Currently, the actual test used appears to be that a portion of the heap known as *Generation 0* (I'll explain generations in the "Understanding Generations" section) is full, but you can expect that these details will certainly be tweaked for performance as future versions of .NET are released.

Besides this automatic invocation of the garbage collector, it's also possible to explicitly request a collection in your code by calling the static method, System.GC.Collect()—you'll examine this scenario in the "Controlling the Garbage Collector Programmatically" section.

Taking Control of the Program

The first thing the garbage collector needs to do once invoked is to take over control of all the other running threads in your program. The collector will be running on whatever thread called new Foo() or GC.Collect(), but it clearly needs to intercept and pause any other threads to prevent them from attempting to access the heap while the garbage collector is doing its job. Precisely how the garbage collector does this is an implementation detail and depends on factors such as whether your application is running on a workstation or server (because of different performance requirements for these platforms), whether the application is running on a multiprocessor system, whether you're using multiple threads, and whether any of the threads are executing unmanaged code at the time the collection starts. You don't really need to worry about the details, other than that one way or another the garbage collector will either suspend or take over all the threads in the process, causing the application to pause while the collection happens. However, I'll briefly mention the main techniques used, just so you can recognize the names if you see them in documentation.

Hijacking: The garbage collector overwrites the return address from a method with the address of one of its own methods. The result is that when some method that's being executed returns, control gets transferred to the garbage collector instead of the invoking method.

Safe points: These are points in the code at which the JIT compiler decides it'd be suitable to suspend the thread so that a garbage collection can take place. The JIT compiler will insert calls at these points to a method that quickly checks whether garbage collection is pending and, if so, suspends the thread.

Interruptible code: This is the simplest technique in concept though probably not in implementation. The garbage collector simply suspends all threads in your application. It then inspects the memory and uses tables produced by the JIT compiler to determine the exact state your application was in when the threads got suspended and therefore which variables are in scope.

Identifying the Garbage

The garbage collector starts with what are known as the *roots* of the program. The roots are those object references that can be immediately and correctly identified as in scope. They can be identified relatively quickly because the JIT compiler creates tables indicating which roots are accessible at specific byte offsets from the start of each method. The program roots consist of the following objects:

- All global variables

- All static fields of classes that are currently loaded

- All variables that are stored on the current stack frame—in other words, the arguments and locals in the current method and in all of its callers, right up to the program entry point

- All references that are sitting in an internal garbage collector data structure called the *freachable queue* (I'll discuss this queue in the "Finalizers and Resurrection" section)

- All member fields of any of the previous items (where the variables concerned aren't primitive types)

Note that only reference types are garbage collected, but value types are still inspected during the search for objects in case they contain embedded references.

The roots form an initial list of objects that are currently accessible to code in the program. The next task is to identify any other objects that can be accessed indirectly through these roots.

The garbage collector then takes the first root and dereferences it (the process is sometimes colloquially called *pointer chasing*). It examines the object so obtained (as well as any embedded value types) to see if any embedded references to any other objects are among the member fields. The garbage collector will check any such references to make sure they aren't already on the list being built of objects in scope—if any reference is already on the list, it means that object in question has already been examined and it doesn't have to be checked again. For those objects that aren't on the list, the garbage collector dereferences each in turn. You can see where this is going—the same process happens recursively for every object identified. At the end of this process, when the garbage collector has completed adding all objects referenced indirectly from the last root, it will have a complete list of objects that are accessible by the program. From this list, it can deduce which memory on the heap now contains garbage—it's simply the totality of memory in the managed heap minus the memory occupied by the accessible objects.

Compacting the Heap

The list now identifies all those objects that have any business existing on the managed heap, so the next task is usually to compact the heap down so it contains *only* these objects. Note that I say *usually*: The large object heap won't be compacted. It's also possible that, based on its analysis of your application as well as its assessment of memory pressure from other applications, and possibly other factors, the garbage collector will decide it has no reason to perform a compaction of the main heap either.

Microsoft hasn't documented exactly how the compaction process is implemented, but the logical principle would work like this: New addresses are assigned to each object so that the objects form a contiguous block starting at the beginning of the managed heap. Each object in turn is then moved to its new location, and any references to that object are updated. (Note that this means that as part of the process of building the list of available objects, the garbage collector will need to have made an additional list, which indicates where all the references to each object are, so it can update them.) In the process, all the objects that aren't referenced from anywhere and are no longer needed will be lost—quite brutally: The garbage collector will simply stomp over the memory they occupy, writing new data to that memory as it wants. Although the logical concept of compacting the heap is quite simple, you can probably see that the internal algorithm is going to be fairly complex, since for performance reasons it will need to be optimized to move as few objects as possible. And things could get hairy when you're trying to update references, when those references themselves may have already been moved if they're members of other objects. It's the kind of algorithm I'm glad I didn't have to code!

One point about identifying the garbage is that this algorithm clearly shows up the need for objects to be self-describing. In Chapter 3, you saw how the second word in each reference object, the method table pointer, can identify the type of the object and hence the meaning of all the data in it. In principle, the garbage collector has to look up this information for each object it discovers, in order to discover how big the object is, and which words of data in its memory will be references to other objects (in practice, this would be too slow, so a compact garbage collector encoding struct is used). In the case of structs that are located in the stack frame, no such object information identifies the type of object that the garbage collector can use. Instead, for this data, the JIT compiler emits various tables of information about the state of the stack frame, which the garbage collector can use to track down the object references it needs.

The two parts of the garbage collection I've just described, identifying the garbage and then collecting it, are sometimes referred to as the *mark* and *sweep* phases.

Understanding Generations

The concept of generations has been introduced for performance reasons. The idea is that you can speed up the process of garbage collection if, instead of trying to look through everything in the program to identify objects that may not be needed, you look only in the places where you're most likely to be able to find free space most quickly. So where are the places most likely to supply free space? Based on a considerable amount of documented research over many years, on both Windows and on other platforms, it turns out that in most applications, the shortest-lived objects are usually the ones allocated most recently—and this principle is especially true for object-oriented applications. So, at any given point in time, the objects that were most recently allocated are actually the ones most likely to have already moved out of scope.

The garbage collector takes advantage of this principle by assigning each object to a *generation*, according to how many times it has survived a garbage collection: The first time that a garbage collection happens within the lifetime of a process, all objects in the program space are subject to the collection. At the end of the collection, you have a set of objects that have now survived their first garbage collection. These are regarded as Generation 1. All objects subsequently allocated will be Generation 0. The garbage collector can easily tell which object is in which generation just from its position in the managed heap, as you can see from Figure 5-1—the Generation 1 objects will be located before whatever the position of the heap pointer was just after the last collection.

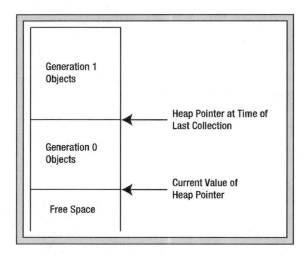

Figure 5-1. *Locations of different generations on the heap*

The next time a garbage collection happens, only Generation 0 variables will be cleaned up. In other words, the first part of the heap, containing the Generation 1 objects, will not be compacted. This is based on the assumption that the Generation 0 part of the heap is where most free space is to be gained. Compacting Generation 1 is on balance of probabilities likely to lead to fewer gains for the work involved. Only if doing a Generation 0 compact doesn't free up sufficient space will the garbage collector turn to Generation 1. And of course, the next time a collection happens, the Generation 1 objects get moved up to Generation 2, and the Generation 0 objects up to Generation 1. This could continue indefinitely, but Microsoft has imposed a limit on the number of generations. At the time of this writing, Generation 2 is the oldest generation permitted, but Microsoft may change that if it decides that performance considerations justify it. Also bear in mind that the concept of generations doesn't apply to objects on the large object heap (from tests, these appear to be automatically categorized as Generation 2).

Finalizers and Resurrection

The process of removing objects that have finalizers is complicated by the need to execute the finalizers. A number of possible ways exist to deal with this. The simplest option would be for the garbage collector, after it has constructed a list of objects that can be removed, to check if each object has a finalizer defined and if so to execute the finalizer before compacting the heap. However, Microsoft has chosen not to do this. One reason is that executing the finalizers during the garbage collection and heap compaction has the potential to dramatically increase the time taken for garbage collection. The garbage collector has no idea how long a given finalizer is going to take to execute—and since finalizers usually do things such as closing database connections or network connections, this time could be large. Moreover, the application is for all practical purposes suspended while the collection is happening. The last thing you want is some finalizer taking ages to close a connection (or perhaps taking ages simply because someone coded it wrong), the garbage collector sitting around doing nothing because it's waiting for the finalizer to exit, your whole program just hanging because it's waiting for the garbage collector to finish and release control of all the program threads, and your user sitting there clicking the nearest Cancel button every few seconds and cursing your application for being so slow. I could go on, but I think you get the picture that executing finalizers during a garbage collection is a very bad idea. So instead, the garbage collector uses an algorithm in which removal of finalizable objects is delayed so that finalizers can be executed on a separate dedicated thread while the program is running normally, in between garbage collections.

Another important reason for running the finalizers on a separate dedicated thread is that the garbage collector executes on whatever thread happened to trigger the collection. If finalizers run on that thread, the developer would have no way to predict what thread a finalizer will run on—if that thread happens to own certain locks on objects, you have a risk of deadlocks occurring (see Chapter 9).

In detail what happens is this: When an object is allocated in the first place, the VES checks whether that object is of a type that has a finalizer defined. (Note that the System.Object. Finalize() method doesn't count here—the VES knows that Object.Finalize() doesn't do anything, and it's interested only in classes that override Object.Finalize()). If an object does have a finalizer, it gets added to a data structure maintained by the garbage collector and known as the *finalization queue*.

Later, during garbage collection, the garbage collector will obtain its list of live objects. I said earlier that any heap memory not occupied by an object on this list can be overwritten. In fact, that's not quite true: There may be objects that have ceased to be referenced from the program but that need to have their finalizers executed—and you certainly don't want to remove these objects from memory before that has happened. To take account of this, the garbage collector will cross-reference the list of objects in the finalization queue with its list of live objects. Any object that's not live but is listed in the finalization queue needs to have its finalizer executed: Any such object is removed from the finalization queue and placed instead on the *freachable queue* that I mentioned earlier (*freachable* means that the object is reachable but ready to be finalized). I listed the freachable queue earlier as one of the places where the garbage collector searches for roots. Objects on the freachable queue are regarded as still alive (albeit on .NET's equivalent of death row), along with any objects they refer to directly or indirectly. Such objects will not be garbage-collected this time around.

The garbage collector then sets about doing its work: It compacts the heap, updates all the pointers in the garbage collector roots and referenced objects, and releases control back to the program. Meanwhile, the separate dedicated thread that's devoted to finalization is woken up. This thread sleeps as long as there are no objects on the freachable queue and is woken when objects get placed there. It processes each of these objects by executing its finalizer and then removing the object from the finalization queue. This means that the next time a collection occurs, that object will be ready to be removed. It all sounds a complex process, but it means that the garbage collector doesn't have to worry about finalizers—they'll be executed in time on their dedicated thread, as shown in Figure 5-2.

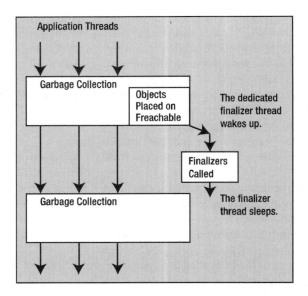

Figure 5-2. *The sequence of calling finalizers and the threads involved*

One point to note from this is that if for any reason a finalizer hangs, this won't in most cases directly affect the rest of the program, but it will mean that no other finalizers will get executed. Ever. Because all finalizers are run on the same thread, each one gets executed only after the previous finalizer has exited. Also, as a minor point, although I've been talking as if the finalizers are executed between garbage collections, the finalization thread runs at a high priority, which means that in most cases each finalizer will be executed as soon as the relevant object is placed on the freachable queue. Only if the finalization code requires the thread to sleep (for example, while waiting for a database connection to close) will execution of the finalizer be delayed (unless, of course, your code attaches a higher than normal priority to one of the other threads under its control).

Controlling the Garbage Collector Programmatically

In most cases it's best to leave the garbage collector to do its job, on the basis that the VES can judge a lot better than you can when more memory is needed. However, sometimes you may feel it's appropriate to force a garbage collection. I should stress that these occasions are rare, so unless you have a good reason to force a garbage collection at a particular time, then my strong advice is to not do so.

In practice, normally it may be appropriate to force a collection in only the following two scenarios:

- You've reached a point in your code where you know your program isn't making heavy demands on the system, but you also know that in a short time your code will be doing some intensive processing that for performance/responsiveness reasons you don't really want to be interrupted. For example, you may be coding a real-time controller that's about to execute a loop that must repeat exactly every ten milliseconds. In this kind of situation you may want to insist that a garbage collection takes place just before the intensive processing starts.

- It's sometimes suggested that calling GC.Collect() can be useful if your code has just stopped using a large number of objects so that you can be fairly sure that a collection will remove lots of memory, forcing a reduction in the program's virtual memory. Unfortunately, the situation here isn't quite so straightforward: It's certainly true that, provided a compaction actually occurs, this *might* improve performance by reducing the number of page faults your application experiences, assuming the objects that would be collected are scattered widely through the heap. However, a collection won't necessarily reduce the program's virtual memory because the garbage collector may choose not to decommit the memory that has been made available. Instead, the garbage collector may decide to hang onto the memory in case it's needed by new objects in the near future, saving on a potentially expensive decommit/commit cycle. The garbage collector will use various heuristic algorithms and statistics to determine in each case whether to decommit memory, so you shouldn't rely on any memory actually being decommitted. I'll explain the process of decommitting memory in Chapter 7.

For situations such as these, Microsoft has provided a programmatic interface to the garbage collector. This interface is available via the System.GC class, which is defined in mscorlib.dll. I won't go over all the available System.GC methods here, since they're documented on MSDN. But I'll show you how to force a garbage collection and how to control finalization.

You can request a plain, ordinary garbage collection—that's to say one that simply collects Generation 0 objects—like this:

```
GC.Collect();
```

Alternatively, you can explicitly specify the generations you want collected; for example, this code will cause Generations 0 and 1 to be collected:

```
GC.Collect(1);
```

If you're in the situation in which you've just released a large number of objects that you want to be collected, and these objects have had a relatively long lifetime, you're probably better off finding out which generations the objects in question had been placed in and then calling GC.Collect(), specifying the appropriate generation. Here's how you'd achieve this:

```
int generation = GC.GetGeneration(someObj);
someObj = null;
GC.Collect(generation);
```

In this code assume that someObj refers to one of the objects you no longer need, and that's representative of the age of the batch you think has recently died. You call the GC method GetGeneration() to find out what generation this object is from. You then make sure you have no outstanding references to this object and ask for a collection.

If you need to know the maximum generation number that the current version of the garbage collector allows, the MaxGeneration property will return this information. Hence, this statement will cause all generations to be collected:

```
GC.Collect(GC.MaxGeneration);
```

You can even find out an estimate of how many bytes of memory are currently occupied in the heap using the `GC.GetTotalMemory()` method.

```
Console.WriteLine(GC.GetTotalMemory(true));
```

Bear in mind, however, that it's not possible to obtain an accurate picture of memory without a performance hit—you can be accurate or quick but not both. The `bool` parameter passed in (`true` in the previous snippet) controls this: A value of `true` means that the collector will take its time, letting finalizers run and forcing a collection in order to compact the memory—possibly several collections in succession, in order to get a stable value for the amount of memory in use. A value of `false` will just take a quick estimated value—not much more than reading an internal field in the garbage collector, which may or may not be accurate.

One other useful thing you can do with the garbage collection concerns finalizers. I've already indicated that if an object has a finalizer defined, the process of garbage collecting that object is much more complex, and you won't be surprised to learn that this can affect performance if a large number of such objects exist. If a given object is of a type that has a finalizer defined but you know that for some reason there's no reason for the finalizer to execute on this particular object, then you can get this object explicitly removed from the finalization queue by calling the `GC.SuppressFinalize()` method.

```
// obj refers to an object that doesn't now need to be finalized
GC.SuppressFinalize(obj);
```

You'd typically do this if your code has just explicitly cleaned up any unmanaged resources referenced by this object (for example, using the `Dispose()` pattern).

You can even get an object added back to the finalization queue if you realize subsequently that it does need to be finalized.

```
GC.ReRegisterForFinalize(obj);
```

Having said that, personally I don't recommend using this method. You may have a use for it, but it's a messy technique, and if you find you're using `ReRegisterForFinalize()` extensively, you should suspect problems with the architecture of your code.

Implementing Dispose() and Finalize()

In the following sections, you'll examine the `Finalize()` and `IDisposable.Dispose` methods in more detail. You'll look at the situations in which you should implement these methods for a type and the general principles you should follow when implementing them.

■**Note** Within this section, I'll use the term *client* to mean any other object that instantiates or invokes methods on the class for which you're implementing `Dispose()` or `Finalize()`. You shouldn't assume that the client is in a different assembly (though if `Dispose()` or `Finalize()` is implemented by a public or protected class in a DLL assembly, it may well be).

Finalize()/Dispose() Semantics

Before you examine how to implement Finalize() and Dispose(), I'll briefly review the respective purposes and semantics of these methods.

Finalize()

There's arguably only ever one reason to implement Finalize() in production code, and that's to clean up unmanaged resources. If you define a Finalize() method, the only thing you should do in it is free any unmanaged resources that are directly referenced by that object and perform any associated operations (for example, you'd probably want to flush an IO buffer prior to closing it). Don't do anything else: Don't try to display a message to the user, and don't try to reference any other objects, because you have no way of knowing whether those other objects still exist. Don't put in any code that's dependent on being called from a certain thread—as I've stated earlier, the finalizer will be executed on a special dedicated GC thread, so it won't be on any thread that's under your control.

The definition for Finalize() in IL looks roughly like this:

```
.method family virtual instance void Finalize() cil managed
{
    // Code
}
```

The CLR will recognize the method as a finalizer from its vtable slot—in other words, from the fact that it overrides Object.Finalize(). This means it doesn't need to have the rtspecialname attribute, which you'd normally associate with methods that are treated in some special way by the runtime. This does, however, mean that if coding in IL, you must take care to define the method as virtual—otherwise it won't occupy the correct vtable slot. Most high-level languages will take care of that for you when compiling finalizers. Also, for correct behavior, the code in the body of the Finalize() method should call the base class implementation of Finalize(), if there's an implementation in the base class. Also, it's good practice always to define Finalize() as protected, since there's really no reason for code external to the object to invoke it. Again, most high-level compilers will take care of these points for you.

The syntax for declaring finalizers in different high-level languages varies, since most high-level languages wrap their own syntax around finalizers to make things easier for the developer. For example, both C# and C++ use the ~<ClassName> syntax, and if coding a finalizer in VB, you should actually explicitly declare the method with the name, Finalize().

```
// C# code
class MyClass
{
    ~MyClass()
    {
        // Finalization code here
    }
    // etc.
}

' VB Code
```

```
Class SomeClass
   Protected Overrides Sub Finalize()
      ' Finalization Code Here
   End Sub
End Class
```

Bear in mind that finalizer syntax in different high-level languages is purely an artifact of each language. It's the IL version I quoted earlier that represents the true picture. Both of the previous snippets will compile to the correct IL.

Dispose()

If your client code is well behaved, then it will be in Dispose() that resources will normally be freed up—whereas the finalizer merely serves as an emergency, point-of-last-recall for the situation that a client fails to call Dispose().This means that, as a good rule of thumb, if you're implementing a finalizer for a class, you should always implement IDisposable for that class too.

Unlike the finalizer, Dispose() will normally clean up managed and unmanaged resources. Why the difference? The answer is that when the finalizer has been called, the garbage collector will be dealing with managed objects anyway, but this isn't the case for Dispose().

Another difference between Dispose() and Finalize() is that, whereas Finalize() is a method that's known and treated specially by the CLR, Dispose() is a plain, ordinary method, which just happens to be a member of an interface (IDisposable), which is commonly understood by client code. The CLR doesn't itself have any intrinsic support for Dispose(), though the syntax of C# has specific support for Dispose() (the C# using statement provides a simple shorthand syntax to ensure that Dispose() is invoked correctly—you'll see using in action shortly).

The fact that Dispose() is defined by the IDisposable interface is important since it gives client code a simple means of checking whether a given object implements Dispose(): Just perform a cast to see if it implements IDisposable. The C# using statement also relies on the presence of this interface.

Some classes define a Close() method instead of Dispose(). Close() is intended to perform the same function as Dispose(), except that it tends to be preferred in situations in which traditional terminology talks of closing an object (such as closing a file). It may also have an implied difference in meaning: Closing a resource is often understood by developers to indicate that the resource may later be reopened, but disposing an object implies you've finished with that object for good. You may want to bear in mind that's how users may understand your code when you write implementations for Close() and Dispose(). Other than that, Close() is for all practical purposes another name for a method that does the same thing as Dispose(). Personally, I prefer Dispose() because it's defined by the IDisposable interface. If you write a Close() method instead of Dispose(), you're clearly not implementing that interface, which means you don't get any of the benefits of the interface (such as the C# using statement). Because of this, if you want to implement a Close() method on a type, it's probably a good rule of thumb to implement IDisposable too, with Dispose() implemented like this:

```
Dispose()
{
   Close();
}
```

Cleaning Up Unmanaged Resources

If your code holds any precious unmanaged resources, it will normally be important that these resources are freed at the earliest possible moment. This is because so many unmanaged resources either come in a limited supply (for example, database connections from a connection pool) or come on a mutual exclusion basis (for example, open file handles). So, for example, a file handle that wasn't freed at the right time could easily be holding up another application that needs to open the same file.

I'll start by presenting a sample that illustrates a typical scenario of an application that holds onto an unmanaged resource. The sample is called DisposeUnmanagedResource, and it shows how you could write code to ensure that the resource is cleaned up properly in two situations: if the resource is being used locally within a method and if it's held on a more long-term basis, as a field of a class.

To start, you need some code that simulates the precious resource itself. This resource could be a database connection, a file, or GDI object, and so on. Of course it's not possible to generalize too much about how a resource is obtained—that will depend on the nature of the resource. However, rather than tying the sample down to a specific resource, I want it to be as generic as possible, so I'll define a class that represents the programming model that's typically used for those resources that are known to the Windows operating system—which covers quite a wide range. These resources are usually represented by *handles*, which are integers that normally index into certain internal data structures maintained by Windows and that identify the particular object being used. Although a handle is just an integer, it's normally represented by the IntPtr class in managed code—recall that this class is intended as a useful wrapper for integers whose size is dependent on the machine architecture.

Here's the class that simulates API functions—you should think of each static member of this class as standing in place of some [DllImport] function:

```
class APIFunctionSimulator
{
   public static IntPtr GetResource()
   {
      // Substitute for an API function
      return (IntPtr)4;
   }

   public static void ReleaseResource(IntPtr handle)
   {
      // In a real app this would call something to release
      // the handle
   }

   public static string UseResource(IntPtr handle)
```

```
    {
        return "The handle is " + handle.ToString();
    }
}
```

The GetResource() method returns a hard-coded number (4), which I'm using to represent some handle. I assume that ReleaseResource() frees the precious unmanaged resource represented by this handle, and UseResource() accesses this resource to obtain some information. This model is pretty typical of the way things usually work with Windows API functions, so you could, for example, easily envisage replacing GetResource() with a call to some API function such as OpenFile(), CreateCompatibleDC(), or CreateBitmap() and such as ReleaseResource() with CloseHandle(), DeleteDC(), or DeleteObject() in real code.

Now for the class that maintains this simulated resource. This class is called ResourceUser and forms the crux of the sample:

```
class ResourceUser : IDisposable
{
    private IntPtr handle;

    public ResourceUser()
    {
        handle = APIFunctionSimulator.GetResource();
        if (handle.ToInt32() == 0)
            throw new ApplicationException();
    }

    public void Dispose()
    {
        lock(this)
        {
            if (handle.ToInt32() != 0)
            {
                APIFunctionSimulator.ReleaseResource(handle);
                handle = (IntPtr)0;
                GC.SuppressFinalize(this);
            }
        }
    }

    public void UseResource()
    {
        if (handle.ToInt32() == 0)
            throw new ObjectDisposedException(
                "Handle used in ResourceUser class after object disposed");
        string result = APIFunctionSimulator.UseResource(handle);
        Console.WriteLine("In ResourceUser.UseResource, result is :" +
                        result);
    }
```

```
~ResourceUser()
{
   if (handle.ToInt32() != 0)
      APIFunctionSimulator.ReleaseResource(handle);
}
}
```

This class maintains the handle to the resource as a member field, which is initialized in the ResourceUser constructor. Notice that the constructor tests the value of the handle, so that if it's zero, an exception will be thrown and the object won't be created (API functions that return handles normally return 0 as the handle value if the attempt to connect to or create the resource failed). The code that's of most interest is of course the code to clean up the resource. The finalizer simply frees the resource (provided a nonzero handle value indicates the code is holding onto a resource) and does nothing else. The Dispose() method is more interesting. I'll start by locking the ResourceUser instance.

```
lock(this)
{
```

The point of this is that it ensures that the Dispose() method is thread-safe by preventing more than one thread from executing it at the same time. If you're not familiar with the C# lock statement, I'll explain it in more detail in Chapter 7. The finalizer doesn't need to worry about thread safety since finalizers are executed on their dedicated thread.

Next the code checks if it's actually holding on to a precious resource and releases it if that's the case.

```
if (handle.ToInt32() != 0)
{
   APIFunctionSimulator.ReleaseResource(handle);
   handle = (IntPtr)0;
   GC.SuppressFinalize(this);
}
```

Note the call to GC.SuppressFinalize()—that's important. Since the resource is now freed, the finalizer of this object no longer has any need to be invoked.

Finally, I've also defined a UseResource() member method of this class, which actually uses the precious resource. Notice that the UseResource() method tests that the handle isn't zero and throws an ObjectDisposedException if a zero handle is detected.

```
public void UseResource()
{
   if (handle.ToInt32() == 0)
      throw new ObjectDisposedException(
          "Handle used in ResourceUser class after object disposed");
```

In this sample class, you can be sure that a zero handle indicates that some client code has already called Dispose()—I've defined the UseResources class in such a way that no other situation can cause the handle to be zero. However, in a more complex class, you may prefer to have a bool variable to test this condition separately so that you can throw a more appropriate exception if the handle somehow becomes zero through some other means.

```
if (disposed)      // bool disposed set to true in Dispose() method
    throw new ObjectDisposedException(
        "Handle used in UseResource class after object disposed");
else if (handle.ToInt32() == 0)
    throw new MyOwnException("Handle is zero for some reason");
```

ObjectDisposedException() is an exception provided in the framework base class library for this explicit purpose. Notice that the way I've coded the Dispose() method means that if Dispose() is accidentally called more than once, all subsequent calls simply do nothing and don't throw any exception—this is the behavior that Microsoft recommends.

Now for the "client" class that tests the ResourceUser class. Here's the Main() method:

```
static void Main()
{
    ResourceUser ru = new ResourceUser();
    ru.UseResource();
    ru.UseResource();
    // WRONG! Forgot to call Dispose()

    using (ru = new ResourceUser())
    {
        ru.UseResource();
        ru.UseResource();
    }
    ru = new ResourceUser();
    try
    {
        ru.UseResource();
        ru.UseResource();
    }
    finally
    {
        ru.Dispose();
    }

    UseUnmanagedResource();
}
```

This method first instantiates a ResourceUser instance and then calls UseResource() a couple of times, but it doesn't call Dispose(). This is bad behavior by the client but doesn't do so much harm in this case because I've followed good practice in supplying a finalizer—which means the precious resource will be freed in the finalizer eventually (sometime soon after the next garbage collection occurs). Next, the Main() method instantiates another ResourceUser object—but does this in the context of a C# using statement. The using statement causes the compiler to automatically insert code to ensure that the object's IDisposable.Dispose() method is always invoked at the closing curly brace of the using block. This is the recommended way in C# of calling objects that implement IDisposable.Dispose().

Finally, the `Main()` method instantiates another `ResourceUser` object and then uses the object inside a `try` block, with the `Dispose()` method being called from inside a `finally` block, which guarantees it will be called even in the event of an exception occurring while the unmanaged resource is in use. This code is equivalent to the previous `using` block and illustrates what the `using` block is expanded to by the compiler and how client code should use objects that define a `Dispose()` method in other languages that don't have the equivalent of C#'s `using` block shortcut syntax. This includes VB and C++—which means that the VB version of this sample with the downloadable code omits that part of the sample.

Finally, the code calls a method called `UseUnmanagedResource()`. I've included this method just for completeness—it illustrates how to use precious resource where the resource is scoped to a method rather than to a member field. Here's the definition of this method:

```
static void UseUnmanagedResource()
{
    IntPtr handle = APIFunctionSimulator.GetResource();
    try
    {
        string result = APIFunctionSimulator.UseResource(handle);
        Console.WriteLine("In EntryPoint.UseUnmanagedResource, result is :" +
                          result);
    }
    catch (Exception e)
    {
        Console.WriteLine("Exception in UseUnmanagedResource: " + e.Message);
    }
    finally
    {
        if (handle.ToInt32() != 0)
        {
            APIFunctionSimulator.ReleaseResource(handle);
        }
    }
}
```

Classes That Contain Both Managed and Unmanaged Resources

I'll now extend the previous sample to illustrate the recommended way of implementing `Dispose()`/`Finalize()` if a class holds onto both managed and unmanaged resources. I stress that, although for completeness this sample shows you how to implement such a class, you'll see in the following discussion that this is rarely a good design. The new sample is downloadable as the `UseBothResources` sample and is obtained by modifying the `ResourceUser` class from the previous sample as follows. I first add a large array that's a member field of the class.

```
class ResourceUser : IDisposable
{
    private IntPtr handle;
    private int[] bigArray = new int[100000];
```

Although I won't actually implement any code that makes use of this array, its purpose should be clear: it serves as a large member field to illustrate how to clean up a large member object when you know that the ResourceUser instance is no longer required.

In principle bigArray is a managed object, and so it will be automatically removed when it's no longer referenced, and a garbage collection occurs. However, since the ResourceUser class has a Dispose() method anyway, I may as well use this method to remove the reference to the array with a statement, like this:

```
bigArray = null;
```

Doing this will ensure that even if some client maintains its (now dead) reference to the ResourceUser object, and then bigArray can still be garbage-collected. The way that I implement this is by defining a new one-parameter Dispose() method and by modifying the Dispose()/Finalize() methods, as follows:

```
public void Dispose()
{
   lock(this)
   {
      Dispose(true);
      GC.SuppressFinalize(this);
   }
}

private void Dispose(bool disposing)
{
   if (handle.ToInt32() != 0)
   {
      APIFunctionSimulator.ReleaseResource(handle);
      handle = (IntPtr)0;
   }

   if (disposing)
      bigArray = null;
}

~ResourceUser()
{
   Dispose(false);
}
```

You should be able to see by following through the logic of this code that the finalizer still does nothing except remove the unmanaged resource—this is important because of the principle that finalizers must not contain any code that references other objects that may have been removed—because you have no way of guaranteeing when the finalizer will execute. It's not the responsibility of finalizers to deal with managed objects—the garbage collector does that automatically. Calling Dispose(false) instead of directly cleaning up the resource from the finalizer gives you an extra method call, but it means you can keep all your resource cleanup code in one method, making for easier source code maintenance.

On the other hand, this new implementation of `IDisposable.Dispose()` cleans up both managed and unmanaged resources—though in the case of managed objects, cleaning up simply means setting references to these objects to `null` in order to allow the garbage collector potentially to do its work more promptly.

Guidelines for Implementing Dispose() and Finalizers

Let's now see what general principles of good practice you can derive from the previous samples.

When to Implement Dispose()

When should you implement `Dispose()`? This question isn't always as clear-cut as it is for `Finalize()`. In the case of `Finalize()`, it's simple: If your class maintains unmanaged resources, implement `Finalize()`. If it doesn't, then don't. Period. But for `Dispose()`, the situation isn't always as clear-cut, since sometimes there's a balance between the benefit that `Dispose()` helps the garbage collector out and the problem that `Dispose()` makes using your class more complicated, since clients have to remember to call it. And if you have a complicated arrangement of classes that refer to each other, figuring out when to call `Dispose()` can be a nontrivial issue.

The situation is easiest to understand if you have wrapper objects that contain references to other objects, as shown in Figure 5-3.

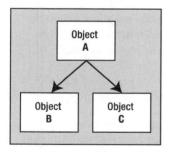

Figure 5-3. *A wrapper object A with references to objects B and C*

In Figure 5-3 I assume that the *only* references held to objects B and C are held by A—in other words, A serves as the only point of access to B and C. The corollary is that the lifetime of A controls the lifetimes of B and C. With this arrangement, the conditions under which you will probably want A to implement `Dispose()` are as follows:

1. If either B or C implements `Dispose()`, then clearly A must implement `Dispose()` to call `B.Dispose()` and `C.Dispose()`—otherwise there's no way for B and C to be disposed of correctly.

2. If A is directly holding onto unmanaged resources, it should implement `Dispose()` (and of course a finalizer) to free those resources. Note that if B or C hold unmanaged

resources, A doesn't need to worry about that directly. But in that case B or C ought to implement Dispose() and the finalizer to clean up those resources—in which case rule 1 forces A to implement Dispose(), though not the finalizer, anyway. Notice therefore how implementations of should Dispose() get propagated back through classes that may store references to IDisposable objects, but this isn't the case for finalizers.

3. If conditions 1 and 2 don't apply now, but you think they may apply for some future version of your A class, it's probably a good idea to implement Dispose() now, even if it doesn't do anything. That way people who write client code will know to invoke it, and you won't end up in a situation two years down the line where lots of legacy client code instantiates what's now the new version of A and doesn't call Dispose() when it should.

4. If none of these cases apply, then you may still want A to implement Dispose() just to set the references to B and C to null, especially if B and C are very large objects (such as arrays). The benefit to doing this is that if for some reason client code holds onto a reference to A long after calling Dispose(), then at least this reference isn't propagated to B and C so that the garbage collector would still be able to remove B and C the next time it occurs. On the other hand, this benefit is more marginal, and you may think it's more than offset by the added complexity involved with using A and therefore choose not to implement Dispose().

That covers the situation in which you have a neat hierarchy of wrapper classes. I still need to discuss the situation where a more complex arrangement of interrelated classes exists. Perhaps, with Figure 5-3, other objects in your code may hold onto references to B and C, so A can't in any way claim ownership of them. Obviously, you should still implement Dispose() on A if A has any unmanaged resources, but A.Dispose() should certainly not call B.Dispose() or C.Dispose(). This illustrates an important principle—that you should normally implement Dispose() only to assist in getting rid of managed objects if you can identify a clear lifetime-containment relationship for the objects. Otherwise, the programming gets complicated, and the code is unlikely to be robust.

Finalizable Class Architecture

The code samples you've just seen covered two means of implementing finalizers, depending on whether the object that directly referenced an unmanaged resource also referenced other large managed objects. I should stress that, although I presented both cases, in most situations the former example shows the best means of designing your classes. It's generally speaking not a good idea to have a finalizable object that contains references to other managed objects, especially large objects. The reason for this is that those other objects will not be garbage-collected as long as the finalizable object is on the freachable queue, which means that those other objects will end up unnecessarily missing a garbage collection—or perhaps many, even hundreds, of collections if the object had been previously promoted to a higher generation. If you find yourself writing an object that needs a finalizer and references other objects, consider separating it into two objects: a wrapper object that references all the other managed objects and a small internal object whose sole purpose is to provide an interface to the unmanaged resource and that doesn't contain references to any other managed objects. Another related point is that it's generally a good idea to arrange your finalizable classes so that each precious unmanaged resource is clearly associated with just one instance of a finalizable class, giving a one-to-one relationship between the lifetime of this class and the lifetime of the resource. Doing this makes finalizers easier to code, and gives a more robust architecture, since you know that at the time of execution of the finalizer, it's definitely OK to free the resource.

This means that with the earlier `DisposeBothResourcesSample`, a more sensible architecture would have involved class definitions similar to the following:

```
// This class does NOT implement a finalizer
class MmanagedResourceUser : IDisposable
{
    private int[] bigArray = new int[100000];
    private UnmanagedResourceUser handleWrapper;
    // etc.
}

// This class does implement a finalizer
class UnmanagedResourceUser : IDisposable
{
    private IntPtr handle;
    // etc.
}
```

In a more general case, if you have more than two managed objects (say E and F) that need to use an unmanaged resource, the actual maintenance of the resource should be the responsibility of a third object (say Y), as shown in Figure 5-4.

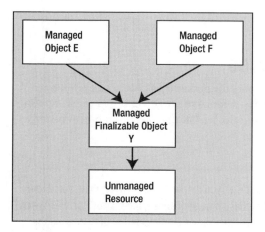

Figure 5-4. *Correct architecture for referencing unmanaged resources*

A corollary of this is that the class that implements the finalizer should keep its reference to the unmanaged resource private, and not expose it to other objects—otherwise you're going to have potential problems because when the finalizer is executed, some other object may still be holding onto the resource.

> ■**Tip** Incidentally, it can be quite an interesting exercise to do a title-only search for `Finalize` in the MSDN documentation to see which classes have finalizers defined. You'll see that they're always the classes that, based on what they do, will need internally to wrap an unmanaged resource such as a windows handle directly. You quite simply have no other conceivable reason for implementing a finalizer. For example, `System.Drawing.Icon` implements `Finalize()` (it will presumably contain an `HICON`), as do `Microsoft.Win32.RegistryKey` (which will contain an `HKEY`) and `System.IO.IsolatedStorage.IsolatedStorageFile` (`HFILE`).

A few Microsoft-defined classes allow the ability for other code to get access to handles—for example, look at the `Graphics.GetHdc()` method, which returns a device context handle, HDC. This looks like it breaks the principle of having only one wrapper class. But you'll find that where this happens, severe restrictions are imposed on the use of such methods; for example, after calling `GetHdc()` on a `Graphics` object, you basically can't use that `Graphics` object again until you've called `ReleaseDc()` to release the device context.

Finalizers and Value Types

I'll finish this topic with a word about the particular problems you'll face if you want to implement a finalizer for a value type. In general, my advice is simple: don't. If a type needs to implement a finalizer, then define it as a reference type instead. The reason is that finalizers on value types will not be executed unless the type is boxed, since only references can be placed on the finalization queue. For this reason, many high-level languages, such as C#, won't permit you to define a finalizer on a value type although doing this is possible if you code directly in IL.

Introducing Weak References

I'll now discuss one last feature that the garbage collector makes available: weak references. A *weak reference* amounts to a way of holding onto a reference to an object but at the same time saying to the garbage collector that if memory gets tight, it's OK to collect that object because you can always re-create it if you need it again.

> ■**Caution** If you're familiar with the weak references in COM, you'll need to forget everything you know about COM weak references. Although the implementation has some similarities, the purpose of .NET weak references is completely different. In COM, weak references are a rather complicated means to avoid the circular reference problem. Weak references in .NET are simpler and exist purely to give the garbage collector extra freedom to clean up objects if memory is limited.

Weak References Explained

The circumstances when you'll consider using a weak reference are if you have some object that's massive in size but that may not be actively in use for some time. Let's say, for example, that you have an application connected to a database on a remote server. This application allows the user to find out geographical information, and some user has used it to download a list (probably via a DataSet) of all the towns and villages in the United Kingdom, complete with information about each town—population, any buildings of interest to tourists, and so on. The user browsed the list for a few seconds and then decided he was particularly interested in Lancaster, so asked the application to download a map of that area from the database. What's going to happen to the list of towns while the user is busily exploring the map or perhaps asking for more maps such as a higher scale one of the area? Now that the application has downloaded the list, it'd be quite nice to keep it locally, ready for when the user wants to come back to it. You certainly don't want to work on the basis of displaying a tiny bit of information from the list and then promptly deleting the whole list—that's going to give poor responsiveness if the user follows up one query with another one concerning the same list, since such a long list will probably take a few seconds to download again from the database. On the other hand, that list is going to be taking up a lot of memory. If the application simply caches everything the user asks for, and the user in succession asks for various similar lists and various accompanying maps, you could easily imagine performance decreasing drastically because the application is hogging too much memory and needs to keep paging.

It looks like this is a no-win situation, but enter weak references to save the day. Once you've downloaded the data, instead of storing a reference object that contains the data, you store a *weak reference* referring to the data—that's to say, an instance of the class System.WeakReference that's initialized to refer to your data. This means that the data will stay in memory, but it's also simultaneously marked as available for garbage collection. Hence, if the garbage collector does get called in, this data will be freed. The WeakReference class exposes a property, Target, which lets you see if the data has been collected. If Target returns null, the object referred to by the weak reference has been collected, and you need to create another copy of it to be able to use it again. Otherwise, the data is still there. Notice that this means that weak references are a suitable solution only if you can, in principle, re-create the original data without too much trouble.

■Tip In contrast to weak references, ordinary .NET references are often known as *strong references*. Bear in mind that a weak reference to an object can function correctly only as long as there are no strong references to the same object. If one strong reference to the object exists, then the object will be completely prevented from being garbage collected.

Let's look at how this is implemented in coding terms. Suppose you have a method, GetTheData(), that calculates some data and returns a reference of type MyData to this data. Ordinarily, you'd have code like this:

```
MyData data = GetTheData();
```

followed later by some method that uses the data, such as this:

```
UseTheData(data);
```

Instead, using a weak reference, you'd do this when first creating the data:

```
WeakReference wr = new WeakReference(GetTheData());
```

Notice that the constructor to WeakReference takes an object reference—so you can pass in any reference type to it.

Then when you want to use the data, you'll do something like this:

```
MyData data;
if (wr.Target == null)
{
   // The data got deleted. Need to recreate it.
   data = GetTheData();
   wr.Target = data;
}
else
   data = (MyData)wr.Target;

UseTheData(data);
data = null;
```

Notice that the data variable has been set to null at the end of this block of code. As I mentioned earlier, it's important that no references to the actual data remain after you've finished actively using it. As long as any such references exist, the garbage collector can't collect the data, which rather nullifies the whole purpose of having the weak reference in the first place!

And that's all there is to it. You've gained a small bit of complexity in your code, but in return you get the peace of mind of knowing that your application will be using memory in a much more intelligent way. (And let's face it, trying to implement something such as a weak reference by hand would be a huge task—especially since the GC doesn't expose any means to inform your code when it's under memory pressure.)

The Weak References Sample

I'll finish this chapter with a sample called WeakReferenceDemo that illustrates how to use weak references. To keep things simple, I won't show accessing a database. Instead, the sample will have an array of 500,000 strings hogging memory. Figure 5-5 shows what the sample looks like when it's running.

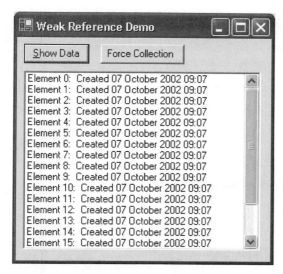

Figure 5-5. *The* WeakReferenceDemo *sample*

The hub of the sample is a Show Data button and a list box. Whenever the user clicks the Show Data button, the list box is refreshed with the first 20 strings from the 500,000-strong array. Each string, as you can see, is initialized to some text that indicates its index in the array and the time of creation for the array.

The second button simulates the effects of lots of other memory-intensive objects being allocated resulting in a garbage collection. Clicking this button forces a garbage collection using the GC.Collect() method. This means that if the user clicks Force Collection and then clicks Show Data, the data will have to be re-created before it can be displayed. Because the data shows its creation time, you can observe that the creation time will get updated. This isn't quite in the spirit of weak references—the real idea is that you're supposed to be able to re-create the identical data exactly as it was before, but having an updated creation time is more illustrative for the sample.

To create the sample, I generated a standard C# Windows Forms application and added the buttons and list box to the form. The controls were respectively named btnShowData, btnForceCollection, and lbData. Then I manually added this code: first a couple of member variables to the Form1 class and then the constants representing the length of the array and the number of elements of it that will actually get displayed in the list box. (I confined it to the first 20 elements since for obvious reasons I didn't really want to have to populate and display a list box with 500,000 items in it!)

```
public class Form1 : System.Windows.Forms.Form
{
    private const int DataArrayLength = 500000;
    private const int ItemsInListBox = 20;
    private WeakReference wr;

    private System.Windows.Forms.Button btnForceCollection;
    private System.Windows.Forms.Button btnShowData;
    private System.Windows.Forms.ListBox lbData;
```

Notice that I've stored the weak reference as a field, but I've been careful not to store any strong reference to the data in any field.

Now for the event handlers. On clicking the Show Data button, a method named RefreshData() gets called. You'll look at RefreshData() in a minute.

```
private void btnShowData_Click(object sender, System.EventArgs e)
{
   RefreshData();
}
```

As described earlier, the other button forces a garbage collection.

```
private void btnForceCollection_Click(object sender, System.EventArgs e)
{
   GC.Collect();
}
```

Here's the RefreshData() method, which does all the work:

```
private void RefreshData()
{
   Cursor.Current = Cursors.WaitCursor;
   lbData.Items.Clear();
   lbData.Items.Add("Retrieving data. Please wait ...");
   lbData.Refresh();
   string[] dataArray;

   if (wr == null || wr.Target == null)
   {
      dataArray = new string[DataArrayLength];
      string text = " Created " + DateTime.Now.ToString("f");
      for (int i=0 ; i<DataArrayLength ; i++)
         dataArray[i] = "Element " + i.ToString() + text;
      wr = new WeakReference(dataArray);
   }
   else
      dataArray = (string[])wr.Target;

   string [] tempStrings = new String[ItemsInListBox];
   for (int i=0 ; i<ItemsInListBox ; i++)
      tempStrings[i] = dataArray[i];

   lbData.Items.Clear();
   lbData.Items.AddRange(tempStrings);
   Cursor.Current = Cursors.Default;
}
```

This method first clears out the list box and replaces its contents with a single entry indicating to the user that the list box will be populated soon. It also changes the mouse cursor to an hourglass wait cursor in accordance with normal UI practice. Then it declares a local object that will hold a strong reference to the array of strings—so the code can manipulate the array locally in this method. The code checks to see if the weak reference currently refers to the array and, if it doesn't, creates it. The if statement tests two conditions.

```
if (wr == null || wr.Target == null)
```

The wr == null condition picks whether this is the first time RefreshData() has been called—in which case wr hasn't been initialized yet. The condition wr.Target == null will pick up the case where the array of strings has been created but has since been garbage collected.

Notice that the code creates a temporary array and uses the ListItemCollection. AddRange() method to populate the list box—that's a lot more efficient than adding the items singly.

The best way to see the sample in action is to watch memory usage with Task Manager while running it (see Figure 5-6).

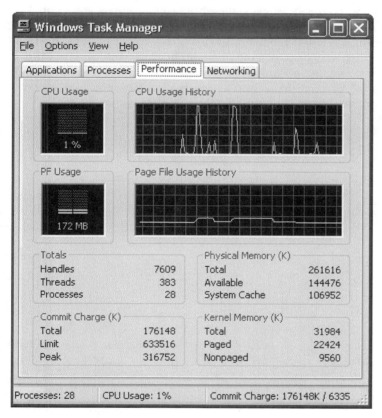

Figure 5-6. *Using Task Manager to monitor the* WeakReferenceDemo *sample*

In Figure 5-6, I started WeakReferenceDemo running with a release build (that's impor-tant—if I'm monitoring memory, I don't want memory being cluttered up by debug symbols and so on). You can clearly see when I first click Refresh Data. The memory usage builds to a new level—you can see it going up gradually as the array is populated, and the CPU Usage hits nearly 100 percent while that happens. A few seconds later, I hit Force Collection, and the memory usage dramatically fell back to its original level as the garbage collector released its memory (it's clear from this figure that in this case the garbage collector actually decommitted the memory). Then I hit Refresh Data again, and you see the same memory buildup. This time, before hitting Force Collection, I clicked Refresh Data a few times. Although this refreshed the list box (I could tell as I saw it flicker), refreshing the data this time had no effect on memory or CPU usage, since the array of strings was already in memory. Then I hit Force Collection again, and you can see the memory usage drop back down. There was also a small drop in memory usage later as I actually exited the program.

Summary

In this chapter, you examined in detail how to get the best from the garbage collection facilities offered by the .NET Framework. You investigated the advantages of garbage collection over other memory cleanup techniques, and you looked at the internal workings of the garbage collector, including the way it uses generations as a way to optimize performance and how it deals with finalizers. I then went discussed the situations in which you'd need to write separate finalizers or `Dispose()` methods for your classes, as well as the techniques you should use to implement these methods in a way that doesn't adversely affect the garbage collection process too much. Finally, you saw how to use weak references to provide an additional means to free up resources.

CHAPTER 6

■■■

Improving Performance

Performance has to be one of the most frequent worries among developers—no one wants their code to run visibly slowly. Despite the huge power of modern processors and large amounts of random access memory (RAM) available, it's still not hard to design an application badly with the result that some bottleneck or piece of inefficient code causes a visible and unnecessary slowdown. As one obvious example, I never cease to be amazed when I ask Windows Explorer to delete one file, and it takes a couple of seconds to do so on my 2GHz-plus Athlon machine! Even without the burden of obviously poor design, some applications place such intensive demands on a system that considering performance when coding them is vitally important. Traditionally, games are the main candidates here, but the same applies to some more complex database queries, to intensive numerical code, and to areas such as regular-expression processing. Any operations that need to be performed over a network can also impact performance.

■Tip Don't confuse performance with responsiveness. Performance is directly concerned with how long the computer takes to do something (including time spent waiting, for example, for network calls), but responsiveness is specifically about how quickly the computer reacts when the user does something. In this chapter, I'll concentrate on performance as a whole, though many of the same techniques I'll discuss will affect responsiveness as well. Generally, however, the user can't perceive time intervals less than about a tenth of a second when judging the time between user input and the computer responding. This is sufficiently long that the performance of code may not be important. Often, what's more important for user responsiveness is that the computer or the thread isn't tied up on some other task when the user does something with the mouse or keyboard. Responsiveness is generally ensured by using correct multithreaded techniques—I'll discuss these in Chapter 9.

The .NET Framework has brought with it the ability to write much more robust and secure code more easily than ever before. But it nevertheless currently presents a layer of code between your application and the Windows operating system, and basic common sense tells you that means it's going to contribute to some overhead. In this chapter, I'll take a critical view of the .NET Framework from the performance perspective. I'll spend some time covering the practical measures you can take to improve the performance of your applications, but I'll also discuss some of the .NET CLR internals that are particularly relevant to performance. In particular, I'll cover the following:

- Is it best to use the .NET Framework or stick with unmanaged code, if performance is an issue?

- The optimizations that the .NET Framework and the JIT compiler perform and how to enable them.

- Various tricks and tips you can use to maximize performance for your unmanaged code.

Should You Write Managed or Unmanaged Code?

It may seem strange in a book about .NET programming that I'm asking this question at all. However, the question of whether you should leverage the .NET Framework at all is an important design decision, and given that .NET puts some overhead in both resource use and performance on any application, it's an issue that will have to be addressed in any application for which performance is an important consideration. Indeed, I have another important reason for discussing this: A point I'll make repeatedly in this chapter is that architectural decisions and high-level design, such as the choice of algorithm, are often far more important factors in influencing performance than are the low-level "Do I recalculate this value inside the loop?" kinds of questions that many developers associate with performance. And you can't get much higher level than asking whether you should be using the .NET Framework in the first place!

In the following sections, you'll examine the issues you should consider when deciding whether to use the .NET Framework for an application. Although I'll focus on performance, it's not possible in this context to cover performance in isolation, so I'll also touch on balancing the conflicting demands of robustness, performance, security, and development time. I can't obviously give any hard advice of the "You must write it this way" form, since every application is different, and you must weigh so many factors—besides the purely technological aspects you'll consider here, you must balance, for example, the skill sets of developers and the prejudices of the managers to which you have to present your decisions. However, I'll discuss the main issues you'll need to bear in mind. I'll start by reviewing the current and likely future status of the .NET Framework, and then I'll assess the issues you're likely to face for new code, before moving onto legacy code.

.NET and the Future

Let's be in no doubt about this: Microsoft regards .NET as *the* future for programming on the Windows platform and wants in a few years time for .NET to be important on other platforms. Roughly speaking, the aim here is that in five to ten years, virtually all new code being written will be managed code, with unmanaged code used only for legacy applications and perhaps a few specialist purposes such as device drivers. Whether this actually happens, only time will tell, but you can be sure that Microsoft's research and development efforts over the next few years will become increasingly focused into helping you write managed rather than unmanaged code.

Currently, what I've heard informally from various developers at Microsoft is that managed code will typically run between five and ten percent slower than the equivalent unmanaged code. This is broadly in line with my own experience, though those figures are only approximate ballpark figures, and they will vary considerably between different applications. For example, code that requires a significant amount of interop marshaling is likely to run considerably slower, and code that's computationally intensive may run faster because of the benefits of JIT optimizations. You also need to recognize that at the time of writing, the .NET Framework has reached only version 1.1—and obviously in getting version 1.x of any product out, priority will tend to be focused on actually shipping a working product and making it robust, rather than on fine-tuning its performance. Within the next year, .NET 2.0 is likely to be released, and as new versions of .NET emerge, you can expect to see performance tuning kicking in, and the small performance loss suffered by running managed code under .NET version 1.x may well diminish or go away entirely. A related aspect of this is that over time more and more of the Windows API will become accessible through .NET. At the moment, one complaint among some programmers is the frequency with which they need to make calls through P/Invoke to Windows API functions to access features that aren't yet directly available through the framework class library. Each P/Invoke call incurs the usual performance hit, as well as compromising security because it means the code has to be granted access permission to run unmanaged code—which for all practical purposes renders all the extra security checks provided by the .NET Framework useless. (What's the point of, for example, .NET decreeing that an application isn't allowed to access the file system if the application can use native code to get around the restriction anyway?) However, given Microsoft's aim of making .NET the universal way of programming, you can expect that, as new versions of .NET are released, coverage of the Windows API will become much more extensive so that the need for those P/Invokes will go away. One obvious example of this is the incorporation of managed wrappers into DirectX 9. When .NET 1.0 was first released, it was necessary for the developer to explicitly resort to unmanaged code in order to use the fast graphics facilities of DirectX. That's no longer the case.

The availability of .NET is also an issue. Some developers are concerned that managed code will run only if the .NET Framework is installed, which means asking customers to install the framework. Installing the framework is easy, but you'll have to decide if your customers will accept it. However, be reassured that Microsoft is taking seriously the issue of getting the .NET Framework placed on as many computers as possible. You can therefore expect that in the near future, the framework will ship as standard with new PCs and many Microsoft products. For example, Windows .NET Server ships with .NET 1.1. In a couple of years, requiring the .NET Framework is unlikely to be an issue.

In general, it's still the case that if you want maximum performance for a given algorithm, you'll need to write in unmanaged code. However, the advantages of .NET in almost every other area are so great that it may be worth sacrificing some performance. I'll quickly review the main options, before covering in detail what the balancing considerations are, including the current and likely future status of the .NET Framework.

Options for Managed Development

In performance terms, the main Microsoft languages of C#, VB, and C++ have little difference, although C++ will have a slight edge in many cases, with VB lagging slightly behind the other languages. This is largely because, on one hand, the C++ compiler performs more optimizations than either the C# or VB ones and because, on the other hand, VB, with its looser framework for types and type conversions, often allows developers to unwittingly write less efficient code that the C# compiler would have rejected. In some cases, the VB compiler can also emit more verbose IL than you'd get from the equivalent C#. Having said that, these differences are small and can often be eliminated with good coding practices. I'll say more about those differences in the section "Performance Tips."

If you have existing code in VB 6, the existence of the VS .NET wizard that will convert much of your code to VB .NET is an extremely good reason for migrating to VB .NET. If you need to use unsafe code, you'll need to choose C# or C++, and if you do often need to call into legacy unmanaged code, C++ is likely to be a better bet.

Options for Unmanaged Development

The options here are the same as they were before the days of .NET. I'll comment only on that if performance is that important an issue, you'll almost certainly be coding in C or C++, using ATL, the Windows API, or just possibly the Microsoft Foundation Classes (MFC).

Options for Interoperability

For mixing unmanaged and managed code, the main three mechanisms are IJW, P/Invoke, and COM interoperability.

P/Invoke can be used from any .NET language and has the advantage that the .NET Framework will marshal the .NET types to/from the unmanaged types, at a slight performance loss.

IJW is the mechanism used by C++ for calling unmanaged code without providing a specific `DllImport` directive. It's not an alternative to P/Invoke but rather an alternative way of using the P/Invoke services. IJW also allows you to write and embed unmanaged code in the same assembly module as your managed code, saving the need for a separate unmanaged DLL, which can provide a slight performance edge.

COM interoperability is the only option if you want to invoke methods on COM objects. However, it will lead to a larger performance hit than for P/Invoke.

In practice, any real product is likely to consist of a number of modules, which means that communication between them is important and also that you may find only some modules are being coded as managed code. As far as out-of-process or cross-machine communication between managed modules is concerned, you'll normally find that Remoting using the Tcp channel will give better performance than the other main techniques provided by the framework (ASP.NET Web services and Remoting using Http).

I'll now summarize some of the main factors you should consider when deciding between managed and unmanaged code for a given module.

Issues to Consider

If you're deciding whether to write a new component for an application as managed or unmanaged code, you should consider the following:

Time scale: If the application is expected to have a lifetime only of a year or two, then it probably won't be around long enough to really see .NET at its best. In this case, you may not lose much by sticking with the Windows API. On the other hand, if this component is intended to last in the long term, programming in .NET is likely to be a good investment for the future. (But equally, if the component has a short life span, you may feel it's not worth the extra development effort to write it as unmanaged code.)

Whether performance is critical compared with development time and other issues: Is this an application where it's really going to matter if it runs five to ten percent slower? For example, if it's basically a user-interface application, then most of its time is going to be spent waiting for user input. In this kind of situation, the ease of programming of .NET, the extra robustness, and the shorter development cycle probably ought to be the prime considerations. A related issue is that, as I've mentioned, that five to ten percent is only an approximation—and one that will vary considerably between different applications. If you need to make frequent calls to Windows API functions, those P/Invokes may add up. In that scenario, your options include the following:

- Putting up with the P/Invokes.

- Using unmanaged code for just a part of your application that needs to call Windows API functions; this allows you to arrange things in such a way that you invoke your unmanaged code less frequently than you'd need to invoke the Windows API functions.

- Writing in managed code in C++, which allows you to access unmanaged code using the IJW mechanism.

Whether the algorithms are complex: Performance has another side: Although a given algorithm may run more slowly under .NET, the availability of the framework class library and the greater ease of programming (for example, that you don't need to worry about memory management) may enable you to use a more complex algorithm, or more complex data structures, which leads to higher performance.

Note that these considerations are additional to the obvious ones—such as the developer skill set.

.NET Performance Benefits

As noted earlier, Microsoft has been making it clear for some time that it thinks eventually .NET code will be able to run faster than the equivalent unmanaged code. Essentially the reason for this is twofold: First, the .NET Framework includes some pretty nifty programming that implements some sophisticated algorithms for various boilerplate tasks such as memory management and thread pooling. You'd be pretty hard-pressed to implement the same algorithms yourself. Second, the JIT compiler is able in principle to perform additional optimizations not available to traditional compilers, including hardware-specific optimizations (although at .NET 1.1, it's not clear that the JIT compiler actually takes advantage of this to any great extent only—this is something that's more likely to become important in later versions). In the following sections, I'll assess in more detail some of the contributions that the .NET Framework can make to performance through two aspects of its design: garbage collection and the JIT compiler.

Garbage Collection

You're probably familiar with the arguments surrounding the relative performance of the managed garbage-collected heap vs. the unmanaged C++ heap, but I'll recap them here for completion, before pointing out a couple of subtleties concerning these arguments that aren't so well known.

The main performance benefit claimed for the garbage-collected heap is that the garbage collection process includes tidying the heap so that all objects references occupy one contiguous block. This has the following two benefits:

- Allocating new objects is much quicker because you have no need to search through a linked list to identify a suitable memory location; all that needs to happen is to examine a heap pointer that will tell the CLR where the next free location is.

- The objects on the heap will be closer together in memory, and that means it's likely that fewer page swaps will be necessary in order to access different objects.

These benefits are of course correct and real. Unfortunately, what the Microsoft sales publicity doesn't tell you is the other side to these points.

In the first place, the implicit assumption being made is that identifying free regions in an increasingly scattered heap is the only way that the unmanaged C++ heap can work. It's more correct, however, to say that this is the default behavior for allocating memory in unmanaged C++. However, in C++, if you want to process your memory allocation more efficiently, you can achieve this simply by overriding the C++ new operator for specific data types. Doing this is probably not a sensible option in the most general scenario because of the amount of work involved, but sometimes you as the developer may have specialist knowledge of the objects that will need to be allocated—for example, of their sizes or where they're referenced from, which allows you to code an override to new without too much effort and which gives you some of the same advantages as managed garbage collection. It's also worth pointing out that many developers discussing the garbage collection issue will assume that the C++ heap allocator works simply by scanning a linked list looking for memory until it finds a block big enough and then splits that block. It's quite easy to see how poor performance will become and how hopelessly fragmented the heap would quickly become if you did things this way. Microsoft hasn't documented how the heap works internally, but I'd be extremely surprised if it used such a primitive and poorly performing algorithm. Without going into details, far more sophisticated algorithms are available for managing a C-style heap—something that should be remembered when assessing the benefits of garbage collection.

In the second place, the number of page swaps is ultimately determined by how much virtual memory your application takes up for both its code and its data. Running as managed code could go either way here as far as code size is concerned. On one hand, a managed application brings in mscorlib.dll and various other DLLs—these DLLs aren't small and will have a big effect on virtual memory requirements. On the other hand, if you're running a number of managed applications that all use the same version of the CLR, then these libraries will be loaded only once and shared across all the applications. The result could be a reduction in total memory requirements compared to the situation if all these applications had been written as unmanaged code. The effect on data size is similarly not easy to predict since there are competing factors; however, it's fair to say that sometimes data size will go up. This is because each reference object in .NET has a sync block index, which takes up a word of memory. The sync block index is there in case you need it for multithreaded applications, but in many cases it's not needed. If you have a large number of reference objects, the memory taken by the sync block indexes will build up—and this will be especially noticeable if you have many reference objects that don't have many instance fields, so the sync block will take up a relatively large proportion of the size of the objects. On the other hand, the .NET Framework is more sophisticated in how it packs fields in classes and structs together, which may reduce data size. This effect will be most noticeable in types that mix data of varying sizes (such as int32 and bool). Of course, if you understand how word alignment works (and this is documented in the MSDN documentation), then you can achieve the same size efficiency by taking care to define the fields in your unmanaged types in the appropriate order.

Having said all this, however, it's also worth bearing in mind that modern machines tend to have so much memory that page swapping is no longer normally an issue for small- or medium-sized applications.

On balance, the issue of page swapping could go either way. If the application is going to be running for a long time, and during that time it will be allocating and deallocating very large numbers of objects, then the benefits of the defragmented managed heap will tend to increase.

In the third place, it's worth recalling that the .NET Framework places quite rigid restrictions on the requirements for value and reference types. Managed structs don't support inheritance and give poor performance when used in data structures such as ArrayLists or dictionaries because of boxing issues. Not only that, but the specification of value or reference type is associated with the type. In managed code, it's not possible, for example, to instantiate the same class on the stack sometimes and on the heap at other times. Unmanaged C++ code has no such restrictions. This means that in some cases you may be using referenced types in .NET where in the equivalent unmanaged code you'd simply be using data structures that are allocated on the stack anyway—and clearly that may cancel out some of the benefits of the garbage collector.

JIT Compiler

The JIT compiler is one worry that newcomers to .NET have for performance. If compilation has to be done at runtime, isn't that going to hurt performance? If you're reading this book, then I guess you've already got enough .NET experience to know that, while it's true that JIT compiling does take time, the JIT compiler is well optimized and works very quickly. You'll also be aware that the compiler compiles only those methods that are required, so not all of a large application gets compiled, and each method is normally compiled only once but then may be executed thousands of times. In the next section, I'll go over the operation of the JIT compiler in more depth.

■**Note** JIT compilation may happen more frequently and therefore contribute more to overhead on mobile devices where memory is often more limited. This is because the JIT compiler is sensitive to memory pressures and may discard compiled methods to save memory and then recompile if the method is called again.

Getting the Best from the JIT Compiler

Many programmers are concerned about compiler optimization. Generally speaking, you don't just want your program to run correctly, but you want it to run efficiently so that it's responsive to the user and doesn't unnecessarily hog processor time or system resources. And this area has been of particular concern to C++ developers, who generally expend the extra effort required to write the code in C++ at least partly in order to gain the claimed performance benefits. Microsoft has countered the argument that the machine cycles taken by JIT compilation will slow the process down by arguing that not only has the JIT compiler been designed to be highly efficient, but it can perform additional optimizations that classic compilers will not able to do. In particular, the JIT compiler knows which machine the application will run on and can therefore perform optimizations specific to that processor. Indeed, Microsoft has argued that this is one reason why JIT-compiled code may one day run faster than native executable code. With hindsight, it certainly seems that the initial fears of many developers at the time of .NET's release that the JIT compiler would significantly affect performance have largely been unfounded.

I'll now discuss how the JIT optimizes your code and show you how you can, to some extent, control the optimizations performed.

Some JIT Optimizations

In this section, I'll review the specific optimizations that the JIT compiler is likely to actually perform on your code.

Before I go onto the actual optimizations, I should stress that the optimizations performed by the JIT compiler are fairly low-level ones—the sort of optimization where you move a variable initialization outside a loop, for example. Those optimizations can affect performance, but it's not often that the effect is particularly dramatic. For most cases, if you want to maximize performance, you're better off looking at higher-level aspects of your program: whether you define a type as a class or a struct, what algorithms you use, and so on. I'll go over what you can do in this regard in detail soon. My reasoning for explaining the low-level optimizations the JIT compiler performs in detail is partly to reassure you that these kinds of optimizations are being done and partly to make it clear that these are optimizations you shouldn't do yourself—because the JIT compiler can do them better. For example, don't waste your time worrying about exactly where to initialize that variable—your time is better spent elsewhere.

■**Tip** I advise against taking the details of specific optimizations in this section as gospel. Microsoft hasn't extensively documented the JIT compiler optimizations for the obvious reason that this is an internal implementation that could change at any time. You can be fairly sure that as newer versions of the compiler become available, more optimizations will be added. I guess it's even possible some optimizations may be removed if they turn out to take longer to process than is worthwhile from the resultant performance improvements. I've pieced the material in this section together from the few snippets of documentation that are available, from a few brief words with Microsoft developers at conferences, and from looking at the native assembly produced by small IL programs. Also, don't assume this list is exhaustive even in .NET version 1.*x*—it almost certainly isn't. But it should give you an idea of what you can expect from the JIT compiler.

For simplicity I'll present these examples in C# rather than IL, even though the actual optimizations will be performed at the IL level.

Evaluating Constant Expressions

The JIT compiler will evaluate constant expressions. In other words, the IL equivalent of this code:

```
int x = 5;
int y = x * 2;
```

will be optimized to the equivalent of this:

```
int x = 5;
int y = 10;
```

Using Registers

The JIT compiler is fairly aggressive in its use of registers to store local variables or frequently used items of data. To explain the significance of this, I need to explain something about the actual architecture of a modern processor. Processors, in a very heavily simplified form, look roughly as shown in Figure 6-1.

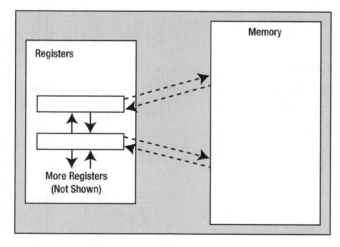

Figure 6-1. *Typical processor architecture*

In this figure, the arrows indicate possible paths for data flow. Solid arrow tails indicate very fast data flow, and dashed arrow tails indicate slower data flow.

Data is stored in two places: memory and registers. In general, variables are stored in memory, but most arithmetic operations will be carried out in the registers. To this extent, you'll notice that the IL virtual machine model, in which data can be operated on only once that data has been moved to the evaluation stack, has similarities to actual machine architecture (these similarities help to explain why JIT compilation can be so fast). The registers differ from the conceptual evaluation stack in that they're each of a fixed size and are usually designed to hold one number (although array-based registers are becoming more common, especially inside graphics cards). There may typically be 10 to 20 registers—as newer machines are released, the numbers are gradually increasing. Some registers are wired up for floating-point arithmetic, and others are for integers. But the point is that operations that involve only the registers are extremely fast. The JIT compiler takes advantage of this by storing a few selected local variables in the registers. According to the documentation, it will perform some analysis of your code to determine which data would be best placed there. Note, however, that this has a couple of restrictions. In particular, it's not possible to take the address of a register, so if your IL code attempts to take the address of any data, then that data has to be stored somewhere in normal memory. Hence, objects will always be stored in normal memory, though the object references can be in stored in registers. (But since a register is designed to store a single number, it wouldn't be practical to store an actual object in one anyway.)

Reusing Results of Expressions

The JIT compiler can reuse results from expressions. This means that this code:

```
int x = 43 * z;
int y = 43 * z;
```

would be optimized to the equivalent of this:

```
int x = y = 43 * z;
```

Moving Unchanging Expressions Outside Loops

If the JIT compiler detects that an expression that can't change is being repeatedly evaluated in a loop, it will move it outside the loop. Thus, this code:

```
for (int i=0; i<myArray.Length; i++)
   DoSomething(i);
```

would probably be optimized to something like this:

```
int len = myArray.Length;
for (int i=0; i<len; i++)
   DoSomething(i);
```

Inlining Methods

This is an important area, since inlining methods is one low-level optimization that can make a significant difference. The philosophy of the JIT compiler here is different from that in unmanaged C++. In C++, the original idea was that the developer got to choose whether a function should be inlined by declaring it in the source code as an `inline` function.

```
// C++ code
inline int GetWidth();
```

This was a flexible system—it worked well and fitted in with the feeling among C++ developers that they knew which functions were going to be called extensively and therefore which were suitable candidates for inlining. However, despite this perception, it's worth remembering that the C++ inline keyword was a suggestion rather than a command, and as C++ compilers have become more sophisticated, they've increasingly tended to ignore inline requests and instead made their own judgments about which methods should or shouldn't be inlined.

.NET has taken this trend to its logical conclusion, in which the compiler is the sole arbiter of what should be inlined. The JIT compiler doesn't support any ability for source files to express a preference for inlining methods: No equivalent of the inline keyword exists in C# or VB, and in C++ it's illegal to use inline for a member of a managed type. Instead, the JIT compiler decides for itself which methods are suitable candidates for inlining. According to Microsoft, it does this aggressively and will inline a large number of functions. So if you have something like this:

```
area = SomeObject.Width * SomeObject.Height;
```

where Width is defined like this:

```
int Width { get { return width; } }
```

and Height is defined similarly, then the JIT compiler will probably compile it into the equivalent of this:

```
area = SomeObject.width * SomeObject.height;
```

This has a limitation, though. Although the JIT compiler may inline aggressively in some cases, it still has its own time constraints, and it won't inline if that's going to take significant time to do. As a result of this, in version 1.*x* the JIT compiler will not inline any method that occupies more than 32 bytes. Thirty-two may sound a lot, until you realize that a simple call instruction occupies 5 bytes (one for the opcode and four for the MethodDef token). You don't have to put much code in a method before it exceeds 32 bytes! I can't help thinking this means a lot of methods in .NET code must exist that are called from inside loops and that ought to be inlined (and would be inlined in the unmanaged C++ model) but that aren't in the .NET Framework.

■Note It should also go without saying that virtual methods called using the IL callvirt instruction aren't inlined. This is no different from the situation in unmanaged C++, for which virtual methods aren't inlined—because it's difficult to tell until the method is actually invoked which override of the method is to be called. In principle, it's not impossible to inline virtual methods—some sophisticated algorithms have been developed, which a compiler could theoretically use to work out at JIT compile time which version of a method is to be called, but I'm not aware of any plans to incorporate this kind of algorithm into the Microsoft's JIT compiler.

On the subject of inlining, I should also mention that the JIT compiler can't inline in a couple of other places.

- Calls to methods in other assemblies in most circumstances. Inlining across assemblies is more problematic than inlining within assemblies for obvious reasons, though it's possible in some cases.

- Calls to methods that cross security boundaries. Inlining methods in this case would lead to the unfortunate situation where one instruction in some method may have different security privileges from the next instruction in the same method, after inlining; it's difficult to write algorithms to manage security that can deal with that, so the compiler won't inline in this situation.

- IL does define a `noinlining` flag—methods marked with this flag will not be inlined.

C and C++ developers will probably be thinking that nothing is particularly exciting here—C and C++ compilers have been routinely doing these kinds of optimizations and much more besides for years. Not only that, but C++ compilers generally have a lot of time at compile time in which to do sophisticated optimizations, and the design of the JIT compiler has to take account of performance while optimizing, which restricts what it can do. The previous list should nevertheless convince you that optimizations are taking place in your code, even if they aren't up to the C++ standard in some respects.

Another issue is that because the JIT compiler has runtime knowledge that isn't accessible to a classic compiler, it can perform extra optimizations. I've already mentioned some of the optimizations Microsoft has claimed in principle that could be done here. These include the following:

- Optimizations based on analyzing the actual execution flow through the program after the program has been running for a while.

- Optimizations based on using machine instructions specific to the actual hardware on which the program is running.

- Certain addresses that aren't known at compile time will be known at runtime. This means that the JIT compiler may be able to replace certain addresses that are coded as variables with constants and then to perform the usual optimizations associated with constants; it may also in some cases be possible to reduce the level of indirection.

Although these optimizations are possible in principle, it's not completely clear which are actually implemented in version 1.x and which may be implemented in future. The likelihood seems to be that the only optimization that's based on runtime knowledge and that as yet is actually implemented is that of replacing addresses.

NGen

Before leaving the subject of the JIT optimizations, it's worth saying a couple of words about ngen.exe. Microsoft has of course provided the native code generator, ngen.exe, as a utility that can precompile your JIT code, leaving an executable that contains roughly the native code you'd get from JIT compiling. Because of this, it's tempting to assume that if you ngen your applications before deploying them, they'll run faster. If you do think that, in most cases you'd be wrong. The problem is that ngen uses the same algorithms as the JIT compiler, but it can't perform as many optimizations because it doesn't have all the runtime information that the JIT compiler has. For example, ngen doesn't know where dependent assemblies are going to be loaded in memory, which means that many cross-assembly calls will have to get ngen'd into code that has an extra level of indirection. And the benefit of not having to JIT compile each method happens only once, and that method may get executed many times, each time without all the optimizations the JIT compiler could have supplied. Some people at Microsoft seem to be of the opinion that ngen'd code is likely in most cases to run a couple of percents slower than code that's JIT compiled in the normal way. Also bear in mind that the ngen'd executable can't be executed on its own—the CLR always expects to load the original assembly first, and the CLR may decide to re-JIT the assembly anyway if it has any reason to suspect the ngen'd file is out-of-date. Not only that, but if your application contains a large amount of code that's never executed, then this code would in the normal course of events never be JIT compiled. But if the application has been ngen'd, then all this code will have been compiled to native executable, which may considerably increase the size of the executable file to be loaded. The native ngen'd file itself is placed in a special area of the assembly cache.

In general, the main reason to ngen code is if your application needs to execute a large amount of startup code once and you think a large startup time is likely to annoy the users—in that case, supplying an ngen'd file may reduce startup time. If you suspect that may be the case for your software, then you should experiment to see whether running ngen on your application will reduce startup time. If you're merely looking for general performance improvements, then my advice would usually be to not use ngen.

Controlling JIT Optimization

In this section I'll explain how you can turn JIT optimizing on or off—it's actually more complex than you may think.

■**Caution** I should say at the outset that, beyond specifying the appropriate flags to instruct the compilers to optimize your code, you can't do much to assist in low-level code optimization. As far as this area is concerned, you're better off viewing the JIT compiler as a black box that handles everything itself and—Microsoft claims—does it better than you could ever do by hand. This section will show how the few flags that are available to control optimization work.

The main difference between .NET compilation and unmanaged compilation to a native executable is of course that for managed code compilation can happen at two stages—compiling from a high-level language to IL and JIT compiling the IL. As you found in Chapter 2, examining the IL produced—at least by the C# and VB .NET compilers—suggests that these compilers rely on the JIT compiler for the bulk of the optimizations. The high-level language compilers themselves (other than the C++ one) will in general perform no more than the most elementary optimizations.

The JIT compiler has the following two options when it compiles your IL:

- It can choose whether to optimize as it converts the IL to native executable.

- It can choose whether to generate tracking information that allows debuggers to figure out which IL instruction corresponds to a given native executable command being executed. This tracking information doesn't have a significant effect on performance but can be important for debugging purposes.

A separate issue also exists—that of whether a program database (.pdb file) should be generated to accompany the assembly. The .pdb file contains information concerning the names of symbols in your source code, as well as which IL instructions correspond to which source code commands. Clearly the presence of this file is essential for debuggers to be able to work at a source code level. However, the .pdb file is entirely separate from the assembly, is of no concern to the JIT compiler, and has no impact on optimization. The .pdb file, if present, will have been generated by the front-end compiler (for example, the C# or VB compiler or ilasm.exe), so the JIT compiler has no control over its presence.

In general, when you're doing a release build you'll want to optimize. When debugging, you'll want nonoptimized code with tracking information (and a .pdb file). Whether you ask for tracking information in a release build isn't such a firm issue. The conventional wisdom would be to not. Personally, I'd be inclined to generate it on the grounds that if some bug later occurs on a client machine and you have trouble reproducing the bug on your system, then you're going to need all the help you can get in tracking down the bug. A small chance exists that in a year you'll be extremely glad you generated tracking information. However, I strongly suggest you don't ship .pdb files, since they contain information about your source code that for obvious confidentiality reasons you won't want to be available to clients.

Tip Although for confidentiality reasons you may not want to ship .pdb files, one situation exists in which shipping nonoptimized executables with .pdb files can be useful: if you're running an ASP.NET Web site, and you have sufficient machine power to cope with any performance losses from running debug software. In this situation, provided you take care with your IIS settings, users can't view the executable directly, so there's no confidentiality issues. I've used this tactic on some sites that I've coded, and the time I've saved from being able to quickly track down the source code at which bugs, in particular unexpected exceptions, have occurred made the decision well worthwhile. Of course, if you're using that tactic, make sure you set up IIS to prevent users from downloading the .pdb files or the DLLs!

The choices the JIT compiler makes are actually determined by information in the assembly itself, in particular by the presence or absence of the assembly-level attribute, System.Diagnostics.DebuggableAttribute.

Using the Debuggable Attribute

In C# terms, the syntax for declaring this attribute is this:

```
[assembly: Debuggable(true, true)]
```

DebuggableAttribute has two properties: IsTrackingEnabled and IsJITOptimizerDisabled—these respectively form the first and second parameters in the attribute's constructor. The previous declaration sets both these properties to true, which means that tracking information will be generated, and optimization will be disabled—the classic debug situation. For a release build, the conventional wisdom would be to set the debugger attribute, like this:

```
[assembly: Debuggable(false, false)]
```

This code sets IsJITOptimizerDisabled to false, which means optimizing isn't disabled (that is, the JIT compiler will optimize). The double negative is a little unfortunate, but it at least means that the two classic debug and release scenarios have easy-to-remember syntaxes.

■**Tip** If this attribute isn't present in your assembly, then the JIT compiler will assume that it must optimize and shouldn't generate tracking information. In other words, the classic release scenario is the default.

Although I've presented the code to illustrate the attribute syntax, in most cases you won't explicitly declare the Debuggable attribute in your source code but instead will use compiler options to have this attribute placed in the assembly. The actual situation for what compilation options give what results isn't totally clear-cut, so you may find you need to experiment a bit to get the precise results you want. I'll take the case of C# and version 1.*x* of the CLR to illustrate the main points—the situation is similar in other languages.

If you compile from the command line, specifying the /o+ flag (csc /o+ MyProgram.cs) to turn on optimizations, then the compiler won't add the Debuggable attribute. By default, this means you'll get optimized code without tracking information. Because the compiler doesn't add the Debuggable attribute, however, you're free to define it yourself in the source code. For example, if your code contains this:

```
[assembly:Debuggable(true, false)]
```

and you compile with /o+, then you'll get optimized code that has tracking information in it. This is what I hinted earlier I'd be inclined to do.

If you compile without any options (or equivalently, specifying /o-), then the compiler will automatically insert [assembly:Debuggable(true, false)] to your assembly, resulting in code that isn't optimized but also doesn't have tracking information—so you can't debug it. This is arguably the most useless possible scenario. Not only that, but in this case it's not possible for you to separately define the Debuggable attribute in your source code with your own preferences specified, since the compiler will just complain that this attribute isn't allowed to be present twice.

If you compile specifying the /debug flag, the compiler will generate a program database file, ProgramName.pdb, and will also insert extra IL code into the assembly that assists with debugging. This extra code may itself slow the application down considerably, quite apart from the effect of not having optimization. Not only that, but this flag appears to override any choice you may make in the /o flag and forces the compiler to add [assembly:Debuggable (true,true)] to the assembly—so you always get an unoptimized build with tracking information—this is the sensible choice for most debugging scenarios, but it's unfortunate that you can't change this preference if for some reason you do need to do so. Again in this case, you'll get a compilation error if your source code contains an explicit Debuggable attribute declaration that conflicts with the one the compiler inserts.

If you're using VS .NET instead of the command line, similar principles hold, except that, short of editing your project properties, you have even less control over the compilation flags. Table 6-1 summarizes the main options you have using VS .NET.

Table 6-1. *Optimization Options When Using VS .NET*

To Achieve This...			Do This...
IL Containing Extra Debug Code and a .pdb File?	**JIT Optimizes?**	**Tracking Information?**	
Yes	No	Yes	Compile in debug mode.
Yes	Any other choice		Compile in release mode, but make sure the Debug symbol is #defined (you won't get a .pdb file).
No	Yes	No	Compile in release mode.
No	Any other choice		Compile in release mode, but declare the Debuggable attribute in your source code with your choices.

One other extra point is that you may separately have a symbol such as Debug #defined in your code, in order to conditionally compile extra source code instructions. If you do, any such symbol works independently of the compilation and optimization options I've been discussing.

In the end, as long as you're doing a conventional debug or release build, you have no problem. If you have slightly different requirements, you'll have to think carefully about how to arrange your build process.

Introducing the PerfTest Sample

I'll now present a short sample program that illustrates the use of the Debuggable attribute and JIT optimization. The sample uses reflection to check whether its own assembly contains the Debuggable attribute and if so displays the results. Then it enters two loops in succession. For the first loop it accesses an int property of a class and does some repetitive processing on it inside the loop, using the System.DateTime class to measure how long the whole loop takes. Then it does the same thing but instead of using the property, it directly accesses the underlying field. The theory is that if you're not optimizing, then going through the property should take longer, but if you're allowing the JIT compiler to optimize, then it really ought to inline a simple property call, and in that case you'll see the two loops taking roughly the same amount of time. You'll do two things with the sample: First, you'll run it with and without JIT optimization and examine the execution times to see what effect optimizing has. Second, you'll use the cordbg debugger to hack into and examine the actual native code generated by the JIT compiler, so you can see in detail just what the JIT compiler is doing in terms of optimizing.

So let's look at the sample. To start with, this is the class containing the property and field that the code is going to access:

```
class TestClass
{
   public int x;

   public int X
   {
      get
      {
         return x;
      }
      set
      {
         x = value;
      }
   }
}
```

As you can see, it's a carefully designed class, which strictly follows all the best practices about giving descriptive, meaningful names to items and never defining public fields!

Now for the loop that accesses the property: The following method is defined in the same class that contains the Main() method. I've called this class EntryPoint.

```
static void ProfileProperty(int numIters)
{
   TestClass test = new TestClass();
   DateTime startTime, endTime;
   startTime = DateTime.Now;
   for (int i=0; i<numIters; i++)
   {
      test.X += i;
      test.X /= 2;
   }
   endTime = DateTime.Now;
   Console.WriteLine("Using property: " + (endTime - startTime).ToString());
   Console.WriteLine(test.X);
}
```

In the ProfileProperty() method, the loop continually adds the loop counter to the property and then divides by two. Notice that I've carefully designed the loop to make sure that you have to keep explicitly accessing the property, so any inlining will have maximum impact.

The code for the field is similar apart from the obvious difference of accessing test.x instead of test.X.

```
static void ProfileField(int numIters)
{
```

```
        TestClass test = new TestClass();
        DateTime startTime, endTime;
        startTime = DateTime.Now;
        for (int i=0 ; i < numIters ; i++)
        {
            test.x += i;
            test.x /= 2;
        }
        endTime = DateTime.Now;
        Console.WriteLine("Using field: " + (endTime - startTime).ToString());
        Console.WriteLine(test.x);
}
```

Finally, here's how I display the DebuggableAttribute and invoke the profiling loops:

```
static void Main(string[] args)
{
    // Find out whether the CLR thinks optimizations
    // are supposed to be on or off
    Assembly asm = Assembly.GetExecutingAssembly();
    object[] attrs = asm.GetCustomAttributes(typeof(DebuggableAttribute),
                                             false);
    if (attrs != null && attrs.Length >= 1)
    {
        for (int i=0; i<attrs.Length; i++)
        {
            DebuggableAttribute da = attrs[i] as DebuggableAttribute;
            Console.WriteLine("IsJITOptimizerDisabled: {0}",
                            da.IsJITOptimizerDisabled );
            Console.WriteLine("IsJITTrackingEnabled: {0}",
                            da.IsJITTrackingEnabled);
        }
    }
    else
        Console.WriteLine("DebuggableAttribute not present.");

    int numIters = 100000000;
    ProfileProperty(numIters);
    ProfileField(numIters);
    ProfileProperty(numIters);
    ProfileField(numIters);
}
```

You may wonder why I've called each loop twice. It just provides an extra check on the results and also eliminates any effects because of the time the JIT compiler takes to compile the code the first time around each loop. I don't seriously believe the JIT compile time is going to be of any significance for such a small piece of code and a loop that iterates 100 million times, but if I don't double-check, I can guarantee someone will come back to me saying, "Your test isn't valid because of the JIT compile time."

Now you'll see the results. If I do a nonoptimizing compile, like so:

```
C:\ExpertDotNet\Performance>csc perftest.cs /o-
Microsoft (R) Visual C# .NET Compiler version 7.10.3052.4
for Microsoft (R) .NET Framework version 1.1.4322
Copyright (C) Microsoft Corporation 2001-2002. All rights reserved.

C:\ExpertDotNet\Performance>perftest
IsJITOptimizerDisabled: True
IsJITTrackingEnabled: False
Using property: 00:00:01.0815552
99999998
Using field: 00:00:00.9814112
99999998
Using property: 00:00:01.1015840
99999998
Using field: 00:00:00.9713968
99999998
```

then this shows the presence of the Debuggable attribute, and you can clearly see that the code takes longer when the code is using the property, as expected. Now I'll do the same thing but enabling JIT optimizations and not changing anything else.

```
C:\ExpertDotNet\Performance>csc /o+ perftest.cs
Microsoft (R) Visual C# .NET Compiler version 7.10.3052.4
for Microsoft (R) .NET Framework version 1.1.4322
Copyright (C) Microsoft Corporation 2001-2002. All rights reserved.

C:\ExpertDotNet\Performance>perftest
DebuggableAttribute not present.
Using property: 00:00:00.9413536
99999998
Using field: 00:00:00.9814112
99999998
Using property: 00:00:00.9413536
99999998
Using field: 00:00:00.9713968
99999998
```

These results show that the time using the field hasn't changed, but amazingly, the time to access the property has not only improved but is now even better than the time using the field!

What does this prove? I should point out that performance results can be hard to reproduce exactly. The previous results are typical of quite a few runs on my machine (an Athlon single-processor machine), but you may find you get different results on your machine. While I was investigating optimization, I ran not only the `perftest` sample but also various variants of it quite a lot of times. The results overall showed me that JIT optimizing has some beneficial effect, though it tends to be of the order of percentage points—I'm not talking about doubling the speed or anything dramatic like that. Remember too that I've carefully engineered this sample to emphasize the effects of inlining a single property. It's unlikely that real production code would have such an obvious example for optimization that would have such a significant effect on the entire program; in that context, the apparent performance improvements shown here don't look overly great. Of course, one small sample isn't necessarily characteristic of a larger, "real" application, and optimizing is a pretty rough science that's full of unpredictable results.

You still have the puzzle of why accessing via the property appeared to be *faster* than via the field with optimization: On the face of it, this makes no sense. I'll show you the native executable code that generated the previous results next, and you'll see then that the generated native code is slightly different for accessing via a property, even when optimized. The differences you'll see don't really account for the speed difference—the property accessor code actually looks marginally slower when looking at the raw executable instructions. However, it's possible that a small program such as this could be affected by byte alignment issues on the actual hardware (which wouldn't be so important on a larger application, since any such effects would be more likely to average out over the entire program). This, however, confirms how low-level optimizations can easily be swamped by other effects.

Examining Native Code

I'll now work through the actual native executable instructions generated by the JIT compiler for the `perftest` sample. I'll do this by running the sample in a debugger, setting breakpoints in the `ProfileProperty()` and `ProfileField()` methods, and examining the surrounding native code. To do this, however, I need a `.pdb` file; otherwise I won't be able to use the source code to set breakpoints. That looks at first sight like an insuperable problem, since you saw earlier that generating a `.pdb` file in C# will automatically disable optimizations—and I specifically want to examine optimized code. Fortunately, the `cordbg` command-line debugger can come to your rescue here. `cordbg` has the ability to control the JIT settings and can instruct the JIT compiler to generate optimized code irrespective of what the assembly attributes placed in the assembly by the C# compiler may be. This means you can debug at a source-code level but still be running optimized code.

■**Tip** It's of course possible to use VS .NET to examine the native executable code, and using the techniques I discussed in Chapter 2, you can even match native executable statements to IL statements, but I'm going to stick with `cordbg` here just to make absolutely certain the native code is fully optimized.

To examine the optimized version of `perftest.exe`, you compile the code at the command line, specifying the `/debug` flag to ensure that a program database `.pdb` file is generated. I've also specified `/o+` on the basis that it can't do any harm and just in case this makes any difference to the assembly.

csc /o+ /debug+ perftest.cs

Then I run `cordbg` and issue the command `mode jit 1`; this tells `cordbg` to allow JIT optimizations (overriding any settings placed in the file when the source code was compiled).

C:\ExpertDotNet\Performance\PerfTest>cordbg perftest
```
Microsoft (R) Common Language Runtime Test Debugger Shell Version 1.1.4322.573
Copyright (C) Microsoft Corporation 1998-2002. All rights reserved.

(cordbg) run perftest
Process 4036/0xfc4 created.
Warning: couldn't load symbols for
c:\windows\microsoft.net\framework\v1.1.4322\mscorlib.dll
[thread 0xd2c] Thread created.

015:                         Assembly asm = Assembly.GetExecutingAssembly();
```
(cordbg) mode jit 1
```
JITs will produce optimized code
```

Now I'm ready to set breakpoints and examine the code (note that the instruction `dis` is the instruction you need to type in at the `cordbg` command prompt to show the disassembled native code).

To keep things as simple as possible, I'll show only the code for the actual loop that occupies the time. In other words, the loop in the `ProfileFields()` method is shown in bold:

```
static void ProfileProperty(int numIters)
{
   TestClass test = new TestClass();
   DateTime startTime, endTime;
   startTime = DateTime.Now;
   for (int i=0 ; i < numIters ; i++)
   {
     test.x += i;
     test.x /= 2;
   }
```

Now, although this is an advanced book, I'm not assuming you're familiar with native assembly code. However, native assembly isn't that different from disassembled IL code, so I've presented the native code here but with enough explanation that you should be able to see what's happening.

To make things as simple as possible, Table 6-2 shows the native code for this method (with JIT optimizations)—I've added comments with brief explanations of the instructions.

Table 6-2. *Native Code for the Loop in the* ProfileProperty() *Method*

Instruction		Effect
[002e] xor	ecx,ecx	i = 0;
[0030] cmp	edi,0	Checks if numIters <= 0; if so, jumps out to next instruction following loop
[0033] jle	00000017	
[0035] add	dword ptr[esi+4],ecx	test.x += i;
[0038] mov	eax,dword ptr[esi+4]	Copies test.x into the EAX register
[003b] sar	eax,1	Divides register contents by 2
[003d] jns	00000005	
[003f] adc	eax,0	
[0042] mov	dword ptr[esi+4],eax	Stores result back in test.x
[0045] inc	ecx	++i;
[0046] cmp	ecx,edi	Checks if i < numIters; if that's the case, jumps back to the start of the loop (the add instruction)
[0048] jl	FFFFFFED	

■**Tip** Bear in mind that the JIT compiler will emit different code on different hardware. The previous code is what I obtained on my Athlon machine—but don't necessarily expect the same results on your computer.

The hexadecimal number in the square brackets that precedes each instruction is simply the relative offset of that instruction in the procedure (yes, even native executable has the concept of procedures that you call and return from, although native procedures are rather more primitive than their IL or high-level language equivalents). The actual instruction consists of the instruction itself (represented by a mnemonic, just as in IL assembly), possibly followed by one or two operands. Where two operands exists, the first one is always the *destination*, and the second is always the *source*. The operand may be a constant hex number or the name of a register. If the operand appears in square brackets, then it means the operand is a pointer to be dereferenced. A couple of examples from the previous code should make all this clearer. Let's look at the first xor instruction:

```
xor    ecx,ecx
```

Now xor is the instruction to perform a bitwise exclusive OR operation. It will take the destination and source (the two operands), XOR them together, and store the results in the first operand (the destination). The previous instruction has the same destination and source: Both operands are indicated to be the contents of a register known as the ECX register. Using the same operand twice may look odd but is actually a clever trick to zero out a register. If you XOR any number with itself, the result is always zero. So the effect of the previous instruction is to store zero in the ECX register. ECX is the location that happens to be used in this procedure to store the variable i, so this instruction is the assembly equivalent of i=0; aside from the clever trick of initializing to zero without actually having to load the constant zero from anywhere, what you see here is an example in action of the JIT compiler optimizing by using registers to store local variables.

As another example, look at that first add instruction:

```
add    dword ptr[esi+4],ecx
```

You won't be surprised to learn that add takes the two operands, adds them together, and stores the result in the first (destination) operand. Understanding the second operand is easy—it's the ECX register, corresponding to the variable i. The first operand is in brackets, so it's an address to be dereferenced. It actually turns out to be the field test.x. The variable test, like i, is stored in a register—in this case a register called ESI. However, test itself is just an object reference. Now recall from Chapter 2 that the address stored in an object reference is actually the address of the method table of the object. The first actual field of the object is stored 4 bytes (one word) later. dword ptr[esi + 4] identifies this field, since it takes the contents of ESI, adds four to it, and then dereferences the resultant address in memory. So the add instruction adds the contents of ECX to the value stored at that location in memory and then stores the result back to that same memory location. Amazingly, you have the complete encoding of the C# statement test.x += i; in one native executable instruction! This feat is even more impressive when you consider that this operation will have been represented in IL by several instructions. This kind of efficiency should start to give you an idea of the potential capabilities of the JIT compiler.

Now let's run through the code for the loop. I've already indicated that, of the local variables, i is stored in the register ECX and the test reference in the register ESI. You also need to be aware that the argument numIters is stored in a register called EDI. (This choice of registers isn't magical—it simply happens to be the registers the JIT compiler chose for this particular code.) After initializing i to zero, the code examines numIters to see if it's less than or equal to zero. If that's the case, the loop shouldn't get executed at all. You normally think of a for loop as having the condition for continuing the loop at the start of each iteration. The code generated by the JIT compiler works a bit differently: it places the test at the end of each iteration, with an additional test before you first enter the loop to see if the loop should be executed at all.

Assuming the execution flow is in the loop, the computer first executes that add instruction to add i onto test.x. Then it needs to divide test.x by two. The code for the division is more complex—and the actual division is performed on an in-register copy of the data. The test.x value is first copied into a register called the EAX register (that's the mov instruction). Instead of dividing by two, the JIT compiler has gone for right-shifting the value (that's the sar instruction). However, sar may in principle introduce an error if a one got shifted into the high-value bit of the register. The following jns and adc instructions check for this and correct if necessary. Presumably the reasoning here is that right-shifting is faster than doing a full division, even after checking for errors. Finally, the new contents of EAX are copied back into the memory location that holds the test.x field.

Finally, the code must test to see if it needs to go around the loop again. It increments i (or ECX, depending how you look at it), tests whether the result is less than numIters and, if it is, jumps back to the start of the loop.

So that's the loop for the field. Now let's see what happens when the code has to deal with a property. In other words, what does the JIT compiler generate that corresponds to this C# code?

```
for (int i=0; i<numIters; i++)
{
   test.X += i;
   test.X /= 2;
}
```

In fact, despite the optimizations, the code generated on my machine *isn't* identical to that for the field access. Examining the native code shows that the calls to the X property have indeed been optimized into straight field accessors, but a couple of minor differences exist in how the registers are used (though these differences are unlikely to significantly impact execution times). Here's the optimized native code for the previous loop. The instructions that are different from those in the previous loop are shown in bold.

```
[002f] xor    edx,edx
[0031] cmp    edi,0
[0034] jle    0000001C
[0036] mov    eax,dword ptr[esi+4]
[0039] add    eax,edx
[003b] mov    dword ptr[esi+4],eax
[003e] mov    eax,dword ptr[esi+4]
[0041] sar    eax,1
[0043] jns    00000005
[0045] adc    eax,0
[0048] mov    dword ptr[esi+4],eax
[004b] inc    edx
[004c] cmp    edx,edi
[004e] jl     FFFFFFE8
```

Some of the changes compared to the previous code represent the relatively trivial facts that i is now stored in the register EDX rather than ECX and that the relative offsets in the jle and jl branch instructions are different because the number of bytes occupied by the instructions in the new loop is slightly greater. The significant difference is in the treatment of the test.x field. For a start, instead of adding i to this field in memory, the field is first copied into the EAX register (the first mov instruction), where the contents of EDX (= i) are added to it. The result is immediately copied back to test.x in the following mov instruction—rather senselessly in this case, since the value will get overwritten again a couple of instructions later. Even more senselessly, this same value is then copied back from test.x into the EAX register again! After that, the code carries on as for the ProfileField() method.

So what can you learn from this? Well, evidently, the JIT compiler has optimized the property accessor away, but in the process it's missed a couple of other possible optimizations having to do with copying data. Future versions of the JIT compiler will probably improve on that performance, but in the meantime it's clear that code gets optimized to a reasonable extent.

Finally, just for comparison, here's the native code for the same for loop, in the ProfileProperty() method, but with JIT optimizations switched off:

```
[004c] mov    dword ptr[ebp-1Ch],0
[0053] nop
[0054] jmp    00000045
[0056] mov    edi,ebx     (This is where we jump back to)
[0058] mov    ecx,ebx
[005a] cmp    dword ptr[ecx],ecx
[005c] call   dword ptr ds:[003F5298h]
[0062] mov    esi,eax
[0064] mov    edx,dword ptr[ebp-1Ch]
[0067] add    esi,edx
[0069] mov    edx,esi
[006b] mov    ecx,edi
[006d] cmp    dword ptr[ecx],ecx
[006f] call   dword ptr ds:[003F529Ch]
[0075] mov    esi,ebx
[0077] mov    ecx,ebx
[0079] cmp    dword ptr[ecx],ecx
[007b] call   dword ptr ds:[003F5298h]
[0081] mov    edi,eax
[0083] sar    edi,1
[0085] jns    00000005
[0087] adc    edi,0
[008a] mov    edx,edi
[008c] mov    ecx,esi
[008e] cmp    dword ptr[ecx],ecx
[0090] call   dword ptr ds:[003F529Ch]
[0096] inc    dword ptr[ebp-1Ch]
[0099] mov    eax,dword ptr[ebp-1Ch]
[009c] cmp    eax,dword ptr[ebp-4]
[009f] jl     FFFFFFB7
```

I won't go over this code in detail, but you can see that not only is it a lot longer but that the four call statements (instructions 005c, 006f, 007b, and 0090) that invoke the test.X property are clearly visible. Two of these calls invoke the get accessor, and the other two invoke the set accessor. Clearly you can pay a heavy price for not optimizing!

I haven't shown the native assembly code for the loop in ProfileField() without optimizations, since it's virtually identical to the code with optimizations.

Performance Tips

This is where I get to cover what I suspect you've been waiting for most of this chapter—a list of specific things you can do to improve performance in your managed applications.

First some general points: for developers concerned about optimizing managed code, much of the advice largely remains the same as it did before the days of .NET.

- Turn on compiler optimizations when you've finished debugging and are close to ship-ping. (And of course—this is very important—make sure you do a final debug of your code in the optimized configuration so those Debug preprocessor symbols and condi-tionally compiled function calls didn't have some side effect you hadn't noticed. Although it's unlikely to affect managed code, certain rare situations exist in which bugs in your code, such as certain buffer overruns, can be masked in debug builds and appear only when the code is optimized.)

- Profile your code to identify for certain which routines are the ones eating processor time and if necessary rewrite the code just for those routines. (I'll cover profiling in the next chapter.) Without profiling, it's easy to guess which method you think is using the time, guess wrong, and then waste development time optimizing some code that's not actually going to make any difference to your application.

- Performing low-level optimizations manually has no point (such as inlining a small method or moving a variable declaration from inside to outside a loop). Virtually all compilers these days are pretty smart and will do all that stuff quite happily themselves without any help from you. The optimizations you should be thinking about are high-level ones (not drawing unnecessarily or using an appropriate algorithm for the task at hand).

You may be able to carry out one additional step for managed code—which is to pass your assemblies through a commercial obfuscator. The real purpose of an obfuscator is to make assemblies harder to decompile by—among other things—mangling private and internal type and variable names. However, some obfuscators are also able to optimize memory layout and reduce name lengths, which makes the assemblies smaller. This is unlikely to affect the time to run the file significantly, but it may be important if your assem-blies are intended to be downloaded on an intranet or the Internet and time to download is a significant factor in performance.

I'll now conclude the chapter by presenting some miscellaneous tips for performance that are worth bearing in mind when writing your source code. Since not all tips are relevant to all languages, I indicate in each section title to which of the three main high-level Microsoft languages the tip mostly applies.

Don't Waste Time on Optimizing (All Languages)

I know I've said this already, but you should remember that your development time and code robustness are important—often more important than performance. Users tend not to be impressed by applications that run like lightning and present the results they wanted before they have even had a chance to blink, immediately followed by an Unhandled Exception dialog box. Yeah, I know, users are fussy. But they're your customers.

Remember too that the biggest killers of performance are usually the following:

- Network calls

- Page swapping

- Inappropriate algorithms and data structures

In most cases, the detailed low-level flow of your code has a relatively minor effect compared to these factors. In most cases, you don't have to go through your code with a fine-tooth comb trying to pick out places where you can improve the performance by changing your control flow, and so on. All you're probably doing is wasting your time (as well as creating code that may look more complex and therefore is less maintainable). You can improve code performance by making sure you minimize network calls, keep your working set down to reasonable levels, and use appropriate algorithms (for example, don't use a bubble sort to sort 50,000 words). To a lesser extent it also helps to minimize calls that don't go across processes but that do cross managed-unmanaged or application domain boundaries. Also, I can't emphasize enough that if your code isn't performing satisfactorily and the work on optimizing is going to take a while, then you should do research to find out where the problem is, so you can concentrate on finding the correct code to optimize (though obviously you should be sensible about this: if a method has a potential performance problem that stands a good chance of being significant and that's going to only take 30 minutes to fix, then it's probably worth fixing it anyway).

Use StringBuilder Sensibly (All Languages)

You're no doubt aware of the existence of the StringBuilder class and of the recommendation that using the StringBuilder will give a higher performance than using the straight String instances if you're concatenating strings together. This advice is true most of the time but not necessarily all the time. It depends on what manipulations and how many concatenations you're doing. You have to be doing at least several string concatenations before the benefits outweigh the initial overhead of instantiating the StringBuilder in the first place. On occasions I've seen people use a StringBuilder just to join two strings. That's madness—in that case using a StringBuilder will actually reduce performance! On the other hand, if you have a large number of concatenations (or other operations that won't affect a substantial number of characters at the beginning of the string), then using a StringBuilder will give a vast improvement.

As a rough guide, if you can perform your operation using one String.Concat() method call, then use that. StringBuilder can't do that faster. And bear in mind that some String.Concat() overloads take two, three, or four strings as parameters, and the Microsoft high-level compilers are fairly good at noticing when they can use those overloads. This C# code will compile into a single Concat() call:

```
result = s1 + s2 + s3 + s4;
```

If you can arrange to do all the concatenations in a single high-level language command, then that's by far the best and most efficient solution. But of course if it's impossible in a given situation for you to do that, you have to consider whether to use StringBuilder. At twoString. Concat() calls, StringBuilder is probably marginally more efficient, though it depends to some extent on the relative sizes on the strings. Thereafter, StringBuilder rapidly gets the edge. But you'll have to balance any performance gains against the reduced readability of code that involves StringBuilders. (For example, you can't use the + operator with a StringBuilder in C# or VB. In C++ this is less of a factor, since C++ doesn't have any shorthand syntax or operator overloads for System.String, which can make C++ System.String manipulations look pretty inscrutable anyway.) Also, StringBuilder implements only a fraction of the string manipulation functions offered by String. Personally, if my code is in a performance-important area (for example, in a loop), I'll probably use StringBuilder if I need three or more calls to String.Concat(). If it's not a piece of code that's important for performance, it'll take a few more calls before I use StringBuilder, because I like code that's easy to read (and therefore easy to maintain). But different developers will probably draw the boundary at different places. If it's an absolutely performance-critical piece of code, I'll start doing rough calculations of how many characters will typically get copied and how many objects will get instantiated with each approach so that I can get a more accurate idea whether a StringBuilder is likely to increase or reduce the processor workload. For the remainder of this section, I'll present an algebraic calculation of numbers of characters copied to illustrate this approach.

I'll use algebra here, using symbols without substituting any actual numbers, because I've taken a general case, but if you want to avoid algebra, you can just substitute in the actual numbers that will be used in your code. The calculation will give you a graphic example of how much better StringBuilder is when doing a lot of calculations and will also show you the principles behind comparing the efficiency of different approaches.

For our purposes, let's suppose you have N strings, which your code will concatenate together into one string. And let's suppose that on average each of the strings contains L characters—so the final string will contain something like $N \times L$ characters (or, as you write it in algebra, NL). In fact, to keep it simple I'll assume that every string contains exactly L characters. To get an idea of performance, I'll work out the total number of characters that will be copied without and with a StringBuilder, because this is the factor that will have the most impact on performance.

Suppose you have code such as the following (I'll assume some other intermediate code isn't shown that will prevent the compiler from emitting IL code that calls the three- and four-parameter overloads of String.Concat()):

```
string result = string1;
result += string2;
result += string3;
// etc.
result += stringN;
```

Roughly how many characters will need to be copied if you use strings to perform the concatenation? You know that each concatenation creates a new string, which means that all the characters in the two strings to be joined will get copied across with each concatenation. This means that for the first concatenation you have $2 \times L$—that is, $2L$ characters. For the second concatenation, you have to join a string of length $2L$ to a string of length L—so there are $3L$ characters to copy. For the third concatenation, it's $4L$ characters, and so on. This means the total number of characters copied is $2L+3L+\ldots+NL$. Using some algebra, that sum turns out to equal $NL(N+1)/2-L$ (if you want to keep things approximate, you can say that's roughly half of $L \times N$ squared). Those are scary figures. If you have, say, 10 strings of average length 20 characters that you want to join to make a single 200-character string, doing it that way will involve the equivalent of copying 2,180 characters! You can see how the performance loss would add up.

Now let's try using StringBuilder. Assume you know in advance roughly how long the final result will be, so you can allocate a StringBuilder with a big enough capacity in the first place. So you're looking at code rather like this:

```
StringBuilder sb = new StringBuilder(x);    // x initialized to
// combined length of all strings
sb = string1;
sb.Append(string2);
// etc.
sb.Append(stringN);
result = sb.ToString();
```

To start with, the StringBuilder will be allocated. It's a fair guess that this is a relatively atomic operation. Then all that happens is that each string in turn needs to be copied into the appropriate area of memory in the StringBuilder. That means a straight $N \times L$ characters will be copied across, so the final answer is NL. Ten strings with an average length of 20 characters gives you 200 characters copied, less than a tenth of what was worked out without using StringBuilder. Note that the StringBuilder.ToString() method doesn't copy any of the string—it simply returns a string instance that's initialized to point to the string inside the StringBuilder, so no overhead exists here. (The StringBuilder will be flagged so that if any more modifications are made to the data in it, the string will be copied first, so the String instance doesn't get corrupted. This means that any further operations on either the String or the StringBuilder will cause another NL characters to get copied.)

One other point to remember: The performance benefits of using StringBuilder apply only for concatenating strings within the existing capacity of the StringBuilder instance. Go beyond the capacity, or perform an operation inside the string, such as deleting a couple of characters (which will force all subsequent characters to move position), and you'll still end up having to copy strings around (although in most cases not as often as you would do with String).

Use foreach Loops on Arrays Sensibly (C# and VB)

You're probably already aware that the standard advice in this situation is to use for loops instead of foreach loops where possible, because foreach will hurt performance. In fact, although this advice is often correct, the difference between the two loops for the specific case when you're dealing with arrays isn't nearly as great as you may imagine, and in many cases using foreach to iterate through the elements of an array will make little or no difference.

The particular question is, does it make any difference whether you write something like this (in C#, or the equivalent in VB)?

```
// arr is an array - we assume array of int for the sake of argument, but
// the same principles apply whatever the underlying type
for (int i=0; i<arr.Length; i++)
{
    // Do processing on element i
}
```

Or like this?

```
foreach(int elem in arr)
{
    // Do processing on elem
}
```

The traditional thinking is based on that internally a foreach loop in principle causes an enumerator to be instantiated over the collection—and this would presumably cause a significant performance loss if the collection were actually an array that could easily be iterated over without an enumerator, just by using a simple for loop instead. However, it turns out that the two previous pieces of code have virtually identical performance in both C# and VB. The reason is to do with compiler optimization. Both the C# and the VB compilers know that the two pieces of code are identical in their effect, and they will therefore always compile a foreach loop over an array into the IL equivalent of a for loop—as you can easily verify by compiling a simple loop and using the ildasm.exe to inspect the emitted IL code. Generally, I've noticed the code isn't quite identical. In many cases a foreach loop will generate slightly more verbose IL code but not in any way that's likely to have too dramatic an effect on performance. So in this case you're probably better off using whichever loop gives maximum readability and not worrying too much about performance. On the other hand, if performance is absolutely critical, then you probably won't want to risk even a small performance deficit.

I should also mention one case in which using for may be a lot more efficient: If you know at compile time how big the array is going to be, that shifts the balance in favor of the for loop. The reason is that this code:

```
foreach (int x in arr)                    // arr is arry of ints
{
```

will be treated by the compiler as this:

```
for(int i=0; i<arr.Length; i++)
{
```

Clearly you're going to give the JIT compiler more scope for optimizations if you're actually able to write something like this:

```
for (int i=0; i<20; i++)
{
```

Bear in mind also that if you're using some high-level language other than VB or C# but that supports a foreach construct, then you should be careful about using foreach unless you know that your compiler will optimize it away. Just because C# and VB do that, it doesn't mean that a third-party compiler will do so.

Use Appropriate String Types (C++)

In managed C++, if you append an S in front of literal strings in your source code, the strings will be treated as System.String instances instead of C-style strings. Buried in the C++ documentation for this feature is the suggestion that you should use such strings for performance. It may be a small thing, but it really can make a difference. Take a look at what happens when you compile this C++ code, which uses the S-syntax:

```
Console::WriteLine(S"Hello World");
```

This compiles on my machine to this IL:

```
IL_0000:  ldstr      "Hello World"
IL_0005:  call       void [mscorlib]System.Console::WriteLine(string)
```

That's about as good as you get for performance.

Now look what happens if you change that S to an L, the normal way you'd traditionally represent Unicode strings in C++.

```
Console::WriteLine(L"Hello World");
```

L"" means Unicode characters—the kind of characters .NET expects. So you may not expect this small change to make much difference. But when I tried compiling it, I got this:

```
IL_0000:  ldsflda     valuetype $ArrayType$0x76a8870b
??_C@_1BI@JBHAIODP@?$AAH?$AAe?$AAl?$AAl?$AAo?$AA?5?$AAW?$AAo?$AAr?
$AAl?$AAd?$AA?$AA@
IL_0005:  newobj      instance void [mscorlib]System.String::.ctor(char*)
IL_000a:  call        void [mscorlib]System.Console::WriteLine(string)
```

What has happened is that the C++ compiler has assumed from your code that you want an array of _wchar_t—after all, that's what L"" normally means. So it's given you exactly that and used the trick I described at the end of Chapter 2 to embed the unmanaged string literal into the metadata. Of course, Console.WriteLine() needs a String instance, so the code has to create one—which it does by using the fact that String has a constructor that can take a pointer to a zero-terminated character array. It works, but for your pains you've got a slightly bigger assembly (both because of the extra opcodes and because of the extra type with the funny name) and slower code.

Of course, sometimes an unmanaged char array is what you want, in particular if you're passing strings to unmanaged functions that expect ASCII strings. In this case, you'd be much better off keeping the strings as char* (that's C++ 8-bit char*, not managed 16-bit char*), because you'll save having to convert between string formats during marshaling.

Be Careful About Crossing Boundaries (All Languages)

By boundaries, I mean anything where the environment changes and work has to be done. That can mean the following:

- Network calls

- Calling unmanaged code from managed code and vice versa

- Making calls across application domains or—even worse—processes

Obviously, of all these "boundaries," making network calls is going to hit your performance hardest. If you do need to make network calls, it may be worth doing the calls asynchronously or using multithreaded techniques so you can do background work while waiting for the call to return.

Increasingly for network calls, bandwidth itself isn't a problem. For example, many intranets have very fast connections between computers. In this scenario, provided you're not transmitting huge amounts of data, it may not be the amount of data going over the network that hits you so much as the number of separate network calls, with a fixed delay for each one. (Incidentally, that's one reason why it's now considered acceptable to use XML so widely, even though XML is a relatively verbose format, and why some .NET classes, such as the DataSet, have been designed to transmit large amounts of data in one single call.) For the Internet, you may have to be more careful, especially if an application will be run on machines with 56Kbps dialup connections. (Yes, many end users do still have 56Kbps connections, even in industrialized countries. Don't be hypnotized by those megabyte connections available in your office. Think of the end user in a rural location where the local telecoms provider has decided it's not cost-effective to allow broadband.) What all this means of course is that you should consider carefully what your application is doing and where data will be used, and you may find that it makes more sense to make fewer network calls even if that means transmitting more data overall.

For calls across application domains or to unmanaged code, similar principles hold true. However, in this case the factors to watch are the number of individual calls and the total amount of data that needs to be marshaled—or, even worse, converted from one format to another, such as Unicode to ANSI strings.

For calls from managed to unmanaged code, Microsoft has suggested the figures shown in Table 6-3 for the time to make the transition.

Table 6-3. *Managed-Unmanaged Transition Times*

Technique	Time
P/Invoke	Typically 30 × 86 instructions; under absolutely ideal conditions, perhaps 10 instructions
COM interop	Typically 60 × 86 instructions

COM interop takes longer than P/Invoke because more processing has to be done to go through the COM layer. Effectively you have two boundaries to go through: managed to unmanaged and then through the COM runtime.

If you're using P/Invoke, try to keep marshaling down to a minimum. Although Microsoft has suggested 10 to 30 x86 instructions per call, that's an average figure. If you pass in types that don't need to be marshaled (which includes all primitive types), then it'll be faster.

C++ developers have the additional option of using the IJW mechanism. This can be marginally faster than using DllImport, since the CLR needs to make slightly fewer checks during the transition (moreover, you can use IJW within the same assembly, so in some cases you also get a savings from that). C++ also gives you better ability to design data types that can be used with minimal marshaling across the unmanaged-managed boundary. However, even with C++, calling unmanaged code isn't free. The CLR will still have to carry out various admin tasks, such as marking your thread to prevent the garbage collector from intercepting it, before it can hand over to unmanaged code. One suggestion I've seen is to allow perhaps eight x86 instructions under ideal conditions.

Use Value Types Sensibly (All Languages)

Using value types can make a real difference. This is both because such types can be instantiated and initialized faster and because each instance takes up less space in memory. The difference on a 32-bit machine is currently three words (value types don't need the reference, method table index, or sync block index), so if you have a large number of objects of a certain type, the memory savings may be significant from the point of view of your working set. On the other hand, you'll be aware of the performance penalty because of boxing that results if value types need to be passed as objects to methods. If you're writing in C++, you can circumvent this performance loss to some extent because C++ is more explicit about requiring you to perform individual boxing and unboxing operations, instead of the compiler guessing what you want.

When deciding whether to declare a type as a value type or a reference type, you'll need to consider carefully how the type is going to be used. In some cases you may even decide it makes more sense to define two types—one value, one reference—that have the same purpose.

You need to be aware of one catch. You'll be aware that classes should normally be specified as auto layout, since this allows the CLR to arrange its fields however it sees fit in the optimal manner for performance and class size, taking account of byte alignment issues. For classes you declare in high-level languages, this is the default, but for valuetypes (struct in C#, Structure in VB, and __value class or __value struct in C++), the default is sequential layout. In other words, this C# code:

```
public struct MyStruct
{
```

compiles to this IL:

```
.class public sequential ansi sealed beforefieldinit MyStruct
       extends [mscorlib]System.ValueType
{
```

Sequential layout is good for structs that are going to be passed via P/Invoke to unmanaged code, since it corresponds to the layout in unmanaged code and is therefore likely to cause less marshaling work. However, it may be less efficient inside your managed code. So if you're declaring structs purely for performance reasons, and not intending to pass them to unmanaged code, consider declaring them like this:

```
[StructLayout(LayoutKind.Auto)]
public struct MyStruct
{
```

This will compile to this IL:

```
.class public auto ansi sealed beforefieldinit MyStruct
       extends [mscorlib]System.ValueType
{
```

Don't Use Late Binding (VB)

It has always been good programming advice to use the most specific type possible, and this is just as true in .NET programming. It's possible in any language to cause performance problems by using less-specific types than necessary—for example, declaring a variable as type object when you actually want an integer. Now C# and C++ developers are extremely unlikely to do this, because the culture in C-style languages for many years has been one of type safety. Generally speaking, to someone with a C++ background transferring to C#, it'd simply make no sense to write this:

```
object x;
```

in place of this:

```
int x;
```

even though the former syntax is quite correct in C#.

However, the situation in VB, before the days of .NET, was different. In VB 6, the Variant class was commonly used as a general-purpose type. You saw some performance loss associated with this, but this loss was often relatively small, and many VB 6 developers thought the flexibility offered by Variant more than made up for that. Besides, VB syntax favors using Variant. Typing in the following:

```
Dim x
```

involves less finger work than this:

```
Dim x As Integer
```

If you're inclined to do that in VB .NET, then I have one word for you: don't. In VB 6, saying Dim x meant you got a variant, which would hurt performance a little bit. In VB .NET, saying Dim x means you get a System.Object instance, which will hurt performance a *lot*. Object is a reference type. Treat an int as an object, and you get boxing. And that's not all; in fact, you probably won't believe just how bad it gets. Let's do some IL-investigating. Here's a snippet of VB code that adds two numbers together:

```vb
Sub Main()
    Dim o1 As Integer = 23
    Dim o2 As Integer = 34
    Dim o5 As Integer = o1 + o2
    Console.WriteLine(o5)
End Sub
```

Simple enough. If you type this in and compile it, the emitted IL is also pretty simple.

```
.method public static void  Main() cil managed
{
  .entrypoint
  .custom instance void
[mscorlib]System.STAThreadAttribute::.ctor() = ( 01 00 00 00 )
  // Code size  17 (0x11)
  .maxstack  2
  .locals init (int32 V_0,
                int32 V_1,
                int32 V_2)
  IL_0000:  ldc.i4.s    23
  IL_0002:  stloc.0
  IL_0003:  ldc.i4.s    34
  IL_0005:  stloc.1
  IL_0006:  ldloc.0
```

```
  IL_0007:  ldloc.1
  IL_0008:  add.ovf
  IL_0009:  stloc.2
  IL_000a:  ldloc.2
  IL_000b:  call        void [mscorlib]System.Console::WriteLine(int32)
  IL_0010:  ret
}
```

This code loads the constant 23 and stores it in local variable 0. Then it stores 34 in local 1, loads the two variables, adds them, stores the result, and prints it. Notice especially the add.ovf instruction—one simple IL instruction to perform an add operation, which will almost certainly be JIT compiled into *one* executable instruction, followed by an overflow check.

Now let's make one change to the VB code. Assume that the developer forgot to explicitly declare one of the Integers as an Integer but left it as unspecified type—in other words, System.Object.

```
Sub Main()
    Dim o1 As Integer = 23
    Dim o2 = 34
    Dim o5 As Integer = o1 + o2
    Console.WriteLine(o5)
End Sub
```

Let's see what that does to the IL. In the following code, I've highlighted in bold everything that has changed:

```
.method public static void  Main() cil managed
{
  .entrypoint
  .custom instance void
[mscorlib]System.STAThreadAttribute::.ctor() = ( 01 00 00 00 )
  // Code size       36 (0x24)
  .maxstack  2
  .locals init (int32 V_0,
                object V_1,
                int32 V_2)
  IL_0000:  ldc.i4.s   23
  IL_0002:  stloc.0
  IL_0003:  ldc.i4.s   34
  IL_0005:  box        [mscorlib]System.Int32
  IL_000a:  stloc.1
  IL_000b:  ldloc.0
  IL_000c:  box        [mscorlib]System.Int32
  IL_0011:  ldloc.1
  IL_0012:  call       object [Microsoft.VisualBasic]Microsoft.VisualBasic.
                           CompilerServices.ObjectType::AddObj(object, object)
  IL_0017:  call       int32 [Microsoft.VisualBasic]Microsoft.VisualBasic.
                           CompilerServices.IntegerType::FromObject(object)
```

```
IL_001c:   stloc.2
IL_001d:   ldloc.2
IL_001e:   call        void [mscorlib]System.Console::WriteLine(int32)
IL_0023:   ret
}
```

The first constant, 23, gets loaded OK. But the second constant, 34, has to be boxed into an object before it can be stored in local 1. Now the code gets set up for the addition. It loads that 23 back onto the evaluation stack, but you can't add an integer to an object, so it has to box that integer, too! So you get two objects. IL won't let you add two objects, but one method will. It's buried away in that Microsoft.VisualBasic.CompilerServices namespace—it's a static method, called ObjectType.AddObject. Of course, since you're calling this method across an assembly, it's less likely to be inlined at JIT compile time. Internally, this method will have to unbox those objects, work out from their types what type of addition is required, add them, and then box the result so it can return the result as an object. Then it goes and calls another method from the VB Compiler Services library to convert that object into an integer.

But you get the point. Those missing two words, As Integer, in the VB source file has cost you two direct boxing operations, two calls into a library (in place of the add.ovf command), and almost certainly further boxing and unboxing operations inside those library calls. Have I done enough to convince you that using late binding in VB .NET sucks? (And it's not often I use language like that.)

■**Note** If you're wondering if the situation is as bad in C#, the answer is that C# has stricter type-safety requirements and won't let you write code analogous to the VB code I just presented. In C#, you can declare a variable of type object and set it to an int value, but you have to explicitly cast it to an int before you can use it in arithmetic operations. That explicit cast gives the C# compiler the information it needs to generate more efficient code (though not as efficient as it would have been if all variables were properly defined as int in the first place).

I have another reason for bringing up this issue. Even if you're careful always to write VB code that uses early binding (in other words, declaring variables of the correct type), you may encounter issues with code that has been imported from VB 6 using VS .NET's automatic conversion process. The VS .NET converter will do the best it can, but if you've declared something without an explicit type in your VB 6 code, the best the converter can do is to declare it as Object in your VB .NET code. So something that was perhaps a little dodgy but considered acceptable programming practice for some purposes has been autoconverted into some VB .NET code that's highly suboptimal. Of course, adding integers isn't the only potentially problematic scenario. The Visual Basic Compiler Services library is full of classes and methods that are designed to implement features that are only there for backward compatibility but where the preferred, and almost certainly more efficient, solution in .NET is different. Although this section of the book is specifically about late binding, it's worth a quick detour to emphasize in general that if you're moving from VB 6 to VB .NET, then you should be wary of using programming methodologies from the VB 6 programming model. And if you've used the VB .NET wizard to transfer code across, look at that code carefully for cases where the code ought to be changed to the .NET way of doing things. Late binding is the most obvious case in point. File handling is another example: You may consider changing all those `Print #` commands to `StreamWriter.WriteLine()` calls. It's not clear from the documentation whether you'll get better performance in this particular case, but you'll almost certainly gain greater flexibility and a more powerful, object-oriented, programming model with more maintainable code. (Of course, if the newly generated code works, that's a big plus, and you may have other priorities than fiddling with it to improve performance or improve your object model—such as debugging some other code that doesn't work yet! But since you've gotten this far through a chapter about performance, I have to assume that you do have time to play with your code for performance reasons!)

■Tip Some of these problems disappear if you use `Option Strict`—this will prevent you from declaring variables without supplying a type and will prevent you from performing arithmetic operations on `Object`, as well as a few other dodgy practices. It's really intended to make your code more robust, but it's quite useful in improving performance by preventing late binding. If you'd declared `Option Strict On` in the previous code, then you would have gotten a compilation error, alerting you to the problem of the late-bound variable.

Don't Use VB 6 Constructs (VB)

In the previous section, I covered VB late binding and pointed out that late binding is really just one of a number of VB 6 constructs that were suitable for VB 6 but are not really suitable for VB .NET. They'll work—VB .NET syntax allows them for backward compatibility—but they won't perform as well as the VB .NET equivalents. Table 6-4 lists some of the more important performance issues related to this point.

Table 6-4. *VB 6 Constructs to Avoid*

Don't Use This...	Use This Instead...
`CType()` and similar cast keywords on reference types	`DirectCast()`
`Mid()` assignment in strings	`StringBuilder` methods
`Redim Preserve`	`ArrayList` instances for dynamic-length arrays (makes a huge performance difference since `Redim Preserve` always copies the entire existing array, but `ArrayList` doesn't, provided the `ArrayList` has sufficient existing capacity)
`On Error`	Exceptions, with `Try`, `Catch`, and `Finally` blocks; not only gives higher performance than `On Error`, but also makes your code more readable

Use C++ If Appropriate

You saw in Chapter 2 when I covered the IL code produced by different compilers that the C++ compiler will tend to perform more optimizations than compilers in other languages. The C#

and VB compilers perform relatively few optimizations of their own, relying on the JIT instead—which is in many ways limited in the optimizations it can perform. Moreover, the C# compiler is a new application, so you perhaps wouldn't expect it to be particularly sophisticated. The C++ compiler, on the other hand, is the latest version of a compiler that has been around for quite a few years and has been specifically designed to generate high-performance applications. This means that if you code in managed C++, you get the same JIT compiler optimizations as for C# and VB, as well as the C++ compiler optimizations. This is significant because the JIT compiler and the C++ compiler are designed for different circumstances and therefore will perform different types of optimizations. Earlier in this chapter I gave examples of the optimizations the JIT compiler performs. In general, it's geared for a speedy compile. That means it can't perform optimizations that require extensive analysis of the code. On the other hand, it can perform optimizations specific to the hardware on which the program is running. The C++ compiler knows nothing about the end processor, but it has a lot of time to perform its compilation. Remember that it's designed for a market consisting of developers who generally don't care if the compiler takes a few extra seconds to compile, as long as the generated code runs quickly. This means that the C++ compiler can look at the program as a whole and optimize based on a fairly sophisticated analysis of the program. Unfortunately, Microsoft hasn't documented what optimizations it does, beyond that it will perform whole-program optimizations. This benefit is of course in addition to the ability to mix managed and unmanaged code, use the IJW mechanism, and speed up your code through sophisticated use of pointers at a source code level.

On the other hand, using C++ will lead to more complicated source code, demands a higher skill set from developers, and can be used only if you know that your software will only run in an environment in which your users are happy to give it full trust, because the code will be unverifiable (though this may change in future versions of .NET).

If you do code in C++, be careful about using C++ function pointers to call methods. This is slow, and if you think you need to do this, consider using delegates instead. When managed code calls another managed function through a function pointer, you'll have a transition from managed to unmanaged and then from unmanaged to managed. This also applies to managed virtual methods in __nogc types.

Keep Your Virtual Memory Requirements Small (All Languages)

I mention this really because of the point I made about page swapping being an important factor behind performance loss. Unfortunately, if you're using an extensive number of libraries, keeping your virtual memory requirements small may be largely beyond your control. The following are the main things you can do to help in this area:

- Call Dispose() where this method is available on your objects as soon as possible.

- Make sure you don't reference objects once you no longer need them, since this will prevent the garbage collector from removing them from your program's memory.

- Move rarely used types in your assemblies into separate modules that can be loaded on demand. The same applies to large resources; keep them in separate files rather than embedding them in the main assembly file.

- If you're using a large assembly just for one or two useful methods contained in it, you may consider implementing your own version of those methods to save having to load the assembly.

- C++ developers who are invoking unmanaged DLLs could also consider using LoadLibrary() to load DLLs on demand rather than statically loading them. This advice doesn't apply to managed assemblies, which are loaded on demand anyway. It's unfortunate that currently the .NET Framework doesn't provide any way for the developer to request dynamic unloading of assemblies (though if necessary you can achieve this effect by loading assemblies into a separate application domain, and then unloading the application domain). You may be able to reduce the numbers of assemblies loaded by moving code that invokes an assembly in a way so as to ensure that code is called only if it's really needed (one example, it may be not performing some initialization until the user has selected the relevant menu options—though this may impact your program's responsiveness).

Summary

In this chapter, I covered the question of performance as it relates to .NET applications. I pointed out that the factors under your control that have the most influence on performance are chiefly related to high-level program architecture—even including the question of whether you should write code that targets the .NET runtime in the first place. You also saw a variety of tips for better programming practices in various .NET-compliant languages, which (if followed) will help to make your programs more efficient. As well as looking at the practical ways you can improve performance, you saw in detail how aspects of .NET in general, and the JIT compiler in particular, help with performance under the hood. In this context, I explained some of the specific JIT optimizations that can occur and also how to enable or disable JIT optimizations.

The other side to performance is that you often need to find out where the bottlenecks are before examining how to improve the performance of your code. In the next chapter, you'll look at profiling managed code in detail.

CHAPTER 7

■ ■ ■

Profiling Your Applications and Using Performance Counters

In the previous chapter, you examined some of things you can do in your code to improve performance. In this chapter, you'll continue along the same theme, but the focus in this chapter will be on the facilities that are available to assist in *monitoring* the performance of a managed application—in other words, identifying what particular factors may be preventing an application from performing well so that you know which parts of the code to concentrate on when you're trying to improve its performance. Along the way, I'll cover some of the tools that are available for profiling and the underlying APIs. You'll also acquire some necessary background information, including in particular the principles behind how Windows manages memory.

Specifically, the topics I'll cover are as follows:

- **Virtual memory management**: I'll explain how Windows manages virtual memory and shares the available RAM between the running processes. You'll also explore the performance implications of this and how to use the Task Manager to monitor the memory an application is consuming.

- **Performance counters and PerfMon**: I'll define what performance counters are and cover how to access them programmatically from managed code as well as how to implement your own counters. You'll also look at the PerfMon tool, which provides a rich user interface for monitoring any chosen performance counters on your system.

- **Profiling**: I'll present the principles behind how commercial profilers work, using the Compuware profiler as an example to illustrate the information you can extract from a profiler. I'll also cover the CLR profiler, which you can use to obtain detailed information about the operation of the garbage collector, and show you how to implement your own code to monitor the performance of other applications with high resolution.

Performance monitoring is one area in which it's well worth a look around the Web for utilities you can use—countless third-party tools and utilities are available that provide convenient user interfaces from which to monitor the performance and resource usage of applications. Much of this software is freeware, but for the most sophisticated profilers you'll have to pay. Because of the number and variety of third-party tools available, it'd be pointless trying to show how to use them in detail here. So instead, in this chapter I'll mostly work with the main utilities provided by Microsoft—including the Task Manager and PerfMon—and use these to illustrate the basic principles behind performance monitoring. This should give you the background you need to assess the usefulness of some of the more sophisticated tools on the Internet.

Tip Good places to start looking for other performance monitoring utilities are `http://www.sysinternals.com` and `http://www.gotdotnet.com`.

How Windows Supports Performance Monitoring

Although large number of third-party profiling and performance monitoring tools are available, almost universally they will be implemented using one of two underlying technologies; the data that they present to you will either be derived from performance counters or from the profiling API.

- You can think of *performance counters* as components that continually record information about some aspect of the state of the computer or of the processes running on it. In most cases, the performance counters will store the data they obtain in memory-mapped files where it's available to other processes.

- The *profiling API* is a facility supplied by the CLR whereby an external unmanaged COM component can request to receive notifications of events that occur as a managed program is being JIT compiled and executed. Typical events include method calls, class instantiations, and the throwing and catching of exceptions. The external component will normally analyze the information retrieved and present it to the user via some user interface.

In general, utilities that use performance counters usually are referred to as *performance monitors*, and those that hook up to the profiling API are referred to as *profilers*. Both types of applications are important because they tend to supply different types of information. Performance counters excel at providing data about resource usage—how much memory an application is using, how many exceptions are being thrown, how many threads have been created, and so on. Profilers, on the other hand, are able to use the notifications they receive to monitor the actual flow of execution in a program, thereby gaining more specific information about which code is being executed at which times. For example, a sophisticated profiler can tell you how many times a method has been called and—very importantly—how much central processing unit (CPU) time is being spent executing each method.

The fact that profilers are more intimately hooked into the actual execution flow of an application is reflected in their complexity. You'll typically find that performance monitors tend to exist as simple stand-alone utility applications—the Task Manager is an example of this. Profilers, on the other hand, are more usually complex applications that are designed to integrate into VS .NET, allowing you to obtain profiling information as you execute the code from VS .NET. In general, profilers are much larger, more sophisticated applications than performance monitors, and they're correspondingly far less likely to be available as freeware or shareware.

■**Note** Developers who came to .NET from a background of Visual Studio 6 will remember that in those days, Visual Studio came with an integrated profiler. Sadly, one feature was lost in the move to .NET. For the time being at least, it appears that Microsoft has decided to rely on third parties to supply .NET-compliant profilers.

Before you start to look in more detail at profiling and performance-counting facilities, I'll point out one important piece of advice about release and debug builds.

RELEASE AND DEBUG BUILDS

Be careful to do your profiling on release builds of your applications where possible. I know it sounds obvious, but accidentally profiling a debug build is an easy mistake to make. Debug builds contain a lot of extra code that among other things may bloat memory, hang onto resources for longer, and will certainly change the relative amounts of time spent executing different methods. Sometimes you may have a specific reason to want to examine a debug build, but in most cases the information you get won't accurately reflect what the shipped version of your application is doing.

If you're responsible for compiling and profiling code, then it's relatively simple to make sure you do a release build. If you've been handed an assembly for profiling that someone else has built, then you can check whether it's a release build by examining the assembly contents with `ildasm.exe`. Look for the assembly-level attribute `DebuggableAttribute`. In a release build, this attribute either will not be present or, if present, will have been passed values of `false` (or equivalently, a zeroed block of memory) to its constructor. If this attribute is present in the assembly and has been passed nonzero data, then chances are you have a debug build.

Understanding Memory

I'll start with this topic because the memory used by an application can have a big impact on performance, and the details of how Windows manages memory is something that's often misunderstood.

One of the first things that gets ingrained into developers who start working with pointers and memory allocation in Windows is that ever since 32-bit Windows emerged, every running process has had available a virtual address space of 4 gigabytes (GB). (It's more than that on a 64-bit machine—but the principles are unchanged, so we'll stick to a 32-bit analysis here.) On Windows NT/2000/XP, and so on, only the first 2GB of this are available for your application (3GB on some server platforms), with the remainder being reserved for system use. On Windows 95/98/ME, the situation is more complicated, with several specific areas of memory being reserved.

Of course, few machines have that much RAM available. For example, the machine I'm currently writing this chapter on has 256MB of RAM—less than a tenth of the address space seen by every application I run on it. The way that this discrepancy is resolved is of course through Windows's virtual memory system, in which the addresses that the code in an application refers to (the values of pointers) are transparently mapped by Windows into pages of memory in RAM. A *page* here simply means a block of memory. The size of the page is system dependent, but on x86 machines it's 4KB; to keep this discussion simple, I'll work with that page size.

Although your application can see 4GB of virtual address space, only a tiny fraction of this is ever actually going to be used in most applications. The ranges of virtual memory that a process actually wants to use will be known to Windows (either because Windows reserved that memory when it loaded the process or because the process asked Windows for that particular block of memory), and these ranges of memory will have been allocated in 4KB chunks to pages of physical memory. Whenever the code in the process refers to any address in memory, Windows will under the hood map this address onto the appropriate page in RAM so the correct memory is accessed. That's why the addresses that an application sees are known as *virtual addresses*.

■Note Although I'll loosely refer to Windows mapping addresses onto an appropriate page, it's worth bearing in mind that this process of mapping virtual addresses is implemented directly by the hardware rather than by software on many machines, including x86-based machines.

To get a better feel for how this works, let's suppose that because of some dynamic memory allocation (for example, you just instantiated some new objects on the managed heap), your application has asked the operating system for another 1,000 bytes of memory to start at virtual address 0x10000fce (I'll keep the numbers simple for the sake of argument). Suppose the situation before this request was as shown in Figure 7-1.

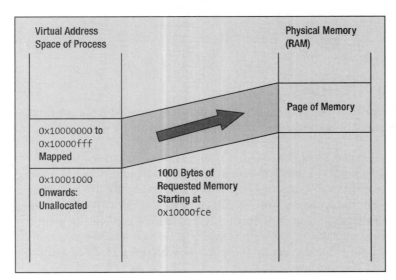

Figure 7-1. *Memory occupied by an application, just before requesting 1,000 additional bytes*

What the figure shows is that the 4KB of memory starting at address 0x10000000 is already mapped to a page of memory. The final 500 bytes of this page (starting at address 0x10000fce) weren't actually in use, but they got mapped anyway because the blocks allocated always come in units of one page. This means that when the new request for memory gets submitted to Windows, the first 500 bytes of this memory can be satisfied from the existing page in RAM. The remaining 500 bytes, however, overrun that page, which means that in order to get those bytes of virtual address space mapped to some physical memory, Windows will have to locate another page somewhere else in RAM that's free to be allocated to the process. Windows will do this, giving your program another 4,096 bytes of memory—it's more than the process asked for, but that doesn't really matter.

Notice that a consequence of this is that consecutive locations in virtual memory that fall on page boundaries probably don't correspond to consecutive addresses in physical memory. That's not a problem because Windows always maps the virtual memory addresses to the correct physical memory—you never have to worry about that in your code.

I can now start introducing some terminology. Virtual addresses in your code that are currently mapped to pages of physical memory are said to be *committed*. Applications can, when requesting memory, indicate whether they need pages to be committed for read-write access or read access only. Requesting a block for read access only is normally done for pages containing executable code and allows Windows to perform optimizations based on knowing that the contents of that page of memory can't ever be modified by the application. (Most notably, if different applications request the same read-only data, then Windows can arrange for them to share one physical copy of the data, saving on physical memory.) Virtual addresses that haven't been allocated to any physical memory are said to be *free*. Another status also exists: *reserved*. Your program can reserve virtual address ranges, which means that these virtual addresses are marked as in use (and can't therefore be the target of dynamic memory allocations), but no physical memory is actually allocated. This happens, for example, when it becomes apparent that a DLL is going to need to be loaded at a certain address, but the DLL hasn't actually been loaded yet. Your application can of course access memory only in the committed address ranges. The usual cause of a memory access violation is an attempt in executable code to access memory, specifying a virtual address that hasn't been committed. Since no such physical memory exists for that address, Windows can't do much other than throw an access violation. The actual process of committing, reserving, or freeing memory is handled by two API functions, VirtualAlloc() and VirtualFree()—these functions lie under the hood in many dynamic memory operations, such as the C++ new and delete operators. You can invoke these methods directly if you want more control over memory.

The procedure I've just described is of course sufficient, provided all the processes running on your system—as well as the Windows operating system itself—don't between them attempt to commit more memory than is available in your RAM. When this happens, some process will request some memory, and Windows won't be able to satisfy the request because of the insufficient physical RAM. In this case, Windows will perform an operation known as *swapping out*. It will identify some pages of memory that haven't been used for a while. These pages may belong to the same process, or they may belong to some other process. These pages will be transferred out from RAM to the hard drive, where they will be stored in a special file, known as the *page file*. That frees some pages in RAM, which can then be allocated to satisfy the request made by your process. If at any point an application references some pages that have been swapped out to disk, Windows will automatically swap those pages back into RAM before they're accessed. Whenever this occurs, the application is said to incur a *page fault*.

Although I've talked about swapping in and out in terms of writing to the hard drive, the hard drive isn't necessarily involved. In fact, Windows routinely swaps pages out of a process even if they aren't immediately needed by anyone else; this ensures that a process doesn't hog too much memory in RAM so that all other processes can get a fair slice of memory according to their needs. However, when this happens, the swapped-out data isn't immediately transferred to disk—the relevant pages are simply marked as available to be grabbed if any process needs it. The data is copied out only if some other application actually takes over that memory. Indeed, it's quite common for pages to be swapped out, left untouched in RAM, and then swapped back into the same process when that process tries to access those pages again. In that case, the performance hit from swapping the pages back in is negligible—it's just the time taken for Windows to update its internal tables of what memory is being used for what purposes. This kind of page fault is known as a *soft page fault* (as opposed to a *hard page fault*, when the data actually needs to be retrieved from the page file). Windows is quite clever when it comes to monitoring whether memory has been modified—and it's quite adept at leaving pages of data lying around as long as possible in order to minimize the number of times that data needs to be copied to or from disk.

At this point it's worth introducing a couple of other terms. You've probably heard the term *working set* thrown around occasionally. Many developers assume that the working set roughly means how much memory the application is consuming. More precisely, the working set is the memory in RAM that's marked as currently belonging to that process. In other words, it's basically that part of the process's memory that hasn't been paged out.

Besides the memory that forms part of a process's virtual address space, Windows maintains some system memory on behalf of the process. This memory contains information that Windows needs in order to be able to execute the process. Some of this memory is so vital that it's never allowed to be swapped out—this memory is referred to as the *nonpaged pool*. Other parts of this memory can be swapped out if needed, and that memory is referred to as the *paged pool*.

The main significance of all this for performance is of course the time consumed by servicing page faults. Every hard page fault takes time to complete, so avoiding page faults is one of the big keys to keeping up performance. Unfortunately, because virtual memory management takes place invisibly to processes, you don't really have any low-level control over memory management. The main technique to avoid page faults is to keep the amount of virtual memory needed by an application to the minimum possible. It also helps if variables that you access together are stored in the same page—that's also not directly under your control, but you can indirectly influence it. Variables are more likely get put on the same pages if dynamically allocated variables are allocated at the same time and if the heap isn't too fragmented; the garbage collector is of course designed to take advantage of this optimization. Other things you can do are to buy more RAM and not to run too many processes at the same time (though that's generally under the control of the user rather than the developer). In general, however, an excessive number of page faults can be a clue that your application is simply using too much memory. You can also get a direct visual and audio clue to this if you hear a lot of disk thrashing on your machine—a clear sign of excessive hard page faults.

Bear in mind as well that I've simplified the previous description considerably. Behind the scenes, Windows is running some fairly sophisticated algorithms that determine, based on how each application is using memory, which pages can be swapped in and out of a process, and how large a working set to maintain for each application. Windows also does some work predicting which areas of virtual memory are likely to be needed by a particular process and swapping them back into RAM before they're required. The main way of doing this optimization is that when a page is requested, neighboring pages (in the process's virtual address space) are automatically swapped in at the same time, on the assumption that pages tend to be accessed in clusters. Another performance gain comes from the shared memory that I mentioned earlier in this section. If two applications load the same DLL at the same address, and neither application is going to alter the contents of the pages into which the DLL is loaded, then Windows has no need to hold two copies of the same data! Instead, both applications will have their relevant pages of virtual address space mapped to the same physical memory. This optimization is particularly important for managed code, since all managed programs need to load mscoree.dll, as well as a number of related DLLs that contain the code that runs the CLR. These files are quite large, and they hit performance at startup time for the first managed program that's executed. You may notice that any managed application typically starts faster if there's another managed application already running. That's because DLLs such as mscoree.dll are already loaded into the first application. So the second managed application can simply share the pages that contain these files already in use—the second application doesn't need to load these files separately.

▪Tip One of the benefits of Windows XP, incidentally, is that XP has considerably more sophisticated algorithms for managing page swapping and virtual memory than do earlier versions of Windows. Among the new things that XP will do is monitor which pages are used by an application at startup, so the next time the application runs, those pages can be loaded more quickly.

Assessing Memory Usage with the Task Manager

The Task Manager provides an extremely convenient and quick way to get information about the resources that a process is using, including its memory usage and the number of handles it's holding. Just about every developer will have opened the Task Manager at some point to kill a process or to quickly check how much CPU time or memory some process is currently taking. However, it's easy to get misled by the information concerning memory usage that's reported by the Task Manager. In the following sections, I'll show you the correct way to interpret the information.

You'll see information about memory usage displayed in the Processes and Performance tabs of the Task Manager user interface; the following sections show both of these in turn.

Using the Processes Tab

The Processes tab really comes into its own when you customize the columns displayed.

You can do this by selecting View ➤ Select Columns. You'll be presented with a dialog box that invites you to modify which information displays for each process. Showing the full set of columns, the Task Manager looks something like Figure 7-2.

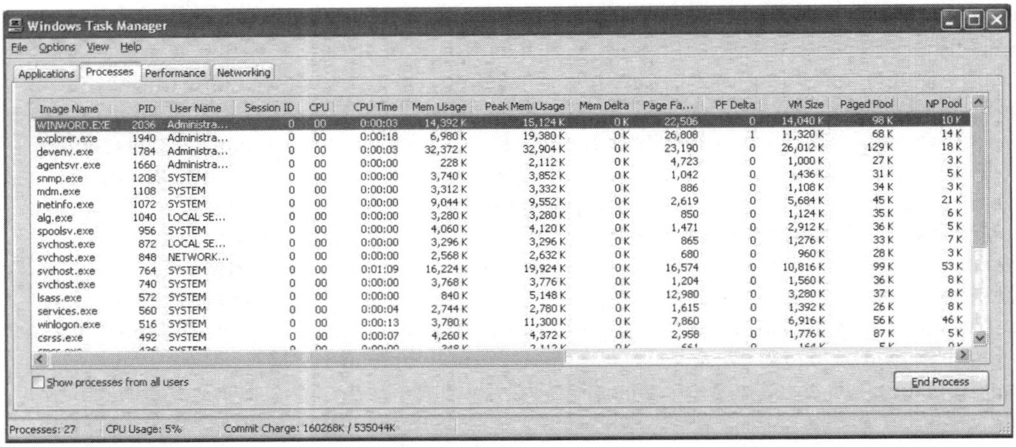

Figure 7-2. *The Task Manager Processes listview with all columns selected*

The Task Manager by default shows a column called Mem Usage—and of course many developers assume that this column tells you how much virtual memory the application requires. In fact, this column tells you the working set of the application; that is, it tells you the amount of space in RAM that has been specifically committed to this process. As you saw earlier, this number excludes all virtual memory that has been swapped out, including memory that the operating system has simply soft-swapped out in case any other applications need it. As a guide to the memory demands that this application is making on the system, this figure is next to useless. A far better indicator of this quantity is the VM Size column, which directly measures the amount of a virtual address space that the application has committed. If you have a large memory leak, it's the VM Size that will steadily increase. If you're interested in using the Task Manager to monitor how much memory an application is consuming, then I strongly recommend you replace Mem Usage with VM Size in your choice of columns that the Task Manager displays. And personally, I'd argue that displaying Mem Usage by default was quite a bad design choice for the Task Manager.

The only potential problem with the VM Size column is that it doesn't take account of shared memory. If, for example, you're running several managed applications, then the memory taken by the CLR's own code (which is quite substantial) will show up separately in all these processes, even though only one copy of this code will be loaded into memory. (The Mem Usage column has the same problem.)

Another indicator that's worth watching is the Page Faults column, since this can tell you if performance is being hit because of memory being swapped in and out of disk too much. Bear in mind, however, that this figure measures all page faults, including soft page faults, which have a negligible impact on performance.

Several other memory-related indicators exist that I normally find less useful but that may still be of relevance in some situations.

- The Paged Pool and NP Pool columns directly measure the memory taken by the system paged and nonpaged pools. Bear in mind, however, that this memory is allocated by the system and not under the control of your application.

- The Peak Mem column indicates the highest figure for Mem Usage that has occurred since the process started.

- The Mem Delta column indicates the change in the Mem Usage column between the last and the previous updates.

You can also get an indirect measure of resource usage by monitoring the columns related to handles. These columns are Handles, Graphics Device Interface (GDI) Objects, and USER Objects. The GDI Objects column specifically indicates those objects committed to your application that are maintained by the graphics GDI system. (GDI has its own resource manager, so these objects are treated by Windows separately from non-GDI objects.) USER Objects indicates certain items related to the windowing system, such as windows, menus, cursors, and so on—these objects also have their own resource manager. You should be aware, however, that the GDI+ library that underpins many System.Drawing classes is independent of GDI, so it's not clear whether GDI+ objects will necessarily show up as GDI objects.

Monitoring how these columns change over time can give you a clue to any problems involving your application not freeing handles—in the case of managed code, that's most commonly caused by failing to call Dispose() on objects you've finished using. By itself, this won't be much of a problem in most cases, but failing to call Dispose() may also be bloating your application's virtual memory requirements and hence causing you extra page faults.

Using the Performance Tab

The Performance tab gives similar information to some of the columns in the Processes tab but aggregates the information over all running processes (see Figure 7-3). It doesn't break down the data by process. Where this tab is useful, however, is that it presents a couple of graphs showing how the two main indicators have varied over time. These indicators are CPU Usage (the percentage of time the CPU has spent actually running processes) and a quantity that's euphemistically called *PF Usage* in Windows XP and *Mem Usage* in earlier versions of Windows. Both these descriptions are misleading—this quantity appears to be the sum of committed virtual memory by all running processes and therefore includes memory in RAM and data that's paged out either to RAM or to the paging file.

The main use of this tab is that, provided you're confident that no other running processes are going to significantly impact the graphs, the graphs give you a feel for the way a process is using memory and CPU time over an extended period of time. It's also useful on multiprocessor machines to check if all CPUs are actually being used.

As far as the data presented below the graphs is concerned, the information under Totals should be obvious. The Commit Charge number just shows the current value of the total virtual memory—the same as the current number in the Page File Usage History graph. The limit is the maximum that can be sustained between RAM and the paging file. If more than this is ever needed, Windows will automatically increase the size of the paging file—though that's usually an indication that some application is misbehaving. Physical Memory simply indicates how much of the RAM on your system is available for use. Kernel Memory indicates the sizes of the paged and nonpaged pools I discussed earlier.

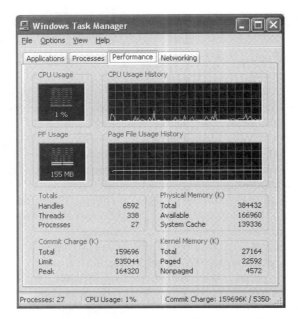

Figure 7-3. *The Task Manager Performance tab*

Working Through the UseResources Example

You'll now look at an example application that uses a large amount of memory so that I can illustrate how you can use the Task Manager to monitor the performance of this application.

Figure 7-4 shows the appearance of the sample application.

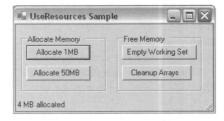

Figure 7-4. *The* UseResources *sample in action*

You can see from the figure that the sample has buttons to allocate memory. Clicking these buttons will cause some large managed arrays to be created that occupy either 1MB or 50MB. This allocation is cumulative, so if you hit the Allocate 50MB button once and the Allocate 1MB button six times, you'll have a total of 56MB of data allocated and referenced from the Form1 object. Clicking the Cleanup Arrays button causes all the references to this data to be removed and also invokes a garbage collection to free up the memory. The Empty Working Set button is somewhat different; clicking this button invokes the native API function EmptyWorkingSet() that causes all nonessential memory in this process to be removed from the working set.

Running this example can teach you quite a bit about memory usage of managed applications. But before you see it in action, though, let's look at the code behind it.

■Tip If you download and run the UseResources example, be careful how much memory you allocate. Clicking the Allocate 50MB button too many times can easily completely fill your RAM and paging file. If this happens, you'll get a dialog box warning you that the system is low on virtual memory, and Windows will then automatically and permanently increase the size of the paging file. Within moderation that's OK, but if your page file size gets too big, you may notice the corresponding reduction in free hard drive space. You may prefer to check the size of the page file before you run the application (it's listed in the Control Panel, under System) so that if it does grow, you can restore it to its original size after running UseResources.

Besides the usual Form1 class that represents the main form, the sample contains a class called MegaByteClass. The class doesn't do anything, except that each MegaByteClass instance occupies 1MB of memory.

```
public class MegaByteClass
{
    int [][] array = new int[100][];

    public MegaByteClass()
    {
        for (int i=0; i<100; i++)
            array[i] = new int[2600];
    }
}
```

The int type occupies 4 bytes, so to occupy 1MB you need 262,144 ints—but since the exact quantities aren't too critical, I've called it 260,000. In this code I've broken that number down into 100 arrays of 2,600 ints each. This ensures that the arrays get placed on the usual heap, not on the special large object heap, which may be treated differently by the garbage collector. Specifically, this ensures that the sample will be backward compatible on .NET 1.0, which featured a bug that sometimes prevented the freeing of memory on the large object heap.

Now you need an extra member field in the Form1 class.

```
public class Form1 : System.Windows.Forms.Form
{
    private ArrayList arrays = new ArrayList();
```

This ArrayList will hold the references to all the MegaByteClass objects you create. Extra memory is allocated using the following method:

```
public void AddArray()
{
    arrays.Add(new MegaByteClass());
}
```

The following are the button Click event handlers:

```
private void btn1MB_Click(object sender, System.EventArgs e)
{
   AddArray();
   this.statusBar.Text = arrays.Count.ToString() + " MB added";
}

private void btn50MB_Click(object sender, System.EventArgs e)
{
   for (int i=0; i<50; i++)
   {
      AddArray();
      this.statusBar.Text = arrays.Count.ToString() + " MB added";
      this.statusBar.Refresh();
   }
}
```

When allocating blocks of 50MB, the sample takes care to display progress information in the status bar, as it goes along. This is because allocating that much memory can take a while, so it's nice to keep the user updated about what's happening.

Cleaning up the memory looks like this:

```
private void btnCleanupArrays_Click(object sender, System.EventArgs e)
{
   arrays.Clear();
   this.statusBar.Text = "No arrays allocated";
   GC.Collect(GC.MaxGeneration);
}
```

Finally, here's the code and associated DllImport declaration for when the user clicks the Empty Working Set button:

```
[DllImport("psapi.dll")]
static extern int EmptyWorkingSet(IntPtr hProcess);
private void btnEmptyWorkingSet_Click(object sender, System.EventArgs e)
{
   IntPtr hThisProcess = Process.GetCurrentProcess().Handle;
   EmptyWorkingSet(hThisProcess);
}
```

The EmptyWorkingSet() API function takes the handle that identifies a process and simply pages out any memory from this process that can be paged out. The data isn't of course actually moved to disk, but any pages that don't form part of the nonpaged pool will simply be marked as no longer a part of the application's working set. My reason for including this facility in the example was because it will provide a clear demonstration of just how meaningless the Mem Usage column in the Task Manager is for most purposes. Calling EmptyWorkingSet() immediately makes your application appear to be occupying less memory, even though the committed virtual memory is unchanged.

Running the UseResources application gives the result shown in Figure 7-5 on my machine when the application first starts.

Image Name	Mem Usage	Peak Mem Usage	Page Fa...	VM Size
devenv.exe	3,792 K	43,032 K	131,100	34,080 K
psp.exe	26,836 K	29,724 K	13,024	19,640 K
taskmgr.exe	2,388 K	4,736 K	2,880	1,272 K
DPNCS.exe	1,532 K	2,848 K	1,391	972 K
WINWORD.EXE	14,852 K	16,788 K	12,650	8,208 K
UseResources.exe	7,260 K	7,284 K	2,117	5,460 K

Figure 7-5. *Memory usage by the* UseResources *sample at application startup*

Now you can do something interesting by minimizing the application, as shown in Figure 7-6.

Image Name	Mem Usage	Peak Mem Usage	Page Fa...	VM Size
devenv.exe	3,792 K	43,032 K	131,100	34,080 K
psp.exe	18,808 K	29,724 K	13,922	11,572 K
taskmgr.exe	2,212 K	4,736 K	3,409	1,272 K
DPNCS.exe	1,532 K	2,848 K	1,391	972 K
WINWORD.EXE	14,956 K	16,788 K	12,676	8,308 K
UseResources.exe	804 K	7,392 K	2,313	5,464 K

Figure 7-6. *Memory usage by the* UseResources *sample on minimizing the application*

And then you can restore it again, as shown in Figure 7-7.

Image Name	Mem Usage	Peak Mem Usage	Page Fa...	VM Size
devenv.exe	2,948 K	43,032 K	131,636	34,068 K
psp.exe	14,648 K	29,724 K	23,713	17,452 K
taskmgr.exe	2,236 K	4,736 K	5,281	1,272 K
DPNCS.exe	368 K	2,848 K	1,474	928 K
WINWORD.EXE	11,792 K	16,788 K	17,260	8,160 K
UseResources.exe	2,932 K	7,392 K	2,830	5,464 K

Figure 7-7. *Memory usage by the* UseResources *sample on restoring the application*

What's going on here? Well, when any managed application starts, it brings in a lot of pages of data required to execute code that initializes the CLR and performs other startup tasks. A lot of this code will never be executed again, but it remains in the process's working set until Windows decides that those pages haven't been touched for a sufficiently long time that it may as well swap them out. Minimizing a form will provoke Windows into swapping out a large number of pages immediately on the basis that if you're minimizing a form, that's usually a good indication that that process is unlikely to be doing anything more for a while. This accounts for the low number in the Mem Usage column when the application is minimized. When you restore the application, Windows will find that some of the swapped-out pages are actually needed and will page fault them back into the working set. If those pages haven't been grabbed by any other application, these will of course be soft page faults that don't impact performance. Hence, on restoring the application, the Mem Usage information goes up again, but not as high as it was when the application started—on my machine, it was 2.9MB instead of 7.3MB. That's because a lot of the code that was originally loaded (presumably that required to initialize the CLR) isn't now required.

The same principles apply to unmanaged applications, except that unmanaged applications don't have the overhead of the CLR to bring into memory (though they may have other libraries such as the MFC or VB 6 libraries). Notice that through all this, the VM size is virtually unchanged.

Now if I click the 1MB button five times to reserve 5MB of memory, you can see the virtual memory grow by 5MB (see Figure 7-8).

Image Name	Mem Usage	Peak Mem Usage	Page Fa...	VM Size
devenv.exe	3,788 K	43,032 K	131,101	34,068 K
psp.exe	19,480 K	29,724 K	14,817	12,232 K
taskmgr.exe	2,592 K	4,736 K	3,503	1,272 K
DPNCS.exe	1,520 K	2,848 K	1,392	948 K
WINWORD.EXE	15,356 K	16,788 K	13,187	8,132 K
UseResources.exe	9,024 K	9,024 K	4,366	10,524 K

Figure 7-8. *Memory usage by the* UseResources *sample on reserving 5MB*

When clicking the 50MB button four times, you'll see Figure 7-9.

Image Name	Mem Usage	Peak Mem Usage	Page Fa...	VM Size
devenv.exe	1,624 K	43,032 K	131,264	34,040 K
psp.exe	1,080 K	29,724 K	16,278	11,584 K
taskmgr.exe	2,116 K	4,736 K	4,125	1,272 K
DPNCS.exe	120 K	2,848 K	1,392	948 K
WINWORD.EXE	604 K	16,788 K	13,609	8,140 K
UseResources.exe	174,496 K	186,976 K	96,736	222,364 K

Figure 7-9. *Memory usage by the* UseResources *sample on reserving an additional 200MB*

As you can see, the virtual memory has grown roughly by the indicated 200MB, but the working set hasn't grown by nearly as much. If you try this, you may see the Mem Usage number fluctuating. This is because allocated memory is always added immediately to the working set, but every so often Windows will decide that the working set is getting too big, so it will swap pages out. The less RAM you have or the more processes running on your system, the sooner this will start happening. Notice also from Figure 7-9 the way that the number of page faults has shot up from about 4,000 to more than 100,000 now that so much more virtual memory is required.

Hitting the Cleanup Arrays button removes the added virtual memory, as shown in Figure 7-10.

Image Name	Mem Usage	Peak Mem Usage	Page Fa...	VM Size
devenv.exe	1,528 K	43,032 K	131,281	34,040 K
psp.exe	5,448 K	29,724 K	19,668	12,264 K
taskmgr.exe	2,144 K	4,736 K	4,729	1,272 K
DPNCS.exe	368 K	2,848 K	1,474	928 K
WINWORD.EXE	10,704 K	16,788 K	16,973	8,152 K
UseResources.exe	8,088 K	186,976 K	105,023	12,564 K

Figure 7-10. *Memory usage by the* UseResources *sample after freeing the memory*

Finally, if you hit the Empty Working Set button, the results look dramatic for the Mem Usage column (though virtual memory is, obviously, unchanged), as shown in Figure 7-11.

Image Name	Mem Usage	Peak Mem Usage	Page Fa...	VM Size
devenv.exe	1,548 K	43,032 K	131,286	34,040 K
psp.exe	9,924 K	29,724 K	21,329	12,972 K
taskmgr.exe	2,196 K	4,736 K	4,742	1,272 K
DPNCS.exe	368 K	2,848 K	1,474	928 K
WINWORD.EXE	10,860 K	16,788 K	17,012	8,152 K
UseResources.exe	720 K	186,976 K	106,371	12,584 K

Figure 7-11. *Memory usage by the* UseResources *sample after emptying the working set*

However, this low memory usage is illusory. If you do anything that causes any code to be executed (for example, you do something that forces a repaint, or you click another button), most of those pages will be immediately brought back into the working set.

Understanding Performance Counters

The Windows operating system supplies a large number of performance counters that monitor such areas as virtual memory usage, I/O and file system operations, network operations, and the amount of CPU time the processor spends on each process. Most of these counters not only supply information about the total resource usage on the system but are also able to break down this information according to which running process owns the resources being monitored. In addition, Windows makes available an API that allows applications to implement and register additional performance counters. You'll typically take advantage of this feature in order to have a counter monitor some items that are specific to your application. The CLR itself registers a large number of performance counters that supply information about the internal operation of the CLR. For example, these counters monitor the work done by the JIT compiler, the operation of the garbage collector, and the amount of memory allocated on the managed heap, data relating to .NET Remoting operations, and so on. Although these counters are implemented by the CLR rather than by Windows, the distinction isn't relevant as far as reading these counters is concerned. You use the .NET counters in the same way you'd use any other counters.

Both the Task Manager and the PerfMon performance-monitoring tool display data that has been read from performance counters. In addition, certain framework classes in the System.Diagnostics namespace allow you to access performance counters easily. The most important of these classes are PerformanceCounter and PerformanceCounterCategory. These objects serve partly as managed wrappers for the native API calls that can be used to read data left by performance counters and partly as a means for you to implement your own performance counters. Indeed, one of the nicest things about PerformanceCounter and related classes is how easy they make it for you to register your own performance counters. If you want to implement your own performance counter, then you can save yourself a huge amount of effort by using managed code to do so, because the .NET PerformanceCounter class pre-implements a lot of the boilerplate code that's normally required of a performance counter. In particular, for obvious reasons, a performance counter should be able to gather its data without consuming any significant resources or CPU time itself—and implementing that ideal takes a lot of work. Remember, I said earlier that performance counters normally tend to be implemented using memory-mapped files. Well, the .NET Framework classes will do all that kind of work for you under the hood, so implementing your own performance counter in managed code is incredibly simple. In this chapter you'll work through examples that show both how to read existing counters and how to implement your own.

Understanding PerfMon

PerfMon is an MMC snap-in designed for performance monitoring. Like the Task Manager, PerfMon is supplied by Microsoft and comes with the Windows operating system on Windows 2000, Windows XP, and later operating systems. It's similar to the Task Manager to the extent that its main purpose is to pull performance data from various performance counters on the system and to display the data in a user-friendly format. However, PerfMon is much more sophisticated, and in particular it allows you complete freedom to choose which performance counters are used. The cost of this flexibility is that PerfMon takes a little longer to learn to use to its full potential, but it's a tool that's well worth using. It can supply a lot of information about the resources used by each running application, but also in some cases you can get hints concerning what the application is doing. For example, you can use PerfMon to find out the rate at which managed exceptions are being thrown.

■**Tip** One other difference between PerfMon and the Task Manager is that PerfMon makes no effort to hide that it's getting its data from performance counters. So, to work with PerfMon, you need to have some understanding of performance counters. In contrast, it's possible to use the Task Manager extensively without ever being aware of the existence of performance counters.

To launch PerfMon, just type `perfmon` at the command prompt. This opens a window that looks something like Figure 7-12.

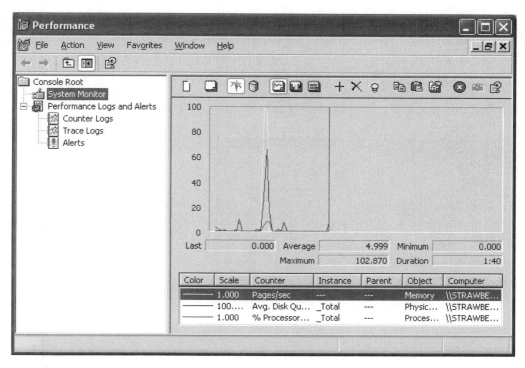

Figure 7-12. *PerfMon*

The System Monitor node in the MMC treeview reveals a time graph that shows how selected performance counter measurements vary with time, similar to the Performance tab in the Task Manager. Although it's not clear in Figure 7-12, the final vertical line in the graph moves steadily to the right as more data is gathered, and the graph restarts as soon as the vertical line reaches the edge of the window. If you run PerfMon, you'll immediately see this happening.

Each line in the graph corresponds to a particular performance counter. You can remove individual counters from the graph by selecting the appropriate counter in the listview and either hitting the Delete key or clicking the X-shaped icon above the graph. You can add new items to be graphed by clicking the plus (+) sign. This opens a dialog box asking which performance counters you want to examine, as shown in Figure 7-13.

In this figure I've selected to examine two counters, which respectively measure the total committed and reserved bytes that the garbage collector has claimed for the managed heap in the process. (It's the same example I presented earlier in the chapter, which I left running for this figure.) The dialog box also illustrates a couple of concepts you need to understand. An individual performance counter monitors just one quantity. Your system has a huge number of performance counters, and these are divided into categories. In Figure 7-13 the selected counters come from the category .NET CLR Memory.

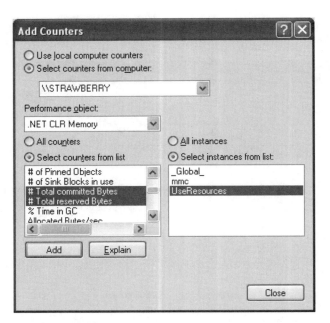

Figure 7-13. *Adding performance counters to PerfMon*

■**Note** Notice that the text accompanying the category drop-down list in Figure 7-13 is *Performance Object*. Some terminology differences exist between .NET and Windows in this regard. In particular, what's referred to in the context of managed code as a *performance category* is referred to by Windows as a *performance object*. Arguably, *category* is a far more meaningful term, and it's therefore the term I'll use.

Once you've chosen the performance counters to use, you also need to indicate the *instance*. You can think of the counter as being analogous to a class and the instance to an object. For example, if you select Total Number of Committed Bytes as the thing you need to monitor, you can roughly think of using the analogy that an object whose purpose is to monitor that particular quantity gets instantiated. When instantiating the object, you need to indicate for which process the number of committed bytes will be monitored. Do you indeed want to look only at the number of bytes for a particular process, or are you interested in measuring the overall number of committed bytes for all processes on the system? The object/instantiation analogy is only an analogy, but if you think along those lines, you'll have a good enough grasp of what's happening. In many cases, an instance called _Global_ exists; this instance doesn't attach to any particular process but monitors the total quantity for all processes. (Note, however, that certain counters may not be appropriate to individual processes.)

Figure 7-13 shows that when I ran PerfMon, it offered a choice of the two running applications—the UseResources example and MMC itself (the application that's running PerfMon).

Note that the system makes no distinction between .NET-related performance counters and other performance counters, so it will allow you to instantiate a .NET-related counter for an unmanaged application—although clearly all .NET-related measurements are likely to be zero for an unmanaged process.

When I OKed this dialog box and waited a short time to allow the measurements to be taken over time, the graph shown in Figure 7-14 developed.

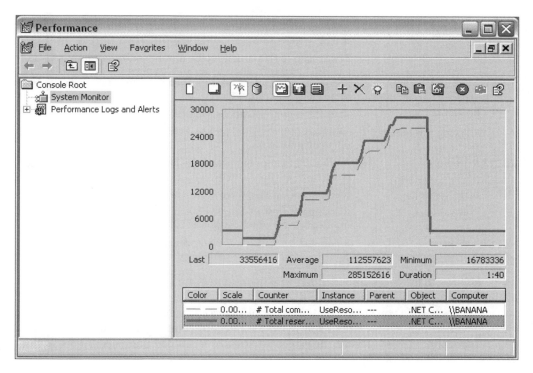

Figure 7-14. *PerfMon, measuring committed and reserved bytes*

The vertical scale is measured in kilobytes (you can change the vertical scale by right-clicking the graph, selecting Properties from the resultant context menu, and then using the Graph tab of the dialog box that appears). While PerfMon was running, I clicked the 50MB button in the UseResource example five times and then clicked the button to free the memory. You can clearly see the five periods when memory was being allocated. It's also clear that the final memory allocation took substantially longer. By this point, the virtual memory required by UseResources was pushing at the limits of the available RAM (the machine this was running on had 256MB RAM), which means that pages would need to be extensively swapped out to the hard drive. This should demonstrate the potential for using PerfMon to get some fairly detailed information about any excessive resource use by an application.

Introducing the .NET Performance Counters

So far, although I've given you a fair idea of how you can use performance counters, I haven't said much about exactly what .NET-specific data you can monitor with the available counters.

In fact, as of .NET version 1.x, the CLR provides nine categories of performance counters (see Table 7-1).

Table 7-1. *The Categories of Performance Counters Implemented by the CLR*

Category	Counters Can Supply Information About...
.NET CLR exceptions	Frequency with which exceptions are thrown, exception-handling blocks are executed.
.NET CLR interop	Frequency with which calls to unmanaged code are made, either by P/Invoke or through COM interop.
.NET CLR JIT	Time taken to JIT compile code, number of bytes compiled. You can use this information to get an idea of whether new code that hasn't been previously executed is being run, since that's the code that will be JIT compiled.
.NET CLR loading	Rate of loading assemblies, classes, and so on.
.NET CLR LocksAndThreads	Numbers of logical and physical threads, the rate at which threads fail to acquire locks.
.NET CLR memory	Amount of memory in heaps, the frequency with which garbage collections are performed.
.NET CLR networking	Numbers of bytes and datagrams sent/received.
.NET CLR Remoting	Numbers of context-bound objects and Remoting objects, frequency with which Remoting calls are made.
.NET CLR security	Frequency with which security checks are made.

In addition to these, a number of performance counters are specifically geared toward ASP .NET.

As you'll see when you start coding with performance counters, to instantiate a particular counter you normally supply strings specifying the category, counter, instance, and possibly the machine name. Table 7-1 listed the category names. You can find the specific counter names by doing the following:

- Looking up the information in the MSDN documentation (at `http://mshelp://MS.VSCC/MS.MSDNQTR.2002APR.1033/cpgenref/html/gngrfperformancecounters.htm`).

- Checking the list of names in the PerfMon Add Counter dialog box or from the VS .NET Server Explorer (just locate the Performance Counter node under the relevant computer name).

- Also, certain methods in the `System.Diagnostics.PerformanceCounterCategory` class enumerate names. I'll cover this in the next section, "Coding with Performance Counters."

I should stress that the previous list indicates only the performance counters that are supplied as part of the CLR. These form a small fraction of the total performance counters available on Windows.

Coding with the Performance Counters

Besides using the performance counters in tools such as PerfMon, it's easy to consume performance counters directly in your code. This means that if you want, your applications can monitor their own performance usage, and you can write code to monitor some other process or aspect of the system. The relevant classes are in the System.Diagnostics namespace, and the key class is System.Diagnostics.PerformanceCounter. You can instantiate a performance counter by specifying the category name, counter name, and instance name in the constructor.

```
PerformanceCounter counter = new PerformanceCounter(".NET CLR Memory",
                                "# Total committed bytes", "_Global_");
```

A number of other constructor overloads exist, including one that allows you to specify the machine the counter is to run on (the default is the local machine).

Once the counter is instantiated, you need to initialize it. You do this by calling BeginInit().

```
counter.BeginInit();
```

BeginInit() sets the initialization process off on a separate thread and returns immediately without waiting for the initialization to complete. If you have some action you want to take but you need to make sure the counter is fully initialized first, you can call EndInit(), which simply waits until the counter is initialized.

```
counter.EndInit();
```

■**Tip** In Chapter 9, when I cover threads, I'll say more about the BeginXXX()/EndXXX() design.

Then, whenever you need to read the value of a performance counter, you invoke the NextValue() method. This method returns a float. That's because some counters return floating-point data while others return integers—so if you know a particular counter returns integer data, you'll need to cast the return value.

```
int numBytesInHeap = (int)Counter.NextValue();
```

If the counter isn't yet fully initialized, NextValue() will block until it has been initialized.

If you want to find out about available performance counters, you can use the PerformanceCounterCategory class. The static GetCategories() method returns an array of PerformanceCounterCategory objects representing the possible categories.

```
PerformanceCounterCategory[] cats =
    PerformanceCounterCategory.GetCategories();
```

Alternatively, if you know the name of the category you want, you can instantiate a category directly. Once you have a PerformanceCounterCategory object, you can find out what instances are available. (The categories are arranged so that all counters in the same category have the same set of instances.)

```
PerformanceCounterCategory cat = new PerformanceCounterCategory(
                                                  ".NET CLR Memory");
string[] instances = cat.GetInstances();
```

You can also obtain an array containing all the counters that are available for a specific instance.

```
PerformanceCounter[] counters = cat.GetCounters("_Global_");
```

Note that some categories can't break up their data by process. Such categories have only one instance, and different overloads of the methods shown in the previous code snippets cover this possibility, as well as different overloads of methods that allow you to instantiate a counter for a remote machine. As always, full details are in the MSDN documentation.

VS .NET also does a lot to make your coding with performance counters easy. In particular, the Server Explorer can show you a list of the registered counters, as shown in Figure 7-15.

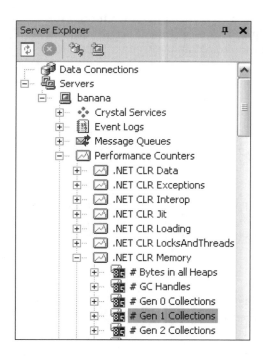

Figure 7-15. *Performance counters, displayed by VS .NET Server Explorer*

This makes it easy to find out the exact strings you need to supply to the relevant constructors to instantiate performance counter–related classes. You can even drag a counter from the Server Explorer to the Design View to get VS .NET to autogenerate the code to instantiate a counter. However, the work you save by doing this is minimal, and the code you get is quite inflexible—in particular since it gives you a counter hardwired to a particular machine name, with all initialization performed in the InitializeComponent() method. I find it easier to just write the code for a performance counter myself, and that's the approach I take in the next example.

Working Through the MonitorUseResources Example

In this section I'll develop a short example that illustrates the use of performance counters. It's a development of the UseResources example, with the additional feature that it monitors and displays one aspect of its own resource use as it runs: the number of generation 0 and generation 1 garbage collections that have been performed.

When running, the example looks like Figure 7-16.

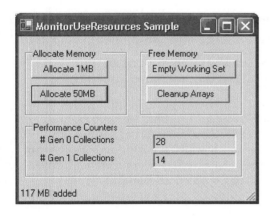

Figure 7-16. *The* MonitorUseResources *sample*

To create the sample, I took the code for UseResources and made a few changes. I used the VS .NET Design View to add the new controls you can see in Figure 7-16. I also added a timer and used the Properties window enable the timer and to set its interval to 1,000 milliseconds (one second). I also set the names of the textboxes to tbGen0Collections and tbGen1Collections.

I then needed a couple of fields in the Form1 class to represent the performance counters.

```
PerformanceCounter pcGen0Collections;
PerformanceCounter pcGen1Collections;
```

Next I added this code to the Form1 constructor:

```
public Form1()
{
    InitializeComponent();


    this.pcGen0Collections = new PerformanceCounter(".NET CLR Memory",
        "# Gen 0 Collections", "MonitorUseResou");
    this.pcGen0Collections.BeginInit();
```

```
    this.pcGen1Collections = new PerformanceCounter(".NET CLR Memory",
        "# Gen 1 Collections", "MonitorUseResou");
    this.pcGen1Collections.BeginInit();

    this.label1.Text = this.pcGen0Collections.CounterName;
    this.label2.Text = this.pcGen1Collections.CounterName;
}
```

You could argue that I may as well have set the text for the labels in the Properties window, but doing it this way makes sure they contain the correct text for the appropriate counter (and makes the name more robust against anyone later changing which counters are displayed).

Finally, I added this code to the timer's `Tick` event handler:

```
private void timer_Tick(object sender, System.EventArgs e)
{
    this.tbGen0Collections.Text =
                        this.pcGen0Collections.NextValue().ToString();
    this.tbGen1Collections.Text = this.pcGen1Collections.NextValue().ToString();
}
```

Running this code, you can watch the garbage collections accumulate as you allocate more bytes of array. You'll notice that generation 1 collections don't start happening too frequently until you've allocated quite a bit of memory—at which point the garbage collector is seriously looking for memory it can reclaim. Although I haven't shown generation 2 collections in the sample, you'd also see the frequency of those collections rising.

Registering Your Own Performance Counter

I'll now develop the MonitorUseResources example to illustrate how you can define your own performance counter. The new example is called CustomPerfCounter and looks like Figure 7-17 when running.

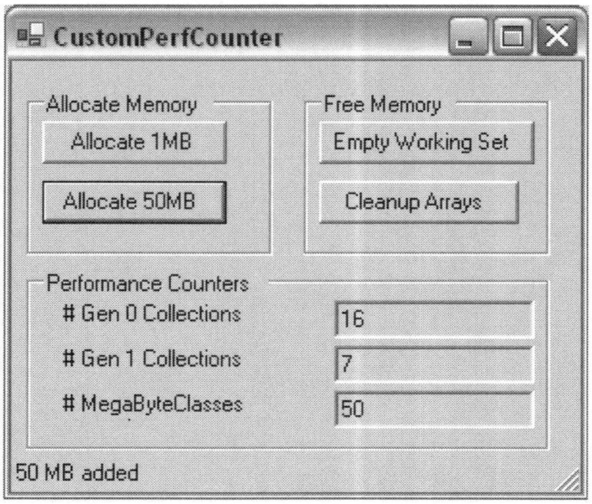

Figure 7-17. *The* CustomPerfCounter *sample*

It's similar to the MonitorUseResources example, except it shows an additional perform-ance counter (category: AdvDotNet, counter name: # MegaByteClasses created, instance name: CustomPerfCtr). This counter is registered and controlled by the sample itself and shows the total number of MegaByteClass instances that have been created since the program started running. To prove that this is a real performance counter that other applications can view, you can start PerfMon while the sample is running and add the custom counter to the counters displayed by PerfMon, as shown in Figure 7-18.

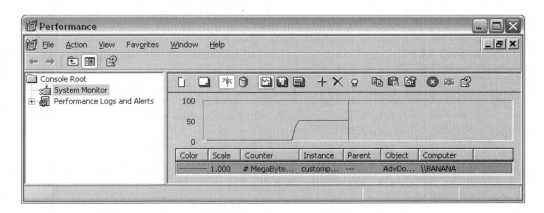

Figure 7-18. *PerfMon, with my custom* MegaByteClass *counter added*

To achieve all this in the code, I first need a new field in the Form1 class to hold the counter (as well as the new textbox and label I added from the Toolbox). I also declared some strings that give the names of the new category, counter, and instance, as well as help text. (If you run PerfMon, you'll see that the help text appears as descriptions when you browse for counters to add.)

```
PerformanceCounter pcGen0Collections;
PerformanceCounter pcCommittedBytes;
PerformanceCounter pcMegaByteAllocs;
string categoryName = "AdvDotNet";
string counterName  = "# MegaByteClasses created";
string categoryHelp = "Advanced .NET Sample Counters";
string counterHelp = "Counts total MegaByteClass allocations";
string instanceName = "CustomPerfCtr";
```

The code to register the new counter, along with the new counter category, AdvDotNet, looks like this:

```
private void RegisterCustomCounter()
{
    if(!PerformanceCounterCategory.Exists(categoryName))
    {
```

```
        PerformanceCounterCategory.Create(categoryName,categoryHelp,
                                          counterName,counterHelp);
    }
    pcMegaByteAllocs = new PerformanceCounter(categoryName, counterName,
                                              instanceName, false);
    pcMegaByteAllocs.RawValue = 0;
}
```

I'm using a couple of new methods on the PerformanceCounterCategory here. Exists() checks whether a category exists—clearly you shouldn't try to register the category if it's already there. Create() registers the specified category as well as one counter in the category (a different overload of Create() exists for registering categories that contain more than one counter). Finally, I use a slightly different overload of the constructor to PerformanceCounter(). The overload I'm using here has an extra bool parameter that indicates whether the access to the counter is to be read-only (the default). I set this to false since the code needs to be able to write to the counter. Finally, I set the data for this counter to initially be zero (no MegaByteClass instances created).

Notice the way that instantiating a PerformanceCounter object really has created a new underlying performance counter instance—that is, genuine Windows object that can be seen by PerfMon, for example. What's actually going on is that the PerformanceCounter constructor checks to see if a performance counter of the named machine, category, object, and instance already exists and has been registered with the performance counter architecture in Windows; if so, it hooks up to that counter. Otherwise it creates a new performance counter instance and registers it.

The RegisterCustomCounter() method is called from the Form1 constructor. The sample also contains a method to remove the counter and the AdvDotNet category, which is called from the Dispose() method of Form1.

```
private void DeregisterCounter()
{
    if (PerformanceCounterCategory.Exists(categoryName))
        PerformanceCounterCategory.Delete(categoryName);
}
```

In a real-world application, you may prefer to leave the counter permanently registered, but this is only a sample. I'm guessing that if you download and run the code, you won't want the extra performance counter cluttering up your system after you've finished playing with the sample! So the AdvDotNet category exists only while the sample is running, which means that if you want to use PerfMon to examine it, then you'll need to launch the sample before you launch PerfMon.

Finally, the code needs to update the counter whenever you instantiate MegaByteClass.

```
public void AddArray()
{
    arrays.Add(new MegaByteClass());
    this.pcMegaByteAllocs.RawValue += 1;
}
```

Strictly speaking, this is updating the counter whenever you add an instance to the array of `MegaBytesClasses` that's stored in the `Form1` class, but you get the picture.

That's all the code needs to do to register and update the counter. However, since the sample is maintaining the counter, I may as well have the code display its value along with the values of the other counters while I'm at it. So here's the new timer tick event handler:

```
private void timer_Tick(object sender, System.EventArgs e)
{
   this.tbGen0Collections.Text =
      this.pcGen0Collections.NextValue().ToString();
   this.tbCommittedBytes.Text =
                              this.pcCommittedBytes.NextValue().ToString();
   this.tbMegaByteAllocs.Text = this.pcMegaByteAllocs.RawValue.ToString();
}
```

The new counter is displayed using the `RawValue` property instead of the `NextValue()` method. I don't have space to go into the distinction in detail here; you can find full details in the documentation. Basically, different types of counters exist. For example, the counter I've developed here has a simple number that's set. Some counters form their values by incrementing or by taking the difference between the last two values. The nature of the counter determines which method/property is most appropriate for retrieving a value.

Understanding Profiling

Although using a profiler can be just as important as using performance counters to identify ways you can improve performance of an application, I won't spend nearly as much time discussing profiling. This is partly because of the lack of Microsoft-supplied profilers—at the time of writing none exist for managed code, other than a couple of samples in the .NET Framework SDK—and partly because you have relatively few new underlying principles to understand concerning the use of profilers. However, I'll use one third-party profiler, the Compuware DevPartner profiler, to demonstrate the general principles of profiling, and I'll briefly discuss the profiling API. I'll also cover the CLR profiler, a profiler supplied by Microsoft that focuses particularly on memory usage.

Choosing a Profiler

Since this is a technology book rather than a sales book, it's not really my purpose to start recommending particular non-Microsoft products. In general, if you think your software will benefit from a detailed analysis of the time spent in various methods, you'll be better off searching the Web for suitable profiling products. Companies I'm aware of that currently offer profilers for managed code include Compuware, AutomatedQA, and Rational. However, there will certainly be others—you'll need to evaluate which is the most suitable product based on your needs and budget. In some cases, companies sell the full profiler but offer a basic version for free.

It's worth mentioning that if you don't want to purchase a commercial profiler, you have a couple of alternative techniques.

Use the Microsoft sample profilers: The .NET Framework SDK contains a couple of sample profilers. One is designed for general profiling, and the other is specifically designed to look for methods that consume too much time. The source code for these profilers is available in the Tool Developers Guide/Samples subfolder in the .NET Framework SDK. These profilers are both quite basic ones, and you'll need to compile them, but they do have the advantage that you have the source code available for them.

Add your own profiling code: Because of the complexity of the profiling API, using the profiling API isn't normally a realistic solution. However, an alternative technique allows you to obtain good-quality information about the execution times of sections of your code: Just take the difference between the times before and after the relevant code is completed. With a little bit of work, you can achieve some quite sophisticated and reasonably automated generation of profiling information based on this technique. If you use this technique, however, you should be aware of inaccuracies because of any time during which threads are sleeping. You'll be measuring wall-clock time, not CPU time.

The next thing I'll do in this chapter is demonstrate how to implement your own code to time some other code.

Writing Your Own Profiling Timer Code

The basic principle of writing a profiling timer is relatively simple: You check what the time is before some operation is carried out, perform the operation, check the time again, and take the difference. That tells you how long the operation took. In this section I'll show you how to write such an application. The disadvantage of this approach compared to using a commercial profiler is that you have to explicitly add calls to your timer code at the points in your profiled code where you want to measure times whereas a commercial profiler will normally retrieve this information for all methods automatically. On the other hand, you get complete freedom to choose exactly which code you want to profile. For example, it doesn't have to be a complete method. Here I'll develop the sample and then use it to measure how long it takes to execute a particular for loop. That kind of fine control may not be available in a commercial profiler, which is more likely to insist you profile a complete method.

To use this technique, you need a high-resolution timer that can accurately measure small intervals of time. Unfortunately, the .NET Framework Class Library doesn't help you here, so for this example I'll have to turn to unmanaged code and a native API method, QueryPerformanceCounter().

■**Note** In this section I use the term *timer* to indicate some code that measures an interval of time for profiling purposes. Don't confuse that with the more usual meaning of *timer*: a component that raises events at regular intervals of time.

Two properties of managed classes look at first sight like possible candidates for a timer, but I don't recommend you use either of them to measure small times (though they will both be fine if you're measuring larger times, say, greater than about a tenth of a second).

System.Environment.TickCount measures the time in milliseconds since the computer started. Unfortunately, one millisecond isn't really short enough for many operations. For example, you may want to profile a method that takes a tenth of a millisecond to execute (such a method may still be significantly affecting performance if it gets invoked a sufficient number of times).

System.DateTime.Now.Ticks is documented as returning the number of 100-nanosecond intervals that have elapsed since 12 a.m., Jan. 1, 1 AD. This sounds more hopeful, since 100 nanoseconds is just one tenth of a millionth of a second. Unfortunately, the accuracy is still not good, since this property appears to increment in large blocks. System.DateTime is just not intended to measure such small intervals, and my own tests suggest that System.DateTime is unable in practice to distinguish time intervals of less than about 1/100 of a second.

Details of the implementations of these properties aren't documented—they both defer internally to IL internalcall methods, indicating that their implementations are supplied internally by the CLR.

So having rejected DateTime.Ticks and Environment.TickCount, let's check out my preferred solution. QueryPerformanceCounter() is an API function that's documented as measuring the tick count of a certain performance counter known as the *high-resolution performance counter*. This counter simply increments a tick count at a given frequency. The frequency itself is undocumented since it's dependent on your hardware, so you need to call another method, QueryPerformanceFrequency(), to obtain that value. To give you some idea of the resolution you can expect, on my 1 gigahertz (GHz) machine, calling QueryPerformanceFrequency() indicates a resolution of 1/3,000,000th of a second—that should be enough for any realistic profiling scenario.

I'll illustrate the use of these methods by developing a small sample, called IntervalTimer. The sample contains a class, also called IntervalTimer, which acts like a stopwatch. You call its Start() method to start measuring an interval of time, and then you call its Stop() method to stop the measurement, after which you can examine how long the interval takes. For this, I've overridden ToString() to display the timing information. Because IntervalTimer uses the high-resolution performance counter, it's extremely accurate even for very small intervals.

I'll start with the test harness that illustrates how to use the IntervalTimer class. The following code measures how long it takes to execute a simple for loop:

```
static void Main()
{
    int quantity = 0;
    IntervalTimer timer = new IntervalTimer();
    for (int numTests = 0 ; numTests < 3 ; numTests++)
    {
        timer.Start();
        timer.Stop();
        Console.WriteLine("Just starting and stopping timer: ");
        Console.WriteLine("     " + timer.ToString());

        timer.Start();
```

```
        for (int i=0 ; i<1000 ; i++)
            quantity += i;
        timer.Stop();
        Console.WriteLine("counting to 1000: ");
        Console.WriteLine("      " + timer.ToString());
    }
    Console.WriteLine("\nquantity is " + quantity);
}
```

The outer `for` loop in this sample means that the test will run three times. Within each test, the code first measures how much CPU time is used just to start and stop the timer and displays the results. This ensures that you can make allowance for this time when assessing the results. Then the code performs the real test—it uses the `IntervalTimer` to measure how long it takes to execute a `for` loop that performs 1,000 additions. At each iteration of the loop, it adds the loop index to a variable called `quantity`. It also displays the value of `quantity` at the end of all the tests (this is just to make sure that the variable is actually used and therefore can't be optimized away by an intelligent JIT compiler).

Running a release build of this code gives these results on my machine:

```
Just starting and stopping timer:
    Interval: 0.000006 seconds (23 ticks)
counting to 1000:
    Interval: 0.000009 seconds (34 ticks)
Just starting and stopping timer:
    Interval: 0.000006 seconds (20 ticks)
counting to 1000:
    Interval: 0.000009 seconds (32 ticks)
Just starting and stopping timer:
    Interval: 0.000006 seconds (21 ticks)
counting to 1000:
    Interval: 0.000009 seconds (32 ticks)
quantity is 1498500
```

I've implemented `IntervalTimer.ToString()` so that it displays the total time in seconds as well as the number of tick counts this represents. For small times, the number of tick counts may be important because if, say, a time was measured to be 20 tick counts, then you know that it's accurate only to within 5 percent (because you can't measure times of less than one tick). The previous results show that the numbers of tick counts is low, so your times won't be especially precise. However, just look at how tiny the times I've managed to measure are: Starting and stopping the timer takes about six-millionths of a second (six microseconds), and starting and stopping the timer and running the loop takes nine microseconds. From this you can deduce that it took approximately three microseconds to execute the loop. A more sophisticated timer would probably do this latter calculation automatically and just show you the final result of three microseconds, but I don't want the sample to get too complicated. You may want to compare this sample with the similar `PerfTest` sample I presented in Chapter 6. In that chapter, I used `System.DateTime` to measure an interval, but that was possible only because the interval was very large—about one second.

Now let's look at the code for the `IntervalTimer` class. First I need to define the P/Invoke wrappers for the unmanaged API functions I'll be using.

```
public class IntervalTimer
{
    [DllImport("kernel32.dll")]
        static extern private int QueryPerformanceCounter(out long count);

    [DllImport("kernel32.dll")]
        static extern private int QueryPerformanceFrequency(out long count);
```

Second, I'll need an enum that indicates whether the timer is started or stopped and some member fields.

```
public enum TimerState {NotStarted, Stopped, Started}

private TimerState state;
private long ticksAtStart;      // tick count when Start() called
private long intervalTicks;     // no. of ticks elapsed until Stop() called
private static long frequency;
private static int decimalPlaces;
private static string formatString;
private static bool initialized = false;
```

The meanings of the instance fields should be obvious. The static fields have to do with storing information about the timer frequency—recall that the frequency has to be determined by calling QueryPerformanceFrequency(). frequency is the frequency (the number of ticks per second). decimalPlaces is used when displaying timing information; clearly, the frequency will determine how many decimal places you can display in the time. Suppose, for example, the timer was a really slow one that fired only every tenth of a second. Then it'd be silly to claim a time of 5.6343442 seconds—the best you could say is that the time is about 5.6 seconds—in other words, you're specifying one decimal place. That's what decimalPlaces stores. formatString contains the formatting string used in IntervalTimer.ToString(). Since the format string will depend on how many decimal places can be shown, you can't hard-code it into the program.

All this information is gathered together the first time an IntervalTimer object is instantiated.

```
public IntervalTimer()
{
    if (!initialized)
    {
        QueryPerformanceFrequency(out frequency);
        decimalPlaces = (int)Math.Log10(frequency);
        formatString = String.Format("Interval: {{0:F{0}}} seconds ({{1}} ticks)",
                                                            decimalPlaces);
        initialized = true;
    }
    state = TimerState.NotStarted;
}
```

You may wonder why I haven't used a static constructor to perform this work. The reason is that using a static constructor appears to distort the timing information the first time

IntervalTimer is used. The reason for this isn't clear. It is, however, difficult to predict the precise timing and order of execution of statements when a static constructor is involved—some multithreading may be at work with static constructors, and this likely has something to do with the problem. To be safe, I've performed the static initialization in an instance constructor.

The implementations of the Start() and Stop() methods are relatively simple.

```
public void Start()
{
    state = TimerState.Started;
    ticksAtStart = CurrentTicks;
}

public void Stop()
{
    intervalTicks = CurrentTicks - ticksAtStart;
    state = TimerState.Stopped;
}
```

The following is the method that works out how many seconds correspond to a given tick count between calling Start() and calling Stop():

```
public float GetSeconds()
{
    if (state != TimerState.Stopped)
        throw new TimerNotStoppedException();
    return (float)intervalTicks/(float)frequency;
}
```

Note that calling GetSeconds() makes sense only if the timer has been started and stopped. This is checked, and if there's a problem, the method throws an exception, TimerNotStoppedException, which I'll define soon.

This is how the timing information is displayed:

```
public override string ToString()
{
    if (state != TimerState.Stopped)
        return "Interval timer, state: " + state.ToString();
    return String.Format(formatString, GetSeconds(), intervalTicks);
}
```

And finally, here's the custom exception:

```
public class TimerNotStoppedException : ApplicationException
{
    public TimerNotStoppedException()
        : base("Timer is either still running or has not been started")
    {
    }
}
```

Now that you've seen how to implement your own profiling timer, I'll cover one commercial profiler to give you a feel for what a full profiler application can achieve.

Working Through the Compuware Profiler Example

To demonstrate profiling in action, I'll use the Compuware DevPartner profiler, which is typical of the features you can expect in a typical profiler. The profiler is available from http://www.compuware.com, and once installed it exists as an add-in to VS .NET. To profile a program, you select Tools ➤ DevPartner Profiler from the main menu to enable the profiler, before running the program normally in VS .NET. After running the program, a new window will open in VS .NET containing profiling information. You can also stop the application at any time using menu options so that you can review the profiling information collected so far.

For this demonstration I'll run the UseResources sample in VS .NET (as a release build, of course). Running on my computer, clicking the Allocate 50MB button four times, freeing the memory, and then closing the form produced the results shown in Figure 7-19.

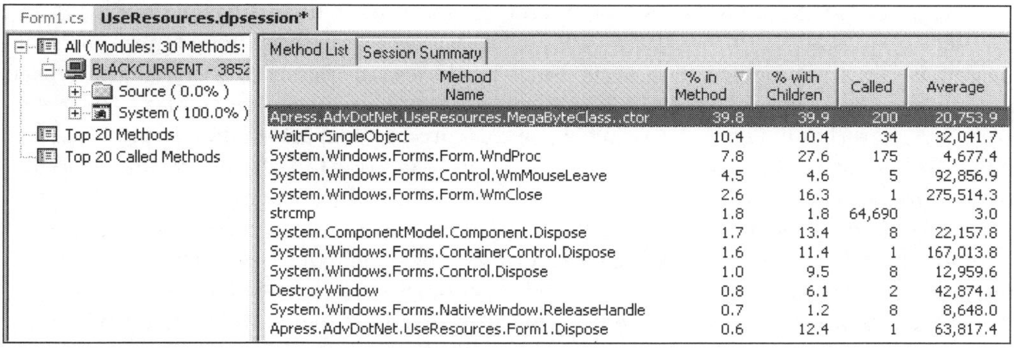

Form1.cs	UseResources.dpsession*					

	Method List	Session Summary				
All (Modules: 30 Methods:	Method Name		% in Method ▽	% with Children	Called	Average
BLACKCURRENT - 3852	Apress.AdvDotNet.UseResources.MegaByteClass..ctor		39.8	39.9	200	20,753.9
Source (0.0%)	WaitForSingleObject		10.4	10.4	34	32,041.7
System (100.0%)	System.Windows.Forms.Form.WndProc		7.8	27.6	175	4,677.4
Top 20 Methods	System.Windows.Forms.Control.WmMouseLeave		4.5	4.6	5	92,856.9
Top 20 Called Methods	System.Windows.Forms.Form.WmClose		2.6	16.3	1	275,514.3
	strcmp		1.8	1.8	64,690	3.0
	System.ComponentModel.Component.Dispose		1.7	13.4	8	22,157.8
	System.Windows.Forms.ContainerControl.Dispose		1.6	11.4	1	167,013.8
	System.Windows.Forms.Control.Dispose		1.0	9.5	8	12,959.6
	DestroyWindow		0.8	6.1	2	42,874.1
	System.Windows.Forms.NativeWindow.ReleaseHandle		0.7	1.2	8	8,648.0
	Apress.AdvDotNet.UseResources.Form1.Dispose		0.6	12.4	1	63,817.4

Figure 7-19. *Compuware DevPartner profiler used to examine the* UseResources *sample*

As you can see, the profiling information is supplied via an extra window in VS .NET. (This window opens automatically when the application being profiled stops running.) The window is divided into two panes, with a treeview to select what data you want to display in the listview. The listview is a property sheet with two tabs.

The Method List tab details the percentage of execution time spent in each method, and the Session Summary tab gives overall statistics as well as indicates the time spent executing code in any unmanaged libraries that have been invoked.

The second column in the listview, % in Method, indicates the percentage of execution time that was directly spent executing code in each method. The results show that the time spent allocating memory (in particular inside the MegaByteClass constructor) was a significant drain on computer time. On this run, the MegaByteClass constructor alone took 16.94 percent of the total processor time. Besides % in Method, the profiler offers a % with Children column. The former column indicates only the time spent executing code inside that method, and the latter indicates the time spent while that method was in the stack frame. For example, if the computer is executing method A, and method A calls method B, which in turn calls method C, then the time spent in B and C will show up in A's % with Children column, but not in A's % in Method column. This means the percentages in the first column will add up to 100 percent (ignoring rounding errors, and minus any time spent executing unmanaged code), but the percentages in the second column won't. When you're using a profiler to look at performance, you'll need to take care to distinguish between those two statistics. The next column in Figure 7-19 is also important—it gives the number of times that the method was called. Pay attention to this column: If you see that a particular method is taking a large proportion of CPU time, it may be because that method takes a long time to execute, or it may be because it's being invoked a large number of times (which may imply it's one of the other methods further up the call stack that needs optimizing). The column Average measures the average amount of time spent executing the code in a method (excluding time spent in child methods).

At this point, having profiled an application and identified the bottlenecks, you'd usually consider what changes in the algorithm you could make to improve performance. Unfortunately, you can't realistically do much to speed up the execution of the UseResources application, other than not allocating so much memory, which would defeat the purpose of this particular sample!

The profiling information for a program reveals some quite interesting details about the internal workings of .NET programs, besides telling you which methods need improvement if the application is to be speeded up. First, notice just how many methods exist that get invoked under the hood during a normal Windows Forms application (you can get an idea from the size of that scroll bar in Figure 7-19). In fact, on this run, a total of 2,001 different managed methods were invoked (you can get that information by clicking the Session Summary tab in the profiling results window). Going back to the Method List, if you click the Called header to sort the items in the listview by the number of times each method was called, the most-called method is revealed to be a method called strcmp, as shown in Figure 7-20. This method is unmanaged and is used within C and C++ code to compare strings. Here I'm not too concerned with precisely why this method got called so many times; it will certainly be well down the call stack and has been invoked by code within the CLR. I just want you to notice that, despite having been called more than 65,000 times, it contributed little more than 1 percent of CPU time.

| Method List Session Summary | | | |
Method Name	% in Method	% with Children	Called ▽
strcmp	1.8	1.8	64,690
RtlLeaveCriticalSection	0.1	0.1	56,244
InterlockedDecrement	0.0	0.0	48,218
RtlEnterCriticalSection	0.2	0.2	46,176
InterlockedIncrement	0.1	0.1	40,011
memset	0.0	0.0	33,928
strncmp	0.0	0.0	21,505
memcpy	0.1	0.1	19,667
RtlAllocateHeap	0.3	0.3	10,233
rotl	0.3	0.3	9,938
strlen	0.1	0.1	9,440
LocalAlloc	0.3	0.3	9,386
System.IO.MemoryStream.ReadByte	0.0	0.0	9,384
RtlFreeHeap	0.0	0.0	9,060

Figure 7-20. *Sorting the profile data by numbers of times a method is invoked*

The information presented in Figure 7-20 is clouded by the amount of information relating to method calls internal to the CLR and unmanaged methods and Windows API calls that are in turn invoked. (You may, by the way, be interested to note how many of the methods indicated in Figure 7-20 have to do with memory management. A number of methods also have to do with threading, a subject I'll cover in Chapter 9.) Seeing all these CLR and unmanaged methods is nice for investigating the CLR under the hood but not so good for trying to find out which of your own methods is taking the CPU time. With the Compuware profiler, this is easy to solve by expanding the treeview. This will reveal a series of nodes that show information based on individual assemblies. Then you simply select the assembly that contains the code you want to investigate, as shown in Figure 7-21.

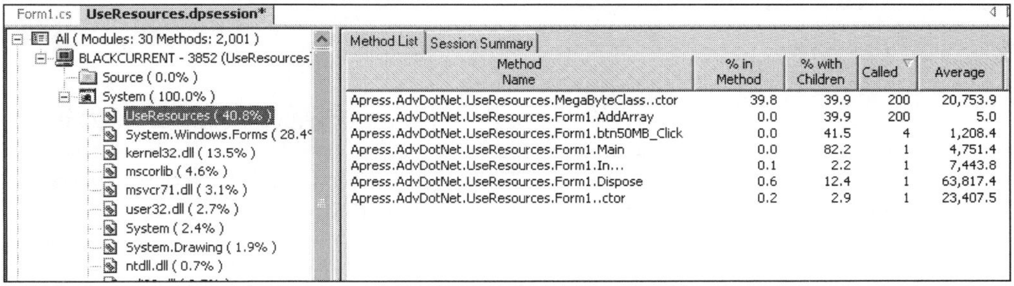

Figure 7-21. *Breaking down information for individual assemblies*

This view makes it clear which methods in your own code are using the bulk of the CPU time. No surprise in Figure 7-21—it's still that `MegaByteClass` constructor!

Although these figures show the Compuware profiler, you'll find that most commercial profilers give you similar features, albeit with slightly different user interfaces.

Using the CLR Profiler

Microsoft supplies the CLR profiler. It works on similar principles to other commercial profilers to the extent that it uses the profiling API to monitor what a program is doing. However, unlike most profilers, the CLR profiler is intended not to profile performance but to profile the allocation of variables in memory and the operation of the garbage collector. It can display full information about what objects have been allocated or freed at what times and even what addresses in memory have been used. The cost of this is that running a program under the context of the CLR profiler will slow it down considerably, so don't try to obtain timing information using this technique. You can obtain both the source and the compiled executable for the CLR profiler from the Microsoft MSDN Web site at `http://msdn.microsoft.com`.

■**Tip** The CLR used to be known as the *allocation profiler* and was available, unsupported, through the GotDotNet.com Web site. Although that version is still available, you should now download the up-to-date version from Microsoft's site.

When you run the profiler, you'll be presented with a dialog box indicating the profiling options, as shown in Figure 7-22.

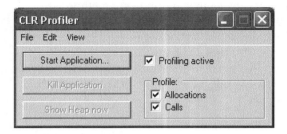

Figure 7-22. *CLR profiler at startup*

If you click the Start Application button, you'll be presented with a standard Open File dialog box that allows you to browse and select an assembly to run. At any time while the application is running, you can click the Show Heap Now button to get a view of the managed heap. Figure 7-23 shows the situation after I've allocated 11MB with the UseResources example.

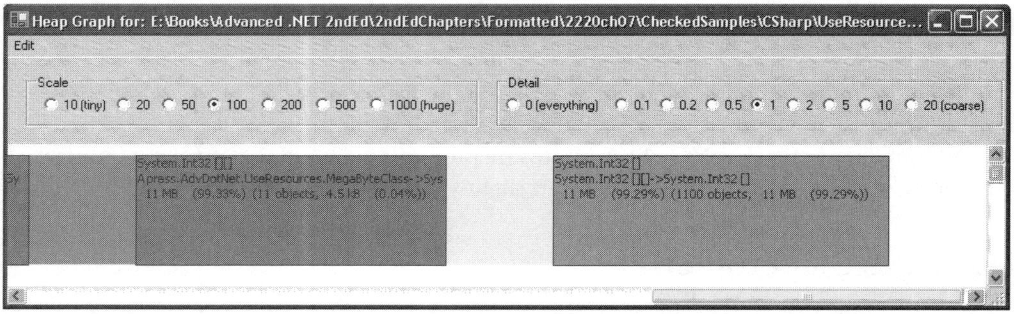

Figure 7-23. *CLR profiler monitoring the* UseResources *sample*

The figure shows that the profiler is able to break up the classes into component fields and has identified, for example, that the memory occupied at the most nested level consists of the int[] arrays contained in the MegaByteClass class. The CLR profiler offers various other views that show, for example, the addresses and ages of objects on the managed heap.

Using the Profiling API

For performance counters, I went into some detail concerning how to access the counters programmatically from your code. In the case of performance counters, that was worth doing because programmatic access is so easy using the performance counter classes. Getting a program to use these classes—for example, in order to monitor its own resource usage—is a relatively simple operation. For the profiling API, this isn't the case. The profiling API is entirely an unmanaged, COM-based API. It's highly complex, and it'd certainly not normally be worthwhile to use it to get code to monitor itself in the way you would with performance counters. Not only that, but because of the way the profiling API hooks into the CLR, it's quite easy to crash the entire CLR if your profiling code contains bugs. This is because for performance reasons the CLR's profiling support does the absolute minimum of error checking. For example, if the CLR has to notify another application whenever the JIT-compiled code invokes a new method, as may happen if you're profiling, then it's imperative that the notification process uses only a few machine cycles; otherwise the profiling process will destroy the timings that it's supposedly measuring. In general, the only reason for using the profiling API is if you're writing a fully-fledged profiler application.

If for any reason you want to use the profiling API, you can find the documentation and samples for it in the Tool Developers Guide in the .NET Framework SDK. You'll need to have a good understanding of COM, and you'll need to code in unmanaged C++. Essentially the procedure involves implementing a COM component that implements the interface `ICorProfilerCallback`. (This interface is defined in the header files `corprof.h` and `corprof.idl`, also supplied with the .NET Framework SDK.) You then temporarily set up a couple of environment variables that indicate that your component is a profiler. As long as you set these environment variables, any managed application that's launched will automatically be hooked up to the indicated profiler.

Summary

In this chapter you examined the facilities that both Windows and the CLR make available for monitoring the performance of managed applications and tracking down bottlenecks that can be impairing performance.

The underlying tools for this purpose fall into two main categories: performance counters and the profiling API. Performance counters monitor the resource usage of an application; for example, they can indicate if memory usage is excessive or if an excessive number of exceptions are being thrown. The Profiling API drills down more specifically into the execution flow of a program, measuring what objects are being instantiated and how long the computer is spending executing various methods. A number of utilities present the information from performance counters in a convenient format, and I've also shown how to access performance counters programmatically from managed code. In the case of profiling, the API is complex, and you won't normally access it programmatically. It's more usual to purchase a commercial profiler—I've used one such profiler to demonstrate the general principles of how to use this kind of tool and what information can be extracted from it.

CHAPTER 8

■■■

Generating Code Dynamically

In this chapter I'll cover a significant, though often underused, feature that's offered by the .NET Framework classes—the ability to generate either source code or IL code dynamically. In other words, you can have your code actually write or manipulate code instead of data. Normally, you'd conceptually imagine that the process of producing a software application involves you writing the source code, compiling it, and shipping it—and that's it. The code and resources your organization wrote constitutes the totality of the shipped product. With dynamic code generation, however, your shipped code can itself actually generate new code to perform additional tasks—this can be useful for performance reasons, among other factors. Alternatively, your code may modify the code in other assemblies (which may be done, for example, to insert calls to create debugging or profiling information). And obviously, if your product is a developer tool that's intended to assist developers in writing code, then it may be called on to generate some source code itself.

This chapter will cover the following:

- **Applications of dynamic code generation**: I'll review the main reasons why you may find it useful to implement dynamic code generation.

- **Architecture**: I'll cover the design of the code generation classes and in particular the different philosophies behind the System.Reflection.Emit classes (which generate straight assemblies containing IL code) and the System.CodeDom classes (which generate source code or assemblies).

- **Examples**: The bulk of the chapter is devoted to a couple of examples that illustrate how to use the dynamic code generation classes. For this part of the chapter, I treat the Reflection.Emit and the CodeDom classes separately.

Dynamic code generation isn't something that has any substantial intrinsic support in the CLR—it's a feature that's supported almost entirely by the associated .NET class libraries supplied by Microsoft. Hence, this chapter focuses almost exclusively on the use of the relevant classes. Note, however, that I won't make any attempt to be comprehensive (for example, to give lists of all the methods implemented by particular classes). You can find out that stuff easily enough in the MSDN documentation. Rather, my aim is to give you a feel for how the classes are used and how they've been designed.

Reasons to Use Dynamic Code Generation

Traditionally, code generation has been associated with compilers. However, the .NET Framework libraries make code generation sufficiently easy that it becomes feasible and potentially useful in a number of different scenarios, which I'll quickly review in the following sections.

Developer Tools

You're probably used to developer tools that can autogenerate code for you; the most obvious examples are Visual Studio .NET's Design View and its Properties window. Other examples from Microsoft include the xsd.exe tool, which can generate a source code file from an XML schema, and the wsdl.exe tool, which can generate client source code for XML services. And of course as I write this chapter Windows Longhorn is on the distant horizon with its Extensible Application Markup Language (XAML) files used to define client user interfaces. I don't personally know how the underlying technology is going to work, but it's a reasonable guess that dynamic code generation may be lurking around there somewhere.

Other situations in which dynamic code generation is important include the following:

Templates: Version 1.*x* of the .NET Framework has often been criticized for not including much support for generics, which offer similar, though more restrictive, features to unmanaged C++ template classes. (This will of course be fixed in .NET 2.*x*.) Since in practice a template isn't really more than a definition that allows the compiler to generate and compile multiple classes (or methods) from the same definition, it should be obvious that a developer tool could use dynamic code generation to implement the same kind of feature.

UML-based coding: Dynamic code generation can be used to implement tools in which developers use some kind of diagram to indicate the code they want to write—and the tool generates the code for them. An obvious example of this is generation of code from Unified Modeling Language (UML) diagrams.

Language conversion: The multilanguage support in the .NET Framework should theoretically reduce the need for source code to be converted between languages, because the source language that an assembly was originally compiled from is to a large extent irrelevant to clients of that assembly. Nevertheless, developers or organizations have an occasional need for applications that can convert source code between languages. Dynamic code generation can assist in the implementation of this kind of application.

Assembly modification: Sometimes you may need to take the instruction stream in an assembly and modify it prior to executing it—for example, to provide notifications of when certain IL instructions are executed. Obfuscators also need to permanently modify the contents of assemblies, and in a similar vein it's conceivable that you may want to write some software that optimizes the IL code in other assemblies (since compilers such as the C# and VB .NET ones perform little optimization of the emitted IL code). Although given how efficient the JIT compiler is at optimizing, I have some doubts whether an application such as this is particularly useful.

For Performance Reasons

Certain types of application exist for which dynamic code generation is likely to be the technique that will give the highest performance. A typical scenario is that the purpose of some method in a library is so general that the actual algorithm that should be used to accomplish the task isn't necessarily known at compile time. A couple of examples that illustrate the kind of situation I'm talking about are as follows:

Eval(): The Eval() function as used in such languages as pre-.NET VBA and VBScript allows the evaluation of an arithmetic expression that's supplied as a string. For example, you can write Eval("10+5"), which would return 15. More complex examples may involve variables or names of functions to be invoked in the Eval expression. In this case, the expression supplied determines the basic algorithm that Eval() needs to implement. If the expression is to be executed a number of times, then it doesn't really make sense to parse the string every time in order to determine what the program is required to do—since parsing the string is going to be significantly more processor intensive than actually doing the calculation. In this case, a more sensible option is to parse the string once and use the results to dynamically generate code that evaluates the expression.

Regular expressions: Regular expressions form another situation in which the actual programming needed to evaluate a particular regular expression is dependent on the actual expression supplied. If you supply a regular expression to some code (such as the relevant classes in the System.Text.RegularExpressions namespace), then a large part of the processing involves parsing the regular expression string and figuring out exactly what you want done. Thus, any code that's generically capable of evaluating any regular expression supplied to it is clearly going to have significantly worse performance than some code that's specifically geared to executing a particular regular expression. So once again on performance grounds, if a particular regular expression is to be executed a number of times, a program will perform better if it dynamically compiles the code needed to evaluate each regular expression the first time it encounters that expression. It turns out that dynamic code generation using System.Reflection.Emit classes does feature in the internal implementation of some of Microsoft's regular expression classes.

Reflection: One of the main benefits of .NET custom attributes is that other code can later read any attributes you define and modify its own execution path based on the attributes. Dynamic code generation based on the values of attributes may play a role here. One example of this is when classes are to be instantiated based on the System.Reflection classes. It's possible to instantiate and use classes using methods such as Activator.CreateInstance() and MethodInfo.Invoke(), but these methods need to use reflection internally to perform their tasks and are therefore much less efficient than invoking the constructor and required methods directly. Once again, you could use dynamic code generation as an alternative technique—which can give performance benefits if the methods are to be invoked many times.

Data access: A program could analyze the structure of the database and then, based on the database structure, dynamically generate IL, C#, or VB code to access the database efficiently.

Understanding the Architecture

The classes that implement dynamic code generation are based on two different methodologies, depending on whether you're generating source code or IL code, as shown in Figure 8-1.

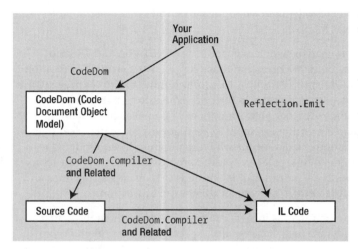

Figure 8-1. *The various ways an application can generate code dynamically*

Figure 8-1 indicates which namespaces contain classes that can make the conversions shown in the arrows. What the figure shows is that the Reflection.Emit classes can be used to directly create an assembly and add IL code to that assembly. The Reflection.Emit classes are based on a similar object model as the System.Reflection classes.

On the other hand, the System.CodeDom classes can create a *document object model* (DOM). This DOM is also sometimes referred to as a *CodeDom* and indicates the structure of program in a source language–neutral way. In other words, it may indicate that the code should define namespace X, which contains class Y. Class Y contains method Z, which contains statements to perform certain operations. However, this is all stored in a way that's independent of the syntax of any given language. (The DOM exists as a tree structure of object references in the System.CodeDom namespace, as you'll see shortly in the section "Coding with the CodeDom.")

■**Caution** The use of the term *DOM* to describe the document hierarchy that represents a particular piece of source code can sound confusing since it's a highly nonintuitive term. Unfortunately, it's the terminology Microsoft has chosen, so you'll have to live with it in this chapter.

Figure 8-1 indicates "CodeDom.Compiler and Related" as the namespaces that contain classes that can operate on the DOM. These classes can convert the DOM into source code and can convert the source code into an assembly; alternatively they can convert the DOM directly into an assembly. What do I mean by *and Related*? Well, the CodeDom.Compiler namespace contains interfaces, abstract base classes, and some supporting helper classes to assist in performing these operations but without reference to any particular language. For example, it contains an interface, `ICodeGenerator`, that defines the methods required to convert a document tree into source code. If you want to actually generate, say, C# source code, then you need a class that actually implements this interface to generate C# code. If you want to generate VB source code, then you need another class that implements the same interface—and so on for the other languages. Microsoft has supplied classes that provide these implementations for several languages, most notably in the `Microsoft.CSharp` and `Microsoft.VisualBasic` namespaces. Of course, other companies can choose to supply implementations for other languages. At the time of writing, managed C++ has no Microsoft-supplied implementation—so you can't dynamically generate C++ source code files.

You've probably gathered from this discussion that dynamic code generation is really founded on two fundamentally different technologies. The underlying object models for the `Reflection.Emit` classes and the `CodeDom` classes are independent of each other, and the classes are used in very different ways. Accordingly, I'll treat the two areas separately in this chapter. I'll cover the `Reflection.Emit` classes first, and then I'll present the `CodeDom` and related classes in the second part of the chapter.

Before I work through some actual code using `Reflection.Emit` and `CodeDom`, I'll point out one other alternative: You can write code that directly outputs the text representing the source code to a file and then, if required, compiles this code. Obviously, if you do that, you won't get the language independence; you'll have to write completely separate code if you want to swap output languages, but this may still be an appropriate technique depending on your project's requirements. When I present the CodeDom examples, you'll see that CodeDom leads to quite long and complex code, so you may decide that ignoring CodeDom and directly figuring out the source code text in your code is a better option. In a similar manner, you could write code that outputs the binary content of assemblies directly, without using the `Reflection.Emit` classes. However, for generating IL, there's unlikely to be much benefit in doing that since the `Reflection.Emit` classes do a lot of work for you in terms of automatically generating the PE and CLR headers and metadata—which would be a major task to do by hand.

Coding Using Reflection.Emit

In most cases, `Reflection.Emit` will be the preferred technique for creating assemblies. Not only is it more efficient, but the programming model is simpler and—provided you have no need for any source code files—more flexible. (If you need to see the emitted code in text form, you can always use `ildasm.exe` to disassemble it.) Also, because you're effectively directly writing IL to the new assemblies, you're not confined to those CLR features that are implemented by any one high-level language in the emitted code. The only proviso is that—obviously—you won't get far with the `Reflection.Emit` classes unless you're familiar with IL.

With `Reflection.Emit`, the newly emitted assembly isn't initially created as a file. Rather, you specify an application domain in which to create the assembly. The assembly is then created in memory, within the virtual address space for that application domain. You can then do one of two things with the new assembly.

- Save it to a file

- Execute it, without ever saving it

Obviously if you don't save the assembly to a file, it will cease to exist as soon as the application domain is unloaded, so it won't be available for any other programs to use. Such an assembly is known as a *transient assembly*.

You'll start the operation of creating a transient assembly like this:

```
// appDomain is a reference to the AppDomain in which the assembly
// is to be created
// assemblyName is an AssemblyName object that gives the name of an assembly
AssemblyBuilder assembly =
            appDomain.DefineDynamicAssembly(assemblyName,
                              AssemblyBuilderAccess.Run);
```

This code uses an enumeration, System.Reflection.Emit.AssemblyBuilderAccess, which defines what you want to do with the assembly. Possible values are Run, Save, and RunAndSave. RunAndSave is the most flexible—it means you'll be able to execute the assembly as soon as you've finished building it, and you'll be able to save it to file, too.

The previous code starts the whole process. The next thing to do is add a module to the assembly.

```
module = assembly.DefineDynamicModule("MainModule");
```

The string passed to DefineDynamicModule gives the name of the module. This method also has a two-parameter version, which is used if you want to save the assembly and which takes as a second parameter the name of the file to which to save this module.

The next step is to define your classes, and so on, that will go in the module. The following code creates a class called MyClass, which is derived from System.Object:

```
TypeBuilder myClass = module.DefineType("MyClass",
                            TypeAttributes.Class,
                            typeof(System.Object));
```

Once you have a type, you'll want to add members to it. Various TypeBuilder methods are defined to do this, with names such as DefineMethod(), DefineConstructor(), DefineEvent(), and DefineField(). For example, to add a method to the class, you can do this:

```
MethodBuilder myMethod = myClass.DefineMethod("GroovyMethod",
    MethodAttributes.Public | MethodAttributes.Virtual,
    typeof(float), new Type [] {typeof(int), typeof(int)});
```

Defining a method is more complex than most operations because you have a lot more information to supply. The first parameter to DefineMethod() gives the name of the method. The second parameter is a System.Reflection.MethodAttributes flag enumeration, which specifies such things as whether the method should be public, private, protected, and so on, and whether it should be virtual. The third parameter is the return type, and the final parameter is a Type[] array that lists the types of the arguments this method will take. So the previous line of code will create a method with the IL equivalent of this signature:

```
public virtual float GroovyMethod(int, int)
```

Adding code to the method is the point at which you need to start getting your hands dirty with IL. The starting point is a method called MethodBuilder.GetGenerator(). The following code returns an ILGenerator object that can be used to add code to the method using an Emit() method:

```
ILGenerator ilStream = groovyMethod.GetILGenerator();
ilStream.Emit(OpCodes.Ldarg_1);
ilStream.Emit(OpCodes.Ldarg_2);
ilStream.Emit(OpCodes.Add);
ilStream.Emit(OpCodes.Conv_R4);
ilStream.Emit(OpCodes.Ret);
```

This code adds the following IL to the method:

```
ldarg.1
ldarg.2
add
conv.r4
ret
```

The emitted method here simply adds the two arguments, converts the result to a float, and returns this result. Notice that the arguments are indexed as 1 and 2 since argument 0 is the this reference.

The ILGenerator.Emit() method deserves a bit more analysis—it has many overloads. However, the first argument is always the IL command to be added. This command is always represented by the type System.Reflection.Emit.OpCodes—a class that's designed to represent the IL opcodes and has a large number of static read-only fields that represent all the different codes. In fact, the class implements only static fields—you can't instantiate it. (You can also use a static method to obtain information about the arguments required by different opcodes.) The names of the fields of this class are basically the same as the mnemonics for the corresponding IL opcodes—except for a couple of modifications to conform to normal .NET naming conventions: The field names each start with an uppercase letter, and any dots in the mnemonic are replaced by underscores. Hence, OpCodes.Ldarg_1 represents the IL opcode ldarg.1, and so on.

I mentioned that other overloads of ILGenerator.Emit() exist. This is to take account of the fact that many opcodes require one or more arguments of different types—the other ILGenerator.Emit() overloads take additional parameters that specify the opcode arguments to be added to the IL stream. You'll see some of these overloads in action in the examples in the next two sections.

Once you've added all the members, IL instructions, and so on, to a type, you actually complete the process of defining the type and making sure the type is added to the module like this:

```
Type myNewType = myClass.CreateType();
```

In other words, you call the TypeBuilder.CreateType() method. You can think of all the stuff up to this point as simply telling the type builder what code and metadata you'll want in the type when it's created. CreateType() is the method that does the work and actually creates the type. The neat thing is that it returns a System.Type reference to a Type object that describes the newly created type. This is a fully working type reference. This means that, provided you created the assembly as a Run or RunAndSave assembly, you can start manipulating this type straightaway. For example, you can instantiate it (provided, of course, that you initially indicated in the AppDomain.CreateDynamicAssembly() call that this assembly was to be run).

```
// paramsList is an object [] array that gives the parameters to
// be supplied to the MyClass constructor
object myNewObject = Activator.CreateInstance(myNewType, paramsList);
```

If, on the other hand, you just want to save the assembly, you can do this:

```
assembly.Save("MyNewAssembly.dll");
```

One other neat thing you'll discover is this: Reflection.Emit classes aren't only based on the .NET type system but in many cases are directly derived from corresponding classes in the Sytem.Reflection namespace. For example, you'll no doubt be familiar with using the System.Reflection.Assembly class, which represents an assembly. The System.Reflection.Emit.AssemblyBuilder class is derived from Assembly and additionally implements methods that allow you to create a new assembly instead of loading an existing one. Similarly, TypeBuilder is derived from System.Type, and ModuleBuilder is derived from System.Reflection.Module. The same pattern applies for most of the Reflection classes that represent items in an assembly. The beauty of this model is the way it permits inline use of transient assemblies. The AssemblyBuilder and related classes you use to create a new assembly already contain all the properties, and so on, that you need to query information about the assembly and its contained types.

Creating a Saved Executable Assembly

I'll now present an example, called EmitHelloWorld. It uses the Reflection.Emit classes to create an executable assembly that contains the usual HelloWorld Main() method. The example will generate an assembly containing this IL code (as viewed in ildasm.exe):

```
.method public static void  Main() cil managed
{
  .entrypoint
  // Code size       11 (0xb)
  .maxstack  1
  IL_0000:  ldstr      "Hello, World!"
  IL_0005:  call       void [mscorlib]System.Console::WriteLine(string)
  IL_000a:  ret
}
```

The code for the example looks like this:

```
public static void Main()
{
    AssemblyName assemblyName = new AssemblyName();
    assemblyName.Name = "HelloWorld";
    assemblyName.Version = new Version("1.0.1.0");
```

```
    AssemblyBuilder assembly = Thread.GetDomain().
            DefineDynamicAssembly(assemblyName, AssemblyBuilderAccess.Save);

    ModuleBuilder module;
    module = assembly.DefineDynamicModule("MainModule", "HelloWorld.exe");

    MethodBuilder mainMethod = module.DefineGlobalMethod("Main",
        MethodAttributes.Static | MethodAttributes.Public, typeof(void), ,
        Type.EmptyTypes);

    Type[] writeLineParams = { typeof(string) };
    MethodInfo writeLineMethod = typeof(Console).GetMethod("WriteLine",
                                                        writeLineParams);
    ILGenerator constructorIL = mainMethod.GetILGenerator();
    constructorIL.Emit(OpCodes.Ldstr, "Hello, World!");
    constructorIL.Emit(OpCodes.Call, writeLineMethod);
    constructorIL.Emit(OpCodes.Ret);

    module.CreateGlobalFunctions();

    assembly.SetEntryPoint(mainMethod, PEFileKinds.ConsoleApplication);

    assembly.Save ("HelloWorld.exe");
}
```

The first thing I do in this code is define the identity for the assembly. The
System.Reflection.AssemblyName class represents an assembly. Next the code uses the
Thread.GetDomain() method to retrieve a reference to the application domain in which
the current (main) thread of execution is running and asks the application domain to create
a new assembly, specifying that the new assembly is to be saved to file.

```
AssemblyName assemblyName = new AssemblyName();
assemblyName.Name = "HelloWorld";
assemblyName.Version = new Version("1.0.1.0");

AssemblyBuilder assembly = Thread.GetDomain().
        DefineDynamicAssembly(assemblyName, AssemblyBuilderAccess.Save);
```

From this, the code creates a module and defines a method. For such a simple application
as I'm creating here, no types need to be defined; the code simply requires to set the Main()
method up as a global method. You do this with the ModuleBuilder.DefineGlobalMethod()
method.

```
MethodBuilder mainMethod = module.DefineGlobalMethod("Main",
    MethodAttributes.Static | MethodAttributes.Public, typeof(void), ,
    Type.EmptyTypes);
```

The four parameters passed to DefineGlobalMethod() are (respectively) the method name, attributes, the return type (void in this case), and an object[] array giving the parameter list. The code passes a special field, Type.EmptyType, for the final parameter to indicate that the method to be created won't take any parameters.

The next step will be to define the IL instruction stream for the new method. Before you can code that, you need a bit of preliminary work. The IL instruction stream is going to contain a call command to call the Console.WriteLine() method. So before you start, you need a MethodRef object that refers to this method. You can use the Type.GetMethod() method to achieve this.

```
Type[] writeLineParams = { typeof(string) };
MethodInfo writeLineMethod = typeof(Console).GetMethod("WriteLine",
writeLineParams);
```

Notice that because here the code is simply retrieving a MethodInfo reference that describes an existing method, you can use the GetMethod() method that's implemented by TypeBuilder's base type, Type; this statement is the same as you'd see in normal reflection calls.

Now the program can write out the instruction stream.

```
ILGenerator constructorIL = mainMethod.GetILGenerator();
constructorIL.Emit(OpCodes.Ldstr, "Hello, World!");
constructorIL.Emit(OpCodes.Call, writeLineMethod);
constructorIL.Emit(OpCodes.Ret);
```

The Reflection.Emit classes can automatically work out the required .maxstack size and insert it into the assembly metadata—so you don't need to worry about that.

The ldstr command is emitted by a two-parameter overload of ILGenerator.Emit(). The second parameter is simply a string, and this method will automatically cause the string to be added to the metadata as a string literal. Similarly, another overload of Emit() can emit the call command. This overload takes a MethodInfo reference as the second parameter to identify the method to be called. Internally, the EmitCall() method will add an appropriate MethodRef field to the metadata and construct the metadata token that will be inserted into the IL stream as the argument to the call opcode.

■**Caution** Unfortunately, although it should be obvious that certain overloads of ILGenerator.Emit() will generate correct IL only if used with certain opcodes, these methods don't appear to perform any checking on the opcodes they've been passed. This means that it's easy to use the overloads of this method to write out an instruction that has an argument type that isn't appropriate to the opcode—for example, emitting an ldc.i4.0 command (which doesn't take an argument) and putting a method token as an argument! Obviously, the JIT compiler won't be able to make any sense of the resultant instruction stream since it'll interpret the "argument" as more IL opcodes! You'll need to take special care to guard against this kind of bug when using the Reflection.Emit classes.

Finally, the code needs to do a bit more. The final three statements in the example create the global Main() function, set it up as the entry point method for the assembly, make sure it's an executable assembly (as opposed to a DLL) that will be emitted, and finally actually save the assembly.

```
module.CreateGlobalFunctions();
assembly.SetEntryPoint(mainMethod, PEFileKinds.ConsoleApplication);
assembly.Save("HelloWorld.exe");
```

ModuleBuilder.CreateGlobalFunctions() does for global functions what TypeBuilder.CreateType() does for types: it finishes the job of writing the methods and accompanying metadata to the assembly.

Notice that the string that's passed as a filename to the Save() method is the same as the filename specified earlier for the module. That ensures the module will be placed in the same file as the assembly itself—as you'd normally expect for a prime module. It may seem odd that you end up specifying the same filename twice, but the distinction is important, since it's possible you may want to create a multifile assembly, in which case some modules would be placed in different files from the main assembly file. Hence, you separately specify the filename of the assembly and the filename of the module.

Creating and Running a DLL Assembly

My second and final Reflection.Emit example, the EmitClass example, is similar to the previous example but illustrates how to create a DLL assembly. In this case, I'll define a class with a constructor and member function instead of a global function; this will require somewhat different code to generate the class. I'll also have the sample both save the assembly and instantiate the class defined in it.

The class I want to have dynamically created will be called Utilities. It's a simple class, but it will suffice for my purposes here. The class will contain an instance string member field, which contains the name of each instance. The value of this field is supplied on construction, and the class overrides Object.ToString() to return this field. The IL emitted, as viewed in ildasm.exe, looks like this:

```
.class private auto ansi Utilities
       extends [mscorlib]System.Object
{
  .field privatescope string a$PST04000001
  .method public virtual instance string
          ToString() cil managed
  {
    // Code size       7 (0x7)
    .maxstack  1
    IL_0000:  ldarg.0
    IL_0001:  ldfld      string Utilities::a$PST04000001
    IL_0006:  ret
  } // end of method Utilities::ToString

  .method public specialname rtspecialname
          instance void .ctor(string name) cil managed
```

```
{
  // Code size        14 (0xe)
  .maxstack  4
  IL_0000:  ldarg.0
  IL_0001:  call        instance void [mscorlib]System.Object::.ctor()
  IL_0006:  ldarg.0
  IL_0007:  ldarg.1
  IL_0008:  stfld       string Utilities::a$PST04000001
  IL_000d:  ret
  } // end of method Utilities::.ctor
}
```

Notice the strange name, a$PST04000001, of the field containing the object's name. This isn't the real name of the field. The actual name is simply a, but ildasm.exe always appends a string starting with $PST to the names of privatescope members when disassembling. This is to make sure no ambiguities exist if the file needs to be reassembled, since as you saw in Chapter 1, you may have identically named privatescope items. I chose to give the field the simple name a, and not anything more meaningful, in order to add more realism. Since this field is intended to be private, you have no need for it to have a human-meaningful name in a shipped assembly.

Tip In general, if you have no need for a variable to have a meaningful human-readable name at the IL level, then for copyright protection reasons, it's best not to give it one, since a human-readable name can aid someone else in decompiling and understanding your code. However, this is an issue only if you're coding in IL or if you're having Reflection.Emit classes generate IL. If you write your code in a high-level language, then as you saw in Chapter 1, the compiler will normally replace the names of private fields, allowing you to safely use meaningful names in your source code.

For the benefit of anyone who isn't yet comfortable with reading such a long snippet of IL, I'll add that the C# equivalent of the previous code is as follows:

```
public class Utilities
{
  private string a;
  public override string ToString() { return a; }
  public Utilities(string name) { a = name; }
}
```

The sample I'll write is designed to create an assembly containing the Utilities class. It then instantiates a Utilities object and calls its ToString() method—just to demonstrate that the dynamically generated code works correctly. Having done all that, it saves the assembly.

Here's the code for the Main() method in the example:

```
public static void Main()
{
```

```
AssemblyName assemblyName = new AssemblyName();
assemblyName.Name = "Utilities";
assemblyName.Version = new Version("1.0.1.0");

AssemblyBuilder assembly = Thread.GetDomain().
   DefineDynamicAssembly(assemblyName, AssemblyBuilderAccess.RunAndSave);

ModuleBuilder module;
module = assembly.DefineDynamicModule("MainModule", "Utilities.dll");

TypeBuilder utilsTypeBldr =
   module.DefineType("Apress.ExpertDotNet.EmitClass.Utilities",
   TypeAttributes.Class | TypeAttributes.Public, typeof(System.Object));

FieldBuilder nameFld = utilsTypeBldr.DefineField("a", typeof(string),
   FieldAttributes.PrivateScope);

MethodBuilder toStringMethod = utilsTypeBldr.DefineMethod("ToString",
   MethodAttributes.Public | MethodAttributes.Virtual, typeof(string),
   Type.EmptyTypes);

ILGenerator toStringIL = toStringMethod.GetILGenerator();
toStringIL.Emit(OpCodes.Ldarg_0);
toStringIL.Emit(OpCodes.Ldfld, nameFld);
toStringIL.Emit(OpCodes.Ret);

Type[] constructorParamList = { typeof(string) };
ConstructorInfo objectConstructor = (typeof(System.Object)).
                                    GetConstructor(new Type[0]);
ConstructorBuilder constructor = utilsTypeBldr.DefineConstructor(
   MethodAttributes.Public, CallingConventions.Standard,
   constructorParamList);
ILGenerator constructorIL = constructor.GetILGenerator();
constructorIL.Emit(OpCodes.Ldarg_0);
constructorIL.Emit(OpCodes.Call, objectConstructor);
constructorIL.Emit(OpCodes.Ldarg_0);
constructorIL.Emit(OpCodes.Ldarg_1);
constructorIL.Emit(OpCodes.Stfld, nameFld);
constructorIL.Emit(OpCodes.Ret);

Type utilsType = utilsTypeBldr.CreateType();
object utils = Activator.CreateInstance(utilsType, new object[] {
               "New Object!"} );
object name = utilsType.InvokeMember("ToString",
                         BindingFlags.InvokeMethod, null, utils, null);
Console.WriteLine("ToString() returned: " + (string)name);

assembly.Save("Utilities.dll");
}
```

This code starts in much the same way as the previous sample. But once it has created the module, instead of creating a global function, it uses the ModuleBuilder.DefineType() method to create the Utilities type, followed by the TypeBuilder.DefineField() method to create the member field.

```
TypeBuilder utilsTypeBldr = module.DefineType("Utilities",
                        TypeAttributes.Class | TypeAttributes.Public,
                        typeof(System.Object));

FieldBuilder nameFld = utilsTypeBldr.DefineField("a", typeof(string),
                        FieldAttributes.PrivateScope);
```

You can similarly define a method using TypeBuilder.DefineMethod() and a constructor using TypeBuilder.DefineConstructor() and use the same techniques I demonstrated in the previous example to add IL code to these members.

When the code has done all this, it uses TypeBuilder.CreateType() to simultaneously actually create the type in the assembly and return a System.Type reference to this type. You can then use this Type reference in the Activator.CreateInstance() and Type.InvokeMember() methods to instantiate a Utilities object and call its ToString() method.

```
Type utilsType = utilsTypeBldr.CreateType();
object utils = Activator.CreateInstance(utilsType, new object[] {
            "New Object!" });
object name = utilsType.InvokeMember("ToString", BindingFlags.InvokeMethod,
                            null, utils, null);
```

One point to watch out for is that, even though TypeBuilder is derived from Type, I've used the Type reference utilsType, which is returned from TypeBuilder.CreateType(), when instantiating the object and invoking methods. Although it looks syntactically correct to use the utilsTypeBldr variable instead of utilsType in these methods, doing so won't work here. This is because the type doesn't actually exist until you call TypeBuilder.CreateType()— which would make it hard to create an instance of it! Using the returned Type object is safe because if you have that object, then you can be certain that the type exists. Indeed, Activator.CreateInstance() has been implemented by Microsoft to check that it hasn't been passed a TypeBuilder reference, and it will raise an exception if it finds one.

When using a dynamically created assembly, you have to use reflection-based methods to invoke members on the types so defined, because the original executing assembly doesn't have the necessary embedded metadata to be able to use these types directly. Thus, you'll get a performance hit whenever execution flow crosses the boundary from the old assembly to the new one. You can minimize the impact of this by making sure the new assembly has methods that perform a large amount of processing and making sure the "interface" between the two assemblies isn't too chatty. In other words, have a few calls across the boundary that perform lots of processing each, rather than lots of calls that each perform only a little processing. These are just the same performance considerations that apply to the managed-unmanaged code boundary or to the crossing of application domains, although the performance hit when using reflection is likely to be greater.

The final action in the sample is to save the assembly for future use.

```
assembly.Save("Utilities.dll");
```

■Tip When developing code that uses Reflection.Emit, it's well worth regularly running peverify.exe on the dynamically emitted assemblies—just to make sure that your code generates correct and valid IL.

Obviously, once the new assembly is saved, any future code you write that depends on this assembly will be able to reference the saved assembly's metadata in the normal way so it won't need to use reflection to access its types.

Be aware that the action of saving the assembly is completely independent of the fact that you've already used the Utilities.dll assembly. Remember that you have a complete choice—you can use the assembly from your code, save it, or do both.

Coding with the CodeDom

In contrast to Reflection.Emit, the CodeDom model isn't specifically based on the .NET reflection architecture. Instead, because CodeDom is really aimed at generating source code, the class hierarchy is based on a document model that contains the kind of item usually found in source code: statements, expressions, type declarations, and so on. Indeed, the underlying philosophy is similar to the Web page document model used in Web page scripting languages.

■Note Although this chapter focuses on the practical, coding side of dynamic code generation, I can't help feeling that perhaps one of the most exciting aspects of CodeDom may in the long term be the way it can be viewed as representing a metalanguage, in terms of which other programming languages can be defined, in much the same way that SGML can be used to define XML or Hypertext Markup Language (HTML).

Creating a DOM

The first stage in generating a program with the CodeDom classes is to create the document object model that represents the code to be emitted.

Although the name CodeDom (or DOM) suggests a kind of document, it's important to understand that the CodeDom representation of a file doesn't exist as a file but rather as a linked set of instances of the CodeDom classes. Strictly speaking, these classes are generally serializable, so if you really need a file representation of a CodeDom, you can get a suitable file by serializing the classes; the file would be quite large and not particularly human readable, however.

Too many CodeDom classes exist to cover more than a small fraction of them in this chapter, but Figure 8-2 shows how some of the more important classes fit into the structure. The figure should also give you an idea of the basic principles behind the CodeDom architecture.

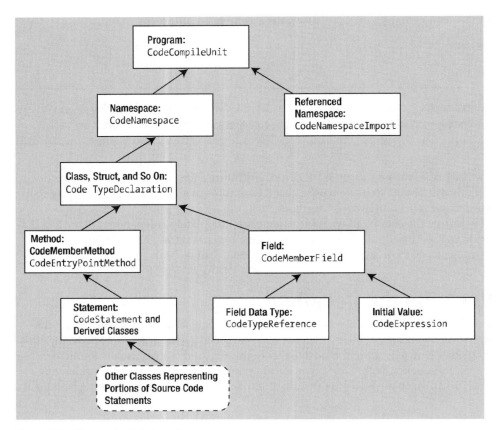

Figure 8-2. *The main* CodeDom *classes*

Each box in the figure indicates the type of item represented, followed by the CodeDom class used to represent this item. For example, the CodeCompileUnit class represents a complete program (something that can be compiled into an assembly as a unit). The arrows should be interpreted in a "contains reference to" sense. For example, the CodeCompileUnit implements a Namespaces property, which contains a collection of CodeNamespace objects (in a CodeNamespaceCollection instance). For simplicity in the figure I haven't drawn in the collection classes. In general, whenever multiple instances of an item are possible, you can surmise that an intermediate collection class is lurking.

Although it's not shown in detail in the figure, a further, fairly complex hierarchy exists below the statement level, depending on the nature of the statement. For example, a statement that calls a method is represented by a CodeMethodInvokeExpression instance. (This class is derived from CodeStatement.) CodeMethodInvokeExpression contains further nested classes that provide information about the method to be invoked, the return type, and the parameters to be passed to it.

The underlying principle of the DOM is relatively simple. It's just a big tree structure, and as you move down the tree, you get closer and closer to the basic items that form a piece of code: the variable declarations and subexpressions within a statement. However, the code needed to implement a DOM is quite complex because so many different types of item can form part of the tree—which means that the System.CodeDom namespace contains a huge number of classes.

Caution Although I say that the CodeDom has a tree structure, you need to be aware of one complication. The items in the "tree" are references, and it's quite possible that multiple references may refer to the same object. For example, suppose the statement x = x*2; is to occur several times in the code. This statement would be represented in the DOM by an instance of the class CodeAssignStatement (which is derived from CodeStatement), but it'd be wasteful to have a separate instance of this class for each statement. Rather, depending on the details of your code, you may choose to have one such instance, with a reference to this instance at each point in the DOM where an x = x*2; statement occurs.

You can create the root of a CodeDom like this:

```
CodeCompileUnit unit = new CodeCompileUnit();
```

The CodeCompileUnit.Namespaces property contains any namespaces you define.

```
CodeNamespace ns = new CodeNamespace("Apress.ExpertDotNet.CodeDomSample");
unit.Namespaces.Add(ns);
```

The CodeNamespace.Types property contains a collection of objects representing the types you define.

```
CodeTypeDeclaration myClass = new CodeTypeDeclaration();
ns.Types.Add(theClass);
```

And so on down the tree. You'll need, for example, to add members to the class declared in this code snippet. I'll present a couple of examples in the section "CodeDom Examples" that illustrate how to do this.

DOM to Source Code

Once you have a CodeCompileUnit object that contains all the details of the program to be generated, the next stage is to convert this "document" into the actual source code file. For this you need the base classes and interfaces defined in System.CodeDom.Compiler and the implementations of these classes defined in various language-specific namespaces.

The programming model is based on the concept of a *CodeDom provider*. A CodeDom provider is a class that provides the entry point into the code generation facilities. Providers must derive from the abstract class, System.CodeDom.Compiler.CodeDomProvider. The providers supplied by Microsoft include Microsoft.CSharp.CSharpCodeProvider, Microsoft.VisualBasic.VBCodeProvider, and Microsoft.JScript.JScriptCodeProvider.

The CodeDomProvider base class defines a CreateGenerator() method, which returns an ICodeGenerator interface reference that can be used to generate the source code from the CodeCompileUnit. Thus, for example, to generate C# source code, you'd do this:

```
CSharpCodeProvider cscp = new CSharpCodeProvider();
ICodeGenerator gen = cscp.CreateGenerator();

// unit is the CodeCompileUnit() reference
// strm is a TextStream (or derived class) used to write out the source code
// opts is a CodeGeneratorOptions instance that specifies code layout options
gen.GenerateCodeFromCompileUnit(unit, strm, opts);
```

You'll see these principles applied in an example soon, when I explain the CodeGeneratorOptions class.

This architecture allows for easy swapping between languages. If, for example, you want to generate VB source code instead, then the only line of this code you need to change is the statement that creates the code provider.

```
VBProvider cscp = new VbProvider();
ICodeGenerator gen = cscp.CreateGenerator();
gen.GenerateCodeFromCompileUnit(unit, strm, opts);
```

Source Code to IL

Dynamically compiling source code works on the same principles as generating source code—you start with the relevant language code provider. Instead of calling CodeDomProvider.CreateGenerator(), however, you invoke another method, CodeDomProvider.CreateCompiler(). This method returns an ICodeCompiler interface reference, through which you can compile code.

```
CSharpCodeProvider cscp = new CSharpCodeProvider();
ICodeCompiler compiler = cscp.CreateCompiler();

// compilerParams is a CompilerParameters object.
// CompilerParameters contains fields that indicate compilation options
compiler.CompileAssemblyFromFile(compilerParams, "MyCode.cs");
```

This code compiles the file MyCode.cs. This code involves another class that you haven't yet seen, CompilerParameters. Using this class is fairly intuitive; it simply indicates various preferences to do with the compilation process. Be aware that, just as for generating source files, if you want to compile a file that's in a different language, you just create a different code provider but don't need to change any other code.

The ICodeCompiler interface offers other methods, among other things, to allow direct generation of an assembly from a CodeCompileUnit, without having to go through an intermediate source code file.

CodeDom Examples

I'll now present a couple of examples that illustrate how to use the CodeDom classes. Because CodeDom typically involves long source code files, I'll keep the examples extremely simple. In fact, I won't get much further than generating simple console applications, but this will be enough to demonstrate the principles of CodeDom.

The CodeDomHelloWorld Example

This example uses the CodeDom classes to generate and then compile a C# application. The application is similar to a simple HelloWorld application, but I'll take advantage of dynamic code generation to vary the generated code based on user preferences. Instead of just displaying *Hello, World!* the example asks the user what string should be displayed and how many times this string should be displayed, and it then generates a custom C# program according to the user's preferences. So, for example, if the user asked for a program that displays *Hello, World!* five times, then the actual source code generated would look like this:

```
//------------------------------------------------------------------------------
// <autogenerated>
//     This code was generated by a tool.
//     Runtime Version: 1.1.4322.573
//
//     Changes to this file may cause incorrect behavior and will be lost if
//     the code is regenerated.
// </autogenerated>
//------------------------------------------------------------------------------

namespace Apress.ExpertDotNet.CodeDomSample
{
    using System;


    public class EntryPoint
    {

        public static void Main()
        {
            for (int i = 0; (i < 5); i = (i + 1))
            {
                System.Console.WriteLine("Hello, World!");
            }
            return;
        }
    }
}
```

The initial comments are automatically added by the C# code generator to every program. You'll notice that some of the constructs aren't quite what you'd probably write if you were coding by hand; for example, the increment operation in the for loop has been emitted as i = i + 1, where most C# developers would more likely write ++i;. Because the CodeDom is intended to be multilanguage compatible, it doesn't support certain constructs that are unique to certain languages, such as the C#/C++ increment operator. Hence, the CodeDom emits the more cumbersome version of the operator.

Now let's examine the code for the CodeDomHelloWorld example, which actually generates the previous file.

As you saw earlier, the process of getting to a compiled assembly through the CodeDom mechanism involves three steps:

1. You create the CodeDom structure.

2. You generate the source code.

3. You compile the source code.

In a real application, it's highly unlikely that all three steps would follow each other in the same program. If that was your intention, you'd get far better performance (and, provided you're familiar with IL, find the code easier to write) if you used the Reflection.Emit classes to generate the assembly directly. However, in order to illustrate all the processes, running through the previous steps is exactly what the example will do.

Let's start with the code that generates the language-neutral CodeDom representation of the generated program. That's implemented in a method that I've called GenerateProgram(). This method returns the CodeCompileUnit instance that represents the program.

```
// generate CodeDOM for code that displays message nDisplays times.
static CodeCompileUnit GenerateProgram(string message, int nDisplays)
{
    // Create Main method
    CodeEntryPointMethod mainMethod = new CodeEntryPointMethod();
    mainMethod.Name = "Main";

    // generate this expression: Console
    CodeTypeReferenceExpression consoleType = new
        CodeTypeReferenceExpression();
    consoleType.Type = new CodeTypeReference(typeof(Console));

    // generate this statement: int i=0;
    CodeVariableDeclarationStatement declareI =
                                new CodeVariableDeclarationStatement();
    declareI.Name = "i";
    declareI.InitExpression = new CodePrimitiveExpression(0);
    declareI.Type = new CodeTypeReference(typeof(int));

    // generate this expression: i;
    CodeVariableReferenceExpression iVar = new
                        CodeVariableReferenceExpression(declareI.Name);

    // generate this statement: i=i+1;
    CodeAssignStatement incrI = new CodeAssignStatement();
    incrI.Left = iVar;
    incrI.Right = new CodeBinaryOperatorExpression(iVar,
            CodeBinaryOperatorType.Add, new CodePrimitiveExpression(1));

    // generate this for loop: for (int i=0 ; i<nDisplays ; i++)
    CodeIterationStatement forLoop = new CodeIterationStatement();
```

```
forLoop.InitStatement = declareI;
forLoop.TestExpression = new CodeBinaryOperatorExpression(iVar,
                         CodeBinaryOperatorType.LessThan,
                         new CodePrimitiveExpression(nDisplays));
forLoop.IncrementStatement = incrI;

// Set up the argument list to pass to Console.WriteLine()
CodeExpression[] writeLineArgs = new CodeExpression[1];
CodePrimitiveExpression arg0 = new CodePrimitiveExpression(message);
writeLineArgs[0] = arg0;

// generate this statement: Console.WriteLine(message)
CodeMethodReferenceExpression writeLineRef = new
    CodeMethodReferenceExpression(consoleType, "WriteLine");
CodeMethodInvokeExpression writeLine = new
    CodeMethodInvokeExpression(writeLineRef, writeLineArgs);

// insert Console.WriteLine() statement into for loop
forLoop.Statements.Add(writeLine);
// add the for loop to the Main() method
mainMethod.Statements.Add(forLoop);

// Add a return statement to the Main() method
CodeMethodReturnStatement ret = new CodeMethodReturnStatement();
mainMethod.Statements.Add(ret);

// Add Main() method to a class
CodeTypeDeclaration theClass = new CodeTypeDeclaration();
theClass.Members.Add(mainMethod);
theClass.Name = "EntryPoint";

// Add namespace and add class
CodeNamespace ns = new CodeNamespace("Apress.ExpertDotNet.CodeDomSample");
ns.Imports.Add(new CodeNamespaceImport("System"));
ns.Types.Add(theClass);

// Create whole program (code compile unit)
CodeCompileUnit unit = new CodeCompileUnit();
unit.Namespaces.Add(ns);

return unit;
}
```

There's quite a lot going on here, so I'll go through it in detail. The code starts by instantiating the classes needed to represent a method and then gives this method the name Main.

```
CodeEntryPointMethod mainMethod = new CodeEntryPointMethod();
mainMethod.Name = "Main";
```

The `CodeEntryPointMethod` class is derived from `CodeMemberMethod` and indicates a method that will form the entry point to an executable.

The next few lines of code have to do with constructing that `Console.WriteLine()` statement. CodeDom truly breaks the source code up into its most basic elements, and the thing you need to deal with first in the code is sorting out a reference to the `Console` type. You don't need to actually define the type here—just somehow indicate that you want to reference an existing type—so the `CodeTypeDeclaration` class that's normally used to declare types isn't appropriate. Instead, the class you need is `CodeTypeReference`. `CodeTypeReference` is little more than a wrapper for the `System.Type` class, but it contains a couple of CodeDom-specific properties related to getting information from an array. The `CodeTypeReference` object needs to be embedded into a `CodeTypeReferenceExpression` instance—this is the class that's used to represent types that are present in expressions in source code.

```
// generate this expression: Console
CodeTypeReferenceExpression consoleType = new CodeTypeReferenceExpression();
consoleType.Type = new CodeTypeReference(typeof(Console));
```

The next task is to generate the statement `int i=0;` that goes inside the `for` loop.

```
CodeVariableDeclarationStatement declareI = new
      CodeVariableDeclarationStatement();
declareI.Name = "i";
declareI.InitExpression = new CodePrimitiveExpression(0);
declareI.Type = new CodeTypeReference(typeof(int));
```

It'll be no surprise to learn that statements that declare variables are represented by the `CodeVariableDeclarationStatement` class. The other new class here, `CodePrimitiveExpression`, represents any constant numeric or string expression, such as 23, 0 or `Hello, World!`.

The code to be generated will refer to the variable i a few times—so to take account of this, the code caches a reference to the following variable:

```
CodeVariableReferenceExpression iVar = new
   CodeVariableReferenceExpression(declareI.Name);
```

This is followed by the increment statement that will go in the loop: i = i + 1.

```
CodeAssignStatement incrI = new CodeAssignStatement();
incrI.Left = iVar;
incrI.Right = new CodeBinaryOperatorExpression(iVar,
   CodeBinaryOperatorType.Add, new CodePrimitiveExpression(1));
```

The `CodeBinaryOperatorExpression` class represents any expression of the form x op y—in this case i+1. The expression (i+1) forms the right side of a `CodeAssignStatement`. (I'm sure you can guess the role of the `CodeAssignStatement` class....)

I'm now ready to put that `for` statement together, using the `int i=0` and `i=i+1` statements just generated, as well as another `CodeBinaryOperatorExpression` that will represent the `i<nDisplays` condition.

```
CodeIterationStatement forLoop = new CodeIterationStatement();
forLoop.InitStatement = declareI;
```

```
forLoop.TestExpression = new CodeBinaryOperatorExpression(iVar,
   CodeBinaryOperatorType.LessThan, new CodePrimitiveExpression(nDisplays));
forLoop.IncrementStatement = incrI;
```

The next thing you need to do is sort out the argument list that will need to be passed to Console.WriteLine(). The argument list should be represented by an array of CodeExpression references. CodeExpression is the base class for a number of classes that can represent different types of expressions in this context. You've already encountered two specific expression classes derived from CodeExpression: CodePrimitiveExpression and CodeBinaryOperatorExpression. In the case of this sample, Console.WriteLine() takes one string argument. As far as CodeDom is concerned, string counts as a primitive type, along with int, float, bool, and so on, so it can be represented as a CodePrimitiveExpression instance.

```
CodeExpression[] writeLineArgs = new CodeExpression[1];
CodePrimitiveExpression arg0 = new CodePrimitiveExpression("Hello, World!");
writeLineArgs[0] = arg0;
```

Now you have all the units necessary to build up the Console.WriteLine() statement.

```
CodeMethodReferenceExpression writeLineRef = new
        CodeMethodReferenceExpression(consoleType, "WriteLine");
CodeMethodInvokeExpression writeLine = new
        CodeMethodInvokeExpression(writeLineRef, writeLineArgs);
```

The previous code starts by defining a reference to the method you need to call—a CodeMethodReferenceExpression instance. CodeMethodReferenceExpression requires a reference to the object or type against which the method is to be called and the name of the method. The first line of the previous code gives you a CodeMethodReferenceExpression that identifies the Console.WriteLine() method. However, by itself that's not sufficient: CodeMethodReferenceExpression doesn't encapsulate any information about how the method is to be used—for example, is it to be invoked or passed as a parameter to a delegate? In this sample, I want to invoke the method, so I pass the CodeMethodReferenceExpression to a CodeMethodInvokeExpression object, along with the parameter list. At this point you at last have an object that represents an expression, which can be used as a full statement. The code therefore has the following statement inserted into the body of the for loop and then inserts the now completed for loop into the Main() method:

```
forLoop.Statements.Add(writeLine);
mainMethod.Statements.Add(forLoop);
```

The remainder of the GenerateProgram() method is relatively easy to follow, so I won't go through it in as much detail. I'll comment, though, that it's necessary to have the return statement added to the method; the CodeMethodReturnStatement class represents a return statement. Then the code instantiates a new CodeTypeDeclaration object and adds the method to this new instance. Finally, it declares a namespace, adds the class to the namespace, and adds the namespace, along with a reference to the System namespace, to the newly created CodeCompileUnit. At this point you can probably see why I haven't gone for a more complicated example!

At this point the code has generated a CodeDom document tree, but it hasn't yet generated any source code. So I'll now present the code that performs this step. It creates the source code from the CodeDom tree. Here's the code:

```
[STAThread]
static void Main(string[] args)
{
    Console.WriteLine("What string do you want the custom program to " +
                                                        "display?");
    string message = Console.ReadLine();
    Console.WriteLine("How many times do you want the program to display " +
                                                    "this message?");
    int nDisplays = int.Parse(Console.ReadLine());
    CodeCompileUnit unit = GenerateProgram(message, nDisplays);

    // Set up options for source code style
    CodeGeneratorOptions opts = new CodeGeneratorOptions();
    opts.BracingStyle = "C";
    opts.IndentString = "\t";

    // Create code generator and write code file
    CSharpCodeProvider cscp = new CSharpCodeProvider();
    ICodeGenerator gen = cscp.CreateGenerator();
    StreamWriter sw = new StreamWriter("MyCode.cs");
    gen.GenerateCodeFromCompileUnit(unit, sw, opts);
    sw.Close();

    CompilerParameters compilerParams = new CompilerParameters();
    compilerParams.GenerateExecutable = true;
    compilerParams.OutputAssembly = "MyCode.exe";
    ICodeCompiler compiler = cscp.CreateCompiler();
    compiler.CompileAssemblyFromFile(compilerParams, "MyCode.cs");
}
```

In this code, you first need a CodeGeneratorOptions object, which specifies options for the layout of code. I use this to set up two options, BracingStyle and IndentString.

BracingStyle indicates how braces should be arranged. It takes a string, and the values of this string will depend on the language to which you're compiling. For Microsoft languages, the options are as follows:

- C, which gives code that looks like this:

```
public class EntryPoint
{
    public static void Main()
    {
```

- Block, which gives code like this:

```
public class EntryPoint {
    public static void Main() {
```

When generating VB code, BracingStyle is ignored. In general, the fact that BracingStyle is a string allows other values to be assigned to it, which may be recognized by different language source code generators.

IndentString is the string that will be used to supply an indent to code in blocks. If you don't assign it explicitly, it defaults to four spaces. For this sample, I've set the IndentString property to the tab character, ensuring that a single tab will be used for indents, as is customary in C#.

Also, two properties exist on CodeGeneratorOptions that are of type bool and that you aren't explicitly assigning to in this example. BlankLinesBetweenMembers controls whether blank lines should be inserted between member and type declarations, and InsertElseOnClosing controls whether if statements should always be terminated with an else, with try blocks followed by a finally block, even if no statements are to be inserted into such blocks.

Having defined the CodeGeneratorOptions, you can instantiate the code generator that implements ICodeGenerator and call its GenerateCodeFromCompileUnit() method to generate the code, passing it a StreamWriter to which the code will be output the following:

```
CSharpCodeProvider cscp = new CSharpCodeProvider();
ICodeGenerator gen = cscp.CreateGenerator();
StreamWriter sw = new StreamWriter("MyCode.cs");
gen.GenerateCodeFromCompileUnit(unit, sw, opts);
sw.Close();
```

The last stage is to get the dynamically generated source code compiled. To do this, I used the provider's CreateCompiler() method to get the interface pointer to a code compiler and call the CompileAssemblyFromFile() method to obtain the assembly. I also passed a CompilerParameters object to this method, which I initialized to indicate I want to create an executable file.

```
CompilerParameters compilerParams = new CompilerParameters();
compilerParams.GenerateExecutable = true;
compilerParams.OutputAssembly = "MyCode.exe";
ICodeCompiler compiler = cscp.CreateCompiler();
compiler.CompileAssemblyFromFile(compilerParams, "MyCode.cs");
```

CODEDOM GOTCHAS

One point to watch about the CodeDom is that it's not particularly good at noticing syntax errors in your program. Although the structure of the CodeDom tree automatically enforces a reasonable structure on the generated code, it's easy to allow absurd syntax errors to creep in undetected. A couple of examples should serve to indicate the kind of problems for which you need to be on the lookout.

You can use the CodeGeneratorOptions.IndentString property with great effect to produce ridiculous source code. Suppose, for example, that you introduce the following bug. Instead of writing opts.IndentString = "\t";, you incorrectly use "t" instead of "\t", thus defining an indent string containing the letter t instead of the tab character. The C# CodeDom generator will (at least at the time of writing) quite happily accept this, impervious to the fact that only whitespace characters should be used in C# to indent strings. When you run the sample with this bug, you get a completely uncompilable file emitted, part of which looks like the following:

```
ttpublic static void Main()
tt{
tttSystem.Console.WriteLine("Hello, World!");
tttreturn;
tt}
t}
```

As another example, you may notice that in this sample I was careful to wrap the CodeMethodReferenceExpression object that indicated the Console.WriteLine() statement in a CodeMethodInvokeExpression. In fact, the code would compile correctly if I omitted this step.

```
// WRONG!
CodeMethodReferenceExpression writeLineRef = new
    CodeMethodReferenceExpression(consoleType, "WriteLine");
mainMethod.Statements.Add(writeLineRef);
```

This works because the CodeMemberMethod.Statements property is of type CodeStatementCollection—and the CodeStatementCollection.Add() method will take either a CodeStatement or a CodeExpression reference. Both CodeMethodReferenceExpression and CodeMethodInvokeExpression are derived from CodeExpression. This flexibility is needed because of the theoretical possibility that any code expression may be valid as a statement in some languages, as is the case in C++ or Perl, for example. However, in C#, the previous code generates the following:

```
public static void Main()
{
    System.Console.WriteLine;
    return;
}
```

The emitted file contains exactly what you've asked for—a method reference. But clearly in this context, the generated source code is meaningless and will not compile.

The lesson from this is that when using CodeDom, you'll need to be careful and precise in your use of the CodeDom classes in order to make sure you request exactly the source code you need.

Caution A related issue is that, although CodeDom is theoretically language independent, in practice the idiosyncrasies and lack of support for some constructs in some languages do get in the way, so it's possible to create a CodeDom that generates correct code in one language but not another.

Generating Files in Multiple Languages

The previous `CodeDomHelloWorld` sample showed you how to use `CodeDom`, but I suspect that it hasn't left you with a positive feeling about the capabilities and ease of use of the `CodeDom` classes, since it took such a huge amount of quite fiddly code to dynamically generate a simple program. In this section I'll develop the sample into a new sample that should rectify that to some extent. The `CodeDomMultiLanguage` sample will show how easy it is to use `CodeDom` to swap between languages. The sample is the same as the previous sample but with the extra feature that it can generate source files not only in C# but also in VB and JScript .NET.

Since the underlying code is the same, the `GenerateProgram()` method is unchanged. You simply need to change the way that the generated `CodeCompileUnit` object is processed. Hence, I made the following changes to the `Main()` method (as usual in this book, the changes are shown in bold):

```
static void Main(string[] args)
{
    Console.WriteLine("What string do you want the custom program to " +
                                                    "display?");
    string message = Console.ReadLine();
    Console.WriteLine("How many times do you want the program to display " +
                                                    "this message?");
    int nDisplays = int.Parse(Console.ReadLine());
    CodeCompileUnit unit = GenerateProgram(message, nDisplays);

    // Set up options for source code style
    CodeGeneratorOptions opts = new CodeGeneratorOptions();
    opts.BracingStyle = "C";
    opts.IndentString = "\t";

    // Create code generators and write code files
    CodeDomProvider[] providers = new CodeDomProvider[3];
    providers[0] = new CSharpCodeProvider();
    providers[1] = new VBCodeProvider();
    providers[2] = new JScriptCodeProvider();
    string[] fileNames = { "MyCodeCS.cs", "MyCodeVB.vb", "MyCodeJS.js" };

    for(int i=0 ; i< providers.Length; i++)
    {
        ICodeGenerator gen = providers[i].CreateGenerator();
        StreamWriter sw = new StreamWriter(fileNames[i]);
        gen.GenerateCodeFromCompileUnit(unit, sw, opts);
        sw.Close();
    }

    string[] assemblyFileNames = { "MyCodeCS.exe", "MyCodeVB.exe",
                            "MyCodeJS.exe" };
    CompilerParameters compilerParams = new CompilerParameters();
    compilerParams.GenerateExecutable = true;
```

```
    for (int i=0; i<providers.Length; i++)
    {
        ICodeCompiler compiler = providers[i].CreateCompiler();
        compilerParams.OutputAssembly = assemblyFileNames[i];
        compiler.CompileAssemblyFromFile(compilerParams, fileNames[i]);
    }
}
```

Instead of creating a single provider, the code creates an array of providers, one for each language. Then it iterates through the array, and for each provider it uses the CodeDomProvider.CreateGenerator() method to instantiate the appropriate code generator. Having done that it repeats the technique to instantiate the required compilers that will generate the assemblies.

For the sake of completeness, the source code files emitted for VB are as follows:

```
Option Strict Off
Option Explicit On

Imports System

Namespace Apress.ExpertDotNet.CodeDomSample

    Public Class EntryPoint

        Public Shared Sub Main()
            Dim i As Integer = 0
            Do While (i < 5)
                System.Console.WriteLine("Hello, World!")
                i = (i + 1)
            Loop
            Return
        End Sub
    End Class
End Namespace
```

The source code files emitted for JScript .NET are as follows:

```
//@cc_on
//@set @debug(off)

import System;

package Apress.ExpertDotNet.CodeDomSample
{

    public class EntryPoint
    {

        public static function Main()
```

```
        {
            for (var i : int = 0;
            ; (i < 5); i = (i + 1))
            {
                System.Console.WriteLine("Hello, World!");
            }
            return;
        }
    }
}
Apress.ExpertDotNet.CodeDomSample.EntryPoint.Main();
```

To save space, in both of these listings I've omitted the initial comments that warn that these are autogenerated files. The VB output is especially informative for the way it shows how the code provider has constructed the loop. It has given you a Do While loop instead of a For loop—you or I would probably have written For I = 1 To 5 . . . Next here. The reason the CodeDom generator hasn't done so is of course that the Do While loop is VB's nearest equivalent in terms of richness to C#'s for loop. Emitting a For loop would require the CodeDom provider to be able to analyze the loop and determine that it's controlled by a simple increment that could be more conveniently represented by a VB For loop. The VB code provider is evidently not quite that sophisticated and takes the easy way out; it uses a loop construct that will always work no matter what the loop condition and increment statements are.

Summary

In this chapter I explored the facilities that are available in the .NET Framework Class Library for generating both source code and assemblies dynamically. You saw that two independent technologies exist for this purpose: CodeDom, which can generate source code or assemblies, and Reflection.Emit, which can generate only assemblies but which is normally the preferred option for directly creating assemblies, on both performance and ease of coding grounds.

CHAPTER 9

■ ■ ■

Understanding Threading

Using multiple threads in a process is a common way of providing greater application responsiveness. On multiprocessor systems, extra threads (up to the number of processors) can increase performance by ensuring that all the processors are contributing simultaneously to the processing being carried out by the application. On single-processor systems, extra threads will not improve performance. Too many threads on any system can decrease performance (because of all the time the processor(s) spends thread swapping), but multithreading will improve responsiveness because the application can quickly swap from background processing to managing the user interface when the user does something. Using multiple threads also means that an application can carry on working while it's waiting for outside events, such as waiting for data to be returned from a Hypertext Transfer Protocol (HTTP) network request.

In this chapter, I'll work through the extensive support that the .NET Framework offers for writing multithreaded applications and go over several examples that illustrate how to code a multithreaded application, taking care of any issues with thread synchronization. In particular, I'll cover the following:

- The difference between operating system threads and managed threads

- The relative benefits of the various available techniques for multithreading

- How to invoke delegates asynchronously

* How to synchronize data access using thread-synchronization objects such as mutexes, events, and so on

- How to use timers

- How to explicitly create worker threads

- How to terminate worker threads to ensure that thread data is cleaned up correctly

Introducing CLR Threading Support

A single thread in managed code can be represented by one of two classes.

- `System.Threading.Thread` represents a managed thread.

- `System.Diagnostics.ProcessThread` represents an operating system thread.

The reason for having two different classes is that the concepts of managed thread and operating system thread aren't the same. A managed thread won't necessarily correspond to a thread in the Windows operating system. In .NET version 1.1, a managed thread is normally simply an operating system thread that happens to be executing managed code and that the CLR knows about. Because of this knowledge, the CLR can maintain some extra data structures about the thread. (For example, the CLR can give textual names to threads, something that Windows doesn't natively support.) However, it's possible that in the future Microsoft may choose to implement CLR threads differently (for example, using some technique based on fibers). It may happen in the future that the CLR will maintain its own logical threads, but under the hood each logical thread will swap between different physical threads according to which threads are available. Although this sounds potentially complex, it could have benefits—for example, it may mean that the CLR is able to use fewer system threads while giving the impression to your code that more threads are available to it. I stress that no guarantee exists that Microsoft will go down this path. However, Microsoft has made sure that the option is available in case it's deemed useful in the future.

Because of this, the framework base classes have been defined in a way that prevents you from directly identifying a CLR managed thread with an operating system thread. One consequence of this is that no cast exists that allows you to convert between Thread and ProcessThread.

For most of this chapter, I'll focus on Thread. My aim is to show you how best to take advantage of the threading facilities offered by the CLR. So you should bear in mind that when I talk about *threads* in this chapter, I'm normally referring to logical, managed, CLR threads unless I explicitly say otherwise. For the most part, directly accessing information about operating system physical threads isn't relevant here. However, I'll briefly cover how to use ProcessThread to access this information, in case you're in a situation where you need to do so (for example, because of compatibility requirements when working with unmanaged code).

You can see the difference between managed and unmanaged threads simply by writing a managed HelloWorld console application, running it, and using the Task Manager to examine the threads in it. You may have imagined that the following code uses only one thread:

```
static void Main()
{
    Console.WriteLine("Hello, World!");
    // The ReadLine() effectively pauses the program so you can use
    // Task Manager to examine the threads
    Console.ReadLine();
}
```

In fact, on my main work computer (a single-processor Athlon machine) this code uses three unmanaged threads when a release build is run from the command line (without VS .NET), as shown in Figure 9-1.

Figure 9-1. *The threads used in a managed* HelloWorld *application*

If you try doing the same test, you may get different results, since the number of threads seems to vary between machines and operating systems. You may also have more threads if you run a debug build.

Bluntly, any managed application is multithreaded as far as Windows is concerned, even if you think you're dealing with only one thread. In Figure 9-1, one of the threads is clearly the one that's executing the Main() method. Although it doesn't document what the other threads are for, I can hazard quite a good guess. One of them is probably the dedicated thread that destructors are executed on, which I discussed in Chapter 5, and the other has something to do with the internal operation of the CLR.

Types of Managed Threads

As far as the managed threads that your code has access to are concerned, any threads that have to do with the internal operation of the CLR may as well not exist. Your code has access to only those managed threads whose purpose is to execute your code. This includes the thread that the Main() method starts executing on and any other threads that are explicitly or implicitly created by your code (plus, for finalizers, the dedicated finalizer thread).

The threads that are visible to your code fall into two categories.

- *Thread-pool threads* comprise the thread on which your entry point method starts executing, and any threads that are created are created behind the scenes by the CLR to perform such tasks as asynchronous processing when you request that a method be executed asynchronously.

- *Non-thread-pool threads* are created explicitly in your code using new Thread (ThreadStart entryPoint).

Thread-Pool Threads

You're probably familiar with the concept of a thread pool from unmanaged code. The idea is simply that a number of threads (a *pool* of threads) are normally sleeping but are available to do work. When some task needs to be done in the background, instead of your code instantiating a thread just for that task, one of these threads is woken up and given the task. When the task is complete, that thread goes back to sleep again. Having a thread pool is potentially an efficient way of doing things, since waking up an existing thread is a lot quicker than explicitly creating a new thread (which involves Windows allocating all the related data structures for that thread). A thread pool means that the number of threads is kept within reasonable limits while at the same time giving your program freedom to perform extensive multitasking. If too many tasks come along at once, then instead of overloading the CPU by trying to run them all at the same time, some of the tasks have to wait until a thread in the pool becomes available. The problem with thread pools in unmanaged code has of course always been that you have to write the infrastructure to implement the pool yourself, and that's a major programming task (although Windows 2000 did introduce thread-pool support). For this reason, thread pools are rarely used in unmanaged code, except in a few cases where Microsoft had supplied specific APIs that implemented them internally (such as OLE DB and MTS/COM+). .NET, by contrast, provides built-in support for a thread pool. For the most part, thread pool threads are invoked implicitly when required; however, some limited explicit access to the thread pool is available via the System.Threading.ThreadPool class.

■Tip One of the biggest differences between multithreading in managed and unmanaged code is arguably the way that the CLR makes it easy (and preferable) to use the thread pool to accomplish tasks that in unmanaged code would usually have been done by explicitly creating threads. If you're used to coding unmanaged multithreaded applications in this way, then you'll do well to shift paradigms and get used to working with the thread pool.

Although a couple of useful static methods on ThreadPool give you information about the pool, you can't create thread pool threads explicitly, and no general mechanism exists to get a Thread reference to a thread pool thread. The idea is that you let the CLR handle the thread pool threads, which gives better performance but means you can't manipulate the threads yourself. In particular, if you ask the CLR to execute some task asynchronously, then it's up to the CLR which thread it picks from the pool to execute it on; you have no control over that.

You can find out how many threads can be placed in the thread pool using the static ThreadPool.GetMaxThreads() method. The method has two output parameters to retrieve the maximum numbers of threads. It has two parameters because the thread pool can contain two types of thread, known respectively as *worker threads* and *completion port threads*.

```
int maxWorkerThreads;
int maxCompletionPortThreads;
ThreadPool.GetMaxThreads(out maxWorkerThreads, out maxCompletionPortThreads);
```

Worker threads are the threads in which you'll mostly be interested. Completion port threads are special threads for asynchronous I/O operations and aren't covered in this chapter.

Running this code on my processor, this method tells me the thread pool can contain up to 25 worker threads and 1,000 completion port threads. (This number will depend on your hardware, version of Windows, and version of .NET.) Note that I say *can contain*. These threads won't actually be created unless they're required—it'd be silly to have so many threads permanently around when most applications will never need that many and when some applications won't use the thread pool at all. A similar method, ThreadPool. GetAvailableThreads(), can tell you how many more asynchronous tasks can be simultaneously executed before the thread pool is full.

You can also explicitly ask a task to be executed asynchronously on a thread-pool thread, using the static ThreadPool.QueueUserWorkItem() method. This method takes a delegate of type System.Threading.WaitCallback that represents the method to be executed.

```
// Assume that void DoSomeWork(object state) is the entry method for
// the task to be performed
WaitCallback task = new WaitCallback(DoSomeWork)
ThreadPool.QueueUserWorkItem(task, state);
```

If no thread-pool thread is currently available to perform the task, the task will wait in a queue until a thread is available; hence, it has the name QueueUserWorkItem(). However, although this method is worth bearing in mind, I won't be using it in the samples in this chapter, since there are other more powerful techniques and concepts available that I want to cover.

Non-Thread-Pool Threads

You'll normally instantiate a non-thread-pool thread if for some reason you need to maintain an explicit reference to the newly created thread—usually this is in order that other threads can maintain some explicit control over this thread.

```
ThreadStart entryPointDelegate = new ThreadStart(EntryPoint);
Thread workerThread = new Thread(entryPointDelegate);
workerThread.Start();

// Later...
void EntryPoint()  // This is the method at which the new thread starts execution
{
```

The previous code snippet shows how you can explicitly create a thread: You first set up a delegate of type System.Threading.ThreadStart, which should refer to the method at which the new thread will start executing. You then instantiate a Thread object, passing it this delegate as a parameter. The thread starts running when you call its Thread.Start() method and normally terminates when its execution flow returns from the method at which execution started.

The important point about the previous code is that it leaves the first thread in possession of the Thread reference that represents the new thread. This means the main thread is able to invoke various methods and properties on this object to find out information about the new thread, as well as perform actions such as terminating the thread. You lose the benefits of having a thread pool, but you do get finer control over the thread you've created.

I won't list all the Thread methods and properties here, as I'm more interested in getting across the basic principles. You're more than capable of looking up the list of methods in the MSDN documentation! However, you'll see various Thread methods in action as you work through the chapter.

I'll mention, though, that if you need a reference to a Thread object that represents the thread your code is currently executing on, you can access it through the Thread.CurrentThread static property.

```
Thread myOwnThread = Thread.CurrentThread;
```

Other Categories of Threads

You can categorize threads in a couple of other ways.

The CLR introduced the concept of *background threads*; these are threads that have no power to hold a process open. The initial thread that starts running your code is a *foreground thread*, which means that as long as that thread exists, so will the process. When you create a new thread, it defaults to being foreground too, but you can explicitly mark it as a background thread.

```
Thread.CurrentThread.IsBackground = true;
```

Windows will terminate a process when no more foreground threads in that process exist—even if background threads are running. In most cases, if you're creating your own threads, it's probably better to leave them as a foreground thread so they can explicitly clean up any data they're using before terminating. Thread-pool threads, however, are all background threads—this makes sense since thread-pool threads will tend to spend most of their time waiting for tasks and aren't under your control.

A *user-interface thread* is a thread that's executing a message loop. A *message loop* is a continuous loop within an application that processes messages sent by Windows (for example, telling the application to repaint itself or to quit). In practice, this means that a user-interface thread isn't continually executing code. Instead, it sleeps most of the time, waking up whenever some message needs to be processed.

■**Note** I'll cover message loops in more detail in Chapter 11, when I cover Windows Forms applications.

In contrast, threads that are simply executing code not inside a message loop (such as the Main() method of a console application) are referred to as *worker threads*. The terms *user-interface thread* and *worker thread* arose because of the traditional architecture of Windows applications. The main thread in a Windows Forms application will normally have a message loop, which is used to process user input. This main thread may instantiate other threads to do certain work—and these other threads traditionally don't have message loops. If you call `Application.Run()` on a thread, that thread will by definition become a user-interface thread, since `Application.Run()` works internally by starting a message loop. However, a thread doesn't have to be processing a user interface in order to have a message loop. For example, COM single-threaded apartment (STA) threads have message loops but no user interface—so to that extent the term *user-interface thread* is a bit misleading.

The distinction between a user-interface thread and a worker thread is purely a terminological one (and the terminology applies equally to unmanaged and managed code). Windows doesn't recognize any formal difference; hence, `Thread` doesn't have any properties to determine into which category a given thread falls.

Thread Identity

Unmanaged threads are normally identified by a thread ID—a number that maps to an operating system handle that identifies the thread's resources. However, the concept of a thread ID isn't defined for managed threads, which will be identified by a hash code or by a name. The hash code is always present and set by the CLR, but the name will be blank unless it's explicitly set by your code.

```
Thread thisThread = Thread.CurrentThread;
int hash = thisThread.GetHashCode();
thisThread.Name = "My nice thread";
```

Note that you can only set the name once—once set, you can't subsequently change it.

Although you can use the hash code to identify a thread, it's not generally possible to obtain a `Thread` reference given its hash code.

If you do specifically need to know the thread ID of the current running thread, then you can use the static `System.AppDomain.GetCurrentThreadId()` method.

```
int id = AppDomain.GetCurrentThreadId();
```

Generally speaking, you'll want to do this only if you need to pass the ID to some native code. Bearing in mind the possibility that physical and logical threads may become separated in future versions of .NET, you should probably avoid caching this value across any points where the CLR takes control over the flow of execution.

Enumerating Unmanaged Threads

It's possible to enumerate over the unmanaged threads in a process using the static `System.Diagnostics.Process.Threads` property. This yields a collection of `ProcessThread` references. I'll show you how to do this for completeness, but in terms of managed code you can't do much with the `ProcessThread` references. The most common reason for using this technique is likely to be to obtain the thread IDs (which are available through the `ProcessThread.Id` property) to pass to some unmanaged code. The fact that the `ProcessThread` is in the `System.Diagnostics` namespace gives a pretty good clue as to the intended purpose of the class; it's there to help with debugging or to perform detailed diagnostic analysis of a process—it's not intended for normal everyday use.

The following sample enumerates the threads in the process, displaying the ID, thread state, and priority level of each:

```
static void Main()
{
    ProcessThreadCollection ptc = Process.GetCurrentProcess().Threads;
    Console.WriteLine("{0} threads in process", ptc.Count);
    foreach (ProcessThread pt in ptc)
    {
        Console.WriteLine("ID: {0}, State: {1}, Priority: {2}", pt.Id,
                        pt.ThreadState, pt.PriorityLevel);
    }
}
```

The code gives the following output on my machine in release mode (you may get different numbers of threads on different machines, and also the results will be different in debug mode because additional threads may be present for debugging purposes):

```
9 threads in process
ID: 3960, State: Running, Priority: Normal
ID: 4080, State: Wait, Priority: Normal
ID: 2700, State: Wait, Priority: Highest
ID: 2312, State: Wait, Priority: Normal
ID: 4064, State: Wait, Priority: Normal
ID: 1808, State: Wait, Priority: Normal
ID: 4004, State: Wait, Priority: Normal
ID: 3444, State: Wait, Priority: Normal
ID: 376, State: Wait, Priority: Normal
```

The ThreadState and PriorityLevel properties are (respectively) instances of the System.Diagnostics.ThreadState and System.Diagnostics.ThreadPriorityLevel enums. Although I've displayed these values for ProcessThread, you can get this data for the Thread class as well—you don't need to go through ProcessThread. However, note that the Thread class's ThreadState and Priority properties have slightly different enums than the ProcessThread equivalents—System.Threading.ThreadState and System.Threading.ThreadPriority, respectively. The state indicates what the thread is currently doing (for example, whether it's sleeping, running, or waiting for a synchronization object).

By the way, although I've shown this sample just to give you an idea of the ProcessThread class, I don't suggest you use this technique to enumerate the physical threads in a real application. My reason? Well you'll notice nine threads have been listed whereas the earlier HelloWorld program had only three threads. The Heisenberg principle applies here: enumerating the process threads actually causes more threads to be created by the CLR to perform the enumeration!

Understanding Multithreading Techniques

Let's say you've decided you're definitely going to use multithreading techniques in an application. You basically have five options available. I'll discuss each of these briefly and then spend most of the rest of the chapter presenting samples that use the main techniques.

Asynchronous Delegate Invocation

Generally speaking, asynchronous delegate invocation is the best technique if you have a number of simple, independent tasks that you want to hand out to another thread. The advantage of this technique is that a thread-pool thread will be used to execute the asynchronous operation, so you get all the performance benefits of the thread pool. If your application needs to do a lot of asynchronous operations, then this performance benefit can be considerable as threads get automatically reused. Not only that, but literally any method can be wrapped in a delegate and invoked asynchronously. All the support for this is already built into delegates by the CLR—you don't need to add any extra support for this in your method whatsoever! That's a powerful argument for this technique.

Explicitly Creating Your Own Threads

Explicitly creating your own threads will be the technique of choice if you need a small number of threads running for a long time and interacting with each other. By explicitly creating your own threads, you don't get to use the thread pool—but as you saw earlier you do get `Thread` references to the threads created, which means you have extra control over the threads. You also get to determine exactly which thread an operation is executed on—something you can't do with the thread pool, since the CLR picks the thread for each asynchronous operation. This will be significant if you need to guarantee that several operations will be executed on the same thread.

Timers

A timer will be the technique of choice if you need to perform some processing at regular repeated intervals—for example, polling an object to see what its state is every few seconds. The `System.Threading.Timer` object that I'll use in this chapter uses the thread pool to make callbacks at regular intervals and is extremely accurate.

Built-in Asynchronous Support

Taking advantage of existing asynchronous support isn't something I'll go into in detail in this chapter. Basically, certain .NET Framework classes, such as `Stream` and `WebRequest`, have intrinsic support for requesting that certain operations can be carried out asynchronously. The pattern for invoking this support closely follows the pattern for asynchronous delegate invocation, but the underlying implementation may be different. I'll briefly mention some of the classes that support this pattern when I cover asynchronous delegates.

Explicitly Queuing Items to the Thread Pool

Queuing an item to the thread pool is also something I won't cover in detail in this chapter. I presented the basic syntax for doing this earlier. It has a similar effect in practice to asynchronous delegate invocation.

Understanding Asynchronous Delegates

Much of the rest of this chapter will be devoted to working through some samples that illustrate most of the previous techniques. The samples are as far as possible based on realistic situations, in order to give you a flavor of the kinds of situation where you'll need to use the main multithreading techniques.

I'll just jump in at the deep end conceptwise by presenting asynchronous delegates first. The reason is that this technique is often the most useful one for asynchronous processing—it allows you to write highly efficient thread pool–based multithreaded applications with very little coding effort. Before you can use this technique, however, you need to understand quite a few concepts, which means the next section is going to be quite top-heavy on theory.

The BeginXXX()-EndXXX() Architecture

In .NET, the usual pattern for implementing an asynchronous method call is for some object to expose two methods, `BeginXXX()` and `EndXXX()`, where XXX is some word that describes the method. Usually a separate unrelated method, `XXX()`, performs the operation synchronously.

`BeginXXX()` is the method that's called to start the operation. It returns immediately, with the operation left executing on a thread-pool thread. `EndXXX()` is called when the results are required. If the asynchronous operation has already completed when `EndXXX()` is called, then `EndXXX()` simply returns the actual return values from the operation. If the operation is still executing, `EndXXX()` waits until it has completed before returning the values. The actual parameters expected by `BeginXXX()` and `EndXXX()` will of course depend on the parameters passed onto the asynchronous operation. If an exception is thrown in the asynchronous operation, this exception will be transferred by the CLR to the `EndXXX()` call, which will throw this same exception on the calling thread.

This design pattern is implemented by various classes, including the following:

- `System.IO.FileStream` (which implements the methods `BeginRead()`/`EndRead()` for reading a stream and `BeginWrite()`/`EndWrite()` for writing)

- `System.Net.WebRequest` (`BeginRequest()`/`EndRequest()` for making a request to a remote server)

- `System.Windows.Forms.Control` (`BeginInvoke()`/`EndInvoke()` for executing any method; however, the underlying implementation here is different—the message loop is used instead of the thread pool for the asynchronous operation)

- `System.Messaging.MessageQueue` (`BeginReceive()`/`EndReceive()` for receiving a message)

However, what's of interest here is that delegates implement this same design pattern. This means you can asynchronously invoke literally any method at all, just by wrapping it in a delegate and invoking the delegate asynchronously. The methods involved here are called `BeginInvoke()` and `EndInvoke()`. Paradoxically, these methods aren't defined in either the `System.Delegate` or `System.MulticastDelegate` classes, but they can be defined, with native CLR support to supply the implementations, in any delegate that derives from these classes—and you'll find that most high-level language compilers, including the C#, VB .NET, and C++ ones, add this support automatically.

To explain how asynchronous delegates are implemented, I first need to go over a couple of other classes and interfaces that are provided by the .NET Framework classes to support asynchronous method calls. I'll first cover the IAsyncResult interface. IAsyncResult is able to hold information about an asynchronous call. You can use this information by calling code to check the status of the operation. IAsyncResult exposes a number of properties, as shown in Table 9-1.

Table 9-1. IAsyncResult *Properties*

Property	Type	Description
AsyncState	object	Extra data that's supplied by the calling method
AsyncWaitHandle	System.Threading.WaitHandle	A synchronization object that can be used to wait until the operation completes
CompletedSynchronously	bool	Gives some indication of whether the operation has completed and, if so, whether it was on this thread
IsCompleted	bool	Whether the operation has completed yet

You'll come across this interface quite a lot in this chapter. Calls to BeginInvoke() on delegates return an IAsyncResult reference, and more generally, calls to BeginXXX() invariably do the same. You use this IAsyncResult by the calling code to check the progress of the operation.

You also need to be aware of the System.Runtime.Remoting.Messaging.AsyncResult class. The significance of this class is that it implements IAsyncResult. In practice, this is the class that the CLR normally uses to provide the implementation of IAsyncResult for asynchronous delegates. Don't worry that this class is in a messaging-related namespace. AsyncResult has uses in connection with messaging (since messaging architecture is full of asynchronous operations), but it happens to be used with delegates as well. AsyncResult implements another property of interest to you, AsyncResult.AsyncDelegate, which contains a reference to the actual delegate that was originally invoked asynchronously, stored as an object reference.

You also need to know about one other delegate, System.AsyncCallback. This delegate is defined as follows:

```
public delegate void AsyncCallback(IAsyncResult ar);
```

AsyncCallback is there to represent a callback method that the CLR should invoke to inform your application that the asynchronous operation has been completed. An initialized AsyncCallback can be passed to BeginInvoke() for this purpose, though you can instead pass in null if you don't want the CLR to call back any method.

That may all sound like a bit much to understand. The best way to see how this pattern works in practice is to look at a specific example.

Example of BeginInvoke()/EndInvoke() Signatures

In Chapter 2, when I covered delegates, I briefly covered the IL that's emitted when a delegate class is defined in C# and showed that it contained two extra methods, BeginInvoke() and EndInvoke(). I indicated in that chapter that I was going to postpone the discussion of these methods until now. I'm afraid you're now going to have to prepare for some more IL code, because the BeginInvoke() and EndInvoke() methods are only defined at the IL level—they don't exist at source code level.

Suppose a delegate is defined in C# like this:

```
public delegate float SomeDelegate(int input, ref int refparam,
                                   out int output);
```

The IL emitted by the C# compiler will look something like this:

```
.class public auto ansi sealed SomeDelegate
       extends [mscorlib]System.MulticastDelegate
{
  .method public hidebysig specialname rtspecialname
          instance void  .ctor(object 'object',
                               native int 'method') runtime managed
  {
  } // end of method SomeDelegate::.ctor

  .method public hidebysig virtual instance float32
          Invoke(int32 input,
                 int32& refparam,
                 [out] int32& output) runtime managed
  {
  } // end of method SomeDelegate::Invoke

  .method public hidebysig newslot virtual
          instance class [mscorlib]System.IAsyncResult
          BeginInvoke(int32 input,
                      int32& refparam,
                      [out] int32& output,
                      class [mscorlib]System.AsyncCallback callback,
                      object 'object') runtime managed
  {
  } // end of method SomeDelegate::BeginInvoke

  .method public hidebysig newslot virtual
          instance float32  EndInvoke(int32& refparam,
                                      [out] int32& output,
                                      class [mscorlib]System.IAsyncResult
                                             result) runtime managed
  {
  } // end of method SomeDelegate::EndInvoke

} // end of class SomeDelegate
```

I've highlighted the key methods by displaying them in bold. What has been emitted is the IL equivalent of this:

```
// Pseudo-code. No method implementation supplied.
IAsyncResult BeginInvoke(
        int input, ref int refparam, out int output,
        ASyncCallback callback, object state);
float EndInvoke(ref int refparam, out int output, IAsyncResult result);
```

Although these methods don't exist in any actual C# source code, the C# compiler knows they're there in the IL, so it will allow you to write code that invokes them. (And although I'm using C# for the discussion, the situation is the same in both VB and C++.) Notice also that the implementations of these methods are supplied automatically by the runtime—hence, you'll see the runtime flags in the IL method signatures.

To invoke the delegate asynchronously, the client code calls the BeginInvoke() method. BeginInvoke() has the same signature as the synchronous Invoke() method, except for its return type and an extra two parameters. The return type is always an IAsyncResult interface reference, which the client code can use to monitor the progress of the operation. The first extra parameter is an ASyncCallback delegate instance, which must have been set up by the client and which supplies details of a callback method that will be invoked automatically when the operation is completed. If you don't want any callback to be invoked, you can set this parameter to null. The second extra parameter is there in case you want to store any extra information about the asynchronous operation for later use. Any value passed in here isn't used by the asynchronous operation but will be passed through to the ASyncState property of the returned IAsyncResult interface—so it's there if the client code needs it later. In most cases, you'll pass in null for this parameter.

EndInvoke() is of course the method that's used to return the result. Its signature is a little different. It has the same return type as the original delegate (that makes sense because EndInvoke() needs to return the result), and it also duplicates any ref or out parameters in the delegate signature. Again, that makes sense because these parameters could contain return values. However, if the original delegate was expecting any value-type parameters passed by value, these won't be present in the EndInvoke() parameter list, since any such values are irrelevant to the question of returned results. EndInvoke() has one other parameter—an IAsyncResult interface reference. The CLR's implementation of EndInvoke() will internally use this parameter to figure out which operation is the one from which you want the return value. In other words, if you've started more than one asynchronous operation using BeginInvoke(), then the IAsyncResult parameter tells the CLR from which of the BeginInvoke() calls you require the return value. Obviously, you'll need to pass in the value returned from the correct BeginInvoke() call here.

The Two Ways to Use Asynchronous Delegates

Notice from the previous discussion that you have a clear choice in how you write your client code. You can do either of the following:

Either arrange for the client thread to call BeginInvoke(), then immediately go off and do some other work, and finally call EndInvoke(). This means that EndInvoke() will be executed on the client thread.

Or call `BeginInvoke()` on the client thread, passing in an `AsyncCallback` that indicates a callback method. The client thread is then free to forget all about the asynchronous operation. This means that `EndInvoke()` will actually be executed on a thread-pool thread, presumably (though that's not documented) the same thread used to perform the asynchronous operation.

Note that you must choose one or the other; you can't do both, since you'll get an exception if `EndInvoke()` is called more than once for the same asynchronous operation.

Which of these techniques you choose depends on which solution best suits your particular situation. The first option has the disadvantage that the client thread has no direct way of knowing when the operation has been completed, other than by polling—that is to say, checking the `IsCompleted` property of the `IAsyncResult` interface every so often. If it calls `EndInvoke()` too early, it will block the client thread until the operation is complete. On the other hand, because it's the client thread that calls `EndInvoke()`, this thread has direct access to the values returned. The second option may be better if the client thread has other important work to do and doesn't directly need to access the returned results (or if it's a method that doesn't return any values). However, if the client thread needs access to the return values, it will still have to poll to find out if the values are there yet. And unless those values are stored in some member fields, it will have to communicate somehow with the callback function to retrieve those values, which brings up thread synchronization issues.

In the following sample I'll demonstrate both approaches, so you can judge their relative merits.

Asynchronous Delegates Sample

Now that you've seen the theory of asynchronous delegates, I'll put it into practice by developing a sample that illustrates the different ways that a delegate can be invoked, both synchronously and asynchronously. For this sample, I'll assume you have a database of names and addresses. I'll define a `GetAddress()` method, which takes a name as a parameter and pretends to look up the addresses in this database. This is the kind of operation that could take a short while to complete if, for example, the database is located remotely. To keep things simple, `GetAddress()` won't actually access any database; it simply pauses for one second (to simulate the delay) and then returns one of a couple of hard-coded values. The sample will involve wrapping the `GetAddress()` method in a delegate. It will then invoke the delegate several times in each of the following three ways:

- Synchronously

- Asynchronously, with the result returned via a callback function

- Asynchronously, with the main thread later calling `EndInvoke()` to retrieve the address

The namespaces you'll need for this sample (and indeed, all the remaining samples in this chapter) are as follows:

```
using System;
using System.Threading;
using System.Runtime.Remoting;
using System.Runtime.Remoting.Messaging;
using System.Text;
```

Before I go over the code for the asynchronous calls, I'll present a quick helper utility class that will be used to display thread information.

```
public class ThreadUtils
{
   public static string ThreadDescription(Thread thread)
   {
      StringBuilder sb = new StringBuilder(100);
      if (thread.Name != null && thread.Name != "")
      {
         sb.Append(thread.Name);
         sb.Append(",  ");
      }

      sb.Append("hash: ");
      sb.Append(thread.GetHashCode());
      sb.Append(",  pool: ");
      sb.Append(thread.IsThreadPoolThread);
      sb.Append(",  backgrnd: ");
      sb.Append(thread.IsBackground);
      sb.Append(",  state: ");
      sb.Append(thread.ThreadState);
      return sb.ToString();
   }

   public static void DisplayThreadInfo(string context)
   {
      string output = "\n" + context + "\n    " +
                   ThreadDescription(Thread.CurrentThread);
      Console.WriteLine(output);
   }
}
```

This code shouldn't need any explanation. It simply means you can call DisplayThreadInfo() to write out quite a bit of information about the currently executing thread so you can see exactly what your code is doing. Unfortunately, System.Threading.Thread.ToString() doesn't appear to have been implemented by Microsoft to do anything intelligent—it simply displays the type name—so I've defined the ThreadUtils class as a substitute.

Now let's look at how you use the delegates. The GetAddress() method, and the various wrapper methods that use delegates to invoke GetAddress() indirectly, are all located in a class that I'll call DataRetriever. The following is the GetAddress() method:

```
public class DataRetriever
{
   public string GetAddress(string name)
   {
      ThreadUtils.DisplayThreadInfo("In GetAddress...");
```

```
        // Simulate waiting to get results off database servers
        Thread.Sleep(1000);
        if (name == "Simon")
            return "Simon lives in Lancaster";
        else if (name == "Apress")
            return "Julian lives in Birmingham";
        else
            throw new ArgumentException("The name " + name +
                                    " is not in the database", "name");
    }
```

As you can see, this method first displays the details of the thread on which it's running. It then returns a string indicating the town in which the named person lives. This simulated database knows about only two people—Simon and Julian. If given any other name, it throws an exception. This will give me the chance to illustrate the catching of asynchronous exceptions.

You also need to define a delegate with the appropriate signature for GetAddress().

```
public delegate string GetAddressDelegate(string name);
```

Based on this delegate syntax, you can call the BeginInvoke() and EndInvoke() methods with the following signatures:

```
// Pseudo-code - these definitions do not actually exist in any source code
public IAsyncResult GetAddressDelegate.BeginInvoke(string name,
                                    ASyncResult callback, object state);
public string GetAddressDelegate.EndInvoke(IAsyncResult result);
```

Now for the wrapper methods; the following calls the delegate synchronously:

```
public void GetAddressSync(string name)
{
    try
    {
        GetAddressDelegate dc = new GetAddressDelegate(this.GetAddress);
        string result = dc(name);
        Console.WriteLine("\nSync: " + result);
    }
    catch (Exception ex)
    {
        Console.WriteLine("\nSync: a problem occurred: " + ex.Message);
    }
}
```

The delegate wrapper methods in this sample don't merely call GetAddress(); they also display the results and catch any errors arising from an incorrect name. The code for GetAddressSync() should be fairly self-explanatory. You'll note that in real production code, you wouldn't use a delegate in quite the way I've done here. GetAddressSync() is in the same class as GetAddress(), and it's known at compile time which method is to be called, so I have no need to use a delegate at all in this particular case! I've done it this way to provide a fair comparison between the synchronous and asynchronous techniques for delegate invocation.

Next, let's examine the way a delegate is called asynchronously using `EndInvoke()` to get the results.

```
public void GetAddressAsyncWait(string name)
{
    GetAddressDelegate dc = new GetAddressDelegate(this.GetAddress);

    IAsyncResult ar = dc.BeginInvoke(name, null, null);

    // Main thread can in principle do other work now
    try
    {
        string result = dc.EndInvoke(ar);
        Console.WriteLine("\nAsync waiting : "+ result);
    }
    catch (Exception ex)
    {
        Console.WriteLine("\nAsync waiting, a problem occurred : " +
                        ex.Message);
    }
}
```

In this method, the delegate is defined in the same way but invoked using `BeginInvoke()`, passing `null` for the callback delegate. I also pass in `null` for the state information. `BeginInvoke()` returns immediately, and at this point the main thread is free to do something else while the background request is processed. Having the main thread free to do something else is of course the main reason for invoking the delegate asynchronously. However, since this is only a sample, the code has nothing else to do, so instead I've simply left a comment in the code reminding you of this. The code in the sample proceeds to call `EndInvoke()` immediately—something that it wouldn't be sensible to do in production code, since if that's all you wanted to do, you would just have called the method synchronously! `EndInvoke()` will block until the asynchronous operation has completed and then return the results. Notice that I've placed the `try` block around the `EndInvoke()` call, since this is the point at which an exception will be raised on the main thread if the asynchronous operation threw an exception.

Finally, I'll cover the technique for using a callback method. You need to actually define a callback method first. This method forms part of the same `DataRetriever` class in the sample, though you can define it in a different class if you want.

```
public void GetResultsOnCallback(IAsyncResult ar)
{
    GetAddressDelegate del = (GetAddressDelegate)
                            ((AsyncResult)ar).AsyncDelegate;

    try
    {
        string result;
```

```
        result = del.EndInvoke(ar);
        Console.WriteLine("\nOn CallBack: result is " + result);
    }
    catch (Exception ex)
    {
        Console.WriteLine("\nOn CallBack, problem occurred: " + ex.Message);
    }
}
```

You also need to retrieve the delegate against which EndInvoke() is to be called. You can get a reference to this delegate from the IAsyncResult interface reference. To do that, you need to cast the interface reference to the AsyncResult class that's actually used to implement the interface. (Why Microsoft didn't define the callback signature so it was expecting an instance of this class in the first place—which would have saved everyone an explicit cast operation—is one of those little mysteries I'll quietly ignore.) Then the code calls EndInvoke() inside the usual try block. The main implementation differences between the callback method and the GetAddressAsyncWait() method arise from the following two points: GetAddressAsyncWait() already has the delegate reference whereas GetResultsOnCallback() has to retrieve it from the AsyncResult object. You know that if GetResultsOnCallback() has been invoked, the asynchronous operation has already finished, so you know that EndInvoke() will not block the thread. This isn't the case for GetAddressAsyncWait().

The following is the code to start the asynchronous operation with a callback:

```
public void GetAddressAsync(string name)
{
    GetAddressDelegate dc = new GetAddressDelegate(this.GetAddress);

    AsyncCallback cb = new AsyncCallback(this.GetResultsOnCallback);
    IAsyncResult ar = dc.BeginInvoke(name, cb, null);
}
```

This code simply sets up an AsyncCallback delegate with the callback method and calls BeginInvoke().

Finally, you need a Main() method that tests the previous code.

```
public class EntryPoint
{
    public static void Main()
    {
        Thread.CurrentThread.Name = "Main Thread";
        DataRetriever dr = new DataRetriever();

        dr.GetAddressSync("Simon");
        dr.GetAddressSync("Julian");
        dr.GetAddressSync("Steve");

        dr.GetAddressAsync("Simon");
        dr.GetAddressAsync("Julian");
        dr.GetAddressAsync("Steve");
```

```
    dr.GetAddressAsyncWait("Simon");
    dr.GetAddressAsyncWait("Julian");
    dr.GetAddressAsyncWait("Steve");

    Console.ReadLine();
  }
}
```

The Main() method first attaches a name to the main thread—so you can easily identify this thread when displaying thread information. Then it sets up a new DataRetriever object and starts obtaining addresses. I'll use three test names: "Simon", "Julian", and "Steve", so the code passes each of these names into GetAddress() using each of the three delegate techniques I've covered. The name Steve should cause an exception to be thrown. Note that because of the way I've implemented the methods in the DataRetriever class, you'll get a message displaying the thread each time GetAddress() is invoked. You'll separately get the result of the operation displayed (without thread information) about a second later.

Running the AsyncDelegates sample gives quite a few results, so I've broken up the results as they appeared on the console, with explanations. The results start like this:

```
In GetAddress...
   Main Thread,  hash: 1,  pool: False,  backgrnd: False,  state: Running
Sync: Simon lives in Lancaster
In GetAddress...
   Main Thread,  hash: 1,  pool: False,  backgrnd: False,  state: Running
Sync: Julian lives in Birmingham
In GetAddress...
   Main Thread,  hash: 1,  pool: False,  backgrnd: False,  state: Running
Sync: a problem occurred: The name Steve is not in the database
Parameter name: name
```

This output is as expected. The program makes three synchronous calls to GetAddress() in succession; in each case the result is returned before the next call is made. If you run the sample, you'll notice the one-second delays before obtaining each result.

Next I obtained this:

```
In GetAddress...
   hash: 3,  pool: True,  backgrnd: True,  state: Background

In GetAddress...
   hash: 4,  pool: True,  backgrnd: True,  state: Background

In GetAddress...
   hash: 5,  pool: True,  backgrnd: True,  state: Background
```

This output shows the first set of three asynchronous calls being made. Each call is delegated to a new thread. On the first asynchronous call, the CLR sees that there aren't yet any threads in the pool, so it creates one (which happens to have hash 3) and sets GetAddress() running on this thread. In fact, the CLR does more than that: The thread pool itself is constructed only when the CLR first sees that it's going to be used, so this is the point at which the thread pool itself will be created, which means that this first asynchronous call will take a little time to set up. Immediately after that, however, the main thread asks for another asynchronous operation. The CLR inspects the thread pool and finds that it contains one thread, but that thread is already occupied. So it creates another one—this time with hash 4. Then the same thing happens again for the third asynchronous call, and you get a new thread with hash 5. It's tempting to see the obvious pattern in the hash values, but remember that the values themselves are irrelevant; in principle you can't deduce anything from them other than that if you get the same hash value twice, you know you're looking at the same logical CLR thread.

Now is when things get interesting. With several threads working at the same time, a lot of scope exists for things to happen in an unexpected order.

```
On CallBack: result is Simon lives in Lancaster
In GetAddress...
    hash: 3,  pool: True,  backgrnd: True,  state: Background
On CallBack: result is Julian lives in Birmingham
Async waiting : Simon lives in Lancaster
In GetAddress...
    hash: 4,  pool: True,  backgrnd: True,  state: Background
On CallBack, problem occurred: The name Steve is not in the database
Parameter name: name
Async waiting : Julian lives in Birmingham
In GetAddress...
    hash: 3,  pool: True,  backgrnd: True,  state: Background
Async waiting, a problem occurred : The name Steve is not in the database
```

The first thing that happens is that, while the CLR has been busy setting up these threads, the first asynchronous result comes through. Simon lives in Lancaster. Hey, I already knew that, but it's nice to get confirmation that I'm currently living in the correct town! This means that the thread with hash 3 is now free, and as you can see from the next In GetAddress... message, the CLR takes advantage of this by directing the fourth asynchronous operation to this thread. Checking against the code, you'll see that this fourth asynchronous operation is the first noncallback one, in which the main thread waits for the result to come back before doing anything else. While the program is waiting, the results for the second asynchronous callback comes through, telling you that Julian lives in Birmingham. Then the asynchronous waiting result for Simon comes through, and the main thread sends the next request off. This one goes onto thread hash 4, as this thread is now free. The final callback, indicating the exception thrown for Steve appears, and the main thread continues to send and wait for the remaining data.

What I've presented here are the results on my machine. If you run the sample on your computer, the results are likely to be different depending on the installed CLR version and also on your hardware, because that will affect how long it takes the CLR to execute the code in the Main() method on your machine. You may also want to experiment with varying the delay time in GetAddress() to see how that will affect your output.

Synchronizing Variable Access

You may have thought that the AsyncDelegates sample was complicated enough. In fact, however, I carefully designed that sample in a way that made it far simpler than most multithreaded applications. Whenever an asynchronous operation was requested, the results would come back, be displayed on the console, and be immediately forgotten about. This meant that when the results were retrieved in a callback method running on one of the thread-pool threads, I didn't have to worry about getting these results stored somewhere where the main thread could access them. I could ignore the whole issue of synchronizing access to variables across threads. In real life it's extremely unlikely that you'll be able to write a multithreaded application without facing this issue—and that's the subject that I'll deal with next. I'll briefly review the principles of thread synchronization and the objects that are available in the .NET Framework for this purpose. Then I'll present a sample that illustrates thread synchronization using the CLR's Monitor class.

Data Synchronization Principles

The reason for needing to worry about data synchronization is fairly well known: In general, the operations of reading and writing large data items aren't atomic. In other words, even if something looks like a single statement in a high-level language (or even in IL), it often actually requires a number of native executable instructions to perform. However, you have no way of telling when Windows may decide that the running thread has finished its time slice and transfer control to another thread. This means, for example, that one thread may start writing some data to an object. While it's in the middle of writing and the object therefore contains half-finished data, Windows could transfer control to another thread, which proceeds to read the value of the same object, happily unaware that it's reading garbage. On a multiprocessor CPU, the situation can get even worse, as two threads running on different CPUs really can try to access the same variable simultaneously. The real problem is that this kind of bug is hard to track down; this kind of data corruption often only manifests itself a lot later, when the corrupt data is used for something else. Not only that, but such bugs are rarely reproducible. It's essentially unpredictable when Windows will swap threads, and this will vary every time you run the application. You could easily end up with completely different behavior every time you run the application, which can make it extraordinarily hard to debug the problem.

■**Tip** Interestingly, although thread synchronization issues can break your code, they won't cause it to fail type safety. This is because loading primitive types such as pointers is always atomic, which means that it's not possible for a thread synchronization bug to cause a managed pointer or an object reference to be corrupted in any way that would cause the application to access memory outside its own area of virtual address space on dereferencing.

The solution to this problem is of course ideally a mechanism that prevents any thread from accessing any given variable while any other thread is already accessing that variable. In practice, it's not practical to have this done automatically. Instead, the Windows operating system provides some mechanisms (for unmanaged code) whereby a thread can ask to wait before proceeding into a potentially dangerous section of code, but this relies on the programmer knowing where the dangerous points of code are and adding extra code that invokes the Windows synchronization mechanisms at those points. For managed code, the same mechanisms are available, plus some extra facilities provided by the CLR itself. I'll now explain the main such mechanisms available to managed code. Bear in mind that, although I'll review all the main thread synchronization objects here so you're aware of their existence, the only ones that I'll actually use in the samples in this chapter are Monitor and ManualResetEvent.

The Monitor

The simplest and most efficient way to synchronize variable access in managed code is normally using something called the *monitor*. Suppose you have some C# code in which some thread is about to access a variable x, and it knows that another thread may want to access x as well. You can ensure that the two threads don't simultaneously access this data like this:

```
lock (x)
{
    // Code that uses x goes here
}
```

You can view the previous code as asking the CLR's monitor for a lock on the variable x. Provided no other thread already has a lock on x, the monitor will freely give this code the lock, which will last for the duration of the block statement associated with the lock (the statements in the braces). However, if another thread has already acquired a lock on x, then the monitor will refuse to grant this thread the lock. Instead, the thread will be suspended until the other thread releases its lock, whereupon this thread can proceed. Provided you're careful to place lock statements around every block of code that accesses the variable x, this will ensure that x is only ever accessed by one thread at any one time, thus ensuring that x isn't the source of any synchronization bugs.

In VB, the corresponding syntax is as follows:

```
SyncLock x
    ' Code that accesses x goes here
End SyncLock
```

A thread that's waiting before starting to execute a potentially dangerous section of code is said to be *blocked*. (Incidentally, blocked threads don't consume any CPU time.) The objects responsible for controlling the blocking of threads are known as *thread synchronization objects* or *thread synchronization primitives*. The sections of code that should not be executed simultaneously, and that therefore will have been coded in such a way that they're subject to the control of thread synchronization primitives, are known as *protected code*.

The C# and VB code you just saw is actually a useful shorthand syntax, which is great for writing code but not so good for seeing what's actually happening. To better understand what's going on under the hood, examine the following C# code. This code is equivalent to the previous snippets; it just explicitly shows what's happening instead of using the lock or SyncLock shorthand syntax.

```
object temp = x;
Monitor.Enter(temp);
try
{
    // Code that uses x (or, equivalently, temp)
}
finally
{
    Monitor.Exit(temp);
}
```

What's actually happening is that the code tells the CLR's `Monitor` class that it wants to acquire a lock on an object, referred to by x. It does this by passing a reference to the object to the static `Monitor.Enter()` method, and it uses the static `Monitor.Exit()` method to inform the monitor when it no longer needs the lock. Notice that the full version of the code caches the original object reference to make sure that the correct reference is passed to `Exit()`, even if the variable x is reassigned. The `Exit()` method is in a `finally` block so that it's guaranteed to execute. If for any reason (such as an exception having been thrown) the thread failed to execute the `Monitor.Exit()` call, you'd have a big problem when another thread tried to grab the lock on that object. The monitor would think the first thread still had the lock, and it'd therefore incorrectly block the other thread. Permanently. Fortunately, the `lock`/`SyncLock` syntax guarantees that `Exit()` will be executed.

■**Tip** C++ has no shorthand equivalent to the C# `lock` and VB `SyncLock` statements. If you're coding in C++, you'll need to invoke the `Monitor` methods explicitly. In that case, take care to place the `Exit()` statement in a `finally` block.

Locks on different objects don't affect each other. In other words, if one thread is executing code inside a `lock(x) { }` block, this won't prevent another thread from executing `lock(y) { }` and entering the protected area of code, provided of course that x and y refer to different objects.

One important point is that, although the statement `lock(x) { }` would normally be used to synchronize access to the object referred to by x, in fact no restriction exists on the code that can be placed in the protected block. Normally you should be wary of placing code in `lock(x) { }` that's unrelated to x, because that will make your code harder to understand, but you'll see later that you may nevertheless sometimes want to do so, normally for reasons having to do with the way you design your thread synchronization architecture.

The `Monitor` class itself represents a special lightweight synchronization object developed specifically for the CLR. Internally, `Monitor` is implemented to use the sync block index of the object passed to the `Enter()` and `Exit()` methods to control thread blocking. Recall from Chapter 3 that the sync block index forms a portion of an `int32` that's stored in the first 4 bytes of each reference-type managed object. This value is usually zero, but if a thread claims the lock on an object, the monitor will create an entry describing that in a table internal to the CLR and modify the sync block index of the object to reference that table entry. However, if the sync block index indicates that the object is already locked by another thread, the monitor will block the thread until the object is released. Bear in mind that you can use the monitor to synchronize access only to object references, not to value types. If you try to pass a value type to `Monitor.Enter()`, the type will be boxed, which will result in no synchronization. To see why, suppose some code such as the following is executed on some thread:

```
Monitor.Enter(v)    // v is  a value type
{
```

v will be boxed, and the boxed object reference will be passed to `Monitor.Enter()`. Unfortunately, if some other thread later attempts the same thing, a new boxed copy of v will be created. Since the monitor will see two different boxed objects, it won't realize that the two threads are trying to synchronize against the same variable, so the threads won't get synchronized. This is potentially a nasty source of bugs—and is another area where the C# `lock` and VB `SyncLock` statements provide additional support. The C# and VB compilers will both flag a syntax error if you use these statements to lock a value type. If you need to synchronize access against a value type, a commonly used technique is this:

```
lock (typeof(v))
{
```

Bear in mind that `typeof(v)` always returns the same object for all instances of v, so using this technique will prevent threads running simultaneously, even if those threads are accessing different, unrelated instances of that type; this may be stronger protection than you need. Other possibilities are to find some convenient reference object you can lock against instead, or to manually box v, so you can synchronize access against the same boxed object.

As a thread synchronization class, `Monitor` is actually quite unusual in two regards: It's implemented entirely within the CLR itself, and it's never instantiated. Most of the other CLR classes used to synchronize threads work by wrapping native Windows synchronization objects, and they also need to be instantiated before they can be used. With a monitor, locking is performed against the reference to the object to which access needs to be protected; by contrast, most of the other synchronization classes require you to instantiate the synchronization object and then perform thread locking against that synchronization object.

Mutexes

A mutex has a similar purpose to the monitor, but the syntax for using it is rather different. Suppose you want to protect access to a variable called X, and you've named the mutex you want to use to do this `mutex1`.

```
// Instantiate the mutex in some manner so that it will be accessible to
// all relevant threads (this normally means it'll be a member field)
this.mutex1 = new Mutex()

// Later, when a thread needs to perform synchronization
mutex1.WaitOne();

// Do something with variable X
mutex1.ReleaseMutex();

// Carry on
```

Calling the WaitOne() method effectively causes that thread to ask for *ownership* of the mutex. If no other thread owns the mutex, then everything is fine; this thread can proceed, and it retains ownership of the mutex until it calls ReleaseMutex() against the same mutex object. If another thread already owns the mutex, the first thread will block until the mutex is released. You can instantiate as many mutexes as you want. If a thread asks one mutex if it's OK to proceed, the result will not be affected by the state of any other mutex; the mutexes all work completely independently.

■**Tip** Although for clarity I haven't explicitly shown it in the previous code, remember to place the ReleaseMutex() call in a finally block to avoid bugs caused by a mutex not being released following an exception being thrown.

Mutexes will give you a much bigger performance hit than using the monitor, and no shortcut syntax exists. So why would you ever use them? The answer is partly because they have an ability to avoid an error condition known as a *deadlock*, which I'll discuss shortly, and partly because they're relatively easy to use cross-process. It's not often that you'll need to synchronize threads running in two different processes (details of how to do this are in the MSDN documentation for Mutex), but the issue may crop up if you're doing some low-level work (such as programming device drivers), for which multiple processes are sharing resources. Another possible reason for using mutexes is if part of your thread synchronization is being done in unmanaged code. Mutex exposes a Handle property that exposes the native underlying system mutex handle, which can be passed to unmanaged code that needs to manipulate the mutex.

■**Tip** Don't try to combine Monitor and Mutex simultaneously to protect any variables. Use either one or the other. The two types work independently. For example, when the monitor checks to see if it's OK to let a thread through to protected code, it won't notice the existence of any mutexes designed to protect the same variables.

WaitHandles

System.Threading.WaitHandle is an abstract class, so you can't instantiate it yourself. I mention it here because it's the base class for several synchronization classes, including Mutex, ManualResetEvent, and AutoResetEvent. It's WaitHandle that encapsulates the underlying thread-blocking mechanism and implements the WaitOne() method, which you've just seen in action for the Mutex class, as well as the Handle property. A WaitHandle instance can be in either of two states: *signaled* or *nonsignaled*. Nonsignaled objects will cause threads that are waiting on the object to be blocked until the object's state is set to signaled again.

Besides WaitOne(), WaitHandle implements a couple of other blocking methods: WaitAll() and WaitAny(). These methods are intended for the more complex situation in which one thread is waiting for several thread synchronization objects to become signaled. WaitAny() allows the thread to proceed when any one of the items is signaled, and WaitAll() blocks the thread until all items are signaled.

ReaderWriterLocks

This is arguably the most sophisticated synchronization object. It's something that has been implemented specially for the CLR—in unmanaged code you'd have to code a ReaderWriterLock by hand if you needed one. The ReaderWriterLock is similar to a Monitor, but it distinguishes between threads that want to read a variable and threads that want to write to it. In general, no problem exists with multiple threads accessing a variable simultaneously, provided they're all just reading its value. Possible data corruption becomes an issue only if at least one of the threads is actually trying to write to the variable. With a ReaderWriterLock, instead of simply asking for ownership of the underlying WaitHandle(), a thread can indicate whether it wants a reader lock or a writer lock, by calling either the AcquireReaderLock() or the AcquireWriterLock() method. If a thread has a reader lock, this won't block any other threads that also ask for reader locks; it will block only threads that ask for a writer lock. If a thread has a writer lock, this will block all other threads until the writer lock is released.

Events

In the context of threading, an *event* is a special thread-synchronization object that's used to block a thread until another thread specifically decides that it's OK for the first thread to continue. This use of the term *event* is quite unrelated to the familiar Windows Forms usage, where *event* denotes a special type of delegate. I'll use events in the TimerDemo sample later in this chapter as a way for a background thread to tell the main foreground thread that it has finished processing its background task.

The way an event works is simple. The thread that needs to wait for something calls WaitOne() to wait until the event is signaled. When another thread detects that whatever the first thread was waiting for has now happened, it calls the event's Set() method, which sets the event to signaled, allowing the first thread through.

Two types of events exist, which are represented by two classes: ManualResetEvent and AutoResetEvent. The difference between these classes is that once a ManualResetEvent is signaled, it remains signaled until its Reset() method is called. By contrast, when an AutoResetEvent is set to be signaled by calling the Set() method, it becomes signaled for a brief instant, allowing any waiting threads to carry on, but then immediately reverts to the nonsignaled state.

Semaphores

A *semaphore* is a thread synchronization object that's similar to a mutex, except that it allows a certain number of threads to execute protected blocks simultaneously. For example, if you want a maximum of, say, three threads to be able to access some resource simultaneously, then you'd use a semaphore. Semaphores are useful for situations such as database connections where some limit may be placed on the number of simultaneous connections. Such limits may be imposed either for license reasons or for performance reasons. Semaphores aren't implemented by the .NET Framework as of version 1.1, so if you need a semaphore, you'll need to fall back on CreateSemaphore() and similar Windows API functions. Because of this, if you do need to use semaphores, you may find it easier to use unmanaged code for that part of your application.

The Interlocked Class

The Interlocked class is a useful utility class that allows a thread to perform a couple of simple operations atomically. It's not itself a thread synchronization primitive as such, but instead it exposes static methods to increment or decrement integers, or to swap over two integers or object references, guaranteeing that the thread will not be interrupted while this process is happening. In some cases, using the Interlocked class can save you from actually having to instantiate a synchronization primitive. Like Monitor, the Interlocked class is never actually instantiated.

Thread Synchronization Architecture

In the following sections, I'll discuss a few issues concerning how you design your thread-synchronization code. I'll concentrate on Monitor and Mutex in this discussion, but similar principles apply to all the synchronization primitives.

Generally, how many primitives you use is going to be a balance between the system resources, maintainability, performance, and code robustness. Robustness is a particular issue because bugs related to thread-synchronization issues are characteristically hard to reproduce or track down. It's not unknown for a thread-synchronization bug to go completely unnoticed on a development machine and then to appear when the code is moved onto a production machine. The only way to avoid this is to take care with the design of your thread-synchronization code. You've already seen the importance of making sure that all access is synchronized to variables that can be seen from more than one thread. You'll also need to take care to avoid introducing deadlocks and race conditions into your code.

Deadlocks

A *deadlock* is a situation in which two or more threads are cyclically waiting for each other. Suppose thread1 executes the following code, where the objects x and y may both be manipulated by more than one thread and therefore need synchronizing:

```
// Needs to manipulate x
lock (x)
{
   // Do something with x
   // Now need to do something with y too...
   lock (y);
   {
      // Do something with x and y
   }
```

Notice that this code features nested lock statements. This by itself is fine—the operation of one lock is completely unaffected by any locks on other objects that may be held by that thread. However, suppose that thread2 is meanwhile executing this code:

```
// Needs to manipulate y
lock(y)
{
    // Do something with y
    // Now need to do something with x too...
    lock(x);
    {
        // Do something with x and y
    }
}
```

The problem is caused by the different order in which the threads claim ownership of the locks. Suppose thread1 claims the lock on x at about the same time as thread2 claims the lock on y. Thread1 then goes about its work and then gets to some code that needs to be protected from y as well. So it calls lock(y), which means the thread is blocked until the second thread releases its ownership of the lock on y. The trouble is that the second thread is never going to release its lock—it's going to get blocked waiting for the first thread to release *its* lock on x! The two threads will just sit there indefinitely, both waiting for each other.

The moral from this is that if you need to start claiming multiple locks, you'll need to be careful about the order in which you claim them. This problem has a number of resolutions. One possibility is simply to use one lock—say, the lock on x—and agree that throughout your code, you'll use lock(x) to synchronize access to both x and y. Since no restriction exists on the code you can place in a lock block, this is fine syntactically but may lead to code that's harder for other developers to understand. Another possibility is to use a mutex. The mutex can avoid deadlocks because of the WaitHandle.WaitAll() static method, which can request a lock on more than one mutex simultaneously. Assume you've declared Mutex variables, mutexX and mutexY, which are used to protect x and y, respectively. Then you can write the following:

```
WaitHandle[] mutexes = new WaitHandle[2];
mutexes[0] = mutexX;
mutexes[1] = mutexY;
WaitHandle.WaitAll(mutexes);
// Protected code here

mutexX.ReleaseMutex();
mutexY.ReleaseMutex();
```

WaitHandle.WaitAll() will wait until all the locks on all mutexes can be acquired simultaneously. Only when this is possible will the thread be given ownership of any of the mutexes; hence, it avoids the risk of a deadlock. But if you use this technique, you'll have to pay a performance penalty, because mutexes are slower than using the monitor.

Races

Race conditions occur when the result of some code depends on unpredictable timing factors concerning when the CPU context-switches threads or when locks are acquired or released. You can accidentally cause a race in numerous ways, but a typical example is where some code is broken into two protected blocks when it really needs to be protected as a single unit. This can occur if you're trying to avoid deadlocks or if you're trying to limit the amount of code that's protected. (This is important because protecting code does hit performance because of the blocking of other threads. The shorter the blocks of code you can get away with protecting, the less the performance hit.)

Let's go back to the code snippet I just used to demonstrate a deadlock, and let's alter the code that the first thread executes in a way that'll prevent the deadlock.

```
// Needs to manipulate x
lock(x)
{
   // Do something with x
}
lock(y)
{
   // Now need to do something with y too...
   lock(x)
   {
      // Do something with x and y
   }
}
```

I've inserted code that releases the lock on x and then reclaims it almost immediately. This means that this thread is now locking the variables in the same order as the second thread, which eliminates the possibility of a deadlock.

Although the deadlock has gone, it has been replaced by a subtler potential problem. Suppose the original protected region of code was there in order to keep some variables in a consistent state while the thread worked on them. For a brief instant after lock(x) has been released for the first time that a different thread could theoretically jump in, execute lock(x), and then have it do its own processing on these variables. Since thread1 was in the middle of working on these variables, they may be in an inconsistent state. That's a race condition. To avoid races, you need to make sure of two points. First, your code should never break out of a protected region of code until it really is completely safe to do so and all relevant variables are in a state in which it's OK for another thread to look at them. Second, when you access variables that need to be protected, make sure that you not only do so from within a protected block of code but also that your code doesn't make any assumptions about the value of the data being unchanged since the previous protected block unless you're certain that no possibility exists for any other thread to have modified that data in the meantime.

You can gather from this discussion that you need to place locks carefully in order to avoid subtle bugs. In general, the more different locks you're using, the greater the potential for problems. Also, a performance/resource problem is associated with having too many synchronization objects in scope simultaneously, since each object consumes some system resources. (By too many, I mean hundreds. Five or ten locks won't be any problem.) This is especially important for objects that wrap underlying Windows structures but is still the case even for the lightweight Monitor, since each active lock occupies memory in the CLR's internal table of sync blocks. At the simplest extreme, you may decide to synchronize all locking against the same object throughout the entire application, effectively using the same lock to protect all variables. (The equivalent, using a Mutex, would be to use just one Mutex for all synchronization.) This will make it impossible for deadlocks to occur—and in general will also make code maintenance easier, which in turn means you're less likely to write code that has synchronization bugs such as races. However, this solution will also impact performance, because you may find that threads can be blocked waiting for ownership of the same lock when these threads are actually waiting to access different variables, so they could have safely executed simultaneously.

In practice, what happens in a real application is that you'll analyze your code and try to identify which blocks of source code are mutually incompatible, in the sense that they shouldn't be executed at the same time. And you'll come up with some scheme that protects these code blocks using a reasonable number of synchronization primitives. The disadvantage now is that working out how to do that is itself a difficult programming task—and one that you'll become skilled at only with practice.

Tip In fact, it'd probably be fair to say that getting a thread synchronization to work correctly in a large multithreaded application is one of the hardest programming tasks you're likely to have to face. And you'll notice this is reflected in the synchronization samples that are coming up soon. You'll find that in the next few samples I'm extremely careful how I use the thread-synchronization objects. In a way, this is the opposite situation to the previous sample. For the AsyncDelegates sample, the concepts you had to learn were quite involved, but once you got through those concepts the code was relatively simple. For the next couple of samples, you won't have many new concepts to learn, but the actual code becomes a lot hairier.

The MonitorDemo Thread Synchronization Sample

I'll now develop the previous AsyncDelegates sample to demonstrate thread synchronization using the CLR's monitor. The new sample works much like the earlier sample, except that now requests are fired off only asynchronously, with a callback method used to retrieve the results on the thread-pool thread—that's the only scenario of interest to you now. However, instead of having the callback method display the results, it now transfers the results into member fields of the DataRetriever class so that the main thread can later display the values. This means that these fields can be accessed by more than one thread, so all access to them needs to be protected. This sample also represents better programming practice; in most cases it's desirable for the user interface always to be accessed through the same thread.

The sample, called MonitorDemo, is going to involve some rewriting of the DataRetriever class, as well as a new enum. Each DataRetriever is now used to obtain the address corresponding to one name, which is supplied in the DataRetriever constructor and which can't subsequently be changed. The enum is used to indicate the status of the fields in DataRetriever—whether results have arrived, are still pending, or whether the address lookup failed.

```
public enum ResultStatus { Waiting, Done, Failed };
```

Here's the new fields and constructor in the DataRetriever:

```
public class DataRetriever
{
    private readonly string name;
    private string address;
    private ResultStatus status = ResultStatus.Waiting;
```

```
public DataRetriever(string name)
{
   this.name = name;
}
```

Notice that the name field is readonly; this means that access to this field will not need to be protected, since as a general rule no thread-synchronization issues exist unless at least one thread can write to a value. (A class is only ever constructed on one thread, and other threads can't access the class until after it has been constructed, so the fact that the field is written to in the constructor doesn't matter.)

The only change I need to make to the GetAddress() method is to its signature—to take account of the fact that name is now a member field rather than a parameter.

```
public string GetAddress()
{
   ThreadUtils.DisplayThreadInfo("In GetAddress...");
   // Simulate waiting to get results off database servers
   Thread.Sleep(1000);

   if (name == "Simon")
      return "Simon lives in Lancaster";
   else if (name == "Julian")
      return "Julian lives in Birmingham";
   else
      throw new ArgumentException("The name " + name +
                                  " is not in the database");
}
```

The GetAddressAsync() method, which invokes GetAddress() asynchronously via a delegate, is unchanged, except that it too no longer takes a parameter, since the name is accessed as a member field instead.

```
public void GetAddressAsync()
{
   GetAddressDelegate dc = new GetAddressDelegate(this.GetAddress);

   AsyncCallback cb = new AsyncCallback(this.GetResultsOnCallback);
   IAsyncResult ar = dc.BeginInvoke(cb, null);
}
```

This change is reflected in a new definition of the delegate.

```
public delegate string GetAddressDelegate();
```

The callback method now looks like this:

```
public void GetResultsOnCallback(IAsyncResult ar)
{
   GetAddressDelegate del = (GetAddressDelegate)
```

```
                              ((AsyncResult)ar).AsyncDelegate;

    try
    {
       string result;
       result = del.EndInvoke(ar);
       lock(this)
       {
          this.address = result;
          this.status = ResultStatus.Done;
       }
    }
    catch (Exception ex)
    {
       lock(this)
       {
          this.address = ex.Message;
          this.status = ResultStatus.Failed;
       }
    }
}
```

I simply set the this.address field to the returned address and update this.status. I do this in protected code because this code is executed on a worker thread, but the results (including the address and status fields) will be read out of the object on the main thread. I don't want the main thread to start reading the results while the worker thread is halfway through writing them.

I also need a new method, which I'll call GetResults(), which can return the name, address, and status to the Main() method for displaying. This is the method that reads the DataRetriever members on the main thread.

```
public void GetResults(out string name, out string address,
                       out ResultStatus status)
{
   name = this.name;
   lock (this)
   {
      address = this.address;
      status = this.status;
   }
}
```

The address and status fields are copied from the member fields, once again in a single protected block, to make sure that no overlap exists between reading and writing this data. I don't copy the name field in the protected block, because name is readonly. This has one extra subtlety. Although I've protected the process of copying out of members, I've copied only the address reference, not the string itself. Given that I want to protect simultaneous access to the data, you may wonder why I haven't actually taken a copy of the string itself, instead of merely copying the reference. The way I've done it, it looks like the main thread and worker thread are both going to end up holding references to the same data. However, this isn't a problem because strings are immutable, so it's not possible for either thread to actually modify this string. In general, however, if you're dealing with references to mutable objects, you'll often have to take copies of these objects in order to ensure that different threads don't try to manipulate the same object.

Finally, the following is the new Main() method. This method sets up an array of three DataRetriever objects, initializes them, and calls GetAddressAsync() on each of them inside a for loop. Then it sleeps for what I hope is a sufficient period of time (2.5 seconds) for all of them to have returned values and calls another method, OutputResults(), which displays the results.

```
public static void Main()
{
    Thread.CurrentThread.Name = "Main Thread";
    DataRetriever[] drs = new DataRetriever[3];
    string[] names = { "Simon", "Julian", "Steve" };

    for (int i=0; i<3; i++)
    {
        drs[i] = new DataRetriever(names[i]);
        drs[i].GetAddressAsync();
    }

    Thread.Sleep(2500);
    OutputResults(drs);
}
```

The OutputResults() method looks like this:

```
public static void OutputResults(DataRetriever[] drs)
{
    foreach (DataRetriever dr in drs)
    {
        string name;
        string address;
        ResultStatus status;
        dr.GetResults(out name, out address, out status);
        Console.WriteLine("Name: {0}, Status: {1}, Result: {2}", name,
                          status, address);
    }
}
```

Running this sample produces the expected output.

```
In GetAddress...
    hash: 2,  pool: True,  backgrnd: True,  state: Background

In GetAddress...
```

```
    hash: 3,  pool: True,  backgrnd: True,  state: Background

In GetAddress...
    hash: 4,  pool: True,  backgrnd: True,  state: Background
Name: Simon, Status : Done, Result: Simon lives in Lancaster
Name: Julian, Status : Done, Result: Julian lives in Birmingham
Name: Steve, Status : Failed, Result: The name Steve is not in the database
```

Using Timers

The MonitorDemo sample I've just demonstrated has one unfortunate problem that you may have noticed: I had to pass in a guessed value of 2.5 seconds as the time that the main thread needed to wait for the results. For the samples, that was a fairly safe bet because I knew exactly how long the results were going to take. However, as a general solution that isn't really satisfactory. If getting the address was really being done by asking a remote database for the value instead of—as in the sample—sleeping for one second and then returning a hard-coded value, it would be hard to know how long to wait.

This problem has two solutions.

- You could set up a timer that polls the DataRetriever objects every so often to see if the results have arrived yet.

- You could have the callback method in the DataRetriever objects somehow notify the main thread when the results are in.

In both cases, the easiest way to inform the main thread of the situation is via a ManualResetEvent.

In the particular situation of the samples for this chapter, the second solution is more efficient. However, I'll go for the first solution because it lets me demonstrate the use of a timer as well as a ManualResetEvent. The first solution also has the advantage that the timer can display regular progress reports to the user.

The CLR Timers

Before I present the sample, I want to say a few words about timers in general. A timer is an object that does something at a specified interval—for example, every half-second or every two seconds—and is invaluable for regularly polling to find out if something has happened. The Windows operating system implements a number of timers that are available to use via Windows API calls, and as you'd expect, the .NET Framework also defines some classes that implement timers, almost certainly by wrapping the Windows API timers. The .NET Framework actually offers three different timer classes, and just to confuse you, they're all called Timer (although they are in different namespaces).

System.Threading.Timer: This is the timer I'll use in the next sample. It works using a callback technique. At the specified interval, it invokes a delegate to a callback method (which will have been supplied to the Timer constructor). The callback method will be invoked on one of the thread pool threads. Bear in mind that, because the thread pool is involved, it's likely that successive callbacks will take place on different threads. This timer has the advantage of accuracy and is the one you should normally use if you're prepared to cope with multiple threads and need an accurate timer.

System.Windows.Forms.Timer: This timer relies on the Windows message loop for its functionality, and it doesn't use multiple threads. It simply raises a `Control.Timer` Windows Forms–style event at the specified intervals, and it's up to you to supply an event handler for this event. Although this timer is easy to use in the Windows Forms environment, it's not very accurate because the timer event handler can be processed only when the user-interface thread isn't doing anything else, which means that although the timer events are raised at accurate intervals, a delay may take place before each event is handled. Also, the timer will work only if the thread on which it's instantiated is a user-interface thread, which in most cases means a Windows Forms application. You should use this timer if accuracy isn't important, you're running a Windows Forms application (or some other application with a message loop), and you don't want to worry about multi-threading.

System.Timers.Timer: I won't say too much about this timer. It's intended for use in a server environment. It's multithreaded and therefore accurate, but it also works by raising events (of the delegate type). This `Timer` is basically the ASP.NET equivalent of the Windows Forms timer. (It isn't restricted to ASP.NET, but it's most useful in a designer environment.)

■Tip Timers represent one of the few cases in .NET where you may need to specify the fully qualified name of a class instead of just the class name.

The TimerDemo Sample

This sample is a development of the previous `Monitor` sample. The `TimerDemo` sample has the added feature that it will use a timer to poll the array of `DataRetrievers` every half-second to see if all results are present. If any results haven't arrived yet, it displays a message indicating how many results it's still waiting for. If all results have arrived, it displays the results, and the program terminates.

This sounds reasonably simple, but the program has a complication. `System.Threading.Timer` callbacks execute on a background thread-pool thread. And background threads don't have any direct influence over the termination of the process. OK, you could do something such as call `System.Diagnostics.Process.Kill()`, but that's a bit of a drastic solution and in general isn't recommended because it doesn't allow other threads to do any cleanup. In the normal course of execution, the process will end when the main thread exits the `Main()` method (provided no other foreground threads exist). If the timer callback were being executed on that thread, this would be trivial to achieve. But it isn't—and that means that for proper program termination, the callback thread will somehow have to communicate to the main, foreground thread to tell it when it's OK to exit the process. The way to do this is using a `ManualResetEvent`.

(Actually, for this particular sample it'd make no difference if I used an AutoResetEvent instead, since I don't care what happens to the event once it's signaled.) The code will work by instantiating the ManualResetEvent and setting it to the nonsignaled state. The main thread, having set up the timer loop, uses the ManualResetEvent.WaitOne() method to block its own execution until the event is signaled. Meanwhile, when the callback function running on the background thread has detected that the results are ready, it calls the ManualResetEvent.Set() method to signal the event. This of course immediately unblocks the main thread, which can proceed to display the results and exit the Main() method, causing the process to terminate.

That's the theory; let's see the practice. The following is the new Main() method, with the changes highlighted in bold:

```
public static void Main()
{
    Thread.CurrentThread.Name = "Main Thread";
    DataRetriever[] drs = new DataRetriever[3];
    string[] names = { "Simon", "Julian", "Steve" };

    for (int i=0; i<3; i++)
    {
        drs[i] = new DataRetriever(names[i]);
        drs[i].GetAddressAsync();
    }

    ManualResetEvent endProcessEvent = new ManualResetEvent(false);
    CheckResults resultsChecker = new CheckResults(endProcessEvent);
    TimerCallback timerCallback = new TimerCallback(
                                        resultsChecker.CheckResultStatus);
    Timer timer = new Timer(timerCallback, drs, 0, 500);

    endProcessEvent.WaitOne();
    EntryPoint.OutputResults(drs);
}
```

Once the main thread has sent off all the queries for addresses, it instantiates the ManualResetEvent. The Boolean parameter passed to the ManualResetEvent constructor indicates whether the event should start off in the signaled state. I don't want it to start signaled here, since the main thread will need to wait for the event to be signaled. Hence, the code passes in the value false.

```
ManualResetEvent endProcessEvent = new ManualResetEvent(false);
```

Next the code instantiates a CheckResults object, passing to its constructor the event just created. CheckResults is a class I'll define to handle the timer callbacks. The code instantiates a timer (a System.Threading.Timer object in this case—it has no name clash since this sample doesn't use either the System.Windows.Forms or the System.Timers namespace). It also defines a delegate that will wrap the callback method (that will be a method in the CheckResults class called CheckResultStatus()) and instantiates the timer.

```
CheckResults resultsChecker = new CheckResults(endProcessEvent);
TimerCallback timerCallback = new TimerCallback(
```

```
                                     resultsChecker.CheckResultStatus);
Timer timer = new Timer(timerCallback, drs, 0, 500);
```

You should note a couple of points about this code. The `Timer` class has a number of constructors, but the one I use here takes four parameters. The first parameter is the delegate that indicates the callback method. This delegate must be of type `TimerCallback`. `TimerCallback` is defined in the `System.Threading` namespace as follows:

```
public delegate void TimerCallback(object state);
```

The delegate returns `void` (as you'd expect—what would the timer do with any return value?) and takes an object as a parameter. This object is the same object that you pass in as the second parameter to the `Timer` constructor. It's there to contain any state information that you want to make available to the callback method. In this case, I'm passing in the `DataRetriever` array; the callback method needs access to this array if it's to be able to check what results are in so far.

The third and fourth parameters to the `Timer` constructor are the delay time and interval time, both in milliseconds. In other words, these represent the number of milliseconds before the first time that the callback method is called (I've indicated zero, so it will be called straightaway) and the frequency with which it will be called; here I've specified every 500 millisecond, or every half a second.

Next the main thread simply sits back and waits for the `ManualResetEvent` to be signaled, at which point it can display the results and exit the program.

```
endProcessEvent.WaitOne();
EntryPoint.OutputResults(drs);
```

Now for the `CheckResults` class. First the code will examine the constructor and the member field that's used to store the reference to the `ManualResetEvent` object created on the main thread.

```
class CheckResults
{
    private ManualResetEvent endProcessEvent;

    public CheckResults(ManualResetEvent endProcessEvent)
    {
        this.endProcessEvent = endProcessEvent;
    }
```

The following is the callback method:

```
public void CheckResultStatus(object state)
{
    DataRetriever [] drs = (DataRetriever[])state;
    int numResultsToGo = 0;
    foreach(DataRetriever dr in drs)
    {
        string name;
        string address;
```

```
            ResultStatus status;
            dr.GetResults(out name, out address, out status);
            if (status == ResultStatus.Waiting)
                ++numResultsToGo;
        }
        if (numResultsToGo == 0)
            endProcessEvent.Set();
        else
            Console.WriteLine("{0} of {1} results returned",
                              drs.Length - numResultsToGo, drs.Length);
    }
}
```

The code in this method is relatively simple. It first loops through the DataRetriever objects in the array, counting how many of them have still got the status set to ResultStatus.Waiting. If this number is greater than zero, it displays a message telling the user how many results are in so far. If the number is zero, then you know the results have all arrived, so the code can signal the ManualResetEvent. This last action is the crucial new piece of code:

```
if (numResultsToGo == 0)
    endProcessEvent.Set();
```

Finally, I'll sneak in one change in the DataRetriever class. Just to make the output from the timer sample more interesting, I'll throw in an extra delay for the case where the name isn't found in the database (a realistic scenario).

```
// In DataRetriever.GetAddress
ThreadUtils.DisplayThreadInfo("In GetAddress...");

// Simulate waiting to get results off database servers
Thread.Sleep(1000);

if (name == "Simon")
    return "Simon lives in Lancaster";
else if (name == "Julian")
    return "Julian lives in Birmingham";
else
{
    Thread.Sleep(1500);
    throw new ArgumentException("The name " + name +
                                " is not in the database");
}
```

Running the TimerDemo sample gives these results:

```
In GetAddress...
   hash: 2,  pool: True,  backgrnd: True,  state: Background

In GetAddress...
   hash: 3,  pool: True,  backgrnd: True,  state: Background
```

```
In GetAddress...
   hash: 4,  pool: True,  backgrnd: True,  state: Background
1 of 3 results returned
1 of 3 results returned
1 of 3 results returned
2 of 3 results returned
2 of 3 results returned
2 of 3 results returned
2 of 3 results returned
2 of 3 results returned
Name: Simon, Status : Done, Result: Simon lives in Lancaster
Name: Julian, Status : Done, Result: Julian lives in Birmingham
Name: Steve, Status : Failed, Result: The name Steve is not in the database
```

Explicitly Creating and Aborting a Thread

Although the previous sample was a considerable improvement on the situation from the point of view of being able to wait until the asynchronous operations were complete, the sample still has a problem. What happens if one of the attempts to retrieve an address simply hangs? In that case, the TimerDemo sample will simply carry on polling the status of the results indefinitely, presumably until the user gives up and kills the process. Clearly that's not an acceptable situation for a real application; you need some way of aborting an operation that's clearly taking too long or going wrong in some way.

You have two possible approaches to this.

- Use WaitOrTimerCallback. WaitOrTimerCallback is a delegate that's provided in the System.Threading namespace. This delegate provides built-in support for methods that are performed asynchronously but where you may want to abort the thread after a fixed period of time. It's normally used in conjunction with the RegisterWaitForSingleObject() method. This method allows you to associate a delegate that's waiting for any object derived from WaitHandle (including ManualResetEvent) with a WaitOrTimerCallback delegate, allowing you to specify a maximum time to wait.

- Explicitly create a thread for the asynchronous task instead of using the thread pool, which means you can easily abort the thread if necessary.

In this chapter I'll take the second approach, because I want to demonstrate how to create and abort a thread explicitly. However, if you find yourself needing to write this kind of code, you should check out the WaitOrTimerCallback delegate in case it provides a better technique for your particular scenario.

Understanding the ThreadAbortException

Aborting a thread that appears to be taking too long to perform its task is quite easy in principle; the Thread class offers an Abort() method for this purpose. The Thread.Abort() method has to be one of the brightest ideas in the .NET Framework. If you use it to tell a thread to abort, then the CLR responds by inserting an instruction to throw a ThreadAbortException into the code that the thread is executing. ThreadAbortException is a special exception that has a unique property. Whenever it's caught, it automatically throws itself again—and keeps rethrowing itself, causing the flow of execution to repeatedly jump to the next containing catch/finally block—until the thread exits. This means that the thread aborts but executes all relevant catch/finally blocks in the process. The result is a completely clean abort that can be instigated from any other thread, which is something that was never possible before the days of .NET. (With the Windows API, aborting a thread always meant killing the thread straightaway and was a technique to be avoided at all costs because this meant the aborted thread could leave any data it was writing in a corrupt state or could leave file or database connections open, since it would have no chance to perform any cleanup.) For managed code, a Thread.ResetAbort() method even exists that an aborting thread can call to cancel the abort!

The Thread.Abort() method and accompanying architecture is great news for anyone writing software in which a chance exists that operations may need to be canceled. However, it requires a reference to the Thread object that encapsulates the thread you want to abort, which means you need to have created the thread explicitly. It's not sensible to do this with a thread-pool thread (besides, the whole point of the thread pool is that operations such as creating and aborting threads is under the control of the CLR, not your code). This is just the trade-off I mentioned near the beginning of the chapter: the performance and scalability benefits of the thread pool come at the expense of the fine control of threads you get with explicit thread creation.

The AbortThread Sample

In this sample I'll modify the TimerDemo sample so that if any of the address retrieval operations take too long, you can just abort the thread by calling Thread.Abort() and display whatever results you have so far. This is going to involve quite a bit of rewriting of the sample, since it will be based on explicitly creating threads rather than on asynchronous delegate invocation.

To start, let's see what you have to do with the DataRetriever class. The fields, the constructor, and the GetResults() method are unchanged. The GetAddress() method that actually returns the address is almost unchanged—except that I'll insert an extra delay for Julian to simulate an asynchronous request hanging.

```
// In DataRetriever.GetAddress()
Thread.Sleep(1000);
if (name == "Simon")
    return "Simon lives in Lancaster";
else if (name == "Julian")
{
    Thread.Sleep(6000);
    return "Julian lives in Birmingham";
}
// etc.
```

You can remove the GetAddressAsync() method that calls GetAddress() asynchronously, as well as the associated callback method; you won't be needing either of them now. Instead, a new GetAddressSync() method will call GetAddress() synchronously and wrap exception handling round it. Notice that no delegate is involved now; it's a straight method call.

```
public void GetAddressSync()
{
    string address = null;
    ResultStatus status = ResultStatus.Done;
    try
    {
        address = GetAddress();
        status = ResultStatus.Done;
    }
    catch(ThreadAbortException)
    {
        address = "Operation aborted";
        status = ResultStatus.Failed;
    }
    catch(ArgumentException e)
    {
        address = e.Message;
        status = ResultStatus.Failed;
    }
    finally
    {
        lock(this)
        {
            this.address = address;
            this.status = status;
        }
    }
}
```

The point of GetAddressSync() is to call GetAddress() and to make sure that no matter what happens inside GetAddress(), even if an exception is thrown, some sensible results get stored back in the address and status fields. With this in mind, GetAddressSync() calls GetAddress() inside a try block and caches the results locally. However, it also catches two exceptions: ArgumentException (which is thrown if the name wasn't found in the database) and ThreadAbortException (which is thrown if the timer callback method decided to abort this thread because it was taking too long). Because this is only a sample, the code doesn't catch any other exceptions—these are the only two exceptions I want to demonstrate. A finally block makes sure that whatever happens, some appropriate data is written to the address and status fields. Notice that I still take the trouble to synchronize access to these fields. (This is necessary because these fields will be read on the timer callback thread, when the timer callback decides to call DataRetriever.GetResults() to retrieve the address.)

Now let's examine the changes to the Main() method.

```
public static void Main()
{
    ThreadStart workerEntryPoint;
    Thread [] workerThreads = new Thread[3];
    DataRetriever [] drs = new DataRetriever[3];
    string [] names = { "Simon", "Julian", "Steve" };

    for (int i=0; i<3; i++)
    {
        drs[i] = new DataRetriever(names[i]);
        workerEntryPoint = new ThreadStart(drs[i].GetAddressSync);
        workerThreads[i] = new Thread(workerEntryPoint);
        workerThreads[i].Start();
    }

    ManualResetEvent endProcessEvent = new ManualResetEvent(false);
    CheckResults resultsChecker = new CheckResults(endProcessEvent, drs,
                                                   workerThreads);

    resultsChecker.InitializeTimer();

    endProcessEvent.WaitOne();
    EntryPoint.OutputResults(drs);
}
```

You'll see quite a few changes here, mostly associated with the fact that Main() is explicitly creating threads and not invoking delegates asynchronously. I start by declaring an array that will hold the Thread references, as well as a delegate that will hold the worker thread entry points.

```
ThreadStart workerEntryPoint;
Thread [] workerThreads = new Thread[3];
```

Then, inside the loop in which the DataRetriever objects are initialized, the code also instantiates the Thread objects, sets the entry point of each, and starts each thread.

```
workerEntryPoint = new ThreadStart(drs[i].GetAddressSync);
workerThreads[i] = new Thread(workerEntryPoint);
workerThreads[i].Start();
```

You'll see a couple of differences around the instantiation of the ResultsChecker object that implements the timer callbacks. This is because ResultsChecker is going to play a more prominent role now and needs more information, so more parameters are passed to its constructor. Also, the Timer will be stored in the ResultsChecker class rather than the Main() method, because the ResultsChecker is going to need access to it later. So the Main() method simply creates a ResultsChecker instance, asks it to start the timer off, and then—as in the previous sample—sits back and waits for the ManualResetEvent to be signaled.

Now for the CheckResults class. The following shows its constructor and member fields and then the InitializeTimer() method:

```
class CheckResults
{
   private ManualResetEvent endProcessEvent;
   private DataRetriever[] drs;
   private Thread[] workerThreads;
   private int numTriesToGo = 10;
   private Timer timer;

   public CheckResults(ManualResetEvent endProcessEvent, DataRetriever[] drs,
                      Thread[] workerThreads)
   {
      this.endProcessEvent = endProcessEvent;
      this.drs = drs;
      this.workerThreads = workerThreads;
   }

   public void InitializeTimer()
   {
      TimerCallback timerCallback = new TimerCallback(this.CheckResultStatus);
      timer = new Timer(timerCallback, null, 0, 500);
   }
```

This code should be self-explanatory. Notice the numTriesToGo field; this field will be used to count down from ten, ensuring that the timer is canceled after ten callbacks (five seconds, since the interval is set in InitializeTimer() to half a second).

Next let's examine the timer callback method.

```
public void CheckResultStatus(object state)
{
   Interlocked.Decrement(ref numTriesToGo);
   int numResultsToGo = 0;
   foreach(DataRetriever dr in drs)
   {
      string name;
      string address;
      ResultStatus status;
      dr.GetResults(out name, out address, out status);
      if (status == ResultStatus.Waiting)
         ++numResultsToGo;
   }
   if (numResultsToGo == 0)
   {
      EntryPoint.OutputResults(drs);
      endProcessEvent.Set();
      return;
   }
   else
   {
      Console.WriteLine("{0} of {1} results returned",
                      drs.Length - numResultsToGo, drs.Length);
```

```
    }
    if (numTriesToGo == 0)
    {
        timer.Change(Timeout.Infinite, Timeout.Infinite);
        TerminateWorkerThreads();
        endProcessEvent.Set();
    }
}
```

You won't see too many changes to this method. The main difference is that the code decrements numTriesToGo. It calls the Interlocked.Decrement() method to do this—just in case execution of the timer callback takes longer than a time slice, in which case this method could be executing concurrently on two different threads. It does contain a new final if block, which catches the situation for which numTriesToGo hits zero but the code is still waiting for one or more results. If this happens, the first thing to do is change the timer interval to infinity, effectively stopping the timer from firing again. You don't want the callback function being called again on another thread while the code to terminate the processing is being executed! The code terminates any outstanding worker threads that are retrieving addresses, using a method called TerminateWorkerThreads(), which I'll go through next. Then it outputs the results and signals the ManualResetEvent so that the main thread can exit and terminate the process.

The TerminateWorkerThreads() method is the one that may in theory take some time to execute.

```
private void TerminateWorkerThreads()
{
    foreach (Thread thread in workerThreads)
    {
        if (thread.IsAlive)
        {
            thread.Abort();
            thread.Join();
        }
    }
}
```

This method loops through all the worker thread references that are present. For each worker thread, it uses another Thread property, IsAlive; this returns true if that thread is still executing and returns false if that thread has already terminated (or if it hasn't started—but that won't happen in our sample). For each thread that's alive, it calls Thread.Abort(). Thread.Abort() returns immediately, but the thread concerned will still be going through its abort sequence, executing finally blocks, and so on. You don't want TerminateWorkerThreads() to exit before all the worker threads have actually finished aborting, because if that happens, then the code may end up displaying the results in the following call to EntryPoint.OutputResults() before the worker threads have finished writing the final data to their address and status fields. So the code calls another method, Thread.Join(). The Join() method simply blocks execution until the thread referenced in its parameter has terminated. So calling Thread.Join() ensures that TerminateWorkerThreads() doesn't itself return too early.

That completes the sample, and I'm ready to try running it. On my computer, it gives the following:

```
In GetAddress...
    hash: 1,  pool: False,  backgrnd: False,  state: Running

In GetAddress...
    hash: 2,  pool: False,  backgrnd: False,  state: Running

In GetAddress...
    hash: 3,  pool: False,  backgrnd: False,  state: Running
0 of 3 results returned
0 of 3 results returned
1 of 3 results returned
1 of 3 results returned
1 of 3 results returned
2 of 3 results returned
2 of 3 results returned
2 of 3 results returned
2 of 3 results returned
2 of 3 results returned
Name: Simon, Status : Done, Result: Simon lives in Lancaster
Name: Julian, Status : Failed, Result: Operation aborted
Name: Steve, Status : Failed, Result: The name Steve is not in the database
```

This output shows the sample has worked correctly. The worker threads have returned the expected results for Simon and Steve. The Julian thread has aborted because of the long delay I put in the code for that case, but the output shows that while aborting it did write the correct "Operation aborted" string to the address field; in other words, it performed the appropriate cleanup before terminating.

Summary

This chapter covered a lot of ground. I started by reviewing the difference between a CLR thread and an operating system thread, and I showed that the two concepts aren't interchangeable and are represented by different, unrelated .NET classes. Then I reviewed the different techniques available for writing multithreaded applications in preparation for demonstrating these techniques in various samples. I started with a sample that demonstrated calling delegates asynchronously—the technique of choice for single methods that you want to be executed on a different thread. A discussion then followed of the principles behind thread synchronization and the classes available to assist with synchronization. I then progressively developed a sample, adding to it first thread synchronization, then adding timers, and then showing how to get one thread to abort a different thread cleanly—a technique that unfortunately can be implemented only if the worker thread has been created explicitly, instead of relying on the CLR thread pool.

■ ■ ■

CHAPTER 10

Understanding Management Instrumentation

In this chapter I'll show how you can use managed code to interact with the Windows Management Instrumentation (WMI) services. The chapter will cover the following:

- WMI architecture

- What kinds of features you can access using WMI

- How to code with the System.Management classes to write WMI clients

- Synchronous and asynchronous requests

- WMI events

WMI has to be one of the most undersold technologies that has emerged over the past few years. It's incredibly powerful and relatively simple to use, but despite this it has never really attracted much publicity, so it's still used by relatively few developers. Because of that, much of the focus of this chapter will be on understanding the principles behind WMI itself, as well as on the techniques for leveraging WMI from managed code.

What's WMI?

WMI is a management technology. It's designed to bring together many of the various APIs used to access the items on your computer system that you may want to manage. Without WMI, you'd have to learn many different APIs in order to write code to perform any extensive systems management. For example, the file system is accessed through the classes in the System.IO namespace (or, in native Windows terms, through the API functions that lie behind these classes). Managing databases is normally done using the unmanaged ADOX API (which doesn't have a managed equivalent). Managed classes and unmanaged API functions exist to control processes and network services. Environment variables are handled through the System.Environment class. In many cases, you'll need to drop back to unmanaged code because the .NET Framework classes aren't yet rich enough to cover all the features that are accessible through Windows API functions. There are even some low-level tasks for which you may need to directly access the corresponding device drivers. WMI provides a way that tasks of this kind can be presented as part of one unified high-level and object-oriented API.

Under the WMI design, various *WMI providers* have been written, each of which wraps some native API and exposes it in a form that can be understood by a service known as the *WMI object manager*. Then, if you want to access the facilities of any of these APIs, you don't need to talk to the API directly; your code simply accesses the object manager instead. That means you have only one API to learn—the API that's used to interact with the object manager. The object manager and the WMI providers handle the rest. And thanks to the .NET Framework classes in the System.Management namespace (these are the classes that handle communication with the object manager), writing WMI-based managed code is extremely simple. Such code will also use the same idioms you're used to for managed code in general—collections, events, and so on. That can hugely reduce the amount of time you need to spend learning new APIs and can lead to more robust code.

A rich callback mechanism also exists. It's common for applications that perform management-related tasks to want to be notified of changes in the state of the system and other significant events. For example, you may want to know if CPU utilization goes very high or if free disk space drops too far. The trouble is that many native APIs don't support any callback mechanism. For example, no Windows API function allows an application to ask to automatically receive a notification if disk space drops too low; the best an application would be able to do in this scenario would be to check the disk space every so often, which gives you a performance hit and also can sometimes be complex to code, especially if you're monitoring the disk space on a different computer. Many other APIs have the same problem. The great thing about WMI is that the object manager implements its own polling mechanism; so if you do want to receive notifications, you can inform the object manager of this fact, and it will handle the rest for you, generating notifications as necessary. Doing it this way, you still get the performance hit associated with polling, but at least you don't need to worry about having to write the polling code yourself.

Microsoft has supplied a large range of WMI providers—enough that you can already use WMI to interact with virtually any aspect of your environment, including both software and hardware. You can, for example, query for information about the processor and any attached devices; you can control running Windows services; you can find out about currently executing processes and threads, as well as drives and file shares on the system; and you can do the same thing remotely for any other computer on the network, provided of course you have sufficient privilege to do so. And as WMI is becoming more widely implemented, the list of possibilities grows. For example, once you have .NET installed, you can use WMI to configure .NET. You can also use WMI to manage the computer's network connections on Windows XP, though not on earlier operating systems. The MSDN documentation contains a full list of the Microsoft WMI providers, but to give you an idea of what's available, Table 10-1 gives a partial list of some of the providers that come with the Windows operating systems.

Table 10-1. *Some of the WMI Providers That Ship with Windows*

Provider	Earliest Windows Version That This Provider Is Supplied With	Allows Access To...
Active Directory Provider	Windows 2000	Active Directory
Disk Quota Provider	Windows XP	Control disk quotas
Event Log Provider	Windows NT 4	The Event Log
IP Route Provider	.NET Server	Network routing information
Performance Counter Provider	Windows 2000	Performance counters
Security Provider	Windows NT 4	NT security settings
Session Provider	Windows NT 4	Network sessions and connections
System Registry Provider	Windows NT 4	The Registry
Win32 Provider	Windows NT 4	Environment variables, the files system, and so on
Windows Product Activation Provider	Windows 2000	Windows Product Activation administration

The .NET Framework itself also supplies a WMI provider, the so-called configuration provider, which is intended to let you configure the CLR. In this chapter I'll be using only providers that have been supplied by Microsoft, but it's possible for anyone to write additional providers; indeed, if you have some large application that's configurable, then you'd normally be encouraged to write a WMI provider that allows clients to configure the application using WMI.

■**Tip** Although WMI has shipped as part of Windows ever since Windows ME, if you're intending to work with WMI, you'd be well advised to download the WMI administrative tools. The kit is currently available for download from `http://www.microsoft.com/downloads/release.asp?ReleaseID=40804&area=s earch&ordinal=6`.

This kit includes CIM Studio and the WMI object browser, two useful HTML files that can be used to browse around and manipulate WMI objects.

Some WMI Demonstrations

To use WMI effectively, it's necessary to have some understanding of the architecture. However, before you get bogged down with too many new concepts, I thought it'd be nice to have a couple of quick demonstrations of the kinds of things WMI and the System.Management classes can do. One of the examples here changes the volume name of the C: drive, and the other lists all the processors on your machine, displaying the processor type and speed of each. Between them these two examples involve just 13 lines of source code (that's counting the number of C# statements I had to put inside the Main() methods).

First, note that all the examples in this chapter require a using directive for the classes in the System.Management namespace. Second, the classes in this namespace are defined in System.Management.dll, so you'll also need to add a reference to this assembly.

Changing the Volume Label of a Logical Drive

By a logical drive, I mean something that the operating system sees as a drive. That includes each partition on your hard drive(s) as well as other drives such as the floppy drive and CD/DVD/CD-RW drives. In other words, this includes everything that appears under My Computer in Windows Explorer.

The following code forms a sample that I've called ChangeVolumeName. It changes the volume label of the C: drive to the string, CHANGED.

```csharp
static void Main(string[] args)
{
    ManagementObject cDrive = new ManagementObject(
                             "Win32_LogicalDisk.DeviceID=\"C:\"");
    cDrive.Get();
    cDrive["VolumeName"] = "CHANGED";
    cDrive.Put();
}
```

The volume label (sometimes called the *volume name*) is the name by which a logical drive is referred to, for example, in the Windows Explorer tree view (see Figure 10-1).

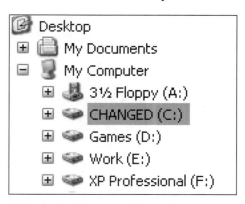

Figure 10-1. *The logical drives on my computer after running the first sample*

■**Tip** Windows Explorer isn't very good at noticing changes in drive volume labels that have been made outside of Windows Explorer itself, so you may find if you run the example that the new volume label doesn't appear for a while. If that happens, you can verify the new label by right-clicking the drive in Windows Explorer and selecting Properties from the context menu. The dialog box that pops up displays the volume label and is always up-to-date.

Let's look at how the code for this example works. The first statement, which instantiates a `ManagementObject` instance, really contains the key to how it all works. The `System.Management.ManagementObject` class is intended to represent any object that can be accessed through WMI.

```
ManagementObject cDrive = new
    ManagementObject("Win32_LogicalDisk.DeviceID=\"C:\"");
```

This statement creates something known as a *WMI instance* or sometimes as a *management object*. A management object is an instance of a special data structure called a *WMI class*, which is defined within WMI and which represents the underlying logical drive. This WMI instance is in turn wrapped by a .NET object—a `ManagementObject` instance. The string passed to the `ManagementObject` constructor is called an *object path* and is sufficient to identify the underlying disk drive you want to access. In the previous code, the WMI class in question is a class called `Win32_LogicalDisk`, and the instance is an instance called `DeviceID="C:"`. Figure 10-2 shows this situation.

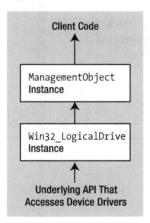

Figure 10-2. *The API layers involved with the* ChangeVolumeName *sample*

■**Tip** Don't confuse WMI classes with .NET classes. Although similarities exist in concept, WMI classes are different entities. I'll explain more about what a WMI class is in the "The WMI Object Model" section. In Figure 10-2, `ManagementObject` is a .NET class, and `Win32_LogicalDrive` is a WMI class.

The next statement in the C# source code merely makes sure that the WMI instance is correctly initialized with the current state of the logical drive:

```
cDrive.Get();
```

Now the volume label of a logical drive is accessible as the VolumeName property of the corresponding WMI instance. You access this property using an indexer, because the .NET class, ManagementObject, defines an indexer that provides access to properties of the WMI instance.

```
cDrive["VolumeName"] = "Changed";
```

Changing the VolumeName property changes only the information in the internal WMI data structure. To actually commit the change to the logical disk itself, you need to call the ManagementObject.Put() method, which updates the underlying object with the current state of the WMI object.

```
cDrive.Put();
```

Listing the Processors on the Computer

The next sample is called ListProcessors, and it lists the processors on the machine. The relevant code looks like this:

```
static void Main()
{
    int totalProcessors = 0;
    ManagementClass processorClass = new ManagementClass("Win32_Processor");
    foreach (ManagementObject processor in processorClass.GetInstances())
    {
        ++totalProcessors;
        Console.WriteLine("{0}, {1} MHz", processor["Name"],
                          processor["CurrentClockSpeed"]);
    }
    if (totalProcessors > 1)
        Console.WriteLine("\n{0} processors", totalProcessors);
    else
        Console.WriteLine("\n{0} processor", totalProcessors);
}
```

Running this on one of my machines gave me this output:

```
AMD Athlon(tm) processor, 1199 MHz
```

```
1 processor
```

Running through the code, it's a bit more complex than the previous example because it needs to enumerate through some WMI instances instead of simply working with a known instance. The WMI class Win32_Processor is the one that's required. However, because the program needs to find out what processors are on the system, it has to work by first connecting to the Win32_Processor class itself instead of to an instance of the class. (Connecting to a class? If that concept surprises you, remember I did say that WMI classes aren't the same as CLR classes). The ManagementClass .NET class represents a WMI class. Once you've connected to a ManagementClass instance, you can call the ManagementClass.GetInstances() method to retrieve a collection of ManagementObject instances, each of which represents one of the instances of this class. In my case, I'm running a single-processor machine, so only one instance is returned. The code uses the Win32_Processor.Name and Win32_Processor.CurrentClockSpeed properties to retrieve the required information.

WMI Architecture

I hinted earlier that WMI is based on a provider model. Figure 10-3 shows the overall architecture.

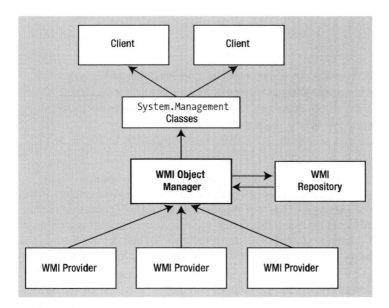

Figure 10-3. *WMI architecture*

At the top of the figure are the clients. These are the programs that want to perform management tasks. Both of the examples I've just worked through are WMI clients. On the other hand, at the bottom of the figure are the WMI providers. These are the components that sit between the underlying objects and WMI. The two samples you've just seen involve a WMI provider that's supplied by Microsoft and that's known as the Win32 Provider.

The heart of WMI is the *object manager*, which acts as the broker between clients and providers. Clients that want to communicate with WMI providers will contact the WMI object manager with their requests. The object manager handles tasks ranging from directing the request to the appropriate provider, obtaining schema information, and handling events. Because of the way that the object manager handles all routing of requests, clients don't even need to know which provider is ultimately responsible for servicing their request.

All the client needs to do is hand a string (the so-called object path) that describes the object or class (such as "Win32_LogicalDisk" or "Win32_Processor") to the object manager and let the object manager do the rest.

The object manager is generally implemented as a Windows service, though this is somewhat dependent on which operating system you're running. Windows 9*x* and ME don't of course support services, so on those machines the object manager is a standard executable. On Windows XP, on the other hand, the object manager has actually been incorporated into the SVCHOST process, so in a sense you can start to regard WMI as part of the operating system itself. The providers are usually instantiated as DLL COM components inside the object manager process, but it's also possible for providers to reside in other processes as .EXE-hosted COM components. All communication with the object manager, from both clients and providers, takes place using COM—various COM interfaces are specifically designed for this purpose. However, if you're coding with .NET, you don't need to worry about that, since WMI clients can use the System.Management classes instead. The System.Management classes are basically managed wrappers over the underlying COM interfaces that the object manager understands.

■Tip It's also possible to write WMI providers using only managed code. The classes in the System. Management.Instrumentation namespace are provided for this purpose. Internally these classes will simply provide implementations of those COM interfaces that the object manager uses to communicate with providers. However, I won't cover writing providers in this book.

One part of Figure 10-3 that I've not yet said anything about is the *WMI repository* (also known as the *CIM repository*). The repository contains definitions of various WMI classes—it's a way of ensuring that the object manager can find out what classes are available, without having to go to the providers for this information every time a new request comes in. Although definitions of commonly used WMI classes are stored in the repository, some class definitions may be supplied by a special type of provider known as a *class provider*. Instances are normally supplied by providers as required and aren't stored in the repository. However, if the data for a particular management object doesn't change frequently, then it may be stored statically in the repository. Although the repository forms an important part of WMI architecture, its existence doesn't really affect anything as far as coding clients is concerned, so I won't say much about it here.

WMI and WBEM

All the discussion so far has referred to WMI as if it's something specific to Windows—which it is. However, WMI also has a basis in a more widely used standard: *Web-Based Enterprise Management* (WBEM) is an industry standard that specifies how information related to management and configuration objects should be made available. WBEM, defined by a group known as the Distributed Management Task Force (DMTF; http://www.dmtf.org), specifies the standards for the representation of classes and objects, as well as some other items that I haven't yet talked about, such as association classes). However, WBEM deliberately doesn't define implementation details—that's up to each company that implements WBEM. WMI, and all the COM-based infrastructure that I've just been describing, is Microsoft's implementation of WBEM. Using COM interfaces was Microsoft's choice for WMI, but other implementations of WBEM on other platforms may use other technologies instead. Just like the WMI repository, the existence of WBEM, while extremely important from the point of view of background information, has little impact on the actual code that you'll write if you write managed WMI clients, so I won't really cover the WBEM standards further in this book.

■**Note** As with all acronyms, it's to some extent a matter of personal taste how you pronounce WMI and WBEM, but most people I've worked with on this technology tend to pronounce WBEM as *wEBem*, and WMI as *wOO-mee* (oo as in book)—which has led to one or two standard "in" jokes about how you're working with or writing about "woomin"—but I won't comment on those.

Security

Given the power of WMI, you may wonder what the security implications are. For managed code to use WMI to access or modify any properties on your system, it has to pass three security checks.

- First, the CLR will prevent code from directly invoking the System.Management.dll assembly in which the System.Management classes are implemented, unless the calling assembly is fully trusted—that's because System.Management.dll is strongly named but doesn't have the AllowPartiallyTrustedCallersAttribute defined. That's a pretty stiff security requirement! I'll discuss this further in Chapter 12. If you need partially trusted code to be able to access WMI, you have to create an intermediate fully trusted assembly that exposes whatever functionality or WMI objects are required by the partially trusted code.

- Second, once code is through to these classes, it hits WMI namespace security. The WMI object manager is able to impose security based on what user accounts are allowed to access which WMI namespaces. (I'll cover WMI namespaces in the section "Namespaces and Servers.") This by itself is a fairly crude security check that I won't be concerned with in this chapter. If you need details, look up the __SystemSecurity class in the WMI MSDN documentation. Suffice to say that if you're running from an administrator account, then you shouldn't have any problems running the examples in this chapter.

- Finally, once you're passed the namespace security check, it's just like using unmanaged code. WMI itself doesn't impose any further security checks, but it simply allows the Windows credentials under which the process is running to propagate to the provider and hence to the underlying API functions. This means that the Windows security system will itself detect whether the account has permission to perform the requested action. Any denial of permission here will be propagated through WMI and manifest itself as an exception in the client process. Hence, it's not possible to do anything with WMI unless the running process has permission to do the same directly.

WMI Object Model

As you saw in the earlier examples, the WMI model is based on classes. For example, when you want to query the information about the CPU hardware, your code actually interacts indirectly through an instance of the Win32_Processor WMI class. However, to understand WMI classes, you'll have to forget a lot of what you've learned about classes in the context of .NET and other programming languages, since the principles behind WMI classes are rather different from classes in typical languages. In the following sections I'll go over the concepts that underpin the object model for WMI objects.

WMI Classes and Instances

When you instantiate a .NET class, what you're doing essentially is reserving a piece of memory in the process, which is going to contain certain data structured in a certain way. No limit exists on how many instances of a given class you can instantiate (unless some restriction has somehow been deliberately written into the program). Also, it's perfectly OK to define and use identical instances. Suppose you wrote some code like this:

```
Point x = new Point(10,20);
Point y = x;
```

In normal coding you wouldn't think twice about doing something such as this. But code such as this is impossible for a WMI class because a fundamental rule of WMI classes is that no two instances can contain identical data. And more surprises are in store for you.

The reason that WMI classes are so different in their behavior is that an instance of a WMI class is a lot more than just a bit of memory with some data in it; it's an abstract representation of some real object on a computer. This object may be a software object (such as a process, a Windows service, or a database connection) or a hardware object (such as a serial port or a CD drive), but it's always some "real" object. And although I said that the WMI instance is a representation of the underlying object, as far as your WMI client code is concerned, you can treat the WMI instance as if it really is the underlying object. That's why you can't have two identical WMI instances—if they were identical, they would in a sense be the same object, which would be silly. Another consequence is that you can't just create or delete a WMI instance in the same casual way you'd create a .NET object. The situation is more like this: When you connect to a WMI provider, the instances are already there. You can call methods on them, or get or set properties, or have them raise events. And that's it. WMI objects have no equivalent of new or of constructors. In a lot of ways, the real analogy isn't between a WMI instance and a .NET instance but between a WMI instance and a .NET static instance—an instance that's returned as a static member of a type, such as Color.Blue.

To make this a bit more concrete, let's take as an example the logical drives on a machine. The computer that I'm writing this chapter on has a floppy drive, a DVD drive, and three partitions on its hard drive. That means the local machine has five logical drives. Each of these logical drives is represented by an instance of the WMI class Win32_LogicalDrive. That means on my machine I have five Win32_LogicalDrive instances. Period. To create another instance would be to create another logical drive, and similarly to delete an instance would be to actually delete a partition—which, unless you have Partition Magic or some similar software installed, isn't something you'd normally do.

Defining Classes: The MOF Language

Let's take a look at the definition of Win32_LogicalDrive. Unfortunately, the definition of this class is complex, so I won't display the whole definition here, but the following is a heavily simplified version showing a few of the properties—enough to give you a feel for the principles:

```
// Simplified from MOF source code. The actual MOF contains many
// more qualifiers etc.
class Win32_LogicalDisk : CIM_LogicalDisk
{
    [read, key] uint16 string DeviceID;
    [read] uint16 boolean VolumeDirty;
    [read, write] uint64 boolean QuotasDisabled;
    [read] string boolean QuotasIncomplete;
    [read] boolean uint32 MediaType;
    // etc.
}
```

This code looks a bit like C++ or C# code, but don't be fooled. It's actually written in a language called *Managed Object Format* (MOF). The MOF language exists for the sole purpose of defining WMI classes and instances. Despite the superficial similarity to C++/C#, you can't write executable instructions in MOF—only class and instance definitions. Also bear in mind that the definitions in this code, which look like field definitions, are more properly thought of as properties. WMI classes can contain only two types of member: properties and methods. No implementations exist for the properties or methods—only definitions—because implementation of members isn't the purpose of MOF. The implementations will be coded in the individual WMI providers.

I won't use MOF in this chapter, other than as a useful syntax for indicating what's inside a WMI class, but it's worth pointing out that even a MOF compiler exists, mofcomp.exe. If you run mofcomp at the command line, it will compile a file that contains MOF source code and place the resultant classes and instances permanently in the WMI repository. If do need to see more information about MOF, refer to http://www.dmtf.org/education/mof/.

The items in square brackets in MOF code are known as *qualifiers*. Despite the different name, they play a similar role to .NET attributes. The [read] qualifier indicates that a property can be read, and [write] indicates it can be written to. The following are a couple of other qualifiers you'll encounter:

- [key] denotes that a property is a key property; key properties are the ones that uniquely identify the instances. A class must have at least one key property, and any two instances must differ in their values of at least one key property.

- [abstract] has the same meaning as the abstract keyword in C#; it indicates that no instances of the class exist, and the sole purpose of the class is to allow other classes to derive from it.

The MOF code snippet I presented earlier shows that Win32_LogicalDisk is derived from a class called CIM_LogicalDisk. This is a common pattern. The WBEM specification included the definitions of a large number of classes (these definitions are known as the *CIM v2 class schema*). The names of these classes are prefixed by CIM_, which stands for *Common Information Model*.

When Microsoft implemented WMI, it defined a large number of classes by deriving from the equivalent WBEM classes and adding extra properties and methods. When Microsoft did this, as a convention it replaced the `CIM_` prefix in the class names by `Win32_`. These `Win32_` class definitions are collectively known as the *Win32 extended schema*.

Inheritance works in much the same way for WMI classes as for other classes—a derived class gets all the properties and methods of its base class and can add others. One point to bear in mind, however, is that a derived WMI class is regarded as conceptually a completely different object from its base class. What this means is that if there are, say, six instances of `Win32_LogicalDisk` on your computer, and you were to ask WMI to retrieve all `CIM_LogicalDisk` instances, then by default none of the `Win32_LogicalDisk` instances would be found (though you can change this by asking WMI to do a deep enumeration). If these were .NET classes, then you'd expect that a `CIM_LogicalDisk` reference could refer to a `Win32_LogicalDisk` object, reflecting the idea that a derived class instance is a base class instance plus a bit more—and that assumption may lead you to incorrectly assume that an attempt to retrieve `CIM_LogicalDisk` instances would also return derived classes. But WMI doesn't take that viewpoint; in WMI derived classes are different classes.

Methods

In general, the WMI object model is heavily based around properties, and for almost all classes the numbers of properties is hugely greater than the number of methods. However, it's worth bearing in mind that some classes have useful methods (for example, to start and stop Windows services or to reset certain hardware devices). In this chapter I'll focus almost exclusively on properties. If you need to invoke methods on WMI objects, you'll need to check out the `ManagementBaseObject.GetMethodParameters()` and `ManagementObject.InvokeMethod()` methods.

Namespaces and Servers

WBEM has a system for placing classes in namespaces that works a bit like .NET namespaces, albeit with some differences in detail and syntax. To illustrate the way it works, here's the full path name for the `Win32_LogicalDrive` class on my machine, `Strawberry`:

```
\\Strawberry\root\CIMV2:Win32_LogicalDisk
```

The path starts with the name of the server—that's the computer on which the item is based. (Although I use the term *server*, it can be any computer, server, or workstation.) Note that WBEM is based entirely around individual computers—rather than around, for example, domains or networks. After the server name, you can see nested namespace names, with backslashes used to separate the namespaces. The first namespace is always called `root`. So the `root` namespace in WBEM serves a similar purpose to the global (unnamed) namespace in .NET. The list of namespaces is separated from the class name by a colon.

As noted earlier, you can also specify individual instances using an object path. Here's the object path of my hard drive:

```
\\Strawberry\root\CIMV2:Win32_LogicalDisk.DeviceID="C:"
```

To specify the instance, you use the class name, followed by a dot, followed by a listing of the values of the key fields.

You can use an alternative syntax for the computer name; just use a dot for the computer name, and this will be understood to specify the local machine.

```
\\.\root\CIMV2:Win32_LogicalDisk.DeviceID="C:"
```

You can also leave the server and part or all of the namespace out of the name altogether, in which case you have a *relative object namespace*. You can indicate the default namespace, relative to which all relative object namespaces are taken. In .NET, this value is known as the *management scope*. The management scope defaults to `\\.\root\CIMV2`, so if you omit the server and namespace in an object path, this is where the class or object will be assumed to be. `\root\CIMV2` is the namespace in which the CIM V2 schema classes are placed. You'll also find many of the Microsoft classes in there too because one of the rules of WBEM is that derived classes must be placed in the same namespace as their base classes when a class schema is being extended.

One point that it's important to understand is that no relationship exists between namespaces and providers. One provider can implement classes in many namespaces, and it's also fine for many providers to implement different classes in the same namespace. This is analogous to the situation for namespaces and assemblies in .NET, whereby no requirement exists for any one-to-one correspondence between a namespace and an assembly.

A WMI client will need to know in which namespace the object it wants resides (otherwise it can't supply the object path needed to tell the WMI object manager which object it's interested in). As remarked earlier, however, the client doesn't need to know which provider implements the class.

System Classes and Properties

One aspect of WMI classes is the presence of a large number of *system classes* and *system propeties*. Certain classes are contained in every namespace, and certain properties are present in every class, automatically, and implemented by the WMI object manager. (The providers don't have to worry about implementing them, and they aren't listed in the MOF descriptions of classes.) These classes and properties are essential to the operation of WMI. There is little point in going over the details of all these classes and properties here—you can find the details in the MSDN documentation at `http://msdn.microsoft.com/library/en-us/wmisdk/wmi/ wmi_reference.asp`, and you'll also be able to browse through them all if you download and run the WMI browser example that I'll present in the section "WMI Browser Sample: Features." But to give you a flavor of what these classes and properties are for, the following are a couple of examples:

- Every namespace contains a class called __namespace. The purpose of this class is to allow enumeration of child namespaces in a given namespace. Each namespace contains one instance of this class for every child namespace, with the Name property giving the name of a child namespace. Hence, enumerating the instances of this class will tell an application what child namespaces are available.

- Every instance contains a property called __path. This property gives the full object path of the object. Also, it contains a system property, __class, that gives the name of the class to which the instance belongs.

You'll have gathered from these examples that system classes and properties are identified by two underscores at the start of their names. It's illegal to name your own classes with names that start with two underscores, so this sequence always identifies system classes.

Association Classes

When using .NET classes, it's perfectly normal for classes to contain references to each other, or even for value types to be embedded directly inside other objects or value types. Although in WMI it's possible to define classes that contain member properties that refer to other WMI classes, this isn't normal practice. In WMI it's more common to use something called an *association class*. The sole purpose of an instance of an association class is to indicate that two classes are associated together, and the usual way of doing this is through the association instance containing properties that give the object paths of the related objects. To give an idea of how this works, consider disks again. You've already seen that the Win32_LogicalDisk class represents a logical disk. There is also a class called Win32_DiskPartition, which indicates a partition. Now since you expect that some of the logical drives on a computer are simply disk partitions, clearly an association exists between instances of these classes. An association class called Win32_LogicalDiskToPartition represents this. A simplified version of part of the MOF definition for this association class looks like this:

```
[dynamic, provider("CIMWin32")]
class Win32_LogicalDiskToPartition : CIM_LogicalDiskBasedOnPartition
{
    [read, key] Win32_DiskPartition ref Antecedent;
    [read, key] Win32_LogicalDisk ref Dependent;
};
```

This code shows that each Win32_LogicalDiskToPartition instance contains two properties: Antecedent and Dependent, which respectively store the object paths of the Win32_DiskPartition and the Win32_LogicalDisk object that are associated. For example, on my machine (as on most computers), the C drive is stored on disk partition 0. This is represented by a Win32_LogicalDiskToPartition instance, which links the two corresponding objects together, as shown in Figure 10-4. The figure comes from the WMIBrowser example that I'll introduce soon, and it shows the values of the properties of a given object.

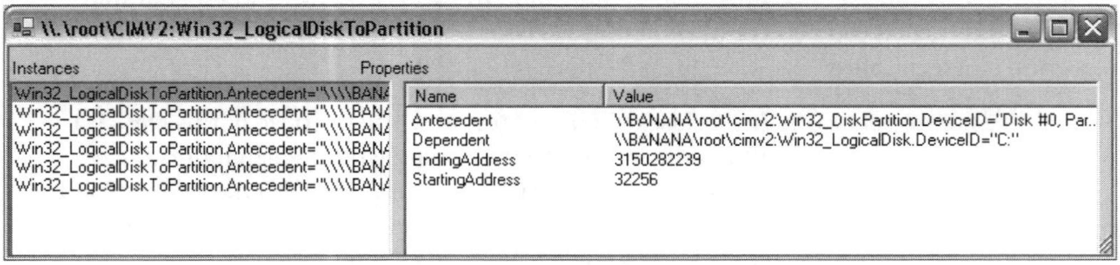

Figure 10-4. *Properties of an association class*

Note that, although Win32_LogicalDiskToPartition uses the names Antecedent and Dependent for the objects it's associating together, no rules say what names should be used, so not all association classes use these particular names. Other WMI association instances map the other disk partitions to their corresponding logical drives. Since other WMI classes represent, for example, physical hard drives, CD drives, floppy drives, other association classes, as you may expect, link these to logical drives.

In this chapter, I won't do any programming that involves association classes, but it's important to be aware of their existence.

Events

WMI defines extensive support for allowing clients to receive notifications when certain events have occurred. Such notifications go by the name *events*, although you should be wary of confusing these with .NET events. WMI events have virtually nothing in common with .NET events when it comes down to underlying architecture, even though WMI events and .NET events serve the same purpose. However, the System.Management classes do an excellent job of encapsulating the WMI event model inside .NET events so that when you write client code, you need to deal only with .NET events and the usual .NET event methodology. Underlying this, the WMI event model is implemented using COM callback interfaces.

WMI events fall into three categories.

Timer events: These simply involve WMI notifying the client at fixed intervals of time. They're implemented by the object manager. Since you can achieve similar functionality with the .NET timers, I won't cover these further.

Extrinsic events: These are wholly custom events and are defined and implemented by providers. When the client registers to be notified of these events, the object manager passes the request on to the provider. When the provider detects that the event has occurred, it notifies the object manager, and the object manager in turn notifies the client.

Intrinsic events: Intrinsic events arguably show the WMI infrastructure at its best. Certain types of events are intrinsically recognized by the WMI object manager, and the object manager implements its own notification mechanism for them, which will function even if the relevant provider doesn't implement callbacks. The events that the object manager recognizes as intrinsic events are creation, deletion, and modification of namespaces, classes, and instances. As an example, suppose some client wanted to be notified when the volume label of a logical drive changed. You already saw that the volume label is a property of a Win32_LogicalDrive instance, so this event falls into the category of modification of an instance. The client would hence pass a request to the object manager to be notified of this event. Now the relevant provider—in this case the Win32 provider—doesn't have any callback mechanism for this scenario, so the object manager will simulate it, by polling the relevant Win32_LogicalDrive instance at an interval specified by the client. If the object manager detects a change has occurred, it will notify the client.

Although these three formal categories exist in the WMI architecture, the distinction between them isn't particularly relevant as far as writing client code is concerned. In a later example, I'll demonstrate how to use WMI events. The example happens to involve an intrinsic event, but the syntax and coding techniques are no different from those for extrinsic and timer events.

WMI Query Language

So far I've covered the principles behind WMI classes, instances, and events, but I haven't really covered the way that WMI expects a client to request a class, an instance, or an event notification. A WMI client hands the object manager some text in a language known as *WMI Query Language* (WQL). The language is based on a subset of the SQL language used for database queries.

It's not absolutely essential to understand WQL in order to perform basic programming in WMI. You've already seen two examples in which no WQL explicitly appeared, but using WQL is essential in order to perform more sophisticated or high-performance queries. WQL is intended solely for queries—you can't use WQL to perform updates to data.

To see how WQL can help you, let's go back to the earlier example in which I requested all instances of the class `Win32_Processor`. There I used the .NET method, `ManagementClass.GetInstances()`.

```
ManagementClass processorClass = new ManagementClass("Win32_Processor");
foreach (ManagementObject processor in processorClass.GetInstances())
{
```

It's possible to perform the same operation using WQL—the following code snippet does the same thing as the previous snippet:

```
ManagementObjectSearcher processorSearcher =
    new ManagementObjectSearcher("SELECT * FROM Win32_Processor");
foreach (ManagementObject processor in processorSearcher.Get())
{
```

The downloadable example code for this chapter includes an example called `ListProcessorsExplicitWQL`, which does the same thing as the `ListProcessors` example but uses explicit WQL syntax.

For the simple case of listing all processors, you have nothing to gain by explicitly putting the WQL statement in the source code; all you'd achieve is to make the source code more complex. However, in general, making the WQL explicit means you get more freedom to narrow down the search parameters to retrieve exactly the data you want—for example, you can specify which properties of the instances you're interested in or impose conditions on which instances you want returned. This brings significant performance gains and also saves you from having to write C# code that filters out the objects you want from the ones that have been returned, assuming you don't just want every instance of a class.

In following sections I'll briefly cover some of the underlying principles of WQL syntax and show you how to construct a few simple WQL statements. I won't attempt to cover WQL in any kind of comprehensive way; I just want to give you a flavor of the language. The full definition of WQL is in the MSDN documentation.

WQL for Queries

Let's examine the WQL query I've just demonstrated.

```
SELECT * FROM Win32_Processor
```

This string requests all instances of the class Win32_Processor.

By comparison, in standard SQL, the basic query has the format SELECT *<column names>* FROM *<table>* WHERE *<condition>*. WQL uses the same format but with properties playing the role of columns and classes playing the role of tables. Any condition is used to restrict which instances are returned. Hence, a basic WQL query has the following syntax:

SELECT *<properties>* FROM *<class>* WHERE *<condition>*

You can write * for the list of properties, which means you get all properties.

Consider the previous ListProcessorsExplicitWQL example. In the query in this example, I asked for all properties, but the example actually uses only the Name and ProcessorSpeed properties. You can make the query more efficient by telling the WMI object manager that these are the only properties you want:

SELECT Name, CurrentClockSpeed FROM Win32_Processor

This query will still return all the Win32_Processor instances, but the WMI instances will have been set up so that these two properties are the only ones available. The full code for the Main() method in the example now looks like this, with the new changes shown in bold (in the download code, this code is available as the ListProcessorsExplicitWQL2 sample):

```
static void Main()
{
    int totalProcessors = 0;
    ManagementObjectSearcher processorSearcher =
        new ManagementObjectSearcher(
        "SELECT Name, CurrentClockSpeed FROM Win32_Processor");
    foreach (ManagementObject processor in processorSearcher.Get())
    {
        ++totalProcessors;
        Console.WriteLine("{0}, {1} MHz", processor["Name"],
                            processor["CurrentClockSpeed"]);
    }
    if (totalProcessors > 1)
        Console.WriteLine("\n{0} processors", totalProcessors);
    else
        Console.WriteLine("\n{0} processor", totalProcessors);
}
```

Explicitly specifying properties does mean that the object manager has slightly more work to do when parsing the query, but this is balanced by the reduced workload involved in retrieving and returning the WMI objects. If properties have to be populated by sending requests to a remote machine, for example, or by using an API that takes a while to return the results, this savings can be significant.

Let's look at a couple of examples that illustrate how to use the WHERE clause to impose conditions on which objects are retrieved. The following code retrieves details of all the Windows services that are currently stopped:

SELECT * FROM Win32_Service WHERE State = "Stopped"

On the other hand, the following query will return the account name and domain name of any user account that's disabled but not currently locked out:

```
SELECT Name, DomainName FROM Win32_UserAccount
WHERE Disabled = true AND Lockout = false
```

WQL for Events

The way that a client notifies the object manager that it wants to receive an event is by passing it a WQL query string in the same way that it requests references to WMI classes and instances. The big difference is that if a client requests an event, the query string will indicate a class name that the object manager recognizes as an event class. To give an example, this is how a client requests to be notified if a modem has been added to the computer:

```
SELECT * FROM __InstanceCreationEvent WITHIN 20
WHERE TargetInstance ISA "Win32_POTSModem"
```

The class __InstanceCreationEvent is a system class that indicates that an instance of some other class has been created. Win32_POTSModem is the class that represents a modem, and the WQL ISA operator specifies that an instance must be an instance of the specified class. The __InstanceCreationEvent class has just one property, TargetInstance, which references the object that has been created. The previous WQL request asks that, if the object manager detects that a new Win32_POTSModem class has appeared in the WMI repository, it should create an __InstanceCreationEvent instance and return it to the client. The WITHIN 20 clause indicates the polling frequency in seconds. Creating instances is an intrinsic event, and as I mentioned earlier, WMI providers don't necessarily support intrinsic events, so WMI may need to poll the WMI repository to check whether there are any new instances. WITHIN 20 indicates that this polling should be done every 20 seconds. Clearly the rate you choose will depend on a balance between performance and how quickly the client needs to be notified of events.

■**Tip** An event request will normally begin with SELECT *. For this type of request, the object manager will ignore any listing of properties that appears in place of the *.

Table 10-2 lists the nine intrinsic events that are represented by classes.

Table 10-2. *The WMI Classes That Represent Intrinsic Events*

Creation Events	Deletion Events	Modification Events
__InstanceCreationEvent	__InstanceDeletionEvent	__InstanceModificationEvent
__ClassCreationEvent	__ClassDeletionEvent	__ClassModificationEvent
__NamespaceCreationEvent	__NamespaceDeletionEvent	__NamespaceModificationEvent

If you're requesting to be notified of an extrinsic event, then the WQL query string will indicate an event class that's supplied by a provider. In this case you have no need to use the WITHIN clause, since the provider will support event notification, and no polling is necessary.

I'll finish this section with a couple of other examples of WQL queries.

The first example is the string that will be used in a sample later in the chapter. It requests to be notified whenever the display resolution of the monitor falls so that the number of horizontal pixels drops below 1024, with a polling interval of 2 seconds.

```
SELECT * FROM __InstanceModificationEvent WITHIN 2
WHERE TargetInstance ISA "Win32_DisplayConfiguration"
    AND TargetInstance.PelsWidth < 1024
    AND PreviousInstance.PelsWidth >= 1024
```

Notice that this query is quite sophisticated. It tests not only the new value of the pixel width but also the old value, so that an event will be generated only if the value of this property falls through 1024. In general, for performance reasons you should construct the query to be as restrictive as possible, so you get only the events in which you're really interested. The following query is similar, but it doesn't test the previous resolution:

```
SELECT * FROM __InstanceModificationEvent WITHIN 2
WHERE TargetInstance ISA "Win32_DisplayConfiguration"
    AND TargetInstance.PelsWidth < 1024
```

This query will generate more events, since it will cause an event to be raised whenever any changes are made to the display configuration properties provided only that the horizontal resolution happens to be less than 1024 after the change, even if the change is unrelated. (For example, an event will be generated if the resolution is 800×600, and the monitor refresh rate is changed.)

Finally, here's an example of a deletion event. This request asks to be notified within ten seconds when any print jobs are terminated. (This could be because a job has finished printing or has been aborted.)

```
SELECT * FROM __InstanceDeletionEvent WITHIN 10
    WHERE TargetInstance ISA "Win32_PrintJob"
```

Performing Queries Using the System.Management Classes

Now that you've seen something of how WMI works internally, I'm ready to cover in more detail how to code clients using WMI. The rest of this chapter is devoted to three examples, which respectively illustrate querying the available classes synchronously, performing asynchronous queries, and receiving event notifications.

The two core classes you'll be using all the time with WMI are ManagementObject and ManagementClass. ManagementObject represents any WMI object—in other words, an instance or a class. ManagementClass represents only those WMI objects that are classes. ManagementClass derives from ManagementObject and implements a couple of extra methods to perform tasks such as obtaining all the instances of a class and obtaining related classes and base classes. In turn, ManagementObject is derived from the class ManagementBaseObject, which implements certain other methods and properties.

You've already seen the use of ManagementClass.GetInstances() to retrieve all instances. This method actually returns a ManagementObjectCollection reference.

```
ManagementClass modemClass = new
    ManagementClass(@"\\.\root\CIMV2\Win32_POTSModem");
ManagementObjectCollection modems = modems.GetInstances();
foreach (MangementObject modem in modems)
{
```

If you need more control over the actual query sent to the object manager, you can use the ManagementObjectSearcher class, in particular the Get() method, as you've already seen. This method also returns a ManagementObjectCollection reference.

Once you have an object, the properties can be returned via an indexer, as you saw in earlier examples.

```
ManagementObject cDrive =
          new ManagementObject("Win32_LogicalDisk.DeviceID=\"C:\"");
Console.WriteLine(cDrive["VolumeName"]);
```

If you want a finer degree of control over the properties, you can use the PropertyData class, which represents an individual property and features methods to obtain the name, value, qualifiers and other data about a property, such as whether it's an array.

You can obtain a collection of all the available properties on an object using the ManagementObject.Properties property. This technique is also useful if you don't at compile time know the names of the properties you'll need.

```
ManagementObject cDrive = new ManagementObject(
        "Win32_LogicalDisk.DeviceID=\"C:\"");
PropertyDataCollection props = cDrive.Properties;
foreach (PropertyData prop in props)
{
    // Note that in real production code you'd check for null values here
    Console.WriteLine("Name: {0}, Value: {1}", prop.Name,
                     prop.Value.ToString());
}
```

Note that the PropertyData.Value property returns an object reference—since the actual data type will vary between properties. Hence, in the previous code snippet I explicitly convert it to a string.

WMI Browser Sample: Features

I'll now present a sample that illustrates how to use the System.Management classes to perform synchronous queries. The WMIBrowser sample is just what its name suggests: it's an application that lets you browse around the various namespaces in WMI and examine classes, instances, and properties. This means that the sample has an added benefit: if you download and run it, you can use it to get a good feel for the kind of things you can do on your computer with WMI.

When you run the example, you're presented with a form containing a large treeview and associated listbox. The treeview shows the complete tree of namespaces. The listbox is initially empty, but whenever any node in the treeview is selected, the listbox is populated with the names of all the classes in that namespace (see Figure 10-5).

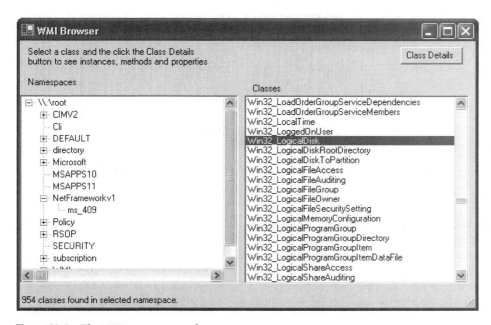

Figure 10-5. *The* WMIBrowser *sample*

Figure 10-5 shows the situation on Windows XP Professional. Which classes you see will depend heavily on your operating system because of the way that WMI is rapidly evolving. On Windows 2000, for example, you'll see fewer namespaces and classes because that was an earlier operating system, so it came with fewer WMI providers. Among the namespaces you can see are the CIMV2 one, which contains the classes defined in the CIM V2 Schema and Win32 Extended Schema. Other namespaces include NetFrameworkv1, which contains the classes that can be used to configure .NET, and directory/LDAP, which allows access to Active Directory configuration.

The form contains a button captioned Class Details. If you click this button, a new form will be displayed, containing more details of the class that was selected in the listbox. On my machine, and with the Win32_LogicalDisk class selected as shown in Figure 10-5, clicking this button gives the form shown in Figure 10-6.

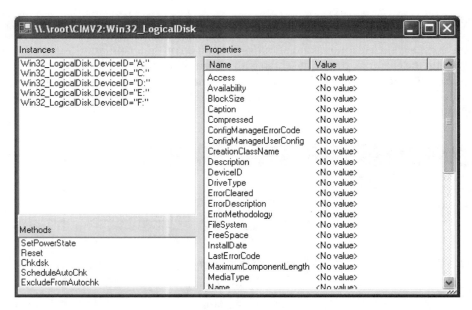

Figure 10-6. *The* WMIBrowser *sample, used to examine the* Win32_LogicalDisk *class*

From Figure 10-6 you can gather that the sample shows the current instances of the selected class, as well as the properties and methods defined for the class. For properties the sample shows the values of each property where available (though for array properties it simply displays the string, <array>). Of course, none of the properties in Figure 10-6 has any values, because at this point the sample is examining a class, not an instance. A few WMI classes have some property values defined statically for the class as a whole, but Win32_LogicalDisk isn't one of them.

To see some property values, you need to select an instance. If you click any instance of the class shown in the upper-left list in Figure 10-6, then the Properties listview changes to show the properties of that instance rather than the whole class (see Figure 10-7).

Now you see that a number of properties have appeared, but still you see a fair number of properties that are either apparently not implemented in Windows or don't currently have any values assigned to them.

The sample doesn't allow you to modify the values of properties or to call methods, but it's enough to give you a fair idea of what's in the WMI namespaces.

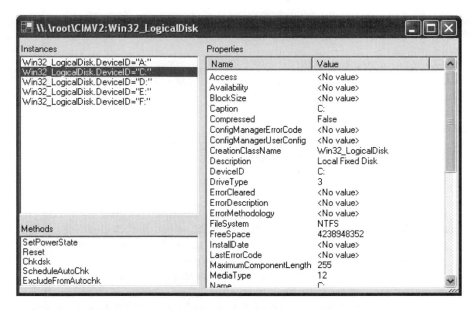

Figure 10-7. *The* WMIBrowser *sample, used to examine an instance*

WMI Browser Sample: How It Works

I'll start by examining the code for the form displayed at application startup, which was shown in Figure 10-5. The controls on this form are respectively named tvNamespaces, lbClasses, btnDetails, and statusBar. When using the Design View to add these controls, I set the Sorted property of the listbox to true.

The Form1 constructor invokes a method called AddNamespacesToList(), which is the method that populates the treeview.

```
public Form1()
{
    InitializeComponent();

    this.AddNamespacesToList();
}
```

The following is the code for AddNamespacesToList():

```
private void AddNamespacesToList()
{
    try
    {
```

```
        string nsName = @"\\.\root";
        TreeNode node = new TreeNode(nsName);
        node.Tag = nsName;
        this.tvNamespaces.Nodes.Add(node);
        RecurseAddSubNamespaces(nsName, node);
        node.Expand();
    }
    catch (Exception e)
    {
        this.statusValue.Text = "ERROR: " + e.Message;
    }
}
```

It's traditional in books to neglect error-handling code in examples because such code usually detracts from the purpose of the example. However, when you start dealing with running through all the WMI namespaces and classes, you'll have a high risk of encountering exceptions, normally because some WMI provider doesn't implement certain features. Because of this risk, most of the substantial methods in this example contain try...catch blocks just to make sure that if an error does occur, an appropriate message is displayed and execution continues. In this case, if any exception is thrown while listing all the namespaces, this will be indicated by a message in the status bar.

As far as the code in the try block is concerned, it starts by placing a root node in the treeview, which represents the root namespace on the current machine. It also sets the Tag property of the node to this string. In this example, the nodes under the root node will only display the name of the namespace represented, but if you're to retrieve details of classes in a namespace, then you'll need to access the full path of the namespace—I solved this issue here by storing that path in the Tag property of each TreeNode object.

Adding the nodes under the root node is the responsibility of a method called RecurseAddSubNamespaces(). After calling this method, the code expands the root node to make the form look prettier (and save the user a mouse click) when the program starts.

RecurseAddSubNamespaces() looks like so:

```
void RecurseAddSubNamespaces(string nsName, TreeNode parent)
{
    ManagementClass nsClass = new ManagementClass(nsName + ":__namespace");
    foreach(ManagementObject ns in nsClass.GetInstances())
    {
        string childName = ns["Name"].ToString();
        TreeNode childNode = new TreeNode(childName);
        string fullPath = nsName + @"\" + childName;
        childNode.Tag = fullPath;
        parent.Nodes.Add(childNode);
        RecurseAddSubNamespaces(fullPath, childNode);
    }
}
```

Essentially, this method takes a namespace and its corresponding TreeNode as a parameter. It finds all the namespaces directly contained in this parent namespace and adds them all to the parent node. Then the method recursively calls itself again for each of the newly added children, thus making sure that any children of those namespaces get added, and so on, until the entire tree of namespaces has been covered.

The real problem is how to find the child namespaces of a namespace—no method in any of the System.Management classes can directly do this. Instead, the procedure that WBEM has defined for this is to go through the special class called __namespace that I mentioned earlier. As I noted earlier, the WBEM standard requires that this class should exist in every namespace, and every namespace should contain one instance of this class for each subnamespace. Thus, by enumerating the instances of this class, you can find the names of the child namespaces— which are available via the Name property of each instance of the __namespace class.

```
ManagementClass nsClass = new ManagementClass(nsName + ":__namespace");
foreach(ManagementObject ns in nsClass.GetInstances())
```

The following is the code that will be executed when the user selects an item in the tree-view:

```
private void tvNamespaces_AfterSelect(object sender,
                System.Windows.Forms.TreeViewEventArgs e)
{
    AddClasses(e.Node.Tag.ToString());
}

void AddClasses(string ns)
{
    lbClasses.Items.Clear();
    int count = 0;
    try
    {
        ManagementObjectSearcher searcher = new ManagementObjectSearcher(
                                    ns, "select * from meta_class");
        foreach (ManagementClass wmiClass in searcher.Get())
        {
            this.lbClasses.Items.Add(wmiClass["__class"].ToString());
            count++;
        }
        this.statusValue.Text = count + " classes found in selected namespace.";
    }
    catch (Exception ex)
    {
        this.statusValue.Text = ex.Message;
    }
}
```

The AddClasses() method uses a WQL query string to obtain all the classes contained in the selected namespace. To retrieve the name of each class, it uses the __class property. This is one of those system properties defined automatically for all WBEM classes. __class always contains the name of the class. Finally, the method updates the status bar with the number of classes in the namespace.

The next action to be considered is the handler for when the user clicks the Show Details button.

```
private void btnDetails_Click(object sender, System.EventArgs e)
{
    string classPath = this.tvNamespaces.SelectedNode.Tag.ToString() + ":" +
                                    this.lbClasses.SelectedItem.ToString();
    ClassAnalyzerForm subForm = new ClassAnalyzerForm(classPath);
    subForm.ShowDialog();
}
```

The handler first figures out the full path to the selected class, by combining the class name with the namespace path obtained from the node in the treeview. Then it instantiates the second form (I've called this form ClassAnalyzerForm) and shows it as a modal dialog box. The controls I added to this form are called lbInstances (the listbox that lists the class instances), lvProperties (the listview that gives the property values) and lbMethods (the small listbox that lists the methods of a class). In addition, the two column headers of lbInstances are respectively called hdrName and hdrValue.

The ClassAnalyzerForm class has several extra member fields that I added by hand.

```
public class ClassAnalyzerForm : System.Windows.Forms.Form
{
    ManagementObject[] instances;
    ManagementClass mgmtClass;
    string className;
    private System.Windows.Forms.ListBox lbInstances;
    private System.Windows.Forms.ListView lvProperties;
    private System.Windows.Forms.ColumnHeader hdrName;
    private System.Windows.Forms.ColumnHeader hdrValue;
    private System.Windows.Forms.ListBox lbMethods;
```

className stores the full path of the class, mgmtClass is a reference to the ManagementClass object that represents this class, and instances is an array of ManagementObject references that represent all the available instances of the class.

Quite a lot has to be done when the form is instantiated.

```
public ClassAnalyzerForm(string className)
{
    InitializeComponent();

    this.className = className;
    this.Text = this.className;
    mgmtClass = new ManagementClass(this.className);
    mgmtClass.Get();
```

```
   AddInstances();
   AddProperties(mgmtClass);
   AddMethods();
}
```

Besides initializing the member fields, the code must call the ManagementObject.Get() method to retrieve data from the underlying object to be managed. It then calls methods to populate the listboxes that will list the instances and methods of the object and similarly to populate the listview that will display its properties. The reason that the AddProperties() method takes a parameter is that in principle I also want to display the properties of instances, if the user clicks an instance. Hence, it needs to be passed details of precisely which WMI object to use. By contrast, AddInstances() and AddMethods() are never invoked after the form has been instantiated and always populate their respective listboxes based on the mgmtClass field.

Let's examine AddInstances() first. You can obtain the instances using the ManagementClass.GetInstances() method. The main complicating factor is the need to store all the ManagementObject instance references—you'll need them later if the user clicks one of them. Unfortunately, although ManagementObjectCollection has a Count property, this isn't currently implemented by Microsoft, which makes it impossible to tell up front how big an array to allocate to store the instances in. The problem is solved in this method by holding the data in a temporary ArrayList, which is transferred to a proper array when the code knows how many instances are available.

```
public void AddInstances()
{
   try
   {
      ManagementObjectCollection instances = mgmtClass.GetInstances();
      ArrayList tempInstances = new ArrayList();
      ArrayList tempIndices = new ArrayList();
      foreach (ManagementObject instance in instances)
      {
         int index = this.lbInstances.Items.Add(
                                       instance["__RelPath"].ToString());
         tempInstances.Add(instance);
         tempIndices.Add(index);
      }

      this.instances = new ManagementObject [tempInstances.Count];
      for (int i=0; i<tempInstances.Count; i++)
         this.instances[(int)tempIndices[i]] = (ManagementObject)
                                                      tempInstances[i];
   }
   catch (Exception e)
   {
      this.lbInstances.Items.Add("ERROR:" + e.Message);
   }
}
```

The `tempIndices` `ArrayList` stores the indices at which each `ManagementObject` is added to the listbox. You need this information so that when the user clicks an item in the listbox, you can work out which `ManagementObject` corresponds to that index. The code uses the `__RelPath` property, another system property implemented by all objects, to retrieve the name of the object (strictly speaking, its relative object path).

The process of adding methods to the appropriate listbox (called `lbMethods`) is far simpler since you have no need to store any information.

```
void AddMethods()
{
   try
   {
      foreach (MethodData instance in mgmtClass.Methods)
      {
         this.lbMethods.Items.Add(instance.Name);
      }
   }
   catch (Exception e)
   {
      this.lbMethods.Items.Add("ERROR:" + e.Message);
   }
}
```

Adding properties is complicated by the need to retrieve the property value of an object. To keep things simple, I didn't write any code to enumerate through the elements of array properties. So as I noted earlier, if a property is an array (indicated by the `PropertyData.IsArray` property), the code just displays the string `<Array>`. If for any reason the code can't retrieve the property value (retrieving it either returns `null` if no value is present or throws an exception if there is a problem in the provider), then it displays the string `<No Value>`. The individual properties are represented by `PropertyData` instances.

```
void AddProperties(ManagementObject mgmtObj)
{
   lvProperties.Items.Clear();
   try
   {
      foreach (PropertyData instance in mgmtObj.Properties)
      {
         ListViewItem prop = new ListViewItem(instance.Name);
         if (instance.IsArray)
            prop.SubItems.Add("<Array>");
         else
         {
            object value =instance.Value;
            if (value == null)
               prop.SubItems.Add("<No value>");
            else
               prop.SubItems.Add(value.ToString());
```

```
        }
        this.lvProperties.Items.Add(prop);
    }
}
catch (Exception e)
{
    this.lvProperties.Items.Add("ERROR:" + e.Message);
}
}
```

Finally, I should mention the event handler that invokes AddProperties() if the user clicks an instance in the lbInstances listbox.

```
private void lbInstances_SelectedIndexChanged(object sender,
                                              System.EventArgs e)
{
    AddProperties(instances[lbInstances.SelectedIndex]);
}
```

And that completes the code for the sample.

Performing Asynchronous Processing

The code I've used in the examples so far in this chapter performs all requests synchronously, which means that the calling thread blocks while the object manager services the request—which can on occasions take a long time. It's alternatively possible to ask for the request to be performed asynchronously on a separate thread—and, unusually for .NET, the mechanism isn't based on the BeginXXX()/EndXXX() design pattern that I discussed in Chapter 9. In the following section I discuss how to perform asynchronous queries using the System.Management classes.

How the CLR Implements Asynchronous WMI Queries

Instead, to request asynchronous processing, you instantiate an object of type ManagementOperationObserver(). Taking the ManagementClass.GetInstances() method and using a query to obtain details of current modems as an example, the code uses a one-parameter overload of GetInstances() and looks like this:

```
ManagementClass modemClass = new
    ManagementClass(@"\\.\root\CIMV2\Win32_POTSModem);
ManagementOperationObserver observer = new ManagementOperationObserver();

// Initialize observer by adding handlers to events.

modemClass.GetInstances(observer);
```

This code works as follows: The ManagementOperationObserver class defines a number of events, and before calling the one-parameter overload of GetInstances(), you should add appropriate handlers to the events in which you're interested. This overload of GetInstances() returns immediately, and the WMI object manager will raise the events as appropriate. The events will be handled on managed thread-pool threads, not on the main application thread.

Table 10-3 shows the events available.

Table 10-3. *CLR Events That Are Available for Asynchronous WMI Queries*

Event	Meaning
Completed	Indicates that the operation is completed.
ObjectReady	This event is raised whenever a new object becomes available as a result of a query.
ObjectPut	A Put() operation has been successfully completed.
Progress	This event is raised at intervals to indicate the progress of the operation.

It should be clear now why Microsoft has chosen not to use the BeginXXX()/EndXXX() architecture here. In the case of asynchronous WMI events, one operation can give rise to a succession of events. For example, a GetInstances() query will cause the ObjectReady() event to be raised each time a new object is returned from the WMI provider. The BeginXXX()/EndXXX() architecture hasn't been designed for this kind of scenario.

You'll notice that the list of events includes an ObjectPut() event, which is clearly appropriate only when writing values to an object—it's not appropriate for a SELECT query. The reason this event has been defined is that the ManagementOperationObserver-based design pattern isn't only used for queries. It's used for quite a few different methods that call up the object manager, including ManagementClass.GetInstances(), ManagementObjectSearcher.Get(), ManagementObject.Get(), and ManagementObject.Put(). For example:

```
ManagementOperationObserver observer = new ManagementOperationObserver();

// Initialize observer by adding handlers to events

// Assume myModem and myModem2 are references to objects that describe modems.
myModem.Put(observer); // Asynchronously writes data to modem
myModem2.Put();        // Do same thing but synchronously
```

Microsoft has also defined suitable event handler delegates for each of events defined by ManagementOperationObserver; for example, the Completed event is of type CompletedEventHandler, which has this definition:

```
public delegate void _CompletedEventHandler(object sender,
                                            CompletedEventArgs e);
```

CompletedEventArgs contains information appropriate to this event (in this case, the status—whether the operation completed successfully or whether it failed and, if so, why).

The other events in ManagementOperationObserver have similar handler and event args. The best way to see this, however, is with an example. In the next section I develop the earlier ListProcessors example so that it retrieves its results asynchronously.

ListProcessorsAsync Sample

This sample retrieves the list of processors on the computer, just like the earlier similar samples, except that it retrieves the list asynchronously. This sample will demonstrate the ObjectReady and Completed events.

This is the code for the Main() method:

```
static void Main()
{
    ManagementObjectSearcher processorSearcher = new ManagementObjectSearcher(
        "SELECT Name, CurrentClockSpeed FROM Win32_Processor");

    ManagementOperationObserver observer = new ManagementOperationObserver();
    CallBackClass callBackObject = new CallBackClass();
    observer.Completed += new
                    CompletedEventHandler(callBackObject.OnAllProcessors);
    observer.ObjectReady += new
                ObjectReadyEventHandler(callBackObject.OnNextProcessor);

    processorSearcher.Get(observer);
    Console.WriteLine("Retrieving processors. Hit any key to terminate");
    Console.ReadLine();
}
```

This code first sets up the ManagementObjectSearcher instance that will make the query request. Then it instantiates the ManagementOperationObserver callback object and supplies handlers to the ObjectReady and Completed events on the callback. The handlers supplied are defined in a class, CallBackClass, which I'll show you shortly. Having done all the preparatory work, the code calls ManagementObjectSearcher.Get() to perform the query. This call returns immediately, and in a real application, the main thread would probably go off and do some other work now. However, since this is only a sample, I've coded it so the main thread simply waits for some user input to terminate the process.

Here's the definition of CallBackClass, which implements the event handlers. Remember that these handlers will be executed on a thread-pool thread, not on the main thread.

```
class CallBackClass
{
    int totalProcessors = 0;

    public void OnNextProcessor(object sender, ObjectReadyEventArgs e)
    {
        ManagementObject processor = (ManagementObject)e.NewObject;
        Console.WriteLine("Next processor object arrived:");
        Console.WriteLine("\t{0}, {1} MHz", processor["Name"],
                                        processor["CurrentClockSpeed"]);
        ++totalProcessors;
```

```
   }

   public void OnAllProcessors(object sender, CompletedEventArgs e)
   {
      if (totalProcessors > 1)
         Console.WriteLine("\n{0} processors", totalProcessors);
      else
         Console.WriteLine("\n{0} processor", totalProcessors);
   }
}
```

As you can see, `OnNextProcessor()` (which I set up as the handler that's called each time a new result is ready) displays details of this processor and increments a count of how many processors exist. `OnAllProcessors()` (the handler for the `Completed` event) simply displays the number of processors returned. To keep this example as simple as possible, I've taken a couple of shortcuts that you probably wouldn't do in a real application. In particular, you'd probably not want worker threads handling user output, and the `OnAllProcessors()` method in particular would be more likely to do something to signal to the main thread that the process is complete.

Running this example on my machine gives this result:

```
Retrieving processors. Hit any key to terminate
Next processor object arrived:
        AMD Athlon(tm) processor, 1199 MHz

1 processor
```

Receiving Notifications

The final topic I'll cover is writing clients that can receive notifications of events. As with the previous section, I'll first explain a bit of the general principles of writing code that receives notifications, and then I'll present a sample to illustrate the concepts.

How the CLR Implements Event Notifications

The general principles for receiving event notifications are identical to those for performing asynchronous queries, but some of the classes used are a bit different. In place of the `ManagementOperationObserver` class is a `ManagementEventWatcher` class. This class doesn't only indicate the callback method but is also responsible for sending the notification request (as a WQL string) off to the object manager. So the first thing you have to do is set up a `ManagementEventWatcher` instance initialized with the appropriate query string. The following code performs this initialization, with a query string that indicates that the client wants to be notified within five seconds whenever any Windows services are registered:

```
string queryString = "SELECT * FROM __InstanceCreationEvent " +
    "WITHIN 5 WHERE TargetInstance ISA 'Win32_Service'";
ManagementEventWatcher watcher = new ManagementEventWatcher(query);
```

Next you have to indicate the handler method that will receive callbacks.

```
watcher.EventArrived += new
    EventArrivedEventHandler(myCallBackMethod);
```

Here, the myCallBack method is a method that you'll have implemented elsewhere and that has a signature corresponding to the EventArrivedEventHandler delegate (yes, Microsoft has defined yet another delegate. . .).

Finally, the ManagementEventWatcher.Start() method sends the notification request off to the object manager. You simply call this method and then sit back and wait (or, more likely, do some other work) while the notification responses come back on a thread-pool thread.

```
watcher.Start();
```

If at some later point you want to cancel the notification request, so the object manager stops sending notifications, you call the ManagementEventWatcher.Stop() method.

```
watcher.Stop();
```

Monitoring Display Settings Example

This example will demonstrate how to use WMI events. It's called MonitorDisplaySettings, and it's a short console application whose purpose is to warn you if for any reason the display settings for the screen area change and fall below 1024¥768 pixels. When the code starts, it sets up a WQL query asking the WMI object manager to notify it if this event occurs. If the display settings do fall below this value, then a warning message displays. The main thread simply waits for some user input so that the application terminates when the user hits the Return key.

The code for the example looks as follows. You'll see the Main() method that sets up the request to be notified of events first.

```
static void Main()
{
    WqlEventQuery query = new WqlEventQuery(
        "SELECT * FROM __InstanceModificationEvent " +
        "WITHIN 2 WHERE TargetInstance ISA \"Win32_DisplayConfiguration\" " +
        "AND TargetInstance.PelsWidth < 1024 AND PreviousInstance.PelsWidth " +
        ">= 1024");
    ManagementEventWatcher watcher = new ManagementEventWatcher(query);
    CallbackClass callback = new CallbackClass();
    watcher.EventArrived += new EventArrivedEventHandler(
                                        callback.DisplayProblemCallback);
```

```
    watcher.Start();
    Console.WriteLine("Monitoring display settings.");
    Console.WriteLine("Hit return to stop monitoring and exit.");
    Console.ReadLine();
    watcher.Stop();
}
```

This code shouldn't need much additional explanation given the explanation of the ManagementEventWatcher class that I ran over in the previous section. Notice that, although the aim is to test if the display resolution falls below 1024¥768, I'm assuming it's sufficient to test only the horizontal resolution. Since the standard screen resolutions normally jump from 800¥600 to 1024¥768, this is a good approximation for the sample, but if you were performing this task in real life, you'd probably want to test the vertical resolution too.

Now here's the callback class, which handles events. The following code simply displays a warning message each time the object manager raises the event to indicate that the horizontal display resolution has fallen below 1024:

```
public class CallbackClass
{
    public void DisplayProblemCallback(object sender, EventArrivedEventArgs e)
    {
        Console.WriteLine("Warning! Display settings have dropped " +
                        "below 1024x768");
    }
}
```

To test the example, you should just start it running. Then, while the example is running, open the properties window for the desktop, locate the Settings property page, and change the screen resolution to something coarser than 1024¥768.

For my test, I picked the next lowest setting, 800¥600. I found that within seconds, the console window in which the example was running displayed the warning message, as shown in Figure 10-8.

If you run this sample and make this change, you'll subsequently find that you can make further changes to the display settings without generating any further warnings. This is because the PreviousInstance.PelsWidth property is now less than 1024, so the conditions in the WQL event query string I supplied in the program aren't satisfied. However, if you change the resolution back to 1024¥768 (or something higher) and then back down again, you'll quickly see another warning appear in the console window.

Figure 10-8. *Detecting a reduction in screen resolution*

Summary

In this chapter, you looked at how to use the classes in the System.Management namespace and at the underlying WMI and WBEM architecture that underpins these classes. You saw that by using WMI, it's possible in just a few lines of source code to interact with the environment, the operating system, the running processes, and the hardware in a powerful way to perform management and monitoring tasks. Besides having a glimpse of some of the things you can do using WMI, you saw samples to browse the WMI namespaces, list the processors on the local machine, and warn the user if the horizontal display resolution falls below 1024 pixels. These examples illustrate sending synchronous and asynchronous WMI queries and receiving notifications of WMI events.

Building Advanced Windows Forms Applications

In this chapter I'll cover some of the techniques you can use to develop Windows Forms applications, and—in accordance with the advanced philosophy of this book—I'm not talking about basic Windows Forms techniques. I'm referring to some of the ways you can make your Windows Forms programs that little bit more sophisticated or look that bit more polished than those of your competitors.

This chapter will cover two broad areas: First, you'll learn how to take full advantage of the message loop—possibly in combination with multiple threads—to perform asynchronous and background processing in a way that keeps your code simple without sacrificing application responsiveness. Second, you'll learn how to give your application the edge in terms of graphics. So the chapter comprises two fairly independent halves, covering each of those areas.

In more detail, the topics I'll cover are as follows:

Message loops: Every Windows Forms application is underpinned by a Windows message loop. The details of the operation of the message loop are largely hidden from you by the System.Windows.Forms classes, but understanding how the loop works is important for writing and debugging any Windows Forms code that performs sophisticated background processing. You'll see how to access the message loop from your code; you may need to do this if you need to handle a situation for which no Windows Forms event is available.

BeginInvoke: The Control.BeginInvoke() method provides a useful way of using the message loop to allow communication between threads without requiring the use of the normal thread-synchronization primitives—and hence without blocking threads. You'll see how to do this, and along the way I'll develop a sample that illustrates how to implement an Abort dialog box that allows the user to cancel an asynchronous operation.

XP-themed controls: I'll show how to add support for XP themes to your controls.

Nonrectangular forms: I'll show how you can create forms and controls with more interesting shapes than the usual rectangles.

Owner-draw forms: It's possible to make the appearance of certain controls—including menus, listboxes, and buttons—much more attractive by taking charge of some drawing operations that are usually handled by the Microsoft-supplied code in these controls. Used in conjunction with nonrectangular controls, this can lead to astounding visual effects. I'll develop a sample that illustrates this.

GDI: Although in almost all cases you'll use the built-in GDI+ classes that come with the .NET Framework for your drawing operations, GDI+ doesn't support certain operations, so you'll need to fall back on GDI. I'll discuss when you may want to do this, and I'll present a sample that illustrates one such case: a form that can take screenshots. Note that I won't be extensively discussing DirectX. DirectX is another option for graphics, but it's much more specialized and can be more complicated to code—and is beyond the scope of this book (since this isn't a graphics book!)

I'll start by covering the Windows message loop architecture and then show how the Windows Forms event architecture has been built to encapsulate the message loop.

Looking at Windows Messages Under the Hood

I'll now show you what's really going on when some standard Windows event is raised in your code. Consider, for example, the Paint event. You probably know that you can add an event handler to this event and that this event is normally raised when Windows detects that some portion of a form or control needs repainting. But under the hood, what's happening? Windows itself has no awareness of .NET and so can't have any knowledge of the .NET events architecture. So clearly, under the hood, Windows must be doing something else to make the control aware of the need to raise the Paint event. And a similar reasoning follows for every other Windows Forms event you may encounter. In fact, Windows informs the control of the need to do painting by sending it something called a *Windows message*, or more commonly known simply as a *message*. A message is a C-style struct that contains some fields. Its actual definition looks like this:

```
// this is unmanaged C code.
struct MSG
{
    HWND     hwnd;
    UINT     message;
    WPARAM   wParam;
    LPARAM   lParam;
    DWORD    time;
    POINT    pt;
};
```

If you haven't programmed in C or C++ on Windows before, don't worry about the unfamiliar data type names. Other than POINT (the unmanaged equivalent of Point), they're all for all practical purposes just different names for integers. In particular, the purposes of the member fields of the unmanaged MSG struct in this code are as follows:

hwnd is a handle that identifies the window that the message is destined for (in this context, a window means either a form or a control).

message is a number (integer) that identifies what the message actually is. Whereas in managed code the nature of an event is identified by the identity of the event that's been raised, by contrast in unmanaged code the nature of a message is determined by the value of this integer. Generally speaking, you don't need to memorize which integer values correspond to the various different messages, as Microsoft has defined symbolic constants for the important messages. (These are defined in a header file called WinUser.h that's supplied with VS .NET and earlier versions of Visual Studio and with the Platform SDK, so just search on your machine for that file if you're curious.) For example, the constant for a paint message is always written as WM_PAINT rather than its actual value of 15. That for a mouse move message is written not 512 but WM_MOUSEMOVE, and the message that says the user has clicked a menu is written WM_COMMAND (actual value, 273).

wParam and lParam are simply two integers that contain more information about the message. Their meaning depends on what the message is. For example, for WM_COMMAND they will contain information about which menu item has been clicked.

time and pt have fairly obvious meanings—they're the system time and the position of the mouse hotspot when the message was raised.

Processing Messages

So that's what a message looks like. How does Windows get the message to the application? Figure 11-1 best answers that question.

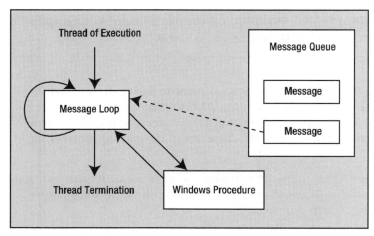

Figure 11-1. *The Windows messaging architecture*

The solid lines with arrows indicate the flow of execution of the main user interface thread in the process. The dashed arrow indicates that messages are pulled off the message queue and read in the message loop.

The *message queue* is a data area used by Windows to store any messages that need to be sent to a window. The *Windows procedure* and the *message loop* are both functions that must be implemented by the application that wants to display windows.

The Windows procedure has the task of processing messages sent to a window. It's the function that comes closest in concept to a .NET event handler. However, where a .NET event handler is specifically geared to one event and is normally only called when that particular event is raised, the Windows procedure is much more general in nature. It's there to handle all messages—paint messages, resize messages, click messages, and so on. This means in practice that Windows procedures normally end up being implemented by big `switch` statements, something like this:

```
// This is C++ code
switch (message)        // message is a UINT (unsigned int32 which
// Indicates which 'event' has occurred
{
case WM_COMMAND:        // User has clicked on a menu item
   ExecuteMenuHandler();
   break;
case WM_PAINT:          // Equivalent to Paint event
   ExecutePaintMethod();
   break;
case WM_MOUSEMOVE:      // Mouse has moved
   ExecuteMouseMoveHandler();
   break;
// etc.
}
```

■**Note** .NET isn't the first API to hide the Windows message loop underneath layers of API code supposedly designed to make the developer's life easier; VB always does this, as does MFC.

The message loop is the thing that links the message queue to the Windows procedures. In Figure 11-1 I've shown the message loop as being the function that the program enters when it starts running—and with good reason. Running the message loop is what the main thread of an application normally spends most of its time doing. The message loop normally does the following:

1. It checks to see if a message is on the queue waiting to be processed. If there isn't, then the thread goes to sleep. The Windows operating system will wake the thread up as soon as any message for it arrives in the queue.

2. When a message is on the queue, the message loop reads the message (popping it off the queue in the process) and then calls the appropriate Windows procedure, passing it the details of that message. This step is known as *dispatching* the message.

3. When the Windows procedure returns control to the message loop, the loop goes back to step 1.

Note that a given thread will by default have just one message loop (although in some situations other loops can be added), but often each type of window (form or control) in the application will have a different Windows procedure. For example, a Windows procedure will exist for all textboxes, one for all buttons, and so on. Microsoft implements the Windows procedures for standard controls, but you implement your own controls and forms. (Or, if you're using an API such as .NET or MFC, the Windows procedures will be implemented under the hood for you by the API.) When a message is dispatched, Windows is automatically able to make sure the correct procedure is invoked. This all happens on the same thread. (The thread that executes the message loop also executes all the Windows procedures.) Other threads are involved only if some code inside a Windows procedure explicitly calls up another thread to do some task. As I remarked in Chapter 9, a thread that's executing a message loop is normally termed a *user-interface* thread.

The whole process normally ends when a WM_QUIT message has been received, which indicates that the application needs to terminate.

In programmatic terms, typical code for a message loop normally looks like this.

```cpp
// This is C++ code
MSG msg;
while (GetMessage(&msg, NULL, 0, 0))
{
    TranslateMessage(&msg);
    DispatchMessage(&msg);
}
```

■Tip If you want to see a real example of this code, just start VS .NET and ask it to generate a new unmanaged C++ Windows application, taking the default settings. This produces a complete working C++ application that displays a form, complete with message loop and Windows procedure and all done using raw Windows API functions. No class library of any kind exists that wraps the API calls, so you see directly what's happening. I'll warn you, though, that you'll find the code looks rather more complicated than what I've presented here.

The GetMessage() API call is implemented as part of the Windows operating system, and it does what its name suggests—it retrieves the next message from the message queue. If no such message exists, then GetMessage() has its thread put to sleep until a message appears (taking virtually no processor time while it sleeps). The details of the message retrieved are returned via the first argument to GetMessage(), which is a MSG struct of the type you saw earlier. The return value from GetMessage() is normally used as a quick way of determining if the message loop should continue. It's zero if the message retrieved was the WM_QUIT message (which indicates the application should close down), and it's one otherwise. Hence, the previous code will always exit the while statement when a WM_QUIT message is received.

While inside the loop, two operations happen to the message—TranslateMessage() is an API call that performs certain changes on messages to simplify processing of text. It's TranslateMessage() that's responsible, for example, for figuring out that a WM_KEYDOWN followed by a WM_KEYUP is equivalent to a WM_CHAR (indicating that a character has been received from the keyboard). Then DispatchMessage() is where the real action happens. This API call examines the message it has been passed and then invokes the appropriate Windows procedure for that message.

That's the basic principle. I should stress that what I've presented here captures the essence of what's going on but ignores quite a few complications. For example, for this to all work and for DispatchMessage() to know which Windows procedure to invoke, the application will have to have informed Windows about which types of form or control it implements and where the message handlers for those controls are. (This process is called *registering a window class*.) I've also been loosely talking about the "next message" on the message queue without questioning which message will be retrieved first if more than one message is on the queue. In general, GetMessage() will retrieve messages in the same order they were posted, with a couple of exceptions. Most notably, if a WM_QUIT message is on the queue, that will always be given priority over all other messages (because if you want to quit the application, there's probably not much point in the application doing anything else).

Messages get put on the message queue in two main ways. First, Windows itself puts messages there when it detects things an application needs to respond to, such as mouse clicks and mouse movements. Second, an application can post a message to the queue by calling the PostMessage() API function.

Windows Forms and the Message Queue

Now that you've seen how the message queue works for unmanaged applications, I can explain how the CLR encapsulates this process. What exactly do the System.Windows.Forms classes do that turns what's really happening (the message loop) into what your application sees (a class that's derived from Control and that raises events whenever something happens)? The answer is relatively simple in principle. Somewhere buried deep within the Sysem.Windows.Forms.Control class there will be some code that implements a Windows procedure. That Windows procedure will invoke the various methods in Control and its derived classes that perform default processing as appropriate. For example, in response to the WM_PAINT event, the Windows procedure implemented by the NativeWindow class (one of the classes internal to Windows Forms) will call the virtual method Control.Paint(PaintEventArgs e). In addition, it will also check whether your code has added any event handlers to the Paint event of the managed Control-derived object and, if so, invoke them. Notice how the managed events arise from this process entirely as a consequence of managed code—the events that you see in the Control class and derived classes are not dependant in any way on the underlying Windows messages, beyond that many of them happen to have been defined with similar meanings. The sequence looks a bit like Figure 11-2. To make the figure more concrete, I've drawn the case for a WM_PAINT message and assumed the receiving control is a System.Windows.Forms.TextBox.

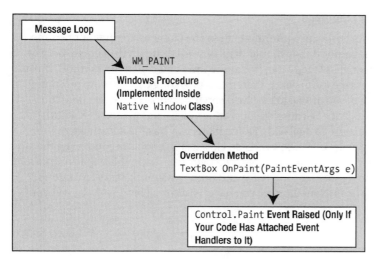

Figure 11-2. *The process of raising a* Paint *event*

Incidentally, this sequence is the reason why some developers regard it as better practice to override Control.OnPaint() and similar methods rather than add an event handler to the Paint event. Overriding OnPaint() will give marginally better performance because it saves raising an event. However, the difference is really too small to be significant in most applications.

That accounts for the Windows procedures. How about the message loop? That comes from the Application object. If you code in C++ or C#, you'll be aware that the Main() method for a Windows Forms application looks like this:

```
// C# code
static void Main()
{
    Application.Run(new Form1());
}
```

The static Application.Run() method takes the form that it has been supplied, locates its Windows procedure, and registers it with Windows. Then it starts executing a message loop.

If you normally code in VB, you may not have seen the Application.Run() method. That's because the VS .NET, working in conjunction with the VB compiler, hides the Main() method and the call to Application.Run() so that these items are not part of the source code that you can see but are instead added implicitly during compilation. But if you use ildasm.exe to examine the emitted IL, you'll see that this code is present in the emitted IL.

Some Message Loop Concepts

Now that you've seen the basic principles underlying the Windows message loop, I'll explain a few concepts and implications in more detail, which will help you to understand some of the samples I'll be presenting later in the chapter.

Understanding When Painting Happens

If you've done a lot of Windows Forms programming, then the chances are that at one time or another you've called some method that should display something on the screen, only to find that the data has only been displayed later, not at the time you called the method. If you don't understand how the message loop works, then this type of bug can be quite puzzling, but with your new knowledge of the message loop you can now work out the explanation.

In general, most painting is done because the operating system has posted a WM_PAINT message for the Windows procedure to deal with. Doing it this way has the advantage that if several paint jobs have to take place, Windows can do clever things such as combining the messages on the queue, which may save some duplicated painting—something that's important since painting is one of the most processor-intensive and time-consuming tasks a Windows Forms application commonly does. Now suppose you have a listbox called listBox1, and you execute this code:

```
void MyMethod()
{
    // Some processing
    listBox1.Items.Add("My new item");
    // Some more intensive processing
}
```

As you can see, during the course of this code, a new item is added to a listbox, and you may deduce that the listbox will need to be repainted as a consequence in order to show the new item on the screen. However, the ListItemCollection.Add() method that's invoked in this code doesn't do this painting directly. Instead, it posts a WM_PAINT message to the queue, with accompanying data that indicates exactly which area of the listbox on the screen needs repainting. Then the Add() method returns control back to the MyMethod() method, which carries on performing its intensive processing. If this intensive processing lasts for several seconds, you won't see the new item appear in the listbox for several seconds, because the required drawing to the screen won't take place until the WM_PAINT message is processed. In a Windows Forms application, if MyMethod() is being executed on the main thread, it must have been invoked by some event handler—that's the only way the main thread in a Windows Forms application ever normally executes any methods. In other words, everything happens in response to an event. The main thread won't get to look at the message queue until the current event handler has completely finished. Once that happens, execution flow will transfer back into the message loop, and, assuming there aren't any other higher priority messages, the WM_PAINT message will be processed and the listbox will be updated on the screen.

This architecture has two consequences. You've just seen the first consequence: Painting can be delayed. But the second consequence is more subtle: The message loop is being executed by the main UI thread, which means that it's always the main UI thread that gets to handle the messages. So even if, in the previous example, MyMethod() was actually being executed on some other worker thread, the actual painting will end up taking place on the main application thread, in the Paint event handler(s). Clearly, if you're writing multithreaded applications, that information is rather important for writing correct thread-synchronization code! Of course, if MyMethod() is executing on a different thread, then the actual painting may take place before MyMethod() exits, if the main thread becomes available to process messages earlier. Incidentally, that the painting takes place on the main thread is normally regarded as a good thing since it's considered good practice to only allow one thread to deal with the user interface. The Windows Forms classes have been designed with this assumption in mind, which means most of their methods aren't thread safe.

The previous reasoning applies to any method on the Windows Forms classes that works internally by posting a message. In general, all drawing operations work this way. So if you do anything to a control that would require it to be redrawn—or for that matter, if you call the Control.Invalidate() method to explicitly request repainting—then the painting won't happen until the WM_PAINT message is processed. (Control.Invalidate() is a method supplied by Microsoft that's designed to cause a control to be repainted. Its implementation basically posts a WM_PAINT message for the control.) If for some reason you want the display to be updated immediately, then you should call the Control.Refresh() method. This method is similar to Invalidate(), but after posting the message, it directly calls the Windows procedure. This bypasses the message loop so that the painting code can execute immediately, but it still means you can take advantage of things such as merging invalidated regions. In that case, the previous code would look like this:

```
void MyMethod()
{
    // Some processing
    listBox1.Items.Add("My new item");
    listBox1.Refresh();
    // Some more intensive processing.
}
```

You can also use the Control.Update() method, which is similar to Refresh(), but Update() just gets the control redrawn without calling Invalidate() first.

■**Note** The previous discussion applies to methods such as Invalidate() that internally post a message to the queue. Don't get confused between this and events. If you define your own event in a control or form and then raise the event, the event handler will be executed inline, just as for events and delegates in any other application. The message loop isn't involved in this process. Remember that Windows Forms events don't themselves have anything directly to do with the message queue.

Applying Multithreading to Windows Forms Applications

One of the neatest things about the message loop is the way it allows threads to communicate with each other in a multithreaded application. When the main UI thread picks up a message from the queue, it doesn't know or care which thread originally left the message there. All it cares about is that a message exists with some data that needs to be processed. This means that if you have worker threads in an application, then these threads can leave data or instructions for the main thread simply by posting a message to the queue. This provides a convenient alternative way of communicating between threads that doesn't involve the thread-synchronization primitives I discussed in Chapter 9. This facility is restricted; it provides only one-way communication, from a worker thread to the UI thread that's running the message loop, and it has the disadvantage that posting and processing a message involves more overhead than, for example, using a Monitor class. On the other hand, posting messages can't block a thread, and it means you can avoid some of the subtle thread-synchronization bugs that occur with traditional means of passing data between threads.

If you want to use this technique to pass data to the main thread (or if you want to get some method called on the main thread), then you'll need to use the Control.BeginInvoke()/ EndInvoke() methods, which I'll cover in the next section.

Another intriguing aspect of the message loop is the way that the message loop gives you many of the benefits of multithreading, but without some of the disadvantages—even just for the single UI thread. Recall that the real gain in a multithreaded program is the way the program can smoothly context switch, as the CPU swaps between different threads, making it appear that several tasks are being executed at the same time. With a message loop, this switching between different tasks happens too. The program responds to one event, and then it responds to another event. Each time it has finished executing one event handler, the thread is free to perform whatever task is waiting next. This actually means that you can have the UI thread of a message loop–based application perform background tasks in a similar manner to having a background thread. Despite this, however, it's normal to use additional threads to perform background tasks in order to avoid blocking the user interface for any time. An important principle of the operation of the message loop is that processing each message should take as little time as possible so that the computer quickly becomes free to respond to the next message; hence, slow non-UI-related tasks will normally be performed by worker threads away from the message loop.

Coding with Control.BeginInvoke()

BeginInvoke() is an incredibly useful method implemented by the Control class to provide a way of getting the main thread to do something. In terms of the way you call this method, it looks on the outside similar to the BeginInvoke() methods that are implemented by many delegates. Like the delegate version, Control.BeginInvoke() comes as part of a method pair; a similar, though less useful, EndInvoke() method, waits for the method executed by BeginInvoke() to return. However, the internal implementation could hardly be more different. BeginInvoke() called against a delegate will cause the specified method to be executed on a randomly chosen thread-pool thread. Control.BeginInvoke() by contrast will execute the specified method on the application's main UI thread. Control.BeginInvoke() appears to work internally by posting a custom message to the message queue, this message being recognized by the Control class as a request to execute the specified method.

In terms of semantics, BeginInvoke() looks like this:

```
// Definition only.
IAsyncResult BeginInvoke(Delegate method, object[] args)
```

The first parameter is a delegate (of any type), which indicates the method to be called. The second parameter contains an array of objects that should be passed to this method. This array will be unpacked and each element passed in; for example, if the method is expecting two parameters, you should supply an array containing two elements. A second override of BeginInvoke() has only one parameter and can be used to invoke methods that take no arguments. You can use the IAsyncResult interface that's returned in the same way as that returned from the delegate implementation of BeginInvoke(); you can monitor the status of the method and supply it to a call to EndInvoke(). Bear in mind that, although BeginInvoke() invokes a method on the main thread, you can still think of it as an asynchronous method call. If you call BeginInvoke() from a worker thread, then the effect is similar—the call is sent off to a different thread. If you call BeginInvoke() from the main thread, then the call still returns immediately, and the method call request is left waiting to execute as soon as the event handler that's currently executing has completed. In this chapter you'll see a couple of samples of how you can use BeginInvoke(), in both a single-threaded and a multithreaded environment.

Bear in mind that, although Control.BeginInvoke() is available, you can still call the delegate-implemented version of BeginInvoke(), if running on a thread-pool thread is what you need.

■Tip It's also worth noting another method, Control.Invoke(). This has a similar operation to BeginInvoke(), but where BeginInvoke() returns immediately, Invoke() will actually block the calling thread until a the main thread has returned a result from the operation. Invoke() will then return this result. Invoke() can be simpler to use but is more likely to hurt performance through thread blocking, and whereas BeginInvoke() can be called from any thread, Invoke() is intended for worker threads.

Understanding Handles

Although handles don't strictly speaking have anything directly to do with the message loop, a quick word about them will be useful here.

Underlying Windows objects such as controls, forms, windows, and so on, are encapsulated in managed code by classes, usually in the Windows.Forms namespace, as is the case for GDI+ objects that are responsible for painting. These objects are encapsulated by classes in the System.Drawing namespace. For example, you have a Pen class, a Brush class, and so on. However, the Windows API was written many years ago, when C was the common language of choice, and object-oriented programming, classes, and C++ represented new ideas that weren't yet in common use. Hence, the Windows API doesn't use classes. Instead, objects such as windows and graphics objects are represented by *handles*. A handle is simply an integer that can identify a resource. If you think of them as indexes into a table of data structures that the operating system knows about, the table being located deep in the bowels of Windows, then you won't be far wrong. Although handles rarely appear explicitly in elementary Windows Forms programming, they're always there under the hood, and when you start to do more advanced stuff, you do sometimes encounter them—and they will crop up in some of the sample code later in this chapter. Recall that I indicated earlier in this chapter that the first field in the MSG structure that represents a Windows message is a handle, which identifies the window for which the message is intended.

In managed code, handles are represented by an instance of the class, System.IntPtr; this is also the type normally used for storing unmanaged pointers and any native integers whose size is determined by the hardware.

Accessing the Message Loop

Although I've said a lot about how the Windows Forms classes normally hide the underlying message loop from you, in fact the `Control` class does define a couple of methods that allow you to tap into the message loop at a relatively low level—to the point at which you can actually alter the processing the Windows procedure performs in response to certain messages. One reason why you'd need to do this is that, although the list of events defined in `Control` and derived classes is quite comprehensive, it's confined to those events relevant to common UI scenarios. A number of more rarely used Windows messages exist for which the `Control` class doesn't define any corresponding events. This list includes, for example, the various nonclient messages that are related to painting and UI events outside the client area of the form. If you, for some reason, need to handle a message for which no corresponding event exists, you'll need to work at a lower level than the usual Windows Forms events. I'll present a sample in the section "Directly Handling Messages" that demonstrates how you can override `Control.WndProc()` to provide custom processing for certain Windows messages.

Idle Processing

Idle processing means you arrange to have the main UI thread call a method known as an *idle event handler* when no messages are waiting on the queue. The idle event handler does some processing, and then it returns control to the message loop. Doing things this way is less flexible than real multithreading (and carries a real risk of destroying application responsiveness if you're not extremely careful), but it does save you from worrying about having multiple threads and all the associated thread-synchronization issues. Doing idle processing used to be a common technique for giving some appearance of multitasking in Windows applications back in the days when writing genuinely multithreaded applications was quite difficult. Since .NET provides such extensive support for multithreaded techniques, there really is little excuse for using idle processing techniques in a Windows Forms application. However, if you for any reason want to do so, then the technique is simple: you simply supply a handler to the `Application.Idle` event in your code.

Examining Message Loop Samples

In the following sections I'll present three samples that illustrate the topics I've been discussing. One sample will illustrate directly handling Windows messages in your code, and the other two samples are concerned with writing multithreaded applications using `Control.BeginInvoke()` to communicate with the main UI thread. The first of these two samples illustrates how to provide information about the initialization of the application where this takes a while, and the second illustrates a long operation performed on a background thread that the user can abort at any time; both of these are common tasks that require using multithreaded techniques in conjunction with the message loop to implement in a way that doesn't interfere with application responsiveness.

Directly Handling Messages

This sample illustrates how you can write code that directly responds to Windows messages in the Windows procedure for a control.

The usual technique for doing this is to override the protected method, Control.WndProc(). WndProc() (and various other methods that it in turn invokes) is the method that provides much of the processing for the control's Windows procedure; it's the method that decides what to do with each message. It's not quite true to say that WndProc() is the Windows procedure for the control, since the actual Windows procedure is always native, unmanaged code. But in the case of managed Windows Forms applications, the real Windows procedure quickly calls into Control.WndProc() to do the processing, so you won't be far wrong if you informally think of WndProc() as the Windows procedure. This method takes an instance of the System.Windows.Forms.Message struct as a parameter; Message directly wraps the C MSG struct.

The message that this sample is going to handle is WM_QUERYENDSESSION, and the sample will be a short program that, depending on the user preferences, may refuse to close itself down either when the system is shutting down or when the user is logging out, thus preventing the shutdown or logout. You may want an application to do this, for example, if it's coming to the end of some long processing or for some reason shutting down now may cause some important data to be lost or corrupted.

The sample is called DontWantToClose, and when running, it looks something like Figure 11-3.

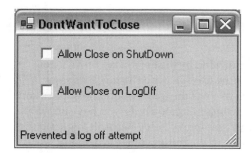

Figure 11-3. *The* DontWantToClose *sample*

If the user explicitly closes the application (such as by clicking the close button in the title bar), the sample always closes normally. However, if the system attempts to shut down or log off the user, then the application will close only if the user has checked the appropriate checkbox. Otherwise, the application will refuse to close; as a result, this will actually prevent the logoff or shutdown attempt and display a message in its status bar explaining what it's just done. Figure 11-3 shows the sample after I started it running and then hit Ctrl+Alt+Del and asked Windows to log off.

To understand the action of the sample, you need a bit of background about how windows applications are normally closed. If the application itself has chosen to close, then it will normally post a WM_CLOSE message to its message queue. The usual handler for this message kicks off the processing necessary to exit the application. The situation is however different if the user is logging off or if the system itself is shutting down and is as a result seeking to terminate running applications. In that case you won't have a WM_CLOSE message. Instead, Windows will post a WM_QUERYENDSESSION message to every running application that has a message loop. (The lParam field of this message indicates whether the end of session is because of a shutdown or logoff. If the user is logging off, then the leftmost bit of the lParam field, the bit with hex value 0x80000000, will be set to one.) The Windows procedure should be implemented to return one if the application is happy to exit and zero if that's not OK. (To keep the earlier discussion simpler, I didn't talk about return values from the Windows procedure earlier. In fact, the Windows procedure does return a value to Windows.) A well-behaved application will normally return one unless it has some unsaved data. If it has any unsaved data, it will most likely display a dialog box asking the user what to do, and its Windows procedure will return zero if the user indicates that the application shouldn't be closed. If just one running application returns zero in response to WM_QUERYENDSESSION, then the system will abandon its shutdown/logoff attempt. However, if all the running applications indicate they're happy to shut down, then Windows will set about posting WM_ENDSESSION messages to them, informing them that it's going ahead and ending the user session.

For Windows Forms applications, the normal way you get to feed in any code into the process of closing is by handling the Closing and Closed events. The Closing event handler takes a CancelEventArgs parameter that you can use to cancel the process of closing the application.

```
private void Form1_Closing(object sender, CancelEventArgs e)
{
    // Probably have code to display a dialog box here
    if (ItsNotOKtoCloseTheApp())
        e.Cancel = true;
}
```

The trouble is that Closing is a high-level event provided by the Form class, and it's not able to distinguish between the different reasons why the form may be closing. This same Closing event will be raised whether the user is trying to close the application, the application has encountered an internal error, or the session is ending. In other words, you have no way to tell from the handler what the situation is. That's an example of how Microsoft has sought to make the Windows Forms classes easy to use by simplifying things somewhat and is arguably quite sensible because for most applications the information about why the application is closing isn't going to be relevant. However, if you need to know the reason why the application is being asked to shut down (and take some custom action depending what the reason is), then you'll need to override the main form's Control.WndProc() method to look for the WM_QUERYENDSESSION message and take appropriate action.

Despite all that long information, the actual coding you need to do for the sample is relatively simple. I just created the sample as a Windows Forms application and add the controls to it that you can see in Figure 11-3. I've named the checkboxes cbAllowCloseShutdown and cbAllowCloseLogOff.

I've also added a couple of constant member fields to the Form1 class.

```
public class Form1 : System.Windows.Forms.Form
{
    const uint WM_QUERYENDSESSION = 0x011;
    const uint ENDSESSION_LOGOFF = 0x80000000;
```

0x11 is the value that identifies that a message is the WM_QUERYENDSESSION, and ENDSESSION_LOGOFF is the bitwise flag that identifies a logoff session in the lParam field of the message. I found these values by inspecting my machine's winuser.h file. As I indicated earlier, this file defines the values for all the common Windows messages, so this is where you'll need to look for these values if you find yourself needing to manipulate messages directly.

Next here's my override of WndProc():

```
protected override void WndProc(ref Message msg)
{
    if (msg.Msg == WM_QUERYENDSESSION)
    {
        if (((int)msg.LParam & ENDSESSION_LOGOFF) > 0)
        {
            if (!this.cbAllowCloseLogOff.Checked)
            {
                msg.Result = IntPtr.Zero;
                this.statusBar.Text = "Prevented a log off attempt";
                return;
            }
        }
        else
        {
            if (!this.cbAllowCloseShutdown.Checked)
            {
                msg.Result = IntPtr.Zero;
                this.statusBar.Text = "Prevented a shutdown attempt";
                return;
            }
        }
    }
    base.WndProc(ref msg);
}
```

And that's all the code you need for the sample. My WndProc() override first tests to see if the message is WM_QUERYENDSESSION; this data is available as the Msg field of the Message structure. If so, then the code needs to check whether the end of session is because of a shutdown or a log off and compare with the state of the checkboxes to see if the user wants the code to permit the end of session request. If it's OK for the session to end, then you have no need for any custom actions; the code just calls the base class's WndProc() method to allow the message to be handled normally, just as happens for any other message. On the other hand, if the code finds it needs to block the shutdown request, then it displays an appropriate message in the status bar and sets the Result field of the Message structure to zero. The Result field is an artifact of .NET, and it doesn't exist in the original message. It contains the return value the Windows procedure should return. Recall that the true Windows procedure returns an integer, but you'll notice Control.WndProc() is defined as returning void; Message.Result is the way that the Control class knows what to do with the "real" Windows procedure.

■Tip If you download and run this sample, you'll need to run it without VS .NET to get the correct results. That's because if you run it from VS .NET and attempt to shut down or log off, you're likely to find that VS .NET receives a WM_QUERYENDSESSION message before the running sample does. And this may interfere with the operation of the sample because VS .NET may itself decide to kill the running application directly in response to the end of session, before the sample has a chance to receive the WM_QUERYENDSESSION.

The InitialUpdate Sample: Initializing an Application

In this section I'll develop a short program that illustrates how you can use Control.BeginInvoke() to have a method processed on the message loop. And this sample actually illustrates a situation in which BeginInvoke() is a useful technique. Let's suppose the application needs to do some processing at startup time. And I'll further assume that because this processing takes a couple of seconds, it's desirable to display progress information so the user is reassured that something is indeed happening. Where could you put the code that displays that information? You could display a dialog box before the main application starts, similar to a splash screen—that's one solution. But you may think a separate, prior dialog box looks messy; in some cases you may think it'd be neater for the application's main form to appear immediately and for the progress information to appear in that window. To achieve that, you'll ideally need to perform the initialization on a separate worker thread—to avoid problems of tying up the user interface by blocking the main thread. You may think that tying up the UI doesn't matter if the application is still initializing, but the problem is that the user may still want to do things such as move or resize the main form. By using a background thread, you ensure that the user can still do that. At the same time, by having the background thread use BeginInvoke() to update the UI to give progress reports, you can ensure that all actual UI operations are performed from the main thread and that you don't therefore run into thread synchronization issues associated with methods on Control not being thread safe.

The sample is called InitialUpdate, and it consists of a Windows form with a listbox called lbInitData and a button called btnDoSomething. I also used the VS .NET Properties window to disable the button. When the application starts, progress reports, as shown in Figures 11-4 and 11-5, appear in the listbox in the first few seconds.

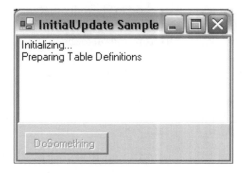

Figure 11-4. *The* InitialUpdate *sample soon after starting*

Notice that the DoSomething button is disabled—representing that until the application is initialized, much of its functionality is going to be disabled. As soon as the initialization is complete, the button is enabled.

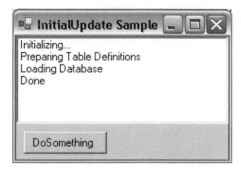

Figure 11-5. *The* InitialUpdate *once initialization is complete*

Of course, no database tables exist in the sample. The sample follows the same trick I used frequently in Chapter 10: it uses Thread.Sleep() to simulate an operation that takes some time to complete.

The form's Load event handler is the ideal place from which to spawn the worker thread to perform the initialization, because the form actually appears as soon as this handler has executed.

```
private void Form1_Load(object sender, System.EventArgs e)
{
   Thread initThread = new Thread(new ThreadStart(Initialize));
   initThread.Start();
}
```

Before I present the Initialize() method used to perform the initialization on the worker thread, you need to be aware of two delegates that I've defined.

```
private delegate void AddItemDelegate(string item);
private delegate void ReadyFormDelegate();
```

These delegate will enable the worker thread to invoke methods on the main thread.
Now here's the Initialize() method:

```
private void Initialize()
{
   this.BeginInvoke(new AddItemDelegate(AddItem), new object[] {
                                                "Initializing..." });
   Thread.Sleep(1500);
   this.BeginInvoke(new AddItemDelegate(AddItem), new object[] {
                                       "Preparing Table Definitions" });
   Thread.Sleep(1500);

   this.BeginInvoke(new AddItemDelegate(AddItem), new object[] {
                                       "Loading Database" });
```

```
    Thread.Sleep(1500);

    this.BeginInvoke(new AddItemDelegate(AddItem), new object[] { "Done" });
    this.BeginInvoke(new ReadyFormDelegate(DoneInitialize));
}
```

Initialize() itself invokes (via the delegates I've just mentioned and Control.BeginInvoke()) two other methods, AddItem() and DoneInitialize(). These methods, respectively, update the progress report and do whatever final processing is necessary in order to make the application ready for use (including enabling the DoSomething button). AddItem() looks like so:

```
private void AddItem(string item )
{
    lbInitData.Items.Add(item);
}
```

Notice that when calling BeginInvoke(), I've packed the string expected by AddItem() into an object[] array; BeginInvoke() will unpack this array. It may look inefficient, but it means that BeginInvoke() can invoke any method, no matter what parameters that method takes.

The following is the DoneInitialize() method:

```
private void DoneInitialize()
{
    this.button1.Enabled = true;
}
```

The AbortableOperation Sample

The sample I'll develop in this section is similar to the previous one to the extent that it involves spawning a background thread and having this background thread call BeginInvoke() to pass UI operations back to the main thread; however, this sample is considerably more complex. It simulates the situation in which the user has asked a Windows Forms application to perform some lengthy operation, and you want the user to have the option to cancel the operation if it's taking too long. The sample looks like Figure 11-6 when it starts.

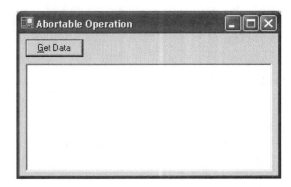

Figure 11-6. *The* AbortableOperation *sample, on startup*

When the user clicks the Get Data button, the form starts a background thread, which retrieves the data. A series of consecutive `Thread.Sleep()` calls means that this operation will take approximately ten seconds. However, the user is informed of the progress of the operation by a dialog box featuring a progress bar control, which is updated frequently (see Figure 11-7).

Figure 11-7. *The* `AbortableOperation` *sample progress dialog box*

When the operation has finished, the dialog box disappears and the data appears in the textbox of the main form. Because this is only a sample, I've put in a hard-coded string as the result (see Figure 11-8).

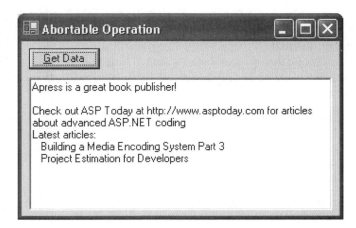

Figure 11-8. *The* `AbortableOperation` *sample after data retrieval*

A progress dialog box by itself isn't that impressive. However, what's novel about this application is that while the asynchronous operation is in progress, the user can at any time abort it by hitting the Cancel button. And just to make it even more realistic, I assume that it's not possible to cleanly abort the operation instantaneously—perhaps database connections need to be closed. So another `Sleep()` statement forces a one-second delay before the asynchronous worker thread can terminate properly. The operation is aborted by using the `Thread.Abort()` method, which will—as you saw in Chapter 9—cause a `ThreadAbortException` to be thrown on the worker thread so that the thread cleans up data. While the thread is aborting, the dialog box remains visible, but with the button now disabled and with a different caption (see Figure 11-9).

Figure 11-9. *The* AbortableOperation *sample, aborting*

In a real application, you may not want the dialog box to remain visible in this situation, depending on whether some reason (such as resources tied up by the aborting thread) would make it difficult for the application to continue normally until the thread has terminated.

The great thing about this application is that because the worker thread uses events (delegate events, not thread-synchronization events) and the Windows message loop to communicate with the main thread, I've been able to design the application in such a way that no member fields are at risk of being accessed simultaneously by more than one thread. Hence, you don't actually need to use any thread-synchronization objects anywhere! The same was true of the previous InitialUpdate sample, but it's more remarkable for this sample in view of the greater complexity of the interaction between the threads.

To create the application, I created a standard Windows Forms application and added the textbox and button to the form. I also used the VS .NET wizards to add a second form and added the progress bar control and button to it.

I'll deal with the code inside the second dialog box, which I've called AbortDialog, first, since that's where the simplest code is. The dialog box has a member field called mainForm that references the main application form, which is initialized in its constructor.

```
public AbortDialog(Form1 mainForm)
{
    //
    // Required for Windows Form Designer support
    //
    InitializeComponent();

    this.mainForm = mainForm;
}
```

I've also added a public method called SetProgress(), which sets the progress bar to indicate the required progress (as a percentage). (The progress bar defaults to the usual values of 0=no progress and 100=maximum.) This method will be called by the worker thread.

```
public void SetProgress(int progress)
{
    int increment = progress - progressBar1.Value;
    Debug.Assert(increment >= 0);
    this.progressBar1.Increment(increment);
}
```

Finally, here's the event handler called if the user clicks the Cancel button:

```
private void btnCancel_Click(object sender, System.EventArgs e)
{
    btnCancel.Enabled = false;
    mainForm.CancelAsyncOperation();
}
```

CancelAsyncOperation() is a method I've implemented in the Form1 class, which—well—does what its name says. I'll present this method in a moment. The following are a couple of member fields:

```
public class Form1 : System.Windows.Forms.Form
{
    private Thread backgroundThread;
    private AbortDialog abortDialog;
    private System.Windows.Forms.Button btnData;
    private System.Windows.Forms.TextBox tbData;
```

I'm sure you can guess what these fields will be storing. This code also tells you the names I've given the button and textbox: btnData and tbData.

Now the following is what's executed on the main thread when the user clicks the button:

```
private void btnData_Click(object sender, System.EventArgs e)
{
    this.tbData.Clear();
    ThreadStart entryPoint = new ThreadStart(RetrieveData);
    workerThread = new Thread(entryPoint);
    workerThread.Start();
    abortDialog = new AbortDialog(this);
    abortDialog.Show();
}
```

Basically, the main thread clears out the textbox and starts the new worker thread, indicating a method called RetrieveData() as the entry point. Then it displays the AbortDialog form as a modeless dialog box. Notice that the dialog box is shown on the main thread—this is important. The new dialog box is being run not only on the same thread but through the same message loop as the main form. Nothing is unusual about this; it's what normally happens for dialog boxes. The fact that I have a separate thread doing background work doesn't change that.

The following is the method that the worker thread has started running to retrieve the data:

```
private void RetrieveData()
{
    try
    {
        for (int i=5 ; i<=100 ; i+=5)
        {
            Thread.Sleep(500);
```

```
            SetProgressDelegate setProgress = new
                SetProgressDelegate(abortDialog.SetProgress);
            BeginInvoke(setProgress, new object[] {i});
        }
        string [] results = new String[1];
        results[0] = @"Apress is a great book publisher!
```

Check out ASP Today at http://www.asptoday.com for
articles about advanced ASP.NET coding
Latest articles:
   Building a Media Encoding System Part 3
   Project Estimation for Developers";

```
        ResultsReturnedDelegate resultsReturned = new
            ResultsReturnedDelegate(this.OnResultsReturned);
        BeginInvoke(resultsReturned, results);
    }
    finally
    {
        // Simulate it takes a short time to and clean up resources
        Thread.Sleep(1000);
    }
}
```

The thread enters a try block, where a for loop ensures that the progress bar is updated every half a second (500 milliseconds). After 20 iterations, or 10 seconds, the result can be displayed. The RetrieveData() method informs the main thread of both the progress updates and the final result by calling Control.BeginInvoke(). Recall that internally this will cause a message to be posted to the message loop that's executing on the main thread, causing the main thread to pick up the method supplied as soon as the main thread can process another message. The method invoked to display the final results is a method called OnResultsReturned(), which you'll see soon. The delegates used to wrap this method and the AbortDialog.SetProgress() method are defined in the Form1 class like so:

```
private delegate void SetProgressDelegate(int i);
public delegate void ResultsReturnedDelegate (string result);
```

Notice that the code passes the string that represents the result into the EventArgs. This means the string has been instantiated on the worker thread and will then be read on the main thread. However, no thread synchronization is required because string is immutable. I discussed this point in Chapter 9.

The finally block of the RetrieveData() method contains the Sleep() call that simulates the time taken. In a real application this may, for example, be the time required to close database connections.

Now, two things can happen: Either the user can cancel the operation or the operation can finish normally, causing the OnResultsReturned() method to be called. Let's examine what happens if the user cancels the operation first. Recall that the event handler for the Cancel button invokes the Form1.CancelAsyncOperation() method. Here's what happens in that method:

```
public void CancelAsyncOperation()
{
   Debug.Assert(abortDialog != null);
   backgroundThread.Abort();

   abortDialog.Text = "Aborting...";
   backgroundThread.Join();
   abortDialog.Close();
   abortDialog.Dispose();
}
```

The first thing that the main thread (which will be the thread executing this method) does is to tell the worker thread to abort. Then it changes the text of the dialog box and calls Thread.Join() to wait for the background thread to finish aborting. Once the background thread has cleaned up its resources and gone, the main thread closes the dialog box.

Now suppose the background thread runs to completion. In that case, the call it makes to Control.BeginInvoke() will cause this method to be executed from the message loop on the main thread.

```
public void OnResultsReturned(string result)
{
   this.tbData.Text = result;
   this.abortDialog.Close();
   this.abortDialog.Dispose();
}
```

As you can see, this method simply displays the result in the textbox and closes the dialog box. Notice that in this case I don't use Thread.Join() to wait for the background thread since the background thread isn't doing anymore lengthy work.

With that I've now completed covering the Windows message loop and shown how to use the message loop in conjunction with multithreading. The remainder of this chapter will switch topics and cover ways in which you can improve the visual appearance of your applications.

Using XP-Themed Controls

Windows XP brought with it a completely new appearance for its forms and controls, with rounded title bars, gradient-filled backgrounds on many controls, and rounded buttons that get highlighted as you move the mouse over them. However, you've probably noticed in the course of your .NET programming that while your applications show the XP-style title bar, the buttons and other controls on your forms have stubbornly continued to be drawn in the old Windows 2000 style. That's also the case for all the samples I've shown so far in this book. In this section I'll quickly go over how you can modify your projects so that your controls are drawn as XP-themed controls where appropriate.

The principle is actually fairly simple: You just need to make sure your application loads the correct version of comctl32.dll. This DLL is the unmanaged library in which the Windows common controls are implemented, and version 5 is the version that's loaded by default in Windows 9x/NT/2000/ME. With XP came version 6, which incorporates an awareness of XP themes and an ability to draw controls in the XP visual style. However, because themes are a new concept and require the application to be set up correctly to use them, Microsoft decided to leave version 5 as the version of comctl32.dll that's loaded by default. Hence, version 6 will only be loaded if an application explicitly indicates that it requires version 6—which presumably implies that it has been tested with themes. You indicate that an application should load version 6 by supplying a manifest. The manifest is an XML file, placed in the same folder as the application's executable file. The name of the manifest file should be the same as the name of the executable, with the suffix .manifest appended, such as MyApplication.exe.manifest. A suitable manifest file looks like this:

```
<?xml version="1.0" encoding="UTF-8" standalone="yes"?>
<assembly xmlns="urn:schemas-microsoft-com:asm.v1" manifestVersion="1.0">
<assemblyIdentity
    version="1.0.0.0"
    processorArchitecture="X86"
    name="Microsoft.Winweb.XPThemes"
    type="win32"
/>
<description>.NET control deployment tool</description>
<dependency>
    <dependentAssembly>
      <assemblyIdentity
        type="win32"
        name="Microsoft.Windows.Common-Controls"
        version="6.0.0.0"
        processorArchitecture="X86"
        publicKeyToken="6595b64144ccf1df"
        language="*"
      />
    </dependentAssembly>
</dependency>
</assembly>
```

This XML file is the one used in the XPThemes sample I'm about to present and is therefore called XPThemes.exe.manifest. To adapt it to other programs, you just need to rename it and change the name attribute to "Microsoft.Winweb.<AppName>".

For most .NET controls, that's all you need to do, but for any class derived from System.Windows.Forms.ButtonBase, you need to set the ButtonBase.FlatStyle property to the value FlatStyle.System. FlatStyle indicates the way in which buttons are drawn and is by default set to FlatStyle.Standard. FlatStyle.Standard draws standard buttons but also allows for owner-draw buttons in which your code takes responsibility for part of the drawing operation. This isn't acceptable for themed controls; for that, it's important that the system controls the entire drawing process.

The XPThemes sample illustrates these principles. It's a simple form with a number of miscellaneous controls and a checkbox that indicates whether to display themes. With the checkbox checked, the sample looks like Figure 11-10—on Windows XP that is. Obviously, if you run the sample on previous versions of Windows, you'll just see standard 9x-style controls.

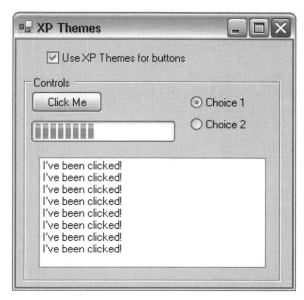

Figure 11-10. *The* XPThemes *sample*

If you uncheck the checkbox marked Use XP Themes for Buttons, the sample immediately redraws itself like Figure 11-11.

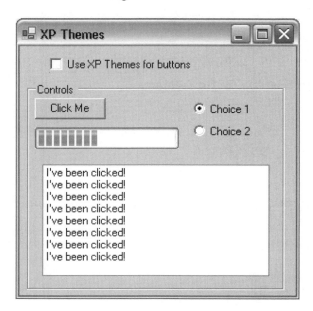

Figure 11-11. *The* XPThemes *sample, with XP themes for controls disabled*

Notice that the progress bar and listbox remain in the XP style; the sample works by modifying the FlatStyle property of the controls that have this property, but it clearly can't change the version of comctl32.dll that it's using, so controls not derived from ButtonBase remain XP themed. The Click Me button, when clicked, increments the progress bar and adds the line *I've been clicked!* to the listbox. The radio button controls don't do anything—they're just there to demonstrate their appearance.

To create the sample, I began with a standard Windows Forms application. To this I added a couple of methods that iterate through all the controls on the form, setting the FlatStyle property of any that it finds are derived from ButtonBase.

```
public void SetXPTheme()
{
    foreach (Control control in this.Controls)
    {
        if (control is ButtonBase)
            ((ButtonBase)control).FlatStyle = FlatStyle.System;
    }
    this.Invalidate();
}
public void SetPreXPStyle()
{
    foreach (Control control in this.Controls)
    {
        if (control is ButtonBase)
            ((ButtonBase)control).FlatStyle = FlatStyle.Standard;
    }
    this.Invalidate();
}
```

Next I added the following event handler for the checkbox to set the style:

```
private void cbXP_CheckedChanged(object sender, System.EventArgs e)
{
    if (cbXP.Checked)
        SetXPTheme();
    else
        SetPreXPStyle();
}
```

Finally, I added the event handler for clicking the button—just so the button does something.

```
private void btnClickMe_Click(object sender, System.EventArgs e)
{
    progressBar.Increment(5);
    lbResults.Items.Add("I've been clicked!");
}
```

For the application to run correctly, you'll need to copy the manifest file to the folder containing its executable—either Debug or Release after the first time you compile it. You'll find the manifest has been included as a text file with the code download.

Creating Nonrectangular Windows

One rather neat but relatively little-used feature of Windows that has been around for a couple of years is the ability to create windows—both forms and controls—that aren't rectangular in shape. This facility is implemented by Windows itself rather than by .NET and is available whether or not you're using managed code. The design of the Windows.Forms classes, however, makes nonrectangular windows particularly easy to accomplish in managed code. Although the feature doesn't seem to be used widely in third-party code, you can see the principle at work in almost every form in Windows XP—in those XP-style title bars with the round corners. I'll now present a couple of samples that show how you can take advantage of this feature, as well as owner-draw controls, to modify your user interface. You may want to do this, for example, if you're writing an application for home use (rather than business use) by non-IT-professionals, and where because of the particular nature of your product, it's important that it has a distinctive appearance. I should warn you, however, that once you start designing your own visual design, it takes a huge amount of work to get something that looks good, original, and professional. Because the samples in this chapter are designed to illustrate the programming principles in as few pages as possible, they won't look particularly professional but will give you an idea of what can in principle be done.

■**Caution** Customizing the appearance of controls risks making your applications harder to use because users who are already familiar with the standard appearance of controls have to get used to the unique appearance designed by your graphics team. For this reason you could also annoy users. You may want to avoid using this feature in applications (notably applications intended for business use) where user familiarity with the appearance of controls is more important than a distinctive appearance.

The Concepts

If you want any form or control to be nonrectangular, the way to do this is to set its Control.Region property to indicate the region within which you want the form to be displayed. For example, if you want a form that's shaped as a downward-pointing equilateral triangle of width 200, you could use the following code inside the Form constructor:

```
GraphicsPath outline = new GraphicsPath();
outline.AddLine(0, 0, 200, 0);
outline.AddLine(200, 0, 100, 174);
outline.AddLine(100, 174, 0, 0);
Region rgn = new Region(outline);
this. Region = rgn;
```

Although this is simple in principle, you need to be aware of a couple of complicating factors. Setting a region will automatically prevent the form from displaying as an XP-themed form, so you'll be back to the Windows 2000/9x title bar, unless of course you take control of the drawing of that area—customizing your UI really is an all-or-nothing thing. When you define the region that you want the form to be confined to, Windows simply sets up a clipper that makes sure that no drawing can take place outside of this region. It also intercepts mouse events so that they're sent to this form only if the mouse is located within the region. However, for all other purposes, Windows still regards the form as occupying the full original rectangle. This means that all drawing and measuring operations take place with coordinates relative to the top-left corner of the original rectangle, and Windows doesn't make any attempt to adjust any drawing to take account of your region. Anything that would have been displayed outside of the region you've defined simply gets clipped. That includes any text in any controls, as well as borders, the title bar, the caption, and the close, minimize, and maximize buttons on a form. This can have unfortunate consequences; users are unlikely to appreciate a form that doesn't have a title bar, especially when they discover they have no way to visually tell if the form has the focus, and they can't click somewhere on the form to move, resize, minimize, maximize, or close it! So if you're going to create nonrectangular forms, you need to be careful how you go about it. You really have two options—make sure your region includes all the important areas of the form, or write your own code to implement your own title bar and other items somewhere that's visible. The latter option is of course a huge task—something to be undertaken only if it's really important for the form to be that particular shape.

■Tip You should also be aware that the Visual Studio .NET Design View draws controls occupying their default rectangular areas and doesn't take account of nonrectangular regions.

The CircularForm Sample

I'll now present a sample in which I develop a form with a semicircular shape, as shown in Figure 11-12.

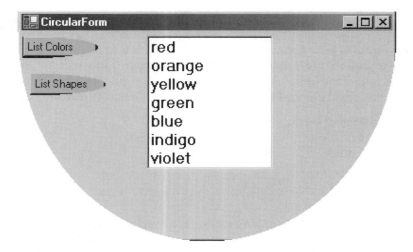

Figure 11-12. *The* CircularForm *sample*

The form has two buttons on the left, one of which populates the listbox in the center of the form with names of the colors of the rainbow and the other with the names of 2D shapes. I've specified that not only the main form but also the two buttons have a half-elliptical shape. The listbox retains its normal rectangular shape for now. The ultimate aim is for the listbox to be the same shape as the form (the lower half of an ellipse), but that would mean much of the text in the listbox wouldn't be displayed since it would lie outside the ellipse. You can solve that with problem an owner-draw listbox—and I'll do that in the next section when I cover owner-draw controls. But for now I'll leave the listbox as a rectangle.

The form is of course resizable, and if the form is resized, the buttons will automatically reposition themselves down the left curve of the form's border, but the listbox will remain central; this means you can freely resize the form, and it'll still keep its unusual, groovy-looking appearance.

Figure 11-12 already illustrates some of the potential problems associated with nonrectangular windows. It's clear that the edges of both the form and the buttons look visibly untidy. You could solve this by manually drawing a border around the curved edge of the form and by setting up the buttons as owner-draw buttons, but since doing so involves a fair amount of work and doesn't demonstrate any new principles, so I'll leave the sample as it is.

The sample is a standard Windows Forms VS .NET project, with the buttons and listbox added as shown. The controls are respectively named btnColors, btnShapes, and lbResults. I've also changed the font size in the listbox to a larger, bolder font as shown in Figure 11-12 and set the form's MinimumSize property to (350,250); any smaller size would make ruin the appearance of the form, since the buttons would overlap the listbox.

I added the following member fields to the form:

```
public class Form1 : System.Windows.Forms.Form
{
    private const int nButtons = 2;
    private Button [] buttons;

    private string [] colors = { "red", "orange", "yellow", "green",
                                 "blue", "indigo", "violet" };
    private string [] shapes = { "square", "circle", "triangle",
                                 "hexagon", "pentagon" };
    private System.Windows.Forms.Button btnColors;
    private System.Windows.Forms.Button btnShapes;
    private System.Windows.Forms.ListBox lbResults;
```

The fields colors and shapes are the string arrays that contain the text to be added to the listbox. buttons is an array that will hold the two Button references—holding these in an array will simplify the code to manipulate them. The array is initialized in the constructor.

```
public Form1()
{
    InitializeComponent();

    buttons = new Button[nButtons];
    buttons[0] = btnColors;
    buttons[1] = btnShapes;
```

```
    SetButtonRegions();
    DoResize();
}
```

SetButtonRegions() is the method that sets the shape of the buttons, and DoResize()
sets the shape of the form and the location of the controls. I'll present the code for these
methods soon. DoResize() needs to be invoked whenever the size of the form changes.
The recommended place to handle updating the layout of controls on a form is in the form's
Layout event handler, so I added the following handler:

```
private void Form1_Layout(object sender,
                             System.Windows.Forms.LayoutEventArgs e)
{
    DoResize();
}
```

DoResize() simply calls a number of other methods to shape the form and lay out the
buttons and listbox in the most appropriate positions given the form's new size.

```
private void DoResize()
{
    SetFormRegion();
    SetButtonLocations();
    SetListBoxLocation();
}
```

The following is the code to set the shape of the buttons: the SetButtonRegion() method.
Note that this method doesn't need to be called from the Layout event handler since the size
and shape of the buttons don't change after form startup—only the locations. This method is
therefore invoked only from the Form1 constructor.

```
private void SetButtonRegions()
{
    int width = this.buttons[0].Width;
    int height = this.buttons[0].Height;
    GraphicsPath outline = new GraphicsPath();
    Rectangle twiceButtonRect = new Rectangle(-width, 0, 2 * width, height);
    outline.AddArc(twiceButtonRect, -90, 180);
    outline.AddLine(0, height, 0, 0);
    Region rgn = new Region(outline);
    foreach (Button button in this.buttons)
        button.Region = rgn;
}
```

This code instantiates a System.Drawing.Drawing2D.GraphicsPath object, which
will be used to define the region. The half-ellipse is added to the path using the
GraphicsPath.AddArc() method. This method needs to be supplied with a Rectangle that
defines the size that the full ellipse would have if it were drawn in full. Since the right half of
the ellipse occupies the full button rectangle, the Rectangle supplied here needs to be twice
that size, stretching out to the left of the button. All coordinates in the regions are given

relative to the top-left corner of each button, which means the same Region can be used for both buttons. The AddLine() call closes the GraphicsPath, so you end up with a path that looks like Figure 11-13.

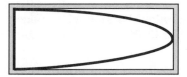

Figure 11-13. *The graphics path used to define the buttons*

In Figure 11-13, the thick line indicates the required graphics path, and the thin line indicates the border of the button.

The code to set up the region for the form is more complex, because the region is more complex in shape. I don't want it to simply be a semi-ellipse because I don't want any of the title bar to be cut out of the region. Instead, I set up a region that consists of a rectangle covering the title bar and of a half-ellipse below it (see Figure 11-14).

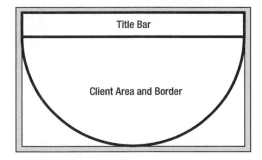

Figure 11-14. *The graphics path for the main form*

The code to set up this region looks like this:

```
private void SetFormRegion()
{
    int titleBarHeight = this.ClientTopLeft.Y;
    int remainingHeight = this.Height - titleBarHeight;
    GraphicsPath outline = new GraphicsPath();
    outline.AddLine(0, titleBarHeight, 0, 0);
    outline.AddLine(0,0,this.Width,0);
    outline.AddLine(Width, 0, Width, titleBarHeight);

    // twiceClientRect covers area below title bar and equal
    // area above it, to set bounds for ellipse
    Rectangle twiceClientRect = new Rectangle(0, titleBarHeight -
                    remainingHeight, this.Width, 2 * remainingHeight);
```

```
      outline.AddArc(twiceClientRect, 0, 180);
      Region rgn = new Region(outline);
      this.Region = rgn;
   }
```

This code uses a small utility property that works out the location of the top-left corner of the client area of the screen relative to the top-left corner of the form; the y-coordinate of this relative offset gives the title bar height.

```
public Point ClientTopLeft
{
   get
   {
      Point pt = PointToScreen(new Point(0, 0));
      return new Point(pt.X - this.Location.X, pt.Y - this.Location.Y);
   }
}
```

Next, the following code sets the listbox location and size; this code is called from the DoResize() method and hence invoked at construction time and whenever the form is resized. The listbox is to be located one-third across the form horizontally and has height two-thirds of the client area height of the form.

```
private void SetListBoxLocation()
{
   this.lbResults.Location = new Point(this.Width / 3, 5);
   this.lbResults.Size = new Size(this.Width / 3,
                                  (this.ClientSize.Height * 2) / 3);
}
```

Setting the button location is more complex since the location depends on the curve of the left side of the form. The following utility method works out how many pixels across from the left side of the form's rectangular area the actual border is at a given number of pixels from the top:

```
private int LeftBorderY2X(int y)
{
   int titleBarHeight = this.ClientTopLeft.Y;
   int remainingHeight = this.Height - titleBarHeight;
   double yOverH = ((double)y) / ((double)remainingHeight);
   double sqrt = Math.Sqrt(1.0 - yOverH * yOverH);
   return (int)((1.0 - sqrt) * ((double)this.Width) / 2.0);
}
```

Don't worry too much about the math. It's basically using Pythagoras's theorem. Now, with the following utility method, it's easy to position the buttons:

```
private void SetButtonLocations()
{
   for (int i=0; i<nButtons; i++)
```

```
   {
      int y = 5 + (int)((double)(this.buttons[0].Height * i) * 1.7);
      int x = LeftBorderY2X(y + this.buttons[i].Height);
      this.buttons[i].Location = new Point(x, y);
   }
}
```

This code places the first button five pixels below the title bar and then separates the buttons by 70 percent of their height. (I assume all buttons are the same size; I made sure of that when I first added the buttons to the main form in the VS .NET Design View.) Each button is inset so that its bottom-left corner just touches the curved border of the form.

That deals with all the code needed to lay out the controls. I'll now go back to more routine Windows Forms stuff; it's also necessary to supply event handlers for the buttons.

```
private void btnShapes_Click(object sender, System.EventArgs e)
{
   lbResults.Items.Clear();
   lbResults.Items.AddRange(this.shapes);
}
private void btnColors_Click(object sender, System.EventArgs e)
{
   lbResults.Items.Clear();
   lbResults.Items.AddRange(this.colors);
}
```

And that completes the application.

Using Owner-Draw Controls

I mentioned in the CircularForm sample that it wasn't sensible to give the listbox a round shape without altering the way it displays its text in order to make sure that the text for each item is placed firmly within the visible region of the listbox. This means writing the listbox as an owner-draw control. That's the subject of this section. I'll enhance the CircularForm sample into a new sample called CircularFormOwnerDraw, which looks like Figure 11-15.

Figure 11-15 ought to give you some idea of how distinctive you can make your Windows Forms applications when you start implementing owner-draw, nonrectangular, controls. Not only do the names of the colors in the listbox line up with its curved boundary, but each one is displayed on a background of the correct color, painted with a gradient brush, so you get a visible rainbow effect. (Unfortunately, you can't see the colors on a grayscale-printed page! You'll have to download the code if you want to see the full effect.) You'll also notice that the heights of the items get slightly bigger as you move down the listbox—compensating to some extent for the reduction in width, so the items appear to occupy something more like the same area. The selected item in the listbox is displayed with a solid rather than a gradient brush. Again, this may be difficult to see in the grayscale-printed book, but Figure 11-15 shows the situation with the green item selected.

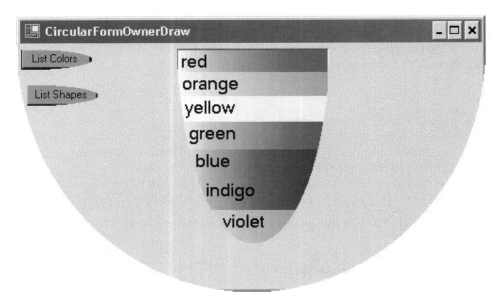

Figure 11-15. *The* CircularFormOwnerDraw *sample*

The different colors and item heights appear only if the listbox currently displays the colors. If it's displaying shapes, then the text of each item is still offset to follow the curve of the listbox border, but the items all have a white background. If you download and run the sample, swapping between the two views will quickly bring home just how boring controls can look if you haven't used the owner-draw facility to spice them up.

Owner-Draw Controls Basics

Although you can draw controls manually by overriding their OnPaint() method, not every control has built-in support for owner drawing. The ones that currently have built-in support are ListBox, ComboBox, MenuItem, TabControl, StatusBar, and classes derived from those. If a control is an owner-draw control, that means when an item in the control needs to be drawn, Windows doesn't draw the control itself. Instead, an event called DrawItem is raised. You can implement a handler for this event, which should do the drawing. You get complete control over what the control looks like. DrawItem is passed a DrawItemEventArgs parameter, which contains all the information you need to do the drawing, including which item is to be drawn, whether this item is selected, what the default foreground and background colors would be for drawing the item if the control weren't owner-draw, and—most important—a Rectangle struct that indicates the bounds within which the item needs to be drawn.

So that's the theory. How do you actually make an item owner-draw? For ListBox and ComboBox you need to set a property called DrawMode. This property is an enum type, also called DrawMode, and can have one of these values:

Normal: This is the default value.

OwnerDrawFixed: This means that the control will be owner-draw, with the DrawItem event being raised.

OwnerDrawVariable: This is similar to OwnerDrawFixed, except that immediately before the DrawItem event is raised, another event, MeasureItem, is raised. MeasureItem gives you the chance to modify the bounding rectangle of the item so that items will be displayed in different sizes. The location of subsequent items is automatically adjusted to take account of any changes in size of previous items.

The OwnerDrawVariable value will be ignored for multicolumn listboxes; variable item size isn't supported for this case.

The CircularFormOwnerDraw Sample

I created the CircularFormOwnerDraw sample by modifying the code for the previous CircularForm sample. First, I used the Properties window to set the DrawMode property of the listbox to OwnerDrawVariable. Second, in code, I used the Region property of the listbox to actually change it to a half-ellipse shape. The logic for doing this follows the same principles as for the form and buttons in the last sample.

```
private void SetListBoxLocation()
{
    int lbHeight = (this.ClientSize.Height * 8) / 9;
    int lbWidth = (this.ClientSize.Width) / 3;
    this.lbResults.Location = new Point(this.Width / 3, 5);
    this.lbResults.Size = new Size(lbWidth, lbHeight);

    int titleBarHeight = this.ClientTopLeft.Y;
    int remainingHeight = this.Height - titleBarHeight;
    GraphicsPath outline = new GraphicsPath();
    outline.AddLine(0, 0, lbWidth, 0);
    Rectangle twiceClientRect = new Rectangle(0, -lbHeight, lbWidth,
                                   (int)(1.9 * lbHeight));
    outline.AddArc(twiceClientRect, 0, 180);
    Region rgn = new Region(outline);
    this.lbResults.Region = rgn;
}
```

This method actually changes the listbox location and size. I've kept the same width for the listbox—one-third the width of the form—but increased its size to eight-ninths of the height of the client area of the form. Now that the listbox has a rounded lower edge, it can be taller without running over the elliptical lower edge of the form.

In preparation for controlling what's displayed in the listbox, you need a couple more member fields of the Form1 class: an enum that defines what the listbox may currently be displaying and an array of Color structs that indicates the background color for each item.

```
public class Form1 : System.Windows.Forms.Form
{
    private enum ListBoxContents { Colors, Shapes, Nothing };
    private ListBoxContents itemSetToDisplay = ListBoxContents.Nothing;
    private const int nButtons = 2;
```

```
private Button[] buttons;
private string[] colors = { "red", "orange", "yellow", "green", "blue",
                             "indigo", "violet" };
private Color[] colorStructs = { Color.Red, Color.Orange, Color.Yellow,
                                 Color.Green, Color.Blue, Color.Indigo,
                                 Color.Violet };
private string[] shapes = { "circle", "triangle", "square", "pentagon",
                            "hexagon" };
```

The button Click event handlers now set the itemSetToDisplay field.

```
private void btnShapes_Click(object sender, System.EventArgs e)
{
   lbResults.Items.Clear();
   itemSetToDisplay = ListBoxContents.Shapes;
   lbResults.Items.AddRange(this.shapes);
}

private void btnColors_Click(object sender, System.EventArgs e)
{
   lbResults.Items.Clear();
   itemSetToDisplay = ListBoxContents.Colors;
   lbResults.Items.AddRange(this.colors);
}
```

And the listbox's MeasureItem event handler is implemented as follows:

```
private void lbResults_MeasureItem(object sender,
                 System.Windows.Forms.MeasureItemEventArgs e)
{
   if (itemSetToDisplay == ListBoxContents.Colors)
      e.ItemHeight += (2 * e.Index);
}
```

MeasureItem works by changing the item height inside the MeasureItemEventArgs that's passed into the event handler; this size is specifically available as the ItemHeight property. An ItemWidth property is also available, but you have no need to fiddle with that here. Notice that I increased the ItemHeight property only if the listbox is displaying colors; as noted earlier, the listbox doesn't change items sizes when displaying shapes.

The following is the DrawItem handler:

```
private void lbResults_DrawItem(object sender,
                         System.Windows.Forms.DrawItemEventArgs e)
{
   switch(this.itemSetToDisplay)
   {
      case ListBoxContents.Colors:
         PaintListBoxColors(e);
         break;
      case ListBoxContents.Shapes:
```

```
        PaintListBoxShapes(e);
        break;
    case ListBoxContents.Nothing:
        return;
    }
}
```

This method simply contains a switch statement, because the way items are drawn differs according to whether the listbox is displaying colors or shapes. If you're displaying shapes, the actual drawing is handled by the PaintListBoxShapes() method.

```
private void PaintListBoxShapes(DrawItemEventArgs e)
{
    e.Graphics.FillRectangle(new SolidBrush(e.BackColor), e.Bounds);
    e.Graphics.DrawString(this.shapes[e.Index], e.Font,
            new SolidBrush(e.ForeColor),
            e.Bounds.Left + GetListBoxLeft(e.Bounds.Bottom), e.Bounds.Top);
}
```

This method is relatively simple; it fills the background with the appropriate color and then draws the text over it. Notice how the colors, bounding rectangle, and item index are taken from the DrawItemEventArgs parameter.

This method also needs to make sure that the text of each item is indented sufficiently so that the curved border of the listbox doesn't cut it off. The principle here is no different from that used in the previous sample for positioning the buttons; it relies on a helper method that can work out how many horizontal pixels right of the original listbox bounding rectangle this border is, given the vertical distance in pixels down from the top of the listbox. This method is GetListBoxLeft(), and just as in the previous sample it uses Pythagoras's theorem to work out the offset.

```
private int GetListBoxLeft(int y)
{
    double yOverH = ((double)y) / ((double)lbResults.Height);
    double sqrt = Math.Sqrt(1.0 - yOverH * yOverH);
    return (int)((1.0 - sqrt) * ((double)lbResults.Width) / 2.0);
}
```

Finally, here's the code for drawing each item if the listbox is displaying colors:

```
private void PaintListBoxColors(DrawItemEventArgs e)
{
    Color leftColor = e.BackColor;
    string text = null;
    Brush brush = null;
    Color rightColor = this.colorStructs[e.Index];
    text = this.colors[e.Index];
    brush = new LinearGradientBrush(e.Bounds, leftColor, rightColor,
                                    LinearGradientMode.Horizontal);
```

```
    e.Graphics.FillRectangle(brush, e.Bounds);
    e.Graphics.DrawString(text, e.Font, new SolidBrush(e.ForeColor),
        e.Bounds.Left + GetListBoxLeft(e.Bounds.Bottom), e.Bounds.Top);
}
```

One point to notice about this code is that you don't need to take any special action for the case where this item is selected. In that case, the e.BackColor value from the DrawItemEventArgs parameter will automatically yield the correct background color for this item state. If, however, you need to know the item state, this is available as the e.State property. Also bear in mind that although I've coded up a drawing routine that displays text, in principle you can add code to draw whatever you want here—for example, you could replace the text with images that identify the item.

Comparing GDI and GDI+ for Graphics

In this section, I'll compare the GDI and GDI+ graphics APIs, and point out a few situations in which it's worthwhile dropping down to GDI for your graphics. I'm confining the discussion to static graphics—in other words, how to create a good still appearance for your form. If your application features animated graphics, then you'll most likely need to use DirectX, which I don't discuss in this book.

A common misconception is that GDI+ has got something to do with the .NET Framework. It's an understandable misconception because the two technologies, .NET and GDI+, arrived at about the same time, and Microsoft's publicity for Windows Forms has promoted that you can use GDI+ for drawing operations. In fact, however, GDI+ is a completely unmanaged API. It's not some kind of managed wrapper around GDI but is rather a completely independent API, implemented in gdiplus.dll, and existing side-by-side with GDI as an alternative means of providing high-level access to the display facilities offered by your graphics card. It's quite possible to instantiate the GDI+ classes and invoke their methods from unmanaged C++ code. The .NET Framework classes in the System.Drawing namespace are for the most part simply managed wrappers around the equivalent classes in gdiplus.dll. And these managed wrappers are very thin; in most cases the .NET classes have the same names and expose the same methods as the equivalent unmanaged classes. This has the rather nice incidental benefit that once you've learned how to use GDI+ in Windows Forms applications, you can directly transfer that knowledge into calling the native GDI+ classes from unmanaged C++, if you so want.

GDI or GDI+?

One question that occasionally arises about Windows Forms applications is, should you ever use GDI for your drawing operations? In almost all cases, you're better off with GDI+. However, the following are two cases in which you may want to drop back to use native GDI.

For functional reasons: To access features not available in GDI+. The GDI and the GDI+ libraries aren't completely equivalent in functionality. Some features are supported in GDI+ but not in GDI (for example, gradient brushes). And other features are supported in GDI but not in GDI+ (for example, Blitting from the screen into memory). If you want to do something such as that, then you can't use GDI+. Period. Another feature that's strictly GDI-only is support for different raster operations when Blitting. By the way, if you're not familiar with the term, *Blt* (short for *bit block transfer*) is the process of copying a rectangular image from one location to another. It's basically the same as calling `Graphics.DrawImage()` in GDI+.

For performance reasons: Now don't get me wrong here. I'm not saying that GDI is faster than GDI+. Indeed, Microsoft actually claims the reverse, that GDI+ offers performance improvements relative to GDI. In practice, however, the situation is more complex. Which API gives the better performance will depend on what you're doing and what hardware you're using. In the vast majority of cases, you'll gain little or no performance improvement from dropping to GDI. However, using GDI may be worth it if your application is to be run on older hardware. Also occasionally you may be able to architect your drawing routines better, and with more efficient algorithms, using GDI, because GDI gives you a finer degree of control over the graphics drawing objects.

I'll say a bit more about performance issues here. GDI and GDI+ are internally implemented very differently. Microsoft hasn't given away much about its internal designs, but I can say that GDI+ is designed much more around today's graphics cards whereas GDI was designed around the graphics cards of yesterday. This means that GDI+ may give better performance on new hardware, with GDI giving better performance on old hardware.

In more detail, GDI+ tends to be based on the assumption that you have a reasonably new graphics card and that you have quite a bit of memory available. For example, GDI+ defaults to working with images that have 32-bit color depth and will tend to internally process images in memory on this assumption, even if the results are sent to the graphics card and displayed using a lower color depth. Incidentally, this isn't just a GDI+ issue. When DirectX 8.0 was released in 2001, it came with redesigned interfaces and objects—the implementation of the new objects being based on the same 32-bit assumptions! Those assumptions have persisted into the latest version of DirectX, version 9. That's fine with modern hardware; modern graphics cards are increasingly being built with the hardware intrinsically designed to favor 32-bit color. However, GDI makes no such assumptions, which is why you may find that if your application is intended to run on older computers with more restricted memory and older graphics cards, you may get better performance with GDI. It's hard to lay down guidelines here, but my own experience suggests that as an extremely approximate rough rule of thumb, you may expect GDI+ not to give very good results on hardware built prior to about 1999–2000. I should stress, however, that because almost every computer system is different, this suggestion is rough. In general, if you're concerned about performance, my advice is to start using GDI+, because that's the quickest way to get your application up and running. If you have, when testing your application on machines at the bottom range of specs typically used by your clients, performance issues with the graphics, then try to identify the code responsible for the bottlenecks and consider swapping this code to GDI (or to DirectX).

One other point to bear in mind is that although GDI+ assumes you have a powerful graphics card from the point of view of Blitting 32-bit pixel depth images, you don't need to worry about the graphics card having any advanced facilities beyond basic Blitting. Many of the new features of GDI+, such as the gradient brushes, are actually implemented by software, so they don't require any intrinsic graphics card support. Essentially GDI+ won't fail because of some feature not being available on a particular graphics card. It's only if you're using DirectX that you may need to start worrying about details of the video card.

Screenshot Sample

The final sample of this chapter, BltFromScreen, illustrates the use of GDI to achieve something that can't be done using GDI+: Blitting from the screen. This sample displays a form with a couple of controls on it and has a menu option to take a screenshot of its own client area. If the user clicks this menu option, the program saves the screenshot in a file called Screenshot.bmp.

Figure 11-16 shows the sample in action.

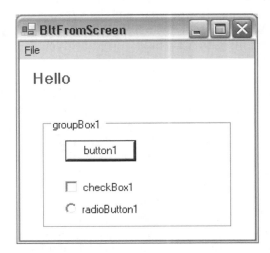

Figure 11-16. *The* BltFromScreen *sample*

As you can see, it just has a couple of random controls on it; it doesn't really matter what the controls are, since they're there only to provide something more interesting than a blank form for the screenshot, so I haven't provided event handlers for them. I have, however, added a Paint event handler to the form to display the *Hello* string that you can see in Figure 11-16.

```
private void Form1_Paint(object sender,
                         System.Windows.Forms.PaintEventArgs e)
{
   e.Graphics.DrawString("Hello", new Font("Ariel", 12, FontStyle.Bold),
                         Brushes.Indigo, new Point(10,10));
}
```

Taking the screenshot happens through the File menu, which has a Get Screenshot menu item. Here's the relevant event handler:

```
private void menuFileGetScreenshot_Click(object sender, System.EventArgs e)
{
   Refresh();
   GrabScreenshot();
}
```

When the user clicks the File menu and then selects Get Screenshot, the code first refreshes the form and then calls a method called GrabScreenshot(), which will actually take the screenshot. Why refresh the form first? The answer is that the expanded File menu will be obscuring part of the client area. This menu is actually removed from the screen before the code in the menu command handler is executed, but the WM_PAINT message isn't sent to the form to get the area where the menu was repainted until after the command handler is executed. So if you don't call Refresh() first to repaint the form, you'll end up with a screenshot that's blank in the area where the menu was.

The GrabScreenshot() method is where the interesting action happens. But before you see the code, I need to define the imported unmanaged GDI functions I'll be using.

```
[DllImport("gdi32.dll")]
static extern int BitBlt(IntPtr hdcDest, int nXDest, int nYDest, int nWidth,
                         int nHeight, IntPtr hdcSrc, int nXSrc, int nYSrc,
                         int swRop);

[DllImport("gdi32.dll")]
static extern IntPtr CreateCompatibleDC(IntPtr hdc);
[DllImport("gdi32.dll")]
static extern IntPtr CreateCompatibleBitmap(IntPtr hdc, int nWidth,
                                            int nHeight);

[DllImport("gdi32.dll")]
static extern IntPtr SelectObject(IntPtr hdc, IntPtr hgdiobj);

[DllImport("gdi32.dll")]
static extern int DeleteObject(IntPtr hgdiobj);

const int SRCCOPY = 0xcc0020;
```

I don't want to get sidetracked into explaining the details of GDI too much—that's not the purpose of this chapter. For the benefit of anyone who hasn't used GDI before, the following is a quick indication of how these functions work.

You need to understand that where GDI+ has objects such as images and graphics objects, GDI uses handles. It works in the same way as the Windows handles that exist beneath managed forms and controls. So where GDI+ has a Graphics object that's used for drawing and for storing all the information about a drawing surface, GDI has a *handle* to a *device context* (or hdc for short). Where GDI+ has an Image object (from which the Bitmap class is derived), GDI has a handle to a bitmap (or hbitmap). By the way, one aspect in which GDI scores higher than GDI+ is that it allows you to create any of these objects independently of any other object; GDI+ has all sorts of restrictions in this regard.

In GDI, an image and a device context exist independently of each other, and you need to specifically select an image into a device context before you can perform BitBlt operations, since BitBlt works from one device context to another. Now here's some background:

- BitBlt() copies a bitmap between device contexts.

- CreateCompatibleDC() creates a memory-based device context. This is something that has no direct equivalent in GDI+ and is the thing that gives GDI so much more flexibility. You can think of it as like a GDI+ Graphics object, but it's not connected to the screen or to any specific device. It exists only in the computer's memory and allows you to do manipulations of images in memory.

- CreateCompatibleBitmap() creates a bitmap; it's GDI's equivalent of new Bitmap().

- SelectObject() selects a bitmap (or other graphics objects such as pens and brushes) into a device context so they can be used for drawing operations.

- DeleteObject() cleans up the memory and resources associated with the handle it's passed. It's the approximate equivalent of the IDisposable.Dispose() method.

- SRCCOPY is a constant that indicates how a bitmap should be copied when it's being Blitted here. In GDI+, when you call DrawImage(), all you can do is have a straight copy, though with the option of color-keying a transparent color. GDI is much more flexible here; it has a huge number of so-called raster operations, which determine how each pixel in the final image should be generated, so when you invoke BitBlt() you have to specify the algorithm, it's the last parameter to BitBlt(). SRCCOPY indicates the simplest raster operation; each pixel is simply copied straight over, just as in Graphics.Draw-Image(). Other possibilities include reversing the color or performing bitwise operations such as And or Or between the source pixel and whatever the previous value of the pixel was in the destination device context; some of these can lead to quite intriguing visual effects.

The following shows the code:

```
private void GrabScreenshot()
{
    int width = this.ClientSize.Width;
    int height = this.ClientSize.Height;

    Graphics screen = this.CreateGraphics();
    IntPtr hdcScreen = screen.GetHdc();

    IntPtr hdcMemory = CreateCompatibleDC(hdcScreen);
    IntPtr hBitmap = CreateCompatibleBitmap(hdcScreen, width, height);
    IntPtr hOldBitmap = SelectObject(hdcMemory, hBitmap);

    int result = BitBlt(hdcMemory, 0, 0, width, height, hdcScreen, 0, 0,
                        SRCCOPY);
    Image screenShot = Image.FromHbitmap(hBitmap);
    screenShot.Save("Screenshot.bmp", ImageFormat.Bmp);

    SelectObject(hdcMemory, hOldBitmap);
    screen.ReleaseHdc(hdcScreen);
```

```
    DeleteObject(hdcMemory);
    DeleteObject(hBitmap);
    MessageBox.Show("Screenshot saved in Screenshot.bmp");
}
```

This code starts by caching the dimensions of the client area, because it'll be using these values a fair bit. It then gets a device context for the screen; the easiest way to do that is to stick with GDI+ and use the `Graphics.GetHdc()` method.

Getting a memory device context isn't possible with GDI+, so the GDI `CreateCompatibleDC()` method is required. Passing in the screen device context as a parameter here ensures that the memory device context will be compatible with the screen when it comes to things such as pixel color depth. Also required is a blank bitmap that will be big enough to hold the screenshot and attach it to the memory DC—that's what the `CreateCompatibleBitmap()` and `SelectObject()` commands are about. Having done all that preparation, the code is ready to copy the screen into bitmap associated with the in-memory device context using the `BitBlt()` function.

At this point, the program now has a bitmap ready to save to a file. GDI+ offers far superior facilities to GDI when it comes to loading and saving images, so it'd be nice to go back to GDI+ here. The `Image.FromHbitmap()` method instantiates a GDI+ `Image` object that contains the image from the GDI bitmap, and I chose to use this method and then call `Image.Save()`. With that the code is basically done; the remaining lines of code are there simply to clean up all the resources. If you download and run the sample, bear in mind that the screenshot taken is only a screenshot of the form's client area, so the title bar and borders, and so on, aren't included in the generated bitmap.

Summary

In this chapter I covered a couple of aspects of Windows Forms that you can use to write more sophisticated, responsive, and visually appealing applications.

In the first half of the chapter, I went under the hood to show the message loop that underpins the event-based architecture of the `System.Windows.Forms` classes. You learned in particular how to integrate this architecture into multithreaded applications, and you saw how to implement a dialog box that allows the user to abort a lengthy operation.

In the second half of the chapter, I covered three topics of relevance to the visual appearance of windows: customizing the shape of forms and controls, customizing the appearance of some controls by implementing them as owner-draw controls, and using GDI to leverage additional graphics features. On one hand, you saw how implementing controls as owner-draw controls with nonrectangular regions can give you controls that look truly spectacular. On the other hand, I presented an example of one of the features that GDI can give you— Blitting from the screen. Then I worked through a sample that showed how you can easily use this feature to programmatically take screenshots.

To some extent, what this chapter has presented are some of the tricks you can use to improve Windows Forms, but it's not possible to be comprehensive in a single chapter. Nevertheless, the concepts presented here should give you some idea of the sort of things you can do to make sure your Windows Forms–based applications are responsive, genuinely multitasked, and look significantly more professional and attractive than many of the applications

CHAPTER 12

■■■

Introducing Code Access Security

The .NET Framework offers a rich security infrastructure based on both the identity of the code (*code access security*, or CAS) and the identity of the account under which the code is running (*role-based security*). In this chapter, I'll cover how CAS works, with a particular focus on looking under the hood. Because security isn't generally a well-understood subject amongst many developers, I don't assume any prior knowledge of CAS and will start by explaining the basic concepts. However, in keeping with the advanced nature of this book, I'll tour through the basic concepts and syntax fairly quickly so that I can get onto presenting some examples of applications that take advantage of CAS in fairly sophisticated ways, including showing you how to define your own custom permissions.

Given that the CLR offers both role-based and code access security, you may wonder why the security chapter of this book is exclusively concerned with CAS. Unfortunately, it's simply not possible in one chapter to do justice to the entire .NET security infrastructure, especially at an advanced level. And although role-based security is important, it to a large extent serves the same role as Windows operating system security—it provides protection based on the identity of the process running an application. It's in CAS that you can find the bulk of the new security concepts introduced by .NET, which is why I'll focus attention there. However, role-based security is exposed to code in a similar manner to CAS, using classes that are specified in XML files, which means that if you have a sound grasp of CAS, you should find it relatively simple to use role-based security as well.

Specifically, I'll be covering the following topics:

- **CAS concepts**: I'll briefly review the concepts behind CAS, as well as its relationship with native Windows security.

- **CAS policy**: I'll cover in some detail the default security policy that's applied when you install .NET. This will lead you to a deeper understanding of the concepts that underpin CAS and how they're implemented. I'll also cover the tools you can use to view and edit security policies, particularly mscorcfg.msc.

- **Coding with CAS**: I'll review the main techniques for taking advantage of the CAS infrastructure in your code, including both imperative and declarative security.

- **CAS under the hood**: I'll cover what actually happens when some code requests a security permission and how the security infrastructure identifies and instantiates the appropriate classes to implement the relevant security policy.

- **Samples**: I'll present a couple of samples that cover how to define custom security attributes and how to use imperative security to demand and assert permissions in order to allow partially trusted code access to resources in a controlled manner or in order to have trusted code perform operations on behalf of less trusted code.

Introducing Code Access Security Concepts

The purpose of CAS is to protect users from code they want to execute but that they aren't absolutely convinced they trust. Traditional Windows security involved allowing or denying access to resources based on the permissions associated with the user account. This worked well in the days before the Internet, when the only software on your computer would normally be programs you had bought from a reputable commercial company (or you had written yourself). But now that it's commonplace just to download code that looks interesting without much knowledge of the author, security based solely on user accounts is clearly inadequate. The problem is well-known; so much code is floating around on the Internet, and much of it is useful, but some of it is either malicious or so badly written that it could damage your system. Even code that comes from reputable companies may have bugs that cause problems—you only have to think of the number of patches Microsoft has had to release to correct problems such as buffer overruns in its software. If you download any of this code so that it executes with the privileges of your account, who knows what it could do, especially if, like many developers, you habitually log in with administrator privileges on your local machine.

The solution is to implement security that restricts access to resources based not only on the identity of the user but also on the extent to which you trust the code. The basic idea is similar to the sandbox under which code in languages such as JavaScript would execute, but CAS is much more sophisticated than the sandbox. It allows a fine degree of control over permissions based on an analysis of the assembly concerned. With CAS, the system will allow an assembly to access a resource only if the assembly containing the relevant code is also allowed access. Working in conjunction with this, additional security based on the identity of the account is of course provided for by both native Windows security and the CLR's role-based security, so to gain access to the resource, both tests have to be passed.

Another aspect of CAS is that the CLR's security infrastructure exposes various hooks that will allow you to define and plug in your own security permissions if the ones defined by Microsoft aren't adequate for your needs. One scenario in which you may do this would be if you had designed your own hardware device and you wanted the systems administrator to be able to control who and what code is allowed access to this device. I'll cover how to define custom permissions in the section "Defining Custom Permissions."

For now, I'll cover how CAS works in practice and the basic concepts behind it. I'll start by showing what CAS means for a single assembly and explaining what happens when you have assemblies invoking methods on other assemblies, where the respective assemblies have been given different sets of permissions and you need to decide whether to allow access to various resources. I'll also cover the permissions available and the way that CAS interacts with Windows security.

CAS for a Single Assembly

A good way to understand the concepts behind CAS is to compare it with the traditional security architecture offered by Windows. Classic Windows security is based on user accounts and groups; the actions that the user can perform are based on the group to which the user has been assigned. Each group is associated with a set of privileges—a list of tasks on the system that members of that group are allowed to do. Typical privileges include the right to debug a process, to increase the priority of a process, or to load a device driver. Users and groups can also be granted access permissions to network resources; the difference between a privilege and a permission in unmanaged code is that a privilege is associated with an account and indicates what actions an account can perform; permissions tend to be associated with particular resources—such as files and folders on the file system. A permission associated with a resource indicates which users should be allowed to access that resource in different ways. The classic example is that each file on an NTFS partition stores details of users allowed to read that file, users allowed to write to it, and so on.

Whenever a process tries to do something that's subject to the control of a privilege, the system will first check and will allow the operation only if the account under which the process is running is allowed to perform the requested operation. In addition, if the user attempts to access some resource that's protected by permissions, the system will similarly check the permissions associated with that resource to verify that the resource is happy to allow that user the required access.

CAS has concepts that are quite analogous to this, but the details are rather different. The reason that Windows defines groups is of course that it makes it much simpler to administer the security policy. For example, if an employee is promoted to a manager and therefore requires more privileges, then rather than editing the details of the privileges for that account, you just add the account to the Managers group. If you want to change what managers are allowed to do, you just change the privileges assigned to the Managers group, and you don't have to edit the properties of each individual manager's account. CAS's equivalent to the group is the *code group*. A code group groups the assemblies that have been given the same set of permissions. However, placing assemblies into code groups works differently than placing users into groups. On Windows, a central database stored on the machine(s) responsible for the security policy indicates the association between users and groups. That's feasible because users tend to exist for long periods of time, and they don't swap groups that often. Further, administrators will in principle know who is registered to use the system and therefore be able to maintain this database. However, that's not the case for assemblies. You'll generate one, perhaps many, new assemblies every time you rebuild a project! So it'd be extremely hard for me to maintain an up-to-date database that says which assemblies should belong to which code groups. Such a solution would clearly be untenable, so instead, Microsoft has introduced the concept of *evidence*. This means that when an assembly is loaded, it's examined for certain characteristics that can be used to identify code groups to which it belongs. In formal terms, each code group has a *membership condition*, which indicates the condition that an assembly must satisfy in order to be a member of that code group. Membership conditions can be based on the following:

- **Signature**: Whether an assembly has been signed with a particular strong name or certificate or whether its hash evaluates to a certain value.

- **Location**: The location of the assembly—for example, its path on the local file system or the URL or Web site from which it was downloaded.

- **Zone**: This is a concept borrowed from Internet Explorer. The world is assumed to be divided into five zones: the local computer, the intranet (in other words, network file shares), Internet sites you've added to your trusted zone in Internet Explorer, Internet sites you've added to your untrusted zone in Internet Explorer, and all remaining sites (the Internet). Membership of a code group can be based on the zone under which the assembly's location falls.

- **Custom**: If none of these possibilities is adequate for your requirements, it's possible to write code to implement your own membership condition and plug this code into the security infrastructure.

The set of code groups and associated membership conditions form part of the CLR's *security policy*. When you first install .NET, you get a default security policy that includes a set of code groups and membership conditions that Microsoft thinks will form a sensible basis on which to implement security. That policy is there without you having to do anything. From the moment you install .NET, every time you load and execute code in an assembly, the CLR is there behind the scenes, checking which code groups that assembly belongs to and ensuring that the current security policy allows that assembly to perform the tasks it's trying to do. However, most systems administrators will obviously want to customize the CLR's security policy for the particular needs of their organization.

Once you've established which code groups an assembly belongs to, you need to sort out which permissions that code has. And again you can probably see an analogy with traditional Windows security. As you've seen, with traditional security each group has an associated set of privileges. Similarly with CAS, each code group has an associated *permission set*, which will contain a number of permissions. At this point, you need to be careful with the analogy. Despite the terminology, a CLR *permission* is more analogous to a Windows *privilege*, since a CLR permission indicates whether code should be allowed to perform a certain type of action. To give you an idea, typical CLR permissions include permissions to call into unmanaged code, to access the file system, or to use reflection to examine a type. However, CLR permissions allow a fine degree of control that's not available to Windows privileges. For example, the CLR file system permission (`FileIO`) allows you to specify exactly the files or folders to which that permission should apply. Thus, in a sense, CLR permissions have a similar flexibility and power to native Windows permissions and privileges combined.

From this discussion, you perhaps have realized that many assemblies will satisfy the membership condition of more than one code group. In this case, the permissions for each code group an assembly belongs to are added together. For an assembly to be allowed to do something, all it needs is for any one of the code groups that it's a member of to grant the relevant permission. Hence, membership of a code group can only ever add permissions, not remove them.

To get a feel for how this all works, let's quickly work through an example. Consider the assembly `System.Drawing.dll`, which contains many of Microsoft's GDI+ classes. Using the default security policy, it turns out that this assembly satisfies the membership condition of the following three code groups:

- **All_Code (all assemblies are a member of this group)**: By default this group gives no permissions.

- **My_Computer_Zone (because the assembly is installed on the local machine)**: Membership of this assembly confers full trust to do anything. The CLR will impose no security restrictions based on the assembly identity (though, of course, that doesn't guarantee the code unlimited access to the machine, since role-based security and native Windows security may still be active).

- **Microsoft_Strong_Name (because this assembly has been signed with Microsoft's private key)**: This code group also confers full trust.

The net result of combining all these groups and their associated permission sets is of course that System.Drawing.dll has full trust.

CAS for Multiple Assemblies

A major complication can occur in CAS. A large amount, perhaps even the majority, of code that's executed by assemblies is being executed because it was invoked by a method in another assembly, and this introduces a whole set of new subtleties. Indeed, a whole chain of assemblies can have contributed to code on the call stack—and you'll need to be careful to ensure that not only is the currently executing assembly permitted to do the exact operation it's attempting to do but that it's not being abused by some other assembly further up the call stack. So the question of what a block of code should be allowed to do depends not only on its own assembly but also on the identities of all the assemblies working up the call stack. This introduces the concept of the *stack walk*, in which the permission sets of all assemblies on the stack are checked. A number of possible scenarios are available here.

Demand: Suppose I write a library that searches the local file system for certain types of files and displays the results. This library will clearly need permission to read the file system (the FileIO permission), so if I want to run this code, I'll need to make sure it has the appropriate permissions. But that's not the end of the story. What if I have some other code that I've downloaded from somewhere and that claims to display nice pictures on my desktop but that I don't trust? And suppose my suspicions turn out to be correct. This other code tries to access my file system library for some reason. In this case, should my library be granted permission to read the file system? Evidently not—for all I know the untrusted code that invoked it may (for example) read the file system and then send back confidential information that it finds to some third party. So it's important not only that my library has the FileIO permission but that every caller in the chain also has this permission. If there's just one assembly on the call stack that doesn't have permission to access the file system, then the security check should fail. This kind of check is known as a *demand* for permission, and this is the type of check that's normally responsible for the stack walk.

Assert: Now suppose I write a library that cleans up my disk by removing certain temporary files I know I don't want. Obviously, this library will also require access to the file system, but notice that here this access is very safe. No matter which methods in this library callers invoke or what parameters are passed to them, the only effect can be to remove certain files that don't matter anyway. I've thoroughly tested this application and am satisfied that it can't affect other files, and it won't ever return confidential information to the caller. This library simply can't be used to damage or compromise the system. It's therefore reasonable to suppose that I'd be happy for other code to invoke this library, even though I may not be happy for that other code to have unrestricted access to the file system. In other words, I'm happy for code that doesn't have FileIO permission nevertheless to be able to invoke this library. In this case, I can have my library *assert* FileIO permission. The way that an assert works is this: My code will presumably call on the System.IO classes to actually delete the temporary files. Somewhere in the implementation of those classes will be code that demands the appropriate FileIO permission. The CLR will respond by walking up the stack to verify that all code on the stack has permission to do this. During the stack walk, it will discover the assert made by my code, and at that point, it will decree the permission asserted and stop the stack walk. This means it won't matter whether the code that invoked my assembly had this permission. Bear in mind that it's possible for an assembly to assert a permission only if the assembly has that permission in the first place. It also needs to have a security permission called Assertion, which indicates that an assembly is allowed to declare asserts.

Deny: Whereas making an assert or a demand is aimed at the assemblies further up the call stack, a deny is aimed in the opposite direction: at protecting code from malicious assemblies that may later be invoked. For example, suppose that someone has written an assembly that claims to clean text files by removing excess whitespace from them. Cleaning up files in this way is a task that your own code needs to do, so you want to use this assembly to save rolling your own code. The trouble is that you're not sure how much you trust this assembly. The solution to this is a *deny*. Your assembly calls a method that informs the CLR that certain specified permissions must not be granted if they're requested by code in any method that's invoked directly or indirectly from the currently executing method, even if a request for those permissions is made by an assembly that would normally have the appropriate permissions. This allows you to prevent called assemblies from performing actions that you think they shouldn't be able to perform.

Permitonly. Permitonly works in much the same way as deny, except that where deny will cause all future requests for the specified permission(s) to be denied, permitonly will only allow the permissions explicitly specified, disallowing all other permissions. You can use these methods to control what a called assembly should be allowed to do and hence to provide additional security.

Incidentally, I've described the demand/assert/deny/permitonly scenarios by reference to code that you may write, but it's easy to see these same concepts at work in the framework class libraries. Take the isolated storage classes, for example; one of the features of isolated storage is that because it represents a private, application-specific area of the file system, you may trust code to use isolated storage where you wouldn't trust that code to have more general access to the file system. Internally, the System.IO.IsolatedStorage.IsolatedStorageFile class is going to be implemented using the System.IO classes to access the file system. This means that the code that implements IsolatedStorageFile is going to need the FileIO permission. Clearly, the only way that isolated storage can be used by code that doesn't have the FileIO permission is if System.IO.IsolatedStorage asserts this permission—and that's exactly what happens. IsolatedStorageFile demands the IsolatedStorage permission and asserts the FileIO permission.

Thus, you can see a subtle situation in which, on occasions, assemblies need to demand permissions, and in other cases, assemblies need to assert permissions in order to carry out some internal work in a carefully controlled manner.

The CLR Permissions

Microsoft has defined a number of specific permissions that indicate whether access to perform some specific task should be allowed. The full list is as follows:

Directory services	DNS	Environment variables	Event log
File dialog box	File I/O	Isolated storage file	Message queue
OLE DB	Performance counter	Printing	Reflection
Registry	Security	Service controller	Socket access
SQL client	User interface	Web access	

The broad purposes of these permissions should be obvious from their names. If you want to find out the exact specifications of what each permission covers, refer to the MSDN documentation.

How the Permissions Work

The idea is that these permissions cover a range of potentially dangerous activities that are enabled by various classes in the framework class library—and they're used by the relevant classes to restrict what code can access those facilities. As an example, suppose you want to use the FileInfo class to read the file C:\boot.ini. Before reading this file, the implementation of FileInfo will at some point execute some code that has the same effect as the following:

```
FileIOPermission perm = new
    FileIOPermission(FileIOPermissionAccess.Read, @"C:\Boot.ini");
perm.Demand();
```

In other words, the FileInfo object will demand the permission to read this file; notice how the permission request is specific, asking for no more than exactly the permission needed to perform the task. The FileIOPermission class implements this permission; every in-built code access permission is represented by a corresponding class, and these classes are implemented in mscorlib.dll, contained in the namespace System.Security.Permissions, and all are derived from System.Security.CodeAccessPermission. The Demand() method is implemented by System.Security.CodeAccessPermission, and it will walk up the stack, inspecting the credentials of every assembly involved. For each one, the permission set that assembly is running under will be examined to make sure that the FileIO permission is contained in that code's permission set. Moreover, if that permission is present, it will be further examined to check that read access to C:\boot.ini is covered. (For example, a FileIO permission that only gives permission to read files on the D:\ drive wouldn't count, but one that gave permission to read the C:\ drive would count, since that implicitly includes C:\Boot.ini.) If you get one failure in this series of checks, the call to Demand() will throw an exception, which means the file won't get read. You'll get an obvious performance hit here, but that's the inevitable price you pay for security.

One point that may surprise you if you're used to Windows security is that I've been talking about the code actively asking for the Security checks. This is different from native Windows security, in which the privileges are just there. Windows will automatically prevent actions that you aren't allowed to do. In .NET the situation is rather different. Each assembly is automatically given the permissions that are determined by its code groups, but (with a couple of exceptions) those permissions are actually checked only if the code explicitly asks the CLR to do so—for example, by calling Demand(). You may think this would expose a security loophole whereby malicious code can just "forget" to demand a permission, but in practice it doesn't—the CLR's security architecture is very secure. You'll see why and how this apparent contradiction is resolved later in the section "Looking at CAS Under the Hood."

The Security Permission

It's worth drawing particular attention to the Security permission because—uniquely amongst the various Microsoft-defined permissions—it contains various subpermissions that are crucial to the operation of any managed code. Figure 12-1 shows the state of this permission for the LocalIntranet permission set.

Permission Viewer (Read-Only)

Security Permission:

Permission	Granted
Enable Code Execution	Yes
Allow Calls to Unmanaged Code	No
Assert any permission that has been granted	Yes
Skip Verification	No
Enable thread control	No
Allow Policy Control	No
Allow Domain Policy Control	No
Allow Principal Control	No
Create and Control Application Domains	No
Serialization Formatter	No
Allow Evidence Control	No
Extend Infrastructure	No
Enable Remoting Configuration	No

Close

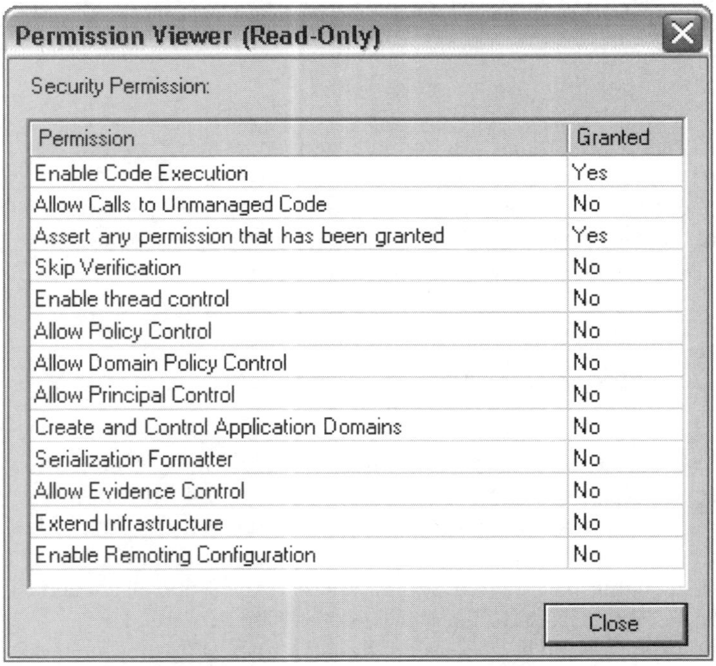

Figure 12.1. *The default security permission for the* LocalIntranet *permission set*

Figure 12-1 has been taken from an MMC snap-in, mscorcfg, which I introduced in Chapter 4.

■Tip Microsoft's chosen terminology is a little unfortunate here. *Permission* is used to refer to a permission object that deals with a certain area; hence, FileIO and Security are both permissions. However, the term *permission* is also used to refer to the subpermissions within each permission, such as the FileIO permission to access a particular file or the Security permission specifically to enable code execution. For clarity, I'll sometimes refer to these as subpermissions (my own term) where there is a risk of confusion.

To execute at all, an assembly must be granted the Enable Code Execution subpermission. You can think of it a bit like this: imagine that before starting to execute code in an assembly, the CLR executes some code that has the same effect as this:

```
SecurityPermission perm = new SecurityPermission(
    SecurityPermissionFlag.Execution);
perm.Demand();
```

If the Demand() call throws an exception, the CLR will simply refuse to execute the code. I emphasize that this is only an analogy. On performance grounds, I very much doubt that any real IL code that has the effect of the previous snippet is executed; it's more likely that this security check will be handled internally within the CLR, but the end result is the same.

Skip Verification is another important subpermission—this permission allows code to run even if it's not verifiably type safe. Skip Verification and Allow Calls to Unmanaged Code are arguably the most dangerous permissions to grant, since code that has either of these permissions can theoretically circumvent all other CLR-based permissions, either by using unmanaged code or by using some cleverly written unsafe code, which makes it impossible for the CLR to detect what the code is actually doing. For all practical purposes, granting code either of these permissions is about as unsafe as giving it FullTrust—which is why, as you'll observe in Figure 12-1, the LocalIntranet permission set grants neither of these permissions! Unlike many CLR permissions, these permissions are enforced by the CLR, irrespective of whether the assembly specifically asks for the permission.

You'll also notice a permission that's listed in Figure 12-1 is Assert Any Permission, which has been granted. This is the permission that allows code to make an assert and therefore to declare that it doesn't care whether calling code has the required permission.

Understanding the Relationship to Windows Security

It's worth saying a couple of words about the relationship between the CLR's security mechanisms and native Windows security. In fact, CLR security and Windows security work completely independently. .NET Framework security is implemented within the DLLs that form the CLR, and Windows security is implemented by the operating system.

Let's say your code requests to perform some action that's covered by both of these security infrastructures, such as accessing the file system. In the first place, the CLR's evidence-based (and in some cases, role-based) security tests whether the code is permitted to perform the requested operation. Then, if that test is passed, Windows itself will check whether the account under which the code is running is permitted to perform the requested operation. This means that a lot of possibilities exist for code to be denied access to something.

Of course, CLR security and Windows security don't cover the same areas. This means that although some operations (such as file access) are subject to both security mechanisms,

Windows doesn't set any security tests in other areas, so the only test is the CLR-based one (this is the case for running unverifiable code), and in other areas the CLR doesn't provide security but Windows does (such as loading a device deriver). In general, you'll notice that despite the overlap between CLR security and Windows security, the CLR-defined permissions often focus on higher-level activities, since the CLR security restrictions tend to apply to activities recognized by the framework and the framework class library (such as using ADO.NET to talk to SQL Server), and Windows security is concerned with basic operations that affect objects known to the operating system (such as creating a paging file or debugging a process). Also, because the action of demanding or asserting a permission is performed from the code within an assembly, there's more scope for CLR security to be sensitive to what the surrounding code is doing, in a way that's not really possible for native security. Take as an example the CLR permission called the FileDialog permission; this permission grants code the right to access a file that has been specified by the user in a File Open or a File Save dialog box, and it can be granted even where code doesn't in general have any FileIO permission. There's no way that kind of sophisticated analysis—to grant permission to access a file based on the fact that this file has been identified by some code that has just executed—can realistically be performed by the operating system's security.

Another point worth noting is that neither the CLR's security nor Windows security operates in all situations. In particular, CLR security works only for managed code and won't, obviously, give you any protection against the actions of unmanaged code. (However, it will prevent managed code from invoking unmanaged code without the Allow Calls to Unmanaged Code subpermission.) Windows security, on the other hand, is operative only on Windows NT/2000/XP and later operating systems. In addition, Windows file permissions are effective only on NTFS-formatted partitions. (The CLR's file-related permissions will work on any partition, since they're implemented within the CLR and not based on information stored with individual files and folders.)

Understanding the CLR Security Policy

Now you'll develop your understanding of CAS security by examining the default security policy that ships with .NET.

Tools for Managing CAS Security

The security policy for the CLR, including all CAS security policy settings, is stored, like most other CLR configuration information, in a set of XML files. This means that in principle you can (provided you have the appropriate rights) change the security policy by directly editing these files. However, because of the risk of breaking the CLR by introducing formatting errors into these files, it's recommended that you do this only as a last resort. Instead, two tools are available that will edit these files on your behalf.

The .NET configuration tool, mscorcfg.msc: As you saw in Chapter 4, mscorcfg isn't intended solely for manipulating security policy—it can control some other aspects of CLR configuration—but security policy is where this tool is at its most powerful. This is the tool I'll mostly use in this chapter, since its rich user interface is helpful for understanding the principles of .NET security.

caspol.exe (the name stands for *code access security policy*): This is a command-line tool that implements similar features, though caspol is able to modify only CAS, not role-based security. The user interface for `caspol` isn't particularly friendly, but it has the advantage that, being a command-line tool, it can be called up from batch files, which simplifies the process of modifying security on a large number of machines (just distribute and run the batch file). I won't be using `caspol` significantly in this chapter, but MSDN documents its various command-line options.

Although `caspol` and `mscorcfg` provide a relatively rich set of features, neither tool is comprehensive, which is why for some specialized tasks you'll need to edit the XML files directly. I won't cover the format of the XML files here; you can fairly easily deduce that for yourself by examining the files. With .NET version 1.1, you can find these files at

- `%windir%\Microsoft.NET\Framework\v1.1.4322\CONFIG\security.config`

- `%windir%\Microsoft.NET\Framework\v1.1.4322\CONFIG\enterprisesec.config`

- `User.config` (This file, if present, will be stored in a folder specific to the individual user.)

Three files exist because the CLR's security policy works at three levels: the enterprise, the machine, and the user. (In some situations, it's also possible to apply security at the AppDomain level.) When you first install .NET, the default out-of-the-box policy really only defines a substantial machine-level policy—that's to say, a policy that applies to the individual computer. Network administrators may then, if they want, add rules to the `Enterprise.config` file. Individual users may also add their own rules to their own `user.config` file. When the CLR evaluates whether some code is allowed to perform a task, it first checks all three policies and calculates the intersection of the policies. Hence, managed code can normally perform some task only if all policy levels allow the operation.

Beyond the differences I've noted here, all three policy levels function in the same way, using the same XML format to define code groups, permission sets, and permissions (or, for role-based security, principals and roles). Since in this chapter I want to focus on how CLR security infrastructure works, and I don't want to get bogged down in questions of domain administration, I'll concentrate exclusively on working with the machine policy.

SECURITY FOR DIFFERENT CLR VERSIONS

You may be wondering how the presence of different versions of the CLR affects security. The answer is that the security policy works completely independently for the different CLR versions. For example, I indicated that the machine-level security policy for .NET 1.1 is defined in the file `%windir%\Microsoft.NET\Framework\v1.1.4322\CONFIG\security.config`. Well, the machine level policy for .NET 1.0 is similarly defined in the file `%windir%\Microsoft.NET\Framework\v1.0.3705\CONFIG\security.config`. These files are of course independent, and if you have both versions of .NET installed, you'll find both files are present. When you're modifying or examining the security policy, you should make sure you're working with correct version of .NET. In the case of the `mscorcfg` MMC snap-in, you achieve this by loading the correct version of the snap-in. You'll find when you first come to load this snap-in into MMC that each version of .NET comes with its own `mscorcfg` tool. The following screenshot shows the situation on my machine when I tried to load the snap-in. My machine has .NET versions 1.0 and 1.1 installed. In this screenshot, the snap-in listed as .NET Framework 1.1 Configuration is used to configure .NET 1.1, and the one listed as .NET Framework Configuration is intended for .NET 1.0. (Evidently at the time of writing the first version of .NET, it didn't occur to Microsoft that version numbers would be useful here!)

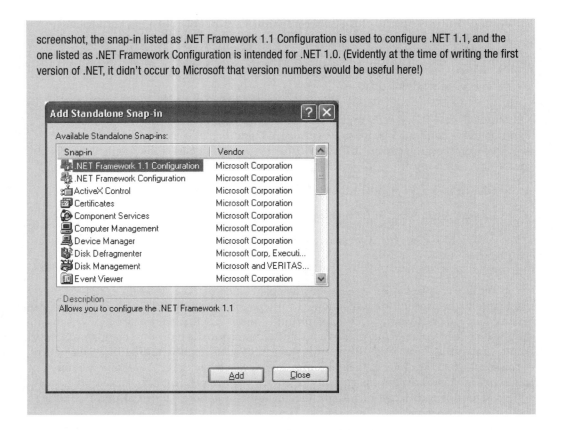

The easiest way to get a feel for a typical CLR security setup is by using the .NET Framework Configuration Tool, `mscorcfg.msc`. In the next couple of sections, I'll use `mscorcfg.msc` to explain the default security policy that ships with .NET, focusing on the default code groups and permission sets. Along the way, this will give you a better idea of how code groups and permission sets are used to enforce CAS security.

The Default Code Groups

Figure 12-2 shows the default situation regarding code groups for a machine policy for a clean install of .NET 1.1.

■Tip It's important to stress that Figure 12-2 and the subsequent discussion is based on the default code groups in the machine configuration that you get when installing .NET 1.1—and so won't necessarily apply if you've already been fiddling with your security policy. You can modify, add, or delete code groups to suit whatever security policy you want on your system, and you also shouldn't expect that future versions of .NET will come with the same default settings. In fact, you'll find some changes, notably to permissions granted for the Internet zone, between .NET 1.0 service pack 2 and .NET 1.1.

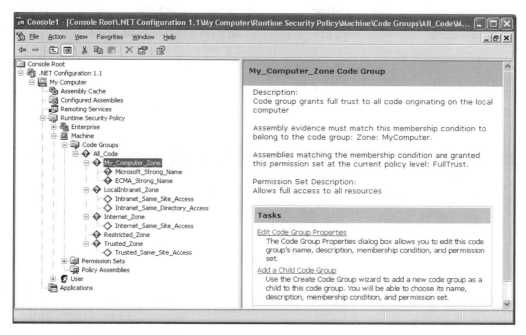

Figure 12-2. *Default situation of code groups for machine policy*

mscorcfg shows that the code groups form a tree structure, with the All_Code group at the top of the tree. It's worth a couple of words of explanation of the main groups.

My_Computer_Zone indicates any code that's stored on the local computer, and LocalIntranet_Zone indicates any assembly that's located on a shared network folder. Between them these zones cover any assembly that's accessed as a file on the local network. In the case of My_Computer_Zone, additional code groups indicate code that has been signed by either the Microsoft or the Microsoft/ECMA strong names. Those assemblies such as mscorlib.dll and system.dll that contain classes defined by the ECMA standard are signed by the Microsoft/ECMA strong name, and the remaining classes supplied by Microsoft are signed with the Microsoft strong name. Chapter 4 discussed strong names.

Of course, with .NET, code can also be executed by someone typing in the path directly to the executable assembly in Internet Explorer, as well as using more traditional means. The remaining code groups between them cover this possibility, as well as any code that has been programmatically loaded with a URL as the path. Downloaded code is divided into three groups: Internet_Zone, Restricted_Zone, and Trusted_Zone. What counts as trusted or as restricted isn't under the control of the CLR; it's an Internet Explorer setting. If you want to add a site to either the trusted or the restricted zones, then you'll find the appropriate menu option in the Security tab of the Internet Options dialog box in Internet Explorer. The Restricted Zone is intended for those Internet sites you especially distrust.

Remember that an assembly isn't restricted to any single code group—it may satisfy the membership condition for several groups. When checking which code groups an assembly is a member of, the CLR will work recursively down the hierarchy of code groups. However, if a particular assembly doesn't satisfy the membership condition for some group, the CLR won't examine child groups. For example, code that has been downloaded from the Internet doesn't satisfy the condition for My_Computer_Zone. Therefore, the CLR will not check whether this code satisfies the `Microsoft_Strong_Name` or `ECMA_Strong_Name` child group. Because these groups are children of the `My_Computer_Zone` group, only code that also falls into `My_Computer_Zone` is allowed to be a member of these groups.

The Default Permission Sets

A permission set is simply a set of permissions. And, just as with the code groups, it's easy to see the default permission sets using the MMC snap-in, as shown in Figure 12-3.

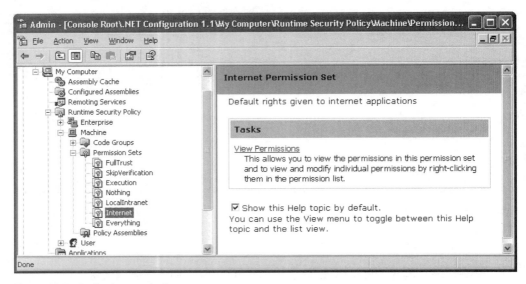

Figure 12-3. *Default permission sets*

Unlike the code groups, most of these default permission sets are fixed by Microsoft and can't be edited. Of the default permission sets, the only one that can be modified is the `Everything` group, though you can freely create new permission sets if for some reason the default ones don't match your needs. The reason for fixing these permission sets is that Microsoft thinks them to represent typical and intrinsically useful sets that should therefore always be available. Table 12-1 indicates the rough purpose of each permission set and indicates which code groups use them by default (as of .NET 1.1). Notice that not all the permission sets are actually used by any code groups; some of them have simply been defined in case you want to use them.

Table 12-1. *The Default CLR 1.1 Permission Sets*

Permission Set	Code Groups That by Default Use this Set	Description
FullTrust	My_Computer_Zone ECMA_Strong_Name Microsoft_Strong_Name	Code with this permission set is completely trusted; the CLR imposes no CAS-based restrictions on what this code does.

Table 12-1. *The Default CLR 1.1 Permission Sets (Continued)*

Permission Set	Code Groups That by Default Use this Set	Description
SkipVerification		Allows code to execute even if it's not verifiably type safe.
Execution		Allows code to execute.
Nothing	Restricted_Zone	This set doesn't contain any permissions whatsoever. Code that has this permission set will not be allowed to execute.
Internet	Trusted_Zone Internet_Zone	Gives a highly restricted set of permissions, allowing code to create top-level windows, present a file dialog box, and use isolated storage, but not much more than that.
LocalIntranet		Gives a restricted set of permissions appropriate to intranet code. This includes Internet permissions plus a couple of others, including the ability to use the DNS service and the Reflection.Emit classes.
Everything		Virtually all Microsoft-defined permissions are assigned, so code can do almost anything covered by these permissions. The exception is the security permission, SkipVerify.

■**Tip** If you need to work with .NET 1.0, you may notice that from service pack 2 onward, the Intenet Zone had no permissions. This was changed to the Internet permission set from .NET 1.1.

Understanding Fully and Partially Trusted Code

One point that confuses developers on occasions is why a permission set called FullTrust exists as well as a set called Everything. Don't the two amount to the same thing? The answer is no. FullTrust is a special permission set, which conceptually indicates to the CLR that this code is *completely* trusted. The CLR will always grant fully trusted code any permission for which the code asks. The FullTrust permission set doesn't even contain a list of permissions to check against—there's no point, since the granting of any permission is automatic. If some code is identified as having any permission set other than FullTrust, then that code is conceptually regarded as *partially trusted*; in other words, that code has been given a set of permissions, and will be permitted to perform all the operations granted by those permissions, but it's nevertheless inherently viewed with suspicion. The Everything permission set happens to include virtually all the permissions that have been defined by Microsoft (which is why it's named as such); however, any code running under the Everything permission set is still regarded as partially trusted. This is significant because of a couple of things the CLR will *never* allow partially trusted code to do, no matter what permissions that code has. Partially trusted code can never do the following:

- Directly invoke an assembly that has been signed with a strong name, unless the strongly named assembly has specifically indicated that it's happy to be called by partially trusted callers. (It can do this by defining an assembly-level attribute, `AllowPartiallyTrustedCallersAttribute`.)

- Register custom security permissions.

Another distinction between `FullTrust` and `Everything` becomes evident if you've registered custom permissions on your system. Any code running under `FullTrust` will of course automatically be granted those custom permissions if it asks for them. On the other hand, these permissions will not be granted to code running under `Everything`, unless you explicitly modify the `Everything` set to include your own permissions. This is the reason why `Everything` is the one default permission set that you're allowed to modify if you want—in case you want to add custom permissions to it. Don't be fooled by the name `Everything`. In reality, this is a permission set just like any other. Microsoft has defined the `Everything` set in case you ever want some code group to have pretty well all the predefined permissions but without that code being formally regarded as fully trusted.

Calling Strong-Named Assemblies

You'll have to deal with one extra security requirement if you have any strongly named assemblies. As an added security precaution, and as noted in the previous section, by default only fully trusted code can invoke methods in strongly named assemblies. The reason for this restriction is that assemblies are normally strongly named so that they can be widely used by different applications (for example, by being placed in the assembly cache). Because such assemblies are more widely available, Microsoft decided that the risk is too great that these assemblies may be invoked by malicious code. Hence, if you sign an assembly with a strong name, it's up to you to make a positive decision that it's OK for partially trusted code to use that assembly. This will normally imply that you think you've tested the assembly sufficiently that you're satisfied it can't compromise the integrity of your system, no matter what methods in it are invoked or what parameters are supplied. If you're happy for that to happen, you need to mark the assembly with the `AllowPartiallyTrustedCallersAttribute` attribute.

```
[assembly: AllowPartiallyTrustedCallersAttribute()]
```

This attribute takes no parameters and is defined in `mscorlib.dll`, in the `System.Security` namespace.

Of course, it may occur to you that you use a lot of shared assemblies in the framework class library all the time in your .NET programming. Does this mean that these assemblies can be called only from trusted code? Well, to some extent, yes. Microsoft has identified certain assemblies as being OK to be called from partially trusted code. According to the documentation, the list is as follows:

- `mscorlib.dll`

- `System.dll`

- `System.Windows.Forms.dll`

- `System.Drawing.dll`

- `IEExecRemote.dll`

- `Accessibility.dll`

- `Microsoft.VisualBasic.dll`

- `System.XML.dll`

- `System.Web.Services.dll`

- `System.Data.dll`

The good news (good if you're writing partially trusted code, that is) is that all the core functionality of the framework (`mscorlib.dll` and `System.dll`) is there, and partially trusted code can also access the Windows forms and drawing features, so you can still get a decent user interface. However, you'll notice that some key assemblies are missing, including these:

- `System.Web.dll`

- `System.Management.dll`

- `System.DirectoryServices.dll`

- `System.ServiceProcess.dll`

- `System.EnterpriseServices.dll`

These assemblies have all been deemed to contain code that's simply potentially too dangerous to allow access to clients that aren't fully trusted, and in most cases you can probably see the reason why; for example, given how powerful WMI is, you probably don't want partially trusted code playing with the management instrumentation classes. Imagine some malicious code running under an administrator account using WMI—the damage such code could wreak on your system doesn't bear consideration. The same holds true for accessing Active Directory with the `System.DirectoryServices` classes. `System.Web.dll` is also excluded from the list of libraries that can be called by partially trusted callers. This would seem to make sense because—well—would you use partially trusted code to run your Web site?

Bear in mind, however, that the restriction on partially trusted callers applies only to the immediate calling assembly, not to assemblies further up the call stack. This means it's possible for partially trusted code to access a strongly named assembly, provided it does so indirectly, via an intermediate assembly that's fully trusted but either has no strong name or (more likely) has the `AllowPartiallyTrustedCallers` attribute set. Figure 12-4 shows this technique.

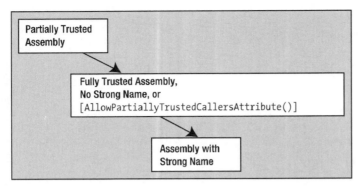

Figure 12-4. *Calling a strongly named assembly from partially trusted code*

Coding with CAS

So far you've learned a lot about the purpose of CAS and the available permissions. However, apart from a few code snippets, you haven't seen too much in the way of code examples. There's a good reason for that—the CLR's security architecture is very well designed to offer protection for code behind the scenes. That means that although it's important to understand how CAS works and how it may affect your code, in practice it's not that often that you'll have to invoke the security infrastructure explicitly from your code. Microsoft, in the implementations of the framework base classes, has largely dealt with the places where you may have had to do that. However, occasionally you'll need to deal with security from your own code (for example, to make an assert or demand). This usually happens if you're writing code that accesses some resources that should be protected, and you need to ensure that your assemblies can't be misused by other assemblies. You may also want to use security-related attributes to publicly declare to the world (via reflection) what permissions your assembly is going to need to execute. The purpose of the following sections is to start explaining some of the concepts you'll need to be aware of when coding with CAS. You can use two fairly distinct techniques, respectively known as *imperative security* and *declarative security,* and it's important to understand those before I start explaining the detailed class architecture that supports CAS. In the next sections, I'll discuss those techniques and also give some tips on good coding practices.

Imperative Security

Imperative security is the name given to the process of actively demanding a security permission (or taking some other action using a security permission) inside the code for a method. All the code snippets you've seen so far in this chapter involve imperative security.

If you want to use imperative security, the first thing you'll need to do is instantiate one of the CodeAccessPermission-derived classes. For example, to instantiate an object that represents the FileDialog permission and grants permission to open (but not save) a file selected by the user in an Open File dialog box, you'd use this code:

```
FileDialogPermission dlgPerm = new
    FileDialogPermission(FileDialogPermissionAccess.Open);
```

▊Note The parameters supplied to the constructor of the various permission classes vary considerably, depending on how each permission can be broken into subpermissions. Some permissions, such as FileDialogPermission and SecurityPermission, have [Flag] enumerations to describe the subpermissions. FileIOPermission, on the other hand, can take a string indicating the file path and an enumeration indicating the kind of access required. Since I'm focusing on the underlying concepts in this chapter, I don't provide parameter lists. If you're in any doubt, you can check in the documentation what the parameters for the permission you require are—or you can just use VS .NET IntelliSense!

Instantiating this object by itself doesn't grant any permissions or indeed have any effect whatsoever on security. However, once you have this object, you can invoke methods on it to request the permission be granted in various ways (or denied, according to your requirements). For example, to demand this permission, you'll add this statement:

```
dlgPerm.Demand();
```

You saw a similar example involving FileIOPermission earlier in the section "The CLR Permissions." The other main actions you can take are supplied by three other methods: Assert(), Deny(), and PermitOnly(). These methods are all defined in a base class, CodeAccessPermission, from which all the specific code access permission classes derive.

For example, suppose I want to demand that this assembly and all callers have permission to both skip verification and execute unmanaged code. I'd use this code:

```
SecurityPermission secPerm = new SecurityPermission(
    SecurityPermissionFlag.SkipVerification |
    SecurityPermissionFlag.UnmanagedCode);
secPerm.Demand();
```

Similarly, to assert that callers need not have this permission, use this:

```
// secPerm defined as above
secPerm.Assert();
```

To deny any future requests for this permission within the currently executing method, use this:

```
// secPerm defined as above
secPerm.Deny();
```

And to ensure this is the only permission granted from now on within the currently executing method, use this:

```
// secPerm defined as above
secPerm.PermitOnly();
```

A subtle difference exists between demanding a permission and the other operations: If you demand a permission, that's a one-off action that may or may not throw an exception. All a demand does is effectively to say to the CLR, "Please throw a security exception if this permission isn't available to me, given the current state of the call stack." On the other hand, the other operations are all designed rather to influence the outcome of future demands. Each of these other methods places what's known as a *stack walk modifier* on the call stack information for the current method. This stack walk modifier will be removed as soon as the current method exits, so it's not possible for a call to Assert(), Deny(), or PermitOnly() to have any effect beyond the method in which it's placed. It's not possible to place more than one modifier of the same type simultaneously in the same method. For example, the following code will throw an exception:

```
SecurityPermission secPerm = new SecurityPermission(
                SecurityPermissionFlag.SkipVerification |
                SecurityPermissionFlag.UnmanagedCode);
FileDialogPermission dlgPerm = new FileDialogPermission(
                FileDialogPermissionAccess.Open);
secPerm.Assert();
dlgPerm.Assert();           // Exception--can't have two Asserts in same method
```

If you need an assert that covers more than one permission, you'll need to construct a permission set and place the assert using the permission set. Details of how to do this are in MSDN; you'll need to look up the PermissionSet class. You'll have no problem, however, using two modifiers of different types in the same method (for example, an assert and a permitonly). Also, you'll have no problem using more than one assert on the call stack provided that they were placed in different methods.

If you need to cancel a stack modifier, you can do this using one of four static methods defined in CodeAccessPermission: RevertAssert(), RevertDeny(), RevertPermitOnly(), and RevertAll(). The reason these methods are static is that since only one modifier of each type can be present for the currently executing method, there's no need to supply any information about the modifier. RevertAssert(), for example, will cancel any assert modifier that's present for this method. As a result, the following code will run happily and not throw any exception:

```
// secPerm and dlgPerm defined as above
secPerm.Assert();
// Do something
CodeAccessPermission.RevertAssert();
dlgPerm.Assert();    // No problem now
```

Before I leave the subject of imperative security, I ought to mention one other point. So far, the discussion has focused entirely on those permissions that control access to resources. Some other permission classes, however, are also derived from CodeAccessPermission and represent not a specific permission but instead represent the conditions used to establish membership of a code group. As an example, remember that one possible membership condition is that code should have originated from a certain Web site. This is represented by the class SiteIdentityPermission. So if I want to check that all the assemblies on the call stack were downloaded from my own Web site, http://www.simonrobinson.com, I could do this:

```
SiteIdentityPermission sitePerm = new SiteIdentityPermission(
                                       "www.simonrobinson.com");
sitePerm.Demand();
```

It's quite instructive to type the previous code into a project that you create on your local machine. You'll find the call to Demand() throws an exception because, obviously, code that's sitting on your machine can't possibly satisfy the specified site identity.

■**Note** In some ways I think it's misleading for Microsoft to refer to the identity permissions as *permissions*—since they aren't really permissions to do anything, just statements of assembly identity. However, you can probably see the advantage of having the classes that implement these statements of identity being derived from CodeAccessPermission; they provide a useful alternative way of checking or controlling which assemblies are allowed to execute code.

Declarative Security

So far the discussion in this chapter has focused entirely on *imperative security*, in which IL instructions in your code instantiate and call methods against the security permission classes in order to enforce security. The CLR also supports *declarative security*, in which the permissions required by an assembly, class, method, and so on, can be indicated by an attribute applied to that item. For example, suppose you've written a method that retrieves boot configurations (this will obviously require FileIO permission to read the Boot.ini file), and you want to demand the FileIO permission in order to gain early information about whether your code has this permission. Using imperative security, the code would probably look something like this:

```
string[] GetBootConfigurations()
{
   FileIOPermission filePerm = new
        FileIOPermission(FileIOPermissionAccess.Read,@"C:\Boot.ini");
   filePerm.Demand();
   // Get the data
```

If you want to do the same thing using declarative security, the code will look more like this:

```
[FileIOPermission(SecurityAction.Demand, Read = @"C:\Boot.ini")]
string[] GetBootConfigurations()
{
   // Get the data
```

Clearly, for declarative security to work, you need the relevant attribute classes to have been defined. If you look in the System.Security.Permissions namespace in the documentation, you'll find that for every CAS permission class, Microsoft has defined a corresponding attribute, derived from System.Security.Permissions.CodeAccessSecurityAttribute (itself derived from System.Security.Permissions.SecurityAttribute). Thus, you'll find a FileIOPermissionAttribute class, a SecurityPermissionAttribute class, and so on.

So what have you gained by using an attribute? Apart from less typing and simpler source code, the permissions this method is going to need are now indicated in the metadata, which means that other code can use reflection to check what permissions this method needs without actually invoking the method. You can also take a few actions with security permissions using declarative security that aren't available using imperative security. With imperative security you can demand, assert, deny, or permitonly a permission. With declarative security, you have further options, as shown in Table 12-2. This is controlled through the first parameter that's passed to the FileIOPermissionAttribute in the previous code. This parameter is an instance of the SecurityAction enumeration.

Table 12-2. SecurityAction *Enumeration Values That Control Possible Declarative Security Options*

Value	Also Available with Imperative Security?	Description
Assert	Yes	Indicates that calling assemblies need not have this permission
Demand	Yes	Checks that all assemblies on the call stack have this permission
Deny	Yes	Future requests for this permission will be refused
InheritanceDemand	No	Requires any class that inherits from this class to have the given permission
LinkDemand	No	Requires the direct calling assembly to have the given permission (but not assemblies higher up the call stack)
PermitOnly	Yes	Future requests for any permission other than this permission will be refused

If an attribute is applied to a method, the relevant security check will be performed whenever that method is invoked. If it's applied to a class, the check will be made when the class is first used.

In addition, it's possible to apply security attributes to an assembly as a whole. This means that the check will be made when the assembly is loaded. In this case the options are as follows:

- **RequestMinimum**: The assembly will load only if these permissions are available.

- **RequestOptional**: The assembly could use these permissions, but that's optional.

- **RequestRefuse**: The assembly doesn't need these permissions; this is similar to a call to Deny() on these permissions. If at any point while the assembly is running, a request is made for a permission that had been listed in a RequestRefuse attribute, then that request will be denied.

Marking an assembly with attributes indicating the permissions that it will require can help systems administrators; for example, it means they will know how to adjust their security policy in order to allow your code to run. Using the `RequestRefuse` option can also help security by preventing your assembly from being abused by malicious code. This has a similar effect to denying a permission but has the advantage that you need to declare it only once for the whole assembly.

Good Coding Practices

While I'm on the subject of using CAS, it's worth saying a couple of words about good programming practices. As a developer, you have a responsibility to decide which security permissions your application really needs to perform its task, to decide which of these should be demanded and which asserted, and also to ensure that you code your application in such a way that it doesn't end up "accidentally" requiring more permissions than necessary. To assist in preventing malicious code from damaging your system, it can also be a good idea to request for permissions to be denied as far as possible if your assembly is to call into other assemblies that you don't trust (this includes callback methods).

When designing your application, you should think about which resources it uses. Don't unnecessarily do something that increases the number of permissions your application needs if an alternative exists. A typical issue here is where an application requires administrator privileges to execute because of careless choice of the files or registry keys it uses to store its internal data. It should go without saying that unless you're writing some kind of administration package, chances are you want your application to be able to run from a normal user's account. The trouble is that a large number of developers work using an administrator account—often the administrator account on their own machine. Let's face it, we developers install new software or otherwise play around with our machines so often that a lot of the time it's just not worth the hassle of not having administrator privileges. The trouble is that many of the applications that are written need to be able to run without admin permissions, and if you're working as an administrator, it's remarkably easy to fail to notice that some avoidable aspect of your design will fail if run from an account without administrator privileges. So the moral is that you should take care not to use a resource that requires high privileges unless it's essential for the operation of your application, and you should test your application at least occasionally from an account with privileges typical of the intended user.

Introducing the ListFoldersC Sample: Security Basics

I'll now present a quick sample that illustrates working with CAS at a basic level and focuses on defensive programming to make sure your code bails out gracefully if it's running in a partially trusted context and is denied permission to do something. In the process you'll see how running code remotely from the Internet works in practice. The sample is called `ListFoldersC`, and its functionality is pretty basic, as you can see from Figure 12-5, which shows the sample running on a local machine.

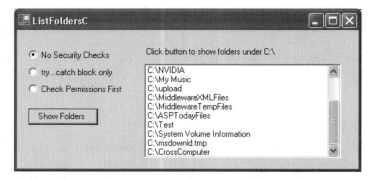

Figure 12-5. *The* ListFoldersC *sample, running locally*

All the sample does is list the folders on the local C drive when the user clicks the button. The interesting functionality is associated with the set of radio buttons, which controls how many security checks take place. The three options are as follows:

- **No Security Checks**: This means what it says—the code presumes it has access and simply lists the folders. This is of course what you'd do if you're absolutely certain that the code will only ever be run in a context where it won't be denied permission (but how often is that going to be?).

- **try...catch block only**: This is almost the same as the option of not having any checks, but the code to list the folders is placed in a try... catch block to catch any security exceptions that occur and display a suitable dialog box.

- **Check Permissions First**: This is the option in which you can start to put into practice what you've learned in this chapter. With this option selected, the code will explicitly check first whether it's going to have permission to read the folders and will display a dialog box if that check fails.

To see what this means in practice, let's check out the code.

Code for the ListFoldersC Sample

I won't show you the click event handler for the button itself—that's just a set of if statements that verifies the status of the radio buttons in order to determine which method to call. So first up, here's the method that lists the folders if no security checks are to be carried out:

```
private void ListFolders()
{
    this.lbFolders.Items.Clear();
    DirectoryInfo c = new DirectoryInfo(@"C:\");
    foreach (DirectoryInfo folder in c.GetDirectories())
    {
        this.lbFolders.Items.Add(folder.FullName);
    }
}
```

No surprises there. The following code adds a try. . . catch block:

```
private void ListFoldersTryCatchOnly()
{
   this.lbFolders.Items.Clear();
   try
   {
      ListFolders();
   }
   catch(SecurityException ex)
   {
      string text = "You do not have permissions to carry out this operation.\n" +
         "Details of failure: " + ex.Message;
      MessageBox.Show( text,
         "Permission denied", MessageBoxButtons.OK, MessageBoxIcon.Error);
   }
}
```

Again, this code should be pretty clear. But now look at the code for the final option, checking the permissions first. This code is similar to the previous case, so I've just highlighted the differences in bold.

```
private void ListFoldersCheckPermissionsFirst()
{
   try
   {
      FileIOPermission perm = new
FileIOPermission(FileIOPermissionAccess.Read, @"C:\");
      perm.Demand();
      ListFolders();
   }
   catch(SecurityException ex)
   {
      string text = "You do not have permissions to carry out this operation.\n" +
         "Details of failure: " + ex.Message;
      MessageBox.Show( text,
         "Permission denied", MessageBoxButtons.OK, MessageBoxIcon.Error);
   }
}
```

As you can see, this code explicitly tries to demand the appropriate FileIO permission first. What difference does that make in practice? Well, to be honest, for this particular sample, it makes virtually no difference. When the DirectoryInfo.GetFolders() method is invoked, about the first thing that will happen is that this method, which was written by Microsoft, demands the appropriate permissions anyway, so the behavior of the code won't be any different. But suppose what I was doing wasn't simply listing files, but some lengthy processing, at the end of which there was a chance that the whole process could be spoiled by some permission being denied. As an example, you may have some code that scrapes information from various Web sites and then stores some of this information in a file. In that case it may make a lot of sense for the program to check that it has appropriate access to the file system *before* it starts hunting round the Internet. Another related point is that if you explicitly check permissions first, that may allow you to better customize the user interface. For example, I could instead have coded the sample to query the relevant permissions at application startup so that the Show Folders button is disabled if the permissions aren't available.

■**Tip** When using the .NET Framework library classes to perform security-sensitive operations, you can be confident that Microsoft has coded the relevant classes so that they demand all appropriate code access permissions first. In general, you have no risk of compromising security by simply using the classes Microsoft has written; I'll discuss that issue in more detail in the section "Declarative Security Under the Hood." If, as in this sample, you write code to explicitly demand the permissions before calling standard framework classes, the reason is almost invariably so you get more information earlier on concerning what permissions are available, thus improving the user interface or application responsiveness.

Running the Sample Remotely

I've talked a bit in this chapter about running samples in partially trusted contexts (for example, on the Internet). Now is where you get a chance to put this into practice. I've actually uploaded the executable for the `ListFoldersC` sample to the Internet, ready for you to try. You can find it at `http://www.SimonRobinson.com/ExpertDotNetSamples/ListFoldersC.exe`.

■**Caution** If you run the sample from here, it's your responsibility to first ensure that your system is set up to safely run CLR executables from the Internet and in particular that it won't run unmanaged executables from your Web browser. Some Web browsers, especially older browsers, can expose this security loophole. While I take all normal security precautions on my Web site, no guarantee exists on any Web site that guards against the possibility of people hacking it. For example, in a worst-case scenario, someone could theoretically hack into the site and replace the file with a malicious file.

If you prefer, you can download and compile the sample and then upload the executable to your own Web site or to a remote location on your own network. To run it from the Internet, you need a Web browser that understands how to run managed executables. Internet Explorer will do nicely there. You just type the URL into Internet Explorer. Under the hood, that will cause the executable to be downloaded and identified as a managed executable and therefore placed in a special section of the assembly cache reserved for downloaded applications. The CLR will then run the application in the appropriate security context to prevent any possibility of damage to your system (provided of course that your CLR security settings are correct). Figure 12-6 shows what happened when I tried doing this.

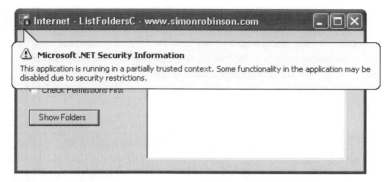

Figure 12-6. *The* ListFoldersC *sample running from the Internet*

Notice how the CLR has identified the context in which the application is running and therefore has displayed a warning bubble. You can get rid of the warning bubble by clicking it. Windows Forms has also stepped in and altered the title bar of the form to indicate that it's running in the Internet Zone and has indicated the Web site from which I downloaded it.

Of course, the Internet Zone doesn't give permission to access my file system, so there's no way the application will now be able to list any folders. The interesting thing is what happens if I try. First, Figure 12-7 shows what happens if I go for a straight listing with no security checks. Of course the DirectoryInfo class throws an exception, and with no exception handling, you get the dialog box shown.

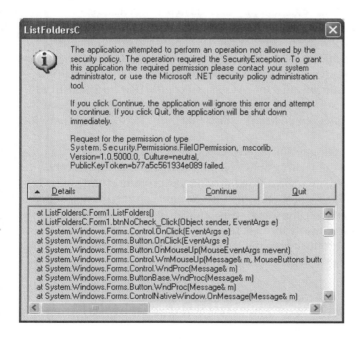

Figure 12-7. *An unhandled security exception in the Internet Zone*

This dialog box has been displayed by the CLR itself. Notice by the way how much information about the method calls in the stack has been provided for free—great news for anyone who wants to hack into or decompile your code and a very good additional reason for handling exceptions yourself! By the way, if you're wondering, I uploaded the release build of the application—that stack trace isn't dependent on having a debug build.

Second, Figure 12-8 shows what happens when I selected either of the two options to do security checks or handle exceptions (both options give the same result).

Figure 12-8. *The* ListFoldersC *sample, gracefully handling a denied permission*

I explicitly coded the sample to display details of the security exception thrown in this dialog box, but, obviously, depending on the sensitivity of your applications, you may decide not to do so in order to avoid giving away too much information.

Granting Permissions to a Remote Application

One disadvantage of the ListFoldersC sample is that, when running remotely, it can't do anything useful because it doesn't have sufficient permissions to perform its intended purpose. In general, applications are distributed remotely for a good reason, most commonly so that updates can be distributed easily. The administrator simply places the updated version at the correct URL, and each user's Web browser, working with the CLR, will each time the application is run automatically check whether a newer version than the version previously downloaded is available and download it if one exists. Of course, that ease of distribution is useless if your applications can't execute because they don't have appropriate security, so you may wonder how, for example, I could have ensured that the sample did have permission to read the C drive.

Here's where a weakness of automatic downloads shows up. To grant the application more security, you need to change the security policy on the client machine. This may be done, for example, by having clients run a setup program. The most common implementation is that you'd have the assembly signed either with a strong name or a certificate, or both, and then set up a code group that grants more trust to assemblies that have been signed by that strong name or certificate. I won't work through that process here, as you'll see an example of setting up such a code group later in the "Defining Custom Permissions" section, where I introduce the WMDDetector sample.

Introducing the ListFoldersAuditing Sample: Asserting a Permission

I'll now modify the ListFoldersC sample to illustrate a situation in which you may want to Assert() a permission. I'll introduce a library that does a form of basic auditing. And by *basic*,

I do mean basic. To keep things simple, I don't use the event log. Instead, the program simply writes out the date and time, along with details of the assembly that invoked it, to a file, `C:\ExpertDotNetAuditText.txt`. (This means that if you download and run the sample, you'll probably want to remove this file afterward.) I'll also have the auditing library invoked from a modified version of the `ListFoldersC` sample so that a record is made whenever that sample is used. In other words, the `ListFoldersAuditing` sample consists of two projects.

- `ListFoldersAuditing`, a Windows Forms, which is similar to the earlier `ListFoldersC` sample

- `AuditLibrary`, which compiles to a simple class library and which is responsible for the auditing

When I ran the new sample from the Internet and subsequently inspected the audit file on my local machine, I found this:

```
Audit invoked at 16/08/2004 11:59:58
   from assembly at
http://www.simonrobinson.com/expertdotnetsamples/ListFoldersAuditing.EXE
   ListFoldersAuditing, Version=1.0.1689.19695,
   Culture=neutral, PublicKeyToken=null
```

Of course, writing this auditing entry involves a problem. The `ListFoldersAuditing` assembly, when running from the Internet, doesn't even have permission to *read* any part of the `C:\` drive, let alone create or append to an audit file there. The auditing library itself is installed locally on my machine so that it has full trust, but by itself that won't do any good because when it attempts to write to the audit file, the CLR will do a stack walk, see that `AuditLibrary` has been invoked by a program running in the Internet Zone that doesn't have this permission, and hence throw an exception. The solution to this is of course to *assert* the permission in the audit library, preventing the stack walk from taking place.

Here's the code for the auditing library. It's quite simple; it consists of just one class with one static method.

```
public class Auditor
{
   public static void DoAudit()
   {
      // Make auditing entries
      string auditFilePath = @"C:\ExpertDotNetAuditText.txt";
      FileIOPermission ioperm = new FileIOPermission(
         PermissionState.Unrestricted);
      ioperm.Assert();
      StreamWriter sw = new StreamWriter(auditFilePath, true);
      sw.WriteLine("Audit invoked at " + DateTime.Now.ToString());
      sw.WriteLine("   from assembly at " +
         Assembly.GetEntryAssembly().CodeBase);
      sw.WriteLine("   " + Assembly.GetEntryAssembly().FullName);
      sw.WriteLine();
      sw.Close();
```

```
    CodeAccessPermission.RevertAssert();
}
```

Although this code is entirely new, I've highlighted in bold only the parts of it that are relevant to asserting the permission. Notice that I've asserted only the minimum permission required—access to one single file. And notice also that I've been careful to revert the assert as soon as the process of writing to the file is complete.

This library needs a little more work before it's ready to compile. Usually when you compile multiproject solutions in VS .NET, all you need to do is ensure that the correct VS .NET project references are in place, and then everything will be ready to run as soon as compilation is complete. However, that's not the case here because I want to run the Windows Forms project in the Internet Zone rather than from a local folder. This means that I'll have to place the auditing library in the assembly cache if the downloaded form is to locate it. This in turn means that the library must have a strong name; also, to be callable from code in the Internet Zone, it'll have to be marked with the AllowPartiallyTrustedCallers attribute. To achieve this I've supplied the sample with a key file, Apress.snk, and made the following changes to assemblyinfo.cs source file for the library:

```
[assembly: AssemblyDelaySign(false)]
[assembly: AssemblyKeyFile(@"E:\Books\Expert .NET 2ndEd\
    Chapters\2220ch12\NewSamples\ListFoldersAuditing\Apress.snk")]
[assembly: AssemblyKeyName("")]

[assembly: AllowPartiallyTrustedCallers()]
```

After compiling the sample, you'll need to run gacutil -i from the command line to install the library into the GAC. You saw how to do this in Chapter 4. You'll also need to change the hard-coded path for the key file that you can see in this code listing, before compilation.

Finally, I'll just show you the modifications to the code for the form. Because I'm not interested in trying different types of security checking, the new sample doesn't feature the radio buttons of the earlier ListFoldersC sample, so now only one method shows the folders. That method looks like so:

```
private void ListFoldersTryCatchOnly()
{
    this.lbFolders.Items.Clear();
    try
    {
        Auditor.DoAudit();
        DirectoryInfo c = new DirectoryInfo(@"C:\");
        foreach (DirectoryInfo folder in c.GetDirectories())
        {
            this.lbFolders.Items.Add(folder.FullName);
        }
    }
    catch(SecurityException ex)
    {
        string text = "You do not have permissions to carry out this operation.\n" +
            "Details of failure: " + ex.Message;
```

```
    MessageBox.Show( text,
        "Permission denied", MessageBoxButtons.OK, MessageBoxIcon.Error);
   }
}
```

I've highlighted the code (actually the one single statement) in bold that's relevant to the auditing. Notice that an exception will still be thrown when the code tries to list the folders, as the application still doesn't have permission to do that. But at the same time, thanks to the assert in the library, the auditing entry will still be made each time you attempt to run the code.

This and the previous sample have (I hope) shown you how to use security at a basic level. The focus of the chapter is now going to shift a bit, as I want to start working toward a much more advanced sample, which will illustrate how to define and use your own custom permissions. To do this, you'll need to understand a bit more about how CAS works under the hood—so that's the topic I'll cover next.

Looking at CAS Under the Hood

I'll now cover in more detail how the implementation of CAS works under the hood. Although I discuss CAS here, many of the principles involved, particularly the way that the underlying security engine exposes numerous hooks that managed classes can plug into to customize security policy, apply equally well to role-based security.

One thing that may surprise you is the extent to which the CLR is divorced from the implementation of security. To see this, let's look once again at that FileIO permission as an example. You know that the FileIO permission is the way that the CLR protects against the unauthorized use of files. It's tempting to conclude from this that there must be some mechanism in the CLR that detects if an application is trying to access a file and therefore checks if it has the appropriate permission. If that's how you've imagined the situation, think again. That's how Windows/NT security works, but it's not how CLR security works. In the CLR, checking that code has sufficient permissions to carry out some operation is (apart from the exceptions noted earlier with regard to the Security permission) the responsibility of the IL code itself, not the responsibility of the CLR. So when you use the System.IO classes to access files and folders, it's those classes that internally are implemented to make sure that the appropriate security is obtained. Returning to the code snippet I presented earlier in the section "The CLR Permissions," I indicated that when accessing the file C:\Boot.ini, code will execute that has the same effect as the following:

```
FileIOPermission perm = new
    FileIOPermission(FileIOPermissionAccess.Read, @"C:\Boot.ini");
perm.Demand();
```

The crucial point to understand is that the CLR has no idea that FileIOPermission has anything to do with file access. All the CLR knows is that some code has called the CodeAccessPermission.Demand() method for this particular permission. It's this method that walks up the stack and checks if each method in turn has this permission. (As you may guess, this process is performed in an IL internalcall method.) The CLR knows only that it must check against the evidence for each assembly to see what code groups that assembly is in and therefore what permission set is available.

I mentioned earlier that this looks at first sight like this exposes a security loophole. If the demanding of permissions is done by the assembly and not automatically imposed by the CLR, what's stopping someone from writing an assembly that does some dangerous operation but without asking for the relevant permissions? For example, suppose someone tried to write an assembly that manipulates the file system but without demanding the FileIO permission first. It's perfectly possible for someone to write such an assembly. However, in general this shouldn't cause problems, and in fact no security loophole exists for the following reasons:

- In practice, under the hood, all the potentially dangerous operations can be accessed only by calling some unmanaged code at some point. This comes back to the point I emphasized in Chapter 3 that no IL instruction exists that can do any more than access the local memory that's available to the application domain. No IL instruction, for example, accesses a file or the registry. You can perform those operations only by calling into unmanaged code. This means that the assembly in question will need to have permission to call unmanaged code—and that's going to happen only if it's a highly trusted assembly. For example, if your assembly wants to manipulate arbitrary files, then it will either have to call the API functions directly (needs unmanaged code permission) or use the System.IO classes (needs the FileIO permission, because those classes will internally call into unmanaged code anyway).

- On Windows NT/2000/XP, the CLR's security sits on top of Windows security. Since Windows security is controlled by the operating system and has nothing to do with the CLR, you still can't do anything in managed code that your account wouldn't have rights to do in unmanaged code (though obviously this doesn't protect against malicious code running under a highly trusted account).

Indeed, the fact that trusted code can arrange for CLR permissions to be circumvented in a controlled manner is a bonus. This ability provides the means by which less trusted code can be allowed to access resources in a controlled and safe manner. And, as you saw earlier, a perfect example of this is sitting in the framework class library: the isolated storage classes. The isolated storage classes also access the file system. However, they don't request FileIO permission. Instead they request IsolatedStorageFile permission, a permission that can be considered less restrictive in the sense that the default security policy allows more code groups to have this permission. That's fine, because the isolated storage classes have been carefully written so that they access only carefully defined areas of the file system. It's simply not possible for client code to, for example, corrupt or damage system files or read private files associated with a different application by calling methods on the isolated storage classes in the same way that it could with the System.IO classes.

Having said all that, I should point out that it'd theoretically be possible to open a security loophole by writing some code that asserts permissions and then allows callers to abuse this fact. For example, if you wrote an assembly whose methods allowed unrestricted access to the file system, but where that assembly invoked the System.IO classes *and* asserted the relevant FileIO permission, and you placed this assembly on a local drive so that it was fully trusted, then partially trusted code would be able to use such an assembly to wreak havoc on your system. But here .NET is no different from classic security. It's hard to guard against some trusted individual opening a security loophole by writing bad code. I hope, once you understand how CAS works, you'll be less likely accidentally to do that through poor use of Assert().

I should also point out one weakness in the whole infrastructure. Often when you install software, you do so by running some `.msi` or similar file from an administrator account. If you do this, then in principle nothing is stopping that file from modifying your CLR security policy, which, if not done carefully, may open a security loophole. I'm already aware of one well-known company that makes software that comes with an MSI file that adjusts the security policy to give full trust to all code signed with that company's certificate—and doesn't warn the user that this change is being made. While I can understand why a large company that's selling sophisticated managed software may want to make that change in order to make life easier for its own programmers, I can't emphasize enough that good coding practice requires that you demand only those permissions your code really needs.

The CAS Security Classes

If security policy is implemented by managed classes, there clearly must be some mechanism by which the CLR can find out which classes it needs to instantiate in order to implement its security policy. This information is indicated in the `.config` XML files that control security. I don't have space here to go into the process in detail, but to get a flavor of it, consider the `LocalIntranet` built-in permission set and in particular its `Security` permission. You saw earlier that this permission set gives code the `Security` permission to execute code and to assert permissions. If you look in the CLR's `machine.config` file, you'll find the following XML tag, which introduces the `LocalIntranet` permission set:

```
<PermissionSet class="NamedPermissionSet"
    version="1" Name="LocalIntranet"
    Description="Default rights given to applications on the local intranet">
```

The `class` attribute of this tag indicates that the class that must be instantiated in order to implement this permission set is a class called `NamedPermissionSet`. This is located in the `System.Security` namespace. The tag contains no indication about where to search for this class. In fact, the CLR's security subsystem will search in those assemblies that have been registered as allowed to implement security policy; you'll see how to do this soon when I work through the final sample of the chapter, the `WMDDetector` sample.

The `<PermissionSet>` element contains a number of child elements, one for each permission defined in this set. Among these elements is the following:

```
<IPermission class="SecurityPermission"
            version="1"
            Flags="Assertion, Execution" />
```

This `<IPermission>` element represents a permission within the permission set, and once again the `class` attribute indicates which class should be instantiated in order to represent this element. This class must implement the `System.Security.IPermission` interface, which defines the `Demand()` method, as well as methods to handle combining permissions. This permission class should also normally implement two other `System.Security` interfaces, `IStackWalk` and `ISecurityEncodable`. `IStackWalk` also defines the `Demand()` method, as well as the `Assert()` method and a couple of other methods that control the process of walking up the stack and checking which assemblies have which permissions. `ISecurityEncodable` defines two methods, `FromXml()` and `ToXml()`, which are respectively able to initialize a class instance by reading from an XML file and writing out the XML element from the state of the object.

All these interfaces are implemented by `CodeAccessPermission`, so it's usual for security classes to derive from this class in order to pick up much of the implementation of these interfaces for free.

Beyond the `class` and `version` attributes, the remaining attributes in the `<IPermission>` element are variable and will depend on the permission class instantiated. The idea is that the CLR will instantiate the named class and then initialize it by invoking that object's `ISecurityEncodable.FromXml()` method, handing it the entire XML element from the security configuration file—so that class must be able to interpret this XML stream. With this XML element, you'll end up with a `SecurityPermission` object that has been initialized to indicate that it should allow requests only for the `Assertion` and `Execution` subpermissions.

You're now in a position to understand better what happens when some code demands a permission. When each assembly is loaded into the process, the CLR will read the XML representation of the security policy defined in the various `.config` files to instantiate permission classes that define the permissions available to that assembly. For the most part, nothing will be done with these objects for the time being, but the CLR will check the `SecurityPermission` object to make sure that the assembly does have permission to execute! However, later, if any code invokes the methods that demand permissions, this set of permission classes is likely to be checked, most commonly as a result of a call to `CodeAccessPermission.Demand()`.

Declarative Security Under the Hood

As I mentioned earlier, the security attributes are all derived from the `System.Security.Permissions.SecurityAttribute` attribute. Knowledge of this attribute has been hard-coded into the CLR, so it knows to take some special action if it encounters it. In particular, after instantiating the `SecurityAttribute`-derived class, it will call the `SecurityAttribute.CreatePermission()` method. All classes that derive from `SecurityAttribute` should implement this method to create an instance of the corresponding security permission class, initialized to the correct state as far as subpermissions are concerned. Once the CLR has this object, it can manipulate it in the same manner as for imperative security.

To enable declarative security, every security permission class should have a corresponding attribute class. If any permission class doesn't have a corresponding attribute class defined, it won't be possible to use declarative security for that class, but you can still use the class for imperative security.

That's really as far as I'll go with exploring the principles of .NET security. I'll now go on to present a couple of samples that will demonstrate how you put these principles into practice.

Defining Custom Permissions

Because .NET security is largely implemented by classes in the framework class library, it's possible to define custom permissions if you're implementing some library that needs to be protected against partially trusted callers but for which the permissions supplied by Microsoft aren't appropriate. Admittedly, defining custom permissions isn't something you should need to do often in the course of normal programming, but I'll use this as the basis for the final sample in this chapter, because defining a custom permission provides considerable insight into how .NET security works under the hood, illustrating many of the principles I've been discussing about how classes are instantiated from XML representations.

Since code access permissions are implemented as classes derived from `CodeAccessPermission`, it follows that defining your own permission normally involves defining your own class, also derived from `CodeAccessPermission`. You also have to take other steps, including adding your custom permissions to the security policy. You'll see all these steps in action as I work through the `WMDDetector` sample.

WMDDetector Sample

This sample will illustrate the process of creating a custom permission. For this sample, I'll assume that Apress, in its noble desire to support the international community, has branched out from publishing into a new business market of searching for weapons of mass destruction (WMDs). Apress's main product in this area is WMD Detector, which can plug into your computer and will detect any WMD in the vicinity. Obviously, this is the kind of device that requires tight security, so Apress sells this device only to selected customers who have been carefully vetted, which is why I consider myself lucky to have been able to pick up my WMD Detector on some Internet auction site, using a false identity. More to the point for this chapter, this story provides the perfect scenario to test creating a custom CAS permission.

For the sample, I assume that the Apress WMD Detectors come with device drivers that can be accessed programmatically only through a managed DLL. Of course, this DLL will be installed on the local system, which means it has full trust and therefore isn't very interesting from the point of view of demonstrating security. However, to make things more interesting, I'll assume that Apress regularly updates some software that processes the data derived from the WMD Detectors and provides reports. As a result, this software isn't normally installed on the local machine but instead is downloaded from a Web site, which means it's running in a low-trust environment. This is where the custom permissions come in. Apress doesn't want the WMD data to be processed by any code other than the code that it has written and signed with an appropriate strong name. You're therefore going to need a new code group to provide membership to assemblies with this strong name. In addition, a custom permission would be most appropriate, since none of the permissions supplied by Microsoft with the CLR is really appropriate to controlling a WMD Detector.

Installing the sample will therefore involve setting up a custom permission set that gives the ability to interface with the WMD Detector, along with a new code group that grants this permission set. The membership condition for this code group is that it must have been signed with the Apress WMD Detector strong name.

I realize that's all quite a bit to take in at once, but don't worry, I'll walk you through the process of setting up the permissions and installing the sample quite carefully.

Tip In real life, an organization would probably sign its software with a digital certificate to provide additional confirmation of its authenticity, and the test for code group membership would involve checking this certificate. However, I haven't covered certificates yet—that's an important topic in its own right that I'll cover in Chapter 13. So instead of certificates, I'll stick with using assembly strong names, which can serve quite a similar purpose. This doesn't change any of the principles of the sample.

What the WMDDetector Sample Does

Before I run through the code for the sample, I'll quickly demonstrate it in action with a couple of figures. Obviously what you're interested in is how the security aspects of the sample work, so I won't code a complicated sample. In fact, the method I wrote that simulates doing a WMD detection simply returns a hard-coded constant result, and the downloadable application simply displays this result in a textbox when a button is clicked. Figure 12-9 shows what the sample looks like if I pretend I'm one of the developers, run the complete sample locally on my machine, and click the button to check for WMDs.

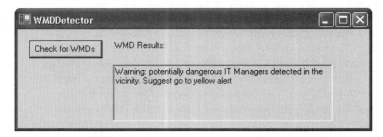

Figure 12-9. *The WMDDetector sample, running locally*

To test the application running remotely, I placed a copy of it at the URL `http://www.simonrobinson.com/expertdotnetsamples/wmddetector.exe`, so you can try it there in the same way as with the previous samples.

Now I mentioned earlier that this sample involves some new custom permissions. First let's confirm what happens if I have the sample running in the Internet Zone and click the Check for WMDs button, but without the sample having the permissions to run properly.

Figure 12-10 simply shows that the sample contains some kind of error handling. I actually obtained this figure by temporarily removing the custom permission from my machine, but you can obtain roughly the same result (perhaps more realistically) by simply recompiling the sample without the strong name and running it from your own Web site.

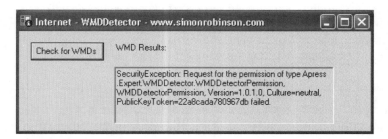

Figure 12-10. *The* WMDDetector *sample, running without the required permissions*

Finally, Figure 12-11 shows the result for when I ran the sample remotely, but with the permissions set up correctly on my local machine.

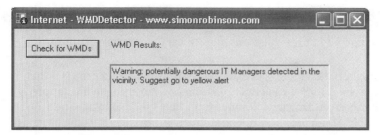

Figure 12-11. *The* WMDDetector *sample, running correctly from the Internet*

The Code for the WMDDetector Sample

The overall architecture of the sample looks like Figure 12-12.

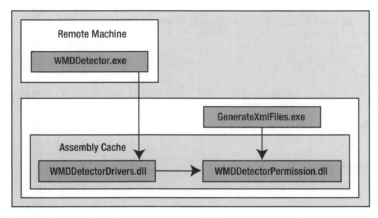

Figure 12-12. *Files that make up the* WMDDetector *sample*

In this figure, the arrows indicate the dependencies of the assemblies. The purposes of the assemblies are as follows:

- WMDDetectorPermission.dll defines the custom security permissions that are needed to control access to the WMD detector.

- WMDDetectorDrivers.dll implements managed classes that can talk to the device drivers and thereby offer a managed interface through which other code can access the WMD detector.

- WMDDetector.exe is a simple Windows Forms application that displays the value read from the WMD detector. Because this file sits on a remote machine, I'll need to configure security to allow it to invoke the relevant methods in WMDDetectorDrivers.dll; as just mentioned, I'll do this by signing WMDDetector.exe with a strong name and setting up a code group to allow access to the light detector by any code signed with this strong name.

- GenerateXmlFiles.exe is a helper assembly that generates the XML representation of the custom permissions used by the application. This is important because you need the XML representation to add the permissions to the local CLR security policy.

Obviously, this sample is simplified relative to any real application. Besides the fact that the WMDDetectorDrivers.dll assembly doesn't actually contain any drivers at all but simply returns a constant string, there's an additional difference from "real life." In real life the GenerateXmlFiles.exe assembly would probably not be shipped out to clients; it'd be used in-house to generate the XML files, which would then presumably be shipped as part of some integrated deployment installation package that installs the files and automatically registers the custom security permissions with the CLR. Since my goal here is to demonstrate CLR security with custom permissions, I'll have the GenerateXmlFiles.exe assembly on the "client" machine and work through the registration process by hand.

The process of compiling these assemblies is relatively complex. You not only need to compile them, but you must also install the two DLLs in the GAC and run GenerateXmlFiles.exe to get the XML files. In view of this, the downloadable version of this sample is supplied not as a VS .NET project but as a set of plain .cs source files, along with a batch file to perform the compilation.

WMDDetectorPermission.dll

This file defines the custom permission. The permission is called WMDDetectorPermission (the same name as the assembly) and has a couple of levels at which it can be granted, which I'll define by the following enumeration:

```
[Flags]
public enum WMDDetectorPermissions
{
    All   = 3,
    Read  = 2,
    Reset = 1,
    None  = 0
}
```

Now you'll see the permission itself. The permission contains one member field, which is used to indicate the level of permission this object represents, as well as two constructors.

```
[Serializable()]
public sealed class WMDDetectorPermission : CodeAccessPermission,
                        IUnrestrictedPermission
{
    WMDDetectorPermissions state;

    public WMDDetectorPermission(WMDDetectorPermissions state)
    {
        this.state = state;
    }
```

```
public WMDDetectorPermission(PermissionState permState)
{
   if (permState == PermissionState.Unrestricted)
      this.state =  WMDDetectorPermissions.All;
   else
      this.state = WMDDetectorPermissions.None;
}
```

```
// etc.
```

The purpose of the first constructor should be fairly obvious. The second constructor is required to support the CLR's security infrastructure. At certain times, the CLR will internally instantiate the permission class and will want to be able to indicate whether the permission object represents unrestricted access (in other words, complete access to all resources controlled by this permission; in our case this is equivalent to the WMDDetectorPermissions.All flag). This concept is represented by the System.Security.PermissionState enumeration, which has just two values, Unrestricted and None. The second constructor in the previous code simply takes a PermissionState and uses it to set an appropriate permission level.

Next I needed to implement a few other methods that are required to support the .NET security infrastructure. These methods are all declared as abstract in the base class, CodeAccessPermission. First, the following is a method that tells the CLR whether this permission object gives completely unrestricted access to its resource. This method is used on occasions by the security infrastructure.

```
public bool IsUnrestricted()
{
   return state == WMDDetectorPermissions.All;
}
```

Second, the following is a method that can return a copy of this permission object, which is cast to the IPermission interface.

```
public override IPermission Copy()
{
   return new WMDDetectorPermission(this.state);
}
```

The sample also requires a method that can deal with the situation in which some code demands two successive WMDDetectorPermissions, which must both be satisfied for the code to run. In this case, the CLR must be able to supply a permission object that represents exactly the set of conditions needed to satisfy both permissions (the *intersection* of the permissions). The CLR does this by calling an override method IPermission.Intersect() on the permission object.

```
public override IPermission Intersect(IPermission target)
{
   WMDDetectorPermission rhs = target as WMDDetectorPermission;
   if (rhs == null)
      return null;
   if ((this.state & rhs.state) == WMDDetectorPermissions.None)
```

```
      return null;
   return new WMDDetectorPermission(this.state & rhs.state);
}
```

Because the possible permission state in the class is represented by a [Flags] enumeration, it's simple to identify the intersection permission by performing a bitwise AND operation on the two state masks. Note that this method should theoretically only ever be called with a WMDDetectorPermission reference passed in as a parameter, but just in case something goes wrong, the code starts by checking the type of the parameter passed in. If it has any problem, it returns null, indicating that any intersection contains no permissions. It also returns null if the intersection of the two permissions results in no permission to do anything.

Another related task is that the CLR will sometimes need to know if a permission represents a subset of another permission. Here's the implementation of the method that the CLR will expect to deal with this task:

```
public override bool IsSubsetOf(IPermission target)
{
   if (target == null || !(target is WMDDetectorPermission))
      return false;
   WMDDetectorPermission rhs = (WMDDetectorPermission)target;

   int subsetFlags = (int)this.state;
   int supersetFlags = (int)rhs.state;
   return (subsetFlags & (~supersetFlags)) == 0;
}
```

Again, my choice of a bitmask to represent the access flags makes this method relatively easy to implement. If the permissions in this object really form a subset of those of the target object, then there will be no bits in the mask that are one (representing a permission granted) in this object and zero (representing a permission denied) in the target object. The bitwise operation subsetFlags & (~supersetFlags) will return zero if that's the case. Obviously, if I had defined a more complicated permission—such as one that could be narrowed down to individual files—then my implementations of IsSubsetOf() and Intersect() would have been considerably more complex.

The Copy(), Intersect(), and IsSubsetOf() methods are defined in the IPermission interface and aren't implemented by the CodeAccessPermission class, which gives a syntactical requirement for WMDDetectorPermission to implement these methods.

Next I needed to implement the methods defined in ISecurityEncodable that allow conversion to and from an XML representation of this permission.

```
public override void FromXml(SecurityElement xml)
{
   string element = xml.Attribute("Unrestricted");

   if(element != null)
   {
      state = (WMDDetectorPermissions)Enum.Parse(
                  typeof(WMDDetectorPermissions), element, false);
   }
```

```
    else
        throw new ArgumentException("XML element does not correctly " +
            "parse to a WMDDetectorPermission");
}

public override SecurityElement ToXml()
{
    SecurityElement element = new SecurityElement("IPermission");
    Type type = typeof(WMDDetectorPermission);

    StringBuilder assemblyName = new StringBuilder(type.Assembly.ToString());
    assemblyName.Replace('\"', '\'');

    element.AddAttribute("class", type.FullName + ", " + assemblyName);
    element.AddAttribute("description", "Apress WMD Detector");
    element.AddAttribute("version", "1.*");
    element.AddAttribute("Unrestricted", state.ToString());

    return element;
}
```

Microsoft has provided a helper class, SecurityElement, to assist in writing an XML element that represents a permission object and that conforms to the XML schema that the CLR's security subsystem can understand. Note that in generating this element I need to remove any double quotes from the assembly name and replace with single quotes. The SecurityElement class automatically handles the <IPermission start of the XML element, which means that the XML emitted by the ToXml() method looks like this:

```
<IPermission class="Apress.ExpertDotNet.WMDDetector.WMDDetectorPermission,
            WMDDetectorPermission, Version=1.0.1.0, Culture=neutral,
                PublicKeyToken=22a8cada780967db"
            description="Apress WMD detector" version="1.*"
            Unrestricted="Read" />
```

Apart from having well-formed XML here, which should be in a format that the SecurityElement class will accept, the main requirement here is that the object should be able to reconstruct itself in the same state. In other words, the result of calling ToXml() and then calling FromXml() should always be an object that has the same state as the original object.

As well as defining the permission class, I also need to define an associated attribute in order to support declarative security. I won't actually be using the following attribute in the sample, but I've included it in the sample to demonstrate how you'd define a permission attribute—because in general you really should always supply one in case it's needed by any client code.

```
[AttributeUsageAttribute(AttributeTargets.All, AllowMultiple = true)]
public class WMDDetectorPermissionAttribute : CodeAccessPermissionAttribute
{
    WMDDetectorPermissions state;
```

```
    public WMDDetectorPermissions Access
    {
        get
        {
            if (this.Unrestricted)
                return WMDDetectorPermissions.All;
            return state;
        }
        set
        {
            this.state = value;
            if (value == WMDDetectorPermissions.All)
                this.Unrestricted = true;
        }
    }

    public WMDDetectorPermissionAttribute(SecurityAction action) : base(action)
    {
    }

    public override IPermission CreatePermission()
    {
        return new WMDDetectorPermission(state);
    }
}
```

Finally, here's the using statements needed for the previous code to work, as well as the AssemblyKeyFile attribute that ensures the assembly will have a strong name:

```
using System;
using System.Security;
using System.Security.Permissions;
using System.Text;
using System.Reflection;

[assembly:AssemblyKeyFile("ApressWMDDetectors.snk")]
[assembly:AssemblyVersion("1.0.1.0")]
```

ApressWMDDetectors.snk is a key file that I generated using sn.exe, and it forms part of the downloadable code for the sample.

GeneratorXmlFiles.exe

Now I'll examine the code that generates the XML file that describes the WMD detector security permission. Strictly speaking, this part of the sample isn't absolutely necessary. I could, after all, decide what the XML representation of the permission is going to look like, make sure that WMDDetectorPermission.ToXml() and WMDDetectorPermission.FromXml() are written so that they emit or read this format correctly, and then independently use Notepad or some similar utility to create a text file with the correct XML in it, which can be shipped with the application. However, doing that carries the obvious risk of typos, and since I've already written a ToXml() method to generate the XML element, I may as well use this method to programmatically create the XML file to be shipped. Then I can be sure the XML is correct. The code I present here will actually generate two files—a file called ReadWMDDetector.xml, which represents a ReadLightPermission initialized to allow read access to the WMD detector, and a separate file, WMDDetectorPermissions.xml, which contains the XML representation of a permission set containing this one permission. First, as usual, here's the namespaces I need:

```
using System;
using System.IO;
using System.Security;
using System.Security.Permissions;
```

This utility doesn't need a strong name, as it's not going to be used in any situation that requires it.

The Main() method is reasonably clear.

```
[STAThread]
static void Main(string[] args)
{
    WritePermission("WMDDetectorPermission.xml");
    WritePermissionSet("ReadWMDDetector.xml");
}
```

The following is the method that writes out a single permission:

```
static void WritePermission(string file)
{
    WMDDetectorPermission perm = new WMDDetectorPermission(
                                        WMDDetectorPermissions.Read);
    StreamWriter sw = new StreamWriter(file);
    sw.Write(perm.ToXml());
    sw.Close();
}
```

WritePermission() simply hooks up the output from WMDDetectorPermission.ToXml() to a StreamWriter to send the XML text to a file.

WritePermisionSet() writes out a permission set.

```
static void WritePermissionSet(string file)
{
    WMDDetectorPermission perm = new WMDDetectorPermission(
                                        WMDDetectorPermissions.Read);
    NamedPermissionSet pset = new NamedPermissionSet("ReadWMDDetector");
    pset.Description = "WMD Detector Permission Set";
    pset.SetPermission(perm);
    StreamWriter sw = new StreamWriter(file);
    sw.Write(pset.ToXml());
    sw.Close();
}
```

WritePermissionSet() uses the System.Security.NamedPermissionSet class, which represents a permission set. I instantiate this class, call the NamedPermissionSet.AddPermission() method to add the custom permission, and then call the NamedPermissionSet.ToXml() method to emit the XML for the whole permission set.

The WMDDetectorDrivers Library

The WMDDetectorDrivers.dll class library is the assembly that exposes managed methods to manipulate theWMD detector. The following is the header information for this file:

```
using System;
using System.Security;
using System.Security.Permissions;
using System.Drawing;
using System.Reflection;
using System.IO;

[assembly: AssemblyKeyFile("ApressWMDDetectors.snk")]
[assembly: AssemblyVersion("1.0.1.0")]
[assembly: AllowPartiallyTrustedCallers()]
```

Notice the AllowPartiallyTrustedCallers attribute; this is important because the library is to be digitally signed and will be invoked by code over the network.

```
public class WMDDetectorDrivers
{
   public Color ReadValue()
   {
      WMDDetectorPermission perm = new WMDDetectorPermission(
                                    WMDDetectorPermissions.Read);
      perm.Demand();
      return Color.FromArgb(255, 40, 30);
   }
}
```

As you can see, I've implemented only one method in this class—that's all that's required for the sample. ReadValue() simulates the process of hooking up to the WMD detector and reading the detected value.

The Remote Client

The remote client is a standard Windows Forms application, with the following using directives and assembly-level attributes:

```
using System;
using System.Drawing;
using System.Collections;
using System.ComponentModel;
using System.Windows.Forms;
using System.Data;
```

```
using System.Reflection;
using System.Security;

[assembly: AssemblyKeyFile("ApressWMDDetectors.snk")]
[assembly: AssemblyVersion("1.0.1.0")]
```

The fact that it has been signed with the `ApressWMDDetectors.snk` file is important, since otherwise the program won't have sufficient permissions to call the `WMDDetectorDrivers.ReadValue()` method. The key code is in the event handler for clicking the button.

```
private void btnRead_Click(object sender, System.EventArgs e)
{
    try
    {
        WMDDetectorDrivers controller = new WMDDetectorDrivers();
        this.tbColor.Text = controller.ReadValue().ToString();
    }
    catch (SecurityException ex)
    {
        this.tbColor.Text = "SecurityException: " + ex.Message;
    }
    catch (Exception ex)
    {
        this.tbColor.Text = "Exception: " + ex.Message;
    }
}
```

Because this sample is aimed at demonstrating security, I've provided separate exception handlers for security exceptions and other types of exception—just to make sure that if there are any problems with the security permissions, this is picked out and a fairly clear message is displayed about the problem.

Compiling the Code

Now that you've seen all the source code, I need to compile it and register the new security permissions. You can compile it by running the following batch file, which compiles the source code, runs the XML generator, and places the two libraries in the GAC:

```
@rem Compile assemblies and add libraries to assembly cache
csc /target:library WMDDetectorPermission.cs
gacutil /i WMDDetectorPermission.dll

csc /r:WMDDetectorPermission.dll /r:System.Drawing.dll
   /target:library WMDDetectorDrivers.cs
gacutil /i WMDDetectorDrivers.dll

csc /r:WMDDetectorPermission.dll GenerateXmlFiles.cs
csc /r:WMDDetectorDrivers.dll /r:System.Windows.Forms.dll
   /target:winexe WMDDetector.cs
```

```
@rem Run app to generate the XML files describing permission and permission set
GenerateXmlFiles

@rem Add permission DLL to full trust list
caspol -polchgprompt off
caspol -addfulltrust WMDDetectorPermission.dll
caspol -polchgprompt on
```

The final statements in the batch file register the WMDDetectorPermissions.dll as an assembly that's allowed to affect security policy. Note that the requirement to register an assembly in this way is additional to the requirement for the assembly to run under the full trust permission set, if the assembly is to define additional permissions.

In principle it'd be possible to use caspol to perform the registration of the new permission set and code group from the batch file. However, I haven't done that because I thought it'd give a clearer picture of what's going on if I use the mscorcfg UI instead.

To start, you need to add a new permission set. That's easily achieved by right-clicking the PermissionSets node in mscorcfg and selecting New Permission from the context menu. You're then presented with a dialog box that asks you to select the permissions to be added to this set. Because you're using a custom permission rather than one of the built-in ones, you need to click the Import button, which opens a file dialog box that allows you to browse for the appropriate XML file. Figure 12-13 shows the situation after I've done that. Note that at the time of writing there seems to be a problem in mscorcfg, which means the description of the newly added permission doesn't appear in a very friendly format, but you don't need to worry about that.

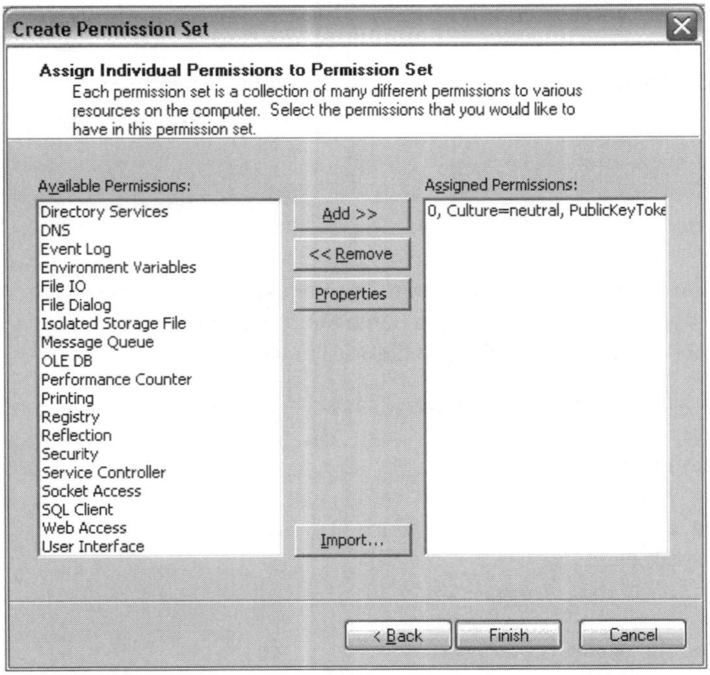

Figure 12-13. *Creating a new permission set with a custom permission*

Now you need to add a code group. You can do this by right-clicking the Code Groups node in the `mscorcfg` treeview and selecting New Code Group from the context menu. This takes you into a couple of dialog boxes that allow you to specify the new code group—its name, its membership condition, and its permission set. The membership condition dialog box looks like Figure 12-14.

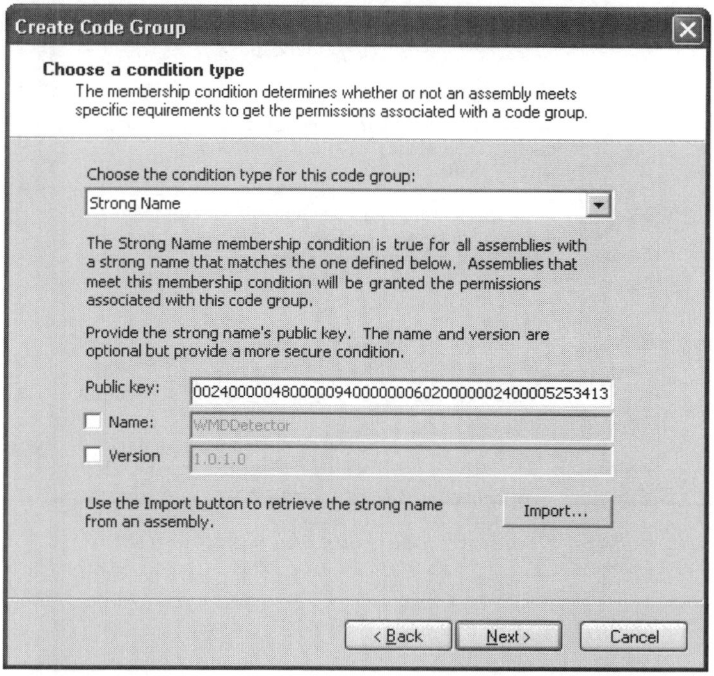

Figure 12-14. *Creating a new code group with a strong name membership condition*

The precise controls that appear in the lower half of the dialog box depend on the condition type for the group. If I select a Strong Name condition, I can use the Import button to browse and select an assembly that's signed with the required strong name; the public key will then be read from this assembly. Figure 12-14 shows the situation after I've opted to read the key from `WMDDetectorPermission.dll`.

After adding the new code group and permission set, `mscorcfg` looks like Figure 12-15.

With security set up in this way, I can then upload the `WMDDetector.exe` assembly to a remote location. (Although I used a trusted internet site when I tested the sample, a file share on the local network will do just as well.) Taking a trusted zone Internet site as an example, if I try to execute the file by typing in its URL in Internet Explorer, the CLR will identify the assembly as matching two zones: `Trusted_Zone`, which gives it permission to do things such as execute and display a form, and `Apress_WMD_Detectors`, which gives it `WMDDetector` read permission—so you'll find it runs successfully.

Bear in mind that if you rebuild the sample, you may need to register the permission again as well, to make sure that the security policy refers to the correct, up-to-date versions of the files.

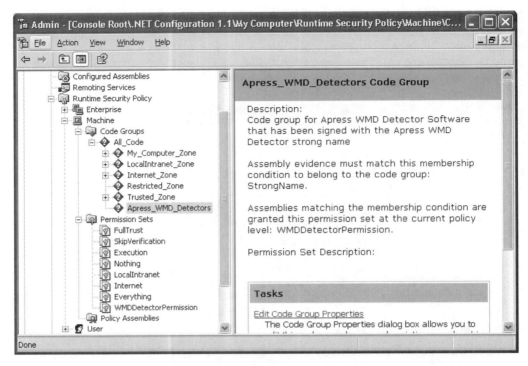

Figure 12-15. *The machine security policy, with the new code group and permission set*

Summary

In this chapter, I covered in some detail certain aspects of security in .NET, focusing in particular on the operation of CAS. I covered the default policy that ships with .NET and used
this to show the relationship between permissions, permission sets, and code groups.
Further, you examined how the permissions are implemented using classes that implement
the IPermission interface. You learned that relatively little of the .NET security architecture is
actually implemented within the CLR; instead, much of this infrastructure is implemented by
classes in the System.Security and related namespaces. This has the advantage that it makes
for a highly extensible architecture, in which you can, for example, define and plug in your
own custom permissions. I also presented a couple of samples that illustrated how to use
CAS, including defining custom permissions.

CHAPTER 13

■■■

Understanding Cryptography

In the previous chapter I covered the facilities that the .NET Framework offers for restricting what an application is permitted to do, based on the evidence provided by the assemblies used by the application. In particular, I covered where the code came from, whether it has been signed, and so on. In short, I covered how much the code itself is trusted. In this chapter, I'll keep on the security theme, but I'll focus on the mechanics of how you can ensure that code and messages passed across the network aren't tampered with and can't be read by unauthorized people. In the process you'll also understand the details of how strong naming of assemblies works and how to digitally sign an assembly with a certificate.

In more detail, I'll cover the following:

- **Theory of cryptography**: I'll cover how both symmetric encryption and public key encryption work under the hood and the differences between these forms of encryption. I'll also work through a sample that illustrates how to use the System.Security.Cryptography classes to encrypt and decrypt data.

- **Code signing**: I'll cover the details of how to sign an assembly with a strong name and what's happening under the hood when you sign an assembly. I'll also highlight the difference between signing an assembly with a strong name and signing it with a digital certificate.

- **Digital certificates**: I'll cover digital certificates and Microsoft's Authenticode technology. I'll also present examples that demonstrate how to sign an assembly with a digital certificate and show how to read the certificate programmatically.

Much of the information in this chapter isn't specific to .NET; the general principles of cryptography on computing networks and the Internet have remained the same for several years. I'll explain those principles in this chapter to make sure you have the necessary background material (if you're already familiar with cryptography theory, you may want to skip the first part of the chapter). However, I'll also focus on how cryptographic principles are applied to managed assemblies in particular, and I'll cover some of the facilities that are made available via the .NET cryptographic classes in the System.Security.Cryptography namespace to allow you to encrypt and decrypt your own messages.

I'll start by going over the basic principles of cryptography as they've existed for much of the past 25 years or so.

The Aims of Cryptography

Let's start by examining in principle what a cryptographic system should be able to achieve. Just as it's traditional for the first program in a new programming language to display *Hello, World* at the command prompt, in cryptography it's traditional to start by introducing three people called Alice, Bob, and Eve. Alice and Bob want to talk to each other, and Eve wants to find out what they're saying or somehow disrupt their conversation (see Figure 13-1).

Figure 13-1. *Bob, Alice, and Eve*

It may sound simplistic, but between them these three people can serve as a model for just about every situation that can occur on a computing network. In the real world, Alice and Bob are likely to be two companies. In the days of the Internet, Alice could correspond to a user browsing with Internet Explorer, Bob could correspond to a Web site, Eve could correspond to a hacker or—even more seriously—perhaps a member of some criminal, terrorist, or similar organization (with apologies to all people who are genuinely called Eve, who I'm sure are very nice really).

The first point to note is that the time of greatest risk is when information is passed over the network (between Alice and Bob). The thing that cryptography is most designed to guard against is data being intercepted when it's in transit—for example, as it's passed from node to node on the Internet, with the sender and receiver having no idea who may be in charge of or monitoring those nodes. For this reason much of cryptography theory is based on this model. However, I can also apply the same principles to data storage on one machine without changing much of the underlying theory—in that case the "sender" is the program that stores the data, and the "receiver" is the program that retrieves the data. Of course, securing your system and your data has many other aspects, including, appropriate firewalls, security policies, and physical security of the actual buildings housing the machines. That's a separate subject, but I won't be covering it here. In this chapter I'll focus purely on cryptography.

Communication should satisfy four classic properties, and you'd rely on the cryptographic system to achieve them: authentication, confidentiality, data integrity, and nonrepudiation.

Authentication means that Alice should be able to be certain that it really is Bob at the other end of the line she is talking to, not Eve pretending to be Bob. Similarly, Bob needs to be able to be certain that the person claiming to be Alice really is Alice. On the Internet, the classic example is that you need to know that those credit card details you think you're sending to Amazon.com really are going to Amazon.com, not to some third party that's spoofed IP addresses in order to make itself look like Amazon.com.

Confidentiality means that Eve shouldn't be able to read the message Alice is sending to Bob. Or, in other words, those credit card details you're sending shouldn't be read en route. This particular guarantee is normally quite easy to spot if you're on a Web browser; you can tell because the `http://` URL has been replaced by an `https://` URL, indicating Secure Sockets Layer (SSL) is at work.

Data integrity is similar to confidentiality, but now I'm looking at Eve's ability to tamper with the message. Note that this is a separate issue from confidentiality, since there may theoretically be a situation in which Eve was unable to read a message but could replace it with one of her own. I need to guard against that, too. The classic example of the issue of data integrity is when downloading some code from a Web site. I want to be sure that it was not only written by a trusted person but that it hasn't been "processed" or even replaced en route by (for example) a virus, which can then use the code to embed itself on your system.

Nonrepudiation is an issue that's sometimes forgotten when learning about cryptography, but it's nevertheless important. You sometimes need to make sure that once Bob has said something to Alice, the proof of that conversation having taken place is available and can be examined in a court of law if necessary. In other words, once you've handed your credit card details in good faith for some goods, and received the goods, you can't run off to your bank and tell them you never made the transaction. Nonrepudiation is closely related to authentication. If you can prove that a message came from a particular person, then that's generally equivalent to having the proof that stops them from denying they sent the message.

Although in this discussion I've been talking about messages, don't think I'm focusing exclusively on text messages. As far as I'm concerned, any data that's transmitted is a message. If you download a file from a Web server, that file constitutes the message that's being sent.

Now that you've seen what a cryptographic system must achieve, I'll cover how you can do this. I'll start by exploring the general principles of cryptography: how messages can be encrypted and decrypted.

The algorithms used in encryption techniques these days are unfortunately (or fortunately, depending on your point of view) based on some fairly complex mathematics, and if I start going into what the algorithms actually are, I'll quickly get sidetracked. It's not really the math that's important so much as what the algorithms can in principle achieve. So instead of working through the actual mathematics, what I'll do instead is use a simple encryption algorithm to illustrate the basic principles on which cryptography is based.

Two types of encryption are around: *symmetric* (*shared key*) encryption and *asymmetric* (*public key*) encryption. Of these, symmetric encryption is by far the easier to understand, so I'll cover that first.

Understanding Symmetric Encryption

I'll explain the underlying theory of symmetric encryption, using a simple algorithm as an example. Then I'll present a sample that illustrates how to perform symmetric encryption in managed code. The algorithm used to explain the theory is so simple that you don't even need a computer to implement it, but it will serve to illustrate all the principles of the (far more complex) symmetric encryption algorithms actually used.

Symmetric Encryption Concepts

Let's suppose that and Alice and Bob want to be able to talk to each other confidentially, so they mutually agreed on the following encryption algorithm for all the messages they send to each other: Each letter of the alphabet will be replaced by the letter three places further on in the alphabet. The scheme will work cyclically so that the letter A is regarded as following the letter Z. Case is preserved, and digits, spaces, and punctuation marks are left untouched. So, for example, if Alice wants to sent this message to Bob:

```
You owe me 100 dollars
```

she will encrypt it first to this:

```
Brx rzh ph 100 grooduv
```

The original message by the way is known as *plain text*, and the encrypted version is known as *cipher text*.

Bob knows therefore that to decrypt a message he has to apply the same algorithm, but replacing each letter by the letter three places further back (or, equivalently, 23 places further forward).

The main thing I want you to notice is that this encryption scheme really has two parts: the algorithm, which is the rule that says you shift each letter by certain number of places in the alphabet, and the number of places, which in this case is three. And that's an important principle. In general, encryption schemes feature an *algorithm*, which tells you in principle how the encryption will be carried out, and a number called the *key*, which has to be inserted into the algorithm at some point. In order either to encrypt or decrypt a message, you need to know both of these things. For example, suppose that Eve wants to eavesdrop on Alice and Bob, and she knows the algorithm but not the key. She knows that each letter gets transposed, but she doesn't know about how much. The only thing she can do is start guessing keys. First she tries using a key of 1 to decrypt the message. This yields the following:

```
Csy sai qi 100 hsppevw
```

That's obviously garbage, so 1 wasn't the correct value. So Eve tries 2. That gives garbage, too. Eventually of course she will get to the value 23 and can recover the original message. The fact that this message isn't garbage tells her she now has the correct key, which also means that she can easily decrypt future messages until Alice and Bob agree to change either the key or the algorithm.

■**Note** I know that for this example I've just mentioned, a lot of clues in the message will assist Eve in decoding it. All the spaces separating words, and the punctuation marks, are still there, so it's not hard to start making educated guesses about some of the simple words or to use frequency analysis on the different letters to help work out likely values. But that's only because this encryption scheme is so simple. Modern computer encryption algorithms don't give you any such clues. If you're faced with something that's encrypted with a modern algorithm, pretty much your only option is to use brute force and start guessing different key values. So by restricting Eve to doing this, I'm keeping the example more related to real computer systems.

The reason that this algorithm is called *symmetric* is partly because Bob and Alice both use the same algorithm and partly because it's easy to work out the decryption key from the encryption key and vice versa. Encryption and decryption are carried out by basically the same method. Bob encrypts messages he sends in the same way Alice does—by replacing letters. Substitute a more complex algorithm, and you have a way of encrypting messages, files, programs, and so. The most well-known symmetric algorithm has probably been *Digital Encryption Standard* (DES), which was developed in the 1970s and which encrypts data in 64-byte blocks. Other algorithms you'll hear about are Triple DES, Rijndael, RC2, and RC4.

Let's write the process a bit more mathematically. I'll call the two keys P and S, and I'll call the original message M. If I encode the message using P, then I get some cipher text that I'll call P(M). If I then decode this using S, I get S(P(M)). If everything's working properly, I know that that gives the original message back. So M = S(P(M)). I could also go the other way round—apply S first, then apply P. That will give me the original message back, too. So in summary:

- $S(P(M)) = P(S(M)) = M$.

- $P(M)$ = encoded stuff that looks like garbage; you have to know what S is to decode it.

- $S(M)$ = encoded stuff that looks like garbage; you have to know what P is to decode it.

It may look like I've just gone out of my way to write something that's obvious, by using unnecessarily complex-looking algebra, but this will be more useful when I come to examine public key cryptography.

One of the principles of cryptography is that it's the key that's kept secret. The algorithm isn't secret; it's largely pointless trying to keep the choice of algorithm secret, because not many good algorithms are available anyway. The requirements of a workable encryption algorithm these days are quite strict, and relatively few algorithms have been developed that fit the bill.

Encrypting a Message with Managed Code

Now that you've learned about the principles of symmetric encryption, I'll demonstrate how to encrypt and decrypt a message using the classes provided in the System.Security.Cryptography namespace. This namespace contains a large number of classes to perform different cryptography-related operations, including classes that will encrypt and decrypt data according to many of the standard algorithms. I'll use the DES algorithm, which means that the class I use will be the DESCryptoServiceProvider class. This class derives from the abstract class DES. Other similar pairs of classes in the System.Cryptography namespace include MD5/MD5CrytpServiceProvider and RSA/RSACryptoServiceProvider, which respectively implement the MD5 and RSA algorithms.

For the sample I'll write two programs to respectively encrypt and then decrypt a message using the DES encryption algorithm.

■**Tip** Bear in mind that although I'm showing you how to write an encryption program, sometimes encryption services are automatically provided (for example, using SSL to talk to IIS). Before rolling your encryption routine, make sure you're not wasting your time duplicating a preexisting service that you could have used. On the other hand, one good reason for writing your own encryption program is to provide secure communications where you don't for example want IIS to be installed on the machines concerned.

The message I'll encrypt is a file called Bloops.txt. This file arose from the fact that I dictated much of this book using speech recognition software. Some of the mistakes the software makes are sufficiently noteworthy that I got into the habit of copying them into the Bloops.txt text file as I corrected the chapters. Since the contents of the file aren't really relevant to the sample, I'll just display a small snippet from the file here. The full file is of course available with the code download on the Apress Web site, and the same information is available on my own site at http://www.SimonRobinson.com/Hum_DragonBloops.aspx. The file consists of line pairs; the first pair lists what the speech recognition software wrote out, and the second line indicates what I actually said.

```
authentic invitation procedures
authentication procedures
```

```
Come into rock
COM Interop
```

Anyway, let's get onto the code. First, I'll show the encryption program.

The Encryption Program

The code is a simple console application, with the encryption being done in the Main() method. It has a small helper method, WriteKeyAndIV(), that writes out the key that's used for the encryption as well as something known as an *initialization vector* (IV) to a file called KeyIV.txt. The initialization vector is simply a random number used to initialize the encryption algorithm. The reason for writing this information to a file is that the encryption program works by generating a random key and vector, and obviously the decryption program needs to be able to read and therefore use the same values of these items so it can perform the decryption correctly! Storing these values in a plain-text file is of course hopelessly insecure; I've just done that here to keep the example simple. In real life you'd most likely use a separate public key encryption method to communicate the key.

The Main() method looks like this:

```
static void Main(string[] args)
{
   DESCryptoServiceProvider des = new DESCryptoServiceProvider();
   des.GenerateKey();
   des.GenerateIV();
   WriteKeyAndIV(des);
   ICryptoTransform encryptor = des.CreateEncryptor();

   FileStream inFile = new FileStream("Bloops.txt", FileMode.Open);
   FileStream outFile = new FileStream("BloopsEnc.txt", FileMode.Create);
   int inSize = encryptor.InputBlockSize;
   int outSize = encryptor.OutputBlockSize;
   byte[] inBytes = new byte[inSize];
   byte[] outBytes = new byte[outSize];
   int numBytesRead, numBytesOutput;
   do
```

```
    {
        numBytesRead = inFile.Read(inBytes, 0, inSize);
        if (numBytesRead == inSize)
        {
            numBytesOutput = encryptor.TransformBlock(inBytes, 0,
                                            numBytesRead, outBytes, 0);
            outFile.Write(outBytes, 0, numBytesOutput);
        }
        else if (numBytesRead > 0)
        {
            byte [] final = encryptor.TransformFinalBlock(inBytes, 0,
                                                numBytesRead);
            outFile.Write(final, 0, final.Length);
        }
    } while (numBytesRead > 0);
    inFile.Close();
    outFile.Close();
}
```

In this code I first instantiate a DESCryptoServiceProvider object and then call methods to generate a random key and initialization vector. Then I call the WriteKeyAndIV() helper method to write these quantities out to a file (I'll examine this method soon).

The following line creates an object that will actually perform the encryption:

```
ICryptoTransform encryptor = des.CreateEncryptor();
```

The details of the encryptor object are hidden; all you know is that it implements an interface, ICryptoTransform, to actually perform the encryption. The encryption is regarded as a transform. (In this case it's from plain text to cipher text, but the transform can go the other way too; the same interface is used for decryption.) The reason for this architecture in which the encryptor object is accessed via an interface is that it allows the same interface to be used with other symmetric encryption algorithms. For example, had you instead wanted to perform encryption using the Rijndael algorithm, then almost the only changes you'd need to make to the source code would be to replace the first line.

```
RijndaelManaged des = new RijndaelManaged ();
des.GenerateKey();
des.GenerateIV();
WriteKeyAndIV(des);
ICryptoTransform encryptor = des.CreateEncryptor();
```

And you'd end up with an encryptor that uses the Rijndael algorithm but that exposes the same interface for actually performing the encryption.

The object that implements ICryptoTransform performs encryption via the TransformBlock() method, which takes five parameters: a byte array containing some bytes to be encrypted (transformed), the index of the first element in the array to be transformed and the number of elements to be transformed, a byte array to receive the transformed data, and an index indicating where to place this data in the output byte array. It also has two properties: InputBlockSize, which indicates how many bytes the encryptor likes to work with at a time (these will be encrypted as one unit), and OutputBlockSize, which indicates how many bytes each block will be mapped to. And finally, you'll see a TransformFinalBlock() method, which acts like TransformBlock, except that it's intended to transform the final block of data in the message. Since the final block may be smaller than other blocks, so it's not known in advance how big the output will be, TransformFinalBlock() places the output in a byte[] return value instead of accepting a reference to an existing array. With this information you can understand how the loop that performs the encryption works.

```
do
{
    nRead = inFile.Read(inBytes, 0, inSize);
    if (nRead < inSize)
    {
        byte[] final = encryptor.TransformFinalBlock(inBytes, 0, nRead);
        outFile.Write(final, 0, final.Length);
    }
    else
    {
        encryptor.TransformBlock(inBytes, 0, nRead, outBytes, 0);
        outFile.Write(outBytes, 0, nRead);
    }
}
while (nRead > 0);
inFile.Close();
outFile.Close();
}
```

Notice that the FileStream.Read() method returns the number of bytes actually read. This will be zero if you've reached the end of the file.

Finally, I need to show you the method that writes details of the key and initialization vector to a file. To keep things simple, I've coded the application so this information is written in text format—slow and insecure, but it makes for easier debugging—and it's, after all, only a sample!

```
static void WriteKeyAndIV(DES des)
{
    StreamWriter outFile = new StreamWriter(@"KeyIV.txt", false);
    outFile.WriteLine(des.KeySize);
    for (int i=0; i< des.KeySize/8; i++)
        outFile.WriteLine(des.Key[i]);
    for (int i=0; i< des.KeySize/8; i++)
        outFile.WriteLine(des.IV[i]);
    outFile.Close();
}
```

To write out the file, you need to know the size of the key (when I ran the program it turned out to be 64 bits). It's possible to set this size, but that involves first querying the DESCryptoServiceProvider object to find out what the allowed key sizes are, so to keep things simple I just accepted the default value. The KeySize property gives the key size in bits, but the actual key and initialization vector (which will be the same size) are returned as byte arrays, so I have to divide KeySize by eight to get the size of these arrays. Incidentally, you may notice one quirk of the interface that Microsoft has designed here. The fact that the Key and IV properties have been implemented as properties runs counter to recommended programming standards; it's not normally recommended to define properties that return arrays, but in this case, the small size of the arrays may make this more acceptable.

The Decryption Program

Now you need to examine the code for the other program in this sample—the Decrypt program that decrypts the file. This code has a similar structure to the encryption program. I'll start by covering the helper method that reads in the file containing the key and initialization vector.

```
static void ReadKeyAndIV(DES des)
{
    StreamReader inFile = new StreamReader(@"KeyIV.txt");
    int keySize;
    keySize = int.Parse(inFile.ReadLine());
    byte[] key = new byte[keySize/8];
    byte[] iv = new byte[keySize/8];
    for (int i=0; i< des.KeySize/8; i++)
        key[i] = byte.Parse(inFile.ReadLine());
    for (int i=0; i< des.KeySize/8; i++)
        iv[i] = byte.Parse(inFile.ReadLine());
    inFile.Close();
    des.KeySize = keySize;
    des.Key = key;
    des.IV = iv;
}
```

This method reads in the values from the file in the same order that the encryption program wrote them out, constructs the byte arrays, and uses the data to set the key size, key, and initialization vector of the DESCryptoServiceProvider instance.

Now you'll see the code to decrypt the file. In the following code, I've highlighted the lines that are different from the Main() method in the encryption program.

```
static void Main(string[] args)
{
    DESCryptoServiceProvider des = new DESCryptoServiceProvider();
    ReadKeyAndIV(des);

    ICryptoTransform decryptor = des.CreateDecryptor();

    FileStream inFile = new FileStream(@"BloopsEnc.txt", FileMode.Open);
    FileStream outFile = new FileStream(@"BloopsDec.txt", FileMode.Create);
    int inSize = decryptor.InputBlockSize;
    int outSize = decryptor.OutputBlockSize;
    byte[] inBytes = new byte[inSize];
```

```
        byte[] outBytes = new byte[outSize];
        do
        {
           numBytesRead = inFile.Read(inBytes, 0, inSize);
           if (numBytesRead == inSize)
           {
              numBytesOutput = decryptor.TransformBlock(inBytes, 0, numBytesRead,
                                                        outBytes, 0);
              outFile.Write(outBytes, 0, numBytesOutput);
           }
           else
           {
              byte [] final = decryptor.TransformFinalBlock(inBytes, 0,
                                                            numBytesRead);
              outFile.Write(final, 0, final.Length);
           }
        } while (numBytesRead > 0);
        inFile.Close();
        outFile.Close();
}
```

As you can see, few lines have changed. Essentially, the only differences are the names of the input and output files and that I use a method called `CreateDecryptor()` instead of `CreateEncryptor()` to return the interface reference through which I can perform the data transform. Also, I read in the key from a file, instead of generating a random one.

The similarity between the two programs demonstrates the convenience of the model in which encryption and decryption are regarded as transforms to be performed through the same interface. However, note that this model applies only to symmetric algorithms. The .NET cryptography classes that perform public-key encryption don't use this architecture, since with public-key encryption, the encryption and decryption algorithms are very different. Public-key encryption is the topic I'll cover next.

Understanding Public-Key Encryption

These days, most authentication procedures—including the way assemblies are signed—take place using public key encryption. You're probably familiar with the fact that public-key encryption involves a public key and a private key and that the public key is allowed to be made public while the private one must be kept confidential. In this part of the chapter I'll provide a deeper look at how public-key encryption works under the hood. This will enable you to better understand how assemblies are signed and how ownership of assemblies is authenticated when they're downloaded.

The *raison d'etre* for using public key encryption is to solve two inherent weaknesses of symmetric encryption. These weaknesses both arise from the fact that both parties to a conversation need to know the key. This means that

- Somehow the key needs to be transmitted. That's a real problem since if the key has to be transmitted over the network, there's a risk that the villainous Eve will discover it.

Of course, in the previous sample, I didn't bother with encrypting the key but just used a plain text file. That's not satisfactory because if the key isn't kept absolutely confidential, then encrypting the message is a waste of time as anyone can decrypt it!

- Key management is a problem. If, for example, Alice wants to talk to someone else, without Bob listening in, then she is going to need a different key for that channel. With a different key for every pair of people (or group of people) who may want to communicate, managing those keys is going to quickly become difficult.

Public-key encryption solves both of those problems. Let's go over how public keys work.

How Public-Key Encryption Works

My earlier example using Alice and Bob demonstrated that encrypting a message required an algorithm and a key. Decrypting a message was different because it required a different key (encrypting with a key of 3 meant decrypting with a key of -3), but the algorithm was the same. In public key encryption, the algorithms associated with the two keys may be different too, but that is going to be irrelevant for this analysis.

Recall that the situation for symmetric cryptography was this:

- $S(P(M)) = P(S(M)) = M$

- $P(M)$ = encoded stuff that looks like garbage; you have to know what S is to decode it.

- $S(M)$ = encoded stuff that looks like garbage; you have to know what P is to decode it.

Now for public-key cryptography I'll add one other requirement to this list. You need to arrange things so that if you know P, then it's easy to calculate S, but if you know S, then it's next to impossible to work out P in a reasonable time. Mathematicians call working out S from P a *trapdoor function*, meaning it's hard to reverse it.

In practice in real algorithms, the trapdoor function is achieved by using prime numbers. If you're given two large prime numbers, multiplying them together is easy. If you're given the product, however, trying to figure out what the two original primes were is a lot harder. So roughly speaking, in real public key encryption, P is the pair of original primes, and S is their product.

So what happens with Alice and Bob? Well, they each have some software that can randomly generate a private-public key pair. Alice keeps her private key to herself (that's what I'll call P) and tells Bob her public key (that key is the S—for *shared*). In fact, she doesn't just tell Bob. She tells everyone who is interested in knowing. She even tells Eve (it's not going to do Eve any good). Bob does the same thing; he doesn't use Alice's P and S but instead generates his own P and S. And he keeps his private key to himself and tells everyone his public key.

■Note Since S is publicly available, you may wonder why I made an issue of it being easy to calculate S from P. Why would anyone need to calculate it? The answer is that it's important when the key pair is initially created. P is usually generated at random and S immediately calculated from it. Alice will generate her P and S on her own computer so that P never needs to get passed around the network and so is kept secure. Similarly Bob generates his P and S on his own computer, keeps his P there, and distributes his S.

Now Alice sends Bob a message. Since she wants to keep the message confidential, she encrypts it with Bob's public key and sends it off. Since the message was encrypted with Bob's public key, it needs Bob's private key to be decrypted. This means only Bob can decrypt it. Bob reads the message and then sends a reply back to Alice. He encrypts the reply with Alice's public key, which means only Alice can decrypt it. Eve has both public keys, but she still can't read any messages. The situation so far looks like Figure 13-2.

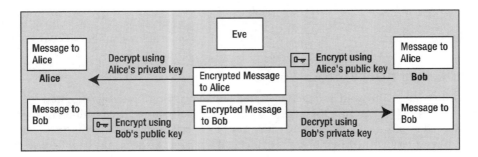

Figure 13-2. *Alice and Bob encrypt messages with each other's public keys.*

A problem exists, however. So far you've gained confidentiality and data integrity. What you don't have is authenticity and nonrepudiation. Eve may not be able to read any messages, but nothing is stopping her from sending a message to Bob and signing it "Alice," and Bob has no way of telling that it wasn't Alice who wrote the message (although Alice may be a bit surprised when she gets a reply). And because Alice knows that Eve can do this, if Alice was dishonest, it'd be quite easy for her to send a message and then deny having sent it. Bob has no way to prove that it really was her.

An easy alternative way to achieve authenticity and nonrepudiation, and keep data integrity, exists. The trouble is that this technique loses confidentiality: If Alice wants to prove her authorship of a message, all she has to do is encrypt it with her own private key. Now Bob can decrypt the message using Alice's public key. The fact that Alice's public key can be used to decrypt the message proves that it was Alice who sent the message. Alice can't deny sending it, because Bob can just hand over the encrypted message to a court and say, "Here—look. It decrypts with Alice's public key! This means it got encrypted with her private key, and no one else can do that." The only snag about this approach is that if the message has been encoded with Alice's private key, and her public key is freely available, that means anyone can read the message. No confidentiality.

So what do you have so far? Well, it seems you can either get confidentiality or get nonrepudiation. But a secure encryption system requires both of those simultaneously. Luckily a very clever trick can achieve that. All Alice needs to do is to encrypt the message with her private key and then further encrypt the cipher text with Bob's public key. To read the message, Bob will have to first decrypt it with his private key—that will still leave him with gobbledygook, but he can then further decrypt it with Alice's public key to get the original message. That meets all the requirements. No one except Bob can decrypt it, and Bob will have the proof that the message really came from Alice. The big win is that the private keys never have to be transmitted over a network. They can be kept strictly confidential, within an organization. You finally have a secure encryption system!

Although this solution looks ideal, the algorithms used for public-key encryption are exceptionally demanding of computer time, so for performance reasons public-key encryption is rarely used to encrypt entire messages. Instead, various techniques can confine the public-key encryption to a small part of the message while keeping security, some of which you'll see later in this chapter. Roughly speaking, the most common scenario is to use symmetric encryption for the bulk of a conversation, as demonstrated in the earlier encryption sample, but to use public key encryption initially to transmit the symmetric key that will be used for that conversation. Something such as this happens with SSL security, the technique that you'll be used to seeing when connecting to secure Web sites. Kerberos security is also based on similar principles.

Key Size

Since the way that messages are cracked is by trying keys at random until you find the right one, the main factor that affects the safety of your encoding is how big the key is. In the simple example I presented earlier that involved transposing letters, only 26 possible values for the key existed. So a computer could try every possibility in a tiny fraction of a second. Modern cryptography algorithms, however, have large keys that would require a cracker to try huge numbers of possible values. For symmetric encryption, traditionally three key sizes have been in common use: 40-bit, 56-bit, and 128 bit. Other sizes are used too, and keys used in public key encryption tend to be larger. Bear in mind that the number of possible key values grows exponentially with key size; a 40-bit number can have up to 2 to the power of 40 (that's one million million) values, although not necessarily all those values are legitimate keys. For every bit you add, you double the number of values.

The following story should give you some idea of the relative risk: In 1997, to test how secure cryptography was, RSA Data Security offered a reward for the first person to crack a message encoded with a 40-bit key. It took a college student, Ian Goldberg, three-and-a-half hours to win the prize. Later in the year, DES issued a similar challenge using a 56-bit key. It took a large team of people working together to pool their computing resources three months to win the prize. To my knowledge, no one has ever cracked a 128-bit key. In general, 40-bit keys will survive a casual attack but not a determined attack. Fifty-six-bit keys are reasonably secure in the short term, and 128-bit keys are for all practical purposes impregnable in the short to medium term. However, in the long run, no key size is going to be secure against time and improvements in computer speed. The bigger the key you choose, the longer your data will stay impregnable.

Many countries impose legal restrictions on the use or export of cryptography software, based on the key size, although in general these restrictions have eased considerably in the previous couple of years. For example, it used to be illegal to export encryption software that used keys bigger than 40 bits from the United States to any other country, which lead to the odd situation that people in much of Europe and Canada could use 128-bit encryption software but only if it was written outside the United States! These days, the regulations are more liberal and are mostly aimed at preventing export of encryption software to countries regarded as representing a high security risk. If you do write encryption software, though, you'll still need to carefully check any legal restrictions your own government imposes on the use or distribution of that software. (Microsoft does, of course, make every effort to comply with those restrictions in the software it places on Windows, so if you have a legal copy of Windows and .NET, you almost certainly don't need to worry about being allowed to do things such as sign assemblies!)

Session Keys

You've seen how, in principle, public-key cryptography can allow completely secure communication of messages, without the need for a key to be transmitted across the network. Although this sounds fine in principle, in practice it's almost never done that way. The reason? Performance. The algorithms in use for public-key cryptography generally involve treating blobs in the message as numbers and raising them to certain powers. That involves lots of multiplication, and it's very slow. In fact, Microsoft claims that encoding a message using one of the public-key algorithms takes about 1,000 (yes, 1,000) times as long as encrypting the same message using a symmetric key algorithm such as DES. Because of this, what almost invariably actually happens is that public-key cryptography is used to encrypt only the most sensitive information, with symmetric encryption being used most of the time. Session keys provide one example of this technique.

If a conversation is to be based on a session key, what happens is that most of the conversation will be encrypted symmetrically. However, prior to the conversation one of the parties will create a symmetric key and send it to the other using public-key cryptography. That key will then be the agreed key to be used for the duration of that conversation (or session) and will be thrown away afterward, which is why the name is *session key*. The result is huge encryption performance gains, but the conversation is for all practical purposes almost as secure as if public key cryptography had been used throughout. The session key is never transmitted in a form that Eve is able to read, so Eve still has to resort to the brute-force technique to figure out the key. The only benefit Eve has is she gets the same performance gains as Alice and Bob when she's trying to decode the messages. The trouble is, that's offset by the fact that the session key is only temporary anyway. Even if Eve has some serious computer power available and somehow does manage to find the key, by then it's too late. Alice and Bob will have ended the session, the messages are probably out-of-date, and that key won't get used any more.

If you connect to a Web site and see from the URL that the HTTPS protocol is being used, that means communications are being encrypted using a protocol based on Windows SSL—and session keys play an important role here.

Understanding Hashing

Hashing is a way of providing a check on message or file integrity. It's not the same as encryption, but as you'll see soon, its use is important as part of the process of signing code. It's based on a similar concept to the old parity and cyclic redundancy checks, common in programming many years ago. (Parity and cyclic redundancy checks are still common, but only in areas such as communications where there's no time to perform more sophisticated checks.) I'll illustrate the principle by quickly defining my own hashing algorithm. Let's suppose I want to check that a file hasn't been corrupted, and I supply an extra byte at the end of the file for this purpose. The byte is calculated as follows: I examine every existing byte of data in the file and count how many of these bytes have the least significant bit set to 1. If this number is odd, I set the corresponding bit of the check byte to 1. If it's even, I set that bit to 0. Then I do the same for every other bit in each byte. Thus, for example, suppose I have a short file containing three bytes with values 0x4d, 0x18, and 0xf3.

Table 13-1. *A Simple Hashing Algorithm*

File Pointer	Value (binary)	Value (Hex)
First byte	01001101	0x4d
Second byte	00011000	0x18
Third byte	11110011	0xf3
CHECK BYTE	**10100110**	**0xa6**

The check byte is my *hash* of the data. Notice that it has the following properties: It's of fixed length, independent of the size of the file, and you have no way of working out what the file contents are from the hash. It really is impossible because so much data is lost in calculating the hash (you should contrast this with the process of working out a private key given the public key—that's not impossible but simply would take too long to be practical). The advantage of hashing the file is that it provides an easy check on whether the file has been accidentally corrupted. For files such as assemblies, the hash will be placed somewhere in the file. Then, when an application reads the file, it can independently calculate the hash value and verify that it corresponds to the value stored in the file. (Obviously, for this to work, you need an agreed file format, allowing the application to locate the hash inside the file. Also, the area of the file where the hash is stored can't be used in calculating the hash, since those bytes get overwritten when the hash is placed there!)

The example algorithm I've just presented is a simple scheme and has the disadvantage that the hash is only 1 byte long. That means that if some random corruption happened, there's still (depending on the types of errors that are likely to occur) a 1 in 256 chance that the corrupted file will generate the same hash, so the error won't be detected. In .NET assemblies, the algorithm used for the hash is known as SHA-1. This algorithm was developed by the U.S. Government National Institute of Standards and Technology (NIST) and the National Security Agency (NSA). The hash generated by SHA1 contains 160 bits. This means that the chance of a random error not being detected is so trivially small that you can forget it. You may also hear of other standard hash algorithms. The ones supported by the .NET Framework are HMACSHA-1, MACTripleDES, MD-5, SHA-1, SHA-256, SHA-384, and SHA-512.

It's also worth bearing in mind that, these days, computer systems are sophisticated enough that files don't get randomly corrupted as often as once was the case. However, what could happen is that someone accidentally replaces one of the modules in an assembly with a different file—perhaps a different version of the same module. This is a more likely scenario that will be detected by the hash, since the hash covers all files in the assembly.

On the other hand, the hash won't protect you against malicious tampering with the file—since someone who does that and understands the file format will simply calculate and store a correct new hash in the file after they've finished their tampering.

Using Digital Signatures

Signing a file with a digital signature is a similar process to hashing. However, signing a file has the additional advantage that it guarantees file authenticity. Digital signatures form the underlying technology behind .NET strong names for assemblies. The next sections will cover both the principles of digital signatures and the implementation for strong names.

Digital Signatures Concepts

Signing a file involves two stages. A hash is embedded into the file as just I've described in this chapter, but in addition, prior to writing the hash into the file, the hash is encrypted using some private key. Often some extra information will be added to the hash before encryption, such as the date when it was encrypted or the name of the company that owns the private key. Notice that this provides an example of the principle I discussed earlier of only using public-key encryption to encrypt small amounts of data for performance reasons. Encrypting the hash is a lot quicker than encrypting the whole file would have been, but it provides virtually the same level of authentication and nonrepudiation security.

When some other software wants to use a signed file, it will first decrypt the encrypted hash using the corresponding public key. Then the software will independently work out the hash value from the file contents. If the two values match, that proves (well OK, not quite by 100 percent, but it comes so close to 100 percent that it's a proof for all practical purposes) that the file was generated by an individual who had access to the private key, and it hasn't been tampered with since. This, provided the organization was keeping its private keys confidential, pretty much proves the authenticity of the file. Notice that all this requires some prior agreement on the format for embedding the signature inside the file. You'll need to have space in the file that's reserved for writing the signature, and those particular bytes shouldn't be used when computing the hash. In practice, various such formats exist, including the format that the CLR uses for strong names, but those details are normally handled by the operating system or the CLR, so that's not something you need to know the details of.

Assembly Strong Names

As noted earlier, assembly strong names are based on digital signatures. The Microsoft high-level compilers will, for example, insert a strong name into an emitted assembly in response to the AssemblyKeyFile attribute in a source file. The strong name is specific to managed code and is therefore stored in the manifest of an assembly. For strong names, the signature is obtained by simply encrypting the hash. Information such as company name isn't added.

The fact that the strong name is an encryption of the hash, rather than the whole file, is particularly important, since the CLR will decrypt the strong name in order to verify the identity of the assembly every time it loads the assembly. Clearly, at this point, performance is very important since loading assemblies is something that happens quite frequently.

Delay-Signing an Assembly

In Chapter 4, I explained how to use the sn tool to create a public-private key pair for an assembly. In that chapter, I presented an example called GreetMe that involved generating a shared assembly with satellite assemblies. However, there was a problem with that example to the extent that it required the public-private key pair to reside in a file to which the developers have access so that each time the project is built, it can be signed again. That's dangerous since private keys really should be kept strictly confidential. If the wrong person gets their hands on the private key, they can start tampering with your code without the users detecting this. So your company really should arrange things so that the .snk file generated by sn is accessible to only a few trusted people.

In this section I'll modify the GreetMe sample so that it meets those criteria, by arranging for assemblies to be delay-signed.

The new-look GreetMe sample has the file structure shown in Figure 13-3.

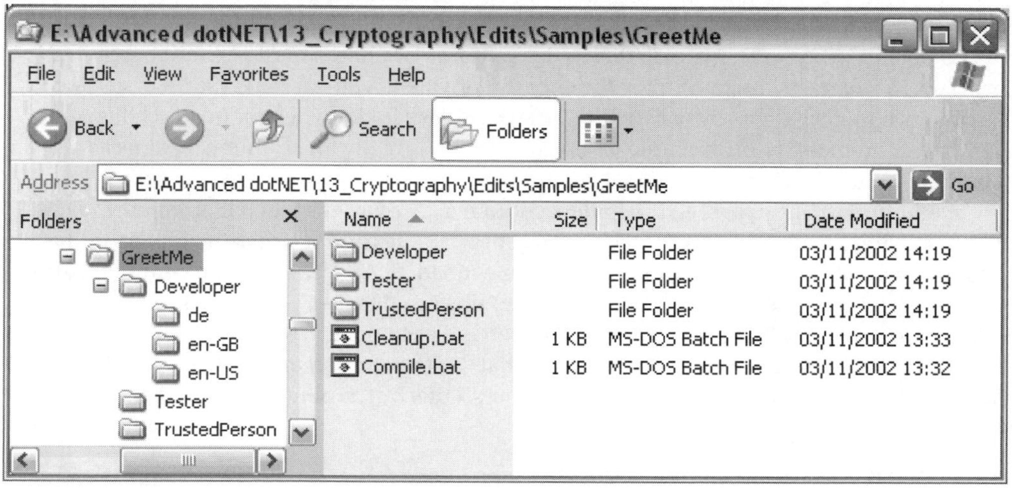

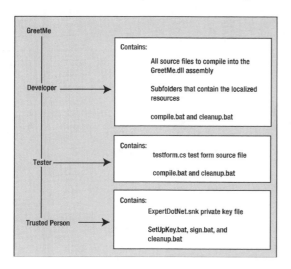

Figure 13-3. *The modified* GreetMe *file structure*

As you can see, there are now three subfolders in the sample, representing the three main roles in the development of the program. The Developer folder contains the files that the developers working on the project should be allowed to see. The TrustedPerson folder represents the folder that's accessible only to those few people who are trusted to have access to your company's private keys. In the example, this folder contains the key file, ExpertDotNet.snk, as well as a couple of batch files. The Developer folder contains the same folders as previously, except that the test form program, TestForm.cs, has been moved into a new folder, Tester. This change is to represent the separation of development and testing.

So, in summary, the folders look like Figure 13-4.

Figure 13-4. *Structure of the revised* GreetMe *sample with delay signing*

To simplify compilation of the project, the Tester and Developer folders both contain compile.bat files that handle the compilation of all the files in their respective folders. The TrustedPerson folder doesn't have a compile.bat file since there are no source files for the trusted person to compile. Instead, this folder contains two batch files. The first batch file, SetUpKey.bat, extracts the public key (but not the private key) from ExpertDotNet.snk and distributes it to developers by copying it to the Developer folder. The second batch file, sign.bat, is intended to be executed when all the code is ready for shipping. It signs all the assemblies and installs them into the GAC.

In addition to these files, all the folders contain a cleanup.bat batch file, which you can use after trying the project; it removes all the generated files and restores the folders to the state they were in when the example was first downloaded. And just to make compiling and cleaning up simple, the main GreetMe folder contains compile.bat and cleanup.bat files, which simply invoke all the compile/cleanup batch files in turn.

The first stage in preparing this project is that the trusted person must give the developers a copy of the public (but not the private) key. You do this by running the batch file, SetUpKey.bat. This is what that file does:

```
sn -p ExpertDotNet.snk PublicKey.snk
copy PublicKey.snk ..\Developer\PublicKey.snk
```

The -p option tells sn to extract the public key from an .snk file and store it separately. So this code simply obtains the public key and stores it in the Developer folder so that the developers can build the files using this key (but they still never get access to the private key).

The developers now develop and test the application, exactly as before. However, a couple of changes are required to the batch file used to build it. For reference, I'll display the complete Compile.bat file here, and highlight the changes in bold as compared to the version of this file I used in Chapter 4.

```
rem COMPILE DEFAULT RESOURCES
rem ------------------------
resgen Strings.txt
resxgen /i:NoFlag.jpg /o:Flags.resx /n:Flag
resgen Flags.resx

rem COMPILE SOURCE FILES
rem -------------------
rem csc /t:module FlagDlg.cs
vbc /t:module /r:System.dll /r:System.drawing.dll
    /r:System.Windows.Forms.dll FlagDlg.vb
csc /addmodule:FlagDlg.netmodule
    /res:Strings.resources /res:Flags.resources /t:library GreetMe.cs

rem COMPILE en-US RESOURCES
rem ----------------------
cd en-US
resgen Strings.en-US.txt
resxgen /i:USFlag.jpg /o:Flags.en-US.resx /n:Flag
resgen Flags.en-US.resx
```

```
al /delay+ /embed:Strings.en-US.resources /embed:Flags.en-US.resources
   /c:en-US /v:1.0.1.0 /keyfile:../PublicKey.snk  /out:GreetMe.resources.dll
cd ..

rem COMPILE en-GB RESOURCES
rem ---------------------
cd en-GB
resgen Strings.en-GB.txt
resxgen /i:GBFlag.jpg /o:Flags.en-GB.resx /n:Flag
resgen Flags.en-GB.resx
al /delay+ /embed:Strings.en-GB.resources /embed:Flags.en-GB.resources
   /c:en-GB /v:1.0.1.0 /keyfile:../PublicKey.snk /out:GreetMe.resources.dll
cd ..

rem COMPILE de RESOURCES Note that there is no de flag
rem because de could mean Germany or Austria
rem ----------------------------------------------------------------------
cd de
resgen Strings.de.txt
al /delay+ /embed:Strings.de.resources /c:de /v:1.0.1.0
   /keyfile:../PublicKey.snk /out:GreetMe.resources.dll
cd ..
rem INSTALL INTO GLOBAL ASSEMBLY CACHE
rem ---------------------------------
sn /Vr GreetMe.dll
gacutil /i GreetMe.dll

sn /Vr en-US/GreetMe.resources.dll
gacutil /i en-US/GreetMe.resources.dll

sn /Vr en-GB/GreetMe.resources.dll
gacutil /i en-GB/GreetMe.resources.dll

sn /Vr de/GreetMe.resources.dll
gacutil /i de/GreetMe.resources.dll
```

The main changes are that I've added the flag /delay+ to the al commands used to create the satellite assemblies (as well as the trivial change of changing the name of the .snk file to match the one I've generated). Adding the delay sign flag means that the public key stored in the key file will be added to the assembly and form part of its identity. However, the assembly won't be signed. The hash of the assembly contents won't be encrypted; you can't encrypt it here since you don't have access to the private key to encrypt it with!

The other big change is the appearance of the sn /Vr commands immediately before I install each assembly to the GAC. sn /Vr registers an assembly for what's known as *verification skipping*. Don't be confused by the name; it has nothing to do with skipping type-safety verification. Instead, it allows the assembly to be installed into the GAC even though it hasn't been digitally signed yet. Normally, gacutil.exe won't allow an assembly into the cache without a digital signature, but this step ensures that these assemblies, which have merely had space reserved for a strong name to be added later, can go in the cache, so that the example can be tested properly.

The example also shows one change to the C# source code. The GreetMe.dll main assembly also needs to be delay-signed. Since this assembly is generated by the C# compiler, not by the al utility, the technique for specifying that it's delay-signed is different. Instead of using a command-line parameter, I use an attribute in the C# source code.

```
[assembly: AssemblyVersion("1.0.1.0")]
[assembly: AssemblyCulture("")]
[assembly: AssemblyDelaySign(true)]
[assembly: AssemblyKeyFile("PublicKey.snk")]
```

The TestForm.cs test program also needs to be compiled. The batch file for this is simple.

```
csc /reference:../Developer/greetme.dll testform.cs
```

The /reference flag here refers to the private copy of GreetMe.dll. Recall from Chapter 4 that it's usual to reference local copies at compile time, but when the program is executed, it will still load the copies in the GAC.

Once the developers have finished with the project and it's ready to ship, the trusted person comes in again and runs the final batch file, sign.bat. This is what sign.bat does:

```
cd ..\Developer
sn -R GreetMe.dll ../TrustedPerson/ExpertDotNet.snk
sn -R en-US/GreetMe.resources.dll ../TrustedPerson/ExpertDotNet.snk
sn -R en-GB/GreetMe.resources.dll ../TrustedPerson/ExpertDotNet.snk
sn -R de/GreetMe.resources.dll ../TrustedPerson/ExpertDotNet.snk

gacutil /i GreetMe.dll
gacutil /i en-US/GreetMe.resources.dll
gacutil /i en-GB/GreetMe.resources.dll
gacutil /i de/GreetMe.resources.dll

cd ..\TrustedPerson
```

This batch file changes the folder into the Developer folder and re-signs all the assemblies with the private key. The -R option on the sn command replaces any previous signature with the specified key. Then the batch file installs the signed files into the GAC (this will overwrite the unsigned copies placed there previously), and you're ready to perform final testing on the application before shipping.

The procedure I've gone through here involves delay-signing the assemblies. As an alternative, you could simply use a temporary test private key to test the assemblies with and then re-sign them with the real key prior to shipping. However, that approach has the minor disadvantage that the assemblies are being tested with the "wrong" identity, since the public key forms part of their identity. That isn't too serious, but it will mean that any dependent assemblies will need to be recompiled to correctly reference the signed assemblies prior to shipping. And if your application is a new version of a library and you want to test it with some other client code to which you don't have access to the source code, you won't be able to use a test key. So in general my preference is the approach demonstrated in this sample.

Using Certificates

Although I've focused so far on signing an assembly with a .NET strong name, there are of course two ways of signing an assembly. The key generated by the sn.exe utility and indicated by the AssemblyKeyFile attribute is stored in a .NET-specific format and is used to sign an individual assembly (or possibly all the assemblies in an application or library). It deals specifically with the CLR-specific information. The support in the CLR for strong names ensures that a strong name is checked every time an assembly is loaded. On the other hand, there has for many years been separate support on Windows for signing any PE file, with a so-called *certificate* using Microsoft's *Authenticode* technology (which I'll cover soon in the section "The Windows Cryptography Model"). The purpose of the two signatures is different. While sn-generated keys are normally used to identify assemblies or applications, Authenticode signatures are used to identify the publisher—the company that produced the assembly. Although the basic public-private key principles and algorithms are the same, the actual file formats used for the keys are different, and different command-line utilities are used to manipulate the keys. Another difference is that Authenticode signatures are designed to provide protection at the time when you download or install an application, by providing confirmation that the company claimed to have written the software did indeed write it. (And as you'll see soon, they provide a far stronger guarantee of this than .NET strong names.)

Nothing is stopping you from signing an assembly in both ways, and for security purposes that is normally a good idea. This means you'll end up with an assembly that looks a bit like Figure 13-5.

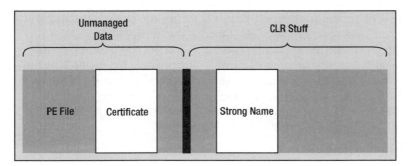

Figure 13-5. *An assembly signed with a certificate and a strong name*

So what exactly is the problem with using only a strong name? Well, if a file has been signed, then that means you can trust that file's integrity to the same extent that you trust the private key with which it has been signed. Are private keys trustworthy? The problem at the moment is that I can easily generate a private key just by running sn or a similar utility to create a private key. What's there to stop me, as a freelance programmer working from home, from creating a private key, sticking the name *Microsoft Corporation* on it, then claiming that I'm the Microsoft Corporation and showing my private key to 'prove' it? Well, OK, claiming to be a huge company such as Microsoft may be stretching it a bit, but you get the point. You may have established that a piece of software was signed with a certain private key, but you still need to be satisfied that that private key really does belong to the person or company indicated. That's where certificates and *certification authorities* (CAs) come in. Let's look at certificates first.

■**Tip** Although certificates and CAs verify all sorts of communications, including e-mails and Web site connections, from now on I'll concentrate exclusively on applying cryptography and certificates for down-loading files—simply because that's the area that's most relevant to .NET assemblies. The same basic principles apply to other areas, though.

What's a Certificate?

A *certificate* is simply a file that contains a public key along with information about to whom that key belongs. Although the concept is so simple, certificates are so important that a couple of industry-standard specifications for certificates exist. The one normally used on Windows is the X.509 certificate, which is stored in a file with extension .cer. The fields included in an X.509 certificate include the algorithm used for the key, the name of the owner, the dates between which the certificate is valid, the public key itself, and any additional information the issuer chooses to add, such as a contact e-mail address or URL. You may, by the way, also encounter .p7b files, which store another type of certificate, known as PKCS #7.

The problem can now be restated as follows: What is there to stop me from creating an X.509 certificate on my computer, putting "Microsoft Corp" in the "owner" field and then passing it around the Internet? Well, the answer is "nothing"—you or I could indeed do that in principle (though it wouldn't be legal in most countries). The problem (or should I say the *solution*) is that no one would trust the certificate because it hadn't been issued by a recognized CA (apart from the fact that Microsoft would probably take an interest in the matter very quickly as well. And Microsoft is a lot bigger than I am. . .).

Certification Authorities

Quite a number of certification authorities exist now. VeriSign is the most well known, but others, such as Thawte, GlobalSign, EnTrust, and PGP (Pretty Good Privacy) exist. These organizations earn a living by checking your identity and vouching for certificates you issue.

The technical details of what happens are fairly complex, but I'll go through the rough principles. If you decide you need a private key and you want to be certified by a CA, then you'll apply to that CA and pay the relevant fee. The CA will then spend some time performing various background checks on you or on your organization. The details of the checks vary depending on what country you're applying from, which CA you apply to, and what fee you pay the CA—the higher the fee, the more checks will be carried out, and the better your certificate will be (because the certificate you get will come categorized according to the level of checks made). They can range from a simple check that you're contactable at your e-mail address up to checks on your physical address, tax returns, and company listings. Once the CA has satisfied itself of who you are, it will issue the certificate. This will normally be done through your browser, over a secure HTTPS Internet connection, and depends on some built-in support from your browser (this support is provided by both Internet Explorer and Netscape). Your browser will generate a private key, work out the corresponding public key, and send it securely to the CA Web server. Notice how this works. The private key is generated locally on your machine and stays there. It's not generated by the CA; if the CA did that, then it'd have to send the key over the wire to you, which would ruin the whole point of private keys! The CA never finds out what your private key is, but it does store the corresponding public key.

How does that help you to sign your software? Well, as soon as your Web browser has sent your public key to the CA, the CA will use this key to generate a certificate. Then the CA will sign the certificate, with its own private key, in just the same way as you sign PE files, and will send the signed certificate back to you. You now have a certificate that indicates the value of your public key, as well as various fields that say who you are, and that has been signed by the CA.

Now, suppose that later, you have reached the point at which you've written some code, you've generated a hash of your PE file, and you want to sign the file. So you encrypt the file with your private key. Now, if you weren't using a certificate, you'd place your public key in the file. However, with a certificate, you can do something better: you can put your certificate in the file.

Now your code gets distributed. At some point someone downloads the code or otherwise tries to run it. Windows sees that the PE file contains a certificate, so one of the first things it does is process the certificate in order to verify file authenticity. Windows will need to decrypt the signature. Now recall that the certificate has been signed with the CA's private key, which means that Windows needs to use the CA's public key to decrypt the signature. At this point the great bonus of signatures comes in to play; certain CAs are called *root CAs* that Microsoft knows about and trusts. And Microsoft has hard-coded knowledge of the certificates that belong to those CAs into Windows (they're stored by Internet Explorer). Thus, when Windows decrypts a certificate that has been signed by a root CA, it does so using one of these hard-coded public keys. Successfully decrypting the certificate in this way proves that it was issued by a root CA and is therefore trustworthy. The point is that because the public keys of the root CA's are hard-coded into Windows, there can be no doubt about the authenticity of the signatures.

Once this check has been made, Windows can verify that your PE file is genuine and hasn't been tampered with. Windows can decrypt the hash of the PE file using your public key, yielding the raw hash value. Windows knows that all the information it read out of the certificate is correct and trustworthy, and that information includes your public key needed to decrypt the hash of the PE file, as well as the details of who you are. Now Windows can perform its own independent calculation of the hash value from the file contents, and if it matches the decrypted value, then the software has been authenticated.

One of the great things about certificates is that they're recursive. You don't have to get your certificates signed directly by a root CA. If you prefer you can use a smaller, CA, which isn't recognized as a root but that has arranged for its certificates to be signed by a larger CA. The whole process can go on until a root CA signs the certificate. As long as a root certificate is at the end of the chain, it doesn't matter how long the chain is. Windows will still be able to confirm whether your PE file is signed and therefore trustworthy.

What happens if the certificate isn't present or not traceable to a root CA? Well, that depends on your policies. The most common situation in which you encounter the use of certificates is when you download an ActiveX control from an Internet site. Windows Explorer will check whether the control has been signed. If IE is running at the medium security level and this is an untrusted site, then you'll get a dialog box like that in Figure 13-6 if the control has been signed with a recognized root public key.

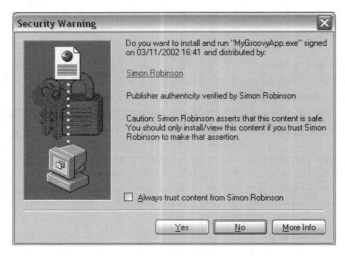

Figure 13-6. *Downloading a signed ActiveX control from the Internet*

If the control doesn't have a key, then you'll see a dialog box similar to the one in Figure 13-7.

Figure 13-7. *Downloading an unsigned ActiveX control from the Internet*

A similar but slightly different dialog box appears if the application has been signed by an untrusted key—that is, a key that can't be traced back to a CA that Windows knows about.

Personally, I don't think these dialog boxes have been that well designed. To someone who doesn't understand the process of generating certificates and the significance of some software having been signed (and let's face it, that'll be about 99.9 percent of Internet users), the dialog box shown in Figure 13-6 looks more like a warning that something may be wrong—when in fact it's your reassurance that the software was definitely written by the company indicated on the dialog box. The dialog box in Figure 13-7 doesn't look that different from the one in Figure 13-6, but the underlying meaning is different—there's no guarantee you can trust this software.

Note that most of the discussion in this section has focused on the general principles of how certification works. The particular implementation of these principles on Windows—the software on your computer that supports checking of certificates—is known as *Authenticode*.

You can see the trusted roots on your machine by running an application called certmgr. (Just type in **certmgr** at the VS .NET command prompt.) You'll get a dialog box with a large property sheet on it. Select the Trusted Root Certification Authorities tab, and you'll see the list, as shown in Figure 13-8.

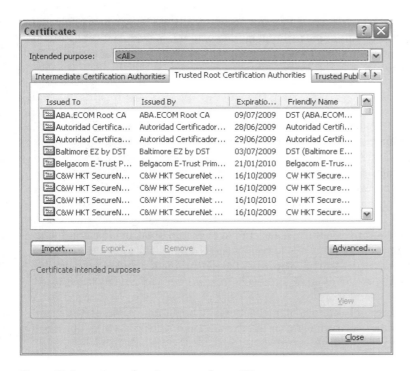

Figure 13-8. certmgr *showing trusted root CAs*

Can Certification Fail?

Now that you've seen how the certification system works, I'll cover how secure the system is. Are there any weak points that make it possible for a hacker to break in and, for example, put some malicious software on your computer?

Can Malicious Code Be Certified?

Could malicious parties get themselves certified and then use their certificates to distribute malicious code? If someone did that, it wouldn't take long before one of their victims figured out which piece of code was interfering with their system and report the fact to the relevant CA. The CA could then test the code to confirm the problem, revoke the certificate, and report the matter to the authorities. Even better, because the code is digitally signed, the nonrepudiation principle cuts in. The malicious party can't deny having written the code because proof is there in the form of the digital signature. Enter lawyers, courts, and (depending on the local laws) a possible jail sentence.

Lost or Stolen Private Key

Private keys are supposed to be kept absolutely secure, but it's possible that the unthinkable may happen—some organization may lose its private key (or worse—have it stolen). This means that whoever stole the key can write code purporting to be from that organization. However, certification will protect against this. As soon as the loss is discovered, the organization can report the loss to the CA, which will expire the certificate and issue a new one. Although I won't go into the details of the technology, I'll say that in principle it's still possible to distinguish code that has been signed and time stamped before the certificate expired and that therefore is still trustworthy.

User Errors and Trojans

In practice, user errors are arguably the means by which problems can most easily occur. Using the various tools concerning security and cryptography require quite a good understanding of cryptography and Authenticode in order to use them properly, so it's not inconceivable that administrators and users can make mistakes in setting up their policies and trusted keys. Add to that the viruses and Trojans that users open in their e-mails, for example. A virus that trashes your system tends to get noticed instantly, but there are also Trojans around that don't have any obvious visible effect. They simply make subtle changes to the security settings on your computer to make it easier for a hacker to break in later—and that may theoretically include adding certificates to your trusted root list. Obviously, the only real protection against this is to ensure you have up-to-date virus protection and to not open suspicious e-mail attachments. But as an experienced programmer, you already take those precautions, don't you. . .?

Then, of course, there are the millions of Internet users who happily download and run executable files and DLLs that have not been certified at all. There's not really a lot that certification can do about that!

The Windows Cryptography Model

Windows has fairly sophisticated cryptography features, which implement all the principles I've discussed in this chapter. It also allows you to do things such as generate public-private key pairs, or symmetric keys, encrypt and decrypt data, sign files, or even create X.509 certificates. (Though, obviously, any certificates you create manually won't be backed up by any certification authority and so won't be regarded as trustworthy outside your organization.)

The Windows cryptography SDK exposes command-line utilities and an unmanaged API known as the *CryptoAPI*. To this the .NET Framework adds the classes in the

`System.Security.Cryptography` and related namespaces. The underlying architecture is based on programs known as *cryptographic service providers* (CSPs). These are the programs that actually implement the cryptographic algorithms. The CryptoAPI invokes CSPs, as shown in Figure 13-9.

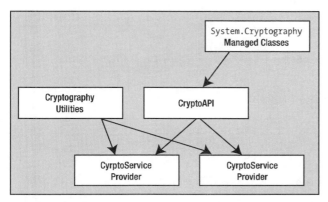

Figure 13-9. *Windows cryptography API and CLR support*

The situation is quite analogous to the architecture of GDI+ (or GDI or DirectX for that matter). Recall that when you use GDI+ to perform drawing, GDI+ will communicate with whatever device drivers are available on your output device to get the drawing done. Similarly, the CryptoAPI is implemented as a set of Windows API functions that are internally implemented to communicate with a cryptographic service provider that actually performs the task. Microsoft has supplied a base CSP, which comes with Windows NT/2000/XP Professional and newer, as standard. If you don't explicitly change the CSP, that will be the one that's called by default when you invoke any CryptoAPI function. However, it's perfectly permissible for third parties to register their own CSPs. Before you ask, though, it's not possible for just anyone to write and install a CSP. (If that were possible, then you could imagine the hackers eagerly queuing up to install rogue CSPs that do bad things such as pass on private keys!) Any CSPs need to be signed by Microsoft before the CryptoAPI will recognize them. And clearly Microsoft will sign a CSP only if it's satisfied as to the integrity of the CSP software and its authors and if the CSP software satisfies all the various legal requirements.

Creating a Certificate

I'll now demonstrate how to attach a certificate to an assembly. This means signing the assembly using various command-line tools that use the default CSP to create a certificate and add the certificate to the list of trusted roots maintained by your computer. You then need to use a tool called `SignCode.exe`, which actually signs the code with the certificate.

■**Tip** Bear in mind that signing with `SignCode` isn't the same as signing with an `sn`-created key. As mentioned earlier, the two processes are similar but are independent of each other. Signing using `SignCode` is intended to verify the publisher rather than the assembly, and it doesn't give the assembly a strong name. In this example I won't be attaching a .NET private key to the assembly created, but the procedure is identical for an assembly that has a strong name.

First, for this sample, you need the program that will be signed. I'll go for another simple AriiteWurld application (a dialect-specific variation of HelloWorld), although this program is a Windows Forms application rather than a console application. Here's the code for it:

```
using System;
using System.Windows.Forms;
using System.Drawing;

namespace Apress.ExpertDotNet.SignedForm
{
   public class EntryPoint
   {
      static void Main()
      {
         Form form = new Form();
         form.Text = "Ariite, Wurld!";
         form.Size = new Size(200,200);
         Application.Run(form);
      }
   }
}
```

I've kept the code as simple as possible because it's not the code I'm interested in here—it's the signing procedure.

To create a certificate, you need a batch file. Here it is:

```
MakeCert -sv TestRoot.pvk -r -n "CN=Simons Test Root" TestRoot.cer
Cert2SPC TestRoot.cer TestRoot.spc
CertMgr -add -c TestRoot.cer -s root
```

There's quite a lot going on here, so I'll go over this file carefully. And you'll also find that when you run this code you'll get a few dialog boxes asking you for passwords.

The first command, MakeCert, is the command-line utility that creates a certificate. In the process, it also creates an appropriate public-private key pair in the process.

```
MakeCert -sv TestRoot.pvk -r -n "CN=Simons Test Root" TestRoot.cer
```

This command will place the certificate in a file called TestRoot.cer. The certificate file contains only the public key, so you need to store the private key somewhere else. The -sv option indicates the file in which the private key should be stored. The key is actually stored in an encrypted, password-protected form, and MakeCert will pop up a dialog asking you to choose the password. This password won't be stored anywhere, so you'll need to remember it. The -r option indicates that this certificate will be self-signed. That basically means it's not going to be signed by any CA—it can exist at the end of any chain of certificates. -n gives the name by which the certificate will be known, in LDAP format.

Tip Note that if you create a certificate in this way, then under the terms of the Windows license, you're not permitted to use the certificate to publicly distribute software. You may use it only for testing purposes within an application. For certifying software for shipping, you must omit the step just described and obtain a .cer file from a CA instead.

Cert2SPC simply copies the .cer file into a different file format that's specifically intended for signing code (as opposed to authenticating a Web site, for example).

CertMgr is more interesting. This is the command that actually manipulates the store of registered certificates. You've already encountered the CertMgr utility in this chapter; I showed that if you run the utility without any parameters, it pops up a form that allows you to manipulate the store from a user interface. Running it with parameters causes it simply to perform the requested task and exit, but you still get a dialog box (shown in Figure 13-10) asking you to confirm the adding of the key to the store. I guess Microsoft decided that adding trusted keys was such a potentially dangerous operation that they put this in as a safeguard.

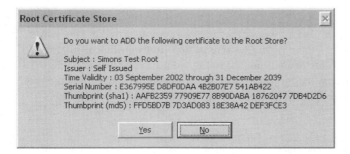

Figure 13-10. *The dialog box that pops up when using* CertMgr *to add a trusted key to the store*

Incidentally, MakeCert works the same way. You can invoke MakeCert without any parameters, in which case you'll get a form that guides you through a wizard to make the certificate. For this sample, however, I pass CertMgr the options -add, which tells it to add the specified item to the store; -c, which tells it that it's a certificate file I want to add; and -s root, which tells it to make the certificate a trusted root. This is important: if you don't do that, then the following call to SignCode.exe will sign the file, but Windows won't recognize the signed file as in any way trusted because it won't be able to link the certificate to a trusted root.

Now that the certificate has been created and installed, you're ready to build and sign the executable. Here's the batch file to do that:

```
csc AriiteWurld.cs
SignCode -v TestRoot.pvk -spc TestRoot.spc AriiteWurld.exe
```

SignCode.exe is used to actually sign the executable with the certificate. Notice that you need to pass it the certificate itself (in the form of a .spc file) and also the private key. Because the TestRoot.pvk file is password-protected, you'll be prompted for the password when this instruction is executed. Just as with the previous sample, you won't normally want developers to have access to the .pvk file, so the process of signing the code will be performed by some

trusted individual, but for this sample I won't worry about that. In the case of digital certificates, there's no facility to delay-sign an assembly. It's not needed since the certificate doesn't
form any part of the assembly's identity. The previous code will sign but won't time stamp the
assembly. To time stamp it you need to supply the option -t and give the path of a DLL
capable of performing the time stamping. Various such DLLs are available to provide this
service on the Internet. I've opted to use one provided by VeriSign, which means that the
command required looks like this:

```
signcode  -v PrivKey.pvk -spc TestRoot.cer
     -t http://timestamp.verisign.com/scripts/timstamp.dll ariitewurld.exe
```

■**Tip** If you explore the MSDN documentation for the .NET command-line utilities, you'll find MakeCert,
SignCode, and related tools listed as .NET utilities. Don't be fooled by this; these utilities are part of the
cryptography SDK and have been around since the days of Internet Explorer 4. They will work equally well
on any PE file, whether or not it's an assembly.

Now that you've signed the assembly, but what difference is it going to make? One way to
tell is to run the utility ChkTrust on it. (Just type in **ChkTrust** *<filename>* at the command
prompt.) ChkTrust will examine any certificate attached to the file it's inspecting and will
display the appropriate message box warning you about its contents—the same message box
that's displayed in Windows Explorer. For this sample, when I tried it, I got the dialog box
shown in Figure 13-11.

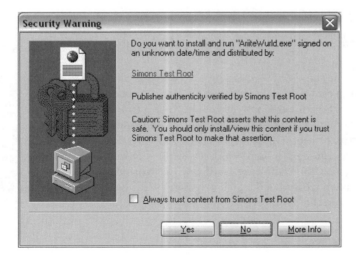

Figure 13-11. *Running* ChkTrust *on the assembly generated from the sample*

It's also possible to use a tool called SecUtil to extract the public key from an assembly, as shown in Figure 13-12.

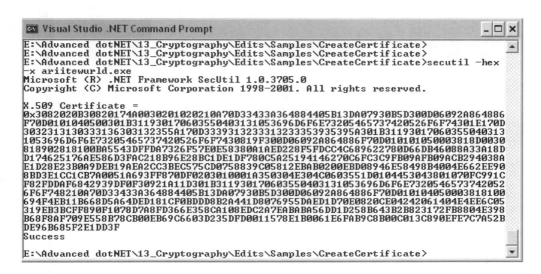

Figure 13-12. *Running* SecUtil *on the assembly*

SecUtil will retrieve the key only if the file has a valid Authenticode signature, which can be traced to a trusted root; otherwise it'll display an error message. Thus, SecUtil not only provides one way of retrieving the public key if you need it for any reason but also serves as a way to check that the signing process was successful. SecUtil by the way is CLR aware. Instead of typing in **-x** (which retrieves the X.509 key), you can pass it the option -s, in which case it'll retrieve the strong name for the assembly, if it exists.

However, the final proof of the pudding is whether the CLR's code-based security mechanism will recognize the certificate. To check this, you should move the AriiteWurld.exe file to some location on a remote machine, from which it wouldn't normally be trusted to run. Placing it on the Internet is ideal. Then try downloading it from Internet Explorer and see the result—a security policy exception dialog box. Now use your favorite tool—either caspol or mscorcfg.msc that I explained in Chapter 4—to add a new code group that gives full trust to code that's signed with your newly created certificate. Personally, I find this easier using the mscorcfg.msc snap-in, since you can click to add a new code group and then select a membership condition based on publisher for the new group. Then you get a dialog box asking you to browse down to the .cer file that contains the certificate. This means you don't have to manually copy and paste the public key; mscorcfg.msc will read it from the certificate file. In Figure 13-13, the Import from Certificate File has the focus. Clicking this button will open the standard File Open dialog box to allow you to search for the certificate file.

Figure 13-13. *Using the* mscorcfg *snap-in to create a code group based on a certificate*

With this code group added, you should find that AriiteWurld.exe will now successfully download and execute, even from an untrusted location.

Reading a Certificate Programmatically

I'll finish this chapter by presenting a short example that complements the previous sample. Where the previous sample involved creating an X509 certificate and using it to sign an application, I'll now write a short example that can read the certificate and display information about it. The example uses the X509Certificate class.

The code looks like this:

```
static void Main()
{
   string filePath;
   OpenFileDialog dlg = new OpenFileDialog();
   if (dlg.ShowDialog() != DialogResult.OK)
      return;
   filePath = dlg.FileName;
   Console.WriteLine(filePath);
   X509Certificate cert = X509Certificate.CreateFromCertFile(filePath);
   Console.WriteLine("Name:\t\t" + cert.GetName());
   Console.WriteLine("Algorithm:\t" + cert.GetKeyAlgorithm());
   Console.WriteLine("Valid from:\t" + cert.GetEffectiveDateString());
```

```
    Console.WriteLine("Valid to:\t" + cert.GetExpirationDateString());
    Console.WriteLine("Issuer:\t\t" + cert.GetIssuerName());
}
```

The first part of the code opens a standard Open File dialog box to allow the user to select the .cer file to examine. For simplicity's sake, there's no error checking here; I trust the user to pick a file of the appropriate type. Next the code instantiates an X509Certificate instance based on the file. The X509Certificate class is in the System.Security.Cryptography.X509Certificates namespace. It's defined in mscorlib.dll, in common with all the cryptography classes, so you don't have any extra assemblies to link in. You can use the class to read an existing certificate, but you can't use it to create one. (This doesn't appear to be possible with the cryptography classes; to do that you need to fall back on native APIs, but then unless you happen to be a CA, you shouldn't normally want to create certificates anyway).

Finally, the code simply uses various methods on X509Certificate to display various fields of the certificate. Note that the code doesn't display the public key because I don't really want to display another public key figure; public keys are too big and don't make especially exciting reading. . . (if required, the public key is available as a string through the GetPublicKeyString() method). Anyway, the output when I ran the DisplayCertificate sample and select the certificate I created in the previous sample looks like this:

```
E:\Edits\Samples\CreateCertificate\TestRoot.cer
Name:         CN=Simons Test Root
Algorithm:    1.2.840.113549.1.1.1
Valid from:   03/11/2002 08:01:25
Valid to:     31/12/2039 15:59:59
Issuer:       CN=Simons Test Root
```

It's interesting to note that the X509Certificate methods such as GetName() and GetIssuerName() that I used here would normally have been expected to have been implemented as properties (since they return nonvolatile property-like items of information without modifying the class instance). Earlier in the chapter I noted a couple of minor eccentricities in the design of the System.Cryptography classes. My own suspicion is that either these classes were designed in a hurry, or there was some lack of communication between teams at Microsoft at some point. However, this is a minor matter of interface design and of following conventions for .NET coding, not something that should affect your use of the classes.

Summary

In this chapter I took you on a tour of cryptography, covering both the basic theory of how cryptography works and some of the classes available in the .NET class libraries to implement cryptographic algorithms. I covered both symmetric and public key algorithms, and I showed how public-key encryption provides greater security but at a performance cost. Then I covered some of the common techniques for getting the best of both worlds by using public-key encryption for only the most sensitive data. In particular, I focused on how public-key encryption is used to sign files with certificates that are in turn signed by CAs and that therefore confirm the origin of those files. I also went through the procedures for signing an assembly with a strong name and with a certificate.

IL Reference

This appendix summarizes the definition of CIL as of .NET 1.*x*, covering data types, IL assembly language directives and keywords, and all the instruction and prefix opcodes.

The appendix aims to provide a comprehensive quick-reference guide rather than detailed definitions. I hope you'll find it useful if you encounter an unfamiliar instruction in some IL code or if you're wondering what instruction you could use to achieve some task. This means it covers all the IL instructions, but I'll give only limited explanations of each one. To a large extent, I rely on your common sense to figure out the main actions of an instruction and its likely usage restrictions. For example, the shift-left instruction shl requires the operands to be integers; the JIT compiler will reject your code if you try to shift floating-point operands. But I don't say that explicitly because it should be obvious that shifting a floating-point number doesn't make sense. I also don't list the exceptions that may be generated by a particular instruction. For more detailed information concerning the exact definition of each instruction, the conditions for it to represent valid or verifiable code, and exceptions it may throw, you should refer to Partition III of the .NET Framework specifications, which ships with the .NET Framework SDK.

IL Types

CIL recognizes the types shown in Table A-1.

Table A-1. *IL Data Types*

CIL Name	Suffix Name (If Relevant)	CLR Type (If Relevant)	Meaning
bool		System.Bool	True or false
char		System.Char	1-byte integer representing a character
int8	i1	System.SByte	1-byte integer
int16	i2	System.Int16	2-byte integer
int32	i4	System.Int32	4-byte integer
int64	i8	System.Int64	8-byte integer
native int	i	System.IntPtr	Integer of size determined by machine architecture

Table A-1. *IL Data Types (Continued)*

CIL Name	Suffix Name (If Relevant)	CLR Type (If Relevant)	Meaning
unsigned int8	u1	System.Byte	1-byte unsigned integer
unsigned int16	u2	System.UInt16	2-byte unsigned integer
unsigned int32	u4	System.UInt32	4-byte unsigned integer
unsigned int64	u8	System.UInt64	8-byte unsigned integer
native unsigned int	u	System.IntPtr	Unsigned integer of size determined by machine architecture
float32	f4	System.Single	4-byte floating point number
float64	f8	System.Double	8-byte floating point number
&			Managed pointer
obj	ref	System.Object	Reference to an object on the managed heap
typedref		System.TypedReference	Dynamically typed reference
void			Method returns no value

In Table A-1, the CIL name is the text used in IL assembly language to indicate the type in directives—for example, when listing types of local variables, arguments, or return values of methods. The suffix name is the text normally used in mnemonics for particular versions of instructions that apply to a given type; for example, ldc.i4 loads an int32 onto the evaluation stack. However, since these suffixes don't have a set standard, they may vary in their usage. The suffix is relevant only if instructions exist that use that suffix in their mnemonic names.

Notes

bool is generally stored as a 1-byte value, except on the evaluation stack where it's stored as a 4-byte value. CIL will interpret any nonzero value as true and will interpret zero as false. The CLR will, however, always generate 1 for true.

native int and native unsigned int are 4-byte integers (= int32) on 32-bit machines and 8-byte integers (= int64) on 64-bit machines. native unsigned int is the data type used for unmanaged pointers.

No differences exist between integer types and the equivalent unsigned types other than how the most significant bit of the data is interpreted for arithmetic, bitwise, comparison, and overflow operations. If signed, then the value is interpreted as being a two's complement representation.

Floating-point numbers are represented according to the IEEE standard IEC 60559 (1989-01). This standard allows for representations of "not a number" (NaN) and positive and negative infinity. Hence, those are values that a number can legitimately have.

Although all the types listed in Table A-1 are recognized when stored in memory, the evaluation stack isn't capable of storing values that occupy less than 4 bytes. Hence, CIL instructions that load lower precision data types (such as int8 or int16) onto the stack will automatically promote the data to the appropriate 4-byte integer with the same value. Instructions that store smaller types in memory will truncate the data, allowing for the sign, which may result in data loss. This can be detected by using the appropriate `conv.ovf` instruction to perform the conversion explicitly and detect any overflow.

IL Instruction Set

The IL instruction set contains 210 instruction opcodes in total (as well as three prefix opcodes), although arguably only 84 of the instruction opcodes represent distinct instructions—the remainder being variant versions of the same instructions, such as shortened forms, unsigned versions, or versions that perform overflow checking.

HOW TO READ THIS SECTION

This appendix lists all the IL instructions, classified by their purpose. For each group of instructions, I give a brief description of the purpose of the instructions, the meanings of any arguments, and a stack transition diagram. Note that I use the term *argument* to indicate any data that immediately follows the opcode in the assembly and *operand* to indicate data that the instruction pops from the evaluation stack and processes. Hence, arguments are hard-coded into the assembly, but operands can change as the assembly runs.

Next I present a table for each set of instructions. This table indicates for each instruction the mnemonic used in textual IL source files, the opcode and the data type of any arguments, a brief description of the purpose of the instruction, and an indication of whether it is always verifiable when it occurs in valid code. You may also find a brief description on the restrictions of using some instructions. For example, Table A-2 shows the information for the unconditional branch instructions.

Table A-2. *Example: The* br *and* br.s *Instructions*

Mnemonic	Opcode and Argument(s)	Purpose	Verifiable?
br	0x38 <int32>	Branch by	Depends
br.s	0x2b <int8>	specified offset	Depends

Table A-2 indicates that br and br.s have the same action (branch by a specified offset) and that br takes an int32 as an argument and br.s takes an int8. You can deduce that the br instruction will occupy a total of 5 bytes in the assembly. The first byte will contain the number 0x38, which identifies this as the br instruction, and the following four bytes will contain the offset as an int32 represented in little-endian format (all arguments in IL are little-endian). On the other hand, br.s occupies only 2 bytes (one for the opcode and one for the following int8). This table also indicates that this instruction may or may not be verifiable, depending on how it's used (details will be in an accompanying explanation).

Besides the CIL data types, I may also indicate <T> for the argument of an instruction. <T> indicates an integer that will be interpreted as a token (index) into the metadata for the assembly or module and may therefore indicate a typedef, typeref, methoddef, or memberref, and so on.

The Verifiable column of the tables that list opcodes may have one of three values: Yes, No, or Depends.

"Yes" indicates that, provided any indicated conditions required for the instruction to represent valid code have been met, this instruction will pass the algorithm used by `peverify.exe` to check that code is type safe. (Obviously, if the conditions for valid code haven't been met, the JIT compiler will refuse to compile the code anyway.) It's important to understand that a "Yes" in this column doesn't necessarily mean the instruction is always verifiable; it may be that in some situations the instruction isn't verifiable, but in those cases JIT compiler will refuse to compile the code on validity grounds anyway.

"No" indicates that if this instruction is used, the containing assembly will fail the type-safety test of `peverify`. It's possible that future JIT compilers that use more sophisticated type-verification algorithms will pass the code, but this isn't guaranteed, and in general you should expect the code will fail type-safety checks and so will run only if the assembly and user have permission to bypass type-safety verification.

"Depends" means that whether the instruction is type safe according to the `peverify` algorithm depends on how it's used. If one or more instructions indicate "Depends" in this column, then more information will almost always be available in a following "Verifiability Conditions" section.

You should be aware of one other point. In the table, I assume you can recognize the suffixes on the instruction mnemonics (for example, `br.s` as a shortened form of `br`). Table A-3 shows the suffixes used.

Table A-3. *IL Assembly Language Suffixes*

Suffix	Meaning
.s	Shortened form of the instruction. This form will do essentially the same thing as the full instruction, but the IL opcode and argument occupy fewer bytes at the expense of a smaller range of values for the argument.
.ovf	Version of the instruction that performs overflow checking and will throw an `OverflowException` if it detects an overflow.
.un	Unsigned version of instruction; this version will interpret the operands as unsigned rather than signed integers.
.i4, .i8, and so on	Suffixes indicating a data type; these indicate that either the operands or the arguments are assumed to be of this type.

Evaluation Stack Operations

These instructions operate in some way on data on the evaluation stack.

Binary Operations

The instructions listed in Table A-4 perform binary arithmetic, or logical operations on elements of the evaluation stack. They all have the following stack transition diagram:

```
... , value2, value1 → ..., result
```

Table A-4. *Binary Operations*

Mnemonic	Opcode and Argument(s)	Purpose	Verifiable?
add add.ovf add.ovf.un	0x58 0xd6 0xd7	Adds the top two items on the stack.	Depends
div div.un	0x5b 0x5c	Divides the first item by the top item on the stack. Note that there's no .ovf version of div. div will itself throw an OverflowException in some cases.	Depends
mul mul.ovf mul.ovf.un	0x5a 0xd8 0xd9	Multiplies the top two items on the stack.	Depends
rem rem.un	0x5d 0x5e	Works out the remainder on dividing the first item by the top item on the stack using integer division.	Depends
sub sub.ovf sub.ovf.un	0x59 0xda 0xdb	Subtracts the top two items on the stack.	Depends
and	0x5f	Performs bitwise AND of top two items on the stack.	Depends
or	0x60	Performs bitwise OR of top two items on the stack.	Depends
xor	0x61	Performs bitwise XOR of top two items on the stack.	Depends
shl	0x62	Shifts the second value on the stack left by the number of bits indicated in the topmost value.	Depends
shr shr.un	0x63 0x64	Shifts the second value on the stack right by the number of bits indicated in the topmost value.	Depends

Verifiability Conditions

The conditions governing whether these instructions are verifiable are complex and depend on the data types on the stack. For full details, see the Partition III document. Roughly speaking, code will fail verifiability if you mix unmanaged pointers with other types. Mixing obviously incompatible types (for example, an int and a float) will result in invalid code.

Comparison Operations

These instructions are similar to the binary arithmetic and logical instructions, but they work by comparing the top two items on the stack and push 1 (=true) or 0 (=false) onto the stack according to the result of the comparison.

```
..., value1, value2 → ..., result
```

Table A-5 lists the instructions to perform comparison operations.

Table A-5. *Comparison Operations*

Mnemonic	Opcode and Argument(s)	Purpose	Verifiable?
ceq	0xfe 0x01	Returns true if values are equal	Yes
cgt cgt.un	0xfe 0x02 0xfe 0x03	Returns true if first operand > second operand	Yes
clt clt.un	0xfe 0x04 0xfe 0x05	Returns true if first operand < second operand	Yes

Unary Operations

These instructions modify the top element of the stack in some way. The data type of this element must be a type for which the operation is meaningful (for example, it isn't valid to call not if this element is a floating-point number).

```
..., value → ..., result
```

Table A-6 lists the instructions to perform unary operations.

Table A-6. *Unary Operations*

Mnemonic	Opcode and Argument(s)	Purpose	Verifiable?
neg	0x65	Negates the value on the stack by taking its two's complement of integers and toggling the sign bit of floats.	Yes
not	0x66	The bitwise complements the value on the stack. It returns true if first operand < second operand.	Yes

Conversion Operations

The following instructions convert the topmost element of the evaluation stack to a different type. This may involve padding with zeros (or ones for negative numbers) or truncating.

```
..., value → ..., result
```

Table A-7 lists the instructions to perform conversion operations.

Table A-7. *Conversion Operations*

Mnemonic	Opcode and Argument(s)	Purpose	Verifiable?
conv.i	0xd3	Converts the operand to the destination type indicated by the mnemonic	Depends
conv.i1	0x67		
conv.i2	0x68		
conv.i4	0x69		
conv.i8	0x6a		
conv.ovf.i	0xd4		
conv.ovf.i.un	0x8a		
conv.ovf.i1	0xb3		
conv.ovf.i1.un	0x82		
conv.ovf.i2	0xb5		
conv.ovf.i2.un	0x83		
conv.ovf.i4	0xb7		
conv.ovf.i4.un	0x84		
conv.ovf.i8	0xb9		
conv.ovf.i8.un	0x85		
conv.ovf.u	0xd5		
conv.ovf.u.un	0x8b		
conv.ovf.u1	0xb4		
conv.ovf.u1.un	0x86		
conv.ovf.u2	0xb6		
conv.ovf.u2.un	0x87		
conv.ovf.u4	0xb8		
conv.ovf.u4.un	0x88		
conv.ovf.u8	0xba		
conv.ovf.u8.un	0x89		
conv.r.un	0x76		
conv.r4	0x6b		
conv.r8	0x6c		
conv.u	0xe0		
conv.u1	0xd2		
conv.u2	0xd1		
conv.u4	0x6d		
conv.u8	0x6e		

Verifiability Conditions

The conv instructions will cause verification to fail if the item on the stack is a pointer.

Other Stack Operations

The following sections list some additional instructions that operate on the evaluation stack.

ckfinite

This instruction allows you to verify that the top item of the stack, which must be a floating-point number, is finite (that is, not plus or minus infinity or NaN). chfinite throws an exception if the element isn't finite but leaves it unchanged otherwise. Unusually, this instruction examines the contents of this element without popping it from the stack.

```
..., value  →  ..., value
```

Table A-8 shows the chkfinite instruction.

Table A-8. ckfinite

Mnemonic	Opcode and Argument(s)	Purpose	Verifiable?
ckfinite	0xc3	Checks if topmost element on the stack is finite	Yes

dup

This instruction duplicates the topmost value of the stack.

```
..., value  →  ..., value, value
```

Table A-9 shows the dup instruction.

Table A-9. dup

Mnemonic	Opcode and Argument(s)	Purpose	Verifiable?
dup	0x25	Duplicates topmost element of stack	Yes

pop

This instruction simply pops the top value off of the stack so that this value is lost.

```
..., value  →  ...
```

Table A-10 shows the pop instruction.

Table A-10. pop

Mnemonic	Opcode and Argument(s)	Purpose	Verifiable?
pop	0x26	Removes topmost element from stack	Yes

Data Transfer Instructions

These instructions are responsible for transferring data between the evaluation stack and the various other data stores available to a method (locals, arguments) or for loading constants onto the evaluation stack. Instructions that transfer data between the stack and member fields or the local memory pool are dealt with separately later in this appendix in the "Accessing Member Fields" section.

Instructions to Transfer Constants

These instructions load hard-coded constants onto the evaluation stack. The constant is in some cases supplied as an argument to the instruction and in other cases embedded in the instruction. Compact instructions that indicate the constant in this way exist for the integers between –1 and 8.

```
...  → ..., value
```

Table A-11 lists the instructions to transfer constants.

Table A-11. *Instructions to Transfer Constants*

Mnemonic	Opcode and Argument(s)	Purpose	Verifiable?
ldnull	0x14	Pushes the null reference onto the stack (as a native int).	Yes
ldc.i4.0	0x16	Pushes the value 0 onto the stack.	Yes
ldc.i4.1	0x17	Pushes the value 1 onto the stack.	Yes
ldc.i4.2	0x18	Pushes the value 2 onto the stack.	Yes
ldc.i4.3	0x19	Pushes the value 3 onto the stack.	Yes
ldc.i4.4	0x1a	Pushes the value 4 onto the stack.	Yes
ldc.i4.5	0x1b	Pushes the value 5 onto the stack.	Yes
ldc.i4.6	0x1c	Pushes the value 6 onto the stack.	Yes
ldc.i4.7	0x1d	Pushes the value 7 onto the stack.	Yes
ldc.i4.8	0x1e	Pushes the value 8 onto the stack.	Yes
ldc.i4.m1 *or* ldc.i4.M1	0x15	Pushes the value –1 onto the stack.	Yes
ldc.i4.s	0x1f <int8>	Pushes the argument onto the stack. ldc.i4.s promotes the value to int32. ldc.r4 and ldc.r8 promote the value to a native float.	Yes
ldc.i4	0x20 <int32>		
ldc.i8	0x21 <int64>		
ldc.r4	0x22 <float32>		
ldc.r8	0x23 <float64>		
ldstr	0x72 <T>	Constructs a string object in the managed heap, holding the characters specified by the metadata token, and pushes a reference to that object onto the evaluation stack. Pushes the string identified by the metadata token onto the stack.	Yes

Instructions to Transfer Local Variables

These instructions copy local variables to or from the stack.

Instructions that load values to the stack have this stack transition diagram:

... → ..., value

Instructions that store values from the stack have this stack transition diagram:

..., value → ...

Table A-12 lists the instructions to transfer local variables.

Table A-12. *Instructions to Transfer Local Variables*

Mnemonic	Opcode and Argument(s)	Purpose	Verifiable?
ldloc.0	0x06	Copies the first local variable (i.e., the one with index zero) onto the stack	Yes
ldloc.1	0x07	Copies the second local variable onto the stack	Yes
ldloc.2	0x08	Copies the third local variable onto the stack	Yes
ldloc.3	0x09	Copies the fourth local variable onto the stack	Yes
ldloc ldloc.s	0xfe 0x0c <unsigned int16> 0x11 <unsigned int8>	Copies the local variable with index given by the argument onto the stack	Yes
ldloca ldloca.s	0xfe 0x0d <unsigned int16> 0x12 <unsigned int8>	Copies the address of the local variable with index given by the argument onto the stack	Yes
stloc.0	0x0a	Pops the top element of the stack in the first local variable	Depends
stloc.1	0x0b	Pops the top element of the stack in the second local variable	Depends
stloc.2	0x0c	Pops the top element of the stack in the third local variable	Depends
stloc.3	0x0d	Pops the top element of the stack in the fourth local variable	Depends
stloc stloc.s	0xfe 0x0e <unsigned int16> 0x13 <unsigned int8>	Pops the top element of the stack in the local variable with index given by the argument	Depends

Verifiability Conditions

The `stloc.*` instructions will fail verification if the type on the stack doesn't match the type of the memory slot to which the value is being stored.

Instructions to Transfer Arguments

These instructions copy method arguments (NB, not IL instruction arguments) to or from the stack.

Instructions that load values to the stack have this stack transition diagram:

```
...  → ..., value
```

Instructions that store values from the stack have this stack transition diagram:

```
..., value  → ...
```

Fewer store instructions exist than load instructions, since storing is an operation that will be performed less often. Since arguments are passed by value, values stored in arguments will not be returned to the calling method.

Table A-13 lists the instructions to transfer arguments.

Table A-13. *Instructions to Transfer Arguments*

Mnemonic	Opcode and Argument(s)	Purpose	Verifiable?
ldarg.0	0x02	Copies the first method argument (in other words, the argument with index zero) onto the stack.	Yes
ldarg.1	0x03	Copies the second method argument onto the stack.	
ldarg.2	0x04	Copies the third method argument onto the stack.	
ldarg.3	0x05	Copies the fourth method argument onto the stack.	
ldarg ldarg.s	0xfe 0x09 0x0e	Copies the method argument with index given by the instruction argument onto the stack.	Yes
ldarga ldarga.s	0xfe 0x0a 0x0f	Copies the address of the method argument with index given by the instruction argument onto the stack. This instruction should be used for arguments that have been passed by reference.	Yes
starg starg.s	0xfe 0x0b 0x10	Pops the top element of the stack into the method argument given by the index on the stack.	Yes
arglist	0xfe 0x00	Loads the address of the start of the method argument list onto the stack.	Depends

Verifiability Conditions

The `arglist` instruction can legally be used only in a method that has a variable argument list. It's verifiable only if the result is treated as a `System.RuntimeArgumentHandle` instance.

Indirect Addressing Operations

These instructions use indirect addressing to indicate the memory location that the data should be loaded from or stored to. This means that, depending on the address, the actual effect may be to load data from or to a local variable, an argument, the local memory pool, or any other area of memory. Note that unlike most other data transfer instructions, these instructions actually take the address to which data should be loaded or stored from the stack, not from any hard-coded instruction arguments.

Instructions that load values to the stack have this stack transition diagram:

```
..., address  →  ..., value
```

Instructions that store values from the stack have this stack transition diagram:

```
..., address, value  →  ...
```

Table A-14 lists the instructions that perform indirect addressing.

Table A-14. *Indirect Addressing Operations*

Mnemonic	Opcode and Argument(s)	Purpose	Verifiable
ldind.i	0x4d	Loads the value at the address given by the topmost element of the stack. The value is assumed to be of the data type specified in the mnemonic.	Depends
ldind.i1	0x46		
ldind.i2	0x48		
ldind.i4	0x4a		
ldind.i8	0x4c		
ldind.r4	0x4e		
ldind.r8	0x4f		
ldind.ref	0x50		
ldind.u1	0x47		
ldind.u2	0x49		
ldind.u4	0x4b		
stind.i	0xdf	Stores the value in the topmost element of the stack in the memory location given by the second address in the stack. The value is assumed to be of the data type specified in the mnemonic.	Depends
stind.i1	0x52		
stind.i2	0x53		
stind.i4	0x54		
stind.i8	0x55		
stind.r4	0x56		
stind.r8	0x57		
stind.ref	0x51		

Verifiability Conditions

The `ldind.*` and `stind.*` instructions aren't verifiable if the address on the stack is an unmanaged pointer or if it's a managed pointer but the pointer type doesn't match up to the type being loaded/stored.

Branch Instructions

The following sections list the various branch instructions.

Unconditional Branch

These instructions transfer control. The argument gives the offset in bytes. An offset of zero will cause execution to continue at the following instruction.

This instruction has no effect on the stack:

```
...   →  ...
```

Table A-15 lists the unconditional branch instructions

Table A-15. *Unconditional Branch Instructions*

Mnemonic	Opcode and Argument(s)	Purpose	Verifiable?
br	0x38 <int32>	Branch by specified offset	Depends
br.s	0x2b <int8>		

Verifiability Conditions

The specified offset must lead to a valid IL instruction (and not to data, for example) or to the prefix of an instruction. It isn't permitted to branch to a destination outside the method or into or out of a `try`, `catch`, `filter`, or `finally` block. In general, branch instructions are verifiable, but verifiability may fail if the state of the stack at the destination address isn't consistent with its state when reached by other execution paths.

Conditional Branch

These instructions transfer control provided that some condition is met. If the condition isn't satisfied, then these instructions have no action other than to pop operands off the stack.

Some conditional branch instructions work by comparing the top two values of the stack (binary conditions).

```
..., value1, value2 → ...,
```

Table A-16 lists the binary conditional branch instructions.

Table A-16. *Binary Conditional Branch Instructions*

Mnemonic and Argument(s)	Opcode and Argument(s)	Purpose	Verifiable?
beq beq.s	0x3b \<int32> 0x2e \<int8>	Branches if operands are equal	Depends (same restrictions as for br)
bge bge.s bge.un bge.un.s	0x3c \<int32> 0x2f \<int8> 0x41 \<int32> 0x34 \<int8>	Branches if first operand >= second operand	Depends
bgt bgt.s bgt.un bgt.un.s	0x3d \<int32> 0x30 \<int8> 0x42 \<int32> 0x35 \<int8>	Branches if first operand > second operand	Depends
ble ble.s ble.un ble.un.s	0x3e \<int32> 0x31 \<int8> 0x43 \<int32> 0x36 \<int8>	Branches if first operand <= second operand	Depends
blt blt.s blt.un blt.un.s	0x3f \<int32> 0x32 \<int8> 0x44 \<int32> 0x37 \<int8>	Branches if first operand < second operand	Depends
bne.un bne.un.s	0x40 \<int32> 0x33 \<int8>	Branches if operands aren't equal	Depends

Other conditional branches work by examining only the topmost element of the stack (unary conditions).

```
..., value → ...,
```

Table A-17 lists the unary conditional branch instructions.

Table A-17. *Unary Conditional Branch Instructions*

Mnemonic	Opcode and Argument(s)	Purpose	Verifiable?
brfalse	0x39 <int32>	Branches if operand is zero	Depends (same restrictions as for br)
brfalse.s	0x2c <int8>		
brtrue	0x3a <int32>	Branches if operand is nonzero	Depends (same restrictions as for br)
brtrue.s	0x2d <int8>		

Switch

CIL also defines a switch statement, which provides conditional branches dependant on the topmost element of the evaluation stack. The switch statement is similar in concept to the C/C++/C# switch statement or to VB's Select statement, though less flexible.

Unusually, this statement takes a variable number of arguments. The first argument is the number of possible branches. Then each possible branch has one argument; the second argument gives the offset by which program flow should transfer if the topmost element of the stack is zero, the third argument gives the offset to branch by if the topmost element is one, and so on. If the topmost element of the stack is outside the range (0, ... number of branches – 1), no branching occurs.

```
..., value → ...,
```

Table A-18 shows the switch instruction.

Table A-18. switch

Mnemonic	Opcode and Argument(s)	Purpose	Verifiable?
switch	0x45 <unsigned int32>, <int32> ... <int32>	Branches to appropriate destination	Depends (same restrictions as for br)

Object Instructions

These instructions deal with objects, including instantiating objects and accessing their member fields.

Instantiating an Object

The newobj instruction instantiates an object. Although this instruction can be used to instantiate value types, it's normally used to instantiate reference types on the managed heap. It takes as an argument a metadata token representing the constructor of the object (the constructor will in turn identify the object type). Note that the number of items popped from the stack is variable and will equal the number of arguments to be passed to the constructor. A reference to the new object is also pushed onto the stack.

```
..., arg1, ..., argN → ..., object ref
```

Table A-19 shows the newobj instruction.

Table A-19. `newobj`

Mnemonic	Opcode and Argument(s)	Purpose	Verifiable?
newobj	0x73 <T>	Instantiates an object	Yes

Accessing Member Fields

These instructions copy member fields of a value or reference object to or from the stack. In all cases they take a metadata token as an argument, which identifies the field concerned (and so, implicitly, the type of the containing instance).

Several operations have different stack transition diagrams, so I'll treat them individually.

The `ldfld` and `ldflda` instructions are concerned with loading a field. Note that these instructions can be used for instance or static fields, but clearly the object reference is irrelevant for static fields.

```
..., object  →  ..., value
```

Table A-20 lists the `ldfld` and `ldflda` instructions.

Table A-20. `ldfld` *and* `ldflda`

Mnemonic	Opcode and Argument(s)	Purpose	Verifiable?
ldfld	0x7b <T>	Loads the given field onto the stack	Depends
ldflda	0x7c <T>	Loads the address of the given field onto the stack	Depends

`ldsfld` and `ldsflda` are similar to `ldfld` and `ldflda` but apply to static fields and hence don't need the object address.

```
...  →  ..., value
```

Table A-21 lists the `ldsfld` and `ldsflda` instructions.

Table A-21. `ldsfld` *and* `ldsflda`

Mnemonic	Opcode and Argument(s)	Purpose	Verifiable?
ldsfld	0x7e <T>	Loads the given field onto the stack	Depends
ldsflda	0x7f <T>	Loads the address of the given field onto the stack	Depends

Storing works on pretty much the same principle as loading, except that there are no instructions to store addresses (that operation wouldn't really make sense). First up, here's the version that works for instance or static fields:

```
..., object, value  →  ...
```

Table A-22 shows the `stfld` instruction.

Table A-22. `stfld`

Mnemonic	Opcode and Argument(s)	Purpose	Verifiable?
stfld	0x7d <T>	Stores the specified value in the given field	Depends

And finally here's the simpler instruction for static fields:

```
..., value  →  ...
```

Table A-23 shows the `stsfld` instruction.

Table A-23. `stsfld`

Mnemonic	Opcode and Argument(s)	Purpose	Verifiable?
stsfld	0x80 <T>	Stores the specified value in the given static field	Depends

Conditions

For all instructions to access member fields, the following verifiability condition holds: It's not verifiable to use the instruction on an `initonly` field outside the constructor.

Casting

Two instructions cast an object reference from one type to another type: `castclass` and `isinst`. Both instructions will cast `null` to `null`. They differ in that if the cast is unsuccessful, `castclass` will throw an `InvalidCastException`, but `isinst` will simply return `null`. In both cases the destination type is supplied as a metadata token in the instruction argument.

```
..., object reference  →  ..., object reference
```

Table A-24 lists the instructions to perform casting.

Table A-24. *Casting Object References*

Mnemonic	Opcode and Argument(s)	Purpose	Verifiable?
castclass	0x74 <T>	Casts object to the given type	Yes
isinst	0x75 <T>		

Operations Specific to Value Types

The following instructions are related to initializing, copying, and identifying information about value type instances and aren't intended for use on reference types.

Initializing a Value Type

The `initobj` instruction initializes a valuetype instance, given its address, by zeroing all its fields. The address at the top of the stack must be a managed pointer. The instruction takes a

TypeDef or TypeRef token as an argument, which indicates the type of the object. Note that initobj doesn't call any constructor. If required, a constructor should be invoked explicitly.

..., address → ...

Table A-25 shows the initobj instruction.

Table A-25. initobj

Mnemonic	Opcode and Argument(s)	Purpose	Verifiable?
initobj	0xfe 0x15 <T>	Initializes a value objectvalue type instance	Yes

Copying a Value Type

The copyobj instruction requires the top two items on the stack to be addresses and copies the contents of the object at the top address to the other object. The instruction takes a TypeDef or TypeRef token as an argument, which indicates the type of the object.

..., dest address, src address → ...

Table A-26 shows the copyobj instruction.

Table A-26. copyobj

Mnemonic	Opcode and Argument(s)	Purpose	Verifiable?
cpobj	0x70 <T>	Copies a valuetype instance	Depends

Verifiability Conditions

The addresses on the stack must point to the correct type of object for the code to be valid. Additionally, these must be managed pointers if the code is to satisfy verifiability.

Loading a Value Type

The ldobj instruction loads a value type onto the evaluation stack, given its address. The instruction takes a TypeDef or TypeRef token as an argument, which indicates the type of the object.

..., address, → ..., object

Table A-27 shows the ldobj instruction.

Table A-27. ldobj

Mnemonic	Opcode and Argument(s)	Purpose	Verifiable?
ldobj	0x71 <T>	Loads a value object onto the stack	Depends

Verifiability Conditions

The address on the stack must point to the correct type of object for the code to be valid. Additionally, it must be a managed pointer if the code is to satisfy type safety.

Storing a Value Type

The stobj instruction stores a value type from the evaluation stack, given the address at which it should be stored. The instruction takes a TypeDef or TypeRef token as an argument, which indicates the type of the object.

```
..., address, object → ...
```

Table A-28 shows the stobj instruction.

Table A-28. stobj

Mnemonic	Opcode and Argument(s)	Purpose	Verifiable?
stobj	0x81 <T>	Stores a value object at the given address	Depends

Verifiability Conditions

The address on the stack must point to the correct type of object for the code to be valid. Additionally, it must be a managed pointer if the code is to satisfy type safety.

Determining Object Size

The sizeof object loads the size in bytes of the value type specified in the given metadata token onto the evaluation stack. This instruction is important because the size may not be known when the IL code was generated (for example, if the type is defined in a different assembly, a new version of that assembly may have added more fields to the type, increasing its size).

```
..., → ..., size
```

Table A-29 shows the sizeof instruction.

Table A-29. sizeof

Mnemonic	Opcode and Argument(s)	Purpose	Verifiable?
sizeof	0xfe 0x1c <T>	Returns size of the given type	Yes

Boxing Instructions

The boxing-related instructions box and unbox an object. The box and unbox instructions both require a metadata token identifying the value type of the item to be boxed or unboxed as an argument.

Boxing

The box instruction boxes a value type and pushes an object reference to the boxed type onto the evaluation stack. The top item on the stack must be the value object, and the object reference to the boxed object is pushed onto the stack.

```
..., value → ..., object reference
```

Table A-30 shows the box instruction.

Table A-30. box

Mnemonic	Opcode and Argument(s)	Purpose	Verifiable?
box	0x8c <T>	Boxes the item on the top of the stack	Yes

Unboxing

unbox pops the object reference from the stack and pushes the address of the value object onto it. Note that whereas boxing actually copies the object, unboxing merely returns a managed pointer to the instance (in other words, to the address of the first field in the instance) on the managed heap and doesn't copy any data.

```
..., object reference → ..., address
```

Table A-31 shows the unbox instruction.

Table A-31. unbox

Mnemonic	Opcode and Argument(s)	Purpose	Verifiable?
unbox	0x79 <T>	Unboxes the object referred to by the top item of the stack	Yes

Array Instructions

These instructions deal with arrays (strictly speaking, vectors), including instantiating arrays, determining the length of an array, and accessing its elements.

Instantiating an Array

The newarr instruction creates a new array. The instruction takes a metadata token representing a typedef or typeref as an argument. The size of the array is taken from the stack, and an object reference to the new array is pushed onto the stack.

```
..., no. of elements → ..., array ref
```

Table A-32 shows the newarr instruction.

Table A-32. newarr

Mnemonic	Opcode and Argument(s)	Purpose	Verifiable?
newarr	0x8d <T>	Instantiates array of the given type	Yes

Determining the Length of an Array

The `ldlen` instruction pushes the number of elements in an array onto the stack.

..., array ref → ..., length

Table A-33 shows the `ldlen` instruction.

Table A-33. `ldlen`

Mnemonic	Opcode and Argument(s)	Purpose	Verifiable?
ldlen	0x8e	Pushes the length of the array onto the stack	Yes

Accessing Elements of an Array

These instructions either load a given element of an array onto the stack or store the top element of the stack in an array element.

Load instructions have this stack transition diagram:

..., array ref, index → ..., value

Store instructions have this stack transition diagram:

..., array ref, index, value → ...

Table A-34 lists the instructions to access array elements.

Table A-34. *Accessing Array Elements*

Mnemonic	Opcode and Argument(s)	Purpose	Verifiable?
ldelem.i	0x97	Loads the given element onto the stack. The array must be of the type given in the mnemonic (for example, `ldelem.i1` requires that the array is an array of int8).	Yes
ldelem.i1	0x90		
ldelem.i2	0x92		
ldelem.i4	0x94		
ldelem.i8	0x96		
ldelem.r4	0x98		
ldelem.r8	0x99		
ldelem.ref	0x9a		
ldelem.u1	0x91		
ldelem.u2	0x93		
ldelem.u4	0x95		
ldelema	0x8f <T>	Loads the address of the given element onto the stack.	Yes

Continued

Table A-34. *Accessing Array Elements (Continued)*

Mnemonic	Opcode and Argument(s)	Purpose	Verifiable?
stelem.i	0x9b	Stores the top element of the stack in the given array element; the array must be of the type given in the mnemonic.	Yes
stelem.i1	0x9c		
stelem.i2	0x9d		
stelem.i4	0x9e		
stelem.i8	0x9f		
stelem.r4	0xa0		
stelem.r8	0xa1		
stelem.ref	0xa2		

Instructions to Invoke and Leave Methods

Several instructions are available to invoke a method, depending on whether the method is static, instance, or virtual and whether indirect addressing is to be used. In all cases, the arguments to the method are supplied by popping them off the evaluation stack into the arguments table of the called method in reverse order (that is, the last argument to the method is the first item popped off the stack); this means that the number of items removed from the stack depends on the method signature. You should note that if the method is an instance or virtual method, the number of parameters it takes is one greater than the number explicitly indicated in the method signature, since it will expect as the first parameter the address (or object reference for reference types) of the instance against which the method is to be called (the this pointer). This address must also be pushed onto the evaluation stack before invoking the method.

In all cases, any return value from the method that has just been called will be pushed onto the evaluation stack within the calling method.

Invoking a Method

Two instructions call a method: call and callvirt. The difference is that call identifies the method to be invoked using only the metadata token supplied as an argument to the instruction. callvirt routes the dispatch through the object's method table, which may mean the method actually called is an override of the one specified in the metadata token. You can use call to invoke a virtual method if that's the behavior you require (in other words, if you want to call a base method, not an override). Similarly, you can use callvirt to invoke an instance (in other words, nonvirtual) method.

```
..., arg1, ...argN → ..., result (may not be returned)
```

Table A-35 shows the call and callvirt instructions.

Table A-35. *Invoking a Method*

Mnemonic	Opcode and Argument(s)	Purpose	Verifiable?
call	0x28 <T>	Invokes method specified in the metadata token	Depends
callvirt	0x6f <T>	Invokes specified method, but if an override to this method exists in the object instance being invoked, invokes the override instead	Depends

Verifiability Conditions

These methods aren't verifiable if the types on the evaluation stack don't match the types expected by the method being invoked.

Invoking a Method with Indirect Addressing

The calli instruction uses indirect addressing to call a method, supplying as an operand a pointer to the address of the method. The instruction also takes an argument—a metadata token that identifies the signature of the method. calli may be used to call managed or unmanaged code and is the usual way of calling into unmanaged code.

```
..., arg1, ...argN, method address → ..., result (may not be returned)
```

Table A-36 shows the calli instruction.

Table A-36. *Invoking a Method with Indirect Addressing*

Mnemonic	Opcode and Argument(s)	Purpose	Verifiable?
calli	0x29 <T>	Returns control to calling method. Calls the method with entry point at the given address.	Depends

Verifiability Conditions

According to the docs that define the standards, calli should be verifiable if the address of the method being called was generated using an ldftn or ldvirtftn instruction (see the next section). However, for the first release of the CLR on the Windows platform, calli is never verifiable.

Manipulating Function Addresses

CIL defines two instructions that can push a function pointer onto the evaluation stack that's suitable for use with calli. ldftn and ldvirtftn supply a pointer to the native code for a function. Details of the function are specified in a metadata token supplied as an argument to the instructions. ldvirtftn differs from ldftn in that it also examines an object reference on the evaluation stack to check if a pointer to an override to the function should be supplied instead.

ldftn has this stack transition diagram:

```
..., → ..., method address
```

ldvirtftn has this diagram:

```
..., object reference →..., method address
```

Table A-37 shows the ldftn and ldvirtftn instructions.

Table A-37. *Manipulating Function Addresses*

Mnemonic	Opcode and Argument(s)	Purpose	Verifiable?
ldftn	0xfe 0x06 <T>	Loads function	Yes
ldvirtftn	0xfe 0x07 <T>	pointer	

Exiting a Method

You can exit a method using either the ret or the jmp instruction. ret returns control to the calling method. The evaluation stack must either be empty or contain one value to be used as the return value depending on whether the method you're exiting is defined as void. jmp doesn't return control to the calling method but transfers control straight to a named method. The named method must have the same parameter types as the current method—the current set of arguments will be transferred across. The evaluation stack must be empty when jmp is called.

```
<empty (in old method)> → <empty (in new method)>
```

Or (for ret):

```
return value (in called method) → <previous contents>, value (in calling method)
```

Table A-38 lists the instructions to exit a method.

Table A-38. *Exiting a Method*

Mnemonic	Opcode and Argument(s)	Purpose	Verifiable?
ret	0x2a	Returns control to calling method	Yes
jmp	0x27 <T>	Jumps to specified method	No

Exception Handling Instructions

The following sections list exception handling instructions.

leave

The leave instruction empties the evaluation stack and transfers control out of the containing catch, try, or filter block, ensuring that any appropriate finally blocks are executed. It can't be used to transfer control out of a finally block or into a different method.

```
... → <empty>
```

Table A-39 shows the leave instruction.

Table A-39. leave

Mnemonic	Opcode and Argument(s)	Purpose	Verifiable?
leave	0xdd <int32>	Leaves try, catch, or filter block	Yes
leave.s	0xde <int8>		

endfinally

The endfinally (also called endfault) instruction transfers control out of a finally or fault block in the usual manner. This means that if the finally block was being executed as a result of a leave statement in a try block, then execution continues at the next statement following the finally block. If, on the other hand, the finally (or fault) block was being executed as a result of an exception having been thrown, then execution will transfer to the next suitable block of exception handling code (or to the next finally block working up the stack). This instruction has two mnemonics, and you should use the appropriate one for the location of the instruction.

... → ...

Table A-40 shows the endfinally instruction.

Table A-40. endfinally

Mnemonic	Opcode and Argument(s)	Purpose	Verifiable?
endfinally *or* endfault	0xdc	Leaves a finally or fault block	Yes

endfilter

endfilter is similar to endfinally, except it's designed to leave a filter block. The top item on the stack immediately before executing this instruction is used to determine the action to be taken; a value of zero will cause searching for a handler to continue, and a value of 1 indicates this block has agreed to handle the exception and control will transfer appropriately.

..., 0 or 1 → ...

Table A-41 shows the endfilter instruction.

Table A-41. endfilter

Mnemonic	Opcode and Argument(s)	Purpose	Verifiable?
endfilter	0xfe 0x11	Leaves a filter block	Yes

throw

The throw instruction does exactly what throw does in C++ and C# and what Throw does in VB: it causes execution to transfer to the next catch block that's able to handle the object at the top of the evaluation stack (or to any intermediate finally, filter, or fault block).

..., object reference→ ...

Table A-42 shows the throw instruction.

Table A-42. throw

Mnemonic	Opcode and Argument(s)	Purpose	Verifiable?
throw	0x7a	Throws exception	Yes

rethrow

The rethrow instruction is similar to throw, but it can be placed only in a catch block. It rethrows the current exception. Because the current exception object is known to the JIT compiler, it doesn't need to be on the evaluation stack. Hence, rethrow doesn't change the stack contents.

... → ...

Table A-43 shows the rethrow instruction.

Table A-43. rethrow

Mnemonic	Opcode and Argument(s)	Purpose	Verifiable?
rethrow	0xfe 0x1a	Rethrows current exception.	Yes

Memory Instructions

The following sections list the instructions that manipulate the local memory pool.

Allocating Memory

The localloc instruction allocates memory in the local memory pool. It also initializes it to zero if the initialize flag for the method is true. It pops the size of the memory required in bytes from the evaluation stack.

..., size → ..., address

Table A-44 shows the localloc instruction.

Table A-44. localloc

Mnemonic	Opcode and Argument(s)	Purpose	Verifiable?
localloc	0xfe 0x0f	Allocates memory in the local memory pool	No

Verifiability Conditions

The size of the memory required must be the only item on the evaluation stack when `localloc` is called. `localloc` can't be called from inside `catch`, `finally`, `filter`, or `fault` blocks.

Initializing Memory

The `initblk` instruction sets all bytes in an area of memory to the specified value. The block of memory is identified by its start address and size in bytes.

```
..., start address, value, size → ...,
```

Table A-45 shows the `initblk` instruction.

Table A-45. `initblk`

Mnemonic	Opcode and Argument(s)	Purpose	Verifiable?
initblk	0xfe 0x18	Initializes memory	No

Copying Memory

The `cpblk` instruction copies the contents of memory from one location to another, given the addresses and number of bytes to be copied.

```
..., dest address, source address, size → ...,
```

Table A-46 shows the `cpblk` instruction.

Table A-46. `cpblk`

Mnemonic	Opcode and Argument(s)	Purpose	Verifiable?
cpblk	0xfe 0x17	Copies memory contents	No

Dynamically Typed Referencing

A typed reference is a data type that contains both a pointer (which can be managed or unmanaged) and a `TypeDef` or `TypeRef` token that indicates the object type to which this pointer should point. CIL allows dynamically constructing a typed reference at runtime and passing it to a method that's expecting a typed reference as a parameter, with several instructions devoted to this purpose.

Making a Typed Reference

The `mkrefany` instruction makes up a typed reference, given a pointer and a token (supplied as an argument), and pushes it onto the stack.

```
..., addr → ..., typedref
```

Table A-47 shows the `mkrefany` instruction.

Table A-47. `mkrefany`

Mnemonic	Opcode and Argument(s)	Purpose	Verifiable?
mkrefany	0xc6 <T>	Creates a typed reference	Depends

Verifiability Conditions

For valid code, the address on the stack must point to an object of the appropriate type. In addition for type-safety requirements, it must be an unmanaged pointer.

Retrieving the Data from a Typed Reference

CIL supports two instructions to extract the data that's in a typed reference: `refanytype` retrieves the token that represents the type and pushes it onto the evaluation stack, and `refanyval` similarly retrieves the address.

```
..., typedref → ..., result
```

Table A-48 shows the `refanytype` and `refanyval` instructions.

Table A-48. *Retrieving Data from a Typed Reference*

Mnemonic	Opcode and Argument(s)	Purpose	Verifiable?
refanytype	0xfe 0x1d	Extracts the type from a typed reference.	Yes
refanyval	0xc2 <T>	Extracts the pointer from a typed reference. The type is supplied as an argument to the instruction.	Yes

Instructions to Support Debugging

The following sections list those instructions whose prime purpose is to support debugging.

nop

The `nop` instruction does nothing. It's used to provide points in the IL stream at which a debugger can patch in break statements if required. It doesn't cause any native executable code to be emitted by the JIT compiler.

```
..., → ...,
```

Table A-49 shows the `nop` instruction.

Table A-49. `nop`

Mnemonic	Opcode and Argument(s)	Purpose	Verifiable?
nop	0x00	No operation	Yes

break

The break instruction signals that a debugger breakpoint has been reached. The actual effect of this depends on the environment in which the program is running and any relevant debugger settings; this may, for example, result in no action, result in an exception being triggered, or cause a debugger to be invoked.

..., → ...,

Table A-50 shows the break instruction.

Table A-50. break

Mnemonic	Opcode and Argument(s)	Purpose	Verifiable?
break	0x01	Signals a breakpoint	Yes

Instructions to Support Reflection

Reflection isn't dealt with by IL, because it's implemented by classes within the main CLR class library. However, IL contains one instruction ldtoken, which is intended to support reflection and which carries out an operation (loading a token) that can't be done in verifiable code using other instructions.

ldtoken

The ldtoken instruction loads a handle representing the given token onto the evaluation stack. This value must be treated in subsequent calls as a runtime handle and passed to certain methods concerned with reflection that expect this type (depending on the token type, a RuntimeMethodHandle, RuntimeFieldHandle, or RuntimeTypeHandle). No other IL instructions can do anything with the token, so the only purpose for this method is to support reflection.

..., → ..., handle

Table A-51 shows the ldtoken instruction.

Table A-51. ldtoken

Mnemonic	Opcode and Argument(s)	Purpose	Verifiable?
ldtoken	0xd0 <T>	Loads handle to token onto stack	Yes

Instruction Prefixes

CIL defines three instruction prefixes, whose mnemonics can be identified because they have a trailing dot: tail., unaligned., and volatile.. These prefixes are represented by opcodes in the instruction stream, just as instructions. However, they serve to modify the behavior of the following instruction. Note that if the following instruction (in other words, the instruction to which the prefixed is attached) is the intended target of a branch, the branch must specify the first prefix of the instruction, not the instruction itself.

tail.

Table A-52 shows the `tail.` prefix.

Table A-52. `tail.`

Mnemonic	Opcode	Meaning	Instructions to Which This Prefix Can Be Applied
`tail.`	`0xfe 0x14`	Stack frame can be discarded	`call`, `calli`, `callvirt`

The `tail.` prefix indicates that this call instruction will be the last instruction executed before leaving this method and hence that the method state for the current method (evaluation stack, local variables, and so on) can be discarded prior to executing the `call`, `calli`, or `callvirt`. It requires that the evaluation stack should be empty other than any parameters to be passed to the invoked method. Because of security considerations, the `tail.` prefix will be ignored if you're calling from untrusted to trusted code or vice versa.

Verifiability Conditions for tail.

`tail.` will fail verifiability if any managed pointers to local variables are passed to the method to be invoked (because the local variables are destroyed so the new method would just get pointers to garbage).

unaligned.

Table A-53 shows the `unaligned.` prefix.

Table A-53. `unaligned.`

Mnemonic	Opcode	Meaning	Instructions to Which This Prefix Can Be Applied
`unaligned.`	`0xfe 0x12`	Addresses may not be aligned	`ldind`, `stind`, `ldfld`, `stfld`, `ldobj`, `stobj`, `initblk`, `cpblk`, and abbreviated versions of these instructions

CIL instructions that take addresses as operands normally assume for performance reasons that the data is correctly byte aligned for the machine architecture. The `unaligned.` prefix warns the JIT compiler that the data may not be aligned, so it should generate unaligned native instructions on processors that require this.

volatile.

Table A-54 shows the `volatile.` prefix.

Table A-54. `volatile.`

Mnemonic	Opcode	Meaning	Instructions to Which This Prefix Can Be Applied
`volatile.`	`0xfe 0x13`	Address JIT compiler should assume that this address may refer to volatile memory	`ldind`, `stind`, `ldfld`, `stfld`, `ldobj`, `stobj`, `initblk`, `cpblk`, and abbreviated versions of these instructions

The JIT compiler may optimize by arranging for data at addresses that have been dereferenced to be enregistered (stored in registers) and may also cache data reads, reorder reads and writes, or omit writes (if the data appears not to get read again before a subsequent write). The `.volatile` prefix warns it that this data may be modified through some external source and therefore that these optimizations must not be performed in respect of this particular instruction. The prefix doesn't affect any other instructions that access the same data and so must be applied separately to all CIL instructions that use the volatile data.

IL Assembly Directives and Keywords

IL source code directives and keywords normally indicate items to be placed in the metadata. The number of directives and keywords is huge, so it's not possible to provide an exhaustive list here, but I summarize the most important ones. Partition II details the full list.

Directives all start with a period (`.`). In several cases, keywords (these don't start with a period) are associated with certain directives. Those keywords are presented here along with their corresponding directives.

In these notes, angled brackets `<>` indicate data that should be filled in when using the directive in ILasm code.

Assembly and Module Structure

These directives determine whether the file is assembled to an assembly or module and what other assemblies are referenced in the metadata.

.assembly {}

`.assembly` indicates that this IL source file is to be built into an assembly (as opposed to just a module). Data needed for the assembly manifest, such as strong name data, may be placed in the braces.

.assembly extern <Name> {}

This directive indicates an external assembly that's required by code in this file. The assembly name shouldn't include the `.dll` or `.exe` filename extension.

.module <name> {}

`.module` indicates that the file forms a module within an assembly. The name should be the filename, including any extension.

Assembly Options

The following sections list directives that affect the JIT compilation of the entire assembly.

.subsystem <2 or 3>

This directive informs the JIT compiler of whether an executable assembly should run as a Windows application (2) or as a console application (3, the default).

.data <name> = <data>

`.data` is used to define arbitrary custom data that's placed in the `.sdata` section of the PE file.

.hash <number>

`.hash` indicates the hash algorithm used to generate the hash value for an assembly. This should normally be 0x00080004, indicating the SHA1 algorithm.

.locale <name>

`.locale` defines the culture for an assembly.

.publickey <data>

This indicates the public key used to access an assembly.

Type Definitions

These directives allow namespaces and types to be defined.

.namespace <name> {}

`.namespace` indicates the name of the namespace that should be prefixed to the names of all types defined inside the braces.

.class <name> {}

`.class` indicates the braces contain code that will form part of the named class.

The `.class` directive can be used in conjunction with keywords, including the following.

extends

The extends keyword indicates the name of a base class. If the extends keyword is omitted, the class is assumed to derive from [mscorlib]System.Object. Value types and enums are indicated respectively by being derived from [mscorlib]System.ValueType and [mscorlib]System.Enum. Delegates are indicated by being derived from [mscorlib]System.Delegate or [mscorlib]System.MulticastDelegate.

value

The value keyword provides a shorthand way of indicating that a type derives from [mscorlib]System.ValueType.

enum

The enum keyword provides a shorthand way of indicating that a type derives from [mscorlib]System.Enum.

autochar/ansi/unicode

These keywords indicate the behavior required for string conversion if strings need to be passed to or from native code. autochar means that the behavior is determined by the underlying platform. The meanings of ansi and unicode should be obvious.

You can use .class directives in conjunction with the accessibility modifiers public, private, and so on, as described next.

abstract

Indicates that this type may only be derived from, not instantiated.

sealed

Indicates that this type can't be derived from.

Members of Types

Several directives indicate you're defining members of classes. Any of these directives may be qualified by the accessibility modifiers, as described next.

.field <name>

This directive indicates that you're defining a member field.

.event <name>

This directive indicates that you're defining a member event.

.method <name> (<list of arguments>) {}

The .method directive indicates that you're defining a method. The code for the method will be in the braces.

You can use the following directives and keywords to supply extra information to the .method directive. (In the following sections, mutually exclusive keywords are presented together.)

override

This indicates that the method overrides a method in a base class.

rtspecialname

This indicates that the name of the method has some special significance known to the .NET runtime; for example, it could be a constructor.

specialname

This indicates that the name of the method has some special significance to compilers and tools. This keyword is often (though not always) used in conjunction with rtspecialname.

cil managed/native unmanaged

cil managed indicates that the method contains IL code.

native unmanaged indicates that the method contains native executable code that doesn't need to be JIT compiled.

.property <name>

This directive indicates that you're defining a property.

.custom

This indicates that a custom attribute is to be applied to this item.

Directives That Occur Inside Methods or Properties

The following directives appear in the code for methods or properties.

.maxstack

.maxstack indicates the maximum number of items that can be stored simultaneously on the evaluation stack for that method.

.locals

.locals lists the local variables for that method. The types must be supplied. Optionally, names may be supplied as well. .locals can be used (and in most cases should be used) in conjunction with init (.locals init (..)) to indicate that the local variables must be initially zeroed-out cases.

.entrypoint

.entrypoint indicates that a method is the method at which execution starts. The method must have been declared as static. (It wouldn't make sense for it to be an instance method since no objects have yet been instantiated when the .entrypoint method is invoked.)

.get and .set

These directives apply to properties only and respectively indicate the get and set accessors associated with the property.

pinvokeimpl

This keyword indicates you're declaring an unmanaged method implemented externally and that should be called using the P/Invoke mechanism.

vararg

The vararg can appear in the parameter list to a method and indicates a variable parameter list, similar to unmanaged C vararg functions. Currently, none of the Microsoft languages use IL variable parameter lists. (The C# params statement for example *doesn't* cause a vararg method to be emitted but instead translates into a fixed object [] argument in IL.)

Accessibility Keywords

These keywords indicate the degree to which a class member is visible to outside code. When applied to nested types (as opposed to member fields, methods, and so on), these keywords must all be prefixed with nested (for example, .class nested public, and so on). public and private may also be applied (without the nested qualifier) to top-level types to indicate whether that type is visible outside its containing assembly.

public

All other code can see this item.

family

Only this type and any types derived from this type can see this item.

assembly

Only types defined in this assembly can see this item.

familyorassem

Only types that satisfy either one of the requirements family and assembly can see this item.

familyandassem

Only types that satisfy both of the requirements family and assembly can see this item.

private

Only code defined within this class can see this item.

privatescope

This is similar to private but allows for multiple items having the same name (they're distinguished by having different tokens within the module). This is the default accessibility.

Exception Handling

Exception handling in IL is indicated through the `.try` directive.

.try

The `.try` directive declares a try block for exception handling. Any associated `catch`, `filter`, `finally`, and `fault` blocks are indicated by the corresponding keywords. Two syntaxes are available for the try directive. For simplicity I'll illustrate them assuming only `catch` and `finally` blocks. The syntax for `fault` and `filter` blocks is identical. A fault block is executed if an exception was thrown in the associated try, and a filter block is executed if an exception was thrown and serves to test if an exception should be handled by an associated catch block (for example, as in VB's `Catch When I>0`).

The first syntax is similar to that in C# and requires the code inside the various blocks to be placed in braces.

```
.try
{
    // Put code for try block here
}
catch(Exception ex)
{
    // Code for catch block
}
finally
{
    // Code for finally block
}
```

The second syntax requires all the code for the blocks to precede the `.try` directive. The beginning and end of the various blocks are indicated by labels in the code, and these labels are quoted in the `.try` directive.

```
try <label> to <label>
catch<Exception Type> <label> to <label>
 finally <label> to <label>
```

You'll generally gain no benefit from using the second syntax (unless you really want your code to be hard to read!).

Index